Activities : sea, sand, birds, and ram

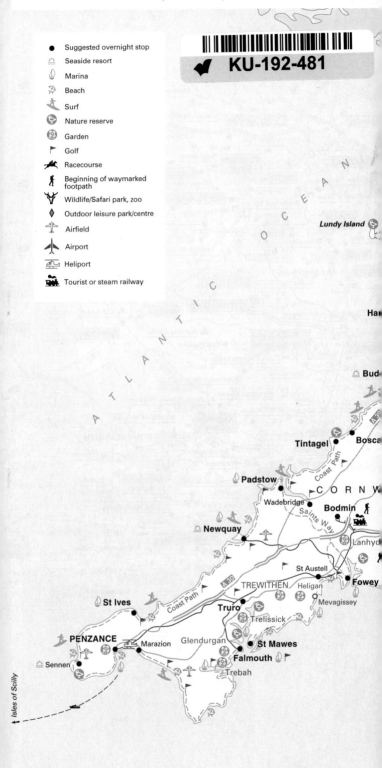

- ● Suggested overnight stop
- ⌂ Seaside resort
- ⛵ Marina
- 🏖 Beach
- 🏄 Surf
- 🌀 Nature reserve
- ❀ Garden
- ⚑ Golf
- 🏇 Racecourse
- 🚶 Beginning of waymarked footpath
- 🐂 Wildlife/Safari park, zoo
- ◆ Outdoor leisure park/centre
- ✈ Airfield
- ✈ Airport
- 🚁 Heliport
- 🚂 Tourist or steam railway

KU-192-481

ATLANTIC OCEAN

Lundy Island

Ha

Bud

Tintagel   Bosca

Padstow

Coast Path

CORNW

Wadebridge

Bodmin

Saints Way

Lanhyd

Newquay

St Austell

TREWITHEN   Heligan   Fowey

Mevagissey

St Ives   Coast Path

Truro

Trelissick

PENZANCE   Marazion   Glendurgan   St Mawes

Sennen   Falmouth

Trebah

Isles of Scilly

Contents

How to use this guide

Maps locating the main towns and star-rated sights are provided on pages 2-7. The **introduction** provides a profile of the different regions including their physical, historical and economic development; the arts cover the development of building, garden design and plant collecting, painting, ceramics and literature. The **sights** section presents the main towns of the West Country, arranged alphabetically, and their surrounding area; all are large enough to have accommodation facilities of one kind or another suited to a weekend break or summer holiday. Cross-references throughout refer to the Michelin sheet map 403 and the Michelin Motoring Atlas of Great Britain and Ireland to assist motorists to locate and schedule attractions in a touring programme. The Channel Islands are listed separately. The **practical information** section gives advice on how to make the most of the region and its varied attractions complete with opening times and admission charges to sites, a calendar of events, bibliography and **index**.

Principal sights

| Worth a journey | ★★★ |

| Worth a detour | ★★ |

| Interesting | ★ |

The names of towns or sights described
in the guide appear in black on the maps.
See the index for the page number.

0 ——————————— 30 km
—————————— 20 miles

UNITARY AUTHORITIES

1. Bath and N-E Somerset
2. Bristol
3. Cornwall
4. Devon
5. Dorset
6. South Gloucestershire
7. Somerset
8. N-W Somerset
9. Wiltshire

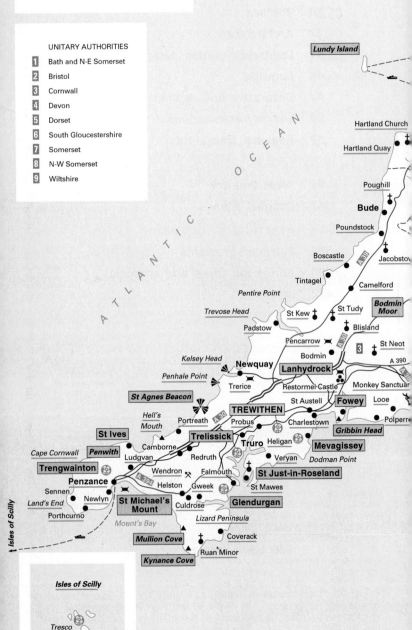

FISHGUARD
A 40

ATLANTIC OCEAN

Lundy Island

Hartland Church
Hartland Quay
Poughill
Bude
Poundstock
Jacobstow
Boscastle
A 39
Tintagel
Camelford
Bodmin Moor
Pentire Point
St Kew
St Tudy
Blisland
Trevose Head
Padstow
3
St Neot
A 390
Pencarrow
A 30
Bodmin
Kelsey Head
Newquay
Lanhydrock
Penhale Point
Restormel Castle
Monkey Sanctuar
Trerice
St Agnes Beacon
TREWITHEN
St Austell
Fowey
Looe
Hell's Mouth
Portreath
Probus
Charlestown
Gribbin Head
Polperr
St Ives
A 30
Trelissick
Truro
Heligan
Mevagissey
Penwith
Camborne
Cape Cornwall
Ludgvan
Redruth
Veryan
Dodman Point
Trengwainton
Wendron
Falmouth
St Just-in-Roseland
Penzance
Helston
Gweek
St Mawes
Sennen
St Michael's Mount
Culdrose
Glendurgan
Newlyn
Land's End
Porthcurno
Lizard Peninsula
Mount's Bay
Coverack
Mullion Cove
Ruan Minor
Kynance Cove

Isles of Scilly

Isles of Scilly

Tresco
St Mary's

Land's End

Introduction

The West Country

BRISTOL AND BATH

Since the demise in 1997 of the former county of Avon, from the Old Celtic word *afon* for a river, the area is now shared by four **Unitary Authorities**: Bristol, Bath and North East Somerset, North Somerset, and South Gloucestershire – *see Principal Sights map*.

Two cities – Bath and Bristol afford infinite variety to the visitor through their contrasting backgrounds and their current atmosphere. Bath (Aquae Sulis) was built for recreation and leisure in the Roman age, revived and vaunted as fashionable in Stuart times and rebuilt again as the supreme example in England of urban planning in the 18C. The City of Bristol (Abone), meanwhile, was granted county status in its own right as far back as 1373 by Edward III, its port having assured the prosperity of venturers, traders, merchants and industrialists who always remained generous to their city. Each has its "great man": Bath in the 18C was transformed by **Beau Nash**; Bristol will always bear the imprint of **Isambard Kingdom Brunel** (1806-59).

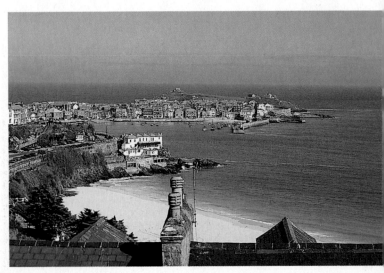

CORNWALL – 1 376 square miles (3 564sqkm)

During the Ice Age, Cornwall was a tundra similar to the Alaska and Siberia of today; when the ice melted, the sea level rose leaving raised beaches, submerged forests and fertile flood estuaries. Isolated from Britain by the Tamar, Cornwall long remained a land of Celtic legend and early saints, of King Arthur and fairy tale giants, of the 'Obby 'Oss (Padstow) and the famous Furry Dance (Helston). It is also a county of "diversified pleasings" as Richard Carew phrased it: of wonderful coastal scenery, jagged headlands, sheer cliffs and offshore needles, of golden sand beaches and picturesque harbours; of rock outcrops and standing stones on the windswept, open moorland; of lush, heron-haunted river valleys with banks densely fringed with oak trees, of glorious gardens contrasting with the stark chimneys of derelict copper and tin mines.

Economy – The Cornish economy long flourished on mining and quarrying, boat-building and fishing. Today tin and copper mining is a dead industry, its engine-houses having been dismantled and its deep shafts flooded; highly industrialised open-quarrying for slate continues at **Delabole** and **Tintagel**, and china-clay is still extracted around **St Austell**. For the present, the shipyard at **Falmouth** thrives and although fishing fleets have been depleted by controversial allocations of territorial waters and fishing practices, **Newlyn** maintains a collection of trawlers which provide employment for a dwindling number of fishermen.

Farming, which at one time consisted of vast sheep flocks to provide wool, has evolved to include cattle holding and crop cultivation including the production of early vegetables and, in the far west and Isles of Scilly, **cut-flowers** (particularly early daffodils and everlasting carnations). The most lucrative business, however, is **tourism**: along the south coast the enchanting sequence of peaceful estuaries blessed with a temperate climate provide ideal conditions for sensitive plants to proliferate and the prospect of the Eden Project entailing the construction of various massive

St Ives

glasshouses outside St Austell before the millennium will further boost interests in horticulture and gardening. The northern coast from Tintagel to Land's End, shaped by wind, rain and sea, attracts hardy ramblers and the more athletic surfers: there is no opportunity for ship-building here as the jagged, granite coastline is ever open to the harshest weather conditions and resists all attempts at sustaining a man-made deep-water harbour; fishing smacks and pleasure boats are berthed inland up river.

Christianity – Local lore relates how Cornwall was converted by saintly men who sailed the sea on millstones and lilypads: **St Piran**, patron saint of tin miners, is reputed to have drifted on a millstone from Ireland to land at Perranporth. In fact Christianity was probably introduced, after the Roman invasion of Britain, by missionaries from Gaul following the ancient trade routes that were established in the 6C BC by Phoenicians buying copper and Irish gold. This is confirmed by the discovery along the main route north-south across Cornwall of early inscriptions with the oldest form of the XP monogram and motifs similar to those found in southern Gaul and on sculpted Irish crosses.

Neither the departure of the Romans nor the Saxon invasion in the second half of the 5C influenced the early Celtic Church which venerated its own saints, until AD 926 when King Athelstan conquered Cornwall, established the English diocese of Cornwall and introduced the doctrine of the Roman Church founded on the teachings of St Augustine – the bishopric endured until 1043 when it was transferred first to Crediton then to Exeter; the See of Cornwall was re-instated in 1876 and Truro Cathedral was erected in celebration.

The Duchy of Cornwall – William of Normandy created his half-brother, Roger of Mortain, first Earl of Cornwall soon after the Conquest. Roger's lands extended far beyond the bounds of Cornwall into Devon, Somerset and even Gloucestershire. In 1337 the Duchy of Cornwall was created by Edward III from the former earldom, for his son Edward, the Black Prince (1330-76). Since 1503 the monarch's eldest son as heir apparent has always succeeded to the title. The lands still extend beyond the confines of Cornwall into Devon (including much of Dartmoor) and Somerset, including some 130 000 acres in the West Country alone.

Until the 19C the Duchy maintained its wealth with the "coinage" dues or stamp with the duchy seal which was required on every smelted block of tin before it could be sold, a duty performed in the Stannary Towns of both Cornwall and Devon until 1838 when the dues were abolished by parliament and compensation paid. Today the Duchy leases complete estates, farm holdings and individual houses to tenants, who manage the land and maintain great tracts of woodland on its behalf.

DEVON – 2 591 square miles (6 710sqkm)

The third largest of the old English counties after Yorkshire and Lincolnshire, Devon is characterised by its open undulating landscape which sustained mining on Dartmoor in Prehistoric times, huge numbers of sheep to provide wool to the cloth trade from the late Middle Ages until the 17C, large military and naval communities for defence purposes stationed at **Dartmouth** and **Plymouth** in the 18C-19C, and fi-

nally, since the advent of the railways in the 1870s, several popular resorts around **Torbay**, **Barnstaple** and **Bideford**. The spectacular cliffs and headlands along the north coast (interspersed with the miles of sand beaches at Westward Ho!, Croyde and Woolacombe) are in contrast with the more gentle coves, headlands and estuaries of the south coast, which are accessible at every point by the South Devon Coast Path. Inland, the green and fertile valleys of its many rivers and the wildness offered by the **Dartmoor National Park**, a granite boss tilted southwards with high tors and free-roaming ponies, have ensured that Devon has remained a perennial favourite.

Clovelly

CLOVELLY ESTATE

American connections – In the early 17C Devon fishermen were not only landing in America to dry their catches and re-supply their boats but had set up trading posts with the Indians for furs. On 14 May 1620, the first permanent English settlement in the New World was established at Jamestown, Virginia; on 6 September 1620 the Pilgrim Fathers aboard the *Mayflower* sailed from Plymouth; three months later they landed at New Plymouth (Plymouth, Massachusetts) on 21 December.

The early history of the United States, it has been claimed, owes more to Devon than to any other English county: for more expeditions, including many emigrant ships, sailed west from Plymouth bound for North America than from all other English ports put together. Indeed, a large number of place-names in the United States derive from towns, villages and counties of England of which around 120-150 of them are from Devon.

In the 19C the traffic divided into bulk traffic through the larger ports for the poorer people, and individual passages on ships using the smaller ports such as Bideford and Torquay. Travel was further transformed in the 20C by ever larger steam-driven ships and the inauguration of regular trans-Atlantic sailings by the ocean liners operated by the likes of Cunard.

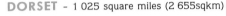

DORSET – 1 025 square miles (2 655sqkm)

The attraction of Dorset lies in the stark contrast of coast and hinterland which quickly feels remote from the sea. Between the North and low-lying South Dorset Downs, so close to the sea that the Osmington White Horse with George III upon it is best seen from offshore, the countryside extends east and north in a series of barren heath-covered moors. The whole area, from **Blackmore Vale** in the west to the part-forested, part-cleared Cranborne Chase in the east, is drained by gentle rivers flowing north-south to the sea – providing enough water to power a broad range of industry (brewing, milling grain, flax, silk and paper, foundries at **Shaftesbury**, Blandford, Dorchester, Chard, Bridport). Southeast of Wareham, the so-called "isle" of **Purbeck** is separated from the "mainland" by a line of hills, the only gap on the skyline being filled by the gaunt outlines of **Corfe Castle**.

The landscape, whose rock has been quarried for centuries to build houses and cathedrals, is windswept on the headlands, steeply undulating and wooded just inland: the chalk downs are used to grow arable crops and to graze sheep, the lush valleys shelter dairy herds. Interestingly enough, dairying was especially stimulated here in the latter half of the 19C when the railways were built and large consignments of cheese, butter and milk could be sent to London more efficiently than before.

Dorset's cliff-lined coast is marked by arches or "doors" in primeval rocks (eg **Durdle Door**), the off-shore chalk stacks known as the Old Harry Rocks, by golden sand beaches, the unique **Chesil Beach**, towering headlands and the long Isle of **Portland**; **Lyme Regis** provides excellent sites for fossil-hunting. Further inland, Dorset boasts Maiden Castle – considered to be the finest earthwork in Britain – the beautiful small abbey at **Sherborne**, and several fine country towns (Blandford Forum, Dorchester, Wimborne, Wareham...).

Dorset Worthies – The classic Dorset Worthies were men of the 17C-early 20C and included the likes of Thomas Hardy; among the contemporary local luminaries there is the glass engraver Laurence Whistler; Reynolds Stone, the letterer and

Fisherman at work, Lulworth Cove

calligrapher on wood and stone who designed distinctive monograms and "logos" used in print, trade-marks, bookplates, programmes and name plates for a generation; John Fowles, the novelist; John Makepiece, the furniture designer...

Cottage industry – The main cloth industries revolved around flax grown for making linen, dowlas (Cerne Abbas) and ticking, sailcloth and sacking (Beaminster), rope and netting (Bridport); in the early 17C broadcloth from Dorchester was produced for the local market and exported to France; in the 18C swanskin, a coarse white flannel used by soldiers and Newfoundland fishermen, was manufactured at Shaftesbury and Sturminster Newton. Undoubtedly in the days before women were employed collectively in workhouses, they would have done piecemeal work notably in the clothes and fashion accessory business. **Button making** (buttony) began in Shaftesbury in the 1680s, but was soon overtaken by Blandford as the main centre: Abraham Case's "High Tops" consisted of a disc of ram's horn with a hole in the centre and a line cone on top decorated with thread. These were made at home and exchanged at specified depots against goods rather than money. Demand dwindled through the 1840s following the invention of a button machine forcing many families to emigrate. Wimborne was an important centre for **silk stockings** whereas Poole was renowned for its knitted woollen stockings – a need born out of the fishing expeditions to Newfoundland: this trade was also killed off by a machine in the early 19C. **Lace-making** is associated with Blandford and Sherborne in the 17C, was introduced to Lyme Regis in the 18C to alleviate hardship and continues in and around Honiton in Devon. **Gloves** were made in Bridport in the early 15C, spreading in time to Beaminster, Cerne Abbas, Bere Regis, Sherborne and Blandford, often adding the finishing touches to goods made in Somerset (Yeovil) on their journey to London: the industry still actively employs out workers in Shaftesbury and Gillingham.

SOMERSET – 1 332 square miles (3 450sqkm)

Somerset derives its name from "summer land" or "land of the summer-farm dwellers": before man's intervention the area stretching from the Mendip and Quantock Hills to Shepton Mallet, Ilchester and Crewkerne largely consisted of barren wet marsh-land. Archeological surveys testify to the fact that the earliest settlers inhabited the hills (Cheddar caves), then learned how to build communities in the bog (Glastonbury Lake Village), and, in the Iron Age, constructed defensible hillforts on the dry outcrops like Glastonbury Tor. With the knowledge of how to drain the "levels" with willow-edged rhines, people began bringing their livestock down from the hills to graze on the rich summer pasture. As long ago as the 12C Henry II was buying Cheddar Cheese; later, careful husbandry as practised on lands belonging to the powerful monastic house at **Glastonbury** helped to establish the large flocks of sheep that were to make Somerset fourth in the production of wool when England was the premier wool producing country in the world.

Somerset rests on a limestone base providing abundant sources of freestone which builders and stone-carvers have exploited with flourish at **Wells** and **Montacute**. Its hill ranges, the Mendips, Poldens, Quantocks, Brendons and Blackdowns catch sufficient rainfall to maintain the excellent agricultural land which includes the Vale of Taunton, one of the great farming areas of England and to provide cavers and potholers with extensive underground complexes (**Cheddar Gorge**, Wookey Hole). In contrast, the coastline is given a gloriously colourful background, edging as it does the heathland and wooded valleys of **Exmoor**.

WILTSHIRE – 1 344 square miles (3 480sqkm)

Wiltshire is a fertile, undulating county, bounded along its eastern border by the distinctive Marlborough Downs; to the south and west lies open country watered by the Avon, which runs some 60 miles from **Malmesbury** to Christchurch in Dorset, the Wylye and its tributaries (Nadder, Ebele, Bourne). The many stretches of woodland include the small but soaring **Savernake Forest**. Great houses and manor houses with their gardens enhance the landscape's natural beauty. Important monuments and what many consider to be England's finest cathedral (**Salisbury**) contrast with small and friendly market towns, picture-postcard villages, tithe barns and village greens.

At the centre of Wiltshire rises the great Salisbury Plain (part of which is used for army training exercises): its range of chalk hills run southwest into Dorset. Throughout the ages the downlands have been farmed as pasture for sheep, and, more recently, as arable land; the area around Calne meanwhile is famous for its bacon and pig farming.

The chalk downlands have their own particular legacy: the chalk figures carved out of the turf are almost unique to this area, as are the abundance of prehistoric monuments probably including the three finest in Europe (**Stonehenge**, Avebury and Silbury) – several being located off the ancient Ridgeway Path, the upland trail which provided access across five counties for contemporary tribesmen.

The network of roads has developed from the Ridgeway Path, through Roman, Saxon and medieval highways and post roads, turnpikes and coaching roads, to the modern trunk roads and M4 motorway; added to these, improved transport was assured by the canal dug early in the 19C and the Great Western Railway. Altogether, Wiltshire has been largely bypassed by modern manufacturing and therefore retains its serene rural character.

Thatcher at work

Historical Notes

Prehistoric and Celtic periods

600 000-10 000 BC	Stone Age invasions from the Continent. Opening of the Irish Channel
6 000 BC	Opening of the English Channel
2950-2300 BC	**Stonehenge**
2000 – 700	Bronze Age, settlements of Beaker people
1500BC	Beaker folk overrun by Urn People
700-33BC	Celtic invasions: trade links with the Iberian Peninsula and Mediterranean Basin, evidence of Phoenicians importing tin and Irish gold via Cornwall. Cornwall and Devon settled by the Dumnonii tribe; Dorset by the Durotriges; Wiltshire by the Belgae

Roman occupation

55 BC	Julius Caesar lands in Britain
AD 43-407	Roman conquest, occupation and withdrawal. Christianity introduced in 313
AD 300	Coastal raids by Saxons begun and increased
432	St Patrick (c389-461), a Romano-Briton undertakes to convert Ireland; Irish missionary monks journeyed to Cornwall

N. Menneer/Bath and North East Somerset Council

Anglo-Saxon Kingdoms; the Danish Kings

500-600	Kingdoms of Northumbria, Mercia and Wessex established
639-709	St Aldhelm
688-726	Ine, King of Wessex
871-901	Wars against the Danes waged by Alfred the Great, King
926	King Athelstan creates Cornish See, ejects the Danes from the Isles of Scilly (930)
973	Edgar crowned first King of all England
979	King Edward murdered at Corfe Castle
1016-1035	Canute the Dane, King

Normans and Plantagenets

1066-1087	King Harold defeated by Duke William of Normandy (crowned William I of England; Conquest completed 1072 with submission of Exeter). Saxon land-holdings given to Norman barons, William's brothers and the church. Compilation of the **Domesday Book** (1086) a national survey of land-holdings, buildings and population (total : 1 000 000 of whom approximately 8 000 were Norman) for taxation purposes
1199-1216	Reign of **John** (Lackland): Normandy is ceded to the French, the Channel Islanders remain loyal to the English Crown in exchange for special privileges (1204); **Magna Carta** imposed by the Barons (1215)
1220-1266	Building of Salisbury Cathedral
1337-1485	The Hundred Years War
1337	Edward the Black Prince made 1st Duke of Cornwall by Edward III
1348-1350	**Black Death** – population reduced by half
1362	French replaced by English as the official language in courts of law

Tudors

1485-1509	**Henry VII**
1492	Discovery of America by Christopher Columbus
1497	Discovery of Nova Scotia and Newfoundland by John Cabot who sailed from Bristol
1498	Advance by Perkin Warbeck, accepted by Yorkists as the real Richard IV, brother of the murdered Edward V, on Exeter and Taunton (executed 1499)

1509-1547	**Henry VIII**: inventory by Thomas Cromwell of all monastic property (1535)
1536-1539	**Dissolution of the Monasteries**; construction of forts along the south coast
1547-1553	**Edward VI**: the "reign" of Edward Seymour, Protector Somerset (executed 1552)
1549	Cranmer's Book of Common Prayer published in English; Prayer Book Revolt in Cornwall
1558-1603	**Elizabeth I**: Age of the Navigators – Sir John Hawkins (1532-1595), Sir Humphrey Gilbert (1537-1583), Sir Francis Drake (c1540-1596), Sir Walter Raleigh (1552-1618)
1577-1580	Circumnavigation of the Globe by Drake in the *Golden Hinde*
1588	Defeat of the Spanish Armada
1600	Foundation of the East India Company (monopoly ended 1813)

Sir Francis Drake, Plymouth

B. Kaufmann

Stuarts and the Commonwealth

1603-1625	**James I**: Authorised Version of the Bible (1611)
1620	Pilgrim Fathers set sail for America
1625-1649	**Charles I**
1642-1645	Civil War. Escape of the future Charles II through the West Country to the Isles of Scilly, and eventually to the Continent, following Cromwell's victory at Naseby (1645)
1649-1660	Trial and execution of Charles I; abolition of the monarchy, establishment of the **Commonwealth**
1651	Escape by Charles II, again via the West Country, to France, following defeat at the Battle of Worcester
1660-1685	**Charles II**: Restoration of the monarchy. Test Act passed: exclusion of Nonconformists and Catholics from civil office (1673: repealed 1828)
1685-1688	**James II**
1685	Monmouth Rebellion: **Battle of Sedgemoor**; Bloody Assizes
1688	Landing of William of Orange (future William III, 1689-1702) at Brixham
1702-1714	**Queen Anne**: Union of England and Scotland (1707)

Houses of Hanover and Windsor

18C	War in Europe (Austrian Succession; Seven Years), in North America and India
1714-1727	**George I**
1727-1760	**George II**
1760-1820	**George III**: conquest of Canada (1760); union of England and Ireland (1800)
1769	First voyage to Australia by Captain Cook
1775-1783	War of American Independence
1793-1815	French Revolutionary and Napoleonic Wars: blockades at sea of France, England and America by England and France: Battle of Trafalgar (1805)
1807	Abolition of the slave trade in British possessions (effectively ended 1833)
19C	**The Industrial Revolution**: migration of industry to the coal-rich areas of the North and Midlands; decline of wool and fishing industries and of tin-mining in the West Country
1807	Completion of the Kennet and Avon Canal linking London to Bristol
1812-1814	Anglo-American War (US revolt against sea-blockade)
1820-1830	**George IV**: Reform Act (1832, final act 1928)

1833	**I K Brunel** appointed engineer to the Great Western Railway
1834	Grand National Consolidated Trades Union launched by Robert Owen; Tolpuddle Martyrs
1837-1901	**Queen Victoria**: advent of the internal combustion engine; coaches and cars. Growth of tourism.
1853-1859	Construction of the Royal Albert Bridge over the River Tamar at Saltash
1914-1918	First World War
1939-1945	Second World War: German occupation of the Channel Islands
1952	**Queen Elizabeth II**
1973	Tate St Ives opened
1984	Collapse of the Tin Exchange pre-empting the end of tin mining in Cornwall
1987	Duchy leases untenanted land to the Isles of Scilly Environmental Trust
1997	Dissolution of Avon and the creation of Unitary Authorities for Bristol, Bath and Northeast Somerset, Northwest Somerset and South Gloucestershire
1998	Automation of all lighthouses in Britain
1999	Monday 11 August, 11.11am: total solar eclipse with the central line passing through St Just, near Land's End, to Falmouth.

New for the millennium

At a time when sustainability and eco-tourism are considered to be important issues, it is of interest to acknowledge several major projects, presently under way, that will enhance future facilities in the West Country.

Bath Spa – A new spa complex is intended to incorporate the historic Cross Bath, Royal Hot Bath and Helting Pump Room in the centre of the town, with a new building on the site of the disused municipal swimming baths. Taking the waters, as described in the neighbouring Pump Room and Roman Baths, is therefore to be given a more modern interpretation.

Bristol 2000 – This is intended to regenerate a derelict site beside the Floating Harbour. The complex is to accommodate a range of state-of-the-art facilities that include a centre for the performing arts and one dedicated to promoting awareness, research and education in science (Science World) and in the conservation of the natural world (Wildscreen).

It is hoped that the new area will become the hub of Bristol. A pedestrian bridge will link the quays and the docks will become the focus of a variety of water-based, boat-related activities.

Eden Project – A 34-acre (15 hectare) abandoned china clay pit near St Austell is scheduled to be transformed into temperate parkland and the most ambitious plant-house to date. This will comprise a series of three biomes that have been designed to provide controlled environments for broad selections of related plant species typical of three climates: humid tropics (tropical rainforest), semi-arid tropics (desert) and temperate (Mediterranean). The massive scale of the enterprise is justified by the scientific research associated with it and the objectives behind its inception. For, faced with the issues of land use in the new millennium, this project aims to highlight the international problem regarding the stewardship of natural habitats and indigenous species in the face of increased pressure to produce enough food to sustain the world's growing population. In short, to research and study man's dependence on plants.

The construction of the biomes – 60m tall and almost 1km in length – is intended to be environmentally friendly using the most modern and, where ever possible, recyclable materials. The architects for the Eden Project are Nicholas Grimshaw & Partners of London. It is intended that the Visitor Centre should open in April 1999 and the biomes be fully operational in April 2000.

St Helier Waterfront – The States of Jersey are committed to developing tourism alongside the island's infrastructure. Ongoing work is providing a modern marina, landscaped gardens graced with sculpture and fountains, cafés, restaurants, conference hotel and leisure complex.

The land

Dating from when kingdoms were considered to be the personal property of a king or chieftain, grants of land were endowed as rewards to favourites, be they secular or episcopal. But soon after coming to the throne in 1042 Edward the Confessor decreed that all royal lands that had been assigned by his forerunners to the Saxon nobility should be returned to the Crown. His successor William I, therefore, owned extensive properties: while retaining very considerable territories, notably the royal chases or forests, he gave great swathes, particularly on the borders of the kingdom, to his half-brothers (including Robert of Mortain, first Earl of Cornwall) and his barons (like the de Redvers, appointed sheriffs and subsequently created the first Earls of Devon). They, in turn, built motte and bailey castles to defend their, and the Conqueror's, land against the Celts and Continental invaders. Other estates were donated to the Church for the foundation of new monasteries which, by their preaching and care of the poor would further the pacification of the kingdom, by their clearance of scrubland, draining of marshlands, farming and animal husbandry, would increase its wealth. Several of these institutions subsequently became dependent houses of existing communities in France as with the Benedictine-owned St Michael's Mount.

By the 14C Edward III considered that the Church should be restrained and passed a statute of mortmain. The Hundred Years War had begun (1327-1453) and although Henry IV rejected a parliamentary petition to disendow the Church, he fined monasteries with overseas connections; his heir, Henry V, under the **Alienation Act** forced all religious houses to sever links with the Continent. The Church, which had reached a peak of learning and husbandry in the 13C-14C, declined: community numbers, decimated as with the national population by the Black Death in 1348-50, never regained their size or energy. The land remained in the Church's possession but fell into neglect.

Dissolution of the Monasteries – Henry VIII, encouraged by Wolsey in the early years of his reign, began by dis-establishing the monastic houses with less than five members; Thomas Cromwell made his inventory. Ambitious and the land-hungry councillors urged further action and Henry, who was by this time (1535) in dispute with the pope over his divorce from Catherine of Aragon and subsequent marriage to Anne Boleyn in 1533, demanded that all churchmen take the Oath of Supremacy, acknowledging him as head of the Church in place of the pope. Their objections were finally silenced when he decreed the **Dissolution**. Over 800 religious houses were dissolved (1536-39), the monarch confiscated treasures for his own coffers and caused a major redistribution of land throughout the realm.

Land formerly held in mortmain or in perpetuity as a possession of the Church returned to the hazards of private ownership, and thereby subjected to division, exchange, sale and, for many centuries, royal attainder. Prosperous Tudor merchants, venturers, newly ennobled second sons were able to purchase tracts of land; those with estates extended them or purchased property in other parts of the country.

So much was available – estimated at one third of the total acreage of the kingdom – that prices were not exorbitant. Commissioners were appointed for each area and sales continued into the latter part of Elizabeth's reign. One condition of sale stated that if the abbey church was not required by the parish (as at Sherborne or Stogursey) it should be razed (as at Glastonbury and Abbotsbury); if the church was preserved then dependent monastic buildings must be obliterated. Either way the new owner frequently found himself the possessor not only of his land but of a quantity of ready dressed stone, ideally suited to constructing a mansion to rival those already in existence listed in Domesday at the Conquest. In many cases, it is a combination of these medieval and 16C elegant residences that make up England's unique heritage of historic houses.

In the West Country, manorial houses tended to be built without fortifications; where towers, crenellations and gatehouses were incorporated, there were also large mullioned windows. The four areas to be exceptions to the generalisation are those within the estates owned by the Duchy of Cornwall where, by definition, there are no "big" houses although there are many farmhouses notably around Bodmin Moor, Dartmoor and Exmoor.

"The history of the change from medieval to modern England" G M Trevelyan wrote, "might well be written in the form of a social history of the cloth trade".

The starting point of that trade was the Black Death: although there had been sheep in Britain since prehistoric times, and Stone and Iron Age men had woven wool into cloth, the Normans improved breeds so as to give better wool which was spun and woven for the home market, and traded in its raw state. In the 1350s, after the plague had ravaged the population, there was insufficient manpower to till the fields, harvest the crops and tend cattle; those freemen who survived put a premium on their labour and villeins demanded their freedom, and so farmers turned to the labour-saving practice of sheep-farming. Soon almost every village in Wiltshire, Dorset and Somerset appeared to have its regular sheep market and annual wool fair where fleeces would be sold. Notable among the early successful farmers were the Cistercian monks of Norton-St-Philip priory which, like others, developed long-term trade arrangements for the export of fleeces to sister houses on the Continent.

Although by comparison with today's breeds the sheep were small and many died or were killed for want of winter feed, flocks numbered many hundreds and the national total many million. The fleeces, more abundant but coarser on the large, valley stock, were lighter and finer on the upland sheep weighing between 3-6lbs as against today's 8-20lbs and even 40lbs. English native cloth remained coarse-woven until the 14C when Edward III brought in Flemish Huguenot weavers, fullers and dyers who gave a new impetus to the industry. Every cottage came to have its spinning wheel and, in some cases, handlooms; cottages were adapted with wide windows for weaving. Fulling mills became common wherever there was water; village greens and fields became quartered with the hooked tenter frames on which cloth was stretched and dried.

By the end of the 14C 5 000 pieces of cloth were being exported annually from England to the Continent in addition to raw wool; by the late 16C the number was 100 000 pieces. By the 15C-16C the wool industry had grown to such an extent that new merchant guilds – the staplers and clothiers – were formed to control the raw wool and cloth-weaving traders. As wool replaced corn as the most important crop in farming, the government began negotiating sales of wool abroad (as with the **Methuen Treaty** of 1703 with Portugal). When raw wool was prohibited from export in order to maintain supplies for home weavers, it was smuggled out on a vast scale; the prohibition was eventually repealed in 1824. In the 17C as a further protection of the industry, parliament passed acts to lessen the import of linen by decreeing that "no material (ie a shroud) unless made entirely of sheep's wool be allowed to be put in a coffin" under penalty of a £5 fine.

Evidence of this long period of considerable prosperity in the West Country appears in the construction of terraced cottages for outworkers (as at Bradford on Avon), and in the embellishment of parish churches in Somerset. The industry that Daniel Defoe in the 18C constantly refers to in his *Tour through the Whole Island of Great Britain* and describes as "the richest and most valuable manufacture in the world" continued as the mainstay of the West Country until textile fashions changed and processes were altered by the coming of the Industrial Revolution in the 19C.

MINING

In the Devonian Period (400 million years ago), the land mass now known as Cornwall lay south of the Equator, in the tropics. Here, fine sediments of sand and mud were deposited on the floor of a sea which was then compressed against the rest of Britain as the tectonic plate comprising southern Europe and Africa moved north. Extreme temperatures transformed the layers of mud into slate; this was folded and faulted by pressure,

St Just Tin Miners by Harold Harvey (1935)

allowing molten rock to break through the crust and harden to form outcrops of granite and serpentine. Trapped water, heated in the process helped form veins of metallic deposits and china clay. Submerged once more by the sea, the land mass was eroded into a new form, rising in stages thereafter.

Cornwall was at one time the most important non-ferrous metal mining county in Britain, responsible for large-scale extraction of tin, arsenic and copper, but also for such minerals as lead, silver, tungsten, zinc, nickel, cobalt, bismuth, antimony, uranium, iron, manganese, pyrite (for sulphur) and fluorspar – extensive collections of specimens are to be seen at the Royal Cornwall Museum (Truro), Camborne School of Mines (Redruth) and Cornwall Geological Museum (Penzance). By 1900, certainly by the outbreak of World War I, the industry had collapsed and almost two thirds of the mining population had emigrated.

Tin (Sn) – This is a highly stable soft base metal: its malleable properties allow it to be easily extruded, drawn, stamped and spun; its ductile qualities are exploited in alloys such as bronze, pewter, Britannia metal and solder (20-80% tin and lead); its stability as a base metal makes it ideal for plating iron to prevent corrosion, for use in distillation equipment and for processing alkali substances where aluminium or lead are impractical; it is also an important component of opaque pottery glazes.

Cornish reserves almost certainly began to be exploited in late prehistory: Diodorus Siculus, the 1C BC Greek historian, wrote that the Cornish "work the tin into pieces the form of knuckle-bones and convey it to an island which lies off Britain and is called Ictis... the merchants purchase the tin of the natives and carry it from there across the Straits of Gaul" to Greece, Rome or Egypt, thereby affirming that trade with the Mediterranean basin existed well before Julius Caesar's invasion of Britain. Initially, the lodes were released by erosion of the parent lodes on the uplands of Bodmin Moor, Dartmoor, west Penwith and Carnmenellis, and would have been easily collected by streaming, the hydraulic mining of tin gravels from beneath riverbeds; this "clean" or nearly pure deposit was then smelted with charcoal. Production was local and with tin so important, by the early Middle Ages the "streamers" or miners had acquired rights and privileges including special courts and a local parliament in four **stannary** or coinage towns chartered by King John – Truro, Helston, Liskeard and Lostwithiel (to which Penzance was added in 1663). The Stannary or Tinners' Parliament convened regularly at Lostwithiel until 1752, regulating the activities of the tinners who were exempt from many laws and most taxes. In the 14C the earldom of Cornwall was made into a duchy and granted to the Prince of Wales (the monarch's eldest son), providing him with a substantial revenue levied from "coinage duty" which in simple terms was a tax on tin. The courts sat, ingots were assayed: as a corner (or coign – hence Coinagehall Street in Helston) was cut off each block it was stamped with the Duchy seal.

As supplies became scarce, the metal was sought from the bedrock, requiring ever deeper excavation with ever increasing problems of drainage. The advent of steam power in the 18C facilitated digging to 3300ft at Dolcoath near Camborne in the late 19C. At the height of the industry (1860s) there were some 600 coal-powered pumping steam-engines in operation within Cornwall; when copper production collapsed, tin (found below the copper) briefly sustained the mining industry.

Decline – At the end of the 19C, the tide turned again: recession spread from America to Europe; new and more accessible deposits were discovered in every continent; prices fell; the mines closed; more than 30% of the miners and their families emigrated until it was said that at the bottom of every hole the world over you would find a Cornish miner. In the 20C tin mining revived until the collapse of the market in 1986. Relics of the old mines, in the form of disused engine houses and sentinel stacks, romantically mark the hills along the north coast and even Cape Cornwall.

Copper (Cu) – Copper-mining technology was adapted from that used for extracting tin, but unlike tin which was largely processed at the mine, copper ore had to be

Pascoe's Whim Engine, South Wheal Frances

transported to smelters in its rough state. This necessitated, in the first half of the 19C, investment in tramways and later railways to take the ore to new ports such as Hale, Portreath and Calstock in Cornwall and Morwelham in Devon. As the Industrial Revolution gathered pace so the demand for copper rocketed. British men o' war were "copper bottomed" to prevent parasites and barnacles attacking the hulls and to increase their speed. A new gentry (the so-called "Mineral Lords") emerged having grown wealthy on mineral royalties, mine dividends, smelting profits and transport dues by rail and sea. In turn Cornish foundries produced the largest steam engines worldwide; soon more steam-pumping engines were employed on Cornish mines than anywhere else.

This investment and subsequent technology assured Cornwall's industrial economy at a time when income from fishing and agriculture dwindled. In Cornwall, 340 mines employed 50 000 men, women and children: one in five of the population. The women and children's job was to crush the mined ore with hammers and pick it over. It has been estimated that, in the 19C, Cornish mining was the unhealthiest occupation in Britain: deaths from accidents and lung diseases were three times higher than among coal miners. 30 million tons of ore were mined in the period of a hundred years, producing 1.5 million tons (5%) of pure copper (smelted with coal in Wales). The peak price reached was £100 a ton. Meanwhile, Cornwall became the greatest single producer of copper in the world.

Winston Graham's novel *Ross Poldark* (later made into a television drama) sets the scene in a mining community, painting a bleak picture of poverty versus wealth.

China-clay – Mining around St Austell, by comparison, is a 19C industry that continues to thrive. Hugely profitable, it has marked the local landscape with green-white slag pyramids and is now Cornwall's economic mainstay.

INDUSTRIALISATION

The 19C witnessed a radical change in working practices. Mechanisation in the textile industry put an end to cottage industry and prompted a boom in large-scale manufacturing. Improved engineering, sponsored largely by private enterprise, revolutionised conditions in the mines and founded a viable transport system. Large fortunes were made and invested in better education, health, housing and social reform at home, propagating an affluent middle class; abroad, military prowess and private banking were underpinning an ever larger Empire and an ever more sophisticated trading network. The two figures who undoubtedly made the greatest impact on the West Country were Richard Trevithick and Isambard Kingdom Brunel, who spanned just two generations.

Richard Trevithick (1771-1833) – It is no surprise that the earliest invention of the Cornish-born son of a mine manager was an improved plunger pole pump (1797) for deep mining, the principles of which he used to build a water-pressure engine. The inventive engineer's next projects involved a working high-pressure non-condensing steam-engine (1800) that was to rival Watt's low-pressure steam-vacuum engine: technology which allowed considerable improvements to be made in the general working conditions in the mines, facilitating output and powering more efficient transport for mineral ore in Cornwall and coal in Wales and the Midlands.

Trevithick's interest in **steam locomotion** prompted in 1801 the first common road passenger-carrying locomotive to be built; on 24 March 1802 he, in association with Andrew Vivian, applied for a patent for steam-engines in propelling carriages, and launched a public service in London. In 1808 he constructed a circular railway from Euston Square, running at some 12-15mph round curves of 50ft or 100ft radius. Meanwhile he managed a team of Cornish miners engaged to tunnel under the Thames between Rotherhithe and Limehouse: when forced to abandon this ambitious scheme by a massive breach in the workings, the civil engineer suggested excavating a ditch along the river bed capable of accommodating a giant **cast-iron pipeline**, laid in sections to provide a tunnel – a far-sighted proposal that was eventually adopted by the Americans for the Detroit River and San Francisco Harbour tunnels. His expertise in the properties of iron also proposed its use in ship-building: ideas that were to influence the future generations of steam-boats.

The Trevithick Trust

Cornwall, besides exporting its valuable minerals, has provided highly-skilled miners to countries worldwide: to maintain the industrial heritage that formed these men, the Trevithick Trust has been set up "to identify, preserve, protect, manage and interpret... whatever the historical, architectural and engineering heritage...". It is named after **Richard Trevithick** (1771-1833), a key figure in the development of steam powered railway locomotives, road carriages and beam engines, many of which were built in Cornwall at Hayle. These same "Cornish engines" were also adapted to pump water and sewage, and to drain Holland's polders.

Meanwhile, Trevithick continued to pioneer the application of his **high-pressure engines** in boring and breaking rock, heavy dredging and in agricultural machinery – constructing a steam-driven threshing machine at Trewithen in 1812. In 1814 he became engaged in a contract to design engines for use in the mines of Peru, emigrating there in 1816 before travelling on to Costa Rica and home in 1827. Having unsuccessfully petitioned Parliament for some financial recompense for his inventions, Trevithick died penniless at Dartford in 1833.

Isambard Kingdom Brunel (1806-59) – To appreciate just how Brunel came to epitomise the spirit of the age, it may be appropriate to describe how his father, Sir Marc Isambard Brunel (1769-1849) came to be so versatile an engineer and inventor. The elder Brunel, born in Normandy, was forced to flee Revolutionary France because of his staunch loyalty to the *ancien régime*. He emigrated to New York, where he gained valuable experience working on a projected canal linking the Hudson River to Lake Chaplain; in 1799 he sailed to Falmouth intent on presenting the British Government with designs that were to radically improve methods of ship-building in the naval dockyards (particularly useful given the pending threat of Napoleon). Subsequent inventions included a round stocking frame or *tricoteur* patented in 1816, machines for winding cotton thread into balls or for duplicating drawings, others for mass-producing nails, preparing tinfoil and for improving stereotype plates in printing; ambitious engineering projects involved steam navigation on the Thames, large span bridges (built at Rouen and St Petersburg), swing bridges and floating landing stages (implemented at the Port of Liverpool). The most important was the first Thames tunnel (1824-43) to be completed between Rotherhithe and Wapping, a feat accomplished by father and son following the attempts thwarted by flooding and quicksand of the Cornish engineers Robert Vazie (1802) and Richard Trevithick.

The younger Brunel was born in Portsmouth, partly educated in Paris (Collège Henri IV) and apprenticed to his father's drawing office from 1823 when plans were being drafted for the Thames tunnel. Here, the brilliant engineer learnt disappointment and failure at first hand in experiences that were to be validated later when called upon to prepare meticulous plans for subsequent projects and strengthen his resolve to succeed. Physical exhaustion accrued during work on the tunnel coupled with stress incurred by financial insecurity eventually led to his collapse; he went to Bristol to recuperate and there became interested in the problems of the constricted shipping lanes and plans for a floating harbour, agreed in 1833 (expertise he was to apply at Monkwearmouth, Plymouth, Brentford and Milford Haven).

Great Western Railway – In March 1833 Brunel, then aged 27, was appointed Principle Engineer to the newly formed Great Western Railway with the specific task of opening a fast and direct line between Bristol and London. Convinced that the standard 4ft 8.5inch gauge developed by George Stephenson for the northern colliery tramways would restrict future development, Brunel eventually persuaded the GWR Board to sanction his use of a 7ft gauge which would allow for spacious, comfortable carriages carrying more commuter traffic (and therefore earning more revenue); he designed a series of distinctive, far-sighted, signals, notably the disc and crossbar. Construction began in 1835: it took eight years to lay 118 miles of track; five years to excavate the 2-mile long Box Tunnel between the Avon valley and the Cotswolds. He designed Temple Meads Station – which became the GWR headquarters in 1840 – and collaborated with the architects of Paddington Station. This terminus, which Betjeman described in the days when today's concrete concourse was laid out as a garden as "a conservatory in a railway cutting", Brunel insisted should be fronted with the first great railway hotel. The first steam locomotive completed its journey between London and Bristol, in 1843. By 1878 the company had incorporated into its network the Bristol and Exeter, South Devon and Cornwall railways, thereby giving it control of all the lines with the broad-gauge track west of Bristol; soon followed moves to extend the network into South Wales, the West Midlands and Birkenhead.

Until the advent of the GWR the West Country was relatively inaccessible except by stage coach, a dangerous mode of travel in the days when coaches were vulnerable to attack by highwaymen. Built largely by a private consortium, the Great Western was designed for speed and comfort if it was to compete with stage coaches: by chance, the deal with a local entrepreneur in **Swindon** to provide refreshment facilities for passengers while engines were changed and refuelled for their onward journeys led to the station becoming the line's principle maintenance depot; soon it had become the main engineering works of the railway employing some 10 000 men, the greatest industrial site in Wiltshire. Meanwhile, the network was extended into Devon, Cornwall, South Wales, West Midlands and Birkenhead. Alas in 1892, the GWR broad gauge was replaced by the more common narrow gauge, after a long and bitter campaign; in 1935 the GWR, nicknamed the "The Holiday Line", celebrated its centenary with the launch of the Cornish Riviera Express with engines and coaches built in Swindon to the highest specifications. These works closed in 1986.

Bridges – When a competition to design a bridge that could span the Avon Gorge was launched in 1831, Brunel was already familiar with the site; his bold Egyptian-style design for the **Clifton Suspension Bridge** was chosen and although

23

altered, was completed posthumously in 1864. Other major suspension bridges built to designs by Brunel include the old Hungerford Bridge (1841-45: displaced in 1862 by the present Charing Cross railway bridge), and the **Royal Albert Bridge** across River Tamar at Saltash which was Brunel's last and greatest railway project (1853-59).

Shipping – As early as October 1835 Brunel suggested to the GWR board that they should extend the London – Bristol railway with a Bristol – New York trans-Atlantic service. The **Great Western** steamship was duly built in Bristol (1838) – the first steamship to run a regular service; she was followed by the **Great Britain**, the largest ship afloat at the time and the first large iron-hull steamship to be driven by a screw propeller, sailing for New York out of Liverpool in 1845. Emboldened by success, Brunel reviewed his conception of a real "great ship", and began work on the **Great Eastern** which was eventually launched on 31 January 1858: alas, Brunel collapsed exhausted days before she put to sea on her maiden voyage on 7 September 1859.

Steam railways

Today, there are several steam engines, on both broad-gauge and narrow-gauge tracks, which have been rescued from extinction by dedicated enthusiasts keen to preserve what some consider to be the very best in mechanical engineering. Painstaking efforts to conserve and restore the smart livery of locomotives and their sometimes luxurious passenger carriages recapture with nostalgia the spirit of a more romantic age of travel. The distinctive smell of steam and the evocative sounds made by the trains are always specially popular with children. Those with published timetables of events include the Bodmin and Wenford Railway and the West Somerset Railway – *see Index for additional information*. The annually-held Great Dorset Steam Fair takes place at Tarrant Hinton (near Blandford) in August.

The sea

TRADE

Trade through itinerant merchants walking the Ridgeway Path, Phoenicians and Mediterranean peoples shipping tin and copper from Cornwall, the Romans transporting lead from the Mendips to Pompeii, was transformed in the 16C-17C by the discoveries of the navigators, the spirit of commercial adventure: "our chiefe desire", Richard Hakluyt the geographer (1552?-1616) declared, is "to find out ample vent of our wollen cloth, the naturall comoditie of this our Realme". He went on to propose the opening of new markets in Japan, north China and Tartary. In the early days boats were small and had only a shallow draft enabling coasters and cross-Channel craft to go far upriver to Exeter, Topsham, Bridgwater; as ships increased in size estuary harbours came into their own and finally the deepwater harbours of Plymouth and Fowey, and Bristol where a constant water level was ensured by the construction of the Floating Harbour in the 19C.

Bristol became the second city in England after London but even so handled only 10% of the national trade (the figure for London until the second half of the 20C was always over 50%). Hampered by the smallness of the local population and the lack of local communications – transport was by pack-horse and cart – the West Country sought to improve facilities with the construction of canals.

These were almost immediately overtaken by the steam railway, but meanwhile the woollen cloth industry had been first mechanised and then removed to the Midlands and North, for which the local port was Liverpool.

THE NAVIGATORS

In the 16C Britain "shifted" from being on the outer edge of navigational charts to being at the centre. When the caravan routes to the Orient, opened up by Marco Polo in the 13C, were suddenly closed, the Venetian Empire and the Mediterranean powers ceased to be at the hub of east-west trade.

The navigators of the Atlantic seaboard, particularly the Portuguese, who were encouraged and guided by Prince Henry the Navigator, and the Genoese, who were financed by Venice and Spain, set out to find a route to the east round Africa; the prize was gold, jewels, silks and the costly spices so much in demand at home to give flavour to poorly preserved or even rotten meat.

Ports on the **Atlantic seaboard**, Lisbon especially, and later Bristol and Plymouth, assumed importance; Madeira and the Azores were discovered; the Portuguese, Bartolemeu Dias rounded the Cape of Good Hope (1488) and Vasco da Gama reached Calicut in southern India (1498); in 1492 Christopher Columbus, a Genoese under

The *Matthew* under sail

the patronage of Ferdinand and Isabella of Castile, set out westwards and discovered **America.** The following year in 1493, under the Treaty of Tordesillas, the pope divided the discovered and the yet to be discovered world between Spain and Portugal along a meridian which, in the event, cuts through eastern Brazil.

John Cabot, a Genoese settled in Bristol, set out westward with his sons in 1497 under letters of patent from Henry VII – all voyages were licensed by the monarch. Cabot sailed in search of the Northwest Passage and discovered Nova Scotia and Newfoundland.

In the 16C Magellan threaded the strait which bears his name (1520), and his ship – he died on the voyage – circumnavigated the world. In the same age, rivalry between the European nations – England and Spain in particular – grew and exploded. The great exploring, trading, warring **English mariners** were mostly Devon men: John Hawkins, Martin Frobisher (c1535-94), Humphrey Gilbert, Francis Drake, Richard Grenville (1541?-1591), Walter Raleigh... There followed two centuries later the Yorkshireman, James Cook, circumnavigator, surveyor and Pacific cartographer (1728-79).

Funds to support the quest of the unknown, the driving force of every navigator, were obtained by patronage and trade – the first often based on the promise of

---

John Cabot

Giovanni (or Zuan) Caboto – the epithet for a coastal seaman – was granted Venetian citizenship in 1476 having successfully established himself, it appears, as a wealthy merchant trading in spices, silks and dyes from the Arab world by venturing into Muslim territories disguised as a pilgrim to Mecca. Between 1482-84 he married Mattea who proceeded to provide him with at least three sons. Records from c1480 confirm the family as being in Valencia (Spain); here "Juan Caboto Montecalunya, the Venetian" earned a reputation as a cartographer and became known as an ambitious navigator who was keen to cross the Atlantic and reach Cathay, the exotic land described by Marco Polo. Sometime between 1493-95, after Columbus' return from what he presumed to be Japan but in fact were the West Indies, Cabot moved his family to Bristol in the hope of persuading English investors to sponsor his attempts to reach Asia and claim valuable territories for the Crown. Contemporary registers list several ships sailing from Bristol with the sole intent of prospecting hitherto uncharted lands like the Isle of Brasil and the Seven Cities, or to seek additional fishing stocks. Cabot's most famous endeavour was on the *Matthew*, a small ship of 50 tons named after his wife it would seem, and manned by a crew of 18. They set sail on 2 May 1497, reached "New Founde Landes" on 24 June and returned to Bristol on 6 August. The following year, attempting a repeat voyage, Cabot perished. To honour the occasion, on 2 May 1997 a modern replica of the Matthew, built at Redcliffe Quay in Bristol, set sail for Bonavista.

the latter. Christopher Columbus sought financial support for years before he was able to set sail; Queen Elizabeth was far from open-handed in support of Drake's ventures; Raleigh was executed for not finding El Dorado.

Already by the 17C the **East India Company** (chartered in 1600), the earlier **Muscovy** and **Turkey** or **Levant Companies** (mid-16C) were in being, and the **Merchant Venturers of Bristol** incorporated (1552); the Hudson's Bay Company was chartered by Charles II in 1670. First raw wool was exported, then cloth; hides, tallow and linen were imported from Ireland; salt from Brittany; wine and brandy from Gascony, also wax, wood, iron and honey; from Spain and Portugal came olive oil, figs, iron and wine. Then after the discovery of the New World, Africa and the Orient, new commodities were traded, namely sugar, tobacco, fish, cotton, cocoa (for drinking chocolate), tea and coffee. Trading posts were established in distant lands – the maxim being "trade follows the flag".

PRIVATEERS AND LETTERS OF MARQUE

A code of practice dating back to the 13C, operated on broadly similar lines by which England, France, Spain, Portugal and Holland took turns to reign supreme: during this period, privately-owned merchant ships under **letters of marque** were licensed to "annoy" the sovereign's enemies of a named nationality in time of war. If war had not been officially declared, ships attacked in recompense for or on the pretext of previously suffered injury and loss under **letters of reprisal.**

Letters in England were originally issued by the monarch, later they were sold to ships' owners by the Lord High Admiral. The rules of this licensed piracy were strict and £3 000 bond had to be left as surety that they would be obeyed. The Admiralty, which judged the value, took 10% of every prize; customs duty (5%) was paid on all cargo captured which, in theory, had to be brought in as captured; two thirds of the remainder were then divided among the ship's promoters and the final third amongst the crew who relied on this "purchase" or booty together with "pillage" of the valuables not forming part of the cargo, as their pay. Under this system Queen Elizabeth, without acknowledgement or expense, was able to ensure almost perpetual harassment of Spanish shipping.

The Spanish galleons were tall and clumsy; the British merchant ships or barques were at first between 50 and 100 tons with crews of 40 to furnish boarding parties and men to sail prizes home. By an Order in Council of 1695 the ships were required to be of not less than 200 tons and 20 guns; half the crew had to be "landmen" so as not to attract sailors, often then impressed, from the navy.

Many owners, masters who sailed the ships, captains who controlled the crews including the lawless boarders, lost all, even their lives in this adventuring; others made sufficient; many turned to cut-throat piracy, for which the penalty, if caught, was death. Drake and several of his contemporaries made fortunes on the Spanish Main and off the shores of Spain capturing the treasure ships which returned home each summer from South America, laden with the treasure of the Incas, gold, silver, precious stones and rich cargoes. Queen Elizabeth's coffers were filled.

Prizes from those times still to be seen in the region include the rose-silk damask furnishings in the drawing room at Pencarrow, the head of Christ in Golant Church, the pillars in the manor house at Bickleigh Castle in Devon, Sharpham House overlooking the River Dart, Tregothnan House overlooking the River Fal built with prize money in the 18C... On a more modest scale are the half-timbered merchants' houses near the quayside in the Barbican in Plymouth – the Elizabethan House and its neighbour – and the district to the rear, erected by speculative builders of the time for returned sea-captains.

PIRATES AND PIRACY

Pirates, 15C-18C highway robbers of the sea, owed allegiance to no one. All men's hands were against them and they were against all men. The crewmen would sign on and, in lieu of wages, receive a specified share of any prize captured. Hard and brutal, each was in it for the adventure and the loot. They plun-

Ship figurehead, Tresco

dered any ship they could overcome in home waters and, when these were too well patrolled, they sailed to the waters around the West Indies and off the North American coast.

Booty was sold to Spanish, French and English colonists, who, in theory, were obliged to trade only with their countries of origin; countless island and mainland creeks became pirates' lairs.

The 15C-16C **Fowey Gallants**, with their raids on the coasts of France and Spain, although sometimes referred to as pirates, were of an altogether different breed, as were the men of Devon who set out to avenge the Plymouth raid by Bretons in 1403, the Cornishmen who sought vengeance on the Spaniards who had burned Marazion – all were land-based groups, pirates for a day or a week only.

WRECKERS AND WRECKING

Wrecking, as every Cornishman, Devonian and coastal dweller will tell you hotly, has nothing to do with decoy lights and leading ships to their doom on the saw-toothed coastal rocks – nature alone has always seen to that. What would happen, and happens even now, is that a ship, seeking shelter from gale-force winds, would come too close in and get caught on underwater rocks or in a race or current, and break up. It has been estimated that, over the centuries, as many as 250 ships have been wrecked along each mile of cliff and cove of the British Isles: Lyme Bay was known as the Bay of 1 000 Wrecks; not for nothing are the Manacles so called... Warned by the watch, the villagers of old would gather in wait, all too often not to rescue the crew, but to seize the ship and her cargo, to loot everything and finally break up the hull until not a spar was left. The cargo of treasure and coin, timber, coal, satins and finery, the provisions, china and glass, the anchors, cordage and sails were regarded by all as a legitimate harvest of the sea, a bumper beach-combing.

SMUGGLERS AND SMUGGLING

In 1784 William Pitt the Younger calculated that 13 million pounds in weight of tea were consumed in Britain annually, 7.5million pounds of which were smuggled in order to avoid the exorbitant taxes imposed so as to finance defence of the realm. The "trade", as smuggling was known along the length of England's south coast, began in the early Middle Ages when customs dues were first levied on incoming and outgoing goods; it flourished from the 16C to the mid-19C, particularly in times of war, and ended when ships of the Royal Navy, freed from the centuries of intermittent war and coastal blockades against France, Spain and America, could patrol the coast in support of the coastguard cutters and small boats of the revenue or "preventive" men. Although everyone, particularly in Cornwall, was against the revenue men, it has been estimated that they succeeded in seizing the contraband of one in three venturers: where the boat was captured and the captain convicted – rarely in Devon or Cornwall – the hull would be sawn in three and sold for firewood together with her equipment and cargo.

The early "free traders" slipped across the Channel in 10-ton fishing smacks to take out raw wool and "bring in" brandy, wine, spices, fine silk and lace for local consumption; by the 19C 300-ton armed cutters were making 7 or 8 voyages a year carrying as much as 11 tons of tea and some 3 000 half-ankers of spirits a time (an anker or keg = 9.5gallon cask; the spirits were usually over proof and diluted on shore by the smugglers' wives). Goods were bespoke, and handling and distribution by pack-horse from the landing place in cove or harbour was conducted by a waiting team. Where necessary kegs would be weighted and dumped overboard to be collected when the coast was clear if not previously discovered by the preventive men. Contraband also came in through cargo ships, including the great tea-clippers. When a trading ship was sighted, pilot gigs manned by 8 oarsmen would race to her, the leading boat gaining the right to pilot her into harbour and handle her cargo, not all of which would pass through the custom house.

With the abolition of many duties and the lowering of many more – a policy instigated by the Younger Pitt as the best means of knocking the bottom out of the illicit trade – with the revolution in official, retail distribution and the different style of living, smuggling (apart from drugs) is now on a small scale: tobacco is imported not by the ton but in cartons, whisky is trans-shipped in bottles as is wine and brandy rather than in casks.

LIGHTHOUSES

There are around 80 lighthouses around the coast of England and Wales, 29 of them in the West Country. Since 1836, by Act of Parliament, lighthouses have been under the jurisdiction of **Trinity House**, a corporation of shipmen or mariners incorporated in 1514 as the regulating authority for pilots in British waters. In 1594 the Corporation acquired the rights of beaconage under which it marked navigational channels and erected waymarks.

Lighthouses, however, were constructed by individual venturers under patents granted by the Crown. The licensee, who was required to pay rent to the Crown, recouped his expenditure at the custom house by levying tolls on passing shipping.

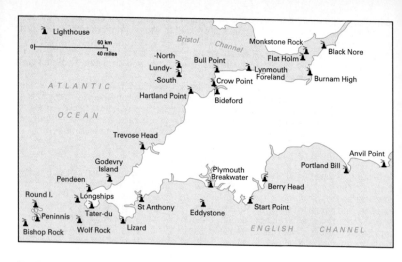

Flat Holm, built for £900 in the 18C with a nominal annual rent of £5-£10, charged 1.5*d* per ton to all Bristol ships; 3*d* to all foreign ships; 1*d* to coasters to or from Ireland; 1*s* to vessels from St David's Head or Land's End (market and fishing boats excepted). Shipping increased so colossally in the 18C and 19C that when Trinity House bought out the owners under the 19C Act, the lighthouse had become so profitable that the remaining 12-year lease cost the corporation £15 838 18*s* 10*d*. In some cases the necessity for a light and, therefore, toll rates was hotly contested by Merchant Venturers, shipmasters and Trinity House, and the granting of a building patent was delayed for years.

Other lights came into existence modestly and personally: the first **Burnham** light is said to have been a candle set in her window by a fisherman's wife; the sexton eventually took over with a light in St Andrew's church tower and in the 19C, the curate, when dues were fixed at 5*s* for British vessels, 10*s* for foreign and 3*s* for coasters. The short remainder lease was purchased in 1829 for £16 000.

Delays in construction were also due to vested interests. For many the ships, which were driven onto the rocks by the winter gales, were a source of rich plunder. Local opposition caused a 50 year delay before the first lighthouse was built on the **Lizard** in 1619.

Eddystone, the Wolf, Longships and the Bishop, standing out to sea, pinned to rocks surrounded by the Atlantic swell, each signal a triumph of engineering construction. The many gales resulted in the first **Bishop Rock** tower being washed away incomplete after two years' work and the second tower taking seven years to construct inside a coffer dam. The feat was accomplished finally by dressing, dovetailing and numbering each of the 1-2 ton blocks of granite before transporting it to the site; the foundations were re-secured, the base re-cased and the light raised to its present position of nearly 160ft above the waves in 1881. It was within a short distance of Bishop Rock that the British squadron returning from the Mediterranean under Admiral Sir Cloudesley Shovel in the *Association* was wrecked with the loss of 1 800 men on 22 October 1707 (the admiral, washed ashore alive, was murdered for his gold ring).

Construction of the **Wolf Rock** began in 1791 with the erection of a 20ft wrought-iron mast held by six stays and topped by a metal model of a wolf. It was immediately swept away. In 1835-39 an iron beacon was built: only 60 hours work could be accomplished in any year; finally in 1861-70 the present 116ft granite tower with walls 7ft 9in thick at the base was constructed and the light shown.

The **Eddystone** light originated as a wooden structure erected by Henry Winstanley, showman and shipowner, who had lost a vessel on the rocks. Problems with the site, the elements, labour, were capped when in 1697 a French privateer kidnapped Winstanley himself and took him across the Channel to Versailles. Louis XIV, however, ordered Winstanley's immediate return to Eddystone, with the words "France is at war with England, not humanity". In November 1698 the Eddystone light was lit for the first time and survived, with improvements, until the worst gale ever recorded in Britain swept away the tower and its designer in November 1703. By 1709 a new wooden tower with a lead roof and massive candelabrum, designed by a silk-merchant, was in operation. It endured for 49 years before it caught fire and burned for 5 days. Its replacement (1879-82) was built by **John Smeaton,** a Yorkshireman, who constructed a tower of dressed granite blocks, dovetailed on all four sides and secured by quick drying cement; the tower stood for 123 years before cracks appeared. The present lighthouse is a stalwart 167ft edifice. The top stage of the Smeaton Tower was subsequently re-erected by public subscription on Plymouth Hoe.

The Trinity House Lighthouse Service is funded, as were the individual light-houses originally, from dues levied on all shipping sailing to and from United Kingdom ports. All 348 are, since 1998, automated. The last rock lighthouse to be manned in the southern British Isles was **Les Hanois Lighthouse**, two miles off Guernsey, built in 1862 and now managed from Harwich – 105ft above water at high tide, its lamp has a range of 23 miles and a fog signal with a 3-mile range.

Eddystone Lighthouse

BIRDING IN THE WEST COUNTRY

Bird watching in the West Country can be highly rewarding given the broad range of habitats that attract residents and migrants alike: rocky crags offshore, fertile river estuaries, wetlands, reservoirs, rich farmland and bleak moorland. National parks, nature reserves, considerate land-owners like the Duchy of Cornwall, food-producers mindful of organic farming methods, together with the careful land management of coastal regions by the National Trust (Lundy, Brownsea Island) has encouraged wildlife to colonise and flourish.

Gannet *(Sula bassana)* – Britain plays host to a large proportion of the world's population of gannets or Solan geese, the largest and most spectacular seabird of the North Atlantic, with a wingspan of up to six feet (1.8m). It "nests" freely in large colonies on cliffs or steep slopes of small isolated islands so that the juveniles can throw themselves down to the sea when required, and embarks on its journey to the West African coast where it will spend a couple of summers before returning. Full maturity is reached at five or six years; mates are chosen for life which averages 20 years. The most endearing features of these powerful birds are their elegant white plumage with black wing tips and yellow nape, and their skill at fishing for mackerel and herring: "dropping" from 10ft (9m) at a speed of 30ft (100kph) to a depth of 60mph (3m). *Illustrated.*

Shag *(Phalacrocorax aristotelis)* – The shag, also known as the green cormorant, is distinguished most easily from the common cormorant by its tufted forehead during the breeding season. It is also more solitary than his taller (by 6 inches) and more timid white-bearded cousin the cormorant, which congregates in large colonies and seems mindless of its evil-smelling nest surrounded by putrefying discarded fish. Both birds often stand with wings folded outwards: this, it has been ascertained, may be to help digest food rather than merely to dry-out feathers after diving through deep water. *Illustrated.*

29

Razorbill *(Alca torda)* – The most distinctive feature of the razorbill is its wide beak with white stripes, otherwise it resembles its cousin the guillemot with its sleek black plumage and startlingly white breast; the black colouring extends up to the beak outside the breeding season, from August to March. The razorbill, one of the auk family is a social bird, happy to nest in colonies alongside guillemots and kittiwakes (a small dark-legged oceanic gull), ever prepared to dispute its territory with neighbours. They somewhat lack manoeuvrability in the air, but make up for it under water through which they are able to swim with wings half open: for this reason they are especially vulnerable to getting caught in fishing nets. *Illustrated.*

Puffin *(Fratercula arctica)* – Britain's most colourful seabird, the naturally inquisitive clown-faced sea-parrot is comical to watch often hopping about its burrow, which it might share in part with Manx shearwaters or feral rabbits (all of which fall prey to the rapacious great black-backed gull). Puffins return to their breeding colonies in March having wintered at sea and stay until mid-August. They lay one egg 3-6ft underground, or, more rarely, in crevices; they roost at sea, sleeping with the bill tucked up under the wing. The single chick sheds its down after three weeks, emerging from the burrow at night at four weeks; at five or six weeks the parents desert their offspring to fend for itself. The distinctive red, yellow and blue serrated bill is equipped with hooks which hold the fish as the bird swims underwater in a zigzag through a shoal, catching its prey in an alternate head to tail arrangement.

This particular member of the auk family was highly regarded for its meat in the Middle Ages (300 birds being paid to the Black Prince in lieu of rent by a tenant-farmer in Scilly in 1337) as it was classed as fish and therefore could be eaten during Lent. *Illustrated.*

Common Tern *(Sterna hirundo)* – Common terns, together with arctic (which migrates, miraculously, from pole to pole), Sandwich, little and black terns – known collectively as sea swallows – frequent most of the West Country coastline and flooded gravel pits. They arrive in April, a harbinger of spring like the swallow, and leave in October. These are particularly streamlined birds, white, with a forked tail and black capped head: distinguishing them from the arctic tern can be difficult, although if compared side by side, the arctic tern has a longer tail, shorter head and bill. These engaging birds penetrate the water with wings outstretched, hence the splash, unlike the gannet which will fold back its wings into a more streamlined profile. *Illustrated.*

Northern Fulmar *(Fulmarus glacialis)* – The large gull-like petrel has a silver-grey back plumage, striking white head and short curved beak (tube-nosed); it is most readily distinguished from the larger herring gull when in flight for it flies stiff-winged like its cousins the shearwater and petrel, literally shearing the surface of the sea. Other peculiar behaviour includes its spitting a foul-smelling oily substance when threatened and its guttural growling, chuckling and grunting when defending breeding sites. Nests in colonies (May/June) on cliffs at the water's edge or inland amongst ruined masonry; fledging and dispersal (August / September); at other times it lives at sea. *Illustrated.*

Peregrine falcon *(Falco peregrinus)* – The indigenous peregrine population has been monitored for years: having symbolised noble privilege in hunting circles in the Middle Ages, the bird was shot by gamekeepers as vermin or trapped for collectors; during World War II numbers were controlled so as to safeguard carrier and homing pigeons released by fallen pilots; after the war numbers dwindled with the increase in the use of pesticides – the toxicity of which accumulated in the birds causing infertility and making the eggshell so fragile as not to survive incubation – and of poaching. Today, the peregrine is protected and population numbers are slowly recovering. Perhaps its most remarkable feature is the speed, estimated between 100-200mph, at which a peregrine will stoop on its prey (game birds, waders, pigeons) winding it with its foot before killing it outright with a talon in mid-flight.

Gannet

Fulmar

J. Brun, S. Cordier, Ph. Prigent, Wild Pat/JACANA

Puffin

Shag

Architecture

We… therefore take this opportunity to express our surprise that so little is known by English men and women of the beauties of English architecture. The ruins of the Colosseum, the Campanile at Florence, St Mark's, Cologne, the Bourse and Notre Dame, are with our travellers as familiar as household words; but they know nothing of the glories of Wiltshire, Dorsetshire, and Somersetshire. Nay, we much question whether many noted travellers, men who have pitched their tents perhaps under Mount Sinai, are still not ignorant that there are glories in Wiltshire, Dorsetshire, and Somersetshire. We beg they will go and see.

Anthony Trollope from his novel *Barchester Towers (1851)*

LOCAL BUILDING STONE

Even without venturing into the many excellent geological sections of each and every local museum, the observant visitor will be aware, almost unconsciously, of the area's complex geological make-up. Not only are the major phases, including the famous Jurassic and Devonian, easily discerned in the contours and colours of the landscape; they are evident, at closer quarters, in the rich variety in texture of the local building materials. In the simplest of terms, the further west one travels, the older and harder are the rocks, the more difficult they are to work, the more straight-forwardly they are incorporated into buildings.

Bath and Bristol – Lime-stone, although of a warmer hue than that used for Salisbury Cathedral, was quarried at Claverton, Box and Corsham to build the magnificent Georgian terraces in Bath designed for Ralph Allen and John Wood.

Bristol, meanwhile, a harbour city strategically situated on the River Avon, imported much of its stone from neighbouring Somerset. The cathedral, St Mary Redcliffe and many of the medieval buildings are built of Dundry limestone. In the Avon Gorge, one layer overlaid upon another, limestone above sandstone, often at steep angles, can easily be seen (most dramatically on the hill-slope, Bridge Valley Drive – watch out for the peregrine falcons at the same time!).

King's Spring, Pump Room

K Porter/Bath and North East Somerset Council

Cornwall – The **granite** which forms the peninsula's backbone appears in the tors on Bodmin Moor, in outcrops north of St Austell Bay, northwest of Falmouth and throughout Penwith. In all these areas, small workers' cottages, solitary inns like Jamaica Inn, isolated farmhouses and outbuildings, and the churches are built of granite. Elsewhere, everything from the houses to the boundary walls is made of **slate schist**, a laterally grained rust-grey stone. Most buildings, however, are roofed in **slate** from Tintagel and Delabole, which supplied enough slate to furnish not only Cornwall but the whole of the south of England. It is also used in the distinctive church towers (which in coastal areas served as identifying landmarks to mariners) with their louvered belfry openings, for biscuit-thin tombstones in churchyards and memorial tablets.

The Lizard has a rare volcanic outcrop of **serpentine rock**, unique in Britain. Cottages and churches alike were built of the dark green rock which when dressed begins to show its colour, when polished the friable marble-like stone reveals its intricate veining which has given it its name.

Devon – Quarries at Beer (west of Seaton) were among the several which provided Cretaceous **limestone** to the building of Exeter Cathedral: now the colours of stone from different sources appear to jar on the eye, but doubtless the arcades were once painted and the vaults at least intended to be plastered and painted as at Salisbury and Wells. This stone, which hardens once it has been cut or carved, is more vulnerable to erosion than the older and harder old Devonian limestone found between the estuaries of the Exe and the Tamar, widely used for buildings in Torquay and Plymouth, and for intricate chimney pieces, church screens and reredos in local parishes.

Exeter's wall, built by the Romans is of locally-quarried **basalt**, as is the Norman Rougemont Castle. **Slate**, another result of volcanic activity in the area around Kingsbridge, besides being used extensively to insulate houses from the weather in Totnes and Dartmouth, was exported from Charleston to Holland in the 15C, later (16C) in exchange for bricks which were used for building fire-proof chimneys and ovens. Incidentally, the same area boasts a number of timber-framed town houses (Dartmouth, Plymouth and Exeter).

Sandstone from Salcombe Regis (greenish) or from Sidmouth (neutral grey-brown) verges on the red around Teignmouth, and between Tiverton and Exeter. This is often considered as the friendliest part of the Devon landscape: a stark contrast to the more insipid veined and striated sandstones on the north coast around Hartland, indicative of considerable geological movement and upheaval. The Exmoor landscape has been altered by erosion as deep snowfalls, sudden thaws and torrential rain have affected even the hardest **granite** outcrops. Dartmoor and Lundy have abundant supplies of granite which has been exploited to build such major complexes as Lutyens' Castle Drogo, the prison at Princetown and the Lundy lighthouse.

Dorset – The coastline of Dorset ranges widely in character: after muddy Poole Harbour come the chalk cliffs, famously eroded at Lulworth Cove, the immense pebbled spit of Chesil Beach and the fossil cliffs of Lyme Regis. From here the famous **Portland** and **Purbeck** stone is cut, some of the hardest fine-grained limestones of the Jurassic period and therefore a highly prized building stone.

On the Isle of Portland everything from the prison to keepers' cottages and garden walls is built of "the fashionable stone" – an even-grained pale, almost white stone. In Purbeck, both houses and churches have dressed stone walls, while inside, their interiors are graced with polished features such as columns and fonts: Purbeck shafts are used to great effect at Salisbury Cathedral.

By contrast, a much more warmly coloured **sandstone** is more local in and around Sherborne, making the abbey a friendly building. The great variety of possible building materials available to masons is nowhere more obvious than at Wimborne Minster built in a mixture of contrasted colours including greenstone and red conglomerate.

Somerset – A sequence of hilly barriers, running east to west, divide Somerset into distinct geological and climatic zones. The scarp slope of Mendip catches the weather, occasionally inflicting a severe winter, while the Quantocks typify a more scenic landscape with a more mellow climate.

The structure of Mendip is famously visible at Cheddar Gorge, where the porous limestone has been eroded to form fantastic caves, as at Wookey (*see* WELLS) – a similar geological formation is to be seen at Kent's Cavern, just outside Torquay in Devon. To the south of Mendip, near Doulting, is the quarry which provided the stone for Wells Cathedral; this is a warm honey colour and ideally suited to being drilled and delicately worked into crisp naturalistic Early English figurative carving (look out for the spoonbill capital in the nave).

Another easily identifiable Somerset stone is the **blue lias** which, when polished, can shine like marble – a local substitute for the more famous Purbeck "marble". Its effect must once have been quite striking in the Lady Chapels of Glastonbury Abbey and Bristol Cathedral (and on the west front of Wells where the original columns have been replaced). It has also been used in blocks as a foil to yellower stones, as on the tower of North Petherton church. Today it is mainly exploited for kitchen flooring.

Dartmoor longhouses

Within the parish of Widecombe are a number of distinctive longhouses, a typical kind of Dartmoor farmstead in the 17C-18C. These shelter from the weather by being dug deep into the ground, often anchored by a natural rock mass which is integrated into the wall; additional protection is provided by a thatch roof which reaches almost down to the ground. Built on a slight incline to facilitate clearance of the shippon drain, one end of the house is used to accommodate livestock and hay, the other for use by the farmer. Often, the stone door- and window-frames are carefully moulded, a leftover perhaps from Tudor halls. Notable examples are to be found at Uppacott, one mile east of Poundstock.

Richer in colour, though rather coarser in texture, is the stone quarried south of Yeovil at Ham Hill, used most effectively at Montacute. Whole villages, like East Coker, are built of the mellow **Ham stone**, as are the innumerable fine church towers, with their unique Somerset tracery in the bell lights, as at Ilminster and Yeovil. The Quantocks, the Brendon and the Blackdown Hills are formations of very hard, **old sandstone**, the stone of the Quantocks veering towards pink and dark red: this sedimentary rock formed by the cementing together of grains of quartz or detritus resulting from the denudation of granite dates from the Devonian period and provides an effective source of building stone for the area, notably in Taunton Deane, where it appears rough hewn for cottage and church walls, dressed for trimming house and church windows and tractable for the decoration and carving of the west towers.

Wiltshire – The rolling downlands are made of chalk – as railway cuttings and the region's white horses will confirm. Chalk is too porous and crumbly to be of much use, but the hard black flints it contains are often integrated into decorative chequer-board patterns that ornament the characteristically picturesque thatched houses. The most common building material is brick and tile which has been traditionally fashioned from a variety of clays found in pockets along the undulating valleys, used with notable success at Littlecote House (*see* MARL-BOROUGH) and, later, to line the Kennet and Avon Canal from Bath to Reading. The high water table, usual in chalkland , also sustains the required conditions for growing reed for thatch and the base elements for cob, an economical material commonly used throughout Wiltshire, Devon and Dorset as at the regimented (and damp) new village at Milton Abbas *c*1780 (*see* DORCHESTER) and very picturesquely at Selworthy (*see* EXMOOR). For the construction of more major monuments, neat blocks of oolitic **limestone** were specially quarried: Salisbury Cathedral

Salisbury Cathedral

is built with a fine-grained greyish stone from nearby Chilmark transported by boat along the River Avon – the way in which the stone is laid to build the east end has rarely been excelled.

CELTIC AND SAXON: 5C – 11C

There is a clear cultural divide between the eastern and western regions of the West Country from the earliest times: to the east survive a number of (fragmentary) Anglo-Saxon crosses – at Colerne, Bath (Abbey Heritage Vaults), Codford St Peter and Ramsbury in Wiltshire for example, and intricately carved slabs as at Bradford on Avon and Britford in Wiltshire. These are in a distinctively different tradition from that apparent on the upstanding Celtic crosses of Cornwall (notable ones at Cardingham, Lanherne, Perranporth) and the Ogham stone of St Kew (*see* BODMIN MOOR) which betray the influence of the Celtic Church in South Wales and Ireland respectively, an association confirmed by the litany of dedications to missionary saints peculiar to Cornwall.

Incredibly, the sites of most cathedrals and parish churches in England were hallowed before the Conquest. Churches originated often as regular preaching stands which, in time, would be marked by a cross, an oratory and eventually a small church built of wood or stone. The fragments of Saxon masonry incorporated into the fabric of Sherborne Abbey suggest that the Anglo-Saxons could build on a grand scale but by far the best-preserved of all churches of the period are much smaller; typical is the main structure of St Laurence at Bradford on Avon. The 11C carved angels here may be compared with another similar one at Winterbourne Steepleton in Dorset, and the Harrowing of Hell relief in Bristol Cathedral: their Byzantine-style is quite independent from the Celtic tradition, reflecting foreign ideas probably brought to Britain in the form of manuscripts.

ANGLO-NORMAN ROMANESQUE: mid-11C – mid-12C

The impact of church reorganisation following the Norman Conquest has been largely obscured by later rebuilding. In Cornwall, despite the survival of St German's and Morwenstowe, the cluster of stupendous fonts – often with bold geometric or organic moulding anchored by primitive bearded heads, once coloured, at the angles – centred on Bodmin indicates that there were many more Norman churches than now remain.

Among the many Norman parish churches, typical examples might include Studland in Dorset; Compton Martin, Lullington and Stogursey in Somerset; St John, Devizes in Wiltshire.

The majesty of this most impressive phase of English architecture, characterised by round-headed window and door openings accentuated by **carved zigzag, dog-tooth or beaked hood mouldings**, is still dominant in several great churches: Christchurch Priory (*see* BOURNEMOUTH), Sherborne Abbey and Wimborne Minster. Exeter is unique amongst English cathedrals in having twin towers at its transepts, as plain as castles until the richly decorated upper parts. Even more highly ornamented, like the north transept at Christchurch, is the Chapter House of St Augustine's Abbey (now Bristol Cathedral): when the interlaced **blind arcading** carved with zigzags was painted, as no doubt it was, the effect must have been outrageous. A distinctive Norman feature that forecasts the horizontal emphasis of the West Country Gothic cathedrals (picked up in the triforium of Wells Cathedral) is the way arches and supports are delineated by a continuous moulding.

By far the most significant West Country monument of the Romanesque period is Malmesbury Abbey, from where a number of decorative elements were borrowed as at Bristol, Glastonbury, Wells, Christchurch, Wimborne... suggesting that there might have been an influential school of masons. Quite unique in England is the huge south porch (*c*1170); its great continuous arch is carved with a concentric set of scenes from the Old and New Testaments, and with symbolic subjects: an ensemble closely linked to the pilgrimage churches in southwestern France, but unparalleled in Britain.

Architectural features found at Malmesbury, such as sub-arches below major arches and paterae (or floral knops) reappear at Glastonbury Abbey but in a context using pointed rather than semi-circular arches. The Lady Chapel represents a transition from the Romanesque of Bristol's Chapter House to the succeeding Early Gothic, as is apparent in the design of the main elevation at Glastonbury where a giant pointed arch encloses the middle storey – something attempted with round arches at Oxford Cathedral. It is a puzzling design and it is clear that the builders were puzzled using round and pointed arches for the same window in the aisles!

GOTHIC: mid-12C – late 16C

Roughly speaking, the period divides into three parts: **Early English** from 1150-1290, **Decorated** from 1290-1350 and **Perpendicular** from 1350-1550. During these centuries church builders developed the use of the pointed arch and the expertise of diffusing weight from a stone vault through ribs to buttressed walls or piers. Spatial clarity is articulated first by lierne and tierceron rib vaulting which will ultimately lead to fan vaulting. Windows were enlarged and elaborated: Early English **lancet windows** consisted of long glass panels divided by a mullion that split at the top to accommodate a diamond shape; this, in turn contained circular sections with **quatrefoil tracery**.

In the following Decorated phase, taller and more complex **transomed windows** were filled with increasingly **flowing tracery**; elsewhere, surfaces were encrusted with elaborate ornament.

In the Perpendicular period the window peaks flattened to produce a wider apex over vast areas of glass; above 5, 7, 9 lights the infilling was simplified to a **geometrical tracery**. Attention became focused on the vaulting, which reached its climax in **fan vaulting**, developed at Gloucester and applied at Sherborne Abbey, Bath Abbey and in many parish churches (as at Cullompton in Devon) especially in porches and towers.

Monastic Houses – All the wealthier monastic houses suffered irreparable damage at the Dissolution: notably Glastonbury, Shaftesbury, Bath, Abbotsbury... St Augustine's in Bristol survived because Henry VIII was persuaded to raise it to cathedral status. Its choir (initiated 1298) was designed in a way unique among English cathedrals, as a hall church with aisles as tall as the central vessel: making it the most adventurous design of its date anywhere in Europe. Just before the Dissolution, the transepts and crossing were rebuilt – the vault roof bosses and contemporary misericords are a rare delight.

At Glastonbury, only the magnificent kitchen survives complete although beyond the abbey precinct are the Tribunal, an inn and the abbey barn. Two tithe barns belonging to Shaftesbury Abbey survive at Tisbury and Bradford on Avon. Another barn stands alongside Torre Abbey and at Abbotsbury –enough to suggest the magnificence of contemporary building expertise in the domestic domain. Otherwise fragments have been integrated over the years to serve different functions: the claustral buildings of Cleeve and Muchelney are listed as "ancient monuments"; the abbey church at Milton Abbas serves as a public school chapel; the church at Buckland Abbey has been converted into a house; at Forde, a proud abbot's porch and hall, together with adjoining domestic quarters, have been ingeniously transformed into a country house.

Cathedrals – The three Gothic cathedrals in the West Country are Wells (begun *c*1185), Salisbury (begun 1220) and Exeter (rebuilding begun 1275). All three share similar fundamental "West Country" characteristics by sharing a preference for internal spatial unity on a longitudinal axis, rather than the vertical as sought by contemporary masons in French cathedrals such as Chartres, Reims and Amiens. This is achieved in the elevation by emphasising the **horizontal** elements, particularly in the middle storey: in the nave at Wells (developing elements used earlier at Malmesbury) there is a continuous band of tightly packed arches and sub-arches decorated with leafy paterae; at Salisbury the middle storey is dramatised by a multitude of dark-coloured Purbeck shafts; at Exeter a similar effect is achieved by the shadowy ripple of shallow arcading. In none of these buildings is there any visual link between the main piers at ground level and the springing of the vault: indeed at Exeter the urge to achieve horizontal unity is fully expressed by

aesthetically foreshortening the height of the vault; instead of allowing the proliferation of ribs to spring upwards, they are anchored into place by a great sequence of carved roof bosses which run along the entire length of the building.

It is evident that innovation in **vaulting** techniques and visual effects at Exeter were soon applied elsewhere: notably in the building of the chapter house, new Lady Chapel, retrochoir and extended choir at Wells. Here the complex interplay of vaults between the polygonal lady chapel and the choir is further enhanced by the fortunate survival of the original richly coloured glass – best seen in morning light.

Meanwhile, all three cathedrals reject the twin-towered façade design used at Notre Dame in Paris and at Amiens, preferring, as at Malmesbury, a screen front (*see* Decorative and applied arts: Sculpture). At Wells the lively **carving**, especially of the capitals, is typical of Early English Gothic; by comparison Salis-

Choir and Lady Chapel vaults, Wells Cathedral

bury seems brittle; no cathedral better deserves the term "Decorated" than Exeter.

Parish Churches – During the Tudor age England enjoyed ever greater prosperity, notably among merchants associated with the wool trade. Parish churches were rebuilt (St Mary Redcliffe, Bristol) and private chapels were endowed with fine glass and Renaissance commemorative monuments (Lord Mayor's Chapel, Bristol; St Mary's, Lydiard Park outside Swindon; Christchurch Priory). Outstanding examples include Edington Priory (*see* TROWBRIDGE), St Cuthbert's at Wells and Ottery St Mary (*see* HONITON); Somerset in particular is a paradise for the church-crawler – Axbridge, Chewton Mendip, Martock, Taunton… with many enjoying the most spectacular setting. Elsewhere, churches boast their own unique feature: the apostle roof at Bere Regis, the angel roof at Ilfracombe, the doom painting at Sarum St Thomas in Salisbury, the richly carved porch at Launceston (*c*1551), the windows at St Neot, the Greenway chapel at Tiverton…

Church building in Somerset – In this county where some claimed that Glastonbury had been founded by Joseph of Arimathea, the medieval wool prosperity coincided with the 13C-16C period of church renewal and rebuilding, the Gothic Perpendicular period, which was aided by the abundance of fine, workable, building stone in the region. The local lord of the manor or squire funded the church chancel and family chapels; the parishioners, the nave, the aisles and transepts. Construction, furnishings and embellishment were executed by bands of travelling masons, stone-cutters and carvers, carpenters and skilled wood workers.

Towers, which in Norman churches rose above the crossing and were crowned with spires, were shifted to the west end and ceased to support often dangerous, tapering cones. They were the last part of the church to be built and marked the triumphant culmination of local enterprise – the objects of considerable local rivalry. The requirement of a west tower to include a belfry was universal but it became evident over time that there was a seemingly infinite number of ways of combining in the upper parts blank lights, bell lights, buttresses, pinnacles, castellations, friezes and panelling, rising tier upon tier, ever higher... A unique ornament was the filling of the upper lights with **Somerset tracery,** uniformly carved screens of the tractable stone.

The church interiors, meanwhile, demonstrate the skill of the woodmen: carpenters for the wagon, hammer-beam, tie-beam, king and queen post roofs; carvers for the moulding, cresting, wall plates, infinitely varied bosses, panelling and tracery, and most notably, the life-size angels.

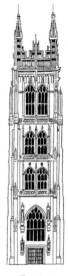

| Bishop's Lydeard | Batcombe | Evercreech | Bristol | Taunton |

Secular and domestic architecture – If churches were built to be ageless, castles and fortresses were conceived as defence works with the latest armouries. It is in this domain, therefore that the origins of secular architecture are to be sought: alas, none among Restormel, Corfe, Launceston, Sherborne, Berry Pomeroy, Nunney is well-preserved but the reinforced artillery forts of the last phase, built by the Crown, namely Nothe in Weymouth, St Mawes (1540) and Pendennis (1544) are most impressively strong, spacious and well appointed, often with details conforming with the Italian Renaissance fashion.

What can be deduced is the way domestic life gradually became more comfortable. Two very rare survivals are the hall of Christchurch Castle (*c*1160) and the "Gloriet" at Corfe Castle (1201-02). The Bishop's Palace at Wells carries the story from the 13C to the late 15C. The architectural features to be noted include the porch, the chapel; the sub-division of the interior into Great Hall, screens passage, solar; oriel windows; and the development of private rooms and the long gallery. Near the fragmentary but elegant remains of the Abbot's Lodging at Muchelney is the 14C-15C Priest's House – a very rare survival. More famous and grander is the "Old Post Office" at Tintagel, in fact a small 14C manor house.

Tudor, Elizabethan and Jacobean Periods – The story of domestic housing, however, is also subject to the political fortunes of individuals and as such is vulnerable to change, alteration and personal taste. Phases are usually simply identified with the reigning monarch. In the 15C-17C, the houses have timber frames with exposed and cruck beams; the timbers, closer together in early work, have plaster or brick infilling. Oversailing upper floors were discontinued in Jacobean times as they were considered a fire-hazard. Great pointed **gables,** imported from the Protestant Low Countries, characterise the roofs. **Chimney stacks** appear for the newly introduced fireplaces; in Elizabethan times they were grouped, set symmetrically, often of brick and fancifully decorated. The **windows** of the period are small, sometimes single casements, but on occasion extend right across a front; the frames have flat-arched heads beneath a hood. Windows in the big houses, illuminating great halls and often the **long galleries** characteristic of the Elizabethan

Old Post Office, Tintagel

age, followed Perpendicular church architecture in comprising great expanses of glass. Inside, the walls (except where clad with tapestries) were **oak panelled**. **Plasterwork** came into its own with ceilings decorated with formal and imaginative patterning and great pendants; friezes and overmantels were often designed to be pertinent to the patron, incorporating the favourite Jacobean strapwork and the display of arms. The **stairs**, whether of monolithic blocks of stone or single timbers, mounted as spirals in the Elizabethan age and as splendid wide staircases, cantilevered and turning in straight flights around open, square wells in the Jacobean period; the **banisters**, of wood inches thick, were often deeply carved, the **newels** heraldic.

It was the rich merchants and landowners who bought the former monastic properties at the Dissolution and converted them into habitable homes as is the case with Lacock, Torre Abbey in Torquay and Hartland Abbey. Others built new (Athelhampton, Longleat, Lanhydrock, Trerice, Wilton), engaging architect-survey-ors and craftsmen who travelled from property to property: in Cornwall, where the most important landowner was the Prince of Wales, there are very few examples.

A simplified chronological list indicates the richness of the area:

Treasurer's House, Martock	13C-14C	Lytes Cary	13C onwards
Clevedon Court	14C and c1575	Dartington Hall	c1388
Old Wardour Castle	14C-16C	Great Chalfield	1467-88
Athelhampton	1493-1550	Cotehele	15C-16C
Berry Pomeroy Castle	1547-1600	Trerice still medieval	1573
Barrington Court arranged symmetrically		1560?	

After these (and several more like them), the exterior of Longleat (1567) comes as a great surprise for its scale, symmetry and Renaissance detailing. Montacute (1588) is widely regarded as one of the most delightful of all the great houses of England, partly on account of its use of distinctly English features like the decorative chimneys and partly for its concession to Renaissance influence. Lanhydrock though mostly destroyed by fire and rebuilt, retains a very late but splendid long gallery of 1636, complete with its original plastered barrel vault: others survive at Dunster Castle (1681).

The Classical phase of English Baroque is most splendidly accessible at Wilton House where six state rooms, designed c1650 by Inigo Jones and decorated with fine pictures (notably the Van Dyck portraits) provide an uplifting expe-rience. Comparison, here, may be made with the formal picture gallery at Corsham Court.

THE CLASSICAL PERIOD: 1700 – 1830s

Queen Anne – The achievement of the 17C was the remarkable development in English architecture which led, by the end of the century, to a new style of domestic architecture which borrowed palatial, Classical proportions and features but attuned them to suit smaller country and town houses. The precepts, as laid down by Palladio and imported by Inigo Jones (1573-1652), were advanced by Sir Christopher Wren (1632-1723), Vanbrugh and others. With a staunchly Protestant monarch opposed to things French, an almost Puritan preference for modesty and simplicity prevailed; however, house **fronts** were plainly contrived with centre doorways and symmetri-cally placed sash windows, the latter introduced in the early 18C. As the period progressed, window frames and glazing bars, at first thick and cumbersome, became ever more slender.

38

Rectangular, brick, box-like houses stood four-square beneath **hipped roofs** (roofs sloping up on all four sides to a flat top) so as to accommodate more rooms (and windows) without the constraints of Classical proportions; additional rooms could be built into the roof and lit by means of **dormer windows.** Articulation and relief was provided by a plain cornice-style decoration at eaves level; the angles were often quoined with dressed stone, and the main accents were sometimes accentuated by a baluster or urn at roof level. The secret of their charm, besides the apparent simplicity of perfect proportion, must be their honest sense of the practical: these houses were primarily designed to function as comfortable homes. More elaborate variations might include a crested or broken pediment, a shell canopy over the porch or some other light fantasy supported on brackets or pilasters.

The prevailing sense of discipline, which underpinned the growth of industry, is also suggested in terraced housing, in the case of Bradford on Avon purpose-built for out-workers.

Georgian – Under the Hanoverians (1714-1837), architecture developed as a refinement of the Queen Anne style and marked its adaptation to the new requirements of crowded urban living. In Blandford Forum a whole town was rebuilt in a largely homogenous style following a fire (1731). The sobriety of the Queen Anne style also engendered an awareness of building materials and thus, a taste for well-cut stone with mellow hues.

Meanwhile, the 18C prided itself on being an "Age of Reason"; accordingly, precepts in architecture were formulated and adhered to. Perhaps the scheme that best encapsulates the period in country house design is Colen Campbell's Stourhead (1721-24) where early Palladian architecture is beautifully set in a gloriously composed landscape inspired by the patron's collection of Continental pictures; this expression of enlightened 18C taste in turn, is complemented by Thomas Chippendale's fine English furniture.

In the design of town-houses, a stricter implementation of Palladian Classicism streamlined the treatment of doorways and windows, their formality, however, could be relieved by ornamental **wrought-ironwork** inserted into balconies, railings and front gates.

Georgian terrace architecture, Bath

The logical consequence of the prevailing influences is the **Georgian terrace**, which defines its own unique specifications in Bath. Following the obligatory rules of proportion, it could rise through several floors because the extent of the terrace gave it width, and each house, as a section of the whole, could, therefore, be provided with sufficient rooms. **Squares** and terraces, designed as single façades, became 18C versions of Classical palaces, complete with central pediments, columns, porticoes and arcades. Some were planned as single fashionable streets ending in a focal point such as St Mary Magdalene, Taunton; some, such as the squares, crescents and the **Circus** at Bath, were designed as elements in the most dignified city plan ever devised in England.

Taste in internal decoration was moulded by the delicate **Classicism** of Robert Adam (1728-92), where every detail is controlled and echoed in ceilings and floors and refracted by mirrors from friezes and frames, carpets, furniture and pictures by

39

Sir Joshua Reynolds. This is particularly illustrated at Saltram outside Plymouth: the fragile Chinoiserie mirrors and wall-papers in the upstairs apartments at Saltram provide a superb parallel to the Classical fantasies in the salon and dining room.

Regency – This period is perhaps the Golden Age of English furniture design and cabinet-making, a period that establishes a distinctively British taste in the decorative and applied arts tailored to the spacious interiors of Georgian buildings. The resolution of the Anglo-American War (1814) and the defeat of Napoleon at Waterloo (1815) might appear of little consequence to the West Country; however, during this time the government invested heavily in expensive foreign campaigns, and Englishmen looked to their own country to provide holidays. A vogue for seaside resorts evolved and communities around Sidmouth, Torquay, Weymouth grew to cater for tourists – these were later superseded when the railways boosted the industry in Victorian times.

Gothick – In the late 18C Horace Walpole announced that he was going "to build a little Gothic structure at Strawberry Hill", Twickenham. Walpole's house was a pastiche, a mixture of the genuine, which he bought at sales in England and on the Continent, and what he had built and decorated in an increasingly extreme manner, so developing what came to be known as the Gothick style. Decoration, ornament, furniture and furnishings in the style became fashionable and were to be seen at one time in many houses. It occurs early in the entry hall at Lacock Abbey: comparison with the genuine Gothic of the cloisters only serves to emphasise the frivolously un-archeological character of the style, especially of the statuary. At Sherborne Castle there is an elegant Gothick library and a Gothick dairy, but the most enchanting application of the style is at St Michael's Mount where the Drawing Room is decorated in the lightest, most delicate form of the style.

VICTORIAN ERA 1837-1901

As Regency gave way to the **Victorian style**, long rows of bay-windowed, steeply roofed, solidly built houses appeared, still to be seen in many seaside towns. Money generated by the Industrial Revolution was invested in restructuring towns and designing new buildings to suit new demands such as railway stations and bridges and in Cornwall to satisfy the need for ever larger churches that could accommodate the growing adherents of Methodism.

Ruskin, to name but one influence in Victorian taste, prompted a new interest in vernacular buildings in England; others such as Gilbert Scott and Street set to the task of restoring them for contemporary usage. When Lanhydrock was devastated by fire, it was rebuilt exactly the same within its 16C granite walls by 19C craftsmen to late 19C standards of taste and comfort (central heating).

In contrast, the Italian Church at Wilton (1843) resembles a folly, built as it is in the Italian Romanesque style and furnished as a depository for Continental medieval glass and antiquarian fragments.

Gothic Revival – A century later, despite ambitious church restoration programmes, the architects' interpretation of Gothic is heavier than the original: Dunster Castle (1876) exploits its magnificent site; at Knightshayes Court (1870) William Burges built an imposingly strong house, but alas most of the schemes for the interior decoration were never executed; Truro Cathedral (begun 1880), however, is an original and authoritative statement of Neo-Gothic by JL Pearson.

20C

The 20C has dealt harshly with many of the cities and towns of the West Country: Bath, Bristol, Exeter and Plymouth all had to be rebuilt after bombing, especially after the Baedecker Raids of 1942. Much of that rebuilding, stretched over long periods of time, was carried out during difficult times and is of poor quality – the Mayflower Theatre in Plymouth being a notable exception.

Tate Gallery, St Ives

40

Besides the Civic Centres (Swindon, Bristol, Poole), purpose-built shopping precincts (outside Plymouth and Bournemouth), signal stations (Goonhilly Satellite Earth Station on the Lizard) and power-generation plants (Delabole wind turbines, Hinkley Point Nuclear Station), two buildings deserve particular attention. These are **High Cross House** at Dartington and the **Tate Gallery at St Ives**, both of which, in a strange way are linked, and provide with the straight-forward Barbara Hepworth Museum at St Ives nearby a most persuasive introduction to modern art.

In a different league is Sir Norman Foster's compelling **Renault Distribution Centre** outside Swindon: here modern building materials have been combined to produce a completely functional modern commercial space.

Landscape garden design

No holiday in the West Country would be complete without a visit to one or more of the great gardens sited amid beautiful valleyed parkland, overlooking river estuaries or the sea where spring extends into the rest of Britain's winter (as in the Scillies), and autumn continues longer. These more temperate climes provide the balmy, frost-free conditions for nurturing **exotic species** imported by travellers from distant parts who landed at Falmouth or Plymouth.

17C

In the earliest gardens, be they formal Elizabethan **knot gardens** enclosed in minute clipped evergreen hedges or the less formal Jacobean **Mount garden**, the main feature of the landscaped garden is symmetry.

As Renaissance ideas spread from Europe, the garden forms of Italy and France were adapted to England. Design remained geometrical but on a large scale: gardens were divided into separate "rooms" each surrounded by a tall hedge; flower-beds, symmetrically arranged and still edged with clipped box, were made larger and were brilliantly, if identically, planted as carpets or **parterres**; openings in the hedges afforded vistas that were punctuated by statuary, or water that had been harnessed into animating a fountain, geometric basin or canal. In all instances, however, compositions must show the hand of the designer; nothing should be left to Nature, that powerful and unpredictable force.

At Versailles, the gardens were laid out as a natural extension of the house; perspectives were delineated as far as the most distant estate boundary; terraces acted as "stepping stones" between formal garden and natural deer park.

18C

The Picturesque – Although there were forerunners, the English genius in large-scale **garden design** dates from the 18C when travel for pleasure began to become popular and an open appreciation of landscape for its own sake could be recognised. On a more intellectual level, the Grand Tour exposed educated diplomats and wealthy men to the philosophy of such thinkers as Aristotle and Plato, revived by the Renaissance, and now discussed among other matters of taste at the royal court, notably at Versailles. Poussin's *Et In Arcadia Ego* shows Man contemplating an antique sarcophagus and becoming aware of his own mortality.

Just as a painter might idolise his sitter in a portrait to conform to the contemporary canon of Beauty, he might represent Nature as ordered and rational according to a system of proportion measured against a human figure. The same rational concept was thus applied to the design of Landscape where trees and water might be arranged in a harmonious composition that exceeded anything found "untamed" in the natural world. As Picturesque novels unfolded their stories of love, betrayal and adventure in contrived settings, so paintings depicted figures in scenery that was evocative of its subject. The Elysian fields, Mount Olympus and tranquil lakesides painted by the likes of **Richard Wilson** (1713-82) were based, in fact upon his observation of the English and Welsh countryside; the landscapes in **Francis Danby**'s Biblical scenes are certainly not realistic representations of the Holy Land. In poetry, the likes of **Thomas Gray** (1716-71) prompted reflection and meditation on the seasons and the countryside well before Wordsworth (1770-1850) and John Clare (1793-1864). This movement swept into garden design as a search to find "the genius of the place", by which was meant enhancing the natural beauty of the site – **Lancelot Brown** (1715-1783) described the task as improving the "capability" of a site (Bowood).

Grand designs – Formal patterning and bedding were abandoned; enclosed spaces were opened out – **William Kent** (1684-1748) invented the ha-ha, an open ditch which enabled the garden to merge visually with the adjoining parkland landscape, at the same time keeping deer and cattle at a distance. It was Kent too who began designing by eye (like a painter) rather than with level and line (like a surveyor).

The Palladian Bridge and Pantheon, Stourhead

Canals became serpentine ponds and lakes; hillsides were planted with trees selected for their leaf colours, their size and shape as clumps or as specimens; cedars of Lebanon, introduced to England in 1676, oaks, ashes and beeches were sited to focus a view, counterpoint a house front.

Poetry and painting were almost literally translated in some cases: landscapes were transformed, lakes excavated, temples, grottoes, follies constructed and situated after the manner of pictures, as may be seen at Stourhead.

Humphry Repton (1752-1818), the next in the line of designers, followed the landscaping precepts of Capability Brown, his famous Red Books giving his clients a detailed idea of how his plans would materialise. His advance on Brown was to re-introduce flowers in beds and on terraces in close proximity to his clients' houses.

19C

Plant hunting, inaugurated in the 16C-17C by the **Tradescants**, father and son, was undertaken on an ever-increasing scale in the 19C-early 20C. Scientific expeditions undertaken by the likes of **Darwin** (1809-82) and other such eminent botanist-naturalists were publicised in journals: Sir Joseph **Hooker**, who explored parts of Nepal, Bhutan, Sikkim in the nether regions of the Himalayas (1847-51) and despatched the seeds of exotic species to Cornwall (*see* ST AUSTELL: Lost Gardens of Heligan), rose to become Director of Kew. Exploration of foreign territories was often sponsored by large trading organisations like the British East India Company in the hope of capitalising on newly discovered commodities that might be exploited in medicine (eg quinine), industrial applications (rubber, turmeric) or, in the tradition of coffee, tea, tobacco, potatoes, sugar and sunflowers, for general consumption (tomatoes). By the late 19C, specialised nurserymen like the Treseders of Truro and Sutton's Earl of Beaconsfield were importing exotics direct from New Zealand and Australia to supply the demands of late Victorian gardeners, while the hot-house manufacturing business of Sir Joseph Paxton was booming.

To accommodate the new ranges of plants, garden design changed again to a labour-intensive formula with flowers over-wintered or raised in greenhouses and conservatories and bedded out each summer; herbaceous borders were crowded with plants; dense shrubberies were allowed to grow; terraces were draped and decorated with climbers and plants in pots. Collections of trees were planted as pinetums and arboretums. In Cornwall especially, sophisticated vegetable gardens were maintained to provide fresh produce throughout the year – a necessity given the county's isolation before the advent of the railways.

MODERN GARDENING

Gradually over the years, gardens became increasingly labour-intensive; tools facilitated the work and schemes became ever more ambitious: however, with the outbreak of World War I gardening practices had to be reformed. Professional gardeners were a luxury and many large estates had to be broken up and sold. Gardens became smaller and contained within hedges that might screen off the neighbours.

Tasmanian tree ferns in Cornwall

Some of the specimens of *Dicksonia antarctica* that populate a number of gardens in Cornwall (Penjerrick, Glendurgan, Heligan, Trebah) arrived in Falmouth from Australia aboard a grain ship in the form of sawn logs. These, after being soaked for two to three days, were successfully planted out.

Latterly, a second major consignment was dispatched from Tasmania this time, as the tree ferns of Australia are now listed as an endangered species. The two positive outcomes of this project are that the Tasmanian variety has proved hardy to temperatures of -13°C and will tolerate snow – this means that it may survive in less temperate zones of mainland Britain – and, secondly, the Tasmanian Government has authorised the export of tree ferns as part of a sustainable conservation programme whereby two are planted for every one cut down.

Reaction produced a less crowded appearance, and, with **Gertrude Jekyll** (1843-1932) a discrimination appeared that gives value to each plant for its flowers, its foliage and as a whole, to produce the plantsmen's and plantswomen's gardens of today. Gertrude Jekyll was a contemporary of the French Impressionist painters who turned to gardening in the 1880s as her eyesight began to fail. For her: "having got the plants, the great thing is to use them with careful selection and definite intention. Merely having them, or having them planted unassorted in garden spaces, is only like having a box of paints from the best colourman, or, to go one step further, it is like having portions of these paints set out upon a palette." Favourite combinations include silver-greys with white and strong purple; she avoided the use of yellow, strong reds, scarlet, orange and hot blues. Her most faithful followers include **Vita Sackville-West** (1892-1962) and Mrs Reis (Tintinhull in Somerset).

Other innovations-cum-revivals of the 20C include the thematic garden which is divided into "rooms" of colour, scheduled to bloom in a particular season, and the maze – notably at Longleat.

The most exciting project for the future, however, is the **Eden Project** which will transform a 37 acre (15 hectare) china clay pit overlooking St Austell Bay into a series of planthouses: three "biomes" designed to provide climatic conditions appropriate to the Mediterranean, humid tropics (tropical rainforest) and semi-arid tropics (desert) have been conceived to harbour plants and trees on a massive scale...

Parks and gardens of the West Country

BATH and BRISTOL: Claverton Manor, Clevedon Court, Prior Park, Bath.

CORNWALL: Cotehele, Glendurgan, Heligan, Lanhydrock, Mount Edgcumbe, Pencarrow, Probus, Trebah, Trelissick, Trengwainton, Trerice, Tresco, Trewithen.

DEVON: Bicton, Cadhay, Killerton, Knightshayes Court, Rosemoor, Sharpitor, Tapeley Park, Ugbrooke.

DORSET: Abbotsbury, Athelhampton, Compton Acres, Cranborne Manor, Mapperton, Parnham House.

SOMERSET: Barrington Court, Clapton Court, East Lambrook Manor, Forde Abbey, Gaulden Manor, Tintinhull House.

WILTSHIRE: Bowood, Heale House, Littlecote, Longleat, Stourhead, Wilton House.

For additional information, consult the index.

Painting

18C PORTRAITURE

One of the first widely acclaimed West Country painters is **Thomas Hudson** (1701-79), who was born in Barnstaple and developed an invariable portrait style in the manner of Lely and Kneller: his fame, however, largely rests upon the fact that he taught Reynolds and endured through the works of other provincial painters like Richard Phelps (active 1729-85) whose works are to be seen at Dunster Castle. Quite a different art is perpetrated by **William Hoare of Bath** (c1707-92), largely as a result of his nine year stay in Italy and close association with Italian painters of the day: Hoare settled in Bath in 1739 and became the leading portraitist there until the arrival of Thomas Gainsborough (1727-88).

Gainsborough in Bath (1759-74) – "Whether he most excelled in portraits, landscapes, or fancy pictures, it is difficult to determine" observed Joshua Reynolds in his Fourteenth Discourse about his contemporary Gainsborough, praising his paintings for their "quality of lightness of manner and effect". Gainsborough was a highly sociable person and a great music lover – qualities that must have helped the artist to settle in Bath before embarking upon the most prolific period for portraiture of his career. In 1768 he was the only portraitist to be invited as a founding member of the Royal Academy, a rare compliment indeed for someone painting so far from London. Shortly after arriving in the West Country, Gainsborough set about modelling his style on that of Van Dyck – visiting Wilton, for example, so as to formulate his art on the contemporary aristocratic idea of elegance. His full-length portraits seem to epitomise the most endearing spirit of English taste: they capture a fleeting light (having been executed for the most part by candlelight), a genial naturalness in their direct, informal appeal (especially with children), and a provocative suggestion of the English landscape (sometimes composed in his studio with arrangements of pebbles and moss). By some, he is considered as continuing the tradition set by Hogarth (as in the portraits of his servants) and preceding the landscapes of Constable. The "fancy pictures", so termed by Reynolds, of this period are informal landscape scenes animated by small groups of figures of idealised peasants; later, after Gainsborough had moved to London, these verge on the Romantic.

John Opie (1761-1807) – Opie, the son of a St Agnes mine carpenter, was launched in London as the "Cornish Wonder" in 1781 by John Wolcot, a former student of Wilson, who had recognised the young boy's precocious talent and encouraged him to study the work of the Old Masters from engravings. Opie excelled at painting elderly women and children in strong chiaroscuro but never succeeded with more formal portraits and history painting.

LANDSCAPE

According to Ruskin with "**Richard Wilson** (1713-82) the history of sincere landscape art founded on a meditative love of nature begins in England": Wilson was born in Wales, trained as a portrait painter, travelled extensively in Italy imbibing the character of the Roman Campagna and assimilating the work of the French painters Claude and Gaspard, before returning to England and satisfying a demand for country-house portraits (*Five Views of Wilton* at Wilton House). Among the artists of successive generations, Joseph Farington (1747-1821), one of Wilson's students, was among the first to embark on making a pictorial survey of English coastal scenery for the book *Britannica Depicta*. A little later, William Daniell (1769-1837) set about painting the coast from the sea for his *A Voyage Around Great Britain*. The Bristol-born sea-captain **Nicolas Pocock** (1740-1821) turned to producing meticulous views of the Avon and its mercantile shipping on retiring from his career piloting ships to the West Indies (on behalf of the porcelain manufacturer Robert Campion). The watercolourist **Samuel Jackson** (1794-1869) and his son Samuel Phillips (1830-1904), both eminent members of the (Old) Royal Watercolour Society, were instrumental in establishing a Bristol School of marine painting; others in the circle include W J Muller, J B Pyne, G A Fripp, Charles Branwhite... The Irish-born **Francis Danby** (1793-1861) settled in Bristol (1813-12) where he evolved a Picturesquely dramatic style of landscape painting complete with thunder and lightning; when he eventually retired to Exmouth, Danby was employed in producing large canvases depicting Biblical and mythological scenes. John Constable (1776-1837) visited the Dorset coast and painted his evocative views of Salisbury Cathedral.

JM Turner (1775-1851) also journeyed through the English countryside, on horseback and on foot, sketching the landscape and studying changes in climate; he travelled to Cornwall on two occasions (1811, 1813) capturing St Michael's Mount, St Ives, Tintagel... Among the artists to settle and regularly paint luminous views of the scenery around Newlyn are Richard Pentreath (1806-69) and Henry Martin (1835-1908). Once Brunel's bridge over the Tamar had been built (1859) and the railway extended (1880), Cornwall was open to mass tourism. It became a popular alternative destination for British artists who had previously studied and worked at Barbizon and in Brittany among the exponents of a new type of "*plein air*" painting, working outdoors and directly from nature. Following the example of these French Barbizon painters (Theodore Rousseau, Jean Corot, Jean-François Millet), the Realist Courbet, and the early Impressionists (Pissarro, Sisley, Manet, Monet, Renoir), these artists sought to express their more naturalistic approach to landscape and "genre" painting. What attracted them particularly to Newlyn and St Ives, where some settled for short periods and others remained for the rest of their lives, was the climate, the ideal quality of light and the ready availability of inexpensive models from among the indigenous population.

NEWLYN SCHOOL

The term "Newlyn School" emerges as a result of works being submitted for exhibition at the Royal Academy during the 1880s and 1890s by artists who worked in Newlyn using the French Impressionist technique of applying paint with a square brush. They chose unassuming subjects – the modest lives of local inhabitants, the fishermen and their families – with which the artists familiarised themselves by living in the community, in order to be able to paint them with penetrating honesty. The results are quiet, dignified pictures full of charm or pathos which avoid the sentimental excesses of much Victorian genre painting.

The artists' colony was led partly by **Stanhope Forbes** (1857-1947; *Fish Sale on a Cornish Beach*, 1885), a prolific painter who was dedicated to the idea of working in the open air. With his wife, Elizabeth Forbes (née Armstrong: 1859-1912), also a painter, they opened a school of painting in Newlyn in 1889 which attracted students from all over the world. Typical of their work is Stanhope Forbes' picture *The Young Apprentice, Newlyn Copperworks* which combines genre naturalistic representations of the common people engaged in some ordinary task) with portrai-

The Young Apprentice, Newlyn Copperworks
by Stanhope Forbes

ture depicting as it does the artist, designer and founder of the Newlyn Industrial Classes John Mackenzie informally overseeing the 15-year old Johnny Payne Cotton *see below:* Silver and copper).

Other painters there included **Walter Langley** (1852-1922): the first figure painter to depict incidents in the life of the fisherfolk, **Frank Bramley** (1867-1943; *A Hopeless Dawn*, 1888), **Norman Garstin** (1847-1926; *The Rain it Raineth Every Day*, 1889), Percy Craft, Harold Knight and his wife Laura, Dod Shaw, Ernest Procter and the Falmouth painter **Henry Scott Tuke** (1858-1929), who began painting in the Newlyn manner but whose use of colour became more vibrant after a trip to the Mediterranean in 1892.

In 1895, the **Newlyn Society of Artists** was founded by **John D Mackenzie, Reginald Dick**, Thomas Cooper Gotch and Percy Craft. During the early years of the new century, Newlyn changed as did tastes in contemporary art; the artistic circle disbanded; John "Lamorna" Birch, Harold and Laura Knight, visited by the likes of Augustus John and Alfred Munnings, settled in the wooded Lamorna Valley, continuing the style and Impressionists and Post-Impressionist styles.

The most notable collections of Newlyn School paintings are displayed at the Royal Cornwall Museum in Truro, the Penlee House Gallery and Museum in Penzance and Falmouth Municipal Gallery. For additional information, consult *The Shining Sands, Artists in Newlyn and St Ives 1880-1930* by Tom Cross (1994).

ST IVES SCHOOL

The other major, though less clearly-defined, school was based at St Ives on the north coast of the Penwith peninsula; the town is still a magnet for artists today. The rugged scenery and clear light around St Ives attracted artists interested in landscapes and seascapes rather than in figure painting.

The town and its surroundings were first brought to prominence by the American **Whistler** and his companions **Sickert** and Menpes who spent the winter of 1883-84 there; others soon followed. The conversion of sail lofts along Porthmeor beach into studios provided the perfect environment for the artists, and the old fishing quarter soon became the centre of the group. **Julius Olsson** (1864-1942), famous for his nocturnal seascapes, ran a school for marine painting in the area; he and several other Royal Academicians formed the Arts Club in 1888. The local artistic community thrived with the result that, in 1926, the **St Ives Society of Artists** was founded to provide a showcase for displaying their art.

Advent of Abstract Art – A new wave of artists, linked by nothing more than a less traditional approach to their art, also began to appear in St Ives after the war. These included the potter **Bernard Leach** (1887-1979), who came to St Ives in 1920 after studying in Japan and whose decorative stoneware pieces masterfully reinterpreted Japanese designs, and the naive artist **Alfred Wallis** (1855-1942), who began painting at the age of seventy following the death of his wife. Wallis painted ships, some from childhood memory, in simplified blocks of colour but with an instinctive feel for abstract design, using decorators' paint on pieces of board given to him by a local shopkeeper. He was "discovered" (1928) by **Ben Nicholson** and Christopher Wood; his apparently crude works only then ever attracted a small following. His tomb in St Ives cemetery is covered with ceramic tiles by Leach. Wallis' flat shapes may, nonetheless, have had a substantial impact on the younger, more dynamic artists in the area who were striving to describe the world in a new, modern way, and whose challenging works soon put them at the forefront of abstract art in this country.

In the late 1930s **Adrian Stokes** (1902-72), the inspired writer on art and painter of subtle, light-filled landscapes, still lifes and nudes, had moved to St Ives with his wife; they invited the couple Ben Nicholson and Barbara Hepworth – later two of the biggest names in British abstract art – to stay, and were joined by the Constructivist sculptor **Naum Gabo** (1890-1977) who remained in Cornwall until the end of the war. Gabo believed that artists had no need to copy the external world as they could work with "absolute forms" to produce pure art works; he was influenced by and in turn influenced both Hepworth and Henry Moore.

Barbara Hepworth (1903-75) had a love of organic shapes and was one of the first artists to work in totally abstract form. Her assured, lyrical sculptures echo nature's generous, sensual shapes and have profound associations with landscape, the coastline, and vegetal forms. Hepworth's house in St Ives is now a museum.

Ben Nicholson (1894-1982) was already known, by the time he joined the Stokes, as a painter of still lifes and abstracted landscapes full of space, light and colour and subsequently as an abstract sculptor who had developed a still-purer aesthetic through the use of light and shade alone *(White Reliefs* series, 1930s). In Cornwall he returned to still-life and landscape painting but no longer made distinction between figurative and non-figurative forms.

St Ives, Cornwall by Ben Nicholson

Penwith Society of Arts – After the Second World War, friction between traditionalists and modernists split the close-knit community which was growing with the influx of a new generation of artists; finally in 1949, shackled by the reactionary views of the president of the St Ives Society of Artists, Sir Alfred Munnings (1878-1968), a group broke away to form the Penwith Society of Arts, with the critic, philosopher and champion of modern art, **Herbert Read** (1893-1968), as its president.

As the 1950s progressed, this group began to fuse abstract ideas and figurative elements more freely, so that the artists of St Ives became less obviously followers of either strictly abstract or strictly figurative tenets.

These artists included **Bryan Wynter** (1915-75) who lived in Cornwall from 1946 to his death; an abstract painter, his romantic and expressive works (usually landscapes) embraced pure colour.

The simplified forms in primary or earth colours with black and white, which typified the abstract works of **Roger Hilton** (1911-75) during the early 1950s, often hinted at landscapes or female figures. From the mid '50s, when Hilton visited St Ives, shallow pictorial space returned to his work and motifs of floating figures or boats were suggested more strongly.

Though the sculptor **Dennis Mitchell** (1912-93) worked exclusively in the abstract idiom – he was Hepworth's assistant for over 10 years – his woodcarvings, and later bronze and slate sculptures, many of which make references to the landscape, were some of the more accessible pieces of the modern movement.

Peter Lanyon (1918-64) was the only Cornishman of the St Ives School. From the 1950s his paintings, heavily influenced by Cubism and by the work of Gabo and Nicholson, were largely abstract but made references to the Cornish landscape and way of life (tin-mining, fishing, farming), as did his reliefs and free-standing pieces. By the later 1950s Lanyon's brushwork had become looser and his paintings included more direct allusions to the sky and weather.

The painter **Terry Frost** (b 1915) worked originally in a style reminiscent of Van Gogh but turned to abstract painting in 1949; gently bobbing boats in harbour are often suggested in his works.

Patrick Heron (b 1920) is also a respected critic of Post-War British Art. Heron admired and was influenced by the works of Braque, and his own works bear some stylistic similarities in their colourful, abstract nature. The new **Tate Gallery at St Ives** (overlooking Porthmeor beach), highlighting works by artists of the St Ives School, features a stained-glass window by Heron, who still lives and works in Cornwall.

Decorative and applied arts

CHURCH FURNISHINGS

Sculpture – Examples of **Saxon** stone sculpture like the *Harrowing of Hell* in Bristol Cathedral (c1050) are rare. The obvious artistry of **Celtic-early Norman** carvers is apparent from the many fonts in Cornish churches to have survived: these huge, square blocks of granite, often standing on five pillars (the five wounds of Christ), are adorned with bearded heads and foliate designs which would originally have been coloured. In contrast, the **Romanesque** stonemasons use geometry to articulate their architecture, grotesque masks and green men on keystones and capitals; the elongated figures at Malmesbury affirm a disregard for realism, conventional perspective or proportion.

The finest complete set of **Gothic sculpture** in England is integrated into the west front of Wells Cathedral: the figures of deacons on the northwest tower, in particular, are endowed with great dignity and humanity. When painted, as recent cleaning has revealed, the impact of the ensemble must have been dramatic: comparison with the sculptures at Exeter is fascinating as the seated kings on the buttresses at Wells reappear in livelier poses as argumentative cross-legged knights in plate armour. From here, it is easy to recognise that the same carvers who cut the Nativity scenes in the south porch at Exeter (the one through which visitors are encouraged to leave) worked also on the great reredos at Christchurch Priory.

Inside, as at Wells, Exeter boasts an outstanding sequence of monumental **effigies** and chantry chapels. The representation of a person either by engraving or with an effigy became general in the Middle Ages. There are stone recumbents of knights in full armour (Sherborne), sometimes accompanied by their wives, of bishops, robed and as cadavers. Many had the monuments which were to adorn their tombs carved in their own lifetime. Others, more modest, are commemorated in fine **brasses**. The Renaissance taste of the Elizabethans and Jacobeans is mirrored in their tombs (Christchurch): the earlier, dignified stone effigies were superseded as the century wore on by ruffed and robed figures presented with their spouses and their

Gallery of the Kings, Exeter Cathedral

children aligned as weepers (Lydiard Park); above were canopies or screens decorated with scrolls and strapwork, eulogies, heraldic devices, achievements, helms and obelisks. Brilliant colours heightened the effect (Lacock).

The Classical influence of the late 17C-18C introduced tombs with figures carved by the fashionable and famous sculptors of the day including Rysbrack, Westmacott and Nost.

Woodwork – Oak wagon roofs, sometimes with carved angles and wall plates mark the long tradition of skill and craftsmanship, especially during the years of prosperity when the trade in wool flourished. Lively **bench-ends** in Cornwall, a few early (15C-16C) ones of oak survive carved with Biblical scenes and/or symbols relating to local legends (like the mermaid at Zennor). In Devon, **rood screens** (the carved and often painted open screen which stands across the entrance to the chancel of a church) for the most part dating from the 15C-16C, embellish many parish churches; in the cathedrals there are **misericords** (the carved bracket under a hinged seat in the choir stalls, which provided support during a long period of standing), **bishops' thrones**, and canopied stalls.

Following Archbishop Laud's (1573-1645) injunction to keep animals away from the altar and to prevent the theft of holy water, splendid **font covers** and **altar rails** were carved in the Jacobean period, also pulpit stair banisters.

In more contemporary times, studio furniture-making is becoming a thriving business once more. Excellent fittings grace the Russel-Cotes Art Gallery in Bournemouth, while elsewhere craft galleries offer individual pieces for sale or on commission. The most notable single furniture-designer, however, is **John Makepiece** (*see* BRIDPORT: Parnham House).

SILVER AND COPPER

The two major West Country towns to have assay offices were Bristol and Exeter, both of which being important centres of banking and commerce, as is reflected in their city museums; at Wells and Salisbury, the best plate was probably made for the church; today trade in antique silver continues to thrive in Bath and Honiton and lavish services grace several of the historic houses in the area, notably Longleat, Wilton and Kingston Lacy...

In 1423 an act licensed seven cathedral cities – which included Bristol – with the authority of registering quality of silver and gold with a "touche" or hallmark. Little West Country silver from the period up to the 17C survives other than apostle and seal-top spoons (Holburne Museum, Bath; Exeter; Truro), as large quantities of plate were confiscated at the Reformation, melted down during the Civil War or sold to finance high-risk ventures overseas.

By 1696, bullion was in short supply and goldsmiths were habitually clipping coin to make up the deficit: the government therefore introduced the Britannia mark for items made of wrought silver of superior quality than coinage, which could only be delivered at Goldsmiths Hall. Before long, fines were considered an easier penalty to bear than the unforeseeable costs of appointing an agent, together with the risks and delays to goods in transit. In 1699, the goldsmiths of Exeter petitioned the government for the repeal of the clause obliging silver to be marked exclusively in London; this was supported by Chester and Norwich so that in the following year a further act was passed authorising the cities of Norwich, York, Bristol, Exeter and Chester to set up assay offices for marking wrought silver conforming to the new standard. Marks were introduced to denote the city and the date; penalties were imposed on those who sold unmarked or substandard plate. Business in Bristol and Exeter boomed. A surge in Exeter registrations coincided with the development of Plymouth Dock as a naval base in preparation for the Napoleonic Wars: demands for buckles, buttons, beltplates, clasps and whistles soared. Interestingly, the influx of Huguenots from France seems to have had little impact on the prevalent styles of the 18C outside London, as designs continued to be sourced from published pattern books.

19C – Fortunes were tested and lost in Bristol as trade declined; Exeter's assay office was closed in 1883 largely as a result of considerable competition from Birmingham and Sheffield. The only thing that reversed the extinction of fine metalwork and jewellery-making in the southwest was the **Arts and Crafts Movement:** largely founded by William Morris and supported by Pugin and Ruskin, it celebrated "the dignity of manual work", "respect for materials" and the concept that "art is the expression of man's pleasure in labour". To advertise their cause exhibitions were organised, guilds were founded, art courses were set up and a whole generation of students went forth to commercialise their skills; they also served to spread a new and radical social awareness. For, as manufacturing processes became mechanised, cottage-industry in rural districts dwindled depriving many (women in particular) of any extra income and forcing ever increasing hardship: mentors of the Arts and Crafts philosophy moved to small communities distant from London with an urge to bring people together and to improve their welfare.

Newlyn Arts and Crafts – Ropework, carpentry, smithying, knitting and sewing kept idle hands busy when adverse weather conditions or depleting fish stocks kept the Newlyn fishing fleet in harbour. In 1890, with financial sponsorship and artistic support, an Industrial Class was established: soon a self-supporting craft workshop specialising in repoussé copper and enamelling was flourishing.

It was the arrival of the already successful artist-craftsman **John Pearson** from Whitechapel, however, which sparked the enterprise into action: Pearson had worked with William de Morgan, bringing to Newlyn a range of designs inspired by Hispano-Moresque lustreware, Persian and Turkish Iznik pottery he would have studied in the British Museum (notably stylised ships, fish, flowers, trees and peacocks painted predominantly in greens, blues and black).

Works designed by Mackenzie and executed by "his fisher lads", the likes of **Phillip Hodder**, William Wright, John Payne Cotton (*note the portrait of Mackenzie and Cotton by Stanhope Forbes illustrated in the section above on painting*), Obed Nicholls are documented in the London exhibitions held by the Home Arts

Repoussé copper charger (1893) by John Pearson

and Industries Association in 1899, 1900 and 1902. By then **The Newlyn Art Metal Industry** offered a range of high-quality objects with well-fitting lids and beautifully finished riveted seams direct from the copperworks, from a selection of shops in Penzance or to order from a catalogue. Mackenzie and a number of his colleagues enlisted for action in World War I; Tom Batten and Cotton survived but found copper (sourced from the Birmingham-based suppliers of the sheet metal used also for stamping coins) in short supply until 1920; Obed Nicholls worked independently; soon machine-made souvenirs and cheap foreign imports proved too much competition.

Enamel – Examples of this intricate art are less common than the copper chargers, picture frames and domestic furnishings. The main exponent was the painter R Dick, who painstakingly evolved designs in blues, greens and amethyst so often associated with the Art Nouveau style of jewellery-making. Perhaps the most skilled of the young "fisher lads" to attend the classes was Francis Charles Clemens (1890-1950) who continued throughout his life to make jewellery for his wife, family and friends.

Ella Naper (1886-1972) must be included although her contact with Newlyn was less formal. She settled in Branscombe (South Devon) to complete her apprenticeship under Fred Partridge, where she met Charles Naper, a landscape painter. Once married, they moved to Lamorna in 1912 near to the painters Harold and Laura Knight. Her exquisite enamelled jewellery and hair combs were closely modelled on studies of plants and flowers, and sold through Liberty's.

An important selection of items by local artists is on permanent display at the Royal Institution of Cornwall in Truro and at Penlee House Gallery and Museum, Penzance. For additional information, consult *Arts and Crafts in Newlyn 1890-1930* by Hazel Berriman (Newlyn Art Gallery 1986).

GLASS AND CERAMICS

Glass – Records affirm that the first glasshouses in Bristol were established in *c*1651 by members of a Genoese factory (Altare) who, unlike contemporary Venetian glassworkers, were obliged to spend time abroad and hence spread their practices to the Netherlands, Germany and Britain; early Bristol clear glass is displayed in the Bristol City Art Gallery and Museum. By 1740, the Bristol works were specialising in a range of decanters, goblets and vases suited to the appreciation of wine-drinking. Also popular was the use of coloured glass which was often decorated with elaborate gilding: the most notable craftsmen associated with the **Bristol blue** were Lazarus and Isaac Jacobs; white glass aping porcelain, complete with delicate Chinoiseries, was perfected by Michael Edkins; other variations include Bristol Green, and amethyst. The demise of blue glass (1780-1820) was largely due to the lack in supplies of the Silesian cobalt oxide required.

The other important glassworks in the area was the one at **Nailsea** (1788 – 1873) founded by one of the partners at the Bristol Limekiln bottle works. This became famous for making crown window glass; sheet window glass from 1844; rolled plate glass from the 1860s. As a side line, it also turned out jugs, vases, flasks and bottles, rolling-pins and ornamental pieces known as friggers (walking sticks, animals, model ships, top hats) often of blue and green glass with trailed or splashed white.

Modern glass is presently made on an industrial scale at Great Torrington (Dartington Glass) and, in a more modest way by artisans in Bristol and Porlock (Exmoor Glass).

Porcelain – Early attempts at developing an English **soft-paste** alternative to the rare and precious hard-paste Oriental porcelain revolved around the Bow and Chelsea factories using clay (unaker) imported from America, a technique patented in 1744. Another technique employed in Bristol by Benjamin Lund between 1749-52 exploited a Cornish soapstone (steatite): this factory sold its shapes and designs to the Worcester factory in 1752.

The first factory in England to succeed in making **hard-paste porcelain** commercially was in Plymouth. This venture, pioneered by the Quaker apothecary **William Cookworthy** (1705-80), followed his discovery in Cornwall of the two vital components of the glassy white stoneware: **kaolin** (found on the estate of Lord Camelford in 1745) and of **petuntse** (silicate of potassium and aluminium), which, when combined, fuse when fired at temperatures of 1250-1350°C. At the end of lengthy experimentation in Bristol, Cookworthy patented his "invention" in 1768, set up the Plymouth factory and then transferred the works to Bristol in 1770; in 1774 he assigned the patent to Robert Champion, who closed the Bristol factory down in 1862 and sold the patent on to the New Hall manufacturers.

Early forms produced in Plymouth include salts in the form of sea-shells, mugs and sauce boats decorated in underglazed blue often modelled on those made by Meissen, Sèvres and Derby; rather crude figurines copied from Bow and Longton Hall. Given that a number of decorators worked both at Plymouth and Bristol, it is difficult to discern one factory type from the other. The best survey is provided by **Plymouth City Museum**; good collections are to be found at Bristol and Truro.

Earthenware – Earthenware consists of earth-coloured clay being shaped and fired to make it more stable. To make it more durable and practical, the object can be given a **lead-glaze** before being fired a second time at a higher temperature, forcing the glaze to fuse with the baked clay giving it a clear glassy surface. One of the cheapest ways of decorating earthenware is by painting or dribbling the plate, cup or pot with liquid clay (slip) of a contrasting colour to produce **slipware**. Typical examples of these often inherently rustic yet charming pieces were produced at a number of potteries in north Devon, notably at Barnstaple, Bideford and Fremington. The tradition of tin-glazed utilitarian slipware like cider jugs, was particularly revived by Michael Cardew (*see below:* Leach Pottery).

The practice of writing pious or moralising inscriptions, which became common from the 17C, continued through to the Victorian era in the form of souvenir giftware from Torquay.

H.K.P. Lines/Burton Art Gallery and Museum Bideford

Slipware by Henry Phillips of Bideford

The other current form of decoration is by applying an opaque **tin-glaze** over which other colours may be added: since earliest times (9C) efforts were made to rival the glossy whiteness of Chinese porcelain by covering earthenware with an opaque white glaze; the practice was transmitted from Persia to Spain and thence to Italy (13C). Biscuit-fired vessels were more durable than simple clay ones; a second firing after an application of glaze (tin and lead oxides with silicate of potash) made them impermeable to liquid. A surface covering of lead glaze produces a bright sheen on which enamel colours can be applied and submitted to a third firing stage: when the inherent danger precipitated by the fumes from this procedure were fully appreciated in the 19C, less noxious alternatives were developed. Collectively these wares are labelled **Delftware** if the painted decoration is underglazed blue (cobalt), and **Maiolica** if coloured with metallic oxides of copper (green), manganese (purple), antimony (yellow) and/or iron (orange).

Several small potteries are linked with Bristol, notably those at Brislington and Wincanton, in the late 17C and 18C: the absence of consistent marking has meant that pieces are often to be confused with factories at Lambeth and Liverpool. Recurring designs include portraits in maiolica colours, floral bunches, and from *c*1720, a series of Chinoiseries in blue and white.

A variation of tin-glazed earthenware is a particular type of **lustreware** which, like Royal Doulton, was adapted in Victorian times to tile and decorate public buildings. **Poole Pottery** is one factory which has managed to develop its range of enamel-coloured products to suit contemporary demands for utilitarian ceramics.

Studio pottery – The Arts and Crafts Movement inspired artists to apply their skills to all disciplines, and ceramics were no exception. While the likes of the Martin Brothers borrowed from German stoneware designs and William de Morgan turned to Persian pottery, others looked to Japanese raku which was often celebrated for its individuality of form, appearance and texture. True studio potters are those artist-craftsmen who decide to practise traditional methods, alone or with an assistant, to produce individual pieces which might be considered as "works of art". This probably excludes those who merely helped to increase an awareness and appreciation of hand-made/hand-decorated ceramics like Gauguin, Picasso and Matisse who took to decorating blanks, and others, like Harold Stabler at Poole, who adapted graphic skills and an eye for "industrial" design to make distinctive types of pottery.

Leach Pottery – Bernard Leach (1887-1979) is considered as the most important English studio potter. Although he trained as a painter and etcher, Leach elected to spend 11 years (1909-20) in China and Japan studying pottery under the last Ogata Kenzan before moving to England and settling in St Ives. There, assisted by Shoji Hamada, Leach went on to produce his hand-made functional "thinking man's" pots drawing inspiration from Chinese, Korean and Japanese (low temperature raku) pottery, and from 17C English slipware. Soon he was gaining particular notice for the simple forms of vases and bowls which relied rather on incised line or an informal splash of colour for decoration than on figurative design: "Pots, like all forms of art, are human expressions" he claimed. In 1927 Leach became involved with the Elmhirsts at Dartington Hall; in 1934 they paid for Leach to travel back to Japan with the American painter Mark Tobey, a follower of the Baha'i faith which advocates a belief in the universal brotherhood of man: a philosophy that profoundly impressed Leach. During his trip, he collected together his thoughts and theories on design, publishing them in *A Potter's Book* (1940), an enduring manual which broadcasts the concept of the potter as an artist-craftsman in his own right as opposed to a "simple" artisan. In 1962 Bernard Leach was made CBE.

The Japanese potter **Shoji Hamada** (1894-1978) worked in stoneware, typically decorating simple shapes with abstract designs in ash and iron glazes. Between 1920-24, he collaborated with Bernard Leach while at St Ives, before returning to Japan. Other names linked with the early years of the pottery include those of **Michael Cardew** (1901-82;who built the Wenford Bridge Pottery at Bodmin) and **Lucie Rie**. The ex-sculptress from New York, **Janet Leach** (1918-1997) became interested in Bernard Leach's philosophy and Japanese-style of pottery after meeting him in 1952 in America. Two years later, she travelled to Japan to study with Hamada before going into the mountains to see folkcraft potteries at work: the only woman to operate a potter's wheel in Japan. In 1956, she came to Britain and married Bernard, then, as a partner in Leach Pottery Ltd she took an active role in organising the showroom and directing foreign students engaged in two-year work training programmes there making standard wares, while producing her own pots. After the death of Bernard, Janet gave up the teaching side of the business to concentrate on her own work: all individually-designed pots are fired reduction stoneware.

David Leach (b 1911) joined his father at the Leach Pottery in 1930 where he set to learning how to throw pots; in 1934 he after a brief stint at teaching near Dartington Hall, David went to Stoke Technical College to study industrial production techniques. On returning to St Ives he began modernising working practices: he introduced an oil-fired kiln, a machine for blending clay, abandoning slipware in favour of stoneware. After the war (1946) David became a partner in the Leach Pottery alongside Bernard; in 1950 John arrived: meanwhile demand for their works increased via Heals, John Lewis and Liberty's. In 1955 the trio disbanded, David moving to Devon to set up his own pottery at Bovey Tracey. David's eldest son **John Leach** continues the Leach legacy: while actively involved in teaching, kindling in others his own enthusiasm and humble appreciation of hand-crafted pots, he produces unique pieces of studio pottery and a range of utilitarian kitchenware. Although traditionally functional and robustly practical, this wood-fired stoneware is also completely modern, prized for its intrinsic balance – achieved by means of painstakingly mastering the art of throwing as advocated by his grandfather and subsequent teachers including David Leach, Ray Finch and Colin Pearson. John Leach has established his own pottery at Muchelney (near Langport),working with Nick Rees.

For additional information, see *The Leach Legacy: St Ives Pottery and its Influence* by Marion Whybrow (1996).

TEXTILES

Since Roman times, wool played a key role in the developing prosperity of the West Country. It provided monastic institutions with a reliable source of income, and after the Dissolution, **woollen cloth** became a major commodity in the trade with Europe and Newfoundland. In Dorset, flax and hemp were grown from Saxon times for making sailcloth, fishing nets and rope; distinctive smocking patterns peculiar to each family were propagated through the generations; **buttons**, **gloves bonnets** and **lace**, continued to be made in Shaftesbury, Yeovil and Honiton well into the 19C. On an industrial scale, **carpet-making** at Axminster and Wilton, serge at Exeter (1750s-1761), silk (later rayon) at Sherborne (Cerne Abbas, Gillingham) have also been important concerns.

Cryséde silk – In 1920 **Alec Walker** (1889-1964) settled in Newlyn intent on building his own business block-printing the Vigil silk manufactured at the family's mills in Yorkshire and making it up as garments to his wife Kay's designs. The new range of over-printed fabric (crêpe-de-chine from Bradford, later from Sherborne and georgette) they called Cryséde.

Kay had been a student of Stanhope Forbes and she went on to design much of the early promotional material for the range. In 1923 Walker went to Paris and met Dufy and Zadkine, both of whom proved to have major influences on him, encouraging him to develop his own designs. Soon a large portfolio of mail-order customers in Paris, New York and Sydney were registered on the books and an ever greater number of local people were trained to cope with the increase in business. In 1926 the company, under the management of Tom Heron, was transferred to yet larger premises at the Island Works in St Ives.

Walker was never formally trained: he used his strong innate sense of colour and natural design flair to his advantage, adapting and repeating patterns and motifs to a flat silk ground that cleverly find movement and depth when incorporated into clothing by being folded or pleated into place. Most designs were adapted from his studies of landscape (St Buryan depicts a local horse race; Zennor includes the church, houses, rocks and sea; Isles of Scilly with palm trees and waves). Instinct attracted him to the visual appeal of poster art, abstraction and the Fauves in France and the Vorticists or English Futurists who included his friends Frank Dobson and Wyndham Lewis.

Displays of Cryséde textiles are on show at the Royal Institution Museum, Truro and at Penlee House Gallery and Museum , Penzance. For additional information, consult *Cryséde: The Unique Textile Designs of Alex Walker* by Hazel Burston (Royal Institution of Cornwall 1993).

Cryséde silk: Welsh Hill Farm block print

S. Tanner/Royal Institution of Cornwall, Truro

Literary associations

DAWN OF ENGLISH ROMANTICISM

Samuel Taylor Coleridge (1772-1834) was born the youngest son of a Devonshire clergyman and schoolmaster at Ottery St Mary (*see* HONITON). His childhood came abruptly to an end when his father died and the young Sam was despatched to the brutal and Spartan Blue Coat School in London (1782). Devon was left far behind, ever after associated with "visions of childhood", yet the notions of poetry, founded on a need for solace from loneliness, nurtured by voracious reading and a perceptive Grammar School master, soon found a voice in the brilliant, precociously eloquent young Coleridge.

Like many contemporaries, STC was fired with idealism by the ideals of Liberty inspired by the French Revolution; he travelled into Wales and Somerset prompted by the Picturesque writings of William Gilpin; socialised with graduates at Oxford, including the Bristol-born radical **Robert Southey** with whom he discussed the founding of an utopian colony in America; they journeyed on foot to Bristol, Bath, Wells, Cheddar and on to Nether Stowey, on the extreme edges of the open Somerset Levels and the more austerely beautiful Quantock Hills. On 4 October 1795 Coleridge was married to Sara Fricker at St Mary Redcliffe; they lived first at Clevedon, then transferred to Bristol where his work was beginning to be published. The last day of 1796, wrought by indecision and insecurity, the penniless STC moved his young family to Stowey (*see* BRIDGWATER), attracted there by the beauty of the countryside and a profound admiration for his dependable friend Tom Poole, a local tanner.

1797 was a crucial year for Coleridge: in June he delighted his friends William and Dorothy Wordsworth by turning up at their garden gate unexpectedly; after some persuasion, they eventually signed a year's lease on Alfoxden Manor (some 3 miles from Nether Stowey). Together, they spent days at a time expounding ideas, encouraging each other in their work, taking long walks into the Quantocks, to Culbone and to Lynmouth, as a result of which Coleridge wrote two of his most brilliant poems: *Kubla Khan* and *The Rime of the Ancient Mariner*. His close collaboration with Wordsworth became more involved as they embarked on the *Lyrical Ballads* collection and formulated the essence of what later became known as Romanticism: "the two cardinal points of poetry," Coleridge wrote were " the power of exciting the sympathy of the reader by a faithful adherence to the truth of nature, and the power of giving the interest of novelty by the modifying colours of imagination". Coleridge turned to subjects "supernatural, or at least romantic", Wordsworth to "give the charm of novelty to things of every day" in incidents and among characters from village life. Meanwhile, financial insecurity, which had always dogged the young poet was finally suspended when Thomas and Josiah Wedgwood, the sons of the highly successful founder of the potteries, offered Coleridge an annuity for life.

Soon the lease on Alfoxden expired; shortly after leaving Somerset, William and Dorothy Wordsworth set out walking in the Wye Valley. There, Wordsworth wrote his famous meditation on *Tintern Abbey* which, in many ways, encapsulated the spirit of Romanticism.

Late in the autumn of 1798, Coleridge left Tom Poole, his wife and two sons in Nether Stowey, joining the Wordsworths at Yarmouth before embarking for Germany: Coleridge was henceforth only to return to Somerset intermittently. In July 1800, he settled the family at Keswick, a few miles from the Wordsworths' Lakeland home at Grasmere; his relationship with Sara deteriorated and disinte-grated. Meanwhile, having fallen passionately in love, Coleridge wrote little, lacking inspiration; he became increasingly addicted to opium. After collapsing in Bristol he realised he must mend his ways however arduous it might be; with resolve, while staying with friends in Calne, he dictated the *Biographia Literaria* (1815), a brilliant thesis which combined autobiography with literary criticism and philosophy. His final 18 years he spent living with a surgeon in Highgate, where he is buried.

> ....And now, beloved Stowey! I behold
> Thy church-tower, and, methinks, the four huge elms
> Clustering, which mark the mansion of my friend;
> And close behind them, hidden from my view,
> is my own lowly cottage, where my babe
> And my babe's mother dwell in peace!
> by S T Coleridge 1797

OTHER POETIC PICTURES

Besides the evocative **Arthurian Legends** by Thomas Malory, Spenser, Tennyson, Swinburne and TH White, pictures of this part of Britain are vividly portrayed in the poetry of **John Betjeman**, Charles Causley (20C Cornish poet).

THE WESSEX OF THOMAS HARDY

Thomas Hardy (1840-1928), who was born in Dorchester and whose heart lies in Stinsford churchyard, took as his literary arena an area approximately that of King Alfred's Wessex. Indeed Hardy popularised the revival of the name of Wessex; he knew its countryside in minute detail : the heaths and vales, towns, villages, the views, lanes and fields, individual houses, the churches... At times his descriptions were "straight", at times combined with place-names disguised to a greater or lesser extent : a few, such as Bath, Bristol, Falmouth, Plymouth, Chippenham, Stonehenge and Wardour Castle and some geographical features, appear under their real names; others use an old form as in Shaston for Shaftesbury.

Dorset County Museum

Thomas Hardy by William Strang (engraving)

Hardy's Wessex extended beyond the borders of this guide : listed below, for those holidaying in Dorset and the surrounding counties, are the geographical name and the disguised place-name, together with the prose works in which these occur. The lexicon below has been compiled with the learned assistance of the Secretary of the Thomas Hardy Society, J C Pentney.

Key to titles

Novels in order of publication

DR	*Desperate Remedies*
UGT	*Under the Greenwood Tree*
PBE	*A Pair of Blue Eyes*
FMC	*Far from the Madding Crowd*
HE	*The Hand of Ethelberta*
RN	*The Return of the Native*
TM	*The Trumpet-Major*
L	*A Laodicean*
TT	*Two on a Tower*
MC	*The Mayor of Casterbridge*
W	*The Woodlanders*
TD	*Tess of the d'Urbervilles*
JO	*Jude the Obscure*
WB	*The Well-Beloved*

Short Story collections

WT	*Wessex Tales*
GND	*A Group of Noble Dames*
LLI	*Life's Little Ironies*
CM	*A Changed Man*
+	*old form of place-name*

Dorset (Hardy's South Wessex)

PLACE-NAME	HARDY'S NAME	NOVEL
Athelhampton	Athelhall	CM
Beaminster	Emminster	FMC TD
Bere Regis	Kingsbere (sub-Greenhill)	FMC RN TM TD WT
Blandford Forum	Shottsford (Forum)	FMC TM MC W JO WT GND LLI CM
Bournemouth	Sandbourne	HE TD JO WB LLI
Bridport	Port Bredy	MC W TD WT LLI
Blackmoor Vale	Vale of Little Dairies	TD
Cerne Abbas	Abbot's Cernel	W TD LLI
Chesil Beach or Bank	The Pebble Bank	WB
Corfe Castle	Corvsgate Castle	DR HE
Cranborne	Chaseborough	TD
Cranborne Chase	The Chase	TD GND
Dorchester	Casterbridge	DR UGT FMC RN TM MC W TD JO WT GND LLI CM
Evershot	Evershead	TD WT GND CM
Fortuneswell, Portland	The Street of Wells	TM WB
River Frome	Froom or Var	UGT MC TD CM
Frome Valley	Valley of the Great Dairies	TD
Gillingham	Leddenton	JO
Hardy's Cottage	Tranter Dewy's	UGT
Higher Bockhampton	Upper Mellstock	UGT
Kingston Maurward House	Knapwater House	DR UGT (the Manor)
Lower Bockhampton	Lower or East Mellstock	UGT
	Carriford	DR
Lulworth Cove	Lulwind Cove; Bay	DR FMC LLI
Lyme or West Bay	Deadman's Bay	WB
Maiden Castle	Mai-Dun (Castle)	TM MC CM
Maiden Newton	Chalk Newton	UGT FMC TD GM

Maumbury Rings, Dorchester	The Ring	MC
Milborne St Andrew	Millpond (St Jude's)	FMC TD
Milton Abbey	Middleton Abbey +	W TD
Poole	Havenpool	HE MC LLI CM
Portland	Isle of Slingers, Vindilia	WB
Portland Bill	The Beal	TM
Poundbury Camp, Dorchester	Pummery +	MC
Puddletown	Weatherbury or Lower Longpuddle	UGT FMC
Puddletown Forest	Egdon Heath	UGT FMC RN TD
Sandsfoot Castle, Weymouth	Henry VIII Castle	WB
Shaftesbury	Shaston +	TD JO
Sherborne	Sherton Abbas	W TD GND
Stinsford	Mellstock	UGT RN TD
Sturminster Newton	Stourcastle	TD
Tincleton	Stickleford	RN TD WT LLI
Tolpuddle	Tolchurch	DR
Wareham	Anglebury	DR HE RN MC TD WT
Waterston Manor, Puddletown	Weatherbury Upper Farm	FMC
Weymouth (and Melcombe Regis)	Budmouth (Regis)	DR UGT FMC RN TM L TT MC W WT GND LLI CM
Wimborne (Minster)	Warborne	TT GND
Woodbury Hill	Greenhill	FMC RN TM TT TD LLI
Yellowham Hill, Wood, nr Higher Bockhampton	Yalbury Hill, Wood	UGT FMC LLI

Lyonesse, Cornwall (Hardy's Off Wessex)

Boscastle	Castle Boterel	PBE
Bude	Stratleigh	PBE
Camelford	Camelton	PBE
Lanhydrock House	Endelstow House	PBE
Launceston	St Launce's	PBE
Penzance	Penzephyr	CM
Redruth	Redrutin	CM
Tintagel	Dundagel	PBE
Truro	Trufal	CM

Devon (Hardy's Lower Wessex)

Barnstaple	Downstaple	GND
Exeter	Exonbury	PBE TM W LLI CM
Sidmouth	Idmouth	CM
Tiverton	Tivworthy	CM
Torquay	Tor-upon-Sea	CM

Somerset (Hardy's Outer or Nether Wessex)

Dunster (Castle)	Markton Steney Castle	L
East Coker	Narrobourne	LLI
Montacute House	Montislope House	CM
Taunton	Toneborough	L GND LLI
Wells	Fountall	LLI CM
Yeovil	Ivell +	W GND LLI

Wiltshire (Hardy's Mid Wessex)

Marlborough Downs	Marlbury Downs	GM
Old Sarum	Old Melchester	LLI
Salisbury	Melchester	FMC HE TT MC TD JO GND LLI CM
Salisbury Plain	The Great Plain	TD LLI

OTHER FICTION

A number of eminent authors have set their novels in the West Country:

Jane Austen	Persuasion; Northanger Abbey
R D Blackmore	Lorna Doone
William Golding	The Spire
Winston Graham	Poldark Novels
Charles Kingsley	Westward Ho!
Daphne du Maurier	Frenchman's Creek; Rebecca; Jamaica Inn; Vanishing Cornwall
Anthony Trollope	Chronicles of Barsetshire
Virginia Woolf	To The Lighthouse

Regional specialities

Come fill ye up the cider cup
And drink to Cheddar Cheese...
Taken from *The Great Cheeses of Britain and Ireland* by Robert Smith

APPLES AND CIDER

The apple season begins in mid-August when Discovery apples, described as strawberry-flavoured, ripen; the Katy and Worcester varieties follow in September; the famous Cox, Lord Lambourne, Orléans Reinette ripen later in the year for eating in October to Christmas. The true Somerset varieties which include many bitter ones grown exclusively for cider, include Dabinetts, porter perfection, royal Somerset, Morgan sweet, Somerset redstreak, golden pippin, Hang me down, slap me girdle and Kingston black (as grown at Burrow Hill – Somerset Cider Brandy Co, Kingsbury Episcopi and Brimblecombe's Devon Cider at Dunsford).

To safeguard and develop traditional varieties of apple, orchards are being planted throughout the southwest and being exploited to provide wholesome pure apple juice. This should be pasteurised (to prevent bacterial infection) and bottled so as to be kept for a period of 12 months or more.

Cider – According to tradition, cider has been brewed from apples since Celtic times when the Glastonbury area was known as the Isle of Apples under the patronage of Rhiannon, the goddess of apples. Cider quite simply consists of apple juice fermented (like wine) with natural yeast and left to mature gently: as may be seen at Countryman Cider at Milton Abbot; or Hancock's Devon Cider at South Molton. Traditionally only bitter cider apples are used in making West Country cider – elsewhere in Britain dessert (cookers and eaters) are also used – it is normally dry in taste, flat (unless dosed with additional yeast or turned as in the *méthode champennoise*), and ranked between beer and wine in alcoholic content (5.5-5.8%). By contrast, modern methods of ensuring that mass-produced cider is standardised involve pasteurisation, additions of sugar, concentrates and/or cultured yeast before being carbonated and casked. The big brewers like Matthew Clarke, Taunton and HP Bulmer (Woodpecker, Strongbow, Scrumpy Jack) hold over 90% of the market: however, the collective competition from independents making full flavoured traditional or "real" ciders has prompted the large manufacturers to return to producing and distributing more authentic types of full-bodied West Country draught cider through their pubs. The industrial scale of cider production has largely been blamed on the drink being tax-exempt until 1976 when Chancellor Dennis Healey imposed a duty on cider of less than 8.5% alcohol; this was and continues to be less than the duty levied on beer, and still manufacturers can make up to 1 500 gallons (7 000 litres) a year for sale duty-free. This fact has encouraged many cottage-producers to engage in cider making, including winemakers who exploit their presses, bottling facilities and know-how in fermenting cider a second time in the bottle as in Champagne-making as in **Bollhayes Cider** from Cullompton in Devon and **Burrow Hill** Bottle-Fermented Sparkling Cider from the **Somerset Cider Brandy Company**.

Other recommended (prizewinning) producers to look out for include Bennett; Bridge Farm; the Cornish Cider Company (near Truro) which make their brew from a mixture of Bramley and Kingston black apples; Cornish Scrumpy; Grays Farm Cider (Tedbury St Mary); Naish's (Glastonbury); Perry's (Dowlish Wake, Ilminster; museum of cider making). Among the more widely distributed ciders, look out for **Rich's Farmhouse Cider** and **Sheppy's** (from outside Taunton).

The greatest collection of cider-making presses, lovingly restored to working order and regularly employed is at **Millhouse Cider**, Owermoigne (near Dorchester).

Few licences have been granted for making a strong Calvados-like **cider brandy** but the Somerset Cider Brandy Company ages its brandy (averaging at 40% alcohol) three years in oak barrels.

Ice-cream parlour, Cheddar

Genuine **perry** is made with bitter perry pears into a pear equivalent of cider: scarcity of the appropriate fruit, smaller holdings, less predictable quality and problems relating to processing pear pulp have made perrymaking a less commercially viable end-product – hence its rarity.

Consult the *CAMRA Guide to Real Cider*, reviewed annually, for more detailed information.

Useful contacts – Classic English varieties grown and picked for quality and flavour sold at **Charlton Orchard** near Taunton (☎ 01823 412 959) and **New Cross Fruitfarm** at East Lambrook (☎ 01460 241 561).

Cider apples (and fuschias) are grown at **Millhouse Cider** and Nurseries, Owermoigne (near Dorchester). They also have a superb collection of well-worn traditional cider-making equipment. ☎ 01305 852 220.

Roskilly's at St Kevern near Helston distributes apple-juice and cider from its farmshop; also home-produced (scrummy) fudge, icecream, clotted cream (mail order service), honeys, jams and preserves... ☎ 01326 280 479.

Keith Goverd at Compton Dando specialises in making a wide range of pure apple juice and real perry, tastings arranged by appointment; technical advice on production. ☎ 01761 490 624.

Thornhayes Nursery is run by an authoritative nurseryman who supplies RHS and NT properties throughout the UK. Broad range of 200+ apple varieties, including some 70 suited to cidermaking (also plums, medlars, pears; advice and mailorder). Located at St Andrews Wood, Dulford, Cullompton EX15 2DF. ☎ 01884 266 746.

CEREALS AND BEER

Plain strong flour is milled in the traditional way at various mills as a tourist attraction at Sturminster Newton, Dunster and Wilton Windmill; the real thing is organically and commercially produced at **Rushall Mill** (near Pewsey) where a variety of excellent breads are baked.

Also in the area are the **Wiltshire Tracklement Company** (Malmesbury), the original manufacturers of English Coarse-Ground mustard, and Louisa Maskell Preserves, Pickles and Sauces (Marlborough) made from fruits, nuts and herbs home-grown or collected from Savernake Forest.

Beer – **Real ale** consists of cask-conditioned beer, which, in other words, means that the fermentation process is allowed to continue until the beer is served up in a pub: the result should be a naturally rounded drink, not too effervescent, dispensed at a temperature of 12.5ºC (55ºF). As the shelf-life of these is limited to two or three weeks, it is tempting for pubs to stock the more profitable **keg beers**, which, for the sake of the foreign visitor who may wish to join in with the bar banter, consists of beer that has been sterilised (ie pasteurised and filtered to halt fermentation) before distribution, and has to be pumped to the bar under pressure. What makes keg beer commercial for the publican is that it has a longer shelf-life; what makes it contentious to the CAMRA (Campaign for Real Ale Ltd) supporter is the reduced value of his pint: in order to control the effect of the added gas, the beer has to be chilled, which reduces its flavour; while the extra fizz, once allowed to settle in a head of spume, reduces the actual pint measure of drinkable beer.

Considerable upheavals in the brewing industry in recent years have radically altered the range of beers available in pubs today. The main players are the nationals, which for the most part are centred in the north of England. In the southwest, the most successful independents, like Ushers, Wadworths and St Austell, rely largely on their portfolio of tied houses grouped in the vicinity of the brewery. Undoubtedly, cost is a major factor in distribution so the names given below are only a fraction of the many young brewers to look out for in good local pubs: for more complete listings consult the annually updated *CAMRA Good Beer Guide*.

The **Bristol Brewery**, established as a Georges brewery in 1788, is now the only real ale brewery owned by Scottish Courage in the south – house Georges Bitter Ale is still produced, but only really distributed in the West Country and southeast Wales; more popular are Courage Best Bitter and Courage Directors. Other brewers include **Butcombe** (founded 1978: standard Bitter) and the Smile Brewing Co.

In Cornwall, there has long been a taste for strong alcohol encouraged no doubt by smuggling and bootlegging. Plymouth has its own gin distillery and breweries (Summerskills, Sutton's...); **St Austell** boasts Cornwall's oldest family brewery (founded 1851; XXXXMild, Hicks Special Draught or HSD); the 15C **Blue Anchor** in Helston is possibly the oldest established brew-pub in England.

Dorset has several successful independent brewers: **Badger's** in Blandford Forum (founded as Hall and Woodhouse in 1777: Dorset Best and Tanglefoot); the **Thomas Hardy Brewery** in Dorchester (founded as the Green Dragon Brewery in 1837; renamed the Eldridge Pope Brewery: Thomas Hardy's Ale, Pope's Traditional, Royal Oak, Country Bitter); and **Palmers** of Bridport.

Two Somerset brewers that are recommended include **Exe Valley** (1984: Dobs Bitter) and **Exmoor Ales** (1980: Exmoor Ale, Exmoor Stag).

Wiltshire is associated with a clutch of names: **Archers** (founded in 1979 and producing Village, Black Jack, Golden bitters); **Arkells** (1843); **Bunces Brewery** in Salisbury (1984: Benchmark, Old Smokey; wheat beers for summer consumption); **Gibbs Mew** (1898: Overlord; Bishop's Tipple barley wine) and **Hop Back** (1987: Mild, GFB; the vegan beer Entire Stout; their original wheat beer Thunderstorm). **Usher's** of Trowbridge (1824: producing keg and bottled beer for Scottish Courage) and **Wadworths & Co** of Devizes (1885: Henry's Original IPA, 6X, Old Timer).

CHEESE

According to one fanciful legend, the history of West Country cheese began when monks on a pilgrimage to Glastonbury took shelter from a terrible storm in the Cheddar caves and found that the milk they were carrying in leather pouches had turned into a delicious cheese: Cheddar has since become synonymous with English cheese, notably abroad. The fanciful element in the story lies in the fact that the Cheddar Caves remained inaccessible to all but climbers until the 19C. The truth of the tale is that itinerant holy men, especially early Celtic monks from Ireland, were instrumental in developing the art of cheese-making not only as a means of saving what otherwise might be wasted milk but also for eating on days of fasting when meat was forbidden: hence the reason for dairy products (and sometimes eggs) being referred to as "white meat". During the times when the wool trade prospered, certainly up until the 16C, cheeses throughout England must predominantly have been made with ewes' milk – those still produced today include Wensleydale and Caerphilly.

Among the many places in the West Country at which to buy excellent cheeses, look out for The Cheese Board in Bath, Country Cheeses in Tavistock, Ticklemore Cheese Shop in Totnes and The Fine Cheese Co in Wells; market traders in Barnstaple (Friday) and Salisbury (Tuesday and Saturday).

Specialist Cheesemakers' Association

In February 1989, in the face of an outbreak of lysteria, the Ministry of Agriculture announced an intended ban on the sale of unpasteurised cheese: with the financial and administrative backup of the Milk Marketing Board, the Specialist Cheesemakers' Association was formed to promote awareness and encouragement for cheesemaking in Britain and Ireland, to uphold standards of quality and underpin a cooperation between producers, distributors, retailers and consumers.

For more information: PO Box 448, Newcastle under Lyme, Staffs. ST5 0BF. ☎ 01782 580 580.

Main types – Most of the hard cheeses produced in Britain such as Cheddar (double Gloucester and red Leicester) are made as **scalded pressed cheese**. This involves raw or pasteurised milk being treated with starter (an acidic agent that curdles the milk) and rennet (the clotting agent, now often derived using synthetic substitutes and therefore classified as "vegetarian"); the curd is then scalded, pitched for piling and turning (a process known as cheddaring), milled and salted; once moulded, the cheese may be handled so as to produce a rind or matured in large blocks, wrapped in plastic for supermarkets.

Mould-ripened cheeses, which include Camembert (or Bath cheese) and Brie, are produced using the same initial processes as for scalded pressed cheese, only at curd stage, instead of being scalded, they are pressed, drained and ladled into moulds; to achieve a soft white skin, these small individual cheeses are often sprayed with a "flora" culture.

The most smelly types are usually **washed rind cheeses**: early preparation is the same as for the other types; the curd is moulded and pressed, and then washed repeatedly with brine, beer, wine or other such liquid.

Cow's cheese – Traditionally, Somerset is where cheese is most respected, its fertile lands providing the ideal rich pasture for grazing dairy herds; in close second place come the other great dairying counties of Devon and Dorset. It was Daniel Defoe who perhaps established the association of cheese with Cheddar in Somerset for in his *Tour Through the Whole Island of Great Britain* (1724-27) he described how the cows were kept communally on the village green there, how the milk was measured and collectively transformed into cheese. Shortly afterwards, demand for cheese from Cheddar outgrew the supplies available, turning it into an expensive luxury. A century later, cheesemaking was transformed by technology: standardised methods of preparation and dairy-hygiene, largely pioneered by Joseph Harding (1808-76) outside Bath, assured a more viable and consistently high quality product (*see* GLASTONBURY: Somerset Museum of Rural Life).

In general terms, one gallon of milk will make a pound of cheese (5litres to 0.5kg). The fat content of milk usually falls from March to June after the cows have been turned out to pasture; it will gradually rise again over the ensuing months until they are enclosed once more through the winter months. Levels of casein, the main protein, drop as the days shorten. The best cheese, therefore is said to be made after autumn calving. In terms of ageing, from the time it is made (hence its name

The Dairy, Lanhydrock

"green") Cheddar is kept for a minimum of eight weeks before being graded; becomes "mild" flavoured after approximately three months, and reaches "mature" status after eight to nine months. It may of course be stored longer.

Under an EU-backed initiative, a scheme to register cheeses under a "Protective Designation of Origin" – a patent-protection policy on the lines of regional cheese denominations in France – includes West Country Farm Cheddar and Single Gloucester (1997).

Caerphilly – Duckett's Caerphilly was once made to sustain the teams of Welsh workers down the mines when most able-bodied men could earn more in the pits than on the farms; severe milk shortages during World War II revived the demand from across the Bristol Channel. Slightly salty with a crumbly texture, Duckett's prizewinning Caerphilly is available at varying stages of maturity.

Cheddar – Varieties of Somerset Cheddar are currently being made by a number of small and large-scale producers in and around Cheddar, Isle of Athelney (Glastonbury Tor), Lydeard St Lawrence, Frome, Shepton Mallet and Crewkerne, to be sold through local stockists and, very often, from the region's market traders; traditional cheese-making may be seen at the Cheddar Gorge Cheese Company and Chewton Cheese Dairy (*see* CHEDDAR GORGE). Flavoured varieties are made by one of the largest exporters of table cheeses to US and Japan, the Ilchester Cheese Co using applewood smoke (Applewood); chopped onion and chives (Abbeydale); Stilton and Port wine (Admirals); Fuller's ale, spices and chives (Ilchester).

Outside Somerset, the only commercial producers of farmhouse Cheddar left in Devon are the prizewinning Quickes at Home Farm, Newton St Cyres, outside Exeter; while in Dorset, the largest producer is the Ashley Chase Estate which operates a dairy making Cheddar and English Gruyère.

Blue cheeses – The name **Dorset Blue Vinney** is a corruption of "veiny": the West Country's alternative to Stilton used to have a notorious reputation as being hard enough to be used to hone axes. This has been dispelled with the revival of this crumbly low fat blue cheese. Variants include **Exmoor Jersey Blue** (made with Jersey cow's milk) and **Somerset Blue** from Exmoor Blue Cheese (Willett Farm, Lydeard St Lawrence), and **Devon Blue** from Ticklemore Cheese.

Miscellaneous – **Cornish Yarg** is named after a Mr Gray; this medium pressed cheese made by the Lynher Dairies near Liskeard has the consistency of Caerphilly. It is wrapped in nettle leaves which stimulate the formation of the edible rind. Best after four to six weeks.

Cream

The fat content of cream makes it rise to the surface of milk, from where it may be skimmed off to provide **half-cream** for coffee and cornflakes, **single cream** for adding to soups and casseroles, **whipping cream** which can be whisked thick for desserts and double cream for sheer indulgence!

Clotted cream, that unctious substance for plates of summer berries and meringues, is in fact 12-hour old cream that is solidified by very gentle cooking (or scalding) for six to height hours.

Crème fraiche, which the French pass off as cream, is cream that has been left to mature and sour naturally without the addition of bacteria or starters; more resistant to withstanding heat before curdling, it is often used in cooking to thicken sauces.

Curworthy is a full-fat, semi hard cheese sold at three months; when matured for five to six months it is called **Devon Oke**, both are produced on the edge of Dartmoor at Stockbeare Farm near Okehampton. The other variant is **Meldon**, made with Chiltern ale and whole-grain English mustard seeds.

Sharpham's soft, scrummy Coulommiers-style cheese from near Totnes is only available from March to December. Gloucester, the crumbly British "territorial" is made countrywide: its colour, which ranges from pale orange to deep red-orange, is gained with the addition of annatto. Made in Devon as **Single Gloucester** and **Double Gloucester** by J G Quicke and Partners (*see* Cheddar, *above*).

Bath Cheese is a soft creamy cheese resembling Camembert: rescued from oblivion by a traditional recipe book, this is a perfect complement to the traditional Bath Oliver Biscuits.

Ewe's cheese – Ewe's milk is sweeter than cow's milk, richer in vitamins, and makes a richer, creamier-textured cheese. At present there is no single English ewe's cheese to compare in international fame with French Roquefort, but enterprise at The Big Sheep (*see* BIDEFORD) is reviving a series of traditional cheeses such as Abbotsdale, Ashleigh (an Italian Pecorino-like cheese) and Friesla. Innovation on a smaller scale is being managed by Mary Holbrook who produces a range of fresh cheeses, soft Greek-style fetta, the mould-ripened creamy Emlett and a fine hard cheese (Tyning) matured over six to twelve months. Note: sheep are sometimes only milked from March to July, so cheeses may be available only seasonally; although frozen milk may be used, this is not considered as good.

Blue cheeses – Ticklemore Cheeses use milk from sheep that graze in the fertile valley of the River Dart for making **Beenleigh Blue** (available from August/September to January/February). **Coleford Blue** and **Quantock Blue** are made by Exmoor Blue Cheeses with milk supplied by The Big Sheep.

Goat's cheese – The cheese made with goat's milk is more digestible than the butterfat in cow's milk, it therefore provides a high protein alternative to those with allergies to cow's milk. Eaten when mild, this family of cheeses is proving to be versatile in its appeal. Milk yields, however, drop to very low levels during the winter months, hence the fluctuation in availability from when the goats are fallow.

Sleight – Mary Holbrook, a highly respected cheesemaker rears both goats and sheep on Sleight Farm at Timsbury overlooking the rolling countryside outside Bath. Her firm, moist, goat's cheeses vary in flavour according to age (two to eight months) and coating (black pepper, rosemary, crushed garlic, herbs). Other types produced include a new selection of Portuguese-inspired cheeses and the soft **Ash Pyramids**, with a dusting of charcoal or wood ash which traditionally was applied to ward off flies.

Blue cheeses – Soft, full fat, creamy **Brendon Blue** is made by the makers of Exmoor Blue (matures at two – four months); **Harbourne Blue** by Ticklemore Cheese (matures at three – four months, available July – February).

Cheese biscuits – Two bakeries in Dorset have become renowned for producing biscuits. **Fudges Bakery** at Leigh (between Sherborne and Dorchester) produces Dorset Cheddar wafers which are just what a cheese-flavoured biscuit should be. **S Moores** at Morcombelake (between Honiton and Bridport) make Dorset knobs, a peculiarity ideally suited to eating Blue Vinney, definitely worth trying (Beware! Baked between January and March, stocks of these are quite depleted by the summer).

ENGLISH WINES AND LIQUEURS

There are several wine makers in the West Country: **Camel Valley Vineyard** produce both red and white near Bodmin in Cornwall; **Sharpham** make dry and sweet whites, and a red near Totnes in Devon; **Staplecombe** (near Taunton) and **Moorlynch** (Bridgwater) in Somerset – *for Somerset winegrowers see* CHEDDAR GORGE.

Whites are often blended from one or more varieties of grape (Madeleine Angevine, Reichensteiner) to produce ranges of light, dry, fruity wines. Unfortunately, high duty levied by the government cripples the English winegrowers who have to compete with cheap imports.

At **Porthallow** (St Keverne) a range of fruit-flavoured liqueurs and wines are made, and sold through various health-food shops and delicatessens. Look out for sloe gin, ginger whisky, whisky mead, raspberry brandy...

FISH

The West Country is blessed with a long coastline and many beautiful rivers free from pollution. **Crabs** have long been associated and continue to be with Dartmouth and Salcombe. **Oysters**, a rare delicacy along the south coast since Roman times, are farmed in the freshest, plankton-rich salt waters of the Helston, Exe, Avon and the Fal rivers: natives are available from September to April from the Duchy of Cornwall Oyster beds at Port Navas, outside Falmouth; Pacific oysters are farmed at Ferrybridge, on the edge of the Fleet lagoon between Portland and Abbotsbury (*see* WEYMOUTH-PORTLAND). **Freshwater fish** are available from trout farms and farmshops: the **Exe Valley Fishery** (founded 1885) at Dulverton operates a hatchery, rearing farm, fishing lake and smokery.

Star-gazy pie is an unusual kind of fish pie in that the filling is arranged so that the heads of the fish are seen poking through the crispy pastry crust. In Cornwall, the most commonly used fish are the locally- caught pilchards which look and taste like small herring, but are, in fact, mature sardines.

Cured fish – Just as cheese was "invented" as a means of using surplus milk, so smoking and salt were used as methods of curing fish. The clear chalk streams of Wiltshire that run down to the south coast are perfect for eel and trout – both of which make succulent fare when smoked. Henrietta Green ranks the trout from the Mere Fish Farm near Warminster as "one of the best in the country".

In Bridport oak sawdust is used to smoke local silver eels, trout, prawns, haddock, Scottish mackerel and salmon – the reason for importing **mackerel** is largely because the fish that is caught off Cornwall tends to be too low in oil-content to be perfect; instead, plumper fish from the colder Scottish waters are preferred for a more moist end-product. In Kingsbridge these are called Salcombe Smokies; they are also available from the Cornish Smoked Fish Company in Charlestown, while the Quayside fish centre in Porthleven (Helston) excels in locally-caught mullet, flat fish, lobster and crab, and home-smoked kippers and haddock.

In Newlyn the practice of curing **pilchards** by hand lives on: these should not be confused, however, with the canned pilchards found on supermarket shelves; Newlyn pilchards resemble and taste very much like anchovies.

PASTIES, BUNS AND SAFFRON CAKE

Cornish pasties – Throughout the region, hot pasties are widely available from bakeries, although the traditional ones, of course come from Cornwall. The Lizard Pasty Shop reveals the secret of its fillings as having beef, turnips (swede in England), potato, onion, salt and black pepper; vegetarian packages contain just vegetables and/or cheese. Definitely best eaten hot on a cold day!

The original Cornish pasties were designed to provide tin-miners with a complete meal with a savoury filling at one end, and jam or a sweetened thick fruit pulp at the other. The thick, crimped edge – which at one time provided a grip for arsenic-covered fingers – was discarded.

Sweet breads – Flour, fat, milk, dried fruit, sugar, salt and baking powder or yeast are used in different proportions to make on the one hand a tea-time delicacy as in **Bath buns** and on the other a dense, sometimes, stodgy, hunger pacifier as in the case of **lardie cake** from Wiltshire that should be avoided by vegetarians and **heavva cake** (or heavy cake) in Cornwall made from a rich combination of flour, butter, cream, sugar and currants.

West Country tea, Lanhydrock

As with many other regional specialities, the original **Bath bun** is shrouded in legend: according to some, they became popular in the 1670s when served in the Pump Room, others claim them to be adapted from a recipe for Sally Lunns by having spice (caraway), lemon and dried fruit added. Basic ingredients include sugar, flour, yeast, butter and lard or margarine and shortening. Traditionally, they should be baked on top of sugar cubes which soften and get absorbed during baking. A variant, the London Bath bun, a completely different thing, was served at the Great Exhibition of 1851.

Saffron cake, meanwhile, is a Cornish peculiarity, left over, some say, from the 17C and 18C when England had its own thriving saffron industry (notably around Saffron Walden in Essex). Different saffron-rich variants are available throughout Cornwall, notably from St Austell, Truro and Penzance.

Another regional speciality is the **Cornish split**, or its smaller Devon equivalent: a Chudleigh. Alas, this traditional element of the West Country cream tea, a yeast-based soft sweet roll, is increasingly being displaced by light scones made with self-raising flour.

For a picnic lunch worth a journey ...

For a morning's boating on the Dart followed by an excursion on the steam railway, pack a hamper of **crab sandwiches** from Dartmouth and a variety of fresh **cheeses** from Ticklemore Cheese, tasty apple pies and home-made **toffee** or fudge from Totnes High Street. The local off-licence (Threshers) also stocks a variety of **wines** from Cornwall and **cider scrumpy** from Devon.

Home-made, rich and unctuous ice-cream is abundantly available to cap the family's good day out!

If spending a day walking the coast path, surfing the waves at Newquay, or fishing offshore from Padstow, **Rich Stein**'s Delicatessen will provide excellent provender (meat pies, fish salads, pasties, breads and cakes) and his famous restaurant *The Sea Shell* will be ample incentive to complete the Saints' Way from Fowey (26miles cross country – see PRACTICAL INFORMATION: The great outdoors).

Further up the coast, Bude is well-stocked with various delicatessens that draw their fare from both Cornwall and Devon.

For a day's birdwatching in the Somerset Levels: a nip of **cider brandy** or eau de vie and a chunk of home-made pork pie will deflect the early morning chill. Lunch might consist of **smoked eel** or duck, and farmhouse cheese accompanied by fresh bread, washed down with local cider (blended as requested) or **apple juice**.

Good regional produce is to be found in Bath (The Cheese Board), Glastonbury, Langport, Taunton and Wells (The Fine Cheese Company).

Somerset Cider Brandy Company: Open Monday to Saturday, 9am to 5pm. Burrow Hill, Kingsbury Episcopi (near Langport). ☎ 01460 240 782.

Brown and Forrest: Traditional smokery (hot and cold methods) using American oak wood and apple sawdust. Open Monday, Tuesday, Thursday, 10am to 1pm; Saturday 9.30am to 12noon. Bowdens Farm, Hambridge (near Curry Rivel). ☎ 01458 251 520.

Charlton Orchards: Home-grown apples from mid-August to end-March. Open Monday to Saturday, 10am to 6pm; Sunday 2pm to 5pm. Creech St Michael, Taunton, TA3 5PF. ☎ 01823 41959

The Post Office: Freshly baked bread and sweetmeats from Bathway, Chewton Mendip BA3 4ND. ☎ 01761 241 325.

For additional information, consult Henrietta Green's current edition of her *Food Lovers' guide to Britain*

Hardy's cottage

Sights

AVEBURY★★

Wiltshire – Population 562
Michelin Atlas p 17 or Map 403 – O 29

Avebury and its surrounding area is extremely rich in prehistoric monuments and earthworks, the earliest dating from *c*3700-3500 BC; even today, discoveries continue to be made around the valley of the River Kennet. All around Avebury itself, a village of small houses, shops, a 17C pub, a square-towered church, a Tudor-Elizabethan manor house and a 17C thatched tithe barn, 30 to 40-ton **sarsen stones** stand silently in the fields.

★ **The Stones** – The plan of the stones is difficult to decipher, the only vantage points being on the circular earthen banks which, reinforced by an inner ditch, enclose the 28 acre site. The earth "rampart", broken at the cardinal points of the compass to provide access to the centre (now the Devizes-Swindon (A361) and the High Street-Downs roads), encloses a **Circle** of 100 sarsens from the Marlborough Downs and two inner rings. From the south exit an **Avenue** of approximately 100 pairs of stones (some of which may be seen), square "male" and slender "female" stones alternating in each file, once led to the site known as the Sanctuary *(1.5 miles)* on Overton Hill (excavated 1930). It has been estimated that Avebury henge took some 1.5 million hours to construct – or, put another way, 200 men working 60 hours a week for 3 years.

The 4500-year old site, after perhaps 1000 years' service, fell into disuse, a convenient source of building stone. John Aubrey, exultant discoverer and designator of the site as a prehistoric monument in the 17C, was able to show Charles II many more stones in position than there are today. It was Aubrey who, having stumbled upon the site whilst hawking, described Avebury "as surpassing Stonehenge as a cathedral doth surpass a parish church".

It appears that one would-be quarryman, a 13C barber-surgeon, was crushed as he toppled one of the huge sarsens; when he was discovered centuries later, he was found to be carrying some Edward I coins in his pouch and what have become the oldest known scissors in Britain.

The Stones, Avebury

Alexander Keiller Museum ⊙ – Models of the site, aerial photographs and excavated finds from Avebury, the West Kennet Long Barrow, Windmill Hill and Silbury Hill are displayed to advantage in the museum named after the pre-Second World War excavator.

★ **Church** – At a first glance St James' appears to be a Perpendicular church with an embattled and pinnacled west tower; a second look identifies the doorway with colonnettes and zig-zag decoration as Norman; but on going inside and into the west end, the two solid walls extending forwards may be identified as the outer walls of a Saxon church. The aisles were added in the 12C.

In the 19C a local builder removed the Norman columns and substituted Tuscan-style pillars, leaving intact the (medieval) arches and the circular clerestory windows which are believed to be Anglo-Saxon. The chancel arch is 13C, but the chancel dates from 19C rebuilding.

Among the furnishings, the **tub font**, with an intricate carving of two serpents and a bishop, is Norman if not Saxon; the rood-screen is topped by its original 15C loft and crocketed parapet of vine leaves.

Avebury Manor ⊙ – *The manor house has been regularly altered since its origins, linked to a monastery. It now consists of buildings dating from the early 16C with fine late 17C alterations. The garden boasts topiary, ancient box hedges and medieval walls framing the flower garden.*

Archeological sites

★ **Silbury Hill** – *2 miles south on north side of A4; lay-by car park; no direct access.* Silbury, which covers 5.25 acres, was built in four stages beginning *c*2500 BC. Only human muscle, red deer antler picks and oxen shoulder-blade shovels were used to pile up its million cubic yards of chalk. The final

Henge monuments, which are unique to Britain, are a type of sanctuary. Originally fairly simple, they consisted of a bank and ditch, nearly always circular, which enclosed a sacred area sometimes containing a ring of ritual pits, or rings of standing stones or posts. The **Beaker Folk** were largely responsible for subsequent, more refined henges, such as Avebury. They also raised monuments to the dead: individual burial under a circular mound replaced the old communal burials in long barrows.

grassy mound (130ft high), with its distinctive flat top (100ft wide), is one of the largest man-made hills in Europe. Despite shafts sunk to its centre in the 18C and tunnels excavated in the 20C, the reason for its construction remains a mystery.

★ **West Kennet Long Barrow** – *3 miles south on south side of A4, plus 0.75 mile field footpath – signposted from lay-by car park; take a torch and boots in wet weather.* No mystery surrounds the earth-covered mound which provides a fine **view** over the countryside; it is England's finest burial barrow (340ft long x 75ft wide) and dates from 3500-3000 BC.

The entrance at the east end is flanked by giant sarsens; on either side are dependent burial vaults and, at the far end, a chamber, roofed with massive capstones supported on upright sarsens and drystone walling. Some 50 skeletons of the early Neolithic builders, farmers and their families were discovered in the vaults.

The Wansdyke – *Access: 4 miles southwest by A361, Devizes road; there is no public right of way along the Wansdyke though many stretches are open.* The frontier earthwork runs for some 60 miles across Somerset, from the Severn and Compton Dando, westwards through Bath as far as Savernake Forest (*see* MARLBOROUGH); rising steeply to 30 feet in places, it has elsewhere been eroded to oblivion. It was built possibly in the 5C or 6C by the Romano-Britons or Saxons of south Wiltshire to protect themselves from incursions by Saxon settlers in the Thames Valley.

Windmill Hill – *4 miles northwest on foot; follow the land beyond the church and a path thereafter.* The hill is famous, archeologically, as the causewayed camp after which the earliest Neolithic culture in Britain is named. It comprises three concentric ditches and embankments in which the livestock were gathered before the annual autumn slaughter.

White Horses

Hackpen Horse – This is said to have been cut in celebration of Queen Victoria's coronation in 1838 by the parish clerk of Broad Hinton. Its dimensions, 90ft x 90ft, may be an attempt to overcome the lack of hillside incline. It is difficult to view the elongated slender figure from the Ridgeway itself; a good impression is to be had from the unnumbered Marlborough road, signposted off the A4361 Avebury to Swindon road.

Broad Town Horse – Best viewed from the B4041 to Wootton Bassett, this horse is said to have been cut in 1864 by a farmer, which perhaps explains its proportions (78ft long by 57ft) and more naturalistic overall appearance.

Cherhill Horse – Best seen from the A4 just east of Cherhill or from the way out of Calne towards Melksham (A3102). This horse, facing north and sited below the ancient earthworks of Oldbury Castle, measures 131ft by 123ft from nose to tail and dates from 1780. The story goes that work was directed by a certain Dr Alsopp of Calne from the road below, who barked his instructions through a megaphone. The eye, 4ft across, was once filled with upturned bottles so as to glisten in the sunshine; these, however, have disappeared.

The obelisk on the skyline beyond its tail was erected by Lord Lansdowne, of Bowood (*see* CHIPPENHAM), in 1845.

Chalk hill figures

Hill figures cut into chalk escarpments are an idiosyncratic feature of the region although they are not unique to it. The oldest include the Uffington White Horse on the Berkshire Downs, Dorset's Cerne Giant (*see* DORCHESTER) and the Long Man of Wilmington in East Sussex; the purpose of the latter two are thought to be related to fertility rites. The Uffington Horse, located as it is below the earthworks of Uffington Castle, may have served as a beacon to people journeying there: this has been proposed following the discovery of Iron Age coins stamped with a similar outline. Interestingly enough, great fairs were held every seven years on the hill from the Middle Ages to 1857, during which time the horse was cleaned.

The seven horses in Wiltshire largely date from the 18C and 19C: *see also* MARLBOROUGH *and* TROWBRIDGE: Westbury.

★★ The Ridgeway

Ancient trade route – Before the Uffington White Horse, Avebury or Stonehenge, before the sea broke through the chalk to form the English Channel and make Britain an island, our prehistoric ancestors were already walking the Ridgeway Path.

The **Paleolithic** and **Mesolithic** peoples were nomadic and able to wander freely to and from the continent, to hunt the forests and scrub that covered all but the chalk uplands which, because they were less overgrown and offered easier going, the nomads began very early to use as regular tracks. In time, the paths penetrated across country following the line of chalk which extends in a swathe from the Norfolk coast, through the Chilterns to the North Wessex and Hampshire Downs where tracks along the North and South Downs also converged. Finally, all led down to the Dorset coast and the sea.

In the **Neolithic** period, by which time the Channel was in being, the huntsmen and herdsmen began to settle, grazing the downlands with sheep and scratching the soil to grow grain. They made pottery and wove cloth; they buried their dead in long barrows and, as they began to come together in tribes, constructed the prehistoric monuments in the Avebury area, notably around Windmill Hill. They also traded their goods, bartering with early, itinerant traders who came along the tracks with fine axe and arrow heads from Cornwall, Cumbria and Wales.

The Bronze Age (2000-700 BC) saw the invasion of the east coast and of Dorset by **Beaker Folk**, who used the chalk upland tracks to penetrate far inland. They fashioned metals for their own use – copper, tin, bronze and gold (from Cornwall and Ireland) – exported bronze tools and weapons and obtained, in exchange, the pottery and weapons from Brittany, Holland, the Mediterranean and central Europe that has been discovered in their graves by modern archeologists. The constant traffic of traders and itinerant smiths, who cast tools and weapons and, resmelting the metal, exchanged new for old, meant that by 1700 BC the Ridgeway and Icknield Way had become regular trade routes.

The Beaker Folk were overcome by the **Urn People**, invading warriors from Brittany (1700 BC) who had a sophisticated taste for luxuries which were brought by new traders along the old upland routes: gold from Ireland, jet from Yorkshire, amber from the Baltic, blue pottery beads from Egypt. Their name derives from their practice of burying the cremated ashes of the dead in urns in the round barrows which may still be seen on the Wiltshire Downs.

The first wave of **Celts** came over in the 8C BC: their weapons were still of bronze although their agriculture was well advanced – their small rectangular field cultivation is even now visible from the air. In turn they fell before a second wave of Celts: the 5C BC men of the **Iron Age**. As invasion followed invasion, Celts already established defended themselves in the hillforts to be seen everywhere in the region.

The **animals** of the early herdsmen – cattle, sheep, horses, hogs – were leaf, tree bark and scrub eaters; the forests became so reduced that the nature of the countryside was changed for ever; the animals became herbivores. Man, however, had reached the Iron Age: not only weapons but tools for clearing scrub and forest had become keener and agricultural implements had begun to evolve.

With the **Romans** began settlement of the valleys and lowlands with paths and even made-up roads linking the towns. The Ridgeway was abandoned except by drovers who, until the advent of rail and road transport, continued to travel the tracks with their cattle and sheep, heading for London.

Length, course, conditions – The modern Ridgeway Path, opened in 1973 and waymarked by Countryside Commission acorns, extends 85 miles from Overton Hill near Avebury via the Uffington White Horse to the Ivinghoe Beacon near Tring. It passes through five counties, Wiltshire, Berkshire, Oxfordshire, Buckinghamshire and Hertfordshire to join the Icknield Way beyond the river

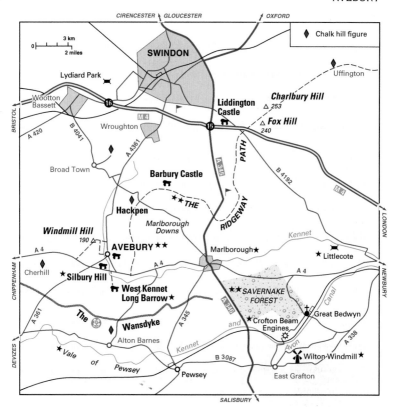

crossing at Streatley, which then runs 120miles to the Suffolk coast, linking up with the 50 mile Peddar Way through Norfolk.

The west section of the Ridgeway is suitable for walking, horse riding and bicycling; car parks are located at intersections with main roads *(for additional information turn to the Practical Information section: Rambling)*. The going is straightforward; the grass and earth track, which occasionally rises to 900ft, is generally wide, passing along downland crests, beside fields, through woods and coppices. It is mostly out in the open, affording wide **views** across the rolling downs – beware the ruts in the path and remember, after heavy rain, that chalk may turn into slippery mud or collect in heavy clods making walking difficult. For those intending to walk a considerable distance or the full length, the 1:50 000 (1.25 inch) Ordnance Survey maps (nos 173, 174, 175 and 165) are recommended.

Rare **downland plants**, as illustrated in the local museum at Devizes, include chalk milkwort, bastard toadflax, clustered bellflowers and low lying stemless thistles; more common species which have struggled to reestablish themselves include the scarlet pimpernel, corn marigold, corn cockles, poppies, pheasant's eye and Venus' looking glass. These in turn attract such **butterflies** as chalk-hill blues and many of the browns, while overhead soar skylarks, and the occasional kestrel or buzzard; the great bustards having long been hunted into extinction.

Iron Age hillforts – The track passes through or alongside several ancient settlements. **Barbury Castle** consists of a triple-embanked earthwork enclosing 11.5 acres with openings to west and east through which the modern path passes. The castle is named after an Anglo-Saxon chief, Bara, who fought a battle in 566 on the slopes to the north. **Liddington Castle** is another Iron Age hillfort.

Fox Hill and Charlbury Hill – The hills are marked respectively by a radio tower and an orange-flashing aircraft beacon.

The star ratings are allocated for various categories:
– regions of scenic beauty with dramatic natural features
– cities with a cultural heritage
– elegant resorts and charming villages
– ancient monuments and fine architecture
– museums and art galleries.

BARNSTAPLE★

Devon – Population 20 740
Michelin Atlas p 6 or Map 403 – H 30

In Alfred's reign Barnstaple became a burgh with defences; in 930 it received a charter. Its long history as the principal agricultural centre, trade and cattle market of the region is recalled in **Butchers' Row** and the 19C cast-iron, glass-roofed **Pannier Market** where stallholders and farmers' wives have traditionally assembled each Tuesday, Friday and Saturday to sell their produce including Devon cream, fruit, vegetables and preserves; cattle market: Friday.

★ **Long Bridge** – The bridge (520ft by 10ft) was first constructed in stone in *c*1273. In 1539 the drawbridge connection, which until then had existed at the town end, was replaced by three arches making a total of 13. The bridge was widened in 1796 – the year a regular coach service to Exeter was inaugurated – and again in 1834.

Parish Church ☼ – The church was rebuilt in 1318 adjoining the older tower, which in 1636 was overlapped with a lead-covered broach spire. Inside, note the 17C **memorial monuments** *(south aisle)* and the large **mayoral pew** with a lion and unicorn.

Horwood Almshouses and Alice Horwood School – The almshouses and school, which were endowed to take "20 poor children for ever", were built in the 17C in the quiet, cobbled and bollarded Church Lane *(courtyard through the arch)*.
It was at the local grammar school, however, which was lodged from 1549 to 1910 in the 14C **St Anne's Chapel** in the High Street, that John Gay (1685-1732) was a pupil under the schoolmaster Robert Luck.

Guildhall ☼– *High Street end of Butcher's Row.* The hall, a 19C replacement, contains the **Dodderidge Parlour**, a room panelled in 17C oak from a wealthy merchant's house, in which the town's famous collection of **corporation plate** is displayed. There are three silver-gilt steeple cups of 1620 – a replica was presented to Barnstaple, Massachusetts in 1939 on the tercentenary of its foundation – maces, lidded tankards and a vast **punch-bowl** used at the proclamation of the annual fair (Wednesday prior to 20 September).

Queen Anne's Walk – *Downriver from the bridge.* The walk was built as the merchants' exchange in 1609, enlarged 20 years later and rebuilt in 1708 to comprise a single colonnade beneath a statue of Queen Anne bearing a gilded crown, sceptre and orb. Note the **Tome stone** on which bargains were struck, and wall tablets about the Armada.

Museum of North Devon ☼ – *The Square.* The old 19C Atheneum Library and Museum beside the river bridge again houses items and artefacts from the local heritage. 'The Story of North Devon' provides an introduction to the area's geology, archeology (flint hand axes, Roman gaming counters) and local industries including the development of north Devon **pottery** (13C-20C). Complementary displays include uniforms and silver belonging to the Royal Devon Yeomanry (1794-1971); pewter; natural history (plants, fossils, shells, **beetles and bugs**, stuffed animals; marine life) – enhanced by special effects and hands-on activities. Changing exhibitions, interactive educational facilities, coin and brass rubbing.

EXCURSION

★★ **Arlington Court** ☼ *8 miles northeast on A39.*

The model ships alone – 36 made by French Napoleonic prisoners of war, 10 Dunkirk Little Ships and some 70 others – would make the Court unique but the ships comprise only one of the collections made by the house's former owner, Miss Rosalie Chichester (1865-1949). This redoubtable lady developed her lifelong fascination with ships from an early age having been on long Mediterranean cruises with her father aboard his 276 ton yacht when three years old. Her father died when Rosalie was 16, leaving the estate so heavily mortgaged that it took the next 47 years to clear the debt. Meanwhile, modestly at first, she began the collections which were to furnish and characterise her home. Uncannily, Miss Chichester died 16 years before her step-nephew, Sir Francis Chichester, made his epic voyage round the world in *Gipsy Moth* (1966-67).

House – *1 hour.* The Classically-styled house, built 1820-23, was altered in 1865 by Miss Chichester's father to accommodate the grandiose staircase and refashion the hall to suit the glittering social life he enjoyed with his wife. Among the photographs in the entrance hall is one of the young Miss Chichester in 1885 in a straw hat.

State Rooms – The 70ft long south front was designed with *scagliola* marble columns to form one long gallery which could be sub-divided into three rooms.

The **Morning Room** contains a typical 19C collection of shells, several ships and a Portuguese pottery bull; the **Ante Room** features a notable collection of silver, English and Irish glass, a Chinese rock crystal cat and small jade, soapstone and crystal animals and scent bottles, a Bristol glass ship of 1851 and the **William Blake** painting *Cycle of the Life of Man* (1821).

The end room, the **White Drawing Room**, has a Donegal carpet and one with the Chichester herons in the corners; English, French and Chinese porcelain; precious snuff-boxes and a unique red amber elephant.

Small Boudoir – The enriched plaster ceiling, faded rose and gold silk hangings, Chinese porcelain and 19C *papier maché* furniture are reflected in the obliquely set mirrors. A display case contains more small animals, snuff boxes and vinaigrettes.

Corridor – The cabinets contain **commemorative mugs** (1887-1937) and an important collection of English pewter from platters to spoons, dominoes and chessmen.

Ship models collection – Pride of place in the fleet of ships assembled in the staircase hall, gallery and lobby is given to the Little Ships that went to Dunkirk and *Gipsy Moth*, which was made as a centrepiece to the collection.

The **Napoleonic prisoners' ships** date largely from 1814. The distinction of the Chichester collection is that it contains examples of almost every class of ship of the Napoleonic period, from three-deckers to sailing frigates.

Some 122 000 prisoners were captured during the Napoleonic Wars between 1793-1815. Almost immediately they were set to constructing prisons and public works – Princetown on Dartmoor, the Floating Harbour in Bristol, a camp in Bideford... Among the men in the south of England were a number of Flemish ivory carvers who, from making and selling small ornaments out of beef and mutton bones, had graduated by 1814 to carving ships which they produced to scale in every detail and embellished with figureheads; the only inaccuracies are the British names and colours given to the otherwise typically French vessels – an intentional inaccuracy so as to make the models more saleable. Other fine examples of ship models are to be found in the Burton museum at Bideford.

Galloping Gig child's carriage, Arlington Court

N. MacKenzie/The National Trust

★ **Carriage Collection** – The handsome 19C stable block, its clock tower dome crowned by a Chichester heron, contains the National Trust collection of 19C-early 20C horsedrawn carriages. They range from Queen Victoria's **pony bath chair** to a hooded buggy, a royal "canoe" landau, hansoms, gigs, phaetons, wagonettes, an omnibus.

Grounds – Paths *(about 1.25 miles)* through the grounds lead down to the lake where an urn marks where Miss Chichester's ashes are buried; in the church a memorial by **John Piper** (1903-92) also commemorates her.

BATH★★★

Bath and North East Somerset – Population 78 689
Michelin Atlas p 17 or Map 403 – M 29

The unparalleled harmony and elegance of Bath's 18C architecture and urban planning combined with its ancient past and its lively present – as the seat of a university, the home of a wealth of museums and a smart shopping centre – makes the city popular with visitors throughout the year.

Legend – According to legend, in 500 BC the leprosy-afflicted **Prince Bladud** had become a wandering swineherd; when his swine appeared cured of their skin ailments after wallowing in the mud, he plunged in himself – and emerged cured. He returned to court, succeeded to the crown, fathered the future King Lear and established his seat at Bath.

History – By the 1C AD, when the Romans had advanced west and were mining lead in the Mendip Hills, the area was already known for its warm springs. Named **Aquae Sulis** after a native Celtic goddess, the Romans transformed the settlement into England's first spa resort; they built baths, a temple, possibly a gymnasium or theatre: developments necessary to make it a leisure centre with minimal military interests.

Following the departure of the Romans in the 5C, the city declined. In the 6C it was taken by the **Saxons** who built a town within the Roman walls and an abbey not far from the Roman temple site. In the 9C Alfred is said to have made Bath into a fortress. In 973 **Edgar**, the first King of all England, was crowned in the Saxon abbey.

In the following century, squabbles between pillaging Norman barons so reduced the city that **John de Villula** of Tours, Bishop of Somerset and Physician, was able

Great Bath, Roman Baths

S. McBride/Bath and North East Somerset Council

to purchase it for £500. He began the creation of a vast Benedictine cathedral priory – the church today occupies only the site of the nave – built a palace, a guesthouse, a new suite of baths, founded a school of science and mathematics and encouraged the treatment of the sick (the Hospital of St John was founded in his name in 1180). His cathedral was never completed. Only in 1499 did building of the present church begin; Bath was by then a prosperous wool town.

At the Dissolution the monks lost their jurisdiction over the baths and sold off lead from the minster's roof, the bells, glass and ironwork. In 1574 Queen Elizabeth ordered that a fund be set up to restore the abbey and St John's Hospital, thereby ensuring that "an unsavoury town... become a most sweet town".

By 1668 Pepys considered it had "many good streets and very fair stone houses"; although he "stayed above two hours in the water" he had reservations about the baths: "Methinks it cannot be clean to go so many bodies together in the same water". Others were less fastidious: where royalty went – Charles II and Catherine of Braganza, Queen Mary of Modena, Queen Anne – crowds followed, until by the early 18C Bath was becoming a place to attend not only for a cure but to be in fashion. In all other respects, however, the city was dull and disorganised.

Beau Nash – "The Beau" arrived in Bath in 1704 (d 1762), then aged 31, in the wake of the fashionable fraternity. He had a flair for organisation and on his appointment as Master of Ceremonies he laid down a programme for the high-flyers to follow: from early morning bathing to evening assemblies, he ordered that the streets be lit and made safe to walk in; that swords be not worn around town and sedan chairmen charge the authorised tariff. He laid down eleven rules, which for fear of ostracism and public ridicule were implicitly obeyed. Within a year he opened the first Pump Room where people might take the waters and meet in civilised society; he organised concerts, balls, cards and gambling. The town prospered, charities benefited, he grew rich and Bath became the most fashionable city in England.

Ralph Allen and John Wood – While Nash refashioned Bath society, Ralph Allen and John Wood undertook the transformation of the city's architecture and entire urban plan.

Allen (1694-1764), a Cornish postmaster, came to Bath in 1710. Thereupon he offered the government £2 000 a year for a seven-year concession to make the region's highly unreliable postal service both efficient and profitable; it became a model and with the fortune he made out of it Allen bought stone quarries at Claverton and on Combe Down, with the idea of building a new city with the honey-coloured stone. **John Wood** (1700-54) was a Yorkshireman who by 1728 had settled in the city: a Classicist inspired by Bath's Roman past, he sought to build principally in the Palladian style (*see* INTRODUCTION: Architecture) using the stone from Combe Down, now known as **Bath Stone**.

★★ LOWER TOWN

(BX) *Half a day*

★ **Bath Abbey** ⊙ – The first abbey, founded during the early reign of King Offa (757-96), later hosted the coronation ceremony of King Edgar (943-75) strategically located, as it was then, on the borders of Wessex and Mercia. During the Middle Ages, the importance of the monastery declined; in 1245 acrimonious rivalry between Bath and Wells was resolved by the pope who declared the see should be allied in electing a bishop.

Sightseeing in Bath

Because of its architectural design, the city is best seen on foot; each of the three walks suggested starts from the Abbey and requires approximately half a day.

If time is short, see: the **Abbey★** (BX) exterior, go into the **Pump Room★** (BX A): view the King's Bath – a full visit to the Roman Baths takes an hour and a half, walk up Milsom and Gay Streets to the **Circus★★★** (AV); bear right to the **Assembly Rooms★** and the **Museum of Costume★★★** (M²) or left to see the **Royal Crescent★★★** (D); return down Gay Street noting, on the way, the many fine **street vistas** closed by perfectly sited houses, often pedimented, and the wealth of individual touches and attractive details: iron railings, lamps, forecourt grass...

The present sanctuary was begun in 1499 by Bishop Oliver King following a dream in which he saw angels climbing to heaven and heard voices commanding that a king, which he took to be himself from his surname, restore the church: from the pillars of the Norman church there eventually arose the pure, late Perpendicular abbey. Incomplete at the Dissolution, the building fell into disrepair; it was purchased in 1572 and given to the city as a parish church, whereupon restoration began. More substantial alterations followed the programme instigated by Sir Gilbert Scott in 1864-76.

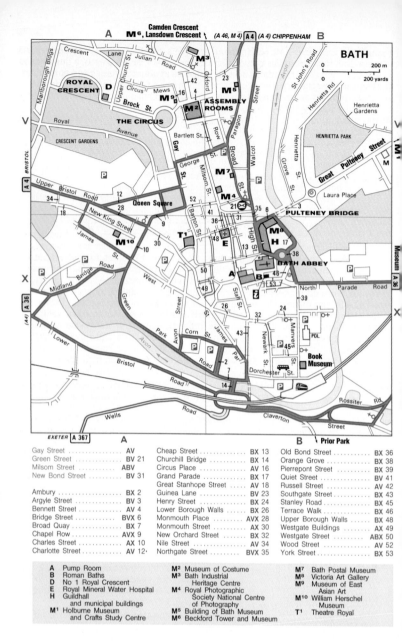

BATH

0 ··· 200 m
0 ··· 200 yards

A	Pump Room	**M²**	Museum of Costume	**M⁷**	Bath Postal Museum
B	Roman Baths	**M³**	Bath Industrial	**M⁸**	Victoria Art Gallery
D	No 1 Royal Crescent		Heritage Centre	**M⁹**	Museum of East
E	Royal Mineral Water Hospital	**M⁴**	Royal Photographic		Asian Art
H	Guildhall		Society National Centre	**M¹⁰**	William Herschel
	and municipal buildings		of Photography		Museum
M¹	Holburne Museum	**M⁵**	Building of Bath Museum	**T¹**	Theatre Royal
	and Crafts Study Centre	**M⁶**	Beckford Tower and Museum		

Outside, five-light windows are framed by flying buttresses, crocketed pinnacles and a castellated, pierced parapet. The fine **west front** which overlooks the Church Yard presents a Perpendicular window, a 17C door and, in the stone, tall **ladders** with angels ascending as in Bishop King's dream. Inside, the nave, chancel and narrow transepts all soar to **fan vaulting** designed by Robert and William Vertue (designers of the vaulting in the Henry VII Chapel, Westminster Abbey).

Heritage Vaults ⊙ – *Entrance from south transept.* Recent archeological surveys have revealed a number of artefacts relating to the use of the site since Saxon times. These, together with fragments of Norman stonework from the fabric of the original cathedral and descriptions of subsequent restoration programmes, are displayed in the context of the history of Christianity in Bath: books and manuscripts, silver plate, memorial tablets commemorating visitors who came to Bath seeking cures from their ills and never left.

★ **Pump Room** ⊙ (**A**) – Set among lines of 17C-18C houses and 18C-19C shopfronts are the Roman Baths complex and Pump Room (1789-1799). These, built after Nash's death, are presided over by his **statue**. The interiors are now elegantly furnished with ornamental pilasters, gilded capitals, coffered ceiling, Chippendale-style chairs and a Tompion long-case clock; musicians play beneath a glass chandelier: altogether the perfect meeting place for Catherine and

Mr Tilney in Jane Austen's *Northanger Abbey* (although then the furniture would have consisted merely of a few rout benches). The rounded bay overlooking the King's Bath contains the drinking fountain from which society may continue to take the waters.

★★ **Roman Baths** ⊘ **(B)** – The baths are fed by a spring which pours out approximately 250 000 gallons of water a day at a temperature of 116°F (46°C). Archeological exploration has recovered Mesolithic flints from the waters which indicate that the area was frequented by early man, long before it was inhabited by the Celtic tribe called the Dobunni who regarded the spring as a sacred site. The Roman complex originally consisted of the **Great Bath**, a large, warm, swimming pool, once covered but now open to the sky, and two baths of decreasing heat to the east. A second building phase installed a *frigidarium* or cold room on the west side with windows at the north end overlooking the **sacred spring** or reservoir, and two heated chambers (the *tepidarium* and *caldarium*) further west. Later alterations enlarged the east end, elaborated the baths at the west end and transformed the *frigidarium* into a cold plunge circular bath. After the Romans had left, the drains soon clogged through lack of attention and mud covered the site. In the early Middle Ages the Normans constructed the King's Bath around the tank which the Romans had lined with Mendip lead. In the 1680s, bathing attire consisted of yellow linen shifts and caps for women, knee-length drawers for men. Children could go naked.

In 1727 workmen digging a sewer in Stall Street found a gilded bronze head of **Minerva**, who was known to have been the presiding goddess of the spring. Since then continuing excavations have revealed that the bath complex was repeatedly remodelled. Items recovered during excavation are displayed in the **museum**; these include a lead curse, altars, coins, vessels, carvings including a **gorgon's head** from the temple façade.

Tour – *45 min.* A tour of the complex below ground begins with two tableaux which set the scene in Roman times; a scale model provides an idea of the main temple surrounded by changing rooms and bathing areas, and the other temple *(tholos)* probably added in the 2C AD to the east on the present site of the Abbey. Equipped with the award-winning audioguide which provides optional commentary to selected sections (included in the entrance charge), the visitor is able to move freely through the site pausing to listen to explanations on items revealed by archeological surveys.

Opposite the main entrance to the Pump Room and Roman Baths, cross Stall Street and continue down Bath Street.

Cross Bath ⊘ – *Bath Street.* The stone cross which until 1789 stood in the centre of the spring, hence its name, superimposed a Christian dedication to St Brigid upon more ancient associations with pagan deity, and with Aesculapius, the son of Apollo and god of healing in particular. Certainly during the Middle Ages, the spring was regarded by pilgrims journeying from Malmesbury to Tetbury to have curative powers. Later, the spring earned further recognition when in 1688, nine months after bathing there, Mary of Modena (1658-1718) gave birth to a long awaited heir to James II.

The elegant urn-topped open screen is all that remains of Thomas Baldwin's building which was remodelled by Palmer in 1797 (facsimile drawings on display inside); in 1885 it was gutted to make way for Victorian changing cubicles and swimming bath, nicknamed the Tuppenny Hot.

From the Pump Room and Roman Baths, turn right up Stall Street, cross Cheap Street into Union Street and continue uphill, over Upper Borough Walls.

★★ **UPPER TOWN** *Half a day*

Before crossing Upper Borough Walls, note the **Royal Mineral Water Hospital (BX E)** built by John Wood in 1738 and the castellated wall opposite, over which cadavers from the hospital used to be thrown.

Continue up Old Bond Street **(BX 36)** (1760-70) into **Milsom Street (ABV)**, the wide shopping street begun by John Wood, which epitomises the carriage, bonneted and beribboned age of the 1770s.

★★ **Royal Photographic Society National Centre of Photography** ⊘ **(BV M⁴)** – The octagonal room that houses the centre was built as a private chapel (1767), hence the gallery supported on Ionic columns. Beneath the 18C chandelier the story of photography unfolds through every stage: from trapping the light, waxed paper and wet plates to the single reflex lens. Elsewhere is a large collection of Leicas and, in three separate galleries, are held changing exhibitions of contemporary artistic, scientific and experimental photographs.

Beyond the arcade next to the Octagon, note the grand curved 18C **Somersetshire Buildings** (now a bank); closing the vista is a range of houses along a raised pavement in **George Street**, which also contains York House *(right)*, an old 18C posting inn.

Turn right along George Street and continue to the Paragon for the Building of Bath Museum – otherwise, bear left up Bartlett Street and left again along Alfred Street to the Assembly Rooms and Museum of Costume.

Building of Bath Museum ⊘ (BV M⁵) – The exhibition explains, illustrates and promotes the architectural design and construction of Georgian Bath: tools, full-scale re-constructions, artefacts and a large-scale model of the city described in 7 languages. The Centre is housed in a Gothick chapel (1765) founded by the Countess of Huntingdon for a Methodist sect.

Plans are afoot to provide an exhibition of internal designs typical of the period in the adjacent building.

Return south; turn right into Hay Hill and Alfred Street.

★ **Assembly Rooms** ⊘ (AV) – The "Upper Rooms"(1769-71) were declared in the 1772 Bath Guide to be "the most noble and elegant of any in the Kingdom". It was here in the 18C that elegant assemblies gathered for an evening's entertainment in the pursuit of several activities – card-playing for the men, tea-drinking for the ladies; both groups would then proceed to the Ballroom for dancing, gossip and scandalmongering: the perfect context for a key scene in Jane Austen's *Persuasion*. During the 19C, Bath's fortunes dwindled as the railways carried people to seaside resorts like Brighton and Bournemouth, and beyond to spas in France and Italy despite such desperate efforts to buck the trend as concert recitals by Johann Strauss and Franz Liszt, and readings by Charles Dickens.

Note: when these rooms are used for private functions access to them may be curtailed.

Ball Room – The pale green-blue room – 105ft 8in long, 42ft 8in wide and 42ft 6in high – was designed so that the dancers in their finery provided the colour below; the decoration therefore is concentrated above at window level where engaged Corinthian columns rise to support a deep entablature and delicately stuccoed ceiling from which are suspended five magnificent crystal **chandeliers**. Evening entertainment was regularly held here once a week: restrained minuets (between 6pm and 8pm) were followed with energetic country dancing, at 9pm the dancers would move to the tea room for refreshment, activities were then resumed until 11pm.

Octagon and Card Room – The 48ft octagonal room was intended as the card room, but as complaints increased about the distracting noise and bustle, a second "card room" was added in 1777. Gambling was a widespread pastime in 18C Britain; according to the contemporary historian William Lecky it was recommended by physicians as a suitably intellectual distraction for house-bound patients. Indeed Beau Nash is said to have lived on his winnings at the gambling tables, owing his eventual ruin to the laws passed in 1739 and 1745 which banned such games as Faro, Basset, Hazard, Ace of Hearts and Even-Odd.

Tea Room – Wood planned a rich and dignified 18C interior for this room where gossip would be rife. At one end stands a screen of superimposed pillars which continue round the sides to support the ornate ceiling. It was here that Thomas Linley directed his subscription concerts, providing a cultural draw to the Assembly Rooms, particularly on Sundays when gambling was prohibited. It was at one such occasion that Captain Wentworth meets Anne Elliot in Jane Austen's novel *Persuasion*.

★★★ **Museum of Costume** ⊘ (AV M²) – Displays selected from the enormous reserves of the national collection of fashionable dress, from the 1580s but dating largely from the 18C onwards, reveal how previous generations might have adorned the streets of Bath during its heyday. Presented within room-settings containing period furniture, groups of figures (some 200 or so) show the fascinating changes in men's, women's and children's dress and how they have evolved to the present day – in shape, texture, colour and adornment.

Crimson satin evening coat
trimmed in black c1894

Spitalfields silks, intricately embroidered bodices typical of court attire, changing hemlines and trouser legs are shown alongside a selection of exquisite accessories (shoes, gloves, purses, buttons, buckles and jewels). The collection is constantly brought up to date with the inclusion of a new Dress of the Year.

Highlights – The museum's oldest complete attire, the **Silver Tissue Dress**, consists of a bodice and skirt from the 1660s with a trim of cream parchment lace; its rare state of preservation is largely due to being made of silk woven with silver thread which supports the natural fibre. The other particularly special display is the selection of the most superb gloves – many of which are from the Spence Collection on loan from the Worshipful Company of Glovers – embroidered, beribboned and printed.

★ **Museum of East Asian Art** ⊘ (AV M') – The museum is designed to encourage interest and understanding of Oriental art and craftsmanship from *c*5000 BC to 1910. Its collections drawn from China, Japan, Korea, Tibet and southeast Asia include a number of exquisite jades, metalwork (gold, silver, bronze, cloisonné, enamel), lacquer, bamboo, wood and ceramics. These are presented in chronological order. The museum regularly publishes its own journal and runs seasons of lectures and workshops alongside major exhibitions.

★ **Industrial Heritage Centre** ⊘ (AV M') – J B Bowler was a turn-of-the-century **brass founder** by trade, but also an engineer-craftsman, businessman and cordial manufacturer (1872-1969). Never known to throw anything away, his small, dark, Victorian shop is still stocked with "new" lightbulbs, period fixtures and fittings, forever stuck in a veritable time warp. Installed in the adjoining rooms are the heavy turning and milling machinery; foundry workshop; drinks-making and bottling plant, complete with Bowler-patented bottles...

The display in the basement relates to the quarrying of Bath Stone and the system used to extract blocks from narrow seams underground. One such quarry that supplied much of the building stone for Bath is **Corsham Underground Quarry** ⊘ (located off the A4 to Chippenham) which may also be visited: those intending to go down into the shaft stone mine should wear suitable shoes and warm clothing as temperatures underground fall to 11°C.

★★ **The Circus** (AV) – The King's Circus, although one of John Wood's earliest concepts, was built in 1754. It comprises a tight circle of identical houses pierced by three equidistant access roads. The houses of pale Bath stone, articulated with coupled columns, rise through three floors to a frieze and acorn-topped balustrade.

No 4 houses the **Fashion Research Centre**, a satellite of the Museum of Costume; it contains the Study Collection and a wide-ranging library.

Royal Victoria Park – Within this large open space is the **Georgian Garden** ⊘ which consists of a walled town garden planted with box, holly and yew topiary, and items listed in Webb's catalogue of 1760. Beyond are the **Botanical Gardens**.

Brock Street (AV) – The street between the Circus and the Crescent, named after Thomas Brock – an early resident, was built by John Wood II in 1767 with houses of differing design. It is only from the very end of the street that the unexpected and stunning sweep of the crescent is finally revealed.

★★ **Royal Crescent** (AV) – The great arc of 30 terrace houses (1767-74), in which the horizontal lines are counterbalanced by 114 giant Ionic columns rising from the first floor to the pierced parapet, is John Wood II's great achievement.

★★ **No 1 Royal Crescent** ⊘ (D) – The narrow Georgian house has been authentically restored showing how wealthy residents of the city would have lived. Inside, the wall coverings and furnishings based on contemporary printing blocks and drawings provide the setting for Chippendale, Sheraton and Hepplewhite **furniture**, porcelain, 18C **glass**, contemporary portraits (Thomas Baker of Bath) and topographical landscape paintings. Peculiarities include the Bristol Giant's chair made for P C O'Brien (1760-1806) who grew to 7ft 9in.

The basement houses the Kitchen Museum.

Cross the road and enter Royal Victoria Park; follow Gravel Walk down and turn left at the bottom to join Gay Street.

Gay Street (AV) – The long street (1734-60) was the work of the two Woods; no 41, on the corner of Old King Street, was designed by the father and lived in by the son and is the Baroque exception to the Classical style of the street.

Next to the recessed bow window on the corner a small, Delft-tiled **powder-cabinet** with a shell niche can be seen inside: this was where gentlemen could powder their wigs before entering the reception rooms.

The author of the popular novel *The School for Scandal*, Richard Sheridan, eloped with Elizabeth Linley from no 11 Royal Crescent in 1772.

Queen Square (AV) – The square was Wood's first example of urban planning. Note the **north side** with its pedimented centre and advanced ends: Wood himself lived at no 24; **Dr William Oliver**, inventor of the Bath Oliver biscuit, at nos 16-18.

Continue by Barton Street to Beaufort Square.

Theatre Royal (AX T¹) – The square of modest 18C houses has been dominated since the early 19C by the Theatre Royal, resplendent inside in an appropriate finery of dark red Regency stripe offset with gilding and plum coloured plush for the horseshoe-shaped auditorium. Sarah Siddons, David Garrick and Mrs Jordan once trod the boards of this elegant establishment where experimental pieces were put on before moving to London's West End.

Adjoining are two houses once occupied by **Beau Nash.**

★ORANGE GROVE, PULTENEY BRIDGE, HOLBURNE MUSEUM *Half a day*

From **Orange Grove (BX 38)** with its 18C houses, walk south to Terrace Walk **(BX 46)**: Bath's oldest shop front is marked Mssrs Eldridge Pope. Round to the right at no **3** North Parade Passage, the former Lilliput Alley, is **Sally Lunn's Refreshment House and Museum** ⊙, dating from 1622, where the famous buns continue to be baked (cinnamon buns and creamy hot chocolate are recommended!). Downstairs may be seen the Roman foundations, medieval masonry and various archeological artefacts recovered during excavation; the kitchen with its Georgian range used by Sally Lunn, a Huguenot refugee, in the 1680s and the ancient stalactite and stalagmite cellars.

While living in the next door house (no 2), Ralph Allen had the **Sham Castle** folly built to complete the landscape on Combe Down.

Continue to Orange Grove; bear northwest into the High Street.

Guildhall and municipal buildings (BX H) – Inside the Classical town hall (1775-79) built by Thomas

Jane Austen (1775-1817)

Jane visited Bath when staying with her aunt and uncle, the Leigh Perrots, at No 1 The Paragon, and it was in Bath that she set much of *Northanger Abbey*.

In May 1799, the Austen family took lodgings at 13 Queen Square; later, they resided at 4 Sydney Place; it was during their time at 27 Green Park Buildings, that Jane's father died in January 1805; on two further occasions, the remaining ladies of the family lived both at 25 Gay Street and in Trim Street.

It is from Jane's letters to her sister Cassandra, however, that the most vivid portrait of Bath is gleaned.

Baldwin to rival the Assembly Rooms in the upper town which opened in 1771, a sweeping staircase rises to the main Banqueting Room upstairs. This and other adjoining rooms (usually closed to the public), are hung with formal portraits. Immediately behind runs the spacious **town market**.

Victoria Art Gallery ⊙ **(BX M⁶)** – The corner building accommodates the city's art collection.

A spacious ground floor area is used for temporary exhibitions held every six weeks while upstairs, the Victorian gallery displays a sample from its permanent collection of British and European Schools of painting, ceramics, glass and watches. Notable artists include Gainsborough, Thomas Barker, JMW Turner, Sickert, John Nash, Mathew Smith...

★ **Pulteney Bridge (BVX)** – During the Middle Ages, a ferry ran a service across the Avon at this point, above the horse-shoe weir that harnessed power for a pair of water mills on either bank. The bridge, apparently based on the Ponte Vecchio in Florence, has a central Venetian window, domed end pavilions and small shops; it was designed in 1769-74 by **Robert Adam** for his friend Sir William Pulteney who hoped to develop a new city area beyond the Avon.

Today, the far bank provides **river boat** moorings: a good starting point from which to explore the six Widcombe Locks that accommodate 74ft x 16ft barges along the Kennet and Avon Canal which rises 65ft uphill out of Bath, past Thimble Mill to Sydney Gardens which were established in 1795.

Pulteney Bridge

A. Taverner

Great Pulteney Street (BV) – The city's longest vista, framed by the classically proportioned terrace houses, extends some 600yds from the end of the bridge. The eye travels along Argyle Street, across the diagonally set Laura Place and down the length of Great Pulteney Street, to rest finally on the Holburne Museum.

★★ **Holburne of Menstrie Museum and Crafts Study Centre** ⊘ (BV **M¹**) – The Sydney Hotel which in the 18C stood at the heart of the Sydney Pleasure Gardens today contains the collection of fine and applied art, largely assembled by **Sir Thomas William Holburne** (1793-1874), who served on HMS *Orion* at the Battle of Trafalgar, and subsequently endowed with bequests and donations.

Holburne, a bachelor, became a reputed connoisseur in his own lifetime, acquiring objects from various sources including the sale of William Beckford's Lansdown Tower collection in 1845; a selection of his possessions were borrowed and displayed at the national exhibitions held in South Kensington (1862) and Leeds (1868).

Among the 16C-18C paintings of the Flemish, Dutch, Italian Schools (Brueghel the Younger, Cornelius Johnson, Francesco Guardi) hang a number of English works predominantly from the 18C-19C by Gainsborough (notably his portrait of Holburne's physician who lived at no 17 The Circus from 1759-74), Romney, Ramsay, Stubbs, Zoffany, Raeburn, George Morland and Thomas Barker of Bath. The silver collection, built on a number of inherited family pieces, includes some exceptionally fine English and Continental signed examples namely the James I Bell Salt and Wine Cup, the embossed and *repoussé* Rosewater Dish of 1616, a selection of 16C-17C Apostle and Seal-top spoons; the odd post 1900 pieces including the Liberty candlesticks are from the Handley-Read Bequest.

Among the ceramics are examples of 16C-17C Italian maiolica from the most famous factories (Castel Durante and Urbino) and a substantial collection of porcelain: Oriental (16C-17C Chinese and Japanese), continental (Sèvre, Meissen) and English (Chelsea, Bow, Derby, Plymouth, Bristol, Swansea, Worcester). Other than the occasional good piece of furniture there are many small items ranging from Roman glass, cameos, seals and coins; Battersea enamels and snuff boxes to Arts and Crafts jewellery.

The **Crafts Study Centre** administered in part by the University of Bath, possesses a unique archive of books, documents, working notes and photographs; it also arranges examples of work by 20C British artist-craftworkers in woven and printed textiles, pottery, ceramics, furniture and calligraphy in its special gallery area on the ground floor. Artists in evidence include Ethel Mairet, Elizabeth Peacock, Rita Beales, Phyllis Baron, Dorothy Larcher; Bernard Leach, Shoji Hamada, Michael Cardew, Katharine Pleydell Bouverie, Lucie Rie; Ernest Gimson, Sidney Barnsley; Edward Johnston and other members of the Society of Scribes and Illuminators.

ADDITIONAL CITY MUSEUMS

Bath Postal Museum ⊙ (BV M⁷) – *Broad Street*. The Post Office from which the world's first stamp was sent (2 May 1840) is now a small museum highlighting the evolution of the postal service, especially since Ralph Allen and John Palmer, "Men of Bath" both, set about reforming the national service to make it more secure and reliable. Displays mark a century of British stamps (1840-1940), the advent of the Air Mail service following the first flight from Bath to London in 1912. A film *(30min)* relates developments over changing times. A library is open to philatelists by appointment.
Also available for consultation is a cabinet of documents listing when notable persons stayed in Bath and the purpose of their visits.

William Herschel Museum ⊙ (AX M¹⁰) – *19 New King Street*. The simply-furnished 18C house of the influential Sir William Herschel (1738-1822), organist at the Octagon Chapel in Bath and composer, is a modest home for a man who was to be appointed King's Astronomer by George III. Following his discovery of the planet Uranus (1781) – thereby doubling the size of the known solar system, Herschel went on to chart the skies, documenting hundreds of double stars, clusters and nebulae, and study infra-red radiation.
The small museum contains some of his telescopes, speculum metal mirrors, eye lenses, prisms, thermometers: his larger pieces of equipment are kept at the Old Royal Observatory, Greenwich. The back garden, from where William and his sister Caroline observed the stars, is planted with herbs and aromatic plants.

George Baytun Book Museum ⊙ (BX) – *Situated opposite the railway station in Manvers Street*. Baytun's bindery and bookshop was founded in 1894, and incorporated the famous Regency firm of Robert Rivière in 1840. Trading from its traditional large Victorian premises, the business has a **Book Museum** arranged in the basement comprising a display on the **Craft of Bookbinding** and one on **Bath in Literature**. The history of the book-making craft from the 16C-20C is explained with examples of beautiful old and new bindings, and includes some important 1st editions. The second section documents the times when Bath attracted such leading lights as Dr Johnson, Samuel Pepys, Burke, Fielding, Goldsmith, Jane Austen, Charles Dickens (whose study is recreated), William Beckford, Disraeli, Lord Nelson, John Wesley and Winston Churchill.

CITY OUTSKIRTS

Go north up Broad Street; fork left into Oxford Row; at the 5-road junction bear centre right.

★ **Camden Crescent** (AV) – The modest crescent, with its wide **view**, was built by John Eveleigh in 1786-92. It was never completed owing to subsidence at the east end, so the pediment above five giant columns is off-centre.

Return to the junction; take Lansdown Road northwest; after 150 yds turn left into Lansdown Place East and the Crescent.

★★ **Lansdown Crescent** (AV) – The serpentine crescent and the continuing, more ornamented, **Somerset Place**★ were built on this site overlooking the abbey and the city centre in 1789-93.
The crescent consists of three-storeyed houses with a rusticated ground floor and pierced balustrade; it is accented at the centre with pilasters and pediment and at either end by bow windows, and the ensemble completed by area railings and graceful lampholders.
Note the **bridge** between no 20 the Crescent and no 1 Lansdown Place West, built by William Beckford.

Return to Lansdown Road and continue north to the tower (left).

Beckford Tower and Museum ⊙ (AV M⁶) – William Beckford (1760-1844), millionaire inheritor with a true 18C collector's taste in books, pictures and art objects, Grand Tour traveller, diarist and MP, was the builder of the fantastic Neo-Gothic **Fonthill Abbey** (now demolished) designed by James Wyatt. In 1882 he left Wiltshire for Bath where he purchased Lansdown Hill and two houses in the crescent. On the hill he erected an Italianate tower (154ft) in local stone, crowned by a lantern of eight cast-iron columns and a domed roof, all gilded. The tower, intended as a library retreat, contains the museum (collection of prints, pictures, *objets d'art*, models) and, at the top of a twisting stairway, a belvedere which affords a **prospect**★ of Bath, the Severn Estuary and Wales, the Cotswolds, Wiltshire and beyond.

EXCURSIONS

Prior Park ⊘ (BX)

Note that there are no car parking facilities in the immediate vicinity to the entrance of the park; visitors are encouraged to take public transport from the city centre and then walk back down.

In the 1730s, when Bath had become fashionable, **Ralph Allen** decided to build himself a seat away from the crowds. He believed that the superbly sited mansion (now Prior Park College), which was designed by John Wood in the Palladian style with giant columns supporting a pedimented portico, would also serve to demonstrate to sceptical London architects that Bath stone from his quarries was supreme for fine construction work. The 28-acre park, inspired by Pope and Capability Brown replaced formal gardens; it is arranged as a "Natural" – in the Picturesque sense – English landscape punctuated with elegant 18C follies. These include a Palladian bridge, a Rock gate, Sham Bridge, Wilderness, grotto, cascade and Gothick temple. Allen kept open house at Prior Park and among his visitors were such leading lights as Alexander Pope, Henry Fielding (who modelled Squire Allworthy in *Tom Jones* upon Allen), Samuel Johnson, Gainsborough, David Garrick and Samuel Richardson.

Claverton *3 miles east of Bath.*

The village extends in name from the River Avon and the Kennet and Avon Canal, up a steep hill to the traditional manor house and beyond, on the down, to the new campus of Bath University created in 1966 out of the Bristol College of Advanced Technology.

★★ **American Museum in Britain** ⊘ – Housed in a compact Classical mansion (1820) designed by Wyattville, architect to George IV, and built of Bath stone, the museum recreates various interiors from wealthy homes of white settlers from the late 17C-mid19C, complete with original furnishings. Besides these, a broad range of treasures and artefacts from a wider cross-section of people (Indians, cowboys, Mexicans) are also displayed.

Museum – The late-17C **Keeping Room** (Massachusetts), with massive fireplace and solid turned and polished furniture, shows the developments made from the modest homes (cabins, wigwams) of the first Puritan settlers: furniture is modelled on English prototypes.

Early 18C rooms present regional differences and changing fashions: the **Lee Room** (1700-30; New Hampshire) has blue-green painted boarding and practical English delftware on show; the small panelled **Borning Room** is functionally furnished for childbirth; the more formal **Perley Parlor** (1763; Massachusetts) has cedar-grained pine panelling and white-washed walls, curving Queen Anne maple and fruitwood furniture. Note the superb array of 18C and 19C American pewter, modelled on European silver shapes fashionable at the time.

In the **Textile Room** are displayed the excellent collection of quilts (18C-20C) illustrating how the craft has evolved into a veritable art form: classical designs contrast with inventive variations. Basic tools and templates are also displayed here as are examples of traditional hooked rugs and Navajo Indian weaving.

The Chalices Quilt (87in x 75in) is one of many such cotton appliqué quilts that would have been made collectively, children and house-servants included, to celebrate the annual visit of the Anglican bishop of New Orleans, in this case to the Mimosa Hall Plantation in Texas. For such special occasions, during which the bishop would carry out baptisms, confirmations and marriage ceremonies, he would stay with a different family each time; after his departure, the quilt would be used in the nursery or in the servants' quarters.

American Museum, Claverton

The late-17C **Deming Parlor** (c1769; Connecticut) has more sophisticated carved cherry-wood and mahogany furniture inspired by Queen Anne and Chippendale reflecting the changing prosperity of the times. The **Deer Park Parlor** (late 18C; Maryland) reveals the influence of Hepplewhite and Sheraton, notably in the use of inlay and veneer; pieces of export Chinese porcelain suggest established trade links with the Far East. The freshness of the stencilled bedroom (1830) exudes simple comfort. A pair of display cabinets in the **Central Hall** contain fine examples of American silver.

Downstairs, the intrepid spirit of the first **pioneers** and the courage of the early traders are suggested in the following galleries dedicated to immigration, whaling, trading with the orient, prospecting for gold, trapping for fur, the advent of the stage-coach and Pony Express, barbed wire and the telegraph. A small display of **North American Indian** artefacts is included to illustrate the diversity of their own traditions (Indian war-bonnet, beaded moccasins, Navajo jewellery, baskets and pottery). Reconstructions of typical **Spanish colonists**' adobe house and Morada chapel interiors suggest the basic level of comfort in New Mexico.

The principal room recreates **Conkey's Tavern**, an original farmhouse tavern (1758) in Massachusetts, complete with kitchen and bar-room: worn cooking utensils and well-used "redware", a cone of sugar, windsor chairs, childrens' toys, travelling gear. This is in stark contrast with the next rooms recreating a spacious **Shaker** and crowded Pennsylvania-German interior: the one with its austerely simple decor, the other cluttered with painted furniture, tinware, chalkware figures and spatterware.

The 19C **Greek Revival** New York dining room (1825-1835) is furnished with pieces by the celebrated American cabinet makers Duncan Phyfe and Ephraim Haines. The richly decorated **New Orleans Bedroom** predates the Civil War; the mahogany bed, carved rosewood seats reflect the influence of French Louis XV.

Grounds – The **New Gallery** is used to house temporary exhibitions. Other amenities include a shop, research library and a display area for items drawn from an extensive collection of rare maps (1472-1600), donated by Dallas Pratt.

Within the gardens overlooking the wooded valley of the River Avon lurk a covered Conestoga Wagon, a copy of a Northern Cheyenne Indian tepee, a 19C milliner's shop with a delightful collection of band-boxes, a splendid arboretum containing native American species subsequently introduced to the British Isles, colonial herb garden, a fernery and a waterfall, George Washington's Mount Vernon garden and a **Folk Art Gallery** with a collection ranging from naive portraits to weathervanes, cigar store to carousel figures, a Mohawk Indian figurehead, tin marriage gifts...

★ **Claverton Pumping Station** ⊙ – *On the east side of A36. Take Ferry Lane across the canal; cross the railway line.*

The pump of 1813 has been restored to raise water from the River Avon into the canal, the other being located just outside Marlborough. Here, the pair of elm paddled, breast shot wheels (each 12ft wide and 17.5ft in diameter) are driven by the headrace, to turn the pitwheel, flywheel, crankshaft, working beams and the pumps, which lift 50 gallons a stroke or 87 000 gallons an hour. These were installed by John Rennie and modified by Harvey's of Hayle in 1843.

Kennet and Avon Canal – Following in the natural wake of the Avon, this section of the canal between Bath and Bradford-on-Avon is particularly attractive, notably so from Dundas (marked by the magnificent Doric **Dundas Aqueduct** which bears the canal over the River Avon – named according to an inscription on the south side, after Charles Dundas, Chairman of the Kennet and Avon Canal) to **Bathampton** where Viscount du Barry (nephew of Louis XV's mistress) was killed in a duel and where the remains of Admiral Arthur Philip, early colonist of Australia and First Governor of New South Wales, lie buried.

★ **Dyrham** *8 miles north of Bath.*

Dyrham Park ⊙ – *45 min.* The house presents a rare contrast in its two 17C-18C fronts. One is an example of formality and symmetry; the other, equally Classical, is lightened by touches of Baroque ornament. Both were built within ten years for the same man, William Blathwayt who inherited Dyrham through marriage. William Blathwayt (1649-1717) was an efficient administrator and diplomat in the service of the Stuart kings and of William III. His taste had been formed by his uncle, Thomas Povey of Lincoln's Inn, who was a connoisseur, man of fashion, *bon viveur,* and friend of Samuel Pepys and John Evelyn. Although he married an heiress and became rich through his appointments, Blathwayt maintained that he "never pretended to any fortune".

Blathwayt's first architect took back the existing Tudor house to the Great Hall and built instead a formal, perfectly regular entrance front of local stone.

In 1698 the second building phase began. Blathwayt chose as architect this time "the ingenious **Mr Talman**", Comptroller of the Royal Works, second to Sir Christopher Wren, a travelled squire, collector and maverick architect. Talman's façade of Cotswold stone, 130ft long with two storeys rising to an attic topped by the same balustrade and urns as on the other side, is relieved by rustication at ground floor level and by a series of quoins, alternate pediments and carved panels above the first-floor windows; Tuscan pillars frame the door.

The orangery, with its round-arched windows, was added in 1701.

Interior – Inside, the contents of the rooms have barely changed since they were recorded in an inventory by Blathwayt's housekeeper.

The **East Entrance Hall** is hung with richly embossed leather purchased at 3*s* a skin when Blathwayt was in the Hague, where he may also have obtained the blue and white delftware.

The **Great Hall** is all that remains, and that only in name, of the Tudor house. The sash windows – though the sills have been raised – and the book presses made to the design of Samuel Pepys were there in Blathwayt's time, as were the pictures of the monarchs he served and portraits by Michael Dahl of himself and Mary Wynter, his wife. The fine set of Dutch walnut "parade" chairs dates from *c*1700.

Note, in the **West Hall**, the delft tile pictures of exotic scenes and fruits by the fireplace, 17C muskets and Blathwayt's own "under and over" holster pistols, the fireside companion "pareing of an apple", and the Cromwellian chairs re-covered in Dutch leather in *c*1700.

By the **White Stair** are licences of 1511 and 1620 to enclose 500 acres as parkland, a Kyp engraving (1712) and a drawing of the grounds after the Repton replanting. The virtuosity of the *Great Perspective* painting at the top of the stairs was much admired by 17C London society, notably Pepys, when it hung in Thomas Povey's rooms.

Among the furniture and furnishings in the other rooms, note in the **Balcony Room** the period blackamoor torchères and delft flowerpot still standing in the chimney as recorded in 1710; in the **Tapestry Room**, the early 18C Flemish tapestries, the bed and its hangings, and the tortoise-shell chest; in the **Drawing Room**, the two Rococo mirrors by John Linnell, the fine gilded side-table, Murillo's *Peasant Woman and Boy* and the most un-Spanish copy painted by the young Gainsborough.

The gilt **Leather Closet** was especially designed to exaggerate the sense of perspective in the illusionist *View down a Corridor* painted in 1662 by Hoogstraeten.

The tapestries in the **Diogenes Room** are from Mortlake, the factory to which Povey served as a director; the state bed was ordered for a proposed state visit by Queen Anne in 1704 when the Carolean stools were re-covered in the same material as the bed hangings.

Garden and park – To complete the house, Talman and the garden designer George Wise laid out formal gardens of parterres, fountains and waterworks including a stepped cascade.

By the turn of the 18C-19C there had been developments in the design of gardens and the Bath to Gloucester road had been improved, exactly reversing the best approach to the house: the fronts were accordingly inverted and **Humphrey Repton** was called upon to replan the park.

Dyrham Village – The village of 17C-18C stone houses and cottages is named in the *Anglo-Saxon Chronicle* as the site of the key battle of 577 after which the West Saxons advanced to the Severn Estuary, dividing the Britons in Cornwall from those in Wales.

Dyrham Church – *Access by road through the village or up from the garden.* The church with an embattled tower, a porch with quatrefoil parapets and Perpendicular windows was rebuilt at different periods in the 15C. The **Flemish triptych** is 15C.

Horton *Follow A46 north: 3 miles northeast of Chipping Sodbury*

This green valley on the northern edge of Horton village just bypassed by the ancient Cotswold Way has been inhabited for centuries; the attractive group of Cotswold stone buildings which comprise the Court consists of the church and manor house, both rebuilt in the 14C-15C, and the hall (12C).

Horton Court ⊘ – In the 16C William Knight was appointed prebendary of Horton; he became protonotary of the Holy See and, in 1527, Henry VIII's envoy to Rome in the unsuccessful divorce negotiations. His advancement is reflected in the highly decorated **doorway** (16C). His **arms**, granted on the prebendaryship, are crowned and flanked by the **protonotary's hat and tassels** (fewer than for a cardinal); the carved **Renaissance columns** recall his visit to Rome.

Hall – The building, a unique link between Saxon domestic halls and later medieval halls, dates from 1100-50. Despite strengthening and rebuilding, the introduction of a Tudor fireplace and conversion to other uses – RC chapel in an inserted upper hall in the 18C when the house belonged to a descendant of the letter-writing **Pastons** – there remain, unscathed, the **south doorway** and, opposite, the **north door** in a wall of early dressed stone.

Ambulatory – The six-arched detached ambulatory, built by Knight in the manner of an Italian loggia, stands opposite a giant **tulip tree** on the south side of the house overlooking the valley garden, which was designed in the medieval manner on several levels.

Church – St James', built in the 14C on the site of the Norman church contemporary with the hall, has been repeatedly altered and restored. It has a 14C arcade, wagon roofs, a re-cut Norman font with 17C cover, a Jacobean pulpit and several Paston memorial tablets.

For BADMINTON *(5 miles southeast by A46 and B4040), see* MALMESBURY

BIDEFORD

Devon – Population 13 066

Michelin Atlas p 6 or Map 403 – H 30

Bideford (pronounced "Biddyford") derives its name from its site at the foot of a hillside "by the ford" across the River Torridge. It achieved fame as a port in the 16C-18C and is always recalled as the town with one of the most "beautiful and stately" **bridges** in the kingdom.

As a port it gained early prosperity having been given by William Rufus to the **Grenvilles** who held it until 1744, by which time they had obtained borough, market and fair charters for the town. During the 16C Bideford established a trans-Atlantic trade largely as a result of Sir Richard Grenville's colonisation of Virginia and Carolina; this was greatly increased in the mid-17C by Newfoundland cod-fishing and, at the turn of the century, by tobacco imports from Maryland and Virginia. At the same time, the local textile industry flourished with imports of wool from Spain and further prosperity from general commerce with the Mediterranean: it is from this period that a number of houses survive. Thereafter business dwindled, except for coastal shipping, until the arrival of the railway in the 19C when the town enjoyed a revival marked by the building of the pannier market in 1883-84: today the area relies on mixed farming, tourism (with excursions to Lundy Island) and light industry.

Market days: Tuesday (includes cattle market) and Saturday all day.

★★ **Bridge** – The original packhorse bridge was built in oak in *c*1280, reputedly paid for by the Bishop of Exeter and later (1459) repaired with funds from the pope. This was eventually replaced by a **stone bridge** using the existing timbers as scaffolding and support during construction; even the width of the arches which had varied according to the length of the original timbers was reproduced according to their prototype. Together, the 24 arches stretch 677ft across the Torridge estuary, each arch spanning a distance of 12ft to 25ft and springing from piers of correspondingly different size. Although repaired (1638) and widened (1865), the bridge remains an impressive feat of civil engineering. A scale model is on view in the Burton Art Gallery.

Overlooking the river is the **Royal Hotel** where Charles Kingsley wrote a great part of *Westward Ho!* in 1855: although originally built as the home of a wealthy merchant, it has also served as the town's workhouse and prison. Inside, fine panelling and decorative plaster ceilings ornament the rooms where a number of American soldiers were stationed between 1940-44.

★ **Burton Art Gallery** ⊘ – The purpose-built gallery (1951, extended 1994) stands in the extensive and brilliantly flowered Victoria Park at the end of the quay – where clay used to be off-loaded to the local potteries.

The spacious, airy exhibition space houses an eclectic collection of things largely donated by two local residents: Hubert Coop (1893-1953) and Thomas Burton. On the ground floor is a case displaying fine examples of English 18C and 19C silver (vinaigrettes, nutmeg graters, tea caddies, snuff boxes) and a selection from a rare bequest of 800 exquisite card-cases.

In the main gallery are displayed an unusual collection of **model ships** made by French prisoners from Napoleon's campaigns (1794-1815); these are painstakingly constructed from wood, mutton bone (salvaged allegedly from dustbins), cotton thread (unravelled from their clothes) and wire.

The collection of **paintings** includes works by Coop and his contemporaries Sir John Lavery, Sir George Clausen and the American E Aubrey Hunt. A later bequest by Judith Ackland and Mary Stella Edwards consists of topographical views in watercolour executed between the early 1920s and the early 1970s.

On the first floor are displayed fine examples of Lambeth drug jars and north Devon pottery: notably some late-18C slipware **harvest jugs** made at the Bideford and Fremington potteries. Separate cases accommodate 17C-19C English porcelain figurines and examples of Judith Ackland's painted cotton-wool Jackanda figures. The museum also has a large area dedicated to temporary exhibitions of works by contemporary craftsmen.

Posset pot

HKP Lines/Burton Art Gallery and Museum, Bideford

The Big Sheep ⊙ – *A39 North Devon Link Road.* This popular family attraction boasts sheep racing, duck trialling, animal milking, cheese-making, sheep shearing, a nature trail through woodland and a woolcraft centre (with demonstrations of spinning wool. Broad range of artisan-made ewe's cheese (*see* INTRODUCTION: Regional specialities).

EXCURSIONS

Westward Ho! *3 miles northwest by A386 and a by-road.*

The golden sands beside the village (renamed in the 19C after Charles Kingsley's book) extend for three miles; the Atlantic rollers bring the surf-riders thunderously towards the shallows then subside harmlessly to wash around the ankles of paddling, squatting toddlers – Westward Ho! being one of Devon's safest beaches. Catering to summer visitors, the resort is equipped with amusements arcades, ice-cream sellers and hot dog vendors...

Backing the sands is a ridge of pebbles and behind these the grass-covered **Northam Burrows** – now a country park and Royal North Devon Golf Club; at the west end of the beach the pebbles end in rocks and pools. Above rise the **Kipling Tors** from which there are views towards Hartland Point, Lundy and, on a fine day, the outline of south Wales.

Rudyard Kipling (1865-1936) spent his schooldays at the United Services College (now the residential Kipling Terrace), "twelve bleak houses by the shore", about which he wrote a highly fictionalised account in *Stalky & Co.*

★ **Appledore** *3 miles north on A386.*

The origins of Tawmutha date back to Saxon times, but it was not until the 14C that its prosperity as a trading and fishing village was ensured when a community of Cistercian monks settled there. In 1588, it was conferred free port status by Royal Charter of Queen Elizabeth I in recognition of the valiant action by local seamen against the Spanish Armada. During the 18C Appledore vied with Bideford as the country's largest importer of tobacco from the New World; another mainstay was the right to fish salmon from the River Torridge.

Today this charming seaside town continues to thrive: art galleries sell local crafts and paintings of topographical scenery while local fishermen ply their trade and land fresh water and sea fish for sale to local restaurants.

Streets – Over the centuries Appledore has evolved into a network of narrow streets and cobbled yards emanating from the quay which was built in 1845 and reinforced in 1941.

Follow the line of the point along the quay, with its views across the Torridge to Instow *(irregular passenger ferry in season)* and north to Braunton Burrows *(see* ILFRACOMBE); wander back along the long **Irsha Street** with its older, vividly painted cottages (one named Smugglers' Run is dated 1664), centre gully and minute courts. In the narrow **Market Street** note the white bow-windowed houses.

North Devon Maritime Museum ⓥ – Odun House (1834) is named after a Saxon chieftain who defeated Hubba the Dane in battle in 878 just outside Appledore. It traces ship development from the building of wooden ships on open beaches to the construction of steel vessels by flow-line production: girthing chains, traverse boards, gammon corners, fiddleheads and carpenter's tools; fishing; ocean rescue; World War II display. A visual aids centre is set in a recreated Victorian class-room.

Northam Burrows Country Park ⓥ – The area overlooking the Torridge and Tor estuary provides an ideal place to watch for migratory birds and study local flora and fauna.

> ### Old and new side by side
>
> It was in an Appledore shipyard that, in 1973, a replica of Drake's *Golden Hinde* was built and launched with a bottle of mead: since then, the ship has sailed the high seas. The same yard builds pleasure-craft and fishing vessels while at the other end of the scale, one of Europe's largest covered yards, Appledore Shipbuilders Bidna complex, produces container ships, sand-dredgers, coasters...

Instow *accessible by ferry*

Tapeley Park ⓥ – *2 miles north on A39, right turn beyond Westleigh.* A long drive banked high with trees and rhododendrons leads to the house which stands in a spectacular **setting** overlooking the Taw and Torridge estuary and a beautiful terraced Italian garden. Other points of interest in the ten acres of "Pleasure Grounds" include an 18C ice house and shell house, an ilex tunnel, dedicated areas of wild and organic gardens. Much of the recent restoration has been undertaken with the assistance of Mary Keen, the designer of the Christies' other gardens at Glyndebourne in Sussex.

The 17C mansion, built of brick with stone dressings, although much altered and enlarged, retains its 18C plasterwork ceilings. Inside, the contents include a range of 18C-19C service memorabilia, fine porcelain and glass, and William Morris furniture.

Great Torrington to South Molton

Great Torrington – Great Torrington, or Torrington as it is known locally, was selected in 1966 by the Trust established at Dartington *(see* TOTNES) as the site for a glass factory which has become a leading manufacturer of plain lead crystal.

Market days: Thursdays and Saturdays.

★ **Dartington Crystal** ⓥ – *Left down School Lane, off New Street opposite the church.* The factory now employs a number of skilled craftsmen, many of whom can be seen from gantry walks at work in small teams, gathering, blowing, shaping the glass, always keeping it turning to produce the well known lead crystal pieces.

Parish Church – "The church was blown up with powder Febre ye 16 ano 1645 and rebuilt in 1651" – a matter of Royalists inadvertently setting off the 80 powder barrels they had been storing in the church when 200 of their men were packed into the building as prisoners of the Parliamentarians. How much of the 14C church, built on an older site – the town dates back to pre-Saxon times – was destroyed is not known but the pillars in the east arcade are decorated with detailed 14C carving while those opposite are square, solid and more utilitarian as though erected at speed in 1651. The spire, unusual in these parts, is 19C. The oak **pulpit** and **sounding board**, carved with cherubs and wreaths, are 17C; the **white ensign** (by the organ) flew at the Normandy Landing in 1944. Note, among the lists of rectors and vicars, the name of Master, later Cardinal, **Thomas Wolsey**.

High Street – The High Street, which is also the market place, extends north from the **Pannier Market** (1842) between the twin-gabled **Black Horse Inn** (1681) and the Georgian-style **Town Hall** ⓥ (museum of bygones).

Castle Hill – *250yds south.* The 12C castle disappeared long ago but the site affords a good **view** south across the River Torridge towards Dartmoor.

★ **Rosemoor** ⓥ – *1 mile south of Great Torrington on B3220 to Exeter.* This 40-acre garden and arboretum, given to the Royal Horticultural Society in 1988 by Lady Anne Berry, was designed to provide inspiration, encouragement and advice to all types of gardeners notably those with similar climatic conditions in the West Country. Since then, the well-tended gardens which nestle in a lovely

Devon valley, have gained national importance for their variety of plants and careful curatorship. Particular points of interest include an extensive collection of roses (200 varieties); thematic use of colour; herbs, vegetables and fruit growing; herbaceous borders; planning seasonal variations.

Atherington – The **church**, much restored in 1884 but with the original wagon roof, has a **rood screen** which at right angles becomes a **parclose screen** with a rare and beautifully decorated gallery.

Chittlehampton – The **church** overlooking the village square has a spectacular 115ft tower which rises in four stages, each underlined by a frieze and pinnacled buttresses, to a crest of pierced battlements, pinnacles and sub-pinnacles in characteristic Somerset style.

South Molton – The old wool town, with colour-washed houses and a Georgian town centre, bustles with life particularly on market day (Thursday).
The guildhall, facing the town square, Broad Street, dates from 1743 and houses the town **museum** ⊘ (historic charters, 18C fire engine, minerals, an old cider press, pewter...). Note also the 19C pannier market next to it, the Medical Hall with an iron balcony supported on columns on an island site and the 15C church with pinnacled tower (107ft).

King's Nympton – *17 miles east by B3227, A377 and left turn before the station.* The hilltop village, which retains a few thatched houses, has a Perpendicular church with a green copper octagonal spire.
The sill, between the porch and the interior, is probably the shaft of a Celtic cross. The carved bosses of the wagon roofs have been enriched above the screen. The box pews, pilastered reredos and communion rails with alternating balusters date from the 18C. The royal arms appear over the south door.

BLANDFORD FORUM*

Dorset – Population 7 957
Michelin Atlas p 8 or Map 403 – N 31

Blandford grew into an important market town in the 13C, strategically situated as it is on the River Stour and at the intersection of several major thoroughfares with connections to London, Exeter, Salisbury, Dorchester and Poole.
Devastated by fire in 1731, the town rose within 30 years "like the Phoenix from its ashes, to its present beautiful and flourishing state". Houses were rebuilt along the old street courses in the latest 18C style; the church, in new guise, rose on its early site...
Across the Stour at Blandford St Mary is the **Blandford Brewery** (Hall and Woodhouse Ltd) which produces Badger Beer, erected in 1900 and still containing an original Gimson of Leicester steam engine of 1899.
Market day: Thursday and Saturday.

Market Place – The square, a wide juncture of West and East Streets with Salisbury Street coming in at the northwest end, is the town centre.
St Peter and St Paul ⊘ – The large green and ashlar stone church dating from 1733-39 has a west tower rising squarely to a pierced balustrade, stone urns and an open wooden lantern.
The interior, which is filled with light from the tall, rounded, typically Georgian windows, has Portland stone columns with Ionic capitals which soar to a moulded entablature and groined vault. Note, amidst the box pews, the canopied, carved and plush lined **Mayoral Chair** (1748), the **17C pulpit** and the **memorial** to the Bastard family who were responsible for much of the rebuilding.
No 26 Market Place – The house on the corner was built by John Bastard for himself and given an integrated façade with the house next door (no 75 East St) which he also built. (East Street itself escaped the fire and contains several older houses.)
Town Hall – The 18C hall (north side) stands over a three-bay arcade, filled with iron gates and lanterns and crowned by stone urns matching those on the church. Opposite stands the **Red Lion**, one of several large coaching inns, with its wide central carriage entrance framed with pilasters and, at the far end of town, the **Old Greyhound** (now a land agent) with its ornate front comprising giant pilasters, a pediment, decorated window frames, plasterwork grapes and a greyhound.
Blandford Museum ⊘ – *Bere's Yard.* The museum is allegedly housed in the Bastard family coach house; it assembles a variety of artefacts of local interest: fossils, archeological fragments; items relating to the Portman family and Bryanston School; examples of lace, hand-made buttons (*see* INTRODUCTION: Dorset) and traditional old-fashioned clothes, tools and domestic vessels; the devastating fire of 1731; militaria, bygones and railwaymania; an assortment of documents relating to the town's schools.

Back streets – North of the main road lies a network of winding streets and alleys with several attractive houses. In Church Lane are Old Bank House and **Legion** (formerly Coupar) **House**, "The finest post-fire building in Blandford", built of purple bricks laid as headers, relieved by a full complement of stone dressings.

Cavalcade of Costume ⊘ – Facing onto the square is **Lime Tree House** which is built of unusual purple brick with red brick dressings and vertical decoration between the windows. Inside is housed an extensive collection of clothes from the 1730s to the 1950s which was acquired by Mrs Betty Penny from various sources including a number of country houses. Displays are regularly changed but always include a broad selection of accessories: children's clothes, underwear, lace, fans, parasols, jewellery, gloves, shoes, Dorset bonnets and buttons, and such like.

Changing faces of fashion	
1550s	Long hair for men became fashionable
1620s	Natural dyes and natural fabrics: linen and cotton (washable) for undergarments; wool and silk for over garments
1660s	Wigs are *de rigueur*
1670	Three piece suit is established, comprising jacket, waistcoat and knee breeches
1720s	Linen petticoats are reinforced with cane hoops
1770s	Sack-back gowns give way to simpler more practical garments
1780s	Trade with India promotes a taste for printed chintz (glaze d cotton) fabrics; hair is worn informally, pinned into a mass of curls and ringlets
1800	Neo Classical elegance is promoted by the Empress Josephine and the likes of Lady Hamilton
1820s	Trousers are accepted as informal day wear; silk returned to fashion following the lifting of the ban on French imports
1830s	Ladies' hair was stiffened, looped and curled with gum arabic and wire
1850s	Introduction of sewing machines and synthetic dyes; launch of department stores point shopping practices to off-the-peg fashion
1856	Invention of the crinoline: light, easy to wear, though very impractical
1860s	Bustles of stiff frills of horse-hair replace graduated hoops of steel
1870s	Suspenders replace garters
1880s	The fringe was made fashionable by Princess Alexandra

The Plocks – *Off to the right.* The street was the gathering place for sheep to be sold in the market.

Old House – *The Close.* The red brick house, which dates from 1660, stands high, rambling and disjointed in an eccentric yet effective way: note how the chimneys are ornamented with a ring of columns supporting an entablature and the roof is tiled with stone and terracotta.

Ryves Almshouses – *Salisbury Street, east side.* The range of 1682 is distinguished by a small centre gable, dominant chimneys and an ornate shield of arms.

Bridge – The stone bridge with six arches spanning the River Stour at the west entrance to the town (A354) dates from 1783.

EXCURSIONS

★ **Royal Signals Museum** ⊘

Blandford Camp. 2 miles northeast off B3082.

Chronologically, there have been smoke and water signals, beacons, heliographs of metal and mirrorglass, despatch riders, pigeons, flags and lanterns to communicate over large distances. The breakthrough came with the Murray Lettering Telegraph which pre-empted the invention of the Morse code (1835), the first electric, single needle telegraph (1837) and, 150 years later, micro-circuit transmitters and receivers.

The first organised military application for an electric telegraph came during the Crimean War (1854); further action in various African campaigns confirmed the need to consolidate a rational system of communication, this led to the foundation of the Telegraph Battalion of the Royal Engineers. The invention of the telephone (1876), followed by Marconi's wireless (1895-98) led to field telephones being used in co-ordinating gun battles at Ladysmith in 1899. During World War I the three-part service of despatch riders, telephone and wireless communications were extensively deployed in Europe and the Middle East: in recognition of the Signal Service's contribution to successful action it was made into a separate Corps of Signals (1920) – six weeks later the "Royal" title was conferred. Expansion, evolution and improved expertise gained while manning colonial outposts of the Empire prepared the Royal Signals for action in World War II, notably in Palestine and Malaya, and thereafter in Korea, Cyprus, Borneo and the Arabian Peninsula. Since then, the Signals have played an integral part in all operations involving the British Army, in the Falklands for example, and on UN Peace Keeping missions (Lebanon, Gulf War, Bosnia).

The history of the Corps is related here with a broad range of equipment from earliest times until the microchip and satellite age; memorabilia is effectively used in tableaux and recreations of active service complete with sound effects and interactive activities; extensive medal gallery; uniforms and paraphernalia; despatch motorbikes, land rovers and specially adapted prototype vehicles: plenty to appeal to interested children and mechanically or engineering-minded adults!

Chettle House ⊙

7 miles northeast by A354; signposted left after the road to Tarrant Hinton.

Chettle comes from the Old English word *cietal*, meaning a deep valley between hills, which describes the tranquil setting of this **English Baroque house** and its surrounding village (described in Domesday as a town).

In 1710 the Elizabethan house on the site was replaced by this small country house designed by Thomas Archer (*c*1680-1743), a pupil of Vanbrugh. The red brick façade has an entablature and capitals of Chilmark stone (Ham stone at the ends) and has rounded corners in the Archer style. In 1846 the house was bought and altered by the Castleman family – note the castles on the skyline – though later returned to its original shape (hence the replacement Ham stone). The interior boasts an impressive **Oak Hall** with a double staircase and a gallery, and a fine spiral stone staircase down to the vaulted basement.

The semi-formal **gardens**, bordered by a vineyard and woodland, are graced by stone urns, lily ponds and a stately cedar.

The banded flint and stone **church**, save for its early 16C **tower** with trefoil-headed lights, was entirely refurbished in the Decorated style in 1849; the 3 old bells (*c*1350) are from an earlier church on the same site. Inside, the two chairs and kneelers *(chancel)* are Victorian, made from decorative panels of the Jacobean 3-decker pulpit. The south transept, which houses the dainty pipe organ (c1870), was originally the Castleman family pew; their crest emblazoned in the stained-glass windows.

★ **Milton Abbas** *9 miles southwest of Blandford by A354; turn right in Winterbourne Whitechurch* ⊙

Henry VIII dissolved Milton Abbey in 1539; Lord Milton, Earl of Dorchester, removed the village with similar autocracy two and a half centuries later. The property was valuable and Henry sold it for £1 000 to his proctor, Sir John Tregonwell, who constructed a house amid the conventual buildings, while the village adopted the abbey as a parish church.

In 1752, the estate was acquired by **Lord Milton**, who would have none of this. He commissioned **Capability Brown** to landscape the park, and finding the village to intrude upon his view, had it rebuilt (1771-90) out of sight as twin lines of identical, 4-room, cob-walled, **thatched cottages**, well spaced on either side of the grass-verged main street.

Marking the centre are the **church** – erected in 1786 with stone and timber from the abbey tithe barn – and the **Tregonwell Almshouses** which were reconditioned from the 16C houses of the original village. The village pub, the Hambro Arms, takes its name from the banking family associated with Milton Abbas in the 19C.

Cob

Old cob cottages have a window facing eastwards "to welcome the rising sun". This ecological building material – dismissed at the turn of the 20C in favour of brick and concrete, has several regional names: mwd, pridd and clom in Wales; tempered clay in Ireland; clay batts and clay lump in East Anglia; mud-and-stud in Lincolnshire; wychert in Buckinghamshire; cob in Devon. The practice consists of breaking down soil to a fine tilth before spreading it out on a layer of straw. Water is then added and the mixture is trodden down and built up in layers, trimmed with a sharp spade when dry. In places the mixture was moulded or contained in wooden shuttering. The product is a building that breathes, in theory eliminating any condensation problems; in ideal circumstances it makes a building warm and cosy in winter, and where whitewashed, cool in summer.

Abbey ⊘ – *30min*. Massive as it is (136ft long), the abbey was never completed. The first church was struck by lightning in 1309 and almost destroyed; building re-started in 1331 in the Early English–Decorated styles but virtually ended at the Black Death in 1348. As a consequence the foreshortened abbey consists of an aisled presbytery, tower and crossing, and transepts.

The contrasting tracery in the windows of the transepts is late Decorated *(south)* and Perpendicular *(north)*. The *Tree of Jesse* is by Pugin; the white marble funeral monument was designed by **Robert Adam**.

The height of the stone vaulted **presbytery** or chancel, together with its size, are a reminder that this was intended to be a great medieval abbey (founded 934). In the 15C the monks erected the reredos of three tiers of canopied niches; Dissolution, Reformation and Puritanism have stripped it of brilliant colour and saintly figures, so that today it stands bone-white, like a piece of starched lace.

Furnishings – The mother-of-pearl **Crucifix**, the tall, hanging **tabernacle** with an octagonal spire of carved and once painted wood, the **panel painting** of King Athelstan, the founder of the abbey, are all 15C; the bust of the pilgrim St James is 16C.

House ⊘ – *30min*. Lord Milton, future Earl of Dorchester, commissioned **William Chambers**, future architect of Somerset House in London, to design his new mansion with a plain exterior to complement the abbey. It now accommodates a school.

The most impressive of the typical 18C staterooms with their plasterwork **ceilings** and white **marble chimneypieces** are the **library**, where the bookcases are framed by paired pilasters, and the **ballroom**, covered by a tunnel vault with Adam-style moulding.

Abbot Middleton's Hall – The hall, the one part of the old monastery to remain, dates from 1498. Above plain panelling, the walls rise through a clerestory, interspaced with angel-supported stone shafts, to a **hammerbeam roof** decorated with panel tracery.

A357 to Sturminster Newton

Fiddleford Manor ⊘ – *A footpath runs along the disused Somerset and Dorset Joint Railway (Bath to Bournemouth) line from the main town car park. 15min.* The 14C hall is abutted by a lateral chamber block consisting of two service rooms on the ground floor and Solar (large chamber) above: the fine plaster ceilings are alleged to have been transferred to Hinton St Mary. The manor was acquired by Thomas White (d 1555) and his wife Ann (note the initials carved into the arched doorways) possibly from land owned by Glastonbury Abbey; after the Restoration the estate was bought by Sir Thomas Freke from whom it passed through his descendants into the Pitt-Rivers family.

★ **Sturminster Newton** – *Take the B3091 southwest*. In 968 King Edgar granted Sturminster to Glastonbury Abbey; the Domesday survey recorded the abbey as having three mills at that time. A major fire in 1708 destroyed most of the older buildings save the White Hart pub.

The modern market town ceased to hold livestock auctions in 1997 although much of the outlying country is dedicated to arable farming. Located on the River Stour, the town was ideally situated for carding and weaving wool, which was then sold for export through Poole to Newfoundland, and leather – the area around the church (built 1486, 15C wagon roof, remodelled in 1825) being known locally as Tanyard: today, the local speciality is Sturminster Newton Cheddar cheese which is produced by J M Nuttalls.

Corn Mill ⊘ – *Located on the far side of town, over the Town Bridge and right, below the A357*. This old **mill**, its weir over 250 yards upstream, rises in a picturesque setting overlooking meadows and the **15C bridge** into town; across the fields sits Riverside, where Thomas Hardy lived (1876-78) and wrote *The Return of the Native*.

The present, largely 17C (stone) and 18C (brick) building dates in part back to the 15C and was still in use commercially until recently. Lovingly maintained in working order, it rises over three floors and has the traditional layout of a corn mill: large wooden bins for storing grain at the top, **milling machinery** on the first floor with millstones, hopper, winnower, crusher etc. and ground floor for bagging, weighing and storing the finished meal. The machinery, all of which is now electrically driven, includes a **water turbine** with a horizontal drive wheel (installed in 1904 and still in working order) controlled by a sluice gate below the water level.

This guide has been designed to help plan short breaks away and longer touring programmes.
Consult the Map of Principal Sights to ensure no major attraction is omitted.

BODMIN

Cornwall – Population 12 553
Michelin Atlas p 3 or Map 403 – F, G 32

Bodmin, founded by St Petroc in the 6C and named as Cornwall's only town in the Domesday Book, described as the "greatest Markett town in the Shere" with a population of 2 000 in Henry VIII's reign, was for centuries the centre of activity in the county. It was too active perhaps for in 1496 its citizens were among the leaders of a protest march on London against an excessive levy on tin – they were massacred; in 1497 they supported the unsuccessful Perkin Warbeck (*see* TAUNTON); in 1549, with Helston, Bodmin took part in the vain Cornish uprising against the imposition of the English Prayer Book.

In the 19C it replaced Launceston as the seat of the County (now the Crown Court). It suffered a major set back, however, when it refused to provide access to the Great Western Railway forcing **Bodmin Road Station** to be built 4.5 miles from the town in the 1870s; as a result it was spared commercialisation, but county offices, the library, museum, the cathedral and businesses established themselves in Truro and as a result Bodmin can seem a little barren.

During the Second World War the crown jewels and the Domesday Book were housed in Bodmin Prison for safe keeping.

★ **St Petroc** – In 1469 the parishioners determined to rebuild their Norman church in the new Perpendicular style. The largest church in Cornwall, 151ft long by 65ft wide, was completed in 1472. Everyone contributed to the cost including the 40 local guilds; the vicar presented a year's salary and others gave materials and labour. The dedication to St Petroc, a Cornish saint (d 564) who lived as a hermit on Bodmin Moor, dates from around 1000 when his shrine, relics, bell and staff were transferred here making Bodmin into the Bode of Monks and therefore an important centre of pilgrimage.

In the churchyard is the holy well of St Goran, Petroc's forerunner.

Interior – Beneath the slim pillars with their small capitals are the free-standing tomb of Prior Thomas Vivian (d 1533) carved in grey marble and black Catacleuse stone. The 12C **font**, "the best of its type in the county" according to Pevsner, is fantastically carved with winged heads (note the eyes: shut before baptism, open after) and deeply undercut foliage, trees of life and weird beasts. Much of the late 15C carved woodwork has been cut down and remodelled during the church's 19C restoration.

> ### Bodmin and Wenford Railway ⊘
> A Great Western branch line built in 1887 extends from the mainline rail network at Bodmin Parkway (footpath to Lanhydrock and Restormel Castle) via Bodmin Central Station (Duke of Cornwall's Light Infantry Museum) to Boscarne Junction (Camel Trail foot and cycle path to Wadebridge and Padstow).

Museum ⊘ – Set on the site of an old Franciscan Friary, the museum concentrates on local history, in particular items relating to cattle and corn markets (weights and measures, the Winchester Bushel, vets' instruments) and items from the old Cornwall County constabulary – the town stocks, a cell door from the old gaol...

EXCURSIONS

★ **Pencarrow** ⊘ – *4 miles northwest of Bodmin, outside the village of Washaway.* The mile-long drive passes through glorious beech woods, past an ancient fortified encampment surrounded by rhododendrons, to the elegant Georgian house with its roofs tiled with Delabole slate. The house, twice remodelled, has been in the Molesworth-St Aubyn family since it was built in the 1770s. It contains numerous family portraits by eminently fashionable painters (Arthur Devis, Joshua Reynolds and his pupil James Northcote), landscapes (Richard Wilson), beautiful porcelain and a variety of furniture by the most admired designers (Chippendale, Adam, Kent, Henri Jacob).

House – A tour of the house begins in the **Music Room** crowned with a Rococo ceiling ornamented with allegories of the four seasons painted by a pupil of Cortese; the walls are painted to simulate maple wood; the Adam furniture was painted black in Victorian times, possibly as a mark of respect during the wake of a deceased member laid in state there; the porcelain is 19C Meissen and Sèvre.

The former Entrance Hall has been adapted into a **Library**: it is lined with family portraits; the glass cabinet displays a rare collection of Kang Hsi *Famille Verte* porcelain and glass pens made specially for the Great Exhibition of 1851 to demonstrate the skill of English glass-blowers.

The **Drawing Room** is furnished with fine giltwood **Adam furniture** upholstered in the same rose silk damask as the curtains – "treasure" from a Spanish ship captured by a relative off the Philippines in 1762. The portrait above the Louis XVI settee is of the "little Cornish baronet", Sir John St Aubyn.

In the grandiose inner hall, hung with two large topographical views of *London Bridge* and *The Tower of London* by Samuel Scott, and a series of seascapes by Charles Brooking, stands a great cast iron stove which once effectively diffused heat throughout the house; today the space is carefully cluttered with Edwardian pushchairs, well-loved teddies and dolls. Further up the stairs hang a portrait of King Charles I painted by Edward Bower from sketches he made in Westminster Hall at the trial, and one of Charles II acquired by the family as rewards for loyal service to the Crown.

On the first floor are the bedrooms furnished with William IV and George IV four-poster beds, bathrooms, nursery and lady's boudoir – many enjoying views over the gardens.

Gardens and grounds – The ambitious remodelling of the gardens was undertaken by Sir William Molesworth between parliamentary sessions until his untimely death whilst Secretary of State for the Colonies in 1855. The sunken Italian garden was replaced with lawns, a rockery was built with boulders from Bodmin Moor on the eastern side. The long drive, a dramatic approach to the house, is lined with exotic conifers acquired indirectly from the botanist-explorers of the day: a specimen of all but ten different kinds known at that time (*c*1848) to thrive in the British climate was planted here including a monkey puzzle tree, Japanese cedar, Caucasian fir, Japanese tiger-tail spruce, pond cypress from South America, deodar cedar... Planting has been maintained by the successive generations and broadened to count some 570 hybrids of rhododendron and 60 different camellias.

St Mabyn – The granite **Church of St Mabena**★ is chiefly notable for its 15C **three stage tower**, abutted partway by a stair turret and unusually decorated with carved figures. Inside, its original wagon roof survives, and is furnished with a Norman font.

★ **St Tudy** – The attractive village's large **Church of St Tudius** was built on Saxon-Norman foundations in the 15C; it has a tall, pinnacled tower. Perpendicular windows, granite **arcades** and **wagon roofs** with foliated wall plates provide the setting for the square Norman font, an earlier carved figure *(facing south door)* and a pre-Norman coped stone carved with interlaced cable and foliage scrolls, used as a gravestone *(in porch)*.

★ **St Kew** – The large **church**★ stands tall with a buttressed and battlemented west tower where the road turns between wooded hillsides. Its only neighbours are the late Georgian vicarage, the St Kew Inn, which is Elizabethan, and the Craftsmen's Barn (studios, workshops).

St Kew church is light inside with slender-columned granite arcades beneath wagon roofs and wall plate angels. There are an Elizabethan **pulpit**, royal arms of 1661, **slate monuments** from 1601 – "All is vanity but vertue" – and glorious 15C **stained glass** in clear colours depicting the Passion from the *Entry into Jerusalem* to the *Harrowing of Hell*.

The Ogham Stone, so called because it is inscribed with the straight lines of Ogham script, also bears a Latin inscription (IUPTI); although an oddity in Cornwall, these occur more frequently in southwest Ireland.

St Endellion – The village's typical Cornish Perpendicular **Church of St Endellienta**★★ is well known as the setting for the major work of the sculptor, the **Master of St Endellion**. Anonymous in all other respects, he lives on through a tomb chest superbly carved in sleek, black Catacleuse stone with small columns and cusped arches, and the stoup inside the south door. The angels mounted on wall plates were carved by villagers just before World War II.

St Teath – The large 15C **church**★ dedicated to St Tetha Virgin was rebuilt around Norman remains. Wagon roofs and font are complemented by a Jacobean **pulpit**, figure painted **almsbox** and a **slate memorial** of 1636 with carved figures *(west end, near porch door)*.

Protected areas with beautiful scenery which may be enjoyed for their peace and tranquillity, for their abundant wildlife, and remoteness include:

Bodmin Moor	*The Ridgeway*
Dartmoor	*Salisbury Plain*
Exmoor	*Somerset Levels*

... consult the index

BODMIN MOOR★★

Cornwall

Michelin Atlas p 3 or Map 403 – F, G 32

Bodmin moor, an elevation of 800-1 400ft covering an area of less than 150 sq miles, is the smallest of the three West Country moors; it is gaunt and wild with rock outcrops, heather, high tors – a savage bleakness in winter and a beauty all its own in summer.

Guarding the moor to east and west are two historic castles, Launceston and Restormel and encircling it, either just on the moor or in the deep wooded valleys which surround it, a number of small villages with attractive churches. The rivers Inny, Lynher, Fowey, St Neot and De Lank flow north-south; the only main road, the A30, runs northeast.

Bolventor – At the centre of the moor stands **Jamaica Inn**, named after the West Indian island where a one-time owner had grown rich on his sugar plantations. This staging post for those making the crossing in the 16C-19C was built of granite and roofed and hung with slate, and in the summer its low beamed rooms are usually crowded; out of season it is worth a visit for its **views**. It is, of course, the setting for Daphne du Maurier's novel, *Jamaica Inn*.

Dozmary Pool – The pool, 1 000ft above sea-level, is associated with the Arthurian sword Excalibur and by tradition is bottomless, although it has been known to dry up.

This stretch of water, together with Colliford Lake (Cornwall's largest man-made reservoir) and the Fowey River nearby, provide varied habitats for long-tailed ducks, dippers, grey wagtails and sand martins.

Jamaica Inn

Altarnun – The main axis of this picturesque village, sheltered in a wooded valley high on the moor, runs between rows of stone cottages down to a stream. It derives its name from St Nona, the mother of St David, who came from Wales in *c*527 – the period of the **Celtic cross** in the churchyard.

The present **church★** of weathered moorstone (outcrop granite) has a 108ft, embattled and pinnacled 15C tower which rises in the usual three stages. Of especial note are the superb large Norman **font** with deeply carved rosettes between once-coloured bearded faces at each angle, the monolithic pillars, capitals and bases, the wagon roofs, rood-screen, full width Jacobean-style **altar-rail** (1684) and the **bench-ends**, 79 in all, carved by Robert Daye (as inscribed on the bench nearest the font) in 1510-30 with the Instruments of the Passion, St Michael, local worthies, a fiddler, bagpipe player, jester: note how several details are Renaissance in origin.

Laneast – The chancel and north wall of the transept of the **church★** are Norman; the rest of the cruciform building is 15C although the two lower stages of the embattled and pinnacled granite tower are undoubtedly 14C; a tall Celtic cross stands nearby. Inside are a robust Norman **font** with corner heads and stylised rosettes as at Altarnun, slate memorials, a tall rood-screen with unusually broad openings, early 16C pulpit and 38 mainly 16C carved **bench-ends**.
There is a holy well in the 16C building south of the church.

★ **Camelford** – The town, beside the River Camel, centres on a small square lined by 18C-19C houses and the old town hall sporting a gilded camel as weathervane. The **North Cornwall Museum of Rural Life** ⊙, in a onetime coach and wagon building, displays the full ranges of tools required by blacksmiths, cobblers, printers, doctors... and domestic exhibits (bonnets, pottery etc).

Michaelstow – The 15C church★, with a 9ft Celtic cross in the churchyard, is known for its furnishings: the wagon roofs rest on granite arcades, the benches are 15C-16C, the octagonal font 15C; the beautifully lettered **slate memorial plates** are embellished with running line engravings of winged heads of cherubim, of young girls or even full-length figures in costume – Jane Merifield 1663.

St Breward – On the edge of the moor among the granite quarries sits St Breward, at 600ft the highest **church★** in Cornwall on a site hallowed since Norman times – 5 fat round columns of uneven height with scalloped capitals remain as testimony inside the present 15C rebuilding.

Note the copy of a watercolour by Rowlandson (c1800), the royal arms, the figured 17C **slate memorial plates** and, outside, the neat granite blocks of the **tower**. The sundial dates from 1792.

Nearby is the stone-built, wind-buffeted **Old Inn**, all beams and fireplaces inside. Some four miles northeast is Rough Tor (*see below*), one of a number of Neolithic or Dark Age monuments.

★ **Blisland** – Church and village stand high on the moor, round a tree-planted green (according to a Saxon layout); the elegant medieval manor house well-preserved in the northeast corner. The main fabric of the **church★** dedicated to St Protus and St Hyacinth is Norman. It has a rectangular three-tier tower and staircase turret abutting the north transept which rises tall above the parapet and pinnacles. Of note there is an 18C slate sundial, the faces (1420) among the **bosses** in the south porch wagon roof, the two fonts (one Norman, circular with herringbone moulding, one 15C, octagonal with shields in quatrefoils), the 17C carved pulpit, a brass of 1410 commemorating a former rector (*chancel*) and **slate memorial** (1624) with six kneeling figures.

Outside the village are a couple of ancient monuments: a 108ft in diameter stone circle on Blisland Manor Common (1mile northeast) comprising eight standing and 12 fallen stones and Stripple Stones Henge Monument on Hawkstor Down (3miles northeast).

Cardinham – The village, close to the wooded Glynn Valley, has a late 15C church★ (St Meubred) with a three-stage granite tower. From earlier sanctuaries there remains one of the best examples of 9C-10C Celtic Cross: 8.5ft tall, three-panelled front, interlaces on the back; a Norman font; a number of 6C-7C inscribed stones (*in and south of the churchyard, and two 0.25 mile northwest of Welltown*); an early (1400) and unusually rare brass to a cleric in civil dress. The wagon roofs above the aisles and porch and the 71 robustly carved bench-ends date from the 15C. Note also the plaster strapwork **royal arms** of 1661.

★ **St Neot** – The approach to the moorland village of houses of tawny stone and a Perpendicular church of 1425 is up a wooded valley, enclosed by sweeping hillsides.

★★ **Parish Church** – St Anietus is strategically positioned to emphasise its battlemented and pinnacled south side, built of regular granite blocks. The oldest part is the west tower with Decorated windows; the rest is Perpendicular, pierced by a series of four-light **windows** of precious 15C-16C English stained glass (often remodelled in 19C). The finest, oldest and the least restored window of **The Creation** (*east window, south aisle*) has God measuring out the universe and, at the end, Noah doffing his cap, having received orders to build the Ark. In **The Flood** (*1st window east, south aisle*), Noah is shown building the Ark, which is a real sailing ship of the period, and the story continues with it surmounting perilous seas.

St George (*west window, north aisle*), St Neot (*5th window east, north aisle*) and **Robert Tubbe**, the vicar from 1508-44 who was responsible for obtaining the glass, all appear, as do the donors, the young men and the young wives of the village, in the lower sections of the aisle windows.

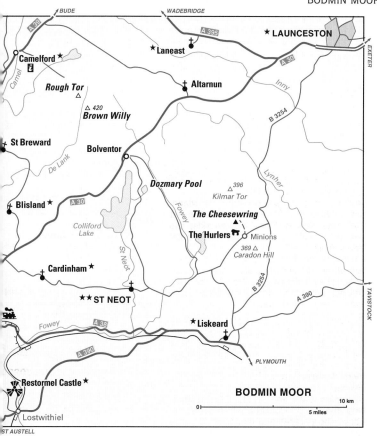

In the churchyard and on Temple Moor stand the shafts of 10C Saxon crosses carved with elaborate interlace work; the latter also bears elements associated with Scandinavian scrolls.

Ancient stones

At 1 375ft, **Brown Willy** is the highest tor on the moor. The granite boss **Rough Tor** (pronounced Rowtor to rhyme with now tor) stands out at 1 311ft as the second highest point on the moor: the Fernacre Stone Circle which comprises 64 stones arranged in a ring 150ft in diameter includes one 4ft 6in high; to the east and north are a number of hut circles.

The stone pile known as **The Cheesewring** is a natural formation which, according to legend, was the dwelling of a druid who offered water to travellers from a cup of gold; its name describes its appearance as a stack of huge farmhouse cheeses wrapped in cloth to drain. From the air, infra-red photography reveals the ghostly shadows of an Iron Age settlement alongside the 19C mining; the nearby quarry provided granite for the Thames Embankment in London.

The Hurlers, the only standing stones on the moor, comprise three circles numbering 9, 17 and 13 stones, in line but of unequal diameter.

EXCURSIONS

★ Launceston

Perched high on the Cornwall-Devon border, Launceston was Cornwall's chief town until 1835 when the assize court moved to Bodmin. In the Middle Ages, the town boasted the most important castle in the province (now a ruin) which was founded in the 11C by William I's brother, **Robert of Mortain**, Earl of Cornwall and the most powerful monastic house in the form of an Augustinian Priory founded in 1136. There are also a number of narrow, twisting streets with houses of all periods ranging from half-timbered Tudor, through 18C and 19C to 20C post-war anonymous styles; a 19C pannier market and a series of

18C-19C shop fronts. Beyond the river, a road leads up to **St Stephen** *(0.5 mile north)*, the mother church of Launceston consecrated in 1259; its tower is later (early 16C), and several Norman fragments have been reintegrated.

★ **St Mary Magdalene** – The Perpendicular church of 1511 gives the lie to the impossibility of carving **granite**: walls, buttresses, two-storey porch, gables are closely patterned with quatrefoils, coats of arms – Henry VII's on the east gable – fleurs-de-lis, roses, thistles, pomegranates and, below the east window, Mary Magdalene. The tower is 14C.

The interior with slender piers, pointed arches and **wagon roofs** contains a pre-Reformation painted **pulpit**, a brass on the south wall and the royal arms of George I. The bench ends are 19C.

St Thomas – Little survives of the Augustinian Priory, although the chapel of ease has a number of Norman features, notably the tympanum in the south porch and a large font of a similar kind to that at Altarnun. The eastern wall of the south aisle has paintings, the ironwork in the door is 13C.

★ **Castle** ⊙ – Walk through the former bailey and up the motte steps to the shell keep; circle the wall before mounting the 13C centre tower for the **view**★ of Dartmoor, Bodmin Moor (Brown Willy and Rough Tor) and the Tamar.

The castle's history is not adventurous: it was visited by the Black Prince, subsequently seized by the rebels in the **Cornish Rebellion** of 1549, and changed hands twice during the Civil War. Until 1840 it served as an assize court and prison, being notorious for imprisoning or executing prisoners on the nod; **George Fox**, founder of the Society of Friends, was incarcerated in it for several months in 1656.

South Gate – The medieval gateway rises through two floors to a castellated parapet; it has served as the former guardhouse and gaol.

> ### Eliot Arms
>
> A creeper-covered ancient house contains a clutter of unexpected paraphernalia: a collection of hundreds of snuffs; 70 or so clocks, gleaming horse-brasses, framed goodies, a miscellany of furniture and facilities for shove-a-ha'penny, skittles, dominoes and darts... Home-cooked food; good beer, wines and whiskys; climbing frame, swing and playhouse! ☎ 01566 772 051

Lawrence House Museum ⊙ – *Castle Street*. The museum arranges changing exhibitions on local life through the ages.

Liskeard

The town rises on two facing hillsides: one with late Georgian (The Parade) and early Victorian houses and a portentous, Italianate town hall (1859), the other with the **Church of St Martin**★, described by Leland as a "fair large thing" being the second largest church in Cornwall after Bodmin. Despite repeated restoration there remain a **chancel arch** (rare in Cornwall), the early-15C Lady Chapel a 16C font, a Jacobean oak pulpit dated 1636, the royal arms of George II, a notice about ladies' pattens, a sundial of 1779 *(south porch)*, a number of consecration crosses – in Cornwall *(north and south walls)* and a small **leper's window** *(west end)* of three equal lights divided by stone mullions (there was a leper hospital for 200 years at Maudlin, 0.5 mile away).

Other local attractions include the modern glassworks in a mill in the main street (Merlin Glass ⊙) and **Dobwells Theme Park** *(signposted off A38 west of Liskeard)* ⊙.

★ **Restormel Castle** ⊙ *0.5 miles north of Lostwithiel.*

The 12C-13C shell keep of local slate shale rock stands on a spur above the River Fowey. Walk through the gate-house and circle the walls to overlook the inner courtyard, the kitchen with its great fireplace, the hall and chapel, and to admire the circular **panorama**★.

This is "by far the most perfect example of military architecture in Cornwall, and in its plan one of the most consummate of England" according to Pevsner. A natural hilltop has been excavated to provide a moat and a platform for a keep and shell keep – as at Launceston and Totnes. Little of the Cardinham castle (*c*1100) exists save the inner gate; the curtain wall is 12C/13C; the rest 13C/14C built when it was inherited by Edmund of Cornwall.

★★ **Lanhydrock** ⊙ *3 miles south of Bodmin. 1 hour.*

The glory of Lanhydrock lies in the combination of the building's fine mid-17C external design complete with battlements and corner pinnacles, and the Victorian-Edwardian interior. **Sir Richard Robartes** accumulated his fortune trading in tin and wool, acquiring the estate in 1620. Construction of the four-sided symmetrical complex around a central courtyard seems to have been initiated immediately; the gatehouses which reflect a hint of the Renaissance were completed in 1658; the eastern wing was removed later. In 1881 a major fire gutted all but the entrance and north wing of the house. It took four years to rebuild the new exterior exactly as it was, while the interior was refurbished to include the latest in Victorian amenities including central heating, plumbed bathrooms and modern kitchens.

House – *Closed Mondays*. Inside the 17C porch, which was not consumed by the fire, the Grand Hall is furnished with family portraits and mementoes.

The wallpaper in the Inner Hall is of a William Morris design.

The stately 19C Dining Room, with its 19C panelling, has a **table** set with fine china and glass and a **centrepiece** made in shining Cornish tin. Note, on a side-table, the hand painted dessert plates.

Lady Robartes' Room is small and cosy with family photographs, books, a desk, a small piano, armchairs, a needlework box and a bobble chenille cloth on the table.

The corridor and Billiard Room, the masculine area of the house, are given character with game trophies on the walls, a fur-lined coat, hat and gloves ready for an outing...

The panelled Smoking Room is furnished with a Turkey carpet, Eton and Oxford favours, a mounted fish and half a dozen easy-chairs.

The bedrooms reflect the owners' personalities: cane furniture and innumerable photographs for the last Miss Robartes; practicality for Lord Robartes; grace for Lady Robartes, from whose room there is a beautiful **view**.

The 116ft Long Gallery, occupying the length of the north wing, is roofed with an outstanding 17C **plaster barrel vault**, hung with elaborate pendants. The surface is divided into 24 sections, each carved in deep relief with an Old Testament scene and separated from its neighbours by bands of decoration filled with every conceivable bird and beast; deeply cut figures grace the panel over the fireplace. Similar ceilings are to be found at Barnstaple and Rashley Barton in North Devon, assumed to be by the same family of master-plasterers.

The servants' quarters on the second floor give a vivid insight into the contrast in lifestyles enjoyed by those above and below stairs at the turn of the century.

Gardens and grounds – **Formal gardens** ornamented with the most beautiful urns are arranged at the front and northern side of the house: a perfect foil of regimented colour and immaculate geometry to the squareness of the speckled granite house and sculptural **gatehouse**. Beyond, a great avenue of beech trees and sycamores planted in 1648 stretches across some of the 950 acres of wooded parkland and rolling farmland down to the medieval bridge at Respryn over the River Fowey.

In complete contrast, the **terraced gardens** at the rear which enfold the unremarkable family church (**St Hyderoc**) are informally planted with specimen and flowering trees including magnolias, azaleas, camellias, rhododendrons and hydrangeas. In spring time, the gardens are a profusion of vivid colour.

Lanhydrock

R. Besse/MICHELIN

Today, it is difficult to determine the extent of Poole, Bournemouth and Christchurch, merged as they seem by straggling conurbation. Poole has an ancient maritime history all of its own and so is listed separately; **Bournemouth** is a Victorian sea-side town and **Christchurch** a small Hampshire village, strangely divorced from yet attached to its larger neighbour: they are therefore listed together.

Bournemouth lies at the mouth of the River Bourne between two pine-covered hills. It began to develop as a summer and winter resort in the mid-19C, when the arrival of the railway made it easily accessible from London. Its popularity increased with the laying out of the **public gardens** and the construction of **two piers**, the pavilion, wintergarden and theatre, elegant arcades and Victorian parades of shops. Another enduring product from this era is the Winter Garden Orchestra (the forerunner of the **Bournemouth Symphony Orchestra**) which was founded in 1893 by the son of a Grenadier Guards bandmaster to provide three daily concerts in the glass-covered pavilion near the Square.

Soon Bournemouth had become the height of fashion – Queen Victoria recommended it to Disraeli – and the population had reached 37 781. Since then the population has multiplied fivefold, the hotels now number several hundred, shops and leisure facilities abound.

★★ **Russell-Cotes Art Gallery and Museum** ⓥ – *Russell-Cotes Road. In 1997 the museum was closed for refurbishment.*

East Cliff Hall was intended by the Russell-Cotes from the outset to act both as a spacious, elaborate home and a museum for their amassed collections, assigning it to the town in 1908, on the understanding that they be free to continue to live there until their deaths.

The house epitomises ornate High Victorian taste furnished as it is with inlaid furniture, painted ceilings, decorative windows, coloured wallpaper (embossed canvas made in

Cosmopolitan Bournemouth tourists

Ill health prompted the prosperous couple Sir Merton and Lady Annie Russell-Cotes to visit the small sea-side resort of Bournemouth, where they stayed at the Royal Bath Hotel. Having been persuaded to buy the hotel in 1876, they set about refurbishing it, thereby developing a keen interest in the fine and decorative arts; gradually Sir Merton became involved in local politics (later to be appointed mayor); the hotel prospered. In 1884 the Russell-Cotes undertook a world tour passing through Australia, New Zealand, Hawaii, San Francisco, Japan; a second trip to the West Indies and the United States followed in 1890; in 1894 they travelled to Egypt and the Mediterranean; to Russia and Scandinavia in 1898: each trip generating its own collection of souvenirs.

Tynecastle), moulded tiles in the closets, large numbers of pictures (William Frith, Landseer, Leighton, Birket-Foster, Rossetti, Alma-Tadema, Edwin Long), fine English china (part of a Rockingham tea-service once owned by the Prince Regent, Coalport and Worcester, Wedgwood plaques, Parian ware), silver and gold plate, mementoes of Napoleon (death-mask), Lady Hamilton (cast of her hand) and of Sir Henry Irving (theatrical memorabilia), a personal friend. Italianate elements were drawn from Queen Victoria's Osbourne House on the Isle of Wight; Oriental influences resulted from the success of Lord Leighton's house in London; the gilded plaster cornice in the stairway is moulded on the Elgin Marbles; delicate Japanese details were taken from Japanese prints...

Souvenirs from abroad include Dresden miniatures, finds from Egyptian tombs, swords, oriental armour, Japanese Noh theatre masks, bronzes, Buddhas, a bronze incense-burner in the style of a cock, a silver and gold elephant with a crystal ball, intricately carved ivory, inlay and lacquerwork, ceramics and lanterns...

The **Art Gallery** extension, opened in 1926, encroaches upon the gardens that overlook the beach. It is presently used to house contemporary exhibitions *(ground floor)*, fine examples of modern craftsmanship and the Joseph Lucas (1851-1924) collection of early Italian religious paintings (Tuscan schools) and portable plaquettes, majolica and delftware; 19C Whitby mourning jet, Toby jugs and Staffordshire figures, 17C Tudor oak furniture, a 16C polygonal virginal, Victorian bygones, African spears, Ghurka kukris, Limoges enamels, hand guns from the 16C-20C, and a Maori Collection including paintings by C F Goldie (1870-1947), hardstone clubs, carvings and a model war canoe...

From the gardens there is a glorious **view**★ of the coast.

Shelley Rooms ⊙ – *Shelley Park, Beechwood Avenue, Boscombe: follow signs to Boscombe Pier, turn left uphill opposite the Seagull pub, continue along the road parallel to the coast.*
The archive collection, in part from Casa Magni, the Italian home of Percy Bysshe Shelley (1792-1822) and his second wife Mary, includes letters, revolutionary leaflets, poems, notebooks, portraits and miniatures, together with a reference library for the Romantic poets Byron and Keats. A video *(30min)* retells the tragic story of the young Romantic poet's death in Italy at the age of 29 and the acquisition of Boscombe Manor by his son Sir Percy Shelley. The property is now managed by Bournemouth and Poole College of Art and Design.

EXCURSIONS

★ **Christchurch**

Christchurch, once part of Hampshire and the New Forest, is now separated from Bournemouth by modern leisure centres and shopping malls. The main features of this prosperous little coastal town, strategically located on the River Stour and River Avon, are to be found at its very epicentre. Here, grouped around the wide, shallow harbour filled with fishing boats and pleasure craft sheltering in a narrow outlet to the sea, are the Norman priory which Henry VIII dissolved and a Norman castle which Cromwell slighted.
20C excavation of the locality that was once surrounded by water meadows has revealed traces of an Iron Age gravel slipway built for beaching and landing small boats; sherds from Roman amphorae and wheel pottery from Brittany suggest a flourishing trading in such commodities as wine and fish paste in 1C BC.

★ **Priory** – *30min.* Ten years after Domesday the village was given by William Rufus to his chief minister, Ranulf Flambard, the builder of Durham Cathedral. He pulled down the existing Saxon church and was about to start the construction of a great Norman church when William II died (1100) and he, Flambard, was put in the Tower. Henry I gave the patronage to his cousin Richard de Redvers, Earl of Devon, who, after Flambard had been pardoned in 1107, encouraged him to complete the church.
Augustine canons worshipped in the choir, allocated the nave to the parish and erected monastic buildings abutting the north wall. In the early 13C the crossing tower collapsed leaving only the nave and the west and end walls of the transepts; rebuilding proceeded slowly until the 16C by which time the church presented a sequence of architectural styles: Norman in the **turret** and the **nave** – note the fish-scale decoration; Early English in the **clerestory**; 14C Decorated for the **choirscreen**, Perpendicular at the east end in the **choir** and **Lady Chapels** with its cusped and pinnacled arcading in the chapel and the canopied reredos with the *Tree of Jesse*. The **choirstalls** are late 15C with an excellent set of **misericords** (one, 13C), depicting everything from a jester to a salmon's head, an angel to Richard III.

Chantry Chapels – The finest memorial, again Perpendicular, is the **Salisbury chantry** *(north chancel aisle)* carved in Caen stone by the Renaissance sculptor, **Torregiano**, with tiers of enriched canopies and fan vaulting but empty because Margaret, Countess of Salisbury, was executed in the Tower by order of Henry VIII in 1541. The traces of paint to be seen on the stonework throughout the interior would once have been a blaze of colour, highlighting every decoration.

Priory precinct – To the east and north of the Priory extends a landscaped garden: bordered by the river which is straddled by an elegant 12C stone bridge with pointed cutwaters, and enclosing a ruined castle keep perched on its artificial mound. The keep would have first been constructed of wood; by the late 13C it had walls of stone 30ft high and 10ft thick; contested in the Civil War, it was razed in 1650.
Beyond the bowling green, the ruined house at the castle's foot is late 12C.

Why Christchurch

It was originally intended that the priory be built on a hill about a mile away but every morning materials taken up the hill the previous day would be discovered mysteriously brought down to the sacred Saxon site until, finally, the builders decided that this was divine intervention. When building began on the town site, the masons and carpenters were joined by an extra, unknown, workman who received no pay and was not seen at meals. One evening it was discovered that a beam had been cut too short and the men went home disconsolate; when they returned in the morning, however, they discovered that it had "grown" in the night; the stranger had vanished. All were convinced it must have been the Carpenter from Nazareth and so the church, and then the town, were renamed Christ's Church.

Red House Museum ⓥ - *Quay Road*. Among the 18C houses round the priory stands the Red House, a long and solid red brick building which was constructed as the Parish Workhouse in 1764. In 1919 it was converted into Christchurch's **local museum** to display a broad range of artefacts relating to the Victorian/Edwardian era, an excellent presentation of archeological finds and the natural history of the region.

The ground floor displays various cumbersome machines (clothes mangle), domestic implements (butter churns, horse-hair carder, wooden dolly tub), 19C toys, the **Herbert David Gallery of Costume** (crinolines, early outfit by Miss Selfridge worn with Russian eiderdown petticoat, modesty skirt *c*1865-1915) and a 1930s room setting with furniture made by Arthur Tomney, a local man.

The first floor provides an insight into the ancient history of the area, notably from **Hengistbury Head** from the Iron Age and Roman times; local resource room. The top floor is dedicated to geology and natural history; the Hart Room recreates a 19C taxidermist shop.

At the back of the building are two gardens, one planted with labelled herbs (witch hazel, apothecary rose, hyssop, meadowsweet, lemon balm, evening primrose...) and the Fishing Gallery which acknowledges the importance of the local fishing industry in fresh and sea water.

Fusée chain-making

In the 15C, the invention of the fusée provided contemporary watch and clock designers with an alternative to interlocking cogs and fly-wheels which became worn and loose with use: these small cone-shaped pulleys, incorporating a spiral groove of variable diameter, were threaded with a belt of cord or gut which transmitted power from the main spring. With the advent of the 1660s, chain began to replace the fragile thread – a practice that was to last until 1875 when Swiss and American watchmakers evolved a completely "modern" design.

The manufacture of these most intricately linked chains, initiated in Christchurch by Robert Harvey Cox in 1790, fell to young girls over the age of nine, first in the workhouse (the present museum), then at home as a cottage industry until the 1820s when demand declined, dwindled and died leaving many of the women completely blind.

Highcliffe Castle ⓥ - *South off the Lymington Road*. Described as "the most important remaining example of the Romantic and Picturesque style of architecture" from the late 18C-early 19C, Highcliffe Castle (1830-35) was built for Lord Stuart de Rothesay, who at one time was the Duke of Wellington's administrator in Europe during the Napoleonic Wars. Of particular note are the fragments of French carved stonework incorporated in the "castle", brought from the Norman Benedictine Abbey of St Peter at Jumièges and from a 16C Gothic manor south of Rouen, La Grande Maison des Andelys. Subject to neglect and then to major restoration, the complex is used for a variety of cultural events.

★ **Hengistbury Head**

7 miles east by the panoramic road from Bournemouth; 4 miles from Christchurch by B3059; bear left at Tuckton for Southbourne.

From the head there is a wide **view**★★ over Poole Bay and east to The Needles and the Isle of Wight (less extensive panorama along the **panoramic road** from Bournemouth).

BRADFORD-ON-AVON★★

Wiltshire – Population 8 815
Michelin Atlas p 17 or Map 403 – N 29

It is the houses of Tory rising tier upon tier up the hillside from the river and the old medieval bridge with its weather-vaned chapel which give the town its character. The larger houses were built in the local creamy-yellow ochre limestone by 17C-18C clothiers some of whom, Daniel Defoe estimated early in the 18C, were worth between ten and forty thousand pounds a man. In the same streets are terraces of weavers' cottages and, in the shopping streets, alleys and shambles, 17C-18C houses above 18C-19C shopfronts. Bradford continues to enjoy prosperity which is sustained not only by tourism but by private small-scale industry: Marcos Cars (manufacturer of British sportscars), Ex Libris Press (established in 1816 and still trading in the Shambles) and such like.
Market day: Thursdays.

Bradford entrepreneurs

By the early 17C, the Dutch had developed improved methods of spinning and weaving that threatened to damage demand for the Bradford white broad-cloth; **Paul Methuen** (d 1667) therefore brought a number of skilled contract-workers from Holland and installed them in houses in Middle Rank, Tory and Newtown.

In 1703, **John Methuen** brokered an important treaty with Portugal: not only did this secure the monopoly of English cloth on the Portuguese markets, it also ensured reduced custom duty on Port and Madeira in the face of competition from French wine producers.

In the early years of the 18C, the invention of Scribbling Engines, Spinning Jennies and Gig Mills saw widespread change in working methods, transforming the centre of Bradford. When the wool trade dwindled, several of these premises were converted by **Stephen Moulton** for producing vulcanised cloth, a process perfected by Charles Goodyear. The waterproof fabric gained widespread usage having been issued to British troops in the Crimean War; the same company was absorbed into the **Avon Rubber Company** in 1956. Today, it is **Dr Alex Moulton**, a contemporary engineer and specialist in suspension systems responsible for the development of the Hydragas shock-absorber suspension in modern cars (pioneered in the Mini) and the Moulton bicycle who continues the tradition of resident-entrepreneurs in Bradford.

Bradford Museum ⊙ – Installed in premises over the purpose-built town library, is the charming museum which assembles artefacts pertaining to the different local industries: woollen mills and dye-works, brewing, iron foundry, mould-making, rubber factories, mushroom growing in disused stone quarries. Pride of place is given to the late 19C-early 20C Miss **Christopher's Pharmacy**, caught in a time warp and transposed in its entirety from Silver Street, complete with its hand-written prescription ledgers documenting every ailment of the local community: note the house brand (Siva) of perfumes, face powders and skin-lotions.

★ **Bridge** – The town developed around the regular passage across the river at the broad ford: the river not only provided the necessary power for fulling woollen cloth – transforming it into felt, it was also essential for the subsequent dyeing process.

The first pack-bridge was built in the 12C. In 1610 when the wool and cloth trades were booming a wider bridge was erected with round arches and incorporating a small, square, domed **chapel**-cum-blind house or lock-up ⊙, furnished with two iron bedsteads and topped by an Avon gudgeon **weather-vane**.

Bradford bridge

Old town – Cross the main bridge into **Silver Street**, the main shopping street. **The Shambles** which once accommodated the town's meat market and slaughterhouse leads through to Market Street where the former town hall (1855) stands, designed by Thomas Fuller of Bath with its elegant domed turret; this was converted for use as a Catholic church in 1955.

Church Street, which forks sharp left past the late Georgian Swan Hotel (a refaced 16C inn) with its Venetian window, leads circuitously uphill; opposite sits Church House. Overlooking the river is **Abbey Mill**, the last woollen mill to be built in Bradford (1857) in complement to the other 31 in town, now converted into retirement homes. Opposite is **Old Church House** (now Holy Trinity Church Hall) built in the 17C by the clothier Thomas Horton (brass in the church); **Dutch Barton** has an 18C front on a 17C foundation; **Hill House** was the home of the Druces, early 18C Quaker clothiers; **Abbey House** with its profusion of pediments is 18C, so too is **Orpin House** *(north of the church)*; midway between the church and the house lies the tomb of Mr Orpin who was parish clerk for 40 years.

The two Chantry Houses beyond Holy Trinity are 16C; Barton Orchard and the terrace of three-storey **weavers' houses** are 18C.

Holy Trinity – The church was consecrated in 1150 having been built possibly because St Laurence was too small, more probably because the 12C was a great period for church building and Bradford was prosperous: Domesday records show that there were 126 burgesses – with their families, labourers and servants; this would mean a township of, possibly, 1 000 inhabitants. In the early 14C the chancel was extended; in the 15C and 19C the entire church was remodelled and embellished. There are, therefore, Norman features (chancel windows, arcade piers), a medieval **wall painting** of the Virgin being taught to read *(north of east window)*, possibly the longest **squint** in England, cut in the 13C when the chancel was lengthened, 16C Flemish glass *(south window in the nave)* presented by an 18C clothier, memorials (Anthony Methuen by Rysbrack) and brasses to clothiers, and at the west end, a 13C **sculpture** of a young girl in a wimple.

★★ **Saxon Church of St Laurence** ⊙ – The church may date from the 7C-8C, the time of St Aldhelm, who is known to have founded a convent on the site between AD 672 and 705. In 1001 church and convent were given to the abbey of St Edward at Shaftesbury by King Ethelred the Unready (apparently to ease his conscience over the murder of his half-brother); by Domesday the convent had disappeared, although records of a leper colony and pilgrims' almshouses suggest these institutions continued to function. From the 12C-19C the church was used as a cottage, a school, a charnel house.

The minute stone building, tall and narrow with steeply pitched roofs and blind **arcading decoration**, is believed to have been erected in a single phase: it survives largely intact, three windows having been inserted at the west end in the 19C. The chancel is slightly "skewed", a feature accentuated by the tapering of the nave (25ft x 13ft) to the end arch (9ft 8in x 3ft 6in). The assembled altar-stones are Saxon; the Byzantine-style "floating" angels (high on the east wall), possible fragments of a rood screen, probably date from a remodelling completed *c*1050.

★ **Tithe Barn** ⊙ – *Follow Barton Orchard behind Holy Trinity and down over the Packhorse Bridge to Barton Country Park.* Barton Farm is probably all that remains of the Manor of Bradford which was given to the Abbess of Shaftesbury in 1001 by Ethelred the Unready. The vast stone barn was probably built early in the 14C to store hay, grain and fleeces. The 14-bay slate-covered cruck-roofed barn has twin gabled doorways and oak doors; it also retains the original threshing floor. This barn, 167.5ft long and 30.25ft wide, is one of a group of similar structures to be found at Glastonbury, Englishcombe (near Bath), Lacock and Tisbury. The neighbouring granary is later.

Newtown, Middle Rank and Top Rank Tory – Above St Laurence are stacked parallel terraces of 17C-18C houses, known as **Newtown**. At the far end, leading into Market Street, is The Priory, once owned by the Methuens, a medieval barn belonging to the same estate, and the Bell Inn, dated 1695.

Middle Rank, a street of largely 17C gabled terrace houses is marked by a Presbyterian church. Above, running along the crest to the town's highest point, is **Top Rank Tory** which consists of 18C houses, terraces, a very special row of 17C weavers' houses and the pilgrim chapel of St Mary Tory (12C rebuilt in 1877). The excellent **view**★ embraces the Marlborough Downs (northeast), Bath, Bristol and the Severn Estuary (northwest) and Somerset (southwest).

It is possible to reach St Mary Tory by car by taking the road at the right (east) end of Newtown, Conigre Hill, and bearing second left into Tory.

EXCURSIONS

Westwood *1.5 miles southwest of Bradford-on-Avon*

★ **Westwood Manor** ⊙ – It is the ensemble which counts in this small, two-storey house which has been continuously occupied and altered since construction began *c*1400 in several phases.

Among the tenants of the manor, owned by Winchester Cathedral from Saxon

Worth a detour...

Across the footbridge from Avoncliffe Station sits the **Cross Guns**, with its splendid view extending along the river, its bridges and aqueducts... Generous portions of home-baked cooking are the order of the day after a good walk and lungfuls of country air! Muddy boots are not welcome. Closed 25 and 26 December. ☎ 01225 862 335. Another Great Western special is the **Quarryman's Arms** situated high on Box Hill which also serves excellent fare. Much frequented by pot-holers, cavers and intrepid walkers. ☎ 01225 743 569.

times to the mid-19C, were Thomas Horton, the clothier from Bradford-on-Avon, who acquired the house in 1515 and benefited the adjoining Perpendicular church by building the splendid **west tower**, crowned with a dome (note the initials TH in the door spandrels) before dying in 1530.

Major alterations were made to the house in the first half of the 17C: the **porch** and **staircase turret** were added, the Great Hall was divided horizontally to create the **Great Parlour** above, **panelling**, including the frieze of landscape scenes, was installed in the Panelled Room, and the Biblical or symbolic **plaster overmantels** (geese hanging a fox, a rose and thistle growing from the same stem) set into the Panelled, Oriel, Dining and King's Rooms.

By the 19C-20C neglect had almost brought the house to ruin before it was bought by a new owner who restored it to life and collected for it the 1537 **Italian virginal**, late 17C-18C **spinet**, 17C English furniture and needlework covers for the chairs.

Iford Manor Gardens ⊙ – *2 miles south of Bradford via Westwood.*

In 1369 Sir Thomas Hungerford acquired this part of Iford together with the Farleigh Hungerford estate; his family granted John Horton a lease for the land on which, it is alleged, he built the late-15C elegant clothier's house *(private)*. The east front was remodelled in Elizabethan times and given its Italianate front in the 1720s, probably by a local architect. Before the close of the 18C, the great cedar was planted on the hillside walk as were great carpets of snowdrops in the wild garden and martagon lilies in the woods.

In 1899 it was acquired by the architect and garden designer Harold Peto, who was responsible for Ilnacullin Island in Bantry Bay, Eire and several gardens on the French Riviera among many. He set about restoring the dilapidated property and creating his very own Italian fantasy with terraces, architectural features (loggia, pool and bridge), Continental antiquarian sculptures (Byzantine roundels, 13C stone lions: all catalogued in the available booklet) and garden furniture (pergola, 18C vases). Into this context he carefully planted trees (placing a yew hedge, symbolising longevity, behind an Italian statue of a youth) and, lastly, colour providers in the form of flowering plants: particularly special are the standard and trained wisteria.

Modern plantings maintain the spirit of Peto where possible, by following his notes collected in *The Boke of Iford*.

Outside, an 18C statue of Britannia (from Dorset) guards the bridge over the River Frome.

★ Great Chalfield Manor ⊙ *2.5 miles northeast of Bradford-on-Avon, off the Melksham road. 45min.*

This fine example of 15C English design, "one of the most perfect examples of the late medieval English manor house" (Pevsner), is made all the more attractive by its mellow warm-grey Corsham stone. The manor complex comprising a dwelling house, farm buildings and parish church is surrounded on all sides by park and farmland; originally it would have been fortified with a moat, curtain wall and bastion. In the 1430s Thomas Tropnell, steward to Lord Hungerford, MP and landowner, entered on thirty years of disputes and lawsuits to possess the house, which had been in his family since the Conquest but had passed to another branch; in 1467 Great Chalfield was his. Two years earlier he had purchased a stone quarry near Box, so that almost immediately he was able to begin work on the house, rebuilding and extending it, and ordering the north face to its present appearance of paired but dissimilar gables, finials, chimneys, buttresses and most particularly two oriels, one three-sided with a small pyramid roof surmounted by his coat of arms with supporters, the other semicircular, poised on corbels and a buttress and coroneted with a strawberry leaf decoration. To complete the forecourt, Tropnell erected a bellcote and added a crocketed spire to the parish church.

House – The main (north) front survives largely intact from 1480; the south side was restored when a south wing was added in 1910. The west wing incorporating farm buildings, was adapted in the 18C.

The **porch** has a fine tierceron-star vault with bosses; note the Tropnell's arms.

The **great hall** (40ft x 20ft x 20ft) is the conventional centrepiece of the medieval manor, standing two storeys high, lit from both sides and flanked by gabled wings with oriel windows. It is unclear, however, what is 15C-16C and what 20C; during those centuries the manor passed from owner to tenant farmer, from being a prize possession to a Parliamentary garrison (1644-6). In 1836 the absentee owner had a survey and drawings made but then lost interest; in 1905, a new owner, using the meticulous 19C drawings, began removing accretions, rebuilding, putting in a carved oak screen and collecting stout examples of

16C-17C refectory tables, benches, stools, chests, Cromwellian chairs, court cupboards, Jacobean small tables, Caroline chairs... Of particular interest are the three **mask-squints** with open eyes and mouths.

The separate **dining room**, an unusual feature for the period, has panelling and a ceiling from 1550. Note the narrow squint to the porch, and the wall painting of a man with five fingers and a thumb.

The **great chamber**, at the top of the stone staircase, includes the three-sided oriel window visible from the front of the house; the chimneypiece is 16C. It is adjoined by a closet built over the porch where a maid or page would have slept.

★ **All Saints** – The spire, the **panelled hood** which forms the porch and the wagon-roofed Tropnell chapel were added to the 14C church in 1470 by Thomas Tropnell, whose arms appear on the 15C crested **stone screen**; the chancel and vestry date from the 16C-18C. Other points of interest are the tub font, the 17C **three decker pulpit**, the 17C-18C chandeliers, the wall paintings of St Katherine (in the chapel) and the consecration crosses flanking the door.

BRIDGWATER★

Somerset – Population 34 610
Michelin Atlas p 7 or Map 403 – L 30

During the Civil War Bridgwater Castle, which was commanded by a Royalist governor with a garrison of 2 000 men, was besieged, captured and slighted and the surrounding area was set on fire. Otherwise the town has enjoyed an uneventful history, growing steadily from a settlement by the first crossing point on the River Parrett to be Somerset's second most important town.

In earlier centuries Bridgwater was surrounded on all sides by marshes, known locally as "levels", which were drained by open ditches known as "rhines" and crossed with tracks surfaced with logs and brushwood. By 1200 the town had a charter, by 1350 a population of 850, a castle, a church rebuilt on older foundations and a flourishing river port trade in saltfish, wine, iron, barley, wheat, peas and wood for dyeing cloth. In the 18C-19C the Bridgwater-Taunton Canal with its dock and quays was constructed but soon superseded by the railway.

Market day: Wednesday all day – includes cattle market.

West Quay – The quay is overlooked by warehouses, a pub and 18C-19C houses.

★ **Castle Street** – *Off West Quay*. The town's most attractive street is lined by 18C houses built of brick with stone trims, segment-headed windows, pillared and pilastered doorways and parapets rising to the street's incline.

King Square – The Square, still incomplete, consists of two ranges of 18C houses and a much-altered farmhouse, built on the site of the slighted 13C castle.

★ **St Mary's** – The day before the battle, the **Duke of Monmouth** climbed the red sandstone tower (60ft) with his spyglass (in the museum) to survey the disposition of the Royalist troops camped on Sedgemoor. The embattled **tower** belonged to an Early English church (*c*1200). The distinctive octagonal **spire** (113ft) of Ham Hill stone was added in 1367 with monies subscribed by the grateful people who had survived the Black Death; it took a year to build and cost £143 13s 5 1/2 d. The weathercock on the summit (2ft 3in) served for centuries as a landmark to shipping on the Parrett.

Interior – A late 17C Bolognese painting of the *Descent from the Cross* provides a striking altarpiece. Also of interest are the octagonal, rose decorated **font** of 1460, the Queen Anne royal arms of 1712 *(west wall)*, the 15C **oak pulpit**, the former rood screen of 1420 now behind the choirstalls, the Jacobean **altar-table**, the marble monument in the chancel of Sir Francis Kingsmill (d 1620) leaning on one elbow.

★ **Admiral Blake Museum** ⊙ – *Blake Street*. The **Commonwealth Jack**, flown by Admiral Blake and adopted by the Commonwealth, often flies above the museum, the house where he was born in 1599. On entering parliament in 1640 **Robert Blake** joined the Commonwealth cause and played an active part in the Civil War. As General-at-Sea he embarked on a campaign against the Dutch admirals Tromp, De Ruyter and De Witt, and fought with pirates off North Africa. In 1657 he sailed his fleet of 12 ships into Santa Cruz harbour in Tenerife, sank 16 Spanish galleons and sacked the port; he died entering Plymouth Sound on 7 August. An audio-visual display of the Battle of Santa Cruz and some of Blake's effects are displayed in the museum.

The Shipping Room displays models of 19C and early 20C sailing rigs. Other rooms are devoted to local history, families, drawings and water colours.

The **Monmouth Room** illustrates the **Battle of Sedgemoor**: weapons, armour and cannon balls, the spyglass and an offer by James II of £5 000 to anyone "Who shall bring in the person of the James, Duke of Monmouth, alive or dead".

Battle of Sedgemoor

James, Duke of **Monmouth**, the natural, illegitimate son of Charles II born in the Netherlands in 1649, returned four months after the death of his father in 1685, landing at Lyme Regis on 11 June with 82 followers. He proceeded to Taunton where he was proclaimed king and advanced, gathering 5-6 000 followers, to Bristol, only to find the royal forces encamped before the city; he turned, fought a rearguard action at Norton-St-Philip, where he stayed at the George, and, with his army reduced to 3 500, confronted the king's force less than three miles from Bridgwater in a night attack on Sedgemoor (6 July 1685).

The aftermath was more cruel than the two-hour battle in which 300 of Monmouth's men and 25 king's men died: summary executions were carried out on the rebels on the field and in the surrounding villages and within a week James II had despatched **Judge Jeffreys** (1648-89) on the notorious **Bloody Assizes**. Monmouth himself was captured two days after the battle and executed on Tower Hill on 15 July 1685.

EXCURSIONS

Barford Park and Fyne Court

Durleigh Reservoir – The 80-acre lake is the haunt of waterfowl and migratory birds.

Barford Park ⊘ – *5 miles west by by-roads.* The Queen Anne house, low-lying by comparison with the trees all round, is extended by wings on either side curving out from the centre. The interior contains earlier kitchens, a modern garden room, and panelled and corniced 18C rooms: hall, dining and big music room, highlighted by contemporary furniture, porcelain and silver.

In the garden the informality of a woodland walk contrasts with a semicircular, walled garden enlivened by peacocks.

North Petherton – Pop 3 177. The silver-grey stone **tower**★★ of the church is outstanding even for Somerset. It rises to 109ft in three stages: a west door surmounted by a frieze and a large window with tracery at the transom as well as the apex; a three-light, decorated window; paired bell openings and a panelled wall area. Finally, there is an embattled parapet from which pinnacles and sub-pinnacles fountain skywards.

Broomfield – *10 miles south and west of Bridgwater by A38 and by-roads.* The **Church of All Saints**, which has a grin of gargoyles and a modest three-stage tower, was built c1440 before the great tower rivalry began. Inside are yellow Ham stone columns and the original **wagon roofs**, supported by 47 angels. Note the 16C bench-ends, Queen Anne's royal arms and, in the porch, a list of charities which includes the provision of free tools to honest workmen who had not pawned previous gifts. The kitchen-type table *(by south door)* with a copper band across it was Andrew Crosse's workbench; his obelisk memorial stands in the churchyard.

Fyne Court – The manor house, built by the Crosse family in the 1600s, later became home to Andrew Crosse (1784-1855), a scientific investigator into the electricity of the atmosphere who was known locally as the "Thunder and Lightning Man". The house, largely destroyed in a fire in 1894, is now leased from the National Trust to serve as headquarters to the Somerset Trust for Nature Conservation: only the Music Room (used for lectures) is open to view; the stables act as an informative interpretation centre for the Quantocks.

The landscaped park was completed in the last part of the 18C: a turretted folly provides sanctuary to a thriving bat colony.

Northwest to Bridgwater Bay

Coleridge Cottage, Nether Stowey ⊘ – Coleridge lived from 1797-1800 with his wife, Robert Southey's sister, and small son in a cottage at the end of the village. It was then a pretty thatched cottage with "a clear brook" running before the door. The former kitchen is now furnished as the parlour containing mementoes, photographs and early editions of the poems and prose works. While at Stowey, Coleridge wrote *The Rime of the Ancient Mariner* and *Kubla Khan* (*see* INTRODUCTION: Literary associations).

Take a by-road north for 3 miles from the far end of Nether Stowey.

Stogursey – This large parish and former borough was given after the Conquest to William de Falaise from whom the manor passed, through his daughter's marriage, to William de Curci. It was Curci who built a castle here in c1100, gave his name to the town which became Stoke (meaning "place" or "dairy farm") Curci, and granted land to the Abbey of Ste Marie de Lonlay in Normandy to found a priory (c1120). Over the ensuing centuries the town grew: a regular Saturday market and fair were established by 1301, shambles were built by 1475.

Today, a ruin of the **castle keep** is all that stands of the establishment, the gatehouse having long been replaced by a house, now owned by the Landmark Trust. The **Priory**, on the east side of the borough, was run as an "alien house" under the authority of the community in France: records from 1326 relate the house as having been reduced to the prior, one monk, servants and "useless folk" to save on costs. War with France caused the estate to be confiscated (1438) and transferred to Eton College, who has appointed the local vicar since 1453; in turn it was leased to the Bristol Merchant Venturers from 1713; most of the buildings were raised over time; the land was sold off in 1921.

★★ **Priory Church** – The outside of St Andrew's Church, with its octagonal, slate-covered spire rising from a superb early crossing tower, gives little indication of its enclosed glory. Substantial sections of masonry mark the first phase of building c1090, notably the lower tiers of the crossing tower and the transepts – once furnished with apses which were removed during the second phase of building c1180 when the choir and aisles was fashioned. It is from this time that the fabulous round headed arches ornamented with elaborate capitals, zig-zags and dog-tooth mouldings date. The nave is Perpendicular, added c1500. A refashioned **Norman doorway** leads to the nave which is lit by Perpendicular windows and furnished with 19C **Friendly Society boards** and 31 **benches** carved in the 1530s with a pelican, a double-headed eagle, a spoonbill, a green man… Four medieval **angels** were retained at the corners of the nave at the time of the 19C restoration; the angel roof was replaced in 1865.

In the north transept is a fossil of an ichthyosaur found locally and laid there in 1944.

Furnishings – The **chandelier** was made in Bridgwater in 1732; the **tub font** (north transept), decorated with cable moulding, four mysterious faces and St Andrew's crosses at the rim, is Norman; the encaustic **floor tiles** are medieval. The **sanctuary ring** was attached to the southeast crossing pier in the 13C when a murderer sought sanctuary in the church but absconded before his trial, leaving the priory liable for his fine (the provision of a ring was intended to enable any future miscreant to be chained to it while awaiting trial. The right of sanctuary was abolished in 1623).

Verney Chapel – Among the 18C wall monuments and tablets are memorials of William Verney (d 1333) who lies holding his heart, and John Verney (d 1472) the local squire, a rumbustious character who was summoned to Canterbury in 1442 to answer charges of interrupting the Latin service and preaching in and out of church in English. Seventy years after his death there is an entry in the accounts of 1540 for the purchase of a Great Bible (Cranmer's Bible) for 10s 6d, and 4d for a chain to secure it safely in the church.

Hinkley Point Nuclear Power Station ☉ – North of Shurton is the one time controversial power station, built in 1957: Hinkley A has two first generation magnox reactors (Magnox Electric); Hinkley B, completed in 1976 has two advanced gas-cooled reactors (Nuclear Electric). The Visitor Centre provides information about the Earth and its energy resource, and includes interactive displays for children. Tours of the stations are also available; nature trails.

Bridgwater Bay National Reserve – *Follow signs to Steart.* This is one of the major inter-tidal areas of the Severn estuary, boasting the largest tidal range in Britain and attracting a large variety of waders (dunlins, black-tailed godwits, grey plovers, curlews, redshanks), wildfowl (mallard, wigeon, teal) and raptors (peregrine, merlin). The best time to visit is within a few hours of high tide.

Inland to Athelney Marshes

Westonzoyland – *Take A372 out of Bridgwater towards Langport.* In the 8C this part of the Levels belonged to Glastonbury Abbey, although few traces of this period survive other than in the **Sedgemoor Inn** and the local church. A **steam-powered grasshopper beam engine**, installed in 1830 to pump water from the Levels in times of flood, has recently been restored.

In 1925 a substantial RAF station was built on the east side of the village; this was upgraded in 1939 and 1943 for use during the wars.

St Mary the Virgin – The Perpendicular parish **church**★★, served as a prison after Sedgemoor for 500 of Monmouth's men, "of which", according to the parish register, "there was 79 wounded and five of them died of their wounds in our church".

The splendid 15C **tower** rises through four stages to 100ft through a west doorway and window, two traceried bays and a triple-light, bell stage, to a crest of pierced battlements, pinnacles and sub-pinnacles.

Inside, the dark oak **roof**, a construction of braces and king-posts on crested beams, dressed overall with panelled tracery, mouchette bosses, pendant posts on bone thin beams, is adorned with hosts of **angels** and **half-angels**... The south transept is lit, in part by good heraldic glass retrieved from the Old Court House.

High Ham – The village, which stands 300ft above the surrounding Sedgemoor levels, is reached by a series of short climbs; from the road and from the village itself there are **views**★★ of the Polden and more distant Mendip Hills *(northeast)*, Bridgwater Bay and the Severn Estuary *(northwest)*, the Quantocks *(west)*, Taunton Vale *(southwest)* and even of Dunkery Beacon on Exmoor.
At the centre is the **village green**, shaded by tall trees and overlooked by a scattering of stonebuilt 17C-18C-19C houses and the parish church.

★ **St Andrew's** – The church is notable for its high **clerestory**, its wide Perpendicular windows above the battlements and the **gargoyles** which mark the aisle roofs – among them are a fiddler, a piper and a trumpeter, a listener with his hand to his ear, a stone thrower and a chained monkey nursing a baby.
The embattled tower is 14C whilst the remainder of the building "was builded anew from the foundation and finished within the space of one yeare, 1476". Inside, with so many windows, the **roof** above the nave can be clearly seen made up of tie-beams, king posts, bosses and arched braces rising from angel figures. The high **oak screen** which widens out into a panelled coving and ornate cornice was carved by Glastonbury monks in the early 16C.
Note also the Ham stone **pulpit** of 1632; the **lectern** with turned balusters and linenfold panelling; the 15C **poppyhead pews** and round Norman **font** with cable moulding.

Stembridge Tower Mill ⓥ – *0.5 mile east along Stembridge Road.* The windmill of 1822, which worked until 1910, is unique in having a **thatched cap** at the summit of its blue lias tower. Inside, the rail on which the cap turned, enabling the sails to face into the wind, is visible at the top of the windmill.
Among the outhouses, note the **bakehouse** with wooden gutters.
From here drive due east to SOMERTON, *south to* LANGPORT *or back to Othery for Burrow Mump and Athelney.*

Burrow Mump – The hillock (250ft) is a major landmark in the flat marshland. A castle stood on the mump in the 12C and before that possibly an Alfredian fort. Today what remains is a church tower, medieval in origin but altered in the early 18C.

Athelney Marshes – **King Alfred's** first encounter with the Danes consisted of a successful skirmish in December 870, a defeat in 871, a victory at Ashdown in Sussex and then further defeats. In 876 and 877 Wareham and Exeter were attacked by the Danes but liberated by Alfred. In 878 he was surprised at his palace in Chippenham and retreated to the marshes near Athelney, where he is supposed to have burned a cottager's cakes while planning his next move. In May 878 he emerged from hiding, defeated the Danes at Edington and signed the Peace of Wedmore which required the Danes to retreat east of the Watling Street and obliged Guthrum and 29 of his chief men to accept baptism. In 884 the Danes invaded again and those who had settled in East Anglia rose in revolt; Alfred moved east. In 885 he recaptured London and signed a second treaty with Guthrum. The Danes returned in 890 and 894; Exeter was again invested and again freed by Alfred. It was his last major battle; he died in 901 at the age of 53 and is buried at Winchester.

Willow and Wetlands Centre ⓥ – *On the edge of Stoke St Gregory at Meare Green.* The willow industry, the wetlands, their flora and fauna are described in the Visitors' Centre which displays a withy boat, old and new examples of willow craft – baskets and artists' charcoal, produced by the Coate family since 1819. Traditional practices include how the willow rods are harvested, bundled and bound, sorted by size, boiled, stripped and dried to produce buff, white or brown willow which is used by the basket-makers in the workshop.

BRIDPORT

Dorset – Population 7 278
Michelin Atlas p 8 or Map 403 – L 31

Bridport is associated with rope-making; as was said as early as 1505, it has been making ships' ropes and cordage "for time out of mind": in the 15C Henry VII decreed that all hemp grown within a five-mile radius of the then river port should be reserved for the king's ships. The trade remains the town's mainstay despite changes over the years in the design of ships' rigging, the evolution of fishing methods, demands for football and tennis nets (like those used at Wimbledon), twine, string, packthread, cordage and rope, and above all, the substitution of nylon for flax and hemp. Most of the extant sheds built to house spinning machines, rope and twine spinning, weaving or net-making date from the late 19C and early 20C.

Bridport is T-shaped, the early, walled Saxon river port (where South Street now runs) expanding north and then east-west in Georgian times along the Dorchester-Exeter road. The other major industry which continues to thrive in the town is the Old Brewery, founded in 1794 and acquired by JC and RH Palmer in 1894, complete with a thatched building and aged iron water-wheel (1879).

Market days: Wednesday and Saturday all day.

South Street – The town's original street is lined by the oldest town houses, seamen's cottages, inns and the Perpendicular St Mary's church with its many 19C additions.

Museum ⊙ – Bridport museum is housed in a 16C stone-fronted house with a prominent porch, known as the Castle. Displays pertain to rural life (agricultural tools) and natural history. The **Local History Centre** provides genealogical and local history records (archive photographs, parish records 1890-1945) and a research facility.

The first floor gallery has changing displays of fine art, decorative arts, costume...

West Street – The Georgian street and its continuation, East Street, are overlooked by imposing houses built for merchants and professional men and former coaching inns.

Note **Granville House**, built in the mid-18C *(north side)* opposite a Venetian windowed house, and, at the bottom end of the street, the late 18C stone **Rope and Net Factory**.

East Street – No 9, opposite the Town Hall, with bow-fronted shop windows and a centre door, smaller, domestic bow windows above and a proud fascia, dates from 1786; the **Unitarian Chapel**, with Ionic columns supporting a semicircular porch, is also 18C; the Classically columned Literary and Scientific Institute, now the **Library**, is 19C.

West Bay – A small harbour **museum** ⊙ (opened 1992) is accommodated in a converted salt house overlooking the harbour: it illustrates the history of Bridport's net and rope-making industry and the maritime history of West Bay.

EXCURSION

Beaminster *8 miles north on A3066*

An undulating countryside of woods and trees surrounds Beaminster (pronounced Bemminster) which, at its centre, presents a triangular square with an old-style, pyramid roofed **market cross** (1906) and a number of thriving old family shops: all rebuilt after fires in 1644, 1684 and 1781 had reduced the town to the "pityfullest spectacle".

St Mary ⊙ – The church has a very tall, castellated **west tower** built *c*1503 in a local ochre stone with a rare number of richly carved canopied niches, gutter heads and a spectacular thrust of crocketed pinnacles. Figures of King Alfred and St Brega adorn the north west corner; on the western face appear a rare composition of Madonna and Child with Saints surmounted by a representation of the Crucifixion flanked by a pilgrim (with staff and scallop badge) and flax merchant holding a fuller's bat and mill.

Inside, the Purbeck font is largely Norman; the western section of the nave arcade is early 15C and has distinctive capitals carved with a continuous grape and vine design, the eastern part being later; the mobile pulpit is predominantly Jacobean (1619); the screen and roof are both 19C; the lectern and candle holder are modern. In the south aisle, beyond the short brass 19C memorial plaque to Sir John Gone, are two imposing monuments dedicated to the memory of Thomas Strode and his nephew George (shown recumbent on his sarcophagus by Scheemakers), resident at Parnham House.

★★ **Parnham House** ⊙ – Parnham combines a mellow stone house set in a wooded valley and beautiful furniture, each of their time: Elizabeth I and Elizabeth II. The E-shaped **house** of Ham stone is gabled, finialled and multiple chimneyed, and emblazoned on the oriel above the entrance.

The house was planned around a Great Hall built in 1540 by Sir Robert Strode, whose coat of arms is emblazoned in the windows there. In the 17C the mansion was overrun by Cromwell's soldiers, who murdered Lady Anne Strode in that same Great Hall. In 1810 John Nash, the architect behind Regent's Park and Buckingham Palace, was employed to remodel the house: he moved the fireplace and inserted windows with panels of 18C Flemish glass. A century later, many of the "most contemptible" Regency additions were replaced with Tudor features: a 17C screen from Surrey was installed, the Library was panelled and the plaster ceiling added.

In 1976 it was purchased by John Makepeace, who set it to rights once more and established it as the **John Makepeace Furniture Workshops**, the School for Craftsmen in Wood; the house provides the most perfect, informal and ageless context and exhibition gallery. Makepeace is considered among the country's foremost contemporary furniture designers: of the commissioned pieces, a few may become prototypes of limited editions, most are unique pieces, often celebratory, as is the fourth centenary table at Longleat.

Gardens – The handsome grounds include formal **gardens** bounded by stone walls and balustrades, courtyards, fountains, topiaried yews, lawns and hedges, a river and a lake – complementary to the highly textured grains and classical line so typical of Makepeace furniture, the plants grown in the gardens are contrasted one with

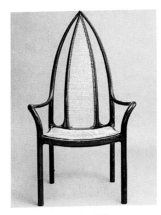

Chair by John Makepeace

another in terms of colour, form and leaf shape. Sculpture also plays its own part in the landscape design.

The other initiative managed by the Parnham Trust is **Hooke Park**, an area of woodland acquired from the Forestry Commission in 1983, which is worked as a sustainable source of renewable wood. Its unconventional, ecological buildings, using spindly but highly flexible Norway spruce thinnings, are conceived as tension and compression structures. *Access along B3163 from Beaminster towards A356.*

★ **Mapperton Gardens** ⊙ – *Signposted 2 miles south of Beaminster, off the B3163.* "There can hardly be anywhere a more enchanting manorial group than Mapperton": so begins Pevsner's entry in his guide to *The Buildings of Dorset*. The integral complex of house (16C-17C) and its medieval church *(both private)* is complementary to the sunken formal gardens which stretch beyond the north lawns. These were laid out in 1926 with architectural features supporting climbers (clematis, wisteria), pools of still water surrounded by box and yew topiary, grottoes, urns and statuary which provide fabulous contrasts of colour, shape, geometric form, gesture and movement. Beyond the gardens extends an arboretum, and the idyllic Dorset landscape of green fields and natural woodland: this is a serene haven for contemplation rather than an inspirational source of provocative effects for the garden designer.

BRISTOL★★

Bristol – Population 376 146

Michelin Atlas p 16 or Map 403 – M 29

Bristol is a lively trading city which originated in the 10C as "Bricgstow" – literally meaning "the settlement by the bridge" located six miles from the coast by the River Avon, at the western limit of the Saxon invasion. By the Middle Ages, Bristol was a flourishing port trading such commodities as timber, wool, fish, leather, wine, iron and tin, with France, Portugal, Spain and Iceland: soon it ranked as England's second city after London, and one of eleven staples in England (a place for the collection of royal fines). Expertise gained from sailing in the north seas, coupled with private enterprise encouraged such adventurers as **John Cabot** to set out for the mythical Cathay portrayed by Marco Polo; regular sailings across the Atlantic exchanged slaves in the West Indies with cargoes of rum, sugar and tobacco – a lucrative business that lasted until the American Wars of Independence (1775-81) and the abolition of the Slave Trade (1833). Prosperity increased until the Industrial Revolution drew interests north, notably to Liverpool, forcing family shipbuilding and carriage works to close.

The city's present affluence and regeneration is underpinned by the electronic age: high technology research and assembly (Rolls Royce, British Aerospace) continues to maintain Bristol's strong tradition in engineering while the shift of major banking and insurance services away from London is providing job security to large numbers of young people in the financial sector (notably Lloyds and TSB banking). Today Bristol continues to be regarded as the capital of the South West.

Historically, the rise in wealth of shrewd merchants and traders can be charted by the changes in the city's architecture: rather than make good, the Bristolian built new. The old was bequeathed to charitable institutions and protected by endowment, hence buildings from the Norman, Gothic – particularly the Perpendicular

---

Tax and duty

In earlier times, when the monarch was personally responsible for the nation's finances, sources of revenue included the sale of royal forests; rents from the royal estates; customs dues; fees, fines, forfeits from the administration of justice; monies extracted on the basis of a vassal's duty to his overlord; and finally the system of licences, patents and charters, all of which had to be granted and purchased from the king or his appointed officer.

Licensing in the Middle Ages became a science: permits, often costly, were required to graze hogs and cattle in the royal forests; to fish, to hunt even the smallest game; to gather fallen branches for fuel; to cut coppice wood; crenellate a house, to keep a dog or hound; to transfer property; charters were needed to hold fairs and markets... Tax-farmers or collectors took their tithe. Others purchased or were granted – usually in return for a gift – export or import licences as was Sir Walter Raleigh (*see* PLYMOUTH) for commodities such as wool and woollen cloth. Even the Elizabethan navigators had to obtain a licence – for instance a letter of marque – or had to present as tribute a proportion of their often hard-won treasure.

– Jacobean and Palladian periods survive – for the most part spared from 19C restoration. The Victorian age is marked by Brunel's exploits in civil engineering and the rise in profits from increased trade with the Americas. In the 20C the centre of Bristol suffered from heavy bombing in 1940-42 and had to be rebuilt.

Trade and Venturing – Bristol trade in the 10C was concerned with Ireland; by the 17C it had expanded to the Canaries, the Spanish American colonies, North America, Africa, the West Indies. In the 18C-19C new industries developed locally: iron, brass, copper, tin, porcelain and glass, chocolate, tobacco.

The merchants, several of whom were Quakers, were incorporated in 1522 as the **Society of Merchant Venturers**; this was granted its charter in 1552. They built and endowed churches – **William Canynges** even paid for the remodelling of the most magnificent of them, St Mary Redcliffe *(see below)*. They bought land freed by the Dissolution and erected great houses; they enabled the corporation to buy the Mayoral Chapel and presented the city with almshouses, hospitals and schools (Queen Elizabeth Hospital or QEH in Jacob's Wells Road, founded in 1590, maintains its traditional uniform comprising belted coats, buckled shoes and breeches). In the early 17C, persecuted Puritans collected together in Bristol before embarking upon the *Mayflower* bound for the New World (1620). By the 18C many were abandoning their houses in the city centre and moving out to Brandon Hill and Clifton where they built great houses like Clifton Hill House, now a university hall of residence.

Dwindling prosperity – Industry and trade depended on effective transport; however, the poor berthing conditions have been a constant problem. Bristol's port has undergone three major transformations in its progress from riparian sailship

Bristol Docks

harbour to tanker and container terminal: in 1240-48, the **Frome Trench** was dug to redirect the course of the River Frome, thereby improving landing facilities and increasing the water depth; in 1804-09 the River Avon was diverted into the New Cut, and the **Floating Harbour**, 2.5 miles in extent, was created to provide a constant water level and an immense quayside in the heart of the city (a system of flood gates allowed this channel to be flushed free of silted mud with high spring tides). This, together with the expansion of the rail network which transported freight more economically, did not provide reason enough to entice business back from Liverpool. In 1877-79 new docks were built at **Avonmouth** and **Portishead** on the Severn Estuary; further capacity was provided in 1977 when the **Royal Portbury Docks** were opened.

★ **OLD CITY** *2.5 hours*

The first merchants turned retailers set up business on Bristol Bridge – the city's main thoroughfare; by the 14C jewellers and mercers had collected together around there, wool drapers in the High Street, linen drapers in Wine Street, butchers at Temple Gate, wine merchants along the harbour front. Not until the close of the 18C did shopkeepers begin to specialise in selling goods made by different manufacturers; perishable provisions meanwhile, were purchased from markets and hawkers well into the 19C.

St Nicholas Church (CDY) – The proud Georgian church was gutted by fire in 1941 and rebuilt with a soaring white stone spire: today it accommodates the **Bristol Tourist Information Centre** and Hogarth's *Ascension* altarpiece formerly from St Mary Redcliffe.

High Street (CDY 39) – The street crosses an area of alleys, lanes and small courts. To its west lies the indoor market (Monday to Saturday) with, at its centre, **The Rummer**, an inn of 1743 and holder of no 1 public house licence in Bristol. It was here that Coleridge launched his magazine *The Watchman* in 1795.

All Saints and Christchurch ⊘ (CY) – Churches have stood here since Saxon times. Although the tower of **All Saints (N)** is 18C, parts of the church *(closed to the public)* are Norman and others early 15C. The austere Georgian **Christchurch (R)** dating from 1791 is to be recognised by its painted wood clock **quarter-jacks** (1728), helmeted, moustachioed, kilted and armed with axes.

Corn Street (CY) – The giant-pilastered and pedimented **Corn Exchange (CY L)** (1740-43) was built by John Wood the Elder of Bath, modelled on mid-16C buildings in Antwerp and London. Outside stand four **brass nails** on which Bristol corn merchants proffered samples of grain, struck deals and paid in cash – hence the expression "to pay on the nail"; the first nail was cast in 1594. Behind the Exchange extends the market, completed in 1745.
Beyond, the columns, coats of arms and exuberant figures along the frieze and in every spandrel mark **Lloyds Bank** (1854-58), designed after St Mark's Library by Sansonvino in Venice; Robert Smirke's sober Greek-style **Old Council House** building is from 1822-27; while the old **Coffee House** is 18C. The Bush Inn, featured in Charles Dickens' *Pickwick Papers*, however, is no more.

★ **St Stephen's City** ⊘ (CY D) – The 15C **west tower** of the city parish church rises 130ft by stages of ogee arched bays to a distinctive crown and two-tier pierced balustrade linking 20ft corner turrets which culminate in fountains of close-standing pinnacles: it was funded entirely by John Shipward, merchant, mayor and MP. In the irregularly shaped interior, supported on shafted piers with gilded demi-angel capitals, are memorials to **Edmund Blanket** *(north aisle)*, a wealthy cloth weaver (d 1371), and **Martin Pring** (1580-1627), merchant adventurer and general of the East India Company, who discovered Cape Cod in 1603, explored Guiana in 1604, the Virginia coast in 1606 and surveyed the Bristol Channel for a fee of £11 1*s* in 1610 – the oval plaque was embellished in the 18C with symbolic figures including the mermaid and merman. Note also the 17C wrought-iron **gates** *(north aisle)* and **sword rest** *(south chancel pillar)* by William Edney, and the medieval **eagle lectern**.
Follow Colston Avenue north and then take Quay Street.

The Conduit – *Nelson Street* (CY 51). The conduit *(right)* used to bring water from Brandon Hill to the old priory and the city in the 14C.
St John's Gate is flanked by the two legendary founders of Bristol: Brennus and Belinus.

★ **St John the Baptist** ⊘ (CY) – The church, including a battlemented tower with a spire, stands over a triple arch, one of the six medieval gateways in the city walls. It was erected in the 14C on older foundations by William Frampton (tomb in the canopied recess, *north chancel wall*), three times mayor: the site determining the narrowness of the nave and chancel. The woodwork and

C Council House
D St Stephen's City
E John Wesley's New Room
K Merchant Seamen's
  Almshouses

L Corn Exchange
M² Industrial Museum
M³ Harveys Wine Cellars
N All Saints
R Christchurch

S Broadmead
  Baptist Church
T Theatre Royal
V Norman Arch
X Hatchet Inn

furnishings are nearly all early 17C including the wooden lectern, **communion table**, the big **hour-glass** intended to curtail sermons. Much earlier is the **brass** (chancel) of Thomas Rowley, merchant and burgess (d 1478) and his wife.

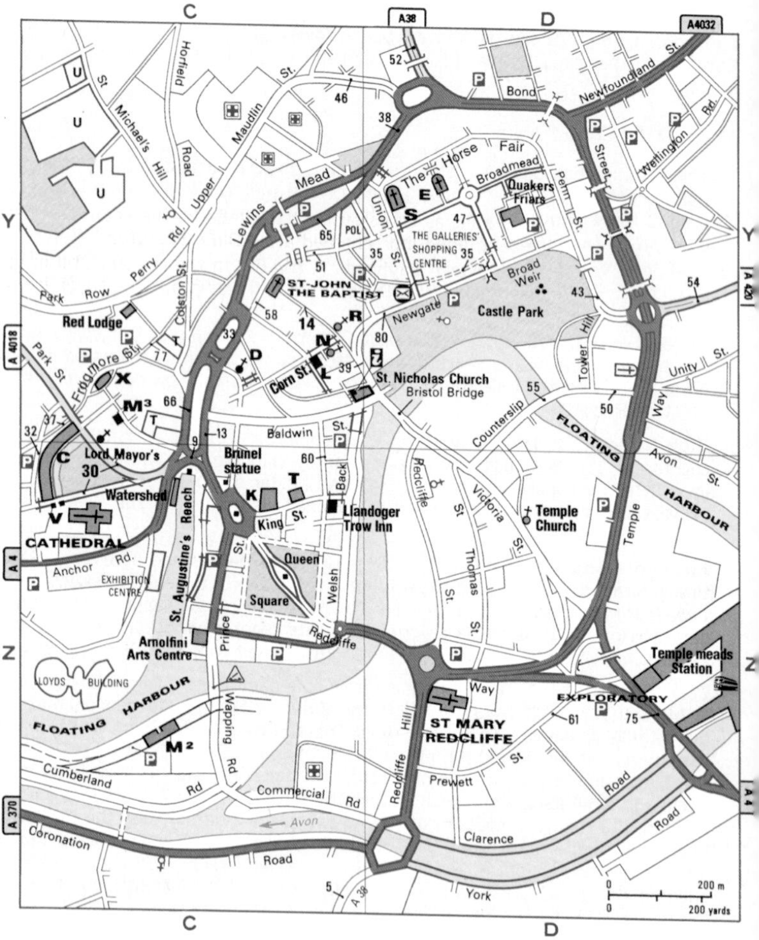

Broad Street (CY 14) – The wide street, which leads to the old city wall, is partly lined by 17C timber-framed houses and shops. The Art Nouveau **Edward Everard building** was designed as a print works: the figures represent Gutenberg and William Morris attended by the Spirit of Light and a figure bearing the attributes of light (lamp) and truth (mirror).

BROADMEAD *45min*

Within the vast new shopping precinct are three religious buildings of contrasting periods.

Broadmead Baptist Church (DY S) of 1967-69 is almost austere in its simplicity.

John Wesley's New Room ⊙ **(DY E)** – The chapel, established in 1739, was the very first Methodist chapel: its two entrances are heralded by statues of John Wesley on his horse and Charles Wesley preaching.

Inside, it is furnished with a two decker **pulpit**, **parliament clock**, mahogany communion table, box pews, graceful **gallery stairs** and former living accommodation (history of Methodism).

It was at the 1771 Bristol Conference, held here, that Francis Asbury was chosen to go to America where he became the first Methodist bishop.

Quakers Friars (DY) – The oldest establishment, takes its name from the Dominicans (Black Friars) who occupied the building from the 13C-16C; it was taken over by the Society of Friends (Quakers) from the 17C to the mid-20C. Today it serves as commercial office space.

KING STREET AND QUEEN SQUARE

King Street (CZ) – The cobbled street has a unique character with the Floating Harbour at one end, 18C and 19C warehouses, the theatre, 17C almshouses and pubs: the **Llandoger Trow Inn**, named after the flat-bottomed barges which unloaded coal on the adjoining Welsh Back quayside and doubles as the Admiral Benbow in *Treasure Island*, was built as three stout, half-timbered merchants' houses in 1663; **The Old Duke** is an aged inn renamed after Duke Ellington.

★★ **Theatre Royal** (CZ **T**) – The oldest playhouse (1764-66) in the country still in use opened to a prologue composed by **David Garrick** and was granted a royal licence by George III in 1778.

Outside, James Paty the Younger's rusticated golden stone ground floor is superimposed by giant Corinthian columns, a cornice and pediment bearing the George III royal arms. Inside, the wide foyers and staircase beneath a decorated ceiling are modern, the small, semicircular rather than the now more common horseshoe auditorium on three levels with boxes on either side of the proscenium stage is original in design, restored in 1800.

It is alleged that the theatre is haunted by a ghost of a lady in black (possibly Sarah Siddons) and one of a man called Richard who moves objects around the theatre's paint shop.

★ **Merchant Seamen's Almshouses** (CZ **K**) – *Northwest end.* The almshouses bear the coloured arms of the **Merchant Venturers** on the outside wall of the pink-washed former quadrangle. The houses were first built in 1544 and enlarged with funds from **Edward Colston** in 1696. The life story of one of the almsmen on the Spanish Main was used by Edgar Allen Poe as the basis for *The Golden Bug.*

Beyond the almshouses, on the other side of the road, stands a more than lifesize, top-hatted bronze of **Isambard Kingdom Brunel**.

Queen Square (CZ) – Bristol's first square laid out like those being built in Bloomsbury, is named after Queen Anne; the houses that enclose it were popular among successful merchants who were keen to leave the ever more noisome city centre and dockside area.

The large, superbly crafted, bronze equestrian **statue of William III** is by Rysbrack.

★★ ST MARY REDCLIFFE AND TEMPLE MEADS *Half a day*

★★ **St Mary Redcliffe** ⊙ (DZ) – The church is known, in the words of Queen Elizabeth, as the "fairest, goodliest, and most famous parish church in England"; Thomas Chatterton, the young Romantic poet born in Redcliffe Way in 1752, named it, more simply "the pride of Bristowe". The pale Dundry stone-faced edifice which ambitiously aspires comparison with a cathedral, represents the most perfect expression of the Gothic style spanning the 13C to 15C evolution of Early English to Perpendicular. Building most certainly was interrupted by the Black Death in the mid-14C.

Exterior – The **spire** (1872) rises 292ft; crocketed pinnacles mark the west end, transepts, porches, the angles of the tower; finialled buttresses separate the wide, pointed windows of the nave and chancel before flying to support the immense clerestory windows, inserted after the original spire collapsed into the roof of the building in 1446.

In the churchyard stands a buckled tramrail embedded in the turf: kept as a reminder of Good Friday 1941 when a bomb fell nearby, missing the church.

Interior – The Decorated **north porch** (1290) highlights the 270ft front's perfect regularity being hexagonal and set, like a jewel, off-centre. It stands with two tiers of decorated gables, saintly figures and a door with a triple, stellate surround as the antechamber to the shrine of Our Lady, situated in an inner, more modest Early English porch, the oldest part of the church (1185). Alms paid by departing seafarers would have been left in the **iron grilled recess**; 10ft from the ground is a ledge and a door to the muniment room which would have accommodated a priest: it was here that the audacious young poet Thomas Chatterton is meant to have found the poems of a Thomas Rowley; when this claim was discovered to be fraudulent, the 17 year old was proclaimed a genius, moved to London, and when fame eluded him there, poisoned himself with arsenic.

Inside, the church is lit by a gloriously tall clerestory which seems to exaggerate the 240ft length of the internal space; in plan, it has aisled transepts, an ambulatory and projecting Lady Chapel; the weight of the great stone-vault is conveyed externally through flying buttresses. Slender shafted pillars sweep up to break into **lierne vaulting** in which every one of the 1 200 and more intersections is masked by a different **boss**, each except those beneath the tower picked out by gold leaf (1740).

In the north transept are displayed the weather-worn statuary that was replaced in 1840-72. In the south ambulatory is a cope chest and a display case in which the Cadbury cope is shown, proof of ongoing endowment by Bristolians, in this instance in memory of Egbert Cadbury, the renowned Quaker chocolate-maker magnate.

American or St John the Baptist Chapel – *northwest end.* Abutting the pillars is a contemporary, painted wooden effigy of **Queen Elizabeth I**, probably a ship's figurehead and a Spanish chair bearing the arms of Isabella of Castile – the sponsor of Christopher Columbus. The stained glass is medieval.

On the nave side of the pillar hangs the full armour of **Admiral Sir William Penn** (d 1670; *tombstone at entrance to south transept*) who was born in Bristol and rose to become Commissioner for the Navy under Charles II; he was also the father of William, the Quaker founder of the American state of Pennsylvania by charter endorsed by Charles II in redemption of his debts to Penn's late father. Note also the medieval stained glass.

Outside the chapel, resting on an Early English corbel that predates the collapse of the tower, rests a whalebone supposedly brought back by Cabot from his expedition of discovery to Newfoundland.

South Aisle – Note the medieval octagonal **font** with an angel on the pillar and a gilded dove; the richly coloured **arms** of Charles II *(over the porch)*; the **stellate tomb recesses**.

South Transept – The transept serves in part as a chapel to **William Canynges** (1400-74), shipbuilder, merchant prince, mayor, MP and benefactor, who paid for much of the rebuilding of the church; in one tomb effigy he lies beside his wife in full colour, in the second in the vestments of the holy order which he joined on his wife's death.

Ambulatory – The ambulatory passes before the Lady Chapel, for 100 years a school screened from the chancel at one time by the Hogarth triptych (now in St Nicholas Church-TIC), and now embellished with contemporary stained glass. Note the 18C brass **candelabra**.

In the chancel, **brasses** commemorate two churchwardens: John Jay (d 1480), merchant, and John Brooke (d 1512), servant-at-law to Henry VIII; at the crossing stands the **lectern**, a fierce 17C eagle, given by James Wathen, "pin Maker".

Temple Meads – Two separate stations were built to serve the city: one for the south west and one for the Great Western Railway to Paddington. The earliest example of a rail terminus in Britain was completed by Brunel in 1842, its symmetrical Tudor-style façade turned towards Temple Gate, for the Bristol to Bath line which opened in 1840; the remainder of the track was opened on completion of the Box Tunnel in 1841. In one of Brunel's subsidiary train sheds, is accommodated the Bristol Exploratory – when this is relocated to the Harbourside, the main area of this complex of Grade 1 listed buildings will house the **British Empire and Commonwealth Museum.**

★ **The Exploratory Hands-on Science Centre** ⊘ **(DZ)** – *Bristol Old Station.* Award-winning displays encourage the young and old to explore 'hands-on' the physical laws of gravity, light, heat, sound, electricity, friction, magnetism, structure and

---

British Empire and Commonwealth Museum

This archive of material has been collected from a variety of sources, namely the Foreign and Commonwealth Office, Military and Colonial organisations, independent societies and companies, collectors and private individuals. The first phase of the museum opened in September 1997 providing a gallery space for temporary exhibitions drawn from national institutions or compiled in-house; the conversion of additional space with display facilities continues. One initiative already well under way is the collation of personal experiences in private recordings: these and material from the archives are accessible to the public.

Pending completion of the Temple Quays development in 2001, information on scheduled events at the museum is available on ☎ 0117 925 4980 or web site: empire museum.demon.co.uk

earth science. Excellent variations on pulling, pushing, balancing, twisting, turning and heat. Interactive displays for younger children disclose the properties of the insect and animal kingdom.

Temple Church (DZ) – Bristol's "leaning tower", a monumental stone belfry dating back to 1300, stands proudly, despite bombing and fire, as a reminder of the medieval Knights Templar. The 144ft structure began to lean at an early stage in its construction and is 5ft out of true (Pisa: 180ft with 15ft "lean").

HARBOURSIDE, INDUSTRIAL MUSEUM and SS GREAT BRITAIN

Floating Harbour (BZ 9) – The lead statue of Neptune on the Bridgehead dates from 1723, marking the point at which the River Frome re-emerges after flowing underground.

The **Watershed** *(below right)* is a media centre and shopping gallery while the area behind is being substantially redeveloped for the millennium: new facilities include a centre for the performing arts, **Wildscreen World** – comprising an electronic zoo, an IMAX cinema, the ARKive which will monitor endangered species of animals, plants and other such living organisms and a museum dedicated to wildlife photography.

> **"Shipshape and Bristol fashion"**
>
> The expression was coined to describe the preparations required before a ship sailed up the river; given the dramatic rise and fall of the tide, ships were often left askew when stranded on the mudflats; if cargo was not properly stowed it was liable to fall or spill. Appropriately enough, it was a Bristol-born man, **Samuel Plimsoll** who came up with the idea of limiting cargo weighting by the elementary concept known as the Plimsoll Line.

Science World will provide the highly successful Exploratory hands-on with bigger and better premises. Details presently on show at the project exhibition centre.

By the waterside, commercial offices (Lloyds and TSB headquarters) and residential units have already been built. Moves to locate the fabulous **ISCA collection of British boats**, formerly housed at the Maritime Museum in Exeter, are also scheduled to provide additional interest in the area (confirmation and exact situation still to be finalised in 1997).

Arnolfini ⊘ (CZ) – This early conversion of an 1830s tea warehouse has been particularly successful, providing an airy, adaptable space dedicated to the promotion of contemporary visual and performing arts, bar and restaurant, video library and bookshop. Elm, ash and sycamore surfaces are muted, carefully blended with the use of Portland stone, slate and marble.

★★ **Industrial Museum** ⊘ (CZ M²) – The 1950s warehouse on the Floating Harbour quayside is a depository for the full range of transport vehicles manufactured in and around the city.

On the ground floor are displayed horse-drawn carriages built until hand-crafted coach-building evolved into panel-beating in the 1920s; this includes the Bristol State Coach (1850). Other vehicles range from broad gauge railway carriages and J F Parker's collection of 1 inch gauge railway models; long-nosed and aerodynamic Bristol 400 and 403 cars; Douglas motorbikes and Bristol-built bicycles; a Bristol lorry (1952) and Lodekka bus (1966).

Upstairs, highly technical displays relate the pioneering developments in the aero-engine industry with factories at Fishponds, Filton, Patchway and Brislington: British and Colonial Aeroplane Co, made private aircraft before switching in 1918 to military applications. Cosmos Engineering, Anglo-American, Rolls Royce, British Aerospace are all included. Subsequent assemblies were perfected to include a complete Olympiad of engine variants (Jupiter, Mercury, Hercules, Titan, Neptune...) before eventually arriving at the jet engines that power Concorde.

The museum steams its engines *Henbury* and *Portbury* (1937) regularly and has restored the 1861 **Mayflower Steam Tug** ⊘.

★ **SS Great Britain** ⊘ (AX B) – Ongoing work to restore the ship to the former glory of her launch in 1843 will continue for a while. Meanwhile this first iron-built, propeller-driven Atlantic liner lies in her original dry dock, a vast 322ft long and 51ft across, with forecastle deck renewed, 43ft bowsprit, reproduction figurehead and gilded trailboards in place, her keel plates exposed inside, her masts shipped once more, the gleaming Dining Saloon ready... Museum and guide describe the innovations of **Brunel's** design, the saga of the ship's history until its return in 1970. Also shown are mementoes of all kinds from both *Great Britain* and *Great Western* and Bristol's maritime history.

Tucked into a workshop behind the boatyard is **Bristol Blue Glassworks** ⓥ, which revives an ancient industry associated with Bristol providing wine merchants with bottles and early settlers in America with window panes.

Maritime Heritage Centre (AX G) – The centre was opened in 1985 to display the collection of ship models and drawings accumulated by the shipbuilders, Hilhouse and his successor, Charles Hill. It illustrates the transition from sail via steam to diesel and from wood via wrought-iron to steel, from 1773 to 1976 when the site was an active shipyard. At the centre is a mock-up of the dredger designed by Brunel to keep the Floating Dock free of mud.

★ **COLLEGE GREEN**
(**CZ 30**) *2 hours*

★ **Bristol Cathedral** ⓥ (**CZ**) – The main body of the cathedral is a 14C-15C Per-

SS *Great Britain*

pendicular Gothic church with a crenellated and pinnacled central tower; the nave and twin west towers were completed by George Street (1868-88). The church was founded as part of an Augustinian abbey in 1140 by Robert Fitzharding, first Lord Berkeley, dissolved by Henry VIII in 1539; three years later it was reconstituted as the Cathedral Church. Its most striking phase of development was initiated by Abbot Knowle and involved a new chancel with aisles and eastern Lady Chapel, a low chapel and antechapel off the south aisle (1298-1330).

Interior – From the crossing look through the screen and the carved and canopied choirstalls (lively **15C misericords**) at the high altar before the 19C reconstructed reredos, then up and obliquely to either side to appreciate the fascinating treatment of space and vaulting arrangement.

The effect is unique in English cathedrals: the east end is a **hall church** with broad chancel and chancel aisles rising to an equal 50ft. Over the choir, the line established by the piers sweeps upwards in an unbroken progression to the ribs of the lierne vault (pioneered at St Stephen's, Westminster in the 1300s), its kite-shaped lozenges emphasised by cusping – a novel feature that was soon copied for the choirs at Wells and Tewkesbury, and St Mary Redcliffe; above the aisles it has been optically lowered for the sake of proportion, by taking the arching to a cross-beam which also serves to spring the roof ribs. This remarkably modern device is conceived as internal flying buttresses, diffusing the weight of the vault across the aisle to the outer wall, and modelled on the tie beams on arched braces in timber roofs. Additional abutment is provided by the transverse tunnel vaults in each aisle bay. Vaults and spandrels are pierced to add a rare perspective while the large aisle windows, arranged in alternating designs, contribute to the spatial clarity of the whole.

Lady Chapels – There are two chapels: off the north transept sits the **Elder Lady Chapel** (1210-20) notable for its sobriety, its stiff-leaf capitals on slender Purbeck columns and small figures – St Michael and the dragon, a fox and goose, a lizard, and pipe-playing monkey carved by a stonemason who also worked on the western parts of the nave of Wells Cathedral; the **East Lady Chapel**, a 100ft extension added when the Norman chancel was rebuilt in 1298-1330, is memorable for its riot of medieval colour highlighting stone carved into cusped arches, gabled niches, friezes, fleurons, heads, crests... This chapel contains one of the cathedral's special features: the 14C **stellate tomb recess**, an interplay of curving lines and gilded ornament, surrounding a 15C gabled tomb chest.

Sacristy – *Off south chancel aisle.* The small, dark chamber has bossaged flying ribs with foliated corbels and three niches, one of them formerly a bread oven. The **Berkeley Chapel** *(down the steps)* contains a Flemish brass chandelier (similar

A. Taverner

to that in St Michael's Mount church) of 1450, transferred from the Temple Church: at the heart stand St George and the Virgin and Child, above a host of golden squares.

In the **Newton Chapel**, note the fine **marble memorial** to Elizabeth Stanhope by Richard Westmacott, together with the 15C, 16C and 17C Newton family tombs and in the south transept the **Harrowing of Hell**; a remarkable carving is a Saxon stone coffin-lid (c1050).

A door on the far side of the transept leads to the cloister and chapter-house.

Chapter-House – A lovely Norman columned vestibule leads to the quite special chapter-house (1150-70), considered one of the finest in the country, where the golden stone walls are patterned with interlacing blind-arcading that would have been painted in hectic colours; the roof is intersected by great, zigzag ornamented ribs.

Norman Arch (**CZ V**) – The abbey precincts, rebuilt in the late 15C, retain the original, robust Norman gateway arch, framed by a collar of zigzag decoration.

Council House (**CYZ C**) – The curved, modern building, the city administration office, is distinguished by high-stepping golden unicorns, supporters of the city arms.

★ **Lord Mayor's Chapel** ⊙ (**CY**) – **St Mark's**, part of the medieval Hospital of the Gaunts founded in 1220, was purchased in 1541 by the City Corporation.

A bird's-eye view from inside the door reveals a narrow 13C nave (orientation north-south) and, to the right, a Perpendicular chapel with **15C-17C tombs**, a large window of English (*St Thomas a Becket* by Benjamin West) and 16C Continental **glass** (largely acquired by the Corporation as a result of the sale of William Beckford's Fonthill collection – *see* BATH) and the 16C flat, black wooden roof highlighted in gold. Note the mayors' hatchments, a fine early 18C gilded swordrest, wrought-iron **gates** *(south aisle chapel)* by William Edney in 1702 formerly in the Temple Church, 16C Spanish tiles in the Poyntz Chapel imported by Bristol merchants, and excellent variety of private memorials, effigies and tomb chests.

Hatchet Inn (**CY X**) – The old gabled farmhouse was first licensed in 1606.

Harveys Wine Cellars ⊙ (**CY M³**) – A video (*9mins*) provides an introduction to John Harvey & Sons (founded in 1796), the famous wine merchants and makers of Bristol Cream Sherry. In the vaulted cellars below the Lord Mayor's Chapel (St Mark's) a museum traces the history of Bristol as a major port, the relationship the city enjoyed with Bordeaux until the Hundred Years War (1453) when interests were switched to Spain and Portugal, the making of sherry – popularised in England after Sir Francis Drake set the Spanish fleet alight in Cadiz and made off with 2900 casks of sack, and of Domecq Port from Portugal. A fine collection of objects associated with wine include silver decanter labels and tastevins, corkscrews (modelled on bullet extractors), funnels, early (17C) bottles which ensured durability, early English lead drinking glasses, ceramic bin labels, traditional coopering equipment.

★★ **BRANDON HILL** (**AX**) *Half a day*

★★ **Georgian House** ⊙ (**AX A**) – No 7 Great George Street was built for John Pinney, a sugar planter, on his return from St Kitts to Bristol where as a merchant he made a second, even larger fortune. It was also here that Coleridge was first introduced to William Wordsworth. The house is now one of the best-preserved museums of its kind.

The Bristol architects **Thomas** and **William Paty** produced for him a typical late 18C design in Bath stone with a pedimented front door and rooms with Adam-style decoration, while Pinney himself attended to every detail: "I desire you send me by the waggon a sufficient quantity of Glass for 4 Chinese doors for Book cases... Let it be the best glass as it is intended for handsome Cases".

Ground floor – The built-in "handsome cases" in the **office** successfully complement Pinney's original rich mahogany **bureau-bookcase** of 1750. The plain mahogany **standing desk** with brass ledger rails and candle brackets was brought back from the West Indies; the fine walnut-veneered moonphase **long-case clock** is by John Jordan of Bristol and dates from c1740.

The arch between the **breakfast parlour and dining room** could originally be closed with folding doors. Mahogany is everywhere: the table, sideboard, chairs, Stilton cheese box, dumb waiter and knife urn. The blue and white Chinese porcelain dinner service bears the Pinney coat of arms.

Upstairs – Note the fine pair of gilded **girandoles** (1775) in the pale drawing room, the enormous Sheraton-style double secretaire bookcase (c1800) and the walnut-veneered collector's cabinet with ormolu mounts in the rich green **library** hung with Piranesi prints. The bedrooms continue the elegant, understated theme.

BRISTOL

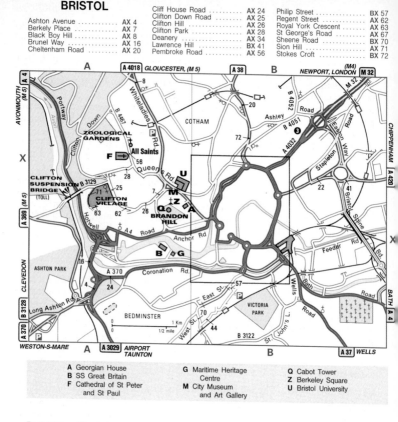

A Georgian House	G Maritime Heritage	Q Cabot Tower
B SS Great Britain	Centre	Z Berkeley Square
F Cathedral of St Peter	M City Museum	U Bristol University
and St Paul	and Art Gallery	

Basement – The basement contains the service rooms necessary for the smooth running of a wealthy 18C household: the pantry, for dirty chores such as cleaning silver; the housekeeper's room *(left)* containing old or unfashionable pieces of the family's furniture, from where an eye could be kept on anyone approaching the front door; the cold-water plunge-bath which Pinney used every morning, finding it to be 'of great service'; the large kitchen with an iron cage-spit in the fireplace, turned by weights as for a clock, a bread oven to its left, and the speaking tubes which were later supplemented by a bell system *(in the hallway)*; the laundry, containing two coppers for boiling washing and a wooden rocker-washer (c1850) but dominated by a late 18C box mangle; the drying room with a large copper warming pan for the floor of a coach.

Cabot Tower ⊙ (AX **Q**) – The slim red tower with a square balcony **(view)** and a white cap was built high upon the hill in 1897 to celebrate the 400th anniversary of the sailing, financed by Bristol merchants, of the navigator **John Cabot** across the Atlantic.

Bristol Guild – *Park Street.* Founded in 1908 by local members of William Morris' Arts and Crafts movement, the Bristol Guild of Applied Art aimed at promoting the works of contemporary British artists and craftsmen. This establishment is now an independent retailer, but remains true to providing quality products with a commercial outlet.

Berkeley Square (AX **Z**) – The handsome square is framed by late 18C terrace houses of ochre stone. John Loudon **McAdam**, Surveyor to the Bristol Turnpike Trust, was living at no 23 when he devised his new method of road surfacing in 1816. The **Cross** at the corner of the green is a 19C replica of the upper section of the former Civic High Cross given to Sir Henry Hoare II and used in the gardens at Stourhead.

Bristol University (AX **U**) – At the top of Park Street sits the **Wills Memorial Building**, a fine example of Neo-Gothic with particularly good sculpture and a city landmark since its completion in 1925. The university was founded in 1876 as the College of Science and Literature, possibly to complement the older Fine Art Academy, later known as the West of England Academy, and the Royal Infirmary which was founded in 1735, one of the earliest provincial hospitals in the United Kingdom. Many of the faculties are accommodated along Woodland Road and in the area of St Michael's Hill (where the city's gallows were situated in medieval times): the oldest building worthy of a mention is the **Royal Fort** (1761) which, according to Pevsner "is one of the finest Georgian houses in Bristol"; opposite is the purpose-built Physics Building (1929) and Library. The **Victoria Rooms** (1839-41), graced with great bronze fountains, marked the now obvious association of Classical architecture with learning and education (reinforced by the École des Beaux Arts in Paris a bit later). The Students' Union is located in Queen's Road near Clifton; **Goldney Hall** (with its unexpected 18C shell grotto) and Clifton Hill House provide accommodation in Clifton; other purpose-built halls of residence are located in Stoke Bishop overlooking the Downs.

Return to Park Street, cross and follow Park Street eastwards to the Red Lodge.

Red Lodge ⊘ (**CY**)– The small entrance gives no indication of the splendours within. The magnificent **Great Oak Room** features its original late 16C **carved panelling** with Italian Renaissance motifs (the American Indians on the **porch** are a reminder of Bristol's trade with America); the imposing fireplace which complements the porch includes alabaster panels personifying Hope, Justice, Charity and Prudence. The pomegranate on the plaster ceiling alludes to the Resurrection; in Classical literature the fruit was associated with Proserpine who returned from the dead. Other rooms – which include a print room, parlour, reception room – feature later styles of decoration and furnishing. Outside, the design for the Tudor **knot garden** was taken from the bedroom ceiling.

Walk back along Park Row, past the Wills Memorial Building.

★ **City Museum and Art Gallery** ⊘ (**AX M**) – The original museum building is in fact next door (1867-71), allegedly designed as a response to Ruskin's high praise of Venetian Gothic.
Limited space and substantial collections of artefacts draws interested amateurs and specialists alike to its galleries. Important study collections of **glass** (pre-Roman; Chinese; Bristol and Nailsea factories; 18C English drinking glasses); **pottery and porcelain** (tin glazed earthenware, hard and soft paste porcelain produced locally; Japanese, Korean and Chinese ware); **silver** (tableware and jewellery); **natural history** (ichthyosaur 'Sea Dragons' and plesiosaur fossils; tableaux of West Country birds, animals, plants, fish, shells and insects; big game); **archeology** of the West Country (4C coins, pewter, tiles); **geology** (specimens of minerals and gemstones with their provenance). The **fine art** collection contains a number of exceptional pieces from the Italian (Taddeo Gaddi, Bernardo Bellotto), 19C French (Delacroix, Courbet, **Vuillard**, Sisley, **Renoir**) and 19C-20C British Schools (Francis **Danby**, **Tissot**, Alma Tadema, Burne-Jones; Winifred Nicholson, Ben Nicholson, Gilbert Spencer, Camden Group). Among the various sculptures (Zadkine, Epstein, Richard Long) is the marvellous terracotta portrait of Edward Colston by **Rysbrack**.
A miscellany of other exhibits includes selections from the Hull-Grundy bequest of **costume jewellery** (of cut steel or Berlin iron, coral, amber, jet, enamel, malachite, seed pearls, fossilised bog oak) and a number of Assyrian and Ancient Egyptian **Antiquities** (sarcophagi and mummies, rare drawings by G Battista Belzoni: 1778-1823).
A series of scale models illustrates the principal locomotives of Brunel's Great Western Railway, maritime history (Poole Collection of 185 Waterline models) and steamships operating from Bristol; in the entrance hall hangs the Bristol Boxkite, one of three models made in Filton, used in the film *Those Magnificent Men in Their Flying Machines* (1963).

★★ CLIFTON (**AX**) *Half a day*

★ **Clifton Village** – The charm of the delightful village, set apart from the bustle of the city, lies in its late 18C and early 19C terrace houses and small shops situated in The Mall, Caledonia Place, Princess Victoria Street, Bellevue, The Paragon (1809-14) and **Royal York Crescent** – begun by William Paty in 1791 and reputedly the longest crescent in Europe: no 2, Eugenie House is named after Empress Eugenie of France who attended a school there. Clifton was incorporated into the city of Bristol in 1835. **Sion Hill**, with its delicate iron balconies and little bow windows is older dating from the 1780s.
Down Hopechapel Hill, beyond Hope Square is Dowry Square: once home to the **Pneumatic Institute** specialising in incurable diseases attended by Humphry Davy (of miner's lamp fame), Peter Roget (of the Thesaurus fame), Coleridge and his fellow poet Southey, the author of *The Three Bears* – both of whom were married at St Mary Redcliffe in 1795.

★★ **Clifton Suspension Bridge** (**AX**) – The 702ft long bridge is amazing, spanning the Avon Gorge like a spider's thread, 245ft above high-water level. It won Brunel the designer's prize in open competition in 1829-31 when he was in his early twenties. (Signed drawings submitted by Brunel for the bridge competition, though not that of the actual bridge as built, may be seen at the GWR Museum in Swindon).

His "first child", "his darling", as he called it, despite "going on glorious" in 1836, suffered long delays and was only completed in 1864, five years after his death. Of countless bridge stories, Sarah Ann Henley's is the happiest: in 1885 a lover's quarrel induced a lover's leap but Sarah Ann's petticoats opened and she parachuted gently down to the mud below – she subsequently married and lived to be 85...

Overlooking the bridge and the gorge is the **Observatory** ⊙, a former windmill which was burnt down and acquired by the landscape painter **William West**. He converted it into a folly in 1829 and installed a *camera obscura* there which he used for his topographical views (several of which are now in the City Art Gallery). 132 steps lead down 190ft to a 200ft long passage and the Giant's Cave: here Roman Catholics used secretly to meet in times of persecution when the only access was up the rock face. Now a balcony provides a **view point**★★ from which to enjoy the bridge and the steep limestone escarpment which provides nesting sites for peregrines and undisturbed habitats for rare plants including the round-headed leek, Bristol rock-cress, spiked speedwell, whitebeam, autumn squill, long stalked orache, dwarf mouse-ear, little robin... The Avon Gorge has attracted naturalists since the 16C.

Take the Hotwell Road through the Avon Gorge for the best view of the bridge. Continue beside the gorge, under the bridge; bear right up Bridge Valley Road.

Clifton Suspension Bridge

Clifton Down (AX) – The steep down was populated by sheep farmers until prosperous merchants came to build substantial residences overlooking the gorge, speculative builders to construct Georgian crescents, Regency squares and terraces and Victorian streets.

In the 18C the area became known through the short-lived Hotwells Spa; in the 19C it acquired fame with the opening of the Suspension Bridge.

Adjacent to the zoo is **Clifton College**, a mid-19C public school built in a Gothic-derived style like other contemporary institutions like Marlborough, Cheltenham, Radley etc..

★★ **Bristol Zoological Gardens** ⊙ (AX) – The famous zoo (opened 1836) features a large selection of animals – from gorillas in their landscaped compound to "Bugworld" – accommodated in various architect-designed houses (Reptile and Ape Houses in particular).

★★ **Clifton R C Cathedral of SS Peter and Paul** ⊙ (AX F) – After three years of construction, the imposing cathedral was consecrated on 29 June 1973 (in place of the 19C pro-cathedral). A white, 165ft, three plane steeple marks the new church: trees and gardens provide a natural contrast to the harsh-sounding materials: white concrete, pink granite agglomerate, black fibreglass, lead and glass.

Inside, the main design motif is the hexagon – elongated to afford a direct view from all sides of the white marble high altar, regular in the flooring, the lanterns, the lights on high, the outline of the organ bay, reduced to a chevron for the flowing stream at the foot of the carved Portland and Purbeck stone font... Warmth and colour are provided by the brown ochre furnishings and wood, and by the limpid blues, greens, greys and jewel reds and yellows in the long, symbolic **windows** of massive glass.

Historic walkways

Perhaps the most picturesque route is to follow the Kennet and Avon Canal towpath from Canon's Marsh behind the cathedral to Keynsham (note the JS Fry chocolate factory that was relocated from the town centre, now Cadbury Schweppes), Bath, Bradford on Avon ...

The area between Bristol and Bath may be further explored on foot or bicycle: the Dramway follows the route taken by Avon and Gloucestershire Railway's horse-drawn tramway (1832) bearing coal from Coalpit Heath near Keynsham to wharves on the River Avon; the Avon Walkway runs some 30 miles from Pill along the river through woodland to Dundas Aqueduct; the Frome Valley is set out as a nature trail starting in Bristol and leading out to Old Sodbury and the Cotswolds Way; the Bristol and Bath Railway Path follows the disused route of the Midland Railway. *Details from the Avon Wildlife Trust, Willsbridge Hill, Bristol BS15 6EX.*

EXCURSIONS

★ **Chew Magna** *Take the A38 south towards Bristol Airport and the B3130.*

Chew Magna was well established by Domesday. In 1546 John Leland, antiquary to Henry VIII, described it as 'a praty clowthing towne' but since then the wool market has moved elsewhere. The straggling main street opens out into a square, which is triangular in shape and bordered by **Harford House** (a pink stone Georgian building), a smaller Georgian town house and a range of cottages, some with white rendering and some of random pink stone.

The 13C-16C church stands back from the road, its pinnacled and gargoyled west tower a proud 99.5ft tall. Inside, the **arcades** have 13C, Early English hexagonal columns *(south)* and 15C Perpendicular columns *(north)*. Note also the fluted Norman **font**; the restored medieval **rood screen**; 15C and 16C recumbents on the tomb chests and, in a niche, a 14C coloured wooden effigy of a knight, smiling benignly as he plants one foot on a surprised, sitting lion (the inscription is Victorian and inaccurate).

At the gate stands **Church House**, a long, early 16C building.

Chew Valley Lake - *4 miles south by B3114.*
The 1 200 acre (4 500 million gallons) reservoir lake lies in a beautiful, drowned valley: it also doubles as a haven for wildfowl.

★ **Stanton Drew Stone Circles** ⊘ - *3 miles east; south of B3130.*
Just before the village bear left down a lane and left again to Court Farm. In a field stand the age-old stones among cows and chestnut trees. The scattered, Bronze Age site consists of **three circles**: the Great Circle, 370ft in diameter with 27 stones in place, 3 of them upright; the Northeast Circle, 100ft in diameter, 8 stones, 4 upright; and the Southwest Circle (on private ground). *Return to the village and bear left, past the church to the Druid's Arms.*

Behind the inn, a group of stones (one fallen and two upright) is known as the **Cove**.

Local legend

Legends connected with the stones abound, the most popular being that "it's a company that assisted at a nuptial ceremony thus petrify'd": the Cove is the parson, the bride and groom, the circles are the company who danced through Saturday and, from midnight, to the tune of a stranger who played ever faster until at dawn the hypnotised dancers turned to stone. The fiddler, the devil in disguise, said he would play again one day to release them but the dancers wait...

★ **Blaise**

★ **Blaise Castle House Museum** ⊘ - *5 miles northwest up A4018 (AX) and B4055.*

The museum is housed in a mansion soberly designed by William Paty of Bristol (1796) for a Quaker banker, and later remodelled by Charles Cockerell; Repton was commissioned to lay out the grounds, complete with grotto, caves, a lover's leap, seat of a giant in complement of the older sham castle of 1766, a Gothick folly fashioned after the Fort Belvedere near Windsor; the Italianate Orangery and Picturesquely English thatched dairy were added by John Nash. The collection illustrates English domestic life in town and country between 1750 and 1900 by way of embroidered waistcoats and Victoriana, dolls, quilted bedcovers, children's and adults' games, bronze wool weights bearing George I's cipher, "dissected" (ie jigsaw) puzzles, a case of Bristol watchmakers' timepieces.

At the far end of the estate, where one set of landscaped grounds folds into those of the **Kings Weston** Estate, there is access to the park, gardens and monumental house designed by John Vanbrugh. This bold, yet engaging, Mannerist complex pile of giant Corinthian pilasters, pedimented portico, vases, arches and large chimney-stacks until recently accommodated a Police Training Centre; today, in the hands of the City Council, its future use remains undecided.

★★ **Blaise Hamlet** – *north side of B4057, Weston Road to Henbury.*
The hamlet was built (1810-12) to house the older servants and tenants of the Blaise Castle estate. Its individually designed nine cottages, which were originally thatched, were designed by John Nash in the cottage *orné* style: Romantic architecture at its most enchanting. Each one is different and stands in its own garden facing the central green; no front door is overlooked by its neighbour; the top-heavy effect of the various chimneys is to provide a picturesque roofline!

BUDE

Cornwall – Population 3 681

Michelin Atlas p 6 or Map 403 – G 31

Bude, a haven in the cliffs standing tall against the incoming Atlantic, offers a popular beach of pale gold sand sheltered by the grass-topped headlands and braided by a long line of beach huts sprucely painted purple, mauve, blue, green... Recently it has become popular with surfers who have bolstered tourism throughout the year; this has also encouraged local shopkeepers to become more adventurous in stocking regional cheeses, cured meats and fish.

★★ **The Breakwater** – At high tide, the breakwater beyond the 19C Bude Canal provides a good view and a close feel of the sea. Background information on the history of Bude and Stratton, the canal and its incline plane, is given in the local **museum** ⊙.

Compass Point – *Access by footpath (30min) from the end of Breakwater Road.* From the point, named after the octagonal waymark tower (with out-of-true bearings), there are spectacular **views**★ along the 200-450ft cliffs, marked by offshore reefs. To the south the vista stretches right round the white-sanded Widemouth Bay.

EXCURSIONS

This corner of north Cornwall has many villages with compact granite churches containing robustly carved medieval bench-ends, Norman fonts and brass and slate memorials. The reason for such a number rests on the fact that pilgrims would travel through the area, having crossed from Wales and landed at Clovelly, on southwards through **Morwenstow**, **Kilkhampton**, **Jacobstow**, **Boscastle**, Trevalga – all with churches dedicated to the patron saint of pilgrims St James de Compostella – to Fowey, before embarking on ships that sailed for Northern Spain. Two groups, one to the north, one to the south of Bude, are listed below.

① **Round tour starting from Bude** *22 miles. Leave Bude by A3072.*

Stratton – Stratton is an old market town which was once a port. The **church**★ was built by stages. The north arcade of sea-green-grey Polyphant stone (1348) was followed by the pinnacled **tower** (90ft) – once a landmark – and by the granite south arcade in the mid-15C. The chancel dates from 1544. The font bowl is Norman, the pulpit Jacobean, the bench-ends medieval, the **royal arms** restyled Stuart-Hanoverian; the east window is by **Burne-Jones**. In the porch is the old door to Stratton prison (the clink).

Continue along A3072; bear left at the first turning.

Launcells – The 15C **church**★ stands in a wooded valley, the tall pinnacles of its 54ft tower surpassing the trees. Inside, the arcades are of Polyphant stone and granite, the **chancel** is paved with rare 15C Barnstaple encaustic tiles designed with fleurs-de-lis, Tudor roses, lions, pelicans, flowers. Note especially the 15C **bench-ends**, 60 in all, carved with the Crown of Thorns, the Harrowing of Hell, the empty tomb...

Continue along A3072 for Holsworthy.

Holsworthy – The Devon town, with a lively pannier market (Wednesday), centres on the **square** which is lined by colour-washed and half-timbered shops and pubs. Streets lead off at the corners to the church with a tall ashlar tower and downhill to an old mill.

Return to Launcells and turn right into B3254.

Kilkhampton - The village must have been an important town in Saxon times, situated as it is on the Ridgeway and surrounded by the scarred sites of ancient camps and burial grounds. This is reinforced by the fact that the Manors of Bideford and Kilkhampton were awarded to Robert Fitz Hamon (the subsequent founder of Tewkesbury) by William Rufus in recognition of his support during Odo's revolt (1088); in turn these territories passed to his brother Sir Richard de Granville, who founded the church in Bideford. The elegantly tall Perpendicular **church**★ with its 90ft embattled and pinnacled granite **tower** was rebuilt on a Norman site in 1485 - of the original building little re-

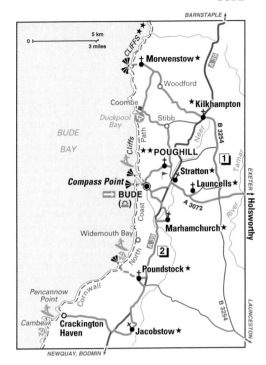

mains other than the Norman **south door** with three orders, zig-zag and beaked bird decoration. Inside, of the 157 carved **bench-ends** two of the finest date from 1380; the remarkable **monuments** sculpted in wood, stone and slate are by **Michael Chuke** (1679-1742), a Kilkhampton boy sent to London as a pupil to Grinling Gibbons.

By way of cross-country by-roads (Burridge, Woodford) make for the coast.

Morwenstow - Morwenstow was the parish of **Parson Hawker**, poet and preacher, who "lived a life made up of eccentricities", travelling this corner of his beloved Cornwall from 1834-75 in purple frock coat, white cravat, fisherman's jersey and boots, rescuing shipwrecked sailors and giving Christian burial to the drowned.

The **church**★, which stands in a dell, the pinnacled and embattled tower a landmark to those at sea, was referred to as 'ancient' in a document of 1296. It has a Norman **south door** with zig-zag moulding on small columns, two interior **arcades**, one with Norman and Early English piers supporting an arch with chevron, ball and headed orders and at the base an antelope and other animal masks. Beneath the original bossaged wagon roofs are a Saxon **font** with cable moulding of *c*800 and mid-16C bench-ends.

The spectacular **cliffs**★★ (450ft high) reach out to offshore rocks.

Take the by-road south to Coombe; turn inland to Stibb then right.

★ **Poughill** - For centuries the kernel of Poughill (pronounced Poffil) has been St Olaf's Church and Church House (opposite) which dates from 1525.

The **church**★★, a Norman foundation, has a 14C Perpendicular granite tower, square and embattled with crocket pinnacles. Inside, two arcades, one 14C sandstone and tall, the other 15C, granite and short, march beneath late 15C wagon roofs with carved bosses. On the walls two medieval St Christopher frescoes were graphically repainted by Frank Salisbury in the 1920s; the **royal arms**, incorrectly dated 1655, are of Charles II. The deeply carved, oak **bench-ends** (nearly all late 15C) are polished each Epiphany to dark translucence with elbow grease, linseed oil and melted down candle-ends from Christmas - note Jonah and the Whale, Biblical and local characters.

Continue south to Bude.

② **Bude to Crackington Haven**

12 miles. Leave Bude by A3073 going south.

Marhamchurch - Stone houses with slate or thatched roofs stand round St Morwenne's **church**★ (14C-15C) with its square tower abutted by a staircase turret. Of interest in the single arcade interior beneath the old wagon roofs are the oak door with its **sanctuary knocker**, the Jacobean **pulpit** with a sounding board, the **royal arms** by Michael Chuke *(see* Kilkhampton *above)* and, in the west wall, the window of a 15C anchorite's cell.

Join A39 and drive south.

★ **Poundstock** – Church, lychgate and unique guildhouse form a secluded group in a wooded dell. The 13C-15C **church**★ with a square unbuttressed tower was restored in the 19C. It retains a nail-studded **south door**, a Jacobean **communion table** *(back of nave)* and pulpit, a square granite **font** (1300), an early 16C oak chest, 17C **slate memorials**, wall paintings, the Trebarfoote **wall monument** *(behind font)* depicting a dapper man in Stuart dress with flowing moustaches.
The **guildhouse**★, sturdily built in the 14C, probably as quarters for the masons constructing the church, passed to the parish guilds as a place of meeting and festivity until such revelries were suppressed by the Puritans; it has also served as a poorhouse and a school. Of cob and stone on two floors with buttresses, wooden mullions and a slate roof over stout timbers, the guildhouse stands as an example of once-common, non-secular building.
One mile west is the Atlantic, pounding the 400ft high cliffs from which the **view**★★ extends south to Trevose Head and north even to Lundy.

Return to A39; continue south for 1 mile; bear left.

Jacobstow – The 15C **church**★ stands in a hollow, its pinnacled granite tower emerging from the trees. A granite **porch** leads to the earlier nave and aisles. The 12C **font** is carved with faces at the angles; the pulpit was made from bench-ends.

Rejoin A39, immediately bearing right into the by-road to the coast.

Crackington Haven – A wide, lush valley leads down to the resort village and dark sand beach. On either side the headlands rise hundreds of feet out of the sea.

CAMBORNE – REDRUTH

Cornwall – Population 31 311

Michelin Atlas p 2 or Map 403 – E 33

The continuous conurbation which lines the main road (A3047) west to east comprises two towns, Camborne and Redruth, and the important mining settlement of Pool and Tuckingmill: at the height of the productive mining period, the area became highly prosperous; since the closure of the mines it has become run down with high unemployment. The abandoned mines serve an awful reminder of hardship and social deprivation. Now it is time to regenerate the local community and surrounding land, and to preserve the technological innovations of 1800-1850 before it is too late. To this end local district and county councils, aided by government funding, have secured large parts of the neighbouring countryside which, with its striking industrial monuments, provides ideal habitats for wildlife and scope for exploration via footpaths, cycle routes and bridle-ways.

Camborne – The oldest community aligned along the main road is marked by 18C-19C houses and backstreets made up of miners' terraced housing, the Tuscan-style granite Literary Institute (1829) and a rambling half-timbered inn, once a posting house. Among the several Methodist chapels sits a 15C granite church with a distinctive west tower, containing an inscribed 10C Saxon stone **altar slab** (originally from Chapel Ia in Troon), a marble reredos (1761) and 18C chandeliers.

Tuckingmill – This settlement around the Bickford Smith fuse factory became the world capital for the production of safety fuses, invented by **William Bickford** in 1830, and broadly used in many Hollywood films and *Mission Impossible* as dynamite fuses. The last fuseworks closed in the 1960s.

Pool – The middle town is distinguished by past and present mining landmarks
Mineral Tramways Discovery Centre ⊘ – This provides a central and highly accessible reference point for information about the area and the efforts being made to develop a network of off-road trails to link the various industrial sites. It outlines a history of the old mineral tramways which were built to transport copper ore from the mines to the ports of Portreath, Hayle and Devoran for export to the copper smelters in South Wales, and to return with supplies of imported coal to fuel the steam-driven beam engines and timber (scarce in Cornwall after the 17C),for use in the mines and the new housing being built.

Mineral tramways – The **Portreath Tramroad**, built in 1812 and active until the 1860s was the first surface tramroad in Cornwall serviced by horse-drawn vehicles; the **Redruth to Chasewater Railway** (1825-1915) converted from horse-power to steam in 1854: separated by a short distance, it is proposed to link these routes to provide a coast-to-coast trail. The **Hayle Railway Network** was incorporated via the

West Cornwall Railway system into the Great Western Railway; its Portreath and Tresavean lines, part of the mineral tramways network, were always steam-powered.

Cornish Industrial Heritage Centre ⓥ – This information centre, accommodated in the old compressor house and winding engine house at **Taylor's Shaft**, is intended to provide a comprehensive introduction to Cornwall's history, natural history and industrial history. Displays are presented in various formats (audio-visual, Braille) and addressed to children, interested amateurs and specialists alike.

Taylor's Shaft is the largest pump engine left in Cornwall; this 90in pump engine with a 52-ton beam and 7.5ft diameter cylinder, exemplifies the use of high pressure steam, patented in 1802 by Richard Trevithick (1771-1883), one of the great Cornish engineers and "father of the locomotive engine".

East Pool Whim ⓥ – **Mitchell's Winder** rotative beam engine (the last to be built in Camborne and installed in a Cornish mine in 1887) was used for bringing ore to the surface from a depth of over 1 600ft. The cylinder is 30in in diameter; the piston is 9ft in length; the engine runs at 17 revolutions per minute. Today it is powered by an electrical motor.

Whim refers to the winch or winding device powered by horse, water or steam, used to haul ore and men up the mine shaft. Its objective was to be as economical as possible: it therefore comprises a double-acting engine with steam applied at the top then the bottom sides of the piston before being driven into a condenser rather than being expelled into the atmosphere.

Camborne School of Mines – Much of the driving force behind providing specialist education to Cornish tin miners stemmed from the energy of Robert Hunt and it is to his memory that a **museum of minerals** ⓥ was instigated at the world-famous Mining School established at Camborne in 1887. In 1909, the school was amalgamated with similar establishments at Redruth and Penzance, thereby also benefiting from additional reference material. Today, the school, under the auspices of the University of Exeter Cornwall College, boasts an extensive collection of geological specimens from the UK and abroad.

Redruth – The most easterly town, like Camborne, was almost entirely dependent on mining for its prosperity; its main street is punctuated by Nonconformist chapels and a granite clock tower. It was here that **Richard Murdoch**, a Scottish-born inventor, first pioneered and equipped his home in Cross Street with coal gas-fired lighting.

Carn Brea – *1.5 miles southwest of Redruth and 500yds south of Carnbrea or Brea village – last 150yds up a field track.*

Crowning the 740ft, boulder-strewn hilltop is a 90ft granite **monument** (1836): a landmark for miles around, marking a remarkable **viewpoint★★** over the length and breadth of Cornwall. The monument and the ruins of a 15C castle (now a restaurant) – probably built as a hunting lodge by the Bassets of Tehidy, a wealthy land-owning family with major interests in local mining – lie within the rubble ramparts of a massive Neolithic hillfort covering over 40 acres.

Marriott's Shaft, Basset Mines

To the south stretches the **Great Flat Lode**, perhaps one of the best examples of a surviving mining landscape punctuated by a substantial number of buildings associated with the Basset, Grenville and Condurrow mines, including King Edward training mine.

Gwennap Pit – *1 mile southeast of Redruth, off A393.*
The Pit is a natural amphitheatre originally formed by the subsidence of an old mine-shaft. In the mid-18C, when Revivalism was strong in the West Country, it was the setting for meetings numbering as many as 30 000 miners and their families on the 18 occasions when **John Wesley** came to preach between 1762-89. In 1805-06 the amphitheatre was remodelled to its present 12 grass tiers; each Spring Bank Holiday it is the scene of a Wesleyan revival meeting *(see also Carn Brea chapel).*

★ **Poldark Mine, Wendron** ⊙ – *7 miles south of Redruth on B3297.*
One mine among the 50 in production from the 15C-20C in the Wendron district has been reopened to allow visitors to see the underground workings and 18C-19C machinery in place. To entertain young families, there are a number of additional facilities in the open and under cover: play areas, computer games, remote-controlled boats, steam locomotives, traction and beam engines...
Mine tunnels – *Safety helmets provided must be worn. No smoking underground.*
A series of metal stairways leads down into the mine shafts that have been excavated to 150ft below ground; water drips down through the rock smoothed by the action of innumerable loaded buckets being heaved to the surface. Twelve marked viewpoints indicate bright blue chloride "lodes" or a seam in the roof, an access-ventilation shaft of 1730, exposed tin lodes. An underground postbox provides a service from the depths of the earth opposite a tableau highlighting the working conditions of the men at the seam, many of whom started work underground at the age of nine and died from malnutrition before the age of 35.
Museum – Luminous mineral deposits, rock drills, a stamping machine, water-wheel and a collection of models illustrating the differences between the various Cornish beam engines relate to the mining industry: atmospheric recreations of life as a miner; collections of dated electrical gadgets such as flat irons.

CHARD

Somerset – Population 10 770

Michelin Atlas p 7 or Map 403 – L 31

The town has long been known as a market centre: for tanning in the 13C, woo cloth in the 15C, coarse linens, cloths and serges for the East India Co in the 17C-18C, lace early in the 19C and now engineering, food processing, textiles and animal feed. The local foundry was renowned for agricultural machinery and iron tombstones typical of those found in the vicinity.
Market day: Saturday all day.

St Mary the Virgin – The church stands in the oldest part of town; local wealth in the 15C-16C is reflected in the Somerset tracery, battlements and pinnacles of the tower.

Fore Street and High Street – The town's prosperity in the 17C-19C is reflected in several substantial buildings: the town hall (1834) with a two-storey portico, the **George Hotel**, the Elizabethan **Manor Court House**, Waterloo House and the Grammar School *(east end, north side),* founded in 1671 in a house built in 1583.
★ **Museum** ⊙ – *Godworthy House, High Street.* Local history centres on lacemaking and the "lace workers riot" of 1842; on **John Stringfellow** (1799-1883), who in 1848 pioneered powered flight following experiments on gliding models and light steam engines with inventor William S Henson (1812-88); on **artificial limbs** which were the creation of local man James Gillingham. Treasures include a facsimile of the Gough map of England and Wales (*c*1360), 17C **embroidery** (*petit point* and stumpwork), a cider mill and press, a **costume gallery** (19C dresses), an old kitchen, toys and puppet theatres. A "Touch-n-handle" table is designed for children. **Net lace-making machines**, farm and road-making machinery made by Chard-based manufacturers, and a recreated early garage are housed in the modern annexe.

EXCURSIONS

Cricket St Thomas

Wildlife Park ⊙ – *3 miles east by A30.* The wildlife and leisure park lies amid the rolling south Somerset countryside, extending along the banks of a tributary of the River Axe and up towards Windwhistle Hill. Its popularity can make it crowded in season.

House, church and gardens – The handsome early 19C colonnaded house *(private)* and the small church are fronted on the river side by trees, tall dark hedges and colourful flower gardens.

Birds and animals – The animals – elephants, big cats, monkeys, deer, wallabies, llamas (the females produce 6.5-9lbs of wool a year), sheep, camels, wapiti and performing sea-lions, otters, birds and reptiles are in enclosures in the house and church area, in the old walled vegetable garden and in large paddocks on either side of the stream. Cows from the home farm are milked each afternoon in the **milking parlour** off the walled garden *(enquire as to time)*.

There is also a **Heavy Horse Centre** with working shires, a **miniature railway**, a tropical aviary, a Craft Centre with working blacksmith, woodturner and potter, a rare breeds farm, an adventure trail, jungle safari rides, a children's playground, a 'Victorian' Shopping Arcade with an original merry-go-round, restaurants, a pub... Special events are held throughout the year.

Crewkerne

The town centres on the wide Market Street and the **Market Square** (market day: Wednesday all day), overlooked by the Jacobean-style Victorian Hall and Georgian houses.

The **parish church★** is a Perpendicular rebuilding with immense windows of an older church. At the time of rebuilding, the substantial piers at the crossing were kept to support a new 80ft tower which includes Somerset traceried bell openings extending through two stages to gargoyles, pinnacles and a pinnacled stair-turret. Battlements and gargoyles appear along the main rooflines and gargoyles in close frills around the twin **octagonal turrets** which mark the west front.

Inside, the piers are tall and slim beneath a wagon roof with angel figures while the north transept and chapel have rich panelled ceilings. Beneath the tower there is a fan vault. Note at the west end the early 19C galleries, the square Purbeck marble font which is Norman and in the chancel *(south wall)*, a brass to the knight Thomas Golde at prayer in 1525.

★ **Clapton Court** *11 miles east by A30 and B3165.*

Gardens ⊘ – The ten acre garden comprises formal terraces, spacious lawns, a rockery, rose and water gardens and a woodland garden with natural streams and glades. Clapton Court is a garden for all seasons, providing blooms throughout the spring and summer and rich autumn colour.

★ **Forde Abbey** ⊘ *4 miles southeast on south bank of the River Axe. 45min.*

The abbey is a synthesis of three major building phases and stands in a garden which has taken owner-gardeners three centuries, notably the 20C, to perfect. The 12C Cistercian monastery was still very much under construction under its 32nd abbot, **Thomas Chard**, when it was dissolved in 1539; the following century of neglect ended in 1649 when the estate was bought by **Sir Edmund Prideaux**, Cromwell's Attorney-General. In the next seven years he saved, knocked down and rebuilt Forde Abbey until it looked much as it does now. The abbey was acquired by the present family in the 19C.

The remoteness of the site very much appealed to a series of writers, notably Wordsworth, who sojourned in Marshwood Vale with his sister at a country house owned by the Pinneys of Bristol, Jane Austen and Thomas Hardy.

Exterior – The range extends from west to east with the main entrance at the centre beneath the Perpendicular **tower;** to the left lies the **Great Hall** with its tall windows; beyond were the abbot's lodgings, remodelled by Prideaux in the 17C when he also castellated the front. Right of the entrance lay the cloisters of which the north gallery remains, now glazed and surmounted by an upper storey; between the tower and cloister gallery Prideaux inserted, on the site of the west cloister, a loggiaed and balconied two-storey block where he placed his **saloon.** On the far right is the **chapel.**

Note the 16C tower's **two-storey oriel** with its mullioned and transomed windows and friezes matching those above the Great Hall.

Interior – The fan vault visible from just inside the entrance remains unfinished as at the Dissolution. The **Great Hall** has its original panelled ceiling but has lost its early proportions, the west end having been walled off in the 17C to create a separate dining room. Furnishings include an oak refectory table (1947), the royal arms, an 18C chandelier, 16C-17C chairs.

The **Grand Staircase** is spectacular, having an enriched plaster ceiling (1658) and a carved banister, a mirror image of which has been painted on the surrounding walls.

The **Saloon** has an ornamental ceiling, moulded with fruit and flower garlands, small pendants and the Prideaux arms enriched with gold. The side panels portray *The Slaying of Abel* and *The Sacrifice of Isaac* with everyone in

Commonwealth dress. The **Mortlake tapestries** are woven after the Raphael Cartoons (intended for the Sistine Chapel and now in the Victoria and Albert Museum, London).

The **Library** occupies the second refectory which was added in the 15C when the Cistercian order was permitted to eat meat; as not all the monks approved the concession, the community had two refectories. Note the recess for the reader's desk, and the 15C roof; the 19C Gothick windows and fireplace and the end screen made out of Breton box-bedsteads.

The **Monks' Dormitory** range, above an 11-bay undercroft, is 160ft long with lancets along the outer wall. It was divided down the centre in the 19C when it was also given a new vaulted ceiling. The gun is an 18C French pinnace gun.

Back at ground level, the former chapter house, remodelled most vigorously in the 17C, now serves as the **Chapel** complete with Norman rib vaulting, round columns and scallop capitals.

★ Ilminster

The word "Minster" originally alluded to a hedged or stockaded piece of land given by a Saxon king to a group of clerics. Here, in the days before regions were subdivided into parishes, they would build accommodation for themselves, a church from which to preach the Gospel and a school where they might train young boys to follow in their footsteps.

The Ham stone town on the south side of the London-Exeter road (A303) originated in Saxon times, was listed in Domesday as possessing both a minster and a market; it grew to prosperity in the 15C-16C on wool – Ilminster being named cloth. New houses were built, old houses refronted in Georgian times, the town's well-being depending, as it still does, on being at the heart of some of England's best agricultural land, both dairy and arable.

R. Besse/MICHELIN

The Minster, Ilminster

Market day: Thursday morning.

★★ **Minster** – The climax of St Mary's late exterior is its 90ft **crossing tower**, modelled on that of Wells Cathedral, and guarded by four angels on the chancel roof. It rises through two stages of bell openings – paired and three abreast with intervening shafts, transoms, tracery and Somerset tracery; up to a crest of gargoyles, fountains of pinnacles and a spirelet on the stair turret. The 15C Perpendicular building consisted initially of a simple nave, transepts, chancel and tower; the aisles were added in the 16C. The main body of the church underwent considerable alterations in 1824-25 when the nave and aisle roofs were raised so that galleries could be introduced to accommodate ever larger congregations.

Inside the main space is covered with a tie-beam and king-post **roof**; **fan vaults** are inserted at the crossing and St Catherine's Chapel, more commonly known as the **Wadham Chapel** (north transept) – this remarkable "glass lantern" was built in 1452 to contain the **tomb chests** (inlaid on the lids with large brasses) of Sir William Wadham (d 1452), and Nicholas (d 1618) who founded Wadham College, Oxford. Note the four splendid 18C brass **candelabra** which are lit at Christmas for Midnight Mass.

Market Square – The square is characterised at its centre by the single-storeyed Market House, open on all sides and last rebuilt in 1819.

For Tintinhull and Montacute, see YEOVIL; *for Barrington Court, East Lambrook Manor and Martock see* SOMERTON.

CHEDDAR GORGE★★

Somerset

Michelin Atlas p 16 or Map 403 – L 30

The "deep, frightful chasm in the mountain, in the hollow of which the road goes", as Defoe described it in the 18C, has been a tourist sight since the 17C.

★★ **Gorge** – *2 miles, 1:6 gradient – car and coach parks near the bottom.* The gorge, which is best approached from the east end, descends from the Mendip Hills, twisting and turning between limestone cliffs which are lush with greenery or gaunt and grey where the fissured walls and pinnacles rise vertically (350-400ft). The rift is probably a dry river-bed; the Romans seem to have exported lead from the Mendip Hills, transporting it by barge from quays in Cheddar down the Yeo and the Axe to Uphill on Severn and from there to Italy.

Jacob's Ladder ⓥ – From almost the foot of the gorge a staircase *(274 steps; rest benches)* leads up to the plateau level from which there is a panoramic **view**★ of the Mendips, the Somerset moors and the Quantocks.

★ **Cheddar Showcaves** ⓥ – *2 hours.* The caves are near the gorge bottom on the south side *(left going down).* Cox's Cave was discovered in 1837 by George Cox when quarrying limestone, Gough's Cave in 1890 by Richard Cox Gough. Both caves were opened to the public soon after their discovery.

A series of chambers follows the course of underground streams through the porous limestone; the formations increase by 1 cubic inch in every 400 years.

Cheddar Gorge

In **Gough's Cave**, the stalagmites and stalactites, the lace curtains, frozen falls and pillars coloured by the minerals in the limestone are each a different, glistening hue from white to alabaster, amber, rust-red (iron), green (manganese) and grey (lead). Among the fancifully named, but nonetheless beautiful formations are the nine-tier Fonts, the Swiss Village and Aladdin's Cave, both with mirror pools, King Solomon's Temple with its stalagmite cascade and the blue-spotlighted Black Cat – the only feature in the caves not lit with a white light. Among the formations of note in **Cox's Cave** are the Transformation Scene, the Marble Curtain, the ringing stalactites known as the Peal of Bells, and the Speaker's Mace. The **Fantasy Grotto** contains an assortment of fountains, coloured lights, melodramatic moving models and a hologram display.

Heritage Centre – Weapons, utensils in flint, bone and antler horn, iron and bronze, pottery and the skull of Cheddar Man indicate that the caves were inhabited intermittently from the Paleolithic to the Iron Age – 20 000-500 BC – and even in Roman times.

Cheddar – The village, which extends from the foot of the gorge to the parish church at the south end of the main street, gave its name to the English national cheese: in 1170 Henry II bought 80cwt of Cheddar declaring it the "best cheese in England".

Hannah More (1745-1835), writer and philanthropist who spent her later life improving the physical and mental welfare of the people of the Mendips, opened her first school in a cottage in Venns Close in the centre of the village.

Market Cross – The cross was originally a preacher's cross round which a hexagonal colonnade was built in the 16C converting it into a small covered market; travelling merchants paid rent to sit under cover.

★ **St Andrew's** – The Perpendicular church, the fourth on the site, dates from 1380-1480. The typical Somerset **tower** rises 110ft through four stages from a west door and window, flanked by carved heads believed to be those of Henry IV and his queen (1367-1413), to a pierced and pinnacled parapet and a staircase turret with a spirelet roof; the east and west faces of the tower are marked with the figure of St Andrew and *The Annunciation*.

Inside, the coffered **oak roofs** on arch braces are supported on **corbels** carved with kings' and bishops' heads – possibly an allusion to Mendip Forest having been a royal manor until sold by King John in 1204 to Hugh, Archdeacon of Wells, who, in turn, passed it to his brother Jocelin, Bishop of Bath and Wells. Othe fine woodwork is to be found in the choir stalls, bench ends (especially in the north aisle) and nave front pews. Among the furnishings are an early 14C **font** with a Jacobean cover, a 15C stone **pulpit** coloured as in medieval times, an **altar-table** of 1631, the tombchest and large brasses of Sir Thomas Cheddar and his wife (dd 1442, 1474) and, in the 15C Fitzwalter Chantry *(off south aisle)*, a pre-Reformation **altar-stone** and a painting of *The Last Supper* by Jan Erasmus Quellinus of Antwerp (1629-1715).

EXCURSIONS

★★ **Axbridge** *3 miles east; bear left off the by-pass (A371).*

The Cheddar road leads directly into the irregular Square, used since Saxon times as the market place and now ringed by tall 17C-18C houses, the pedimented, early 19C town hall, several 18C refronted pubs of earlier vintage and, on the far corner, two half-timbered houses with oversailing upper floors – the legacy of highly prosperous medieval wool and cloth merchants who specialized in knitting stockings.

More recently the town's prosperity has been linked, in part, to strawberries – the surrounding area is known for the quality of the fruits it produces.

★ **King John's Hunting Lodge** ⊙ – The house, an example of a timber framed building, dates from the late 15C but the name is purely notional; it derives from the fact that the Mendip Forest was once a royal hunt and the town's first royal charter was granted by King John. The king's head carving outside, at the angle, probably dates from the 17C-18C when the building was the King's Head Alehouse. The lodge is now a **museum** with exhibits including a "nail" (like those outside the Corn Exchange in Bristol) and two early mayoral maces.

The house is most interesting, however, for the revelation inside of its structure. It stands on a stone sill from which it rises through a ground floor, once an open arcade of shops, to upper living and bedroom floors and, finally, an open timber roof of collar beams, wind braces and rafters made from trees from the onetime royal forests.

Note the all-important **corner post**, the wall plates, peg-holes and slots, wattle and daub partition walls, panelling, the original windows and doorways and the 15C staircase with oak stairtreads round a slim, one-piece **newel**, where the 500 year-old carpenters' adze marks remain visible on the beams.

★ **St John the Baptist** – The church, on a mound on the north side of the square, was rebuilt in the Perpendicular style at the height of the town's prosperity in the early 15C: aisles, nave and transepts were built tall with wide windows, the crossing tower was raised to three stages and crowned with a pierced parapet and pinnacles.

Inside, through the notable **south porch**, the eye is immediately attracted to the nave **ceiling** – a rare example in a church of the moulded plasterwork which decorates the great houses of the early 17C: George Drayton, a local craftsman, was paid ten guineas for the roof in 1636. In contrast to the snowflake pattern, the crossing is fan vaulted; the enamelled wrought-ironwork was bought in Bristol in 1729 at a cost of 21 guineas.

Also of interest are the mid-15C **font** with its circle of carved angels, hidden during the Commonwealth in a plaster casing and only rediscovered centuries later when a sexton, waiting for a baptism, idly picked away some of the cracked plaster; the charity **bread cupboard** where loaves are placed every Saturday in accordance with the 1688 Will of William Spearing *(west of south door)*; the brass to Roger Harper (d 1493) and his wife *(south chapel)*; the **altar frontal** of 1710 embroidered with contemporary altar furnishings.

Town Hall – The balconied building on the south side of the square dates from 1833. Inside, artefacts relating to bull-baiting, which occurred here right up to the 19C, are on show.

Chewton Mendip *8 miles east by B3135 and north by A39.*

Chewton Cheese Dairy ⊙ – Traditional methods are still used by this Cheddar cheese producer: from the corner of the dairy or from the restaurant above, visitors can watch the cheese-making process: filling the vat with milk, starter and rennet, curd cutting, pressing and bandaging the cheese truckles. Work begins at 7.30am and continues until 3pm.

Chewton Priory retains the name of the former Benedictine abbey it replaces, which was given to Sir Edward Waldegrave by Mary I in 1553.

Somerset vineyards

Vines have been grown in Britain since Roman times. Once the domain of monasteries and royal courtiers, the marriage of Henry II to Eleanor of Aquitaine boosted a trade in wines from Bordeaux and damaged the home industry; the Black Death and the Dissolution brought further devastation. Since World War II, interest in viticulture has been consistently growing. The grape varieties that are best suited to these northern latitudes tend to be those grown in Germany which produce a fresh, crisp flavoured wine: these include Müller Thurgau, Seyval (a French hybrid), Reichensteiner, Bacchus, Schönburger, Madeleine Angevine, Huxelrebe…

Those wineries which are open to the public include **Moorlynch Vineyard** at Bridgwater (shop and visitor centre, restaurant in season. ☎ 01458 210 393); **Staplecombe Vineyards** outside Taunton (vineyard walk, winery. ☎ 01823 451 217); **Wootton Vineyard**, outside Shepton Mallet, makes white wines and *eau-de-vie* (☎ 01749 890 359). Other names to look out for: Avalon Vineyard, Bagborough Vineyard, Whatley Vineyard: for more detailed information contact the Somerset Visitor Centre on ☎ 01934 750 833.

CHIPPENHAM

Wiltshire – Population 25 376
Michelin Atlas p 17 or Map 403 – N 29

People have come to Chippenham, the first settlement at the bend in the River Avon, since Saxon times to trade; initially by packhorse and then from 1474 along Maud Heath's Causeway; since 1837 by the railway steaming west along the high striding viaduct, and nowadays by way of main roads and the M4 motorway. At the top end of the town stand the church, a street of houses of every degree and age, and the half-timbered town hall.

★ **Yelde Hall** ⊙ – The 15C timber-framed hall in the Market Place, near to which once stood the local gallows, pillory, stocks and whipping post, served as the office of the bailiff and burgesses of the Hundred (the collection of villages dependent upon Chippenham in the Middle Ages). Inside are a panelled courtroom over a blind-house or lock-up and adjoining, beneath an open timber roof, the old town hall. Items on display relate to the social history of the area.

St Andrew's – The many times remodelled Perpendicular church stands on the site of the Saxon church in which Alfred's sister, Aethelswitha, married the King of Mercia in AD 853. Inside, note the flatly **carved effigy** of a beautiful, mysterious 13C woman *(south chapel)*, the 13C **vestment chest** with bird and animal carved panels and the outstanding 1730s oak **organ case**, pedimented, turreted, intricately carved and surmounted by trumpet-blowing angels.

St Mary's Street – The long street behind the church is lined with cottages, terrace and large town houses, timber-framed, small windowed and low-lying, or tall and ashlar-faced with graceful doors and windows, pediments and parapets.

Maud Heath's Causeway – Maud Heath, 15C widow, farmer's wife or spinster property owner, no one knows, left houses and land in the town for the construction and, most importantly, the maintenance of a causeway so that local producers could come to market dryshod. The 4.5 mile long pathway still exists, running from Wick Hill, where an inscribed stone and 19C pillar crowned by a statue of Maud Heath mark the start, through East Tytherton, Kellaways and Langley Burrell to the former outskirts of the town. A 1698 end stone is now in Barclays Bank in the Market Place; a film-strip about the causeway may be seen in the Yelde Hall *(see above)*.

EXCURSIONS

★★ Corsham Court

Corsham Court, an Elizabethan house of 1582, was bought by Paul Methuen in the mid-18C to house, in due grandeur, a collection he was to inherit of 16C and 17C Italian and 17C Flemish **master paintings and statuary**. At the end of the 19C the house was enlarged to receive a second collection, purchased in Florence at the end of the Napoleonic Empire, principally of fashionable Italian masters, rare Italian primitives and stone-inlaid furniture.

Paul Methuen (1732-95) was a great-grandson of Paul Methuen (d 1667) of Bradford-on-Avon and a grandson of John Methuen (1650-1706), ambassador and negotiator of the **Methuen Treaty** of 1703 with Portugal – a treaty which gave the United Kingdom its "oldest ally", permitted the export (formerly prohibited) of British woollens to Portugal and allowed a preferential 33.3% duty discount on imported Portuguese wines – so bringing about a major change in English drinking habits. Field Marshal Lord Methuen (1845-1932), who became famous in the wars in Africa against the Ashanti and the Boers, was the father of 4th baron, Paul Methuen (1886-1974) the painter.

The architects involved in the alterations to the house and park were successively **Lancelot "Capability" Brown** in the 1760s, **John Nash** in 1800 and Thomas Bellamy in 1845-49.

Brown set the style by retaining the Elizabethan stables and riding school (now occupied by the Bath Academy of Art) but rebuilding the gateway, retaining the great, gabled, Elizabethan stone front and doubling the gabled wings at either end and, inside, by designing the east wing as stateroom-picture galleries... He planned the park to include a lake, avenues and specimen trees such as the Oriental Plane, now with a 200yd circumference.

Nash's work, apart from embellishments such as the octagonal corner towers and pinnacles, has largely disappeared; Bellamy's stands fast, notably in the hall and staircase.

House ⊙ – *30min*. Four state rooms, music and dining rooms provide the setting for the outstanding collection of over 150 paintings, statuary, bronzes and furniture.

The elegant triple cube **Picture Gallery** (72 × 24 × 24ft) is hung with crimson Spitalfields damask, the same that is used to upholster the Chippendale furniture; pier-glasses and tables by the Adam brothers, the girandoles attributed to Chippendale and the white marble fireplace reinforce the air of splendour. Among the glorious paintings are works by Fra Bartolomeo, **Caravaggio** *(Tobias and the Angel)*, Guido **Reni**, Strozzi, Salvator Rosa, **Tintoretto** *(Adoration of the Shepherds)*, **Veronese** *(Annunciation)*, **Rubens** *(Wolf Hunt)*, **Van Dyck** *(Christ's Betrayal)* and by Sofonisba – a portrait of the *Three Caddi Children*.

In the **Cabinet Room** hang **Fra Filippo Lippi's** *Annunciation* (1463) and Cesari's cartoon of a *Flying Cherub*; the side tables with porphyry tops are attributed to Chippendale, the pier-glasses are by Adam and the inlaid commode and torchères by the cabinet maker James Cobb.

The **State Bedroom** is dominated by Chippendale's four-poster bed and serpentine mahogany chests; the oval mirrors framed with vines and bushy-tailed squirrels are by Thomas Johnson; the 18C bracket clock is Italian. Note also the games table and two pictures: the *Infant Christ* by Guercino and the *Duke of Monmouth* by Lely. The most striking feature of the **Octagon Room**, designed by Nash in 1800, is **Michelangelo's** *Sleeping Cupid* (1496), surrounded as it is with paintings by **Claude**, **Bruegel the Elder**, a Caracci self-portrait and an extraordinary allegorical portrait of *Queen Elizabeth* as a seated old woman with death close by and cherubs bearing off the emblems of sovereignty.

The **Music Room** is furnished with a pianoforte (1807) made by Clementi, an aeolian organ and harps; Regency chairs made of mahogany complement a horseshoe-shaped winetable with a hinged coaster.

The showcase, topped by 19C medicine chests, contains porcelain from Derby, Rockingham and Minton; the big "tea-pot" is, in fact, a rare 18C Liverpool or Derby creamware punchpot. The **Dining Room** is hung with the finest family portraits: *Paul Methuen*, the purchaser of the house, and the two delightful children's portraits are by **Reynolds**; one of the girl twenty years later by **Romney**.

★ Sheldon Manor ⊙ *1.5 miles west of Chippenham.*

The stone exterior of the **manor house** with its several additions was complete by the late 17C.

The oldest parts of the house, the sole survivor of a deserted medieval village, are the **Plantagenet porch** of 1282 and the massive wall behind it. Building phases in c1431 and 1659 added new fronts and the **detached chapel**, and introduced Tudor **fireplaces**, linenfold **panelling**, the Jacobean **staircase**...

Inside, among the splendid, massive 16C-17C **furniture** are refectory tables, 17C chests, a four-poster bed with a 17C embroidered cover, a **17C embroidery** of a Tree of Life with an elephant in the corner and a 15C plank chest in the Priest's Room, which has a **13C roof.**

In addition there are small collections of Nailsea glass, Eltonware and William de Morgan ceramics, a Bruegel in the dining room, 19C sporting prints, cartoons and family mementoes from far and wide...

Outside, high yew hedges enclose a pond garden, a flower garden, an orchard and a garden filled with old fashioned and climbing roses.

★★ Castle Combe *6 miles northwest of Chippenham by A420 and B4039.*

The way to the tidied, picture-postcard village is along a wooded valley, as the trees give way the road leads into **The Street** which is lined with stone cottages. Among these stand the **Dower House** of c1700 with a shell hood above the door, the Manor House (c1664), mounting blocks and a **market cross** with a solid pyramid roof: the perfect film set, used, in fact in the making of *Doctor Doolittle* in the late-1960s.

Castle Combe

A. Taverner

St Andrew (largely but faithfully rebuilt in 1851), with a tall pinnacled tower in the Somerset tradition, was initiated in 1434 when the village was a rich wool market. Inside are a 13C/14C font with an integral lectern, a 16C Perpendicular pulpit, a royal coat of arms with seated lion and unicorn supporters, a wall tablet of 1588 in mixed Latin and English, and an early 14C tomb-chest commemorating a medieval knight.

Still further along The Street are the **pack bridge** and, opposite, **Water Lane** circling a widening out of the stream into a pool which mirrors the former weavers' gabled cottages bordering the lane. Gardens, trees, flowers and the stream complete the picture.

The **Castle Inn** is perhaps the most picturesque of the pubs.

★ Biddestone

The village centre is a large green complete with a duck pond; all around, 16C-18C houses and cottages, many with stone mullioned windows, are set in spacious array. One, behind 18C wrought-iron gate and railings, stands in a modest perfection of two storeys with angle quoins, segmented bays and, above the door, an open pediment framing the date, 1730.

The manor house just off the green is 17C, with stone walls and roof, gables ending in ball finials, mullioned windows and a brick gazebo poised upon the garden wall.

CLOVELLY★★

Devon – Population 439
Michelin Atlas p 6 or Map 403 – G 30, 31

The picture-postcard village, which was mentioned in the Domesday Book, is reached via a **visitor centre** ⊙ which outlines the history of this charming, estate-owned, fishermen's community and its preservation in a short video.

Clovelly itself consists of a very steep, stepped and cobbled **High Street** which is known, depending on the direction being faced, as **Down-a-long** or **Up-a-long**. Lining it are whitewashed 18C and 19C slate-roofed cottages decked with pots and window-boxes filled with fuchsias, geraniums and lobelia. Their state of preservation is largely due to the late Christine Hamlyn who undertook an ambitious restoration programme during the 1890s until her death in 1936, hence the initials and dates on the houses: her portrait hangs in the New Inn Restaurant. A **fisherman's cottage** has been arranged as a museum to provide an insight into life and its conditions in the 19C; another house has a display about **Charles Kingsley** who lived in the village while his father served as curate at the church. Donkeys, which are still today the only form of transport up and down the high street, are available for rides (a Landrover does shuttle through the woods between the top car park and the Red Lion at the bottom for a fee ⊙).

In season, the village is best visited early in the morning, or better still, combined with an overnight stay.

Quay Pool – The port, one of the only safe havens between Boscastle and Appledore, once harboured fishing and pilot boats who quickly learnt how to manoeuvre in the treacherous Hartland Race.

Overlooking the restored 14C harbour, which is protected from the open sea by a curving breakwater offering **views** extending from Lundy to Baggy Point, are stone-built fishermen's cottages and balconied houses, the old harbour lime kiln, boats drawn up on the pebble beach (short trips up the coast and to Lundy in season) and the inn, home of the mounted head of the large (478lb) **porbeagle shark**, caught from the waters off Hartland Point in June 1992; ten men helped bring the shark ashore. A short walk along the beach *(15min over the pebbles)*, beyond the lifeboat store, leads to a cascading waterfall.

Clovelly Church – At the top of the hill, down a tree lined path, the Perpendicular church is a haven of peace on the outskirts of the village itself. The imposing church gates lead through to a lush, shaded graveyard overlooked by the square, unadorned tower which rises in three parts to a gently-crenellated skyline. The church was mentioned in the Domesday Book.

Inside, note the Norman font, Jacobean pulpit (1634) and contemporary benches. The church is, however, remarkable for its **monuments** which include a brass of 1540, 17C epitaphs and 18C sculptures.

Hobby Drive ⊙ – *3 miles from A39 to the car park.* The private toll road *(closed to vehicles)* meanders 500ft above sea-level through the woods, affording sudden, open **views** of the coast and cliffs. It was laid in 1811-19 by the owner of Clovelly Court *(private)* partly to give employment to the Clovelly men during the years after the Napoleonic Wars; it is so named because its construction became his hobby.

CLOVELLY ESTATE

The harbour, Clovelly

EXCURSIONS

Hartland

This most remote corner of Devon lies behind a ridge (750ft) which is the watershed for small, local streams which leap spectacularly from the cliffs into the sea, and for Devon's major western rivers the Torridge and the Tamar. Beyond the ridge the wooded valleys give place to almost bare rock which rises as it approaches the sea and at Hartland Point reaches 350ft before plunging vertically into the ocean.

The **Devon Coast Path**, as it follows every indentation of the rugged cliffs, affords breathtaking **views★★★** of the pointed offshore rocks projecting out of the swell as far as the eye can see.

Hartland Village itself consists of a small collection of houses arranged along narrow streets leading to a small square; in North Street a well-established local potter produces and sells his practical wares.

Hartland Abbey ⓥ – The Augustinian abbey was founded in 1160 to serve the church dedicated to St Nectan at Stoke, the parish church of Hartland. It was dissolved at the Reformation and given by Henry VIII to the sergeant of his cellar William Abbott – allegedly after losing at a game of tennis. In 1600 Catherine Abbott married Nicholas Luttrell of Dunster Castle (*see* DARTMOOR); in 1709 the estate passed to the Orchard family of Aldercombe, Kilkhampton (again by marriage). It was this dynasty that raised the abbey buildings and built the present Georgian house, fashioning the interior in the then popular Gothick of Strawberry Hill. Victorian modifications were undertaken by Sir George Stucley with the assistance of George Gilbert Scott.

The ground floor reception rooms are the most interesting: the **Drawing Room** has an ornately carved doorway and fireplace surround, the light oak panelling is decorated with linenfold after that in the House of Lords, the narrative panels depicting events in the history of the family date from 1852, the portraits are by Reynolds, Northcote and Beechey. The **Billiard Room**, formerly the entrance hall, is ornamented with an elaborate fireplace carved from Maltese stone landed at Hartland Quay; the cabinet displays blue and white porcelain made by Meissen for Marie Antoinette of France. The **Dining Room** is dominated by the rare Victorian Jupe table; the walls are hung with portraits of the Royalist Grenville family several of whom were instrumental in the Restoration of the Monarchy; the panels on either side of the door were painted after frescoes found at Pompeii. The **Little Dining Room** constitutes part of the Queen Anne section of the house and is typical of that period: fine portrait, by Kneller, of Dr William Kneller who was instrumental in rallying support to save Stonehenge, Avebury and Hadrian's Wall for the nation. The green **Library** has a fine ogee fireplace; it is furnished with Chippendale chairs and Ramsay portraits. The **Alhambra Corridor** was inserted by Gilbert Scott and was so decorated following Sir George Stucley's visit to Spain: note the fine topographical views of the abbey before 1769.

In the basement servants' quarters is a display of documents relating to the abbey and its estate from 1160; these were found in 1952 and provide, with an extensive collection of Victorian and Edwardian photographs a complete history of the place.

Grounds – Lush parkland surrounds the house which sits in the valley: rhododendrons, and azaleas are particularly beautiful in late April. Peacocks, Jacob sheep and donkeys provide added interest to visitors to the private house.

★ **Hartland Church** – The 14C-15C church, the "Cathedral of North Devon", has a four-staged, buttressed and pinnacled tower, 128ft tall with a niche containing the figure of St Nectan, a Celtic hermit-missionary. Like its predecessor, the conspicuous tower serves as a landmark for ships at sea – the earlier tower, legend has it, was erected in the 11C by Gytha as a thank-offering for the safe passage in a storm of her husband, Godwin, Earl of the West Saxons and father of King Harold.

The slate seat outside the south porch commemorates John Lane, the "inventor" of the paperback book, and his adopted son Sir Allen Lane who lived in the parish. Inside, the tall nave with wide arcades is covered by ceiled, carved, painted and gilded **wagon roofs** – the best section being over the Lady Chapel. A 45ft intricately carved **rood screen**, in typical Devon style, extends across the full width of the church, the nave arcades having had to be raised to accommodate its 13ft height and the 6ft wide gallery above the crested cornice and multi-ribbed coving.

Note also the square Norman **font** with zig-zag carving on the shaft, arcading on the bowl and faces at each angle, a small **brass** of 1610 and the late 14C carved tombchest in Cornish Catacleuse stone (against north wall of chancel) which came from the dissolved Hartland Abbey.

★ **Hartland Quay** – *1 mile west of Stoke.* During fierce storms at the end of the 19C the Atlantic swept away the centuries-old quay built to receive cargoes of fertiliser, coal, lime and building materials in exchange for locally-produced malt and corn. Today a row of cottages, a hotel and shipwreck museum mark the main street, while the quay foundations afford a **viewpoint★★** from which to look at the striated cliffs, inlets and offshore rocks which characterise the beautiful, wild length of coast.

Docton Mill ⊘ – The mill's delightful cottage garden nestles in the lea of the valley, sheltered from strong prevailing winds. The mill, which appears to originate in the 1100s, was used commercially until 1910 when it fell into disrepair, was acquired by Molly Duncan, a protégé of Ezra Pound in the 1930s, and was eventually restored in 1980. Highlights of this charming garden include the bog garden (ligularias, primulas, ferns), areas of Saxon woodland (bluebells), a broad range of spring bulbs and summer-flowering shrub roses underplanted with perennial geraniums.

A footpath runs from the bottom of the garden down to the sea and the 54ft waterfall at **Spekes Mill Mouth** (20mins on foot). From here, a path climbs up to an upland plateau and on to **Welcombe** offering spectacular **views★★** (this track hugs the cliff edge in places, and is therefore not recommended for vertigo-sufferers). Below, mangled metal recalls the demise of the *Green Ranger* shipwrecked on the rocks of Longpeak in November 1962.

DARTMOOR★★

Devon

Michelin Atlas p 4 or Map 403 – H 132

Dartmoor is the largest of the five granite masses which form the core of southwest England; it covers 365 sq miles and offers a marvellous sense of space. The centre is **open moorland** at a height of approximately 1 000ft; to the north and west are the **tors**, with another small group in the south, the highest rising to 2 000ft; to the east and southeast lies a pattern of **wooded valleys**, with hanging oakwoods above cascading streams, fields, farms and small villages. This area of outstanding natural beauty is also home to lizards and adders; Dartford warblers, linnets, whitethroats, tree pipits and stonechats; high brown fritillaries; yellow gorse, bracken, purple moor grass, heather, violets, bluebells... The moor is traversed by two roads – the Ashburton-Tavistock road (B3357) running east-west and the Moretonhampstead-Yelverton road (B3212) running northeast-southwest. Both developed from ancient **trackways** intersecting at Two Bridges *(see below)*, the site of the famous **clapper bridge** similar to the one at Postbridge nearby.

Dartmoor is a **National Park** which means that it belongs to the nation as a heritage and cannot be despoiled; it does not mean that the public have a right of access any and everywhere – on enclosed land, access is by public footpaths and bridleways (Note: it is an offence to drive or park more than 15yds off a road). The land is not common ground: much, about 70 000 acres, is owned by the Duchy of Cornwall, the rest by farmers and other landowners including Devon County Council, the

Forestry Commission, the Water Authority and the Ministry of Defence. A **Commoner**, the occupier of land in a parish or manor which possesses Common Rights, may graze cattle, ponies and sheep, dig for peat, take heather for thatching and stone and sand to repair his house. All **livestock** on the open moor is owned by farmers; animals are rounded up once a year, branded or tagged and culled, with young stock being sold at the famous Widecombe and other fairs.

Of these, the **ponies** are probably descended from domesticated stock turned out to graze on the moor perhaps as early as the Iron Age. Do NOT feed them – it encourages them to approach cars and the roads where they get run down. The original white faced Dartmoor **sheep** has been replaced by Cheviots which have prick ears and a cumbersome dignity, and the blackfaced Scotch, which were introduced in the 1880s for their hardiness and agility. The most common breeds of **cattle** are the black, stocky and hornless Galloways and belted Galloways; there are also occasional groups of shaggy, long horned Highland cattle and local farms stock Welsh blacks and south Devons (as opposed to the more petite red north Devons, or ruby reds).

The number of visitors annually to the moor has been calculated at 8 million; the number of people who live and work in the villages and towns on the moor's edge and the few small villages upon it, 30 000.

Dartmoor pony

Landmarks, towns, villages on the moor

★★ **Lydford** – The long village on the western edge of Dartmoor straggles down from the main road towards the River Lyd and the gorge, the buildings getting ever older as far as the group of cottages and the castle.

From the 7C-13C Lydford was of military importance as a Saxon outpost, first against the Celts and later against the Danes. It was sacked in 997. Of **Lydford Castle**, erected in 1195 and rebuilt to hold prisoners and tinners awaiting trial before their own stannary court, little remains of the stronghouse other than the two storeys high ruined keep on top of its mound. By the 14C the court was notorious, "Lydford law" being such, it was said, that "in the morn they hang and draw and sit in judgement after". The castle continued as a prison until the 17C and as a stannary court until 1800.

Alongside is the Tudor **Castle Inn** ⏱ which at one time served as the rector's house. This was built with stout oak timbers in the 16C and retains many original features that are enhanced by its homely country furniture, high-backed settles, big slate flagstones and unique display of coins minted in the village between 978 and 1050, the time of Aethelred the Unready.

St Petroc's – The church, one of 30 possibly founded personally by St Petroc in the 6C, was rebuilt and enlarged on Norman foundations in the 13C, 15C and 19C – the south aisle and tower are 15C; note how the latter was mis-joined on to the earlier nave.

Inside, the plain **tub font** is Norman; the tower-nave arch is decorated with carved Gothic panelling; the **rood screen** in the traditional style is modern as are the 69 **bench-ends** carved in 1923-26 by two men, one for the figures, one for the borders. Outside, by the south porch, is the **tomb** with the entertaining epitaph "Here lies in horizontal position, The outside case of George Routleigh, Watchmaker..."

Lydford Gorge ⊙ – *2 hours for the joint Upper and Lower Path walk. First right over the road bridge or, for those not wishing to walk far, continue 1.5 miles along the road to the Waterfall entrance.*

The gorge is about 1.5 miles long with rock walls in places 60ft high. The cleft narrows and widens by turns, the river swirling at the feet of tall beeches, sycamores and a dozen other varieties of tree. Among the birds to look out for are woodpeckers, dippers, possibly a heron. At the south end of the gorge is **White Lady Waterfall**, a 90ft fall of a single strand of water.

There are three marked paths from the main entrance – two interconnect near the Waterfall, enabling a return by a different route: **Upper Path** (*1.25 miles*) follows the northeast-southwest course of the gorge from above, affording bird's-eye **views** of the river and glimpses of Dartmoor; **Lower Path** (*1.5 miles*) at the water's edge skirts the northwest bank (*handrails in more difficult parts – liable to be wet and slippery after rain*); **Third Path** (*1 mile*) leads in the opposite direction from the Pixie Glen to the Bell Cavern by way of the thundering whirlpool known as the **Devil's Cauldron.**

Brent Tor – The volcanic hill (1 130ft) which rises on the western edge of Dartmoor is distinctly crowned by **St Michael's**, a small stone church with a low stalwart tower which commands a good view★★.

Okehampton – The market town, formerly on the main Exeter to Cornwall road (A30) but now by-passed, sits on the northern boundary of Dartmoor. Saxon in origin but abandoned, Okehampton was refounded as a strongpoint by the Normans. It became a medieval market town and prospered in the great wool period, only to tear itself apart during the Civil War; again it recovered, particularly after the improvements in communications of the 18C-19C.

Okehampton Castle ⊙ – *Castle Lane.* The strategic site, the end of a spur beside the River Okement, was selected by the Normans for a motte and bailey castle, a wooden defence protected at the foot of the mound by a ditch. The Courtenays, Earls of Devon (*see also* TIVERTON) and the owners in the 13C, rebuilt the castle only for it all to be slighted when Henry III executed the Earl of Devon in 1538 and attainted his property. In the 18C-19C the ruined castle was purchased by a politician for the parliamentary benefits it bestowed.

There remain a two-storey **outer gatehouse**, a barbican with the outer bailey behind it, and the **gatehouse** proper with its attendant guardroom, forming part of the high inner wall. The diamond-shaped inner bailey is enclosed by the walls of the 13C residential buildings, notably the hall (*right*) which communicates with the guardroom by steps and, at the far end by means of a service room, with the kitchens. On the other side are lodgings, the chapel and another kitchen.

The square **keep**, part 14C, part older, has a gaunt **stair turret** at the northeast corner leading to the upper rooms.

Fore Street – The **Chantry Chapel**, a chapel of ease on a near-island site at the east end of the main street was rebuilt in 1862 with many embellishments including obelisk pinnacles. The pulpit dates from 1626. The old yard, through an arch behind the chapel, has been turned into professional craftsmen's studios and a shop.

On the corner with Market Street stands the **Town Hall**, a former merchant's town house of 1685.

The refronted **White Hart Inn**, which was given an impressive portico in the 18C, has held a licence since the town gained its charter in 1623. In the 18C-19C it was a posting inn, the centre of local transport, where parliamentary candidates and their supporters schemed and celebrated in the manner described by Trollope and Dickens; Okehampton long boasted two members, including Pitt the Elder for a time.

The short, 19C shopping **Arcade** is typical of the period with its overhead ironwork and black and white pavement.

Red Lion Yard, a small, open-air precinct with statuary and paved courtyard is surrounded by arcaded, two-storey gabled buildings.

Museum of Dartmoor Life ⊙ – *Museum Courtyard off West Street.* The collection is housed in an 1811 mill through a granite archway. It looks at the changing lifestyles, from prehistoric times to the present, of the people who have lived and worked on Dartmoor. Temporary exhibitions and craft demonstrations complement the collection.

For access to **Yes Tor** (2 030ft) and **High Willhays** (the highest tor at 2 038ft) located within the military zone, enquire at Okehampton.

Sticklepath – *4 miles east on A30*. The attractive village with its slate and thatch roofed houses – two dated 1661 and 1694 – gardens, old inn and bridge over the River Taw extends for half a mile along the main road. At the centre are the Foundry and a Quaker Burying Ground (through the arch alongside the Foundry).

Finch Foundry ⊙ – The 19C edge-tool factory and forge has been restored to working order. On display are a variety of high-quality agricultural hand-tools produced there from 1814 to 1960: scythes, billhooks, axes, cleavers, shovels. The machinery is powered by water from the river and still has working waterwheels: one waterwheel drives a pair of trip-hammers and ancillary machinery including shears, a second, the fan from which air passed through underground pipes to the forges, while a third turns the grinding mill where tools are sharpened and finished.

> ## Tally Ho! Country Inn and Brewery
>
> This very special 15C market-town pub is to be found along Hatherley's Market Street (north of Okehampton up the A386: beware of market day Tuesday): wooden floors, well-worn solid timber furniture, oak beam ceiling, wood-burning stoves, home-baked or barbecued food and home-brewed beer with names such as Nutter, Jollop, Tarka Tipple and Master Jack's Mild. Restaurant reservation essential ☎ 01837 810 306.

South Zeal – *5 miles east, just north of A30.* The village, which lies just within Dartmoor's northern boundary, was once a chartered borough. Several interesting buildings from that time still stand in the square and along the main street: the early 16C **Oxenham Arms** built of granite as the manor house, a house dated 1714, another **house** dated 1656 but much restored, a 15C house with a **tower porch**. The 15C church, in the centre, was built as the guildhouse of the local wool trade workers.

Spinsters' Rock – The megalithic tomb chamber or quoit, consisting of three large upright stones surmounted by a capstone, is visible over a gate to a field on Shilstone Farm.

★ **Castle Drogo** ⊙ – *2 miles northeast of Chagford. 1 hour.*
Castle Drogo is the romantic dream of **Julius Drewe** (b 1856), the son of a clergyman. On leaving school Drewe was sent as a tea-buyer to China; on his return he started the Home and Colonial Stores and within ten years had made a fortune. At 33 he retired from active business. He bought himself a country house in Kent, married and bought a larger house, Wadhurst Hall in Sussex, which he took over complete with its tapestries and Spanish furniture.
Drewe's elder brother consulted a genealogist who "proved" that the family was descended from Dru or Drogo, a Norman noble who came over with the Conqueror; his descendant in the 12C, Drogo de Teigne, had settled in Devon and given his name to the village of **Drewsteignton**. On discovering the family history, Julius Drewe began to buy land and a quarry in the area as a first step towards materialising his dream. The second step was his introduction to an imaginative architect at the peak of his career, **Edwin Lutyens** (1869-1944).

Construction – The foundation stone of Castle Drogo was laid in 1911 on a bluff overlooking the Teign Gorge and vast tracts of Dartmoor; the plans for a great medieval fortress were still being evolved, and continued to be so throughout the next 19 years of building.
Constructed of rough-hewn and dressed granite from Drewe's own quarry, the castle presents two three-storey ranges each approximately 130ft long, on different levels, meeting in a wide angle of 160°. Towers mark either end and the centre; windows, in the form of giant canted bays with stone mullions and transoms, pierce the east and southeast fronts overlooking the moor. The gently sloping walls are contrived so as to exaggerate the impression of size and magnitude, their clean profile sculptural against the gently undulating landscape around. Even the gardens are arranged geometrically in levelled terraces enclosed by yew hedges, radiating from a straight path.

Interior – The overriding quality of the place is one of a grand but comfortable castle: characteristic features throughout are the spacious interplay of heights and levels between the ranges, marked where there are changes in direction by saucer domes; the use of bare grey granite; the beautiful **views** from the windows give onto the formal gardens planted with colourful herbaceous borders and rose beds, and to the moors beyond.
In the **hall** are the first of several tapestries (Gobelins) brought from Wadhurst. Also on view are a 17C Spanish chest, 18C English dummy board figures by the hearth and 16C Limoges enamel roundels.

The **library**, used as a billiard and games room, is furnished with Lutyens oak bookshelves decorated with Spanish lustreware; the marquetry bureau is Dutch, the lacquer screens Chinese.

The glorious space within the **main staircase** is ornamented with portraits of Mrs Drewe in her Sussex garden and Mr Drewe in full fishing regalia in Scotland – about which Lutyens commented that "At least he (the artist) could paint boots".

The **drawing room** has windows along three sides offering broad **views** out over the moor. The chandeliers are Venetian. Among the exotic furniture (George II and Chinese Chippendale) and furnishings, note the lacquer cabinets, 18C *famille verte* vases from China, and a French Empire clock (*c*1810).

The panelled **dining room** with its low, ornate plaster ceiling, on the lower ground floor serves as a family portrait gallery. The vaulted service corridor in the basement accommodates a fine **dolls' house** of 1906 that was made for one of Mr Drewe's daughters. The magnificent granite **kitchen and scullery** are equipped with beautifully designed, functional oak cupboards and a round table conceived by Lutyens.

The stone **north staircase**, which rises through five floors, is cantilevered out from the wall, while the oak balustrade is constructed independently round a cage. The Green Corridor, one of three similarly designed, overlooks the Teign Gorge.

The chapel (*access from outside*) lies beneath the south range.

The vaulted **gunroom** is now used to display a number of Lutyens drawings and plans for this extraordinary house.

Fingle Bridge – The three-arched granite bridge, which spans the most picturesque reach of the Fingle Gorge, was built in the 16C and has been a famous beauty spot since the early 19C. The hills rise up all round, the highest (700ft) to the north crowned by the ruins of an Iron Age hillfort (Prestonbury Castle). Riverside paths lead through the water meadows and hanging oakwoods beside the Teign.

Drewsteignton – The village, to which the nearby Castle Drogo is linked, stands high above the **Fingle Gorge** and has thatched granite and white cob houses around a central square. Overlooking the square are an early Perpendicular granite **church** and the mid-16C **Church House**, which when built served the community as a village hall.

Moretonhampstead – Known locally as **Moreton** (Moor Town), this was an old market town on the edge of the moor in the 14C-15C when its granite **church** was erected with a commanding **tower**.

Drinking and birdwatching

The Drewe Arms – The pub on The Square was until 1994 home to the longest-serving landlady in the country (CAMRA *Good Beer Guide 1997*) who retired aged 99. Inside, there is no bar, only racks in the tap room from which glasses are filled. ☎ 01647 281 224.

Warren House Inn – Set on the open moorland (*on B3212 Moretonhampstead to Princetown road*), the abundant heather attracts ring ouzels and red grouse, skylarks, meadow pipits, cuckoos and wheatears...

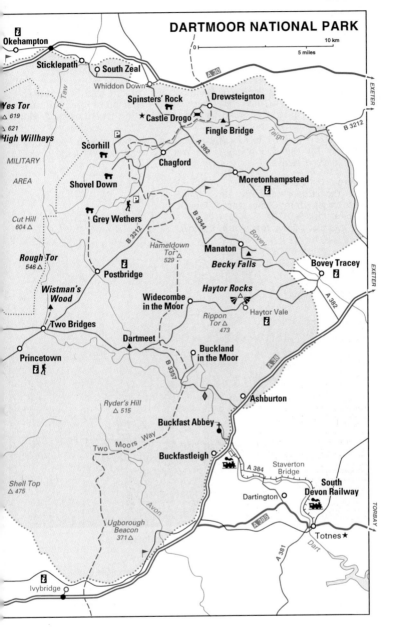

It also possesses a remarkable row of thatched and colonnaded, granite **almshouses** dating from 1637.

The early 19C **White Hart Inn** is a reminder of when Moreton was a coaching stage on the Exeter-Bodmin road.

Chagford – The market town, which in the Middle Ages was one of Devon's four stannary towns and a wool and cloth centre, stands on high ground above the Teign Valley with good **views** of the high tors and Castle Drogo.

A far-seeing vicar in the 19C recognised the town's advantages as a "headquarters for excursions" and encouraged the local people to create the moor's first tourist centre.

Old inns, one built in the 13C-16C as the manor house, and substantial small houses of ashlar granite or whitewashed cob surround the **market square** and its quaint market house known as the Pepperpot.

Overlooking all is the tall, 15C, pinnacled **church tower**. Inside are monolithic granite pillars, carved roof bosses, the tomb of Judge Sir John Whyddon (d 1575).

Scorhill Circle – *4 miles west from Chagford along Teigncombe Road to Batworthy then 1 mile over Teign footbridge and back.* A rare stone circle on the moor.

Shovel Down – *4 miles southwest of Chagford along Teigncombe Road to Batworthy then 1 mile south on foot, there and back.* A single stone and five stone files stand on the down from which there is a wide view.

Postbridge – The **clapper bridge**, doubled by a road bridge in the 1780s, is the largest and most upstanding on the moor, with granite slabs weighing up to 8 tons apiece set on tall piles above the waters of the East Dart River. It is believed to have been constructed when tin-mining and farming were being developed in the centre of the moor in the 13C.

Grey Wethers – *6 miles on foot there and back, northwest from Postbridge via Hartland Tor and White Ridge.* The Wethers comprise two large circles of medium-sized stones.

Mist descending over Two Bridges

Two Bridges – The two bridges, one a medieval **clapper bridge**, mark the crossing of the West Dart River by the two tracks which since time immemorial have traversed the moor. Nearby was the meeting place of the old Tinners' Parliament on Crockern Tor *(northeast). From here the B3357 continues to TAVISTOCK.*

Wistman's Wood – *3 miles there and back from Two Bridges along a marked path from the car park.* The path leads over the moor parallel to the West Dart, a swift stream frequented by dippers. The oak trees of the wood are stunted, primeval; their living trunks, growing out of the boulder-strewn slopes, are draped in grey-green lichen. The trees appear to be self-perpetuating yet there are no saplings.

Rough Tor – 1 791ft. The tor stands out to the north of Two Bridges and Wistman's Wood at the centre of the moor.

Princetown – The town, the highest (1 400ft alt) in England, is dominated by the prison built in 1806-08 to hold Napoleonic prisoners of war – in 1809 some 5 000 men were confined in the then much smaller buildings; by 1813 with the addition of some 2 000 American sailors who refused to join the British against their own countrymen the number had increased to 9 000. After a period as a factory it was reopened as a convict prison in the 1840s (when the practice of deportation ceased).

Burrator Reservoir – The reservoir, an artificial lake ringed by wooded banks against a background of granite tors, was originally constructed in 1891 to supply Plymouth with water. It now has a capacity of 1 026 million gallons.

Dartmeet – The West and East Dart Rivers descend from the open uplands to join forces and flow on through an almost gorge-like valley between wooded hillsides. Footpaths follow the course of the river for some distance.
The swift-flowing streams and the fields and woods on either bank are alive with birds including larks, dippers, green woodpeckers and the occasional heron.

Widecombe in the Moor – The embattled **tower** with tall turreted pinnacles which soars high above Dartmoor makes the church a **landmark** for miles around; Sabine Baring-Gould's ballad about going to the **fair** (still held today on the second Tuesday in September), has made Widecombe itself a popular legend.

> Tom Pearse, Tom Pearse, lend me your grey mare,
> All along, down along, out along lee.
> For I want to go to Widecombe Fair,
> Wi' Bill Brewer, Jan Stewer, Peter Gurney,
> Peter Davy, Dan'l Whiddon, Harry Hawk,
> Old Uncle Tom Cobley and all
> Old Uncle Tom Cobley and all.

The village, a cluster of white-walled, thatched cottages grouped round the church, stands in a shallow valley or wide combe – hence the name – surrounded by granite ridges which rise to 1 500ft with names like Hamel Beacon, Bonehill, Bell, Chinkwell and Honeybag Tor.
The Perpendicular **Cathedral of the Moor**, rebuilt in the late 14C-15C with money from the Dartmoor tin-miners, is denoted by its 135ft-high tower of red ashlar granite added, out of line, in the early 16C. Dedicated to St Pancras, it is a vast building (104ft long) with monolithic arcades rising to plain barrel roofs decorated with a series of well-carved bosses.

Church House, the two-storey stone house fonted by a loggia with seven octagonal columns, dates back to 1537 when it was the village alehouse. It was later converted into almshouses, the village school and finally, the National Trust shop. Pevsner describes it as 'the grandest in the county'. The favourite inn of the village is the **Rugglestone Inn**. Other vernacular buildings in the area include the traditional longhouses, *see* INTRODUCTION: Arts and Architecture.

Haytor Rocks – 1 490ft. *5 miles west of Bovey Tracey.* The by-road from Bovey to Widecombe runs close to the rocks. The **view**★ extends to the coast at Widecombe.

Bovey Tracey – The small town is a gateway to Dartmoor: many of the cottages are built of moor granite but in typical Devon fashion are mellowed by thatched roofs.
St Peter, St Paul and St Thomas of Canterbury★ was founded, it is said, in repentance for his part in St Thomas Becket's murder in 1170 by Sir William de Tracey whose family had long been owners of the village. The slender tower is 14C, the church, comprising Beer stone arcades with well-carved capitals, is 15C and considerably restored. Of especial interest are the Jacobean tombs, the 15C brass eagle lectern with three small lions at the base, the pre-Reformation stone pulpit, carved with ten still-perfect figures all coloured and gilt, and a remarkably carved 15C roodscreen of 11 bays with figures of the saints in the lower panels.

Devon Guild of Craftsmen ⊙ – *Riverside Mill. Across the river from the lower car park.* The Guild was founded in 1954, largely out of craftsmen work-

Stoneware pot, David Leach

Devon Guild of Craftsmen

143

ing in Totnes, Torquay, Exeter and at Dartington Hall. A constantly changing series of exhibitions throughout the year celebrates the work of the Guild's craftsmen: batik, pots and ceramics, needlework, enamelling, furniture, woodwork, glass, weaving, lace, metalwork, silver and jewellery.

House of Marbles and Teign Valley Glass ⊙ - *Pottery Road, 0.25 mile west off B382.* The buildings, an old pottery with listed muffle kilns, now house a glassworks and pottery where craftsmen may be watched at work, and a small museum section outlining the history of the Bovey Tracey pottery, glassmaking and the toys and games made in-house: tools, powders and pigments used for colouring, chunks of cullet used for marble making, Roman bottles, Georgian glasses and probably the largest conceivable variety of marbles...

For Ugbrooke House at Chudley, see TEIGNMOUTH.

Becky Falls ⊙ – Even in dry weather the Becka Brook cascades down from the moor, circling boulders in its rush to descend some 70ft into a wooded glade. This woodland estate, mapped out with nature trails, is a good place from which to plan walks onto the moors to the villages of Manaton and Lustleigh, or to the tors known as Bowerman's Nose, Hay Tor and Hound Tor.
Yarner Wood, nearby, is a National Nature Reserve noted for its research into woodland management; bird-watchers come to spy on the pied flycatchers (May-June), woodpeckers, treecreepers and wood-warblers.

Manaton – The village is centred on the green which is overlooked by a typical 15C moorland **church**, notable inside for its full-width rood screen depicting the Twelve Apostles and other saints on the lower panels.

Buckland in the Moor – The village epitomizes the idyllic Devon village with thatched, stone cottages set in a wooded dell. The late 15C, early 16C moorstone church on older foundations is known for its clockface inscribed MY DEAR MOTHER in place of the usual numerals. Inside is a 16C painted rood screen.

Ashburton - The former stannary town stands on a tributary of the River Dart. When the church with its tall Perpendicular granite tower was built in the 15C, Ashburton was a wool town; the many slate-hung houses date from the 16C-18C when it was a slate mining centre.
Signposted from the town is the **River Dart Country Park**, a popular country park with a range of outdoor facilities for the family and good birdwatching.

> **Dipper** *(Cinclus cinclus)*
> This dumpy bird with a brown head, slate-grey back and brilliant white chin throat and breast, and short tail is to be found in and around fast-flowing upland rivers and streams containing small invertebrates. To catch its food, the dipper has developed an uncanny technique of wading into the water before submerging, swimming or diving for its prey. When underwater, it swims into the current or walks along the stream-bed, wings spread wide to stop itself floating up to the surface, and eyes open – protected by a special white eye-lid adapted for the purpose.

Buckfast Abbey ⊙ - *30min.* The present abbey church was consecrated in 1932, some 900 years after the original foundation made under King Canute. The new church and monastery, built by members of a community of French monks who had fled to England in the 19C, followed in plan the rediscovered foundation of the Cistercian house dissolved by Henry VIII in 1535. The style is Norman in grey limestone relieved with yellow Ham Hill stone; at the centre is the 158ft crossing tower. In the landscaped precincts are two gardens with herbs; fountains and arbours.

Interior – The church of pure white Bath stone rises above the arcades, triforium and clerestory to a plainly vaulted rib roof, 49ft above the nave floor. There is no pulpitum or screen and the eye is immediately drawn the 220ft length of the church to the **high altar**, rich in gold, enamelwork and jewels. Suspended above the altar is a 48-light gilded **corona**.
Continue round behind the altar and east up the steps from the ambulatory.
The modern **Blessed Sacrament Chapel**, dedicated in 1966, features **walls of stained glass.** The chapel was designed by the monks who also built it and made and set the glass in all its shades of blue, purple, red and pale yellow.
An exhibition in the **crypt** traces the history of the Abbey from 1018 to the present with models and photographs. The **Audio-Visual Show** presents the history of the Abbey and the life of the Buckfast community.

Buckfastleigh – The market town on the southeastern edge of the moor, which inspired the Sherlock Holmes mystery *The Hound of the Baskervilles*, was once an important wool and cloth centre.

It is also the northern terminus of the **South Devon Railway** ⊙, a former GWR line, known as one of the most picturesque in England. The centre comprises engine sheds with locomotives and stock, 7.25 in gauge miniature steam railway, steam traction engines and a museum.

The GWR standard gauge line has been re-opened over 7 miles, crossing the river at Staverton Bridge, where the station has been restored, and terminating at Totnes Riverside station *(connection with British Rail)*.

DARTMOUTH★★

Devon – Population 5 712
Michelin Atlas p 4 or Map 403 – J 32

Dartmouth, synonymous with the **Britannia Royal Naval College** ⊙ – the long, turn-of-the-century building on the hill – presents visitors with short and winding streets, steeply stepped alleys, a Butterwalk, a pannier market, pubs, stores and antique shops rather than fine architecture, and of course the River Dart itself. Closely encircled by hills and surrounded by the sea, the town has never grown to unwieldy size. It originated half a mile inland on either side of a creek; as it grew, first the inlet then ever more of the river bank was reclaimed, the final undertaking being the extensive gardens and embankment completed in 1930.

A deepwater tidal inlet almost invisible from the sea, the town grew wealthy on sea trade – land communications even now are tenuous: the railway has never come closer than Kingswear on the opposite bank. There are ferries (one passenger, two car) to Kingswear, the **Paignton and Dartmouth Steam Railway** (*see* TORQUAY: Paignton), boat trips and the **view★** across the estuary in which Defoe declared that 500 ships of any size could "ride with the greatest safety".

From earliest times it served as an embarkation port for the Mediterranean; in the Middle Ages it traded particularly with Brittany, Gascony and Spain (notably wine from Bordeaux), harbouring the fleet while it rallied for the second and third Crusade campaigns; in the 16C its prosperity hinged on the cargoes of cloth and tin from Totnes which was exchanged against linen and manufactured goods from France. When venturing turned to the Spanish Main and the Americas, Dartmouth became the port from which the navigators Sir Humphrey Gilbert and John Davis set out and to which prize Spanish galleons were brought after capture on the high seas.

In the 17C trade concentrated in Bristol and London; Dartmouth became a training centre for naval cadets in 1863. Subsequently, fortunes turned for the worse in the late 18C save for a brief period between 1871-91 when it harboured the fast steamships bound for Australia and South Africa.

Market day: Friday.

Britannia Royal Naval College, Dartmouth

A. Taverner

OLD TOWN

Embankment – The **station pier** (1864) with Victorian cast-ironwork, now the passenger **ferry embarkation point**, was built in hopeful anticipation of the railway coming to the town in the 19C. **Fairfax Place** dates from the 1880s.
The houses along the waterfront are mainly built on land reclaimed from mudflats. Those set back are largely 17C: the timber framed one fronting onto Fairfax Place (no 4) was built for Robert Plumleigh in 1664; its party walls are built of stone so as to contain fireplaces on both sides, serving adjacent houses. **Boatfloat**, until the building of the Embankment, was the town's inner harbour.

Newcomen Engine ⊙ – In the garden just upstream, one of Thomas Newcomen's (1663-1729) atmospheric steam engines, model for 75 years for pumping-engines in many mines, can be seen impressively at work.

Quay – The Quay, fronting the Boatfloat, was constructed in 1584 when it served as the centre of the town's activity. The **Castle Hotel's** facade of 1835 straddles the two merchants' houses of 1639 it occupies.

★ **Butterwalk** – *Duke Street*. The Butterwalk has protected shoppers in Duke Street, at the end of the Quay, since 1635-40 when a terrace of four shops with oversailing upper floors supported on eleven granite pillars was completed (restored 1943) on land reclaimed from the mudflats: at that time trading ships could sail up behind the buildings in order to discharge their cargo (mainly from Newfoundland). Note the ostentatious **woodwork** and carved corbels, the gables of the middle houses. No 12 contains a glorious plaster ceiling decorated with the *Tree of Jesse*, overlooked by the four Evangelists *(ask in the shop for permission to view)*; the ceiling in no 10 is less ornate (ribs and pendants) and its overmantel depicts Pentecost.

Dartmouth Museum ⊙ – *No 6, nearest the Quay*. Outside it is timber-framed; inside, up the newel stair with long post, the main room is panelled and set with a fine **plaster overmantel** bearing the arms of Charles II. The exhibits comprise principally model ships.

Pannier Market – *Victoria Road, continuation of Duke Street*. The general market is on Friday, on other days of the week stalls sell a miscellany of goods.

St Saviour's Church – *Anzac Street*. The tall, square pinnacled tower has been a landmark for those sailing upriver since it was constructed. The church, founded as a chapel of ease under the control of Torre Abbey in Torquay was finally consecrated in 1372. The **chancel** was largely endowed by **John Hawley** (d 1408), who is commemorated between his two wives by an intricate **brass memorial★** *(chancel floor)*: MP and mayor, merchant venturer, buccaneer, property speculator in the town, churchgoer, he was typical of the leading citizens who in the 15C brought prosperity to the town. His fellow townsmen continued to support the church so that it was largely rebuilt in the 1630s. Note especially the **south door** with its two ironwork lions and rooted tree of life; the medieval altar with legs carved like ships' figureheads; the pre-Reformation carved and coloured pulpit; finely carved west gallery in the Elizabethan style; impressively complete **rood screen**, dated 1496; Rococo organ case by Micheau of Exeter (1789).

DOWNSTREAM FROM THE EMBANKMENT

Higher Street – No 1, The shambles has timbers exposed on two upper floors; next door is the four-storey **Tudor House** (nos 3-5) of 1635 complete with oriel windows and slate-hung gables. Further along, on the corner signalled by its coloured and carved emblem, is the half-timbered **Carved Angel** with oversailing upper floors: the only complete house in Dartmouth now an inn, renowned for its typical West Country fare.

Cross Newcomen Road, which was widened in 1864, into Lower Street.

Agincourt House – *27 Lower Street*. The four-storey house around a spacious courtyard was built, as the name suggests, in the early 15C for a rich merchant; it was restored in the 17C and again this century when the courtyard was glazed over.

Continue down to the water's edge.

Bayard's Cove – The "cove", a short cobbled quay, is lined by 18C town houses, the most attractive being the pedimented **Old Custom House** of 1739 with a shell-hooded porch. At the end stood **Bayard's Cove Castle** one of Henry VIII's defences (1536-7), built on an earlier fort that guarded the harbour mouth.

Mayflower Stone – The 180 ton *Mayflower*, accompanied by the *Speedwell*, put into Dartmouth for repairs to the *Speedwell*, which was finally abandoned, leaving the pilgrims to sail on in the *Mayflower* only.

DARTMOUTH CASTLE ⊘

1 mile by Newcomen Road, South Town and (left) Castle Road.

The fort, which commands excellent **views★★★** of the estuary, was built in the late Middle Ages by the merchants of Dartmouth to protect their homes, warehouses and deepwater anchorage from foreign raiders. It is earlier than those ordered by Henry VIII at Falmouth at St Mawes.

Although their ships traded in the regular fashion, it was also the custom of the day for all vessels on the high seas to turn privateer and plunder or capture any prize they might overcome. In addition raids were organised on foreign coastal towns and other English ports. Booty was seized and buildings set on fire. The damage from such raids was often long-lasting. The raiders or pirates might number a single ship's company or several thousand men. Dartmouth suffered two major retaliatory French raids in 1377 and 1400. In 1404 the town was "invaded" by 6 000 Bretons on the rampage.

In 1336 Edward III had ordered the estuary to be protected; in 1374 John Hawley *(see above)* and others were commanded "in consideration of the damage and reproach which might befall the town of Dartmouth through hostile invasion... to fortify the same, array the men of the town and do all other things that may be necessary". By the end of the century 'a fortalice' or **small fortress** had been constructed which was reinforced in 1462 by stretching a chain across the harbour mouth to a fort at Kingswear (visible on the far bank). Twenty years later the townsfolk, still described as 'warlike', began to build the fort standing today. Edward IV and Henry VII both contributed to the cost.

The most interesting architectural fact about the castle, begun in 1481 (altered and added to in the 16C and 18C), is that it was the first in England to be designed to have **guns** as its **main armament.** Gunpowder had been in use in warfare since the mid-14C but gunports were generally inserted in old buildings and took the form of enlarged arrow slits; in Dartmouth the **ports** were splayed internally to allow a wide traverse without an enlarged opening. The guns were strapped to flat wooden beds; 50 years later, in Henry VIII's forts, they would be mounted on wheeled carriages and mobile. Once the castle was built, Dartmouth was never again attacked from the sea.

St Petrox – The Gothic-style church almost abutting the castle dates from 1642 when it was rebuilt on a 12C site. It is believed that in its earliest days it bore a light to guide mariners navigating the narrow estuary entrance.

Of interest inside are two large and outstanding 17C **brasses** *(east end)*, another small brass, the **pulpit** dated 1641, funeral **hatchments**, charity boards and Charles II's arms.

EXCURSION

River Dart boat trips ⊘ – The 12 mile excursion up the River Dart, which the Victorians nicknamed "the English Rhine", to Totnes is an easy way to see the countryside. Exceptional numbers of birds (cormorants, kingfishers, heron), are to be seen on the river banks; note also how the salt water has cut back the lower branches of the trees.

West bank landmarks – Britannia Royal Naval College stands out at the top of the town. The **Anchor Stone** is said to have been used by Sir Walter Raleigh.

Dittisham, pronounced 'ditsum' is an area renowned for fruit farming blessed as it is by a micro-

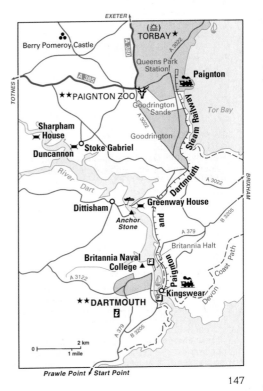

climate all of its own: most special is the Dittisham plum which resembles a large damson in form and a Victoria in flavour and colour; these appear for a short season in mid-August.

Sharpham House was built on an older site in 1770 in a park designed by Capability Brown. The money for the house's building came from exploits such as the capture of the Spanish ship *Hermione* off Cadiz, worth £65 000 in prize money: the 500-acre estate comprises mixed farmland, orchards, vineyards and produces a notable cheese – *see* INTRODUCTION: Regional specialities.

Home Reach, a long and narrow reach, leads to Totnes (*see* TOTNES).

East bank landmarks – The 13C **Kingswear** church tower is a prominent landmark. On occasion the puff of a steam train may be spotted running on the **Paignton and Dartmouth Steam Railway**.

Greenway House, formely Greenway Court, was the birthplace of the navigator Sir Humphrey Gilbert, and for several years the home of Dame Agatha Christie, the murder-mystery novelist.

Stoke Gabriel has a yew tree estimated to be 1 200 to 1 500 years old beside its 15C church: John Davis, who discovered the strait between Greenland and Baffin Island while searching for the North West Passage, was baptised and married in the church.

Duncannon is a hamlet that was once known for its red sandstone quarries.

Start Point

14 miles plus 1 mile on foot; south by B3205 and A379 to Torcross; west to Stokenham and south using by-roads to Kellaton, Hollowcombe Head, Start Farm and the track to the lighthouse car park.

The road follows the curve of the bay fringed by long fine sand beaches and at Slapton rides the low ridge separating the lagoon and the sea. The final few miles inland are typical wooded, undulating farmland. The walk to the point and lighthouse is across open country with an ever increasing **view★**.

The panoramic **views★★★** from **Prawle Point**, beyond, are breathtaking.

For Kingsbury and Salcombe, see SALCOMBE.

DEVIZES

Wiltshire – Population 11 250
Michelin Atlas p 17 or Map 403 – O 29

Modern Devizes is probably best known for its brewery – but from medieval times until the 19C it was an important cloth market which specialised in the narrow woollen suiting known as "drugget" and from the 17C it benefited from widespread tobacco growing – hence the number of well disposed 18C town houses, many on 17C timber framed foundations. Since Cromwellian times, Devizes has also served as a military garrison town equipped with large red-brick barracks on the Marlborough Road.

The name Devizes is thought to originate from the Latin *"ad divisas"* meaning "at the boundaries", which alludes to the town's situation at the edge of three large manorial estates: Potterne, Rowde and Cannings. Evidence of the town's strategic position is confirmed by the Norman castle built by Osmund, Bishop of Salisbury on the spur west of the present Market Place in 1080, which was subsequently rebuilt (1120) by Bishop Roger, Chancellor to Henry I, who had similar fortresses at Malmesbury, Sherborne and Old Sarum (*see* SALISBURY). This fortification eventually became 'ruinated' and was finally demolished by Cromwell's forces in 1646. The castle now on the site is a 19C fantasy *(private, best espied from St John's churchyard)*.

★ **Market Place** – The broad Market Place grew around the flourishing trade in sheep grazed on the Wiltshire Downs; from this evolved the town's medieval **street plan** which, uniquely, has survived largely intact.

Coaching inns – On the road out of town sits **Wadworth Brewery** which was built by Henry Wadworth in 1885: since then Wadworth has risen to become one of the largest brewing concerns in the West Country and the main supplier to the local pubs, many of which started out as coaching inns. The Wadworth drays are often to be spotted delivering supplies of 6X.

At the far end of town, beyond the red brick factory was the King's Arms (**Northgate House**), a brick building with a handsome porch, which later became home to the family for which George Eliot worked as a governess while living next door at the giant-pilastered "Sandcliff".

Facing onto the square itself is the 18C three-storey, pilastered **Black Swan Inn**, **The Pelican** and the **Bear Hotel**. Built in 1599, this was known in the 18C for the portrait sketches of customers drawn by the landlord's young son, **Thomas Lawrence** (1769-1830), later President of the Royal Academy of Arts.

Other establishments once occupied no 32 (The White Hart) and no 40 (The White Swan).

Parnella House – *No 23, between the cinema and Black Swan.* The house was built *c*1740 by a doctor who decorated the front with a somewhat odd, roughly carved statue of Asklepios, the Greek god of medicine (modern copy).

The Shambles – The old dark street known as the Shambles still serves as a regularly-held market (best on Thursdays and Saturdays).

The Brittox, a shopping street which runs off the High Street, once served as the palisaded entrance to the castle (the meaning of the Norman-French *bretasche* from which the name derives); today, modern fronts belie older houses originally built there in 1386.

Corn Exchange – The 19C classical-fronted building, crowned with the figure of Ceres (the goddess of Agriculture bearing a horn of plenty) provides the town with public function rooms (wedding receptions, polling station, concerts and assemblies).

Old Town Hall – The hall, built *c*1750, is fronted by Ionic columns rising to a pediment enclosing a clock and putti. Originally, it was conceived to hold a butter, cheese and poultry market on the ground floor and municipal offices above.

Town Hall – The "new" hall of 1808, designed by Thomas Baldwin of Bath on an island site at the end of St John's Street, is an elegant Georgian building with a rusticated ground floor with arched windows, a rounded back and a wide bow to the front, dignified by tall Ionic columns.

St John's Alley – *Obliquely across from the Town Hall.* The alley is lined with a complete range of half-timbered, compact Elizabethan houses with jettied upper floors.

★★ **St John's** – The parish church through the churchyard, is robustly Norman yet gracefully proportioned. Built by Roger of Salisbury to serve the castle and garrison, it has a mighty **crossing tower**, which inside has round arches towards the nave and chancel, and pointed ones towards the transepts.

Inside, the vaulted east end is typically Norman, decorated with interlaced arches articulated with chevron and zigzag mouldings in contrast with fish-scale-filled spandrels. In 1450 the nave and aisles were rebuilt, and extended in 1863. The side chapels(1483), separated from the chancel and sanctuary by decorative stone screens, have fine lacunar roofs resting on carved corbels.

★ **Devizes Museum** ⊘ – *41 Long Street. 90min.* Founded initially as a show case for the **Wiltshire Archeological and Natural History Society** (founded in 1835 and enriched by early collections made by the likes of Colt Hoare of Stourhead), this delightful, esteemed museum traces the history of the immediate area from Neolithic times with sections dedicated to the Bronze Age, Iron Age, Roman occupation, Saxon and Medieval periods.

The evolving civilisation of Wiltshire is carefully explained in the context of archeological finds: displays of axes and arrowheads, daggers, buckles and beads, jewellery and cosmetic implements, urns, glassware, hoards of coins, the Stourhead Collection of gold ornaments, an outstanding bronze collection, small sculptures and a round, smiling Celtic Janus head.

Particularly fascinating are the rooms dedicated to henge monuments (Stone-henge, Woodhenge, Long Barrow at Avebury, barrows on Salisbury Plain). Scale models illustrate reconstructions, early tools provide an insight into working methods, and, most importantly, a number of pots identify the **Beaker Folk** – the first "Englishmen" to master the use of metal – who proved to be accomplished engineers capable of remodelling henge monuments for their own needs.

An important archive of documentation relating to the discovery, excavation and study of these important sites is preserved in the library upstairs, although consultation of records is restricted to members.

Other departments chart the **geology** (fossils, rock formations) and natural history (flora and fauna). The **art gallery** upstairs, ornamented with a stained glass window by **John Piper** (1982), is used for changing exhibitions; the Recent History Gallery is dedicated to displays of objects relating to Devizes and its prosperity – traditional shops, friendly societies, agriculture, cloth industry, Civil War, transport and Victorian schooldays.

St Mary's – This second Norman church built for the townspeople is more sober than St John's. Sections of the original survive in the chancel and sanctuary which are ornamented with the characteristic blind arcading and geometric patterning; the tall tower, nave and aisles date from 1436. Inside, the royal arms are those of George III.

Further down New Park Street, set back from the road, is **Brownstone House** (1720), a fine, well-proportioned Grade I listed building that is highly praised by Pevsner.

The Wharf – The building of the canal heralded new interests for Devizes such as boat-building, lock-keeping and canal maintenance, although the history of these is difficult to document. Certainly, the railways seized much of the commercial business away from the West Country waterways at the close of the 19C, after which the Avon and Kennet Canal was used to transport heavy military equipment, and as a training ground for handling barges during World War I when British Forces were

Kennet and Avon Canal flight of locks, Caen Hill

operating in Northern France and Belgium. Most of the functional buildings were built for storage and stabling for barge horses. Installed in one such warehouse is the **Wharf Theatre**.

Kennet and Avon Canal Centre ⊘ – The exhibition housed in an old granary (1810) describes the construction (1794-1810) of the waterway which linked Bristol and London engineered by John Rennie, who also designed the bridges and aqueducts, and the two pumping stations at Claverton (*see* BATH) and Crofton (*see* MARLBOROUGH) which topped up the water levels in the locks. Emphasis has been particularly given to the individuals who operated the waterway.

Caen Hill – The impressive **flight of 29 locks** carrying water up 234ft on the two-mile approach to Devizes Wharf is accessible by the **tow path** *(2 miles; 3.5 miles; 4.5 miles on foot)*. Between 1802 and 1810 a temporary horse-drawn tramway hauled the barges up the incline: fortunately, natural deposits of clay suitable for making bricks were located just south of locks 29 to 35. The fastest time for a loaded barge to pass through the 2.25 mile stretch was a mere 2 hours and 30 minutes.

Kennet and Avon Canal

In 1792 an advertisement in a Salisbury journal advertised a scheme to build a canal between navigable sections of the River Avon and the River Kennet, thereby linking Bristol and Bath with Newbury and Reading: private investors welcome. The project's surveyor and engineer John Rennie designed a waterway that could accommodate large barges (3ft 10in – 4.2m in the beam) which were considerably larger than those operating on the Midland canals (6ft 10in – 2.08m). Building work began shortly after Royal Assent was granted in 1794; by 1807 the 57 mile waterway was in operation; in 1810 the flight of 16 locks up Caen Hill was completed. The bulk of the freight was coal from Radstock and Poulton, but with the advent of the Great Western Railway (1841), traffic dwindled forcing the canal authorities to sell up to GWR, who deliberately abandoned the canal. Recently restored (1988-90), the canal is once more open to navigation, threading its way through the Avon Valley, the Vale of Pewsey and on into Berkshire: for details of boat trips and walking the length of the towpath.

EXCURSION

Potterne *2 miles south on A360.*

The village of 18C-19C houses of all shapes and sizes with shops below is aligned along a main street. The 15C thatched cottage, now the **George and Dragon**, was built by the Bishop of Salisbury; it is alleged that when Cromwell billeted his troops in Potterne the pub was forced to feed them.

The **Porch House**★★ *(private)*, at the south end has black and white half-timbering, the beams all vertical, gables with neat ball finials, stone tiles, a two-tier hall window, an oversailing upper floor and the porch itself, well advanced with an oriel window beneath its independent gable. It was built when Henry VIII was on the throne.

Adjoining is a second house, gabled, stone-tiled and with the later 16C "cross-gartered" half-timbering.

George and Dragon at Rowde

Off the road to Chippenham (A342) is a notoriously excellent pub serving a selection of superb treats. Restaurant bookings (closed Monday lunch) ☎ 01380 723 053.

DORCHESTER★

Dorset – Population 15 037
Michelin Atlas p 8 or Map 403 – M 31

The small county town, Hardy's home town, possesses still the house lived in by the Mayor of Casterbridge, the Old Crown Court where the Tolpuddle Martyrs were tried and the half-timbered house known as Judge Jeffreys' Lodgings, where the judge stayed during the Bloody Assizes when he came to "try" 290 of Monmouth's local supporters.

It also bears the imprint of the Romans who in the 3C AD built the hilltop town they named Durnovaria straddling the London-Exeter highway; remains also from the 16C-17C when new houses were erected along the High Street, and of the 18C-19C when those houses were refaced or rebuilt. Every owner decided his own style, producing façades of infinite variety. This spirit has a modern parallel on the outskirts of town *(off A35 to Bridport road)*, where the controversial **Poundbury estate**, endorsed by the Prince of Wales, on Duchy of Cornwall land is in its second phase of development. It comprises a series of individual houses and gardens designed in traditional vernacular styles using brick, tile, slate and stucco – staunchest critics describe the estate as a glorified Tesco-town.

Market day: Wednesday until 3pm.

"Best and finest beer in England"

When, during the war with France in the early 1700s trading in French wine was prohibited, Dorchester established a highly successful concern making the finest malt liquor. The town's very strong beers are described by Thomas Hardy in his novel *Trumpet Major*: anyone found drunk and disorderly and blessed with being foreign to the area would be dismissed by the local magistrate "as one overtaken in a fault that no man could guard against who entered the town unawares"... The Dorchester Brewery maintains the tradition by brewing a strong Hardy's Ale.

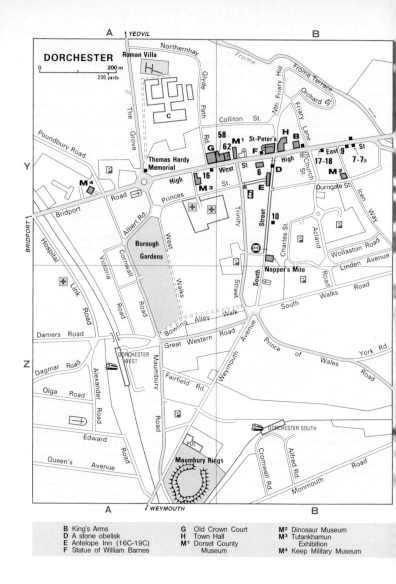

DORCHESTER

B	King's Arms
D	A stone obelisk
E	Antelope Inn (16C-19C)
F	Statue of William Barnes
G	Old Crown Court
H	Town Hall
M¹	Dorset County Museum
M²	Dinosaur Museum
M³	Tutankhamun Exhibition
M⁴	Keep Military Museum

High East Street (BY) – The brick and stone **town hall (H)** with a steepled **clock tower** is 19C.

The **King's Arms (B)** dates from the 17C; it was re-faced with Doric columns during the 19C Classical revival; the house and shop opposite **(no 24)**, is of the same date. As are the **Borough Arms**, nos 45 and 7-7a. Nos 36 and 17-18, although much altered, date back to the 16C.

South Street (BY) – The main shopping street is marked at its opening by **Cornhill**, a pedestrian precinct characterised by a stone **obelisk (D)** marking the town pump and the 16C-19C **Antelope Inn (E)**.

The three-storey, late 18C house **(No 10)** of lustred brick headers with redbrick dressings is where the Mayor of Casterbridge lived in the novel of that name by **Thomas Hardy** who, when he left school, worked at no 62, an architect's office, before he went to London.

The bell-gabled almshouse, the **Napper's Mite**, was founded by Sir Robert Napper in 1615.

High West Street (ABY) – The street opens with the much restored **St Peter's Church**, with its 12C doorway and multi-pinnacled tower and, inside, 14C **military monuments** and 17C **pulpit** and communion table.

Before the church is a statue of **William Barnes (F)** (1800-86), schoolmaster, linguist and pastoral poet in English – *Linden Lea* – and the Dorsetshire dialect; buried in the porch is the Puritan rector **John White** (1575-1648) who organised a refuge for North Atlantic Dorset fishermen which led to many settling in the future Massachusetts.

No 6, Judge Jeffreys' Lodgings – The judge made his way from the house to the assizes at the Antelope by a secret passage, it is said, for fear of the mob. The house with its gabled roofline and jettied upper floor is the town's only half-timbered building.

Old Crown Court ⊘ **(G)** – Inside Thomas Hardwick's Classical Shire Hall of 1797 is the old Crown Court with the dock in which the six **Tolpuddle Martyrs** stood on 19 March 1834. The benches, judge's chair and George III royal arms are 18C. Downstairs are the cells where prisoners were held pending their hearing. Outside, note the distances incised on the pale stone.

Old Ship – The inn was built as a coaching inn in 1600.

Thomas Hardy Memorial (AY) – Right of the West Gate roundabout at the top of the street sits the figure of Thomas Hardy, a posthumous portrait bronze (1931) by **Eric Kennington**.

★ **Dorset County Museum** ⊘ **(BY M¹)** – *High West Street.* Three collections combine to make the museum outstanding: the Thomas Hardy Memorial, the Maiden Castle Gallery and the fossils.

Victorian Gallery – A broad range of artefacts with local associations are collected together in

Thomas Hardy Memorial

this great hall with a tiled mosaic floor and fine ironwork, inspired by the Great Exhibition of 1851 at Crystal Palace.

By the staircase sits an engraved glass panel by Laurence Whistler, the thirteenth – entitled *The Forgiveness Window*, intended for Moreton Church *(see below)* depicting the thirteenth figure at the Last Supper, an ungainly Judas Iscariot portrayed from behind, the pieces of silver slipping from his hand.

A Writer's Dorset – The main section of the six-room display is dedicated to **Thomas Hardy** (1840-1928): it includes original drawings and manuscripts for his novels, books, personal possessions, furniture and pictures from his house, and a reconstruction of his study at **Max Gate**, the house he designed for himself on the Dorchester-Wareham road, where he died on 11 January 1928; an interactive computer terminal provides additional graphics, moving pictures, sound and written word.

The other **Dorset Worthies** celebrated range from St Aldhelm to Sir Walter Raleigh, the novelists John Meade Falkner to the Powys Brothers and Sylvia Townsend Warner. A separate area illustrates the work of William Barnes *(see above)* who wrote poetry in the local dialect (interactive audio-visual unit).

Maiden Castle Gallery – The history of Maiden Castle and the artefacts discovered when it was excavated in the 1930s and 1980s

> ### Thomas Hardy
>
> Born at Higher Bockhampton the son of a stonemason, Thomas trained and worked as an architect (1856-72) before deciding to dedicate himself to writing. A number of his interconnected novels are set in Wessex, which he based on the Saxon Kingdom of Britain which then encompassed Dorset, Wiltshire, Hampshire, parts of Somerset, Oxfordshire and Berkshire: in short, the area linked by the chalk uplands. At the heart was Dorchester, which he renamed Casterbridge *(see* INTRODUCTION: Literature).

are displayed in the context of other sites in the county of the same active period.

Fossils – Lyme Regis is the great fossil area of England: on display are fossil outlines of leaves and fish imprinted on rocks, ammonites, ichthyosaurus and plesiosaurus, the three-toed footprint of an iguanadon dinosaur from Swanage, also maps and diagrams of current prospecting and **oil exploitation** in the county.

Rural Craft Collection – An extensive collection of thatching, ditching, smithing, gamekeeping implements used in Dorset for three centuries to the end of the horse age are displayed alongside the Natural History collection.

Dinosaur Museum ⊘ (BY M²) – *Icen Way*. This small but lively museum reveals all sorts of information on dinosaurs using fossils, skeletons and models; among the array of display panels and videos stand full-size reconstructions of the enormous creatures. A musical video *(upstairs)* traces their evolution and eventual extinction.

Tutankhamun Exhibition ⊘ (BY M³) – Dorset's connection with ancient Egypt lies primarily with the eccentric collector William Bankes of **Kingston Lacy**; this exhibition, however, tries to clarify the mystery of Tutankhamun's identity and houses replicas of some of the treasures found in his grave.

Keep Military Museum ⊘ (BY M⁴) – *Bridport Road. 45min*. Combining the historic, the heroic and the personal, this regimental museum includes battle honours, log-books, despatches and diaries telling of campaigns fought under Clive in India, in the Napoleonic wars, in the War of Independence, in 1914-18, 1939-45, in Ireland, Burma, Korea, Bosnia... Colour is provided in the old barracks gatehouse by dress and battle uniforms – extraordinary headgear – evocative scene sets (military punishment, jungle warfare), audio-visual, kettledrums and cartouche boxes, regimental silver, swords, arms, insignia, trophies and interactive computerised displays. The proud record runs from the raising of 39th Foot in 1702 to the formation of the **Devonshire and Dorset Regiment** – one of the few remaining County Regiments – in 1958 to the present. From the battlements there is a glorious **view** over Dorset.

Archeological sites

Roman Villa (AY) – *North of High West Street, behind the County Hall*. A rich man's town villa – considered as the most extensive and best preserved in Britain – has been excavated to reveal the walls and a number of mosaics.

Maumbury Rings (AZ) – *Weymouth Avenue (A354) – Maumbury Road cross roads*.
The rings, a Neolithic henge, were remodelled by the Romans to provide seating, pens for wild animals and an arena. In the 17C the Parliamentarians converted the rings into a gun emplacement.

EXCURSIONS

★★ Maiden Castle *2 miles southwest off Weymouth Road (A354)*.

The massive, grass-covered **earthwork ramparts** ⊘, the finest in Britain, are three miles long as they follow the hillside contours to enclose about a hundred acres on the saddleback down. They have commanded a **view★** of the surrounding countryside for more than 2 000 years.

Building periods – A Neolithic settlement was established on the site in *c*3000 BC. The existing fort was begun *c*800 BC when 16 acres on the east knoll were enclosed by a single rampart with entrances to east and west. At the end of the century the west knoll was added to the enclosure, now some 47 acres.
In *c*150 BC the rampart was rebuilt to twice its original size and augmented by a 50ft deep ditch; additional fortifications were constructed to north and south.
The **final phase** came in 100-60 BC when the appearance of the sling, with a range of 100yds, caused the outer ditches and ramparts to be remodelled and the gateways, always well protected by inner and outer walls, to be made even more of a chicane. Inside, the walls, huts, storage barns and metalled streets were kept in good order; ammunition dumps of 20 000 beach pebbles for use as sling stones were kept prepared. In **AD 43**, however, the future Roman Emperor, Vespasian, besieged Maiden Castle as part of his campaign to subdue southern England. The Ro-

Aerial view of Maiden Castle

man infantry advanced up the slopes, cutting their way through rampart after rampart until, in the innermost bay, they reached the huts which they fired. Under cover of the smoke, the entrance was forced, the inhabitants put to the sword.

At the end of the 4C a Romano-British **temple** and adjoining priest's house and hut were built (foundations uncovered on the east knoll), since when the site has been deserted. All the finds from the excavations are in the Dorset Museum, Dorchester.

Higher Bockhampton *2.5 miles northeast along A35*

Hardy's Cottage ○ – *Half a mile south up a minor road, then 10min walk from car park.* The "small low cottage with a thatched pyramidal roof, and having dormer windows breaking up into the eaves, a single chimney standing in the midst" was built by Hardy's great-grandfather early in the 19C. Downstairs are the modest living rooms and the office from which the elder Hardy conducted his business as local builder and smallholder; upstairs is the bedroom where Thomas Hardy was born and given up for dead until rescued by the midwife. The garden is pleasant with herbs and simples.

Puddletown

The village lies back in an oasis of calm: the "square" of small houses, neatly white-painted or colour-washed, the grey stone Perpendicular **church★** with a pinnacled and crocketed tower a few yards away.

The interior of the church is remarkable for its **17C furnishings** and its **monuments**: the oak box pews, three-decker pulpit and prayer-desk, Norman beaker-shaped font, the west gallery with the arms of England and France and 16C black-letter texts on the walls.

From 1485, when Sir William Martyn came to Athelhampton, part of the church became a family chantry for which Sir William had his own, very fine, **funeral effigy** carved in alabaster some twenty years before his death in 1503.

★ Athelhampton House ○ *6 miles northeast on A35*

House – *45min.* The house dates from early Tudor times when Sir William Martyn (d 1504), Lord of Athelhampton and Lord Mayor of London, whose family came originally from Tours in France and claimed descent from St Martin, was given permission to enclose 160 acres of deer park and build himself an elegantly towered and battlemented mansion overlooking the River Piddle. To this house with its porch, upper room and great hall were added a gabled parlour wing in the same creamy limestone, new fronts and gables and, as a final embellishment, the gardens – the *Magnolia grandiflora* at the front of the house is believed to be about 200 years old.

Interior – The Great Hall is remarkable for its roof, its **oriel** and its linenfold panelling: the roof is built up on braces and collar-beams, the whole given character by the pointed cusps; the oriel is vaulted with cusped ribs and illumined by tall, two-light, two-transom windows on each side again with the cusp motif – among the medieval painted glass note the Martyn crest: a chained ape, from the traditional French name for a monkey, *Martin*. The ape, now with a Saxon crown and carrying a mace, has been adopted by the present owner as his heraldic badge – the crown being a reference to the manor's situation in the realms of Athelhelm and Athelstan, the mace to the family service in Parliament.

The **brass chandelier** with the Virgin is 15C; the **tapestry** is Flemish; the chests are from the 14C and 15C and from 1681 (dated), the **love-seat** from the time of William and Mary.

In the other rooms, note the oak **panelling**, the Pugin and William Morris **wallpaper** and silk wall hangings and among the medley of treasure, which ranges from 17C furniture to examples of metalwork and manufactures from the 1851 Exhibition, a Henry VIII period **credence cupboard**, a painting on glass, *The Misers*, by the Flemish artist **Quentin Matsys** (1465-1530), a collection of wine glasses, Chinese and Chinese-style cabinets and mirrors, 200 **19C china jugs** and Westminster mementoes.

Gardens – Around the house have been laid a series of interconnected individual gardens (1891), each planned with a fine **vista** punctuated by a fountain, statue fountain or decorative wrought-iron gates. They include a **Great Court Garden** with twin pavilions and 12 giant topiary pyramid yews, a **Private Garden** with lawns and a fishpond, and a **White Garden**. Rarest of all is the **Corona**, an Elizabethan-style circular garden, distinguished by an undulating stone wall topped by slender obelisks and banked with flowers; at the centre an urn gently brims over into a small basin. Collections of tulips, magnolias, roses, clematis and lilies alternate through the flowering season.

On the far side of the house are the **Octagon**, a pleached lime cloister and a circular 15C **dovecote** with a renewed hammerbeam roof and lantern and 1500 nest-holes.

Tolpuddle *8 miles northeast of Dorchester*

The village of Tolpuddle, its name now a symbol of workers' rights to form a trade union, lies at the centre of Dorset's farming country. In 1830 an agricultural labourer's wage was 9s a week; in the next two years it dropped to 8*s* then 7*s*... With threat of a fall to 6*s*, the villagers met, according to tradition, under the now-named **Martyrs' Tree** to form the Friendly Society of Agricultural Labourers, with the blessing of the Grand National Consolidated Trades Union.

Fear of militant trade unionism and riots provoked the arrest of the six ring-leaders on 24 February 1834, their trial at the Crown Court in Dorchester and, convicted under the Mutiny Act of 1797 for administering illegal oaths while founding a trade union, the sentence of seven years transportation. The cause of the Six Martyrs, as they soon became known, was taken up by Robert Owen, by Cobbett in Parliament, and at mass rallies, until in 1836 the men were each granted a full and free pardon, though not before they had worked in Australia in penal settlements and Hammett had been "sold like a slave for £1". They all arrived back between June 1837 and 1839 and were resettled in Essex; in 1845 five emigrated to Canada, and Hammett returned to Tolpuddle, where he died in 1891 (his grave in the parish churchyard is marked by a headstone engraved by Eric Gill).

TUC Memorial Cottages - *North side of A35 just before west end of the village.*
In 1934 the TUC erected the line of six cottages for use by retired agricultural workers to commemorate the six Tolpuddle Martyrs: George and James Loveless, Thomas and his son John Standfield, James Brine and James Hammett. At the centre, below the middle of the gables, is the **Tolpuddle Martyrs Museum** which contains documents relevant to the Labour Movement (Wesleyan sermons, court papers, letters and photographs, press cuttings and pamphlets). In the centre of the village *(just beyond the garage)* is the **cottage** of one of the men, Thomas Standfield *(plaque)*.

Methodist Chapel ⊙ - Five of the six martyrs were Methodists. The **arch** to the chapel bears the affirmation handed to the judge immediately before sentence was passed. An annual service of commemoration is held in July.

St John's Church - The parish church of flint with stone trims retains elements of earlier sanctuaries, despite remodelling in 1855: a Perpendicular tower, Norman doorways, late 13C chancel and transept arches, a Decorated north arcade and a 14C **tie-beam roof** with struts and crown posts.
Earliest of all, in the north transept, is the carved Purbeck **marble coffin-lid** of Philip, a priest of AD 1100.

★ Bere Regis

★ **St John the Baptist** - The Perpendicular church, with its flint and stone chequered square tower (1500), is all that was saved in 1788 when the last in a series of fires devastated the village - the communal iron hooks of *c*1600 which were used to pull away burning thatch from cottages on fire, still hang above the church door.
Inside, the church has the finest wooden **parish church roof** in Dorset. It was the climax in the then 500-year old church's rebuilding, made possible by the gift in 1475 of a huge sum by the locally born Cardinal Morton (1425-1500), Arch-bishop of Canterbury and Lord Chancellor to Henry VII. Note the rare 14C altar slab which was buried during the Reformation to save it from being smashed and the carved oak pew ends. Many of the 19C furnishings date from restoration undertaken by G E Street in 1825.

★★ **Roof** - The nave roof is a structure of oak tie beams and braces, crown posts and queen posts, outlined by cresting, filled with tracery, decorated in gold and rich reds, browns, blues, the meeting points masked with bosses, the not-in-fact hammers disguised by almost lifesize carved figures of the **Apostles**. Easily recognisable are John (holding a book or gospel), Judas (with a money bag), Matthew (holding a book), Philip (with a staff) and Peter (with mitre and keys). In 1738 the entry appears in the churchwardens' accounts "Paid Benjamin Moores for Cleaning and Oyling the Apostles 4*s* 0*d*".
In the roof also are four **bosses** celebrating Cardinal Morton: the head at the east end is said to be a portrait; the arms are of Canterbury of which he was archbishop; the Tudor rose is in honour of Henry VII; the fourth symbolises the marriage Morton arranged between the king and Elizabeth of York. Note the **capitals** in the late 12C arcade with carved figures in an agony of toothache, sore throat...
The chancel roof, meanwhile, is shaped like an inverted ship's roof and decorated with five angels.

Bere Regis Church interior

Since the 14C the south aisle has been the Chapel of the Turbervilles – after whom Hardy modelled the family in *Tess of the d'Urbervilles.*

Clouds Hill ⊘ *9 miles east of Dorchester*

T E Lawrence, alias Lawrence of Arabia, first rented and then purchased the small house among the rhododendrons describing it as "a ruined cottage in a wood near camp". In 1923-25 he was a private in the Royal Tank Corps at Bovington and from 1925-35, in the RAF; throughout this time and in the few weeks before his death in May 1935 in a motorcycling accident, he described in letters to his friends how the cottage became "the centre of my world".

"I put the (Greek) jape, « Why worry » upon the architrave. It means that nothing in Clouds Hill is to be a care upon its inhabitant. While I have it there shall be nothing exquisite or unique in it. Nothing to anchor me" (18/X/32). "I look forward to settling there in a year's time, for good" (26/III/33). "The whole place is designed for just a single inhabitant. Panelling; bookshelves; bare wood and undyed leather. A queer place, but great fun. No pictures and no ornaments" (5/III/34). "Two rooms; one upstairs for music (a gramophone and records) and one downstairs" (23/XI/34). "I think everything, inside and outside my place, approaches perfection" (23/XI/34). "Wild mares would not at present take me away from Clouds Hill. It is an earthly paradise" (8/V/35). (*The Letters of T E Lawrence,* edited by David Garnett; Jonathan Cape, 1938).
The dark house, basically furnished – the bedroom insulated with tin – remains as Lawrence left it.

★★ Moreton Church – *3.5 miles southwest by B3390 and by-roads left.*
St Nicholas is a graceful, small Georgian Gothick church with sparkling windows; it dates largely from 1950. Ten years earlier it lay in ruins, destroyed by a bomb jettisoned by a German aircraft. The new church discarded much done in accordance with Victorian taste and reverted to the 18C church plan.
The entrance is beneath the pinnacled tower, trimmed, like the apse and aisle rooflines, with a narrow, lacelike balustrade. Inside, the wide nave beneath a coloured vault leads the eye to the altar standing at the centre of the semicircular apse. The walls are pierced on all sides so that the church is an ethereal lantern. The engraved **windows** – the first, it is believed, in the outside walls of any church – were executed by **Laurence Whistler** between 1955 and 1984. The design is a celebration, in festive style, of spiritual light and the church's dedication to the patron saint of sailors, children and Christmas: St Nicholas. Within the design are candles, ribbons, the emblems of the Passion, trees, a Christmas tree, the church in ruins and rebuilt, the Cross...
T E Lawrence is buried under the cedar in the cemetery entered through the lychgate off the road.

For the Tank Museum, Bovington and Ape Sanctuary, see SWANAGE.

Charminster *1.5 miles northwest of Dorchester by A37 and first turning right.*

St Mary's – The church has a splendid **west tower** which rises in three stages to battlements and crocketed pinnacles, presented by Thomas Trenchard of Wolfeton House *(see below).* A profusion of gargoyles, grotesques, corbels, angels and the double T monogram of Thomas Trenchard are carved from Ham stone. The body of the church with its round **chancel arch** and massive circular pillars dates from the 11C-12C; note the **nail-head decoration** and, at the northeast end of the nave, the purple-pink **pomegranates** which, being similar to those in Seville Cathedral, are said to have been stencilled by craftsmen sent over after Philip of Hapsburg and his wife, Joanna, daughter of Ferdinand and Isabella of Spain, had sheltered from a storm at sea in Wolfeton House in 1506.

Wolfeton House ⊘ – A **gatehouse** of massive, but dissimilar, round towers guards the entrance to the former Elizabethan manor house, built by Trenchard in the 16C.

The remainder of the main building was remodelled in the Classical style in the mid-1550s. Inside the house, the **screens passage** with a stone-groin vault above linenfold panelling is dominated by a fine **stone staircase** (c1580) with a pierced balustrade and stone caryatid, flanked by two Jacobean doorways, robustly carved with moustachioed Romans in sandals carrying cutlasses and a club carrying ancient Briton.

The stairs lead through a graceful 16C pedimented doorway with fluted pilasters to the **Great Chamber** where a floor-to-ceiling stone fireplace of c1600 exotically carved with Red Indians and Orientals hints at the room's former glory. The Jacobean porches open into the plaster-decorated parlour and dining room.

The garden offers a good view of the early 16C **south front** with its candle-snuffer buttress, stair-turrets, transomed windows...

North of the house sits the **Riding House** thought to be the oldest in the country.

> The village of **Godmanstone** *(off the A352 north of Dorchester)* has what is reputedly the smallest inn in the kingdom: the **Smith's Arms** is a 15C-17C flint and stone building of one room, snug and warmly thatched, overlooking the River Cerne. Antique pews align the wall, a high-backed settle provides a strategic position for toasting the toes before the fire.

★ **Cerne Abbas** 8 *miles north of Dorchester by the Sherborne road (A352).*

The village main street, bordered by shops and a couple of very old inns, intersects with Abbey Street where there stands a beautiful **range of 16C houses**, timber framed upon brick-coursed flint; carved corbels support jettied upper floors.

The Benedictine abbey, after which the street is named, was founded in 987 and dissolved in 1539. The house *(private; much rebuilt after a fire)* aligned to the street, with a centre gable and angle buttresses, was built as the main gateway to the abbey. The ruined porch to the abbot's hall remains in the undergrowth in the wood to the right.

Cerne Abbas Giant

In c1300 the monks gave the village a **church**, St Mary's, from which the Early English chancel survives, complete with 14C paintings; the nave and aisles were rebuilt in the 15C, separated by an arcade with engaged columns and ring capitals. The spectacular Ham Hill stone Perpendicular **tower** with its statue of the Virgin and Child is 16C. Inside, the table altar dates from 1638 *(south aisle)*, the testered pulpit from 1640, the communion rail is Jacobean, the chandelier 18C, the stone screen 15C.

Cerne Giant – The figure outlined in the turf stands 180ft tall and carries a club 120ft long; his head and eye are respectively 23ft 6in and 2ft 6in across; his feet are in profile. Although he is thought, for obvious reasons, to be associated with ancient fertility rites, the giant's origin and date remain unclear.

EXETER★★

Devon – Population 98 125
Michelin Atlas p 4 or Map 403 – J 31

The skyline of Exeter has been dominated by the twin towers of its cathedral since the 12C. The city's history began some 1300 years earlier when a settlement was established by the local **Isca Dumnoniorum** tribe on the westward-sloping hillside at the limit of the navigable waters of the River Exe. In the 1C AD the Romans captured the settlement, built it up as their most westerly strongpoint and brought it out of isolation by extending the London-Silchester-Dorchester road to it.

A monastery was founded in what is now the cathedral precinct during the early peaceful **Saxon** period, developing into a respected centre of learning at which St Boniface (680-755) is alleged to have studied; peace lasted until 876 when, despite the efforts of King Alfred, Danish invaders began a series of raids. After the final devastation in 1003 the city was rebuilt and in 1050 Edward the Confessor authorised the translation of the metropolitan see to Exeter from Crediton.

Further tribulations followed. It was here that Gytha, the mother of the slain Saxon King Harold, had settled rallying the citizens of Exeter to defy William the Conqueror until 1068 when he marched upon them with 500 horsemen; after 18 days they capitulated; the church of St Olave was thereupon entrusted to Battle Abbey. During the **Wars of the Roses** the city changed sides more than once. In 1497 it resisted **Perkin Warbeck's** assault with 600 men; in 1549 it was unsuccessfully besieged by the rebels against the imposition of the English prayer book. In the Civil War Exeter fell first to the Royalists; it was then captured and ransacked by the Parliamentarians and became a minor centre of royalist plots; royal toasts were drunk at an inn in the Blackboy Road. In 1671 the **Black Boy** himself, Charles II, came to Exeter to acknowledge the support he had received. His brother James II, however, was not popular; the citizens gave their support to the **Duke of Monmouth** *(see* BRIDGWATER: Battle of Sedgemoor) – 80 local men were condemned at the Bloody Assizes – and later turned out into the streets to welcome the future William III.

In May 1942, Exeter was targeted by Hitler for one of those devastating "Baedeker" raids: most of the city's medieval fabric was destroyed. Recent archeological investigations have revealed substantial evidence of Roman building (basilica and bath-house), amphora, glass vessels, Samarian and local stoneware (now on display in the Royal Albert Memorial Museum).

Market days: Monday to Saturday in Sidewell Street and St George's Indoor Market; livestock and farming: Friday; horses at Exeter Livestock Centre: second Tuesday in every month.

Guided tours ⊘ of the city are available.

★★ CATHEDRAL ⊘ (z) *1 hour*

Edward the Confessor appointed Leofric as the first bishop in 1050 (d 1072). The builder of the cathedral's distinctive **transept towers** was Bishop William Warelast (1107-37), nephew of the Conqueror; the builder of the cathedral church much as we know it today was **Bishop Walter Bronescombe** (1257-80) who, while retaining the transept towers, remodelled the major part of the 12C building. The work was finally completed a century later under **Bishop John Grandisson** (1327-69) who was buried in a chapel built within the thickness of the wall of the final achievement, the Decorated west front image screen.

Exterior – On the Green in front of the Cathedral sits the figure of **Richard Hooker**, priest and scholar (1553-1600). The cathedral itself, of grey-white Beer stone, rises through buttresses and flying buttresses, windows of five lights and Decorated tracery, to crocketed pinnacles and castellated parapets. The long lines are massively interrupted by the twin but not identical towers which mount solidly through tiers of rounded blind arcading and intersecting arches to castellations and the angle turrets with pepperpot roofs, substituted in the 15C for the traditional Norman pyramids.

At the west end, one good idea was obviously superimposed upon another: the upper gable window is half-hidden by the main window which, in turn, is masked at the base by the pierced parapet edging the splendid late 14C – early 15C **image screen**. This bears 3 rows of fine stone figures: God the Father; Apostles and Evangelists *(top row)*; King Richard II and many unidentified figures.

Nave – The striking tierceron **vaulting** extends 300ft from west to east in an uninterrupted line of meeting ribs with huge gilded and coloured bosses studding the junctures. The ribs fan out from shafts which descend through the triforium stage to important gilded and coloured **corbels** between the pointed arches of the arcade, in turn supported on **piers** of sixteen clustered columns with plain ring capitals.

Note the **minstrels' gallery** *(north side)* with 14 angels playing contemporary musical instruments – bagpipes, a recorder, viol, harp; the west **rose window** with its reticulated

Exeter Cathedral

tracery (20C glass); the great **corbels**, each illustrating as many as three biblical themes.

Except at the crest, the view east is blocked by the pulpitum, a pierced stone screen of 1325, surmounted by a top-heavy organ.

Chancel – The high altar stands before the **Exeter pillar**, the prototype of all the pillars in the cathedral with sixteen shafts and ring capitals.

Through the just pointed arches on either side can be seen the clustered pillars of the ambulatory and the Lady Chapel and, above, the great **east window** (1390) incorporating some original glass from an earlier one (bottom of the three side lights of each side).

The painted corbels at the base of the vaulting shaft, carved with figures and/or foliage predate those in the nave; one is alleged to be a self-portrait of William of Montacute.

Sir Gilbert Scott's canopied choirstalls (1870-77) incorporate the oldest complete set of **misericords** in the country – 49 in number, carved in 1260-80 (a medieval elephant has been moved to a glass case in the south aisle).

The **bishop's throne** (1312) is a fountain of Gothic wood carving in oak, entirely held by pegs – which has enabled it to be twice dismantled in times of danger: during the Commonwealth (17C) and in 1939-45.

The double-canopied, Decorated **sedilia** to the right of the altar are 13C.

Several tombs with recumbent figures arranged with legs crossed, include those of various bishops including Walter Stapeldon, founder of Stapeldon Hall (Exeter College) in Oxford; the 13C effigy in black basalt, on a later gilded and canopied tomb, is **Bishop Bronescombe** *(see above)*.

East End Chapels – The central section is dedicated to the **Lady Chapel**, begun by Bishop Bronescombe (1258-80) between chapels dedicated to St John the Evangelist and St George; St Saviour, St Boniface and St Gabriel.

Transepts – Note the Bishop Grandisson **15C astronomical clock** with the sun and moon revolving round the earth in the north transept; in the south transept are two further tombs, one being that of Sir John Gilbert, the half brother of Sir Walter Raleigh.

Chapter House – The original building having fallen into disrepair, the present fabric dates largely from 1412 when the Early English windows were inserted. The contemporary figures replace those that were removed at the Reformation.

B. Kaufmann

Cathedral Close (Z)

The close is diamond shaped with the cathedral at the centre almost abutted to the southeast by the gabled, red sandstone bishop's palace. Marking the limits are the old **city wall**, a small spired church, a school and some houses, and a curving line of tall 17C-19C shops and houses ending in a white, Georgian four-storey hotel. Pinched into the northern corner of the close is the minute red sandstone **St Martin's Church (Y A)**, dedicated in 1065 and rebuilt in the 15C.

St Martin's Lane (Y 49) – The alley cuts through between the church and the hotel to the street. On one side is the **Ship Inn (Y E)**, half-timbered, heavily beamed, dark and brightly lit and as crowded as in the days when Drake, Hawkins and the queen's admirals used to meet inside.

Cathedral Close Walk (YZ 13) – The northeast side of the close begins at the black and white painted **Mol's Coffee House (Y B)**, a four-storey house of 1596 beneath an ornate gable with windows extending across its full width. It is also reputed to be one of Drake's onetime haunts.
Small shops with bay windows below, oriels above, merge into Tudor beamed houses with oversailing upper floors over possibly older red sandstone ground floors, and beyond, neat, porched, 18C houses of brick with stone trims.

New Cut (Z) – At the east end, New Cut leads out of the close beneath a 19C **cast-iron footbridge** complete with the donors' names.

Southernhay (YZ) – The double terrace of 18C three-storey houses in brick with stone trims, iron railings and tall, rounded ground-floor windows and doorways encloses a broad central garden of trees, lawns and vivid flower-borders.

OTHER SIGHTS

★ **Royal Albert Memorial Museum** ⊙ (Y) – This is a particularly dynamic little museum with superb collections of artefacts and an active educational policy. The four areas of especial interest range from natural history to archeology and ethnography to the fine and decorative arts.

Natural History – The Devon Gallery presents the geological features of the county together with its flora and fauna (including Devon whales); special units, dedicated to local biological and geological research, also monitor changes in the

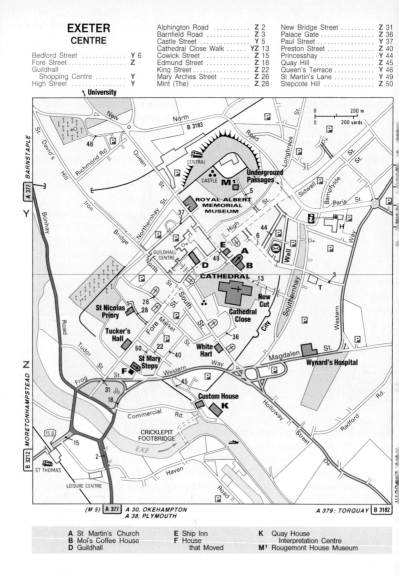

EXETER
CENTRE

A	St Martin's Church	E	Ship Inn	K	Quay House
B	Mol's Coffee House	F	House		Interpretation Centre
D	Guildhall		that Moved	M¹	Rougemont House Museum

ecology of the area. The rest of the collection – one of the largest and most complete outside London – includes a variety of material relating to all five continents between Antarctica and the Arctic: plants, invertebrates, butterflies and moths, beetles, molluscs, sea urchins, starfish, birds, mammals and geological specimens (access to a large reserve study collection on application).

Archeology – The purpose-built Royal Albert Memorial Museum is the depository for the most important **prehistoric material** found in Devon: remains of extinct animals retrieved from Devon cave sites (including Kents Cavern); evidence of early farming practices from New Stone Age settlements (Hembury, Haldon and Hazard Hill); sophisticated examples of cast bronze, gold jewellery and pottery from barrows. This collection is supplemented with large quantities of **Roman artefacts** left over from the occupation of Exeter by the Roman legions (AD55 – AD75): pottery and glass (earliest fragments of mosaic found in Britain), coins, military armour and weaponry. Medieval fragments suggest the continued prosperity of the city.

Ethnography – A number of Exeter families maintained considerable business interests in foreign trade, especially West Africa and the Pacific. Among the considerable specimens of tribal art, including artefacts collected by Captain Cook, are a fine series of Nigerian sculptures (Yaruba ceremonial masks), cast-metal effigies from Benin and a compete mourning dress from Hawaii.

Decorative arts – Exeter was for long an assay town with a large number of gold and silversmiths, jewellers and clockmakers working in the city: fine displays of 18C-19C **clocks** and **watches** from Exeter and Bristol workshops, unique 16C-19C **silver** including communion cups, alms dishes, tankards and flagons,

Apostle spoons, Georgian coffee and chocolate pots, cream jugs and tea pots... The work was little influenced either by the Baroque style of the Huguenots, who did not travel this far west, or by the French Rococo favoured in George II's reign, but retained its purity of line almost until the 19C. A separate case holds a beautiful bequest of 60 **West Country spoons** (16C-17C).

Examples of **Devon pottery** consist of slipware harvest jugs from the Barnstaple-Bideford area and Torquay "art" wares; this is complemented by a rare gift of **Martinware**. The **glass** collection represents the high points in glass-making from Roman times to 18C England, including pieces from Venice and Bohemia.

The **fine art** collection spans the 17C-20C with particular representations of artists associated with Devon: Thomas Hudson, Joshua Reynolds, Francis Hayman, Francis Towne, Samuel Prout, William and Frederick Widgery; also works by the Camden Town Group of Artists, St Ives School, Paul and John Nash, Duncan Grant...

Selections from the museum's substantial collection of topographical works on paper (watercolours, prints and drawings) are often used to supplement displays on the history of the city and county, in Exeter and elsewhere in the region, as is a broad range of 19C-20C scientific and mechanical instruments (microscopes, radios, cameras, typewriters etc).

Rougemont House Museum ⊘ (**Y M¹**) – This elegant Regency house (1760), standing in its garden beside the old castle gate, is used as an education centre for school groups.

Underground Passages ⊘ (**Y**) – *1 hour*. The cut rock or stone built passages were part of an aqueduct system. A video in the Interpretation Centre and a tour explain their history. Given the constraints of the sometimes dark and narrow tunnels, this is not recommended to those suffering from claustrophobia.

Guildhall ⊘ (**Y D**) – The Tudor portico was added in 1593 to, it is believed, the oldest municipal building in the country, erected in 1330 on a possibly Saxon site. The **Chamber** has a timber roof of 1468-70 and outstanding oak **panelling** with no two panels carved alike. Note the bear and ragged staff supporters of Warwick the Kingmaker and the Yorkist cause, the Caroline chairs, the mayoral regalia of several periods, the great 18C brass **chandelier** and the **portraits** of Princess Henrietta daughter of Charles I, born in the city, and of the Devonian General Monck first Duke of Albemarle (1608-70), Parliamentary and later Restoration land and sea general.

St Nicholas Priory ⊘ (**Z**) – The red stone building served once as the domestic and guest wing of a small Benedictine priory founded in 1087 by a small group of monks from Battle Abbey; suppressed in 1536, the church and cloister was pulled down and the remaining buildings were sold by the Crown. During Elizabethan times the place was converted into a wealthy merchant's residence. The **entrance hall, undercroft-crypt** with massive round columns supporting low, stone ribbed vaulting, the kitchen and, upstairs, the large **guest hall** with an arch braced roof, also the adjoining solar and bedrooms, are furnished with 16C-17C tables, chairs, chests, a painted **virginal** of 1697 and a tester bed and cradle. Displays by the Devon and Dorset Regiment.

Tucker's Hall ⊘ (**Z**) – The hall of the Weavers, Fullers (Tuckers) and Shearmen, created in 1638 when a 15C chapel was divided horizontally, is an example of Devon high craftsmanship in oak with its **barrel roof** and carved **panelling.** Note the **royal arms,** the **boards of benefactors,** also the items discovered when the false plaster ceiling was removed – halberds, pikes...

Stepcote Hill (**Z 50**) – The hill with shallow cobbled steps and a centre runnel is lined on either side by small, adjoined stone and half-timbered 16C houses.

St Mary Steps (**Z**) – The 16C, red sandstone church at the bottom of the hill is known for its clock which has **striking jacks.**

House that Moved (**Z F**) – The tall Tudor merchant's house (now a shop) with oversailing upper floors was so named in 1964 when it was transported 75yds.

White Hart (**Z**) – The 14C-15C inn, which has massive beams, flagged floors, dark panelled rooms and a courtyard, was the house of William Wynard, Recorder of Exeter.

Wynard's Hospital (**Z**) – The almshouses *(private)*, an attractive group of cottages surrounding a cobbled courtyard containing a well, were founded by Wynard *(see above)* in 1435 to house 12 poor and infirm citizens and a chaplain.

Quayside (**Z**) *Access by the Butts ferry or the Cricklepit Footbridge.*

The quay dates from earlier days when Exeter was a tidal river port. The period of prosperity was brought to an abrupt end in the 13C *(see Topsham, below)*. When after 300 years of litigation, which Exeter won, the corporation sought to re-open the port in the 16C, the river was no longer navigable so the first ship canal in England was dug (1563-66). The cliffside cellars, which contain a collection of Portuguese fishing boats, are flanked by two **warehouses** (1835). At the north end of the quay, opposite the old fishmarket, stands the **Custom House** (1680), a symbol of the canal trade at the time and one of the first buildings in Exeter to be constructed of **brick** which was probably imported as ballast from Holland. The **Quay House Interpretation Centre** ⊘ (**K**) is housed in another 17C building, on the site of the original 1574 Tudor dock; its projecting roof sheltered goods during loading and unloading. The centre presents models, paintings and artefacts and an audio-visual history of Exeter.

Exeter University (Y) *2 miles north of the city centre via Queen Street and New North Road.*

The campus of the university is mostly situated in new buildings including the Northcott Theatre, on the undulating 350-acre Streatham estate; the grounds are recognised as the most beautiful and botanically interesting of any British university.

EXCURSIONS

Topsham *4 miles south on B3182.*

The small port on the point of land between where the Rivers Exe and Clyst flow into the long Exe Estuary reached the height of its importance in the 13C when Isabella, Countess of Devon, built a weir across the river and successfully diverted all trade from Exeter to Topsham *(see Quayside, above)*. Boat-builders set up yards, craftsmen, dockers and sailors appeared on the waterfront and, in the 17C, merchants built the Dutch gabled houses still to be seen along the Strand. Its heyday has passed but Topsham retains an old-fashioned charm; it is pleasant to stroll along the High Street into Fore Street and the **Strand** to look at the old, half-timbered pubs, the **Shell House** with its hooded doorway, the sailing dinghies on the river and the birds on the mud flats. Housed in a late 17C merchant's house, **Topsham Museum** ⊘ includes period rooms, a sail loft and estuary gardens; it recounts the history of the Exe Estuary, local shipbuilding and maritime trade and includes exhibits on **Honiton lace and lacemaking**.

For Powderham Castle, see TEIGNMOUTH.

Crediton *8 miles northwest along A377*

"When Exeter was a fuzzy town", the old rhyme goes, "Kirton (Crediton) was a market town" and such it remains with a long wide main street of mostly 18C-19C houses with shops at pavement level and, in some of the taller, three storey houses, traces of weaving lofts from when the town was known for its woollen serges (1800-50).

At the lower, east end of the main street stands the vast church built on the site of the earliest cathedral of the See of Devon.

★ **Holy Cross Church** – *30min.* In 739 Aethelheard, King of Wessex, founded a monastery in Crediton, which in the 10C became the seat of the new bishopric of Devon and Cornwall. In 1050 the see passed to Bishop Leofric who transferred it to Exeter, and the church at Crediton became a college of secular canons. In 1539,

> ### St Boniface
>
> The Apostle of Germany, a Benedictine who took the name Boniface, was born in Crediton *c*680 to Anglo-Saxon parents who christened him Wynfrith. In 722 he was summoned to Rome by Gregory II and made Bishop of all Germany east of the Rhine for his missionary work among the Germans. He organised the German and Frankish churches, founded the abbey of Fulda (*c*743) and became Archbishop of Mainz (*c*747). As archbishop, he was responsible for crowning Pepin, the father of Charlemagne, King of France. In old age he returned to Frisia, where he was murdered in 754.

when the college was dissolved, the town raised £300 to "purchase" the former collegiate church and annex the rich Exminster living. The transaction was confirmed in 1547 under a charter granted by Edward VI which incorporated 12 "governors" to supervise the church's temporal affairs including the collection of tithes, providing for the poor and establishing a Free Grammar School (in the Lady Chapel, 1572-1876).

The fabric of the church is built in the local pink volcanic stone which contrasts with the creamy Beer stone used for its Perpendicular window tracery and crossing tower pinnacles.

Interior – The **nave** (1415) is illuminated by clerestory windows (rare in Devon) and covered by a 19C tie-beam roof: its dominant feature, however, is the "period" memorial (1911) in an extraordinary assortment of marble and mosaic. Note the stone benches, the Norman font bowl *(left of the porch)*, the modern wooden statue of St Boniface *(north aisle)* and the lively carving of the 19C wooden eagle lectern.

The **crossing** is the earliest part of the church, dating from *c*1150; among the capitals carved with snakes, scallops and zig-zag decoration, note the pair of solemnly perched birds with spread wings. In the **south transept**, note the 15C human head corbels and 20C armorial window.

In the three-storey Early English building dating from *c*1300 are accommodated the **former chapter house** and governors' room: here the former chapter-house now serves as a vestry; a museum displays a large model of the High Street in 1743; the Governor's Room on the second floor contains 17C armour, a buffcoat, a musket and pair of boots from the Civil War, a 15C angel boss, charity boards and an ingenious vote-casting box.

The **chancel** and aisles contain a number of monuments commemorating Sir John and Lady Sully (full length effigies), he a Knight of the Garter, warrior of Crécy and Poitiers, who is said to have died aged 105 in 1387; Sir William Perryam (d 1650), a judge at Mary, Queen of Scots' trial, leaning on one elbow in his judicial robes above his weeping family; and the 17C Elizabeth Tuckfield, between her be-ruffed husband and father-in-law.

In the **St Boniface Chapel** is a 15C Flemish merchant's chest.

★★ Killerton ⊘ *7 miles northeast by B3181.*

House – *45min.* The house of 1778 stands at the foot of a wooded hillside in glorious parkland on a site purchased by the Aclands in the 17C. After successive remodellings it now houses Acland portraits, contemporary 18C-19C furniture including some pieces especially made for the house, and Paulise de Bush's Collection of 18C-20C Costume.

Ground floor – In the **Music Room**, the chamber organ dates from 1807, the late 18C square piano was made by Clementi, the grand piano is of 1870. The 18C mahogany china cabinet is from Exeter.

The **Drawing Room** is furnished with the portrait and figurine of **Hannah More** who was supported in her work to bring about the abolition of the slave trade by Sir Thomas Acland, the then owner of the house.

The walnut bookcases in the **Library** were especially designed for the house as were the dumb-waiter, pier glasses and marble folio cabinets in the **Dining Room**.

Upstairs – The rooms, which serve as the setting for displays from the Paulise de Bush **Costume Collection**, are peopled with men, women and children in period tableaux: a 1930s cocktail party, a mid-18C musical or painting group, a 1920s nursery, a Victorian mourning group showing one of Queen Victoria's dresses, jet, crêpe, a child in funereal black, a line of 1900s bathing costumes. The displays, historic and sometimes amusing, change every year.

Garden ⊘ – The garden near the house provides colour throughout early spring to late summer with bulbs, early flowering shrubs, clouds of rhododendrons banked along the hillside, magnolias and island beds. Later the wide herbaceous borders on the terrace come into their own and, lastly, the broad-leaved trees with their autumn tints against the silver grey, pale gold and dark green of the conifers. The stables house an exhibition on the history of the family and estate; Markers Cottage (in the nearby village of Broadclyst) is a medieval cob house.

EXMOOR★★

Somerset and Devon

Michelin Atlas p 6, 7 or Map 403 – I, J 30

Exmoor is one of the smaller (267 square miles) National Parks, extending into Devon along its western limits but lying largely in Somerset. Consisting of a 1 200-1 700ft ridged plateau west of the Brendon Hills, the National Park offers a wide range of beautiful scenery from bare upland ridges covered in purple moor-grass, bracken, deer sedge or heather, to great hollows, wide valleys enlivened by streams trickling over stones, or wooded ravines, silent except for birdsong and a rushing torrent – especially those which flow north through waterfalls and gorges into the Bristol Channel.

Exmoor Forest – In the early Middle Ages the forest was one of many unenclosed, uncultivated tracts of land where game, notably red deer, was preserved for the royal hunt; by 1300 the Royal Forest had been reduced to 20 000 acres around the headwaters of the principal rivers; since 1508 much of the land has been leased out to pasture – as many as 30 000 sheep and additional cattle now graze it between March and October, and ponies all the year round. The stock has always belonged to local farmers, for the moor has been settled since prehistoric times.

In 1818 the last 10 000 acres of the Royal Forest were sold at £5 an acre to **John Knight**, a Midlands ironmaster, who set about revolutionizing farming on the moor: by the end of the century a pattern had been set of isolated farmsteads breeding beef and sheep on the uplands for finishing in the valleys. Between 1900 and 1940, when agriculture everywhere in England sank into decline, the moor looked as though it would take over once more; since 1945 however, the pattern has resumed, with owner-occupiers and tenants farming 50-300 acres with flocks of breeding ewes (Exmoor Horn and Devon Closewool having been outnumbered by other breeds such as the Scottish Blackface) and small herds of cattle (horned Devon Reds, known as the "Red Rubies" of the West Country, although these are becoming a rare sight).

Protected species – The **Exmoor ponies**, brown, bay or dun in colour, have a characteristic mealy-coloured muzzle and inside ear. Their quick intelligence and distinctive head show clearly the Exmoor pony's direct descent from prehistoric horses: with only some 500 breeding animals left worldwide, they are amongst the rarest species indigenous to Britain. Herds may sometimes be spotted in the Haddon Hill area, around Winsford Hill, Withypool Common, Dunkery and Molland Moor. The **Red deer** are also descendants of the animals of prehistoric Britain. It is estimated that there are now well over 2 000 on the moor. They live in the woodlands close to the deeper river valleys and are wild, elusive and seldom seen. In 1997, a motion was carried to ban hunting on some Exmoor land owned by the National Trust.

Orientation – Large swathes of land are privately owned and remain inaccessible to the public: other areas are open to exploration along footpaths in the interests of conservation. The Ordnance Survey 1:25000 Outdoor Leisure map marks public Rights of Way; this together with information about cycle routes and bridleways (including where your horse may be stabled), guided walks and nature trails are available from the five National Park Visitor Centres. Fresh water fishing is limited in the main to permit owners.

Exmoor's rugged coastline provides sanctuary to a variety of sea birds (fulmars, kittiwakes, razorbills, guillemots, herring and black-backed gulls, shags, cormorants) which are best viewed from the sea as the high cliffs may be dangerous. Boats from Minehead (*see* MINEHEAD), Watchet, Lynmouth and Il-fracombe *(see* ILFRACOMBE) may also be hired for a day's fishing (bass, cod, whiting, conger, skate). Paths down to the sea provide access to the sheltered habitats of plants and animals, and to rock pools filled with shells, crabs and sea creatures – beware of the tide.

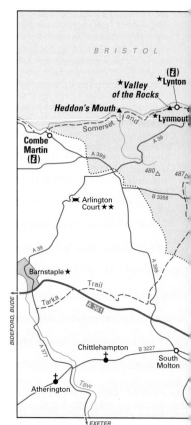

The coast from Luccombe to Combe Martin

★ **Luccombe** – The village consists of attractive cottages clustered around a shop, to the southeast of Porlock. A tall embattled tower rises above the 16C Perpendicular **church**★ which has a barrel **roof** decorated with large bosses carved with solemn faces.

Luccombe is a good centre for walking: to the Dunkery Beacon (*6 miles there and back; see above)*, and by woodland paths to Webber's Post, a well known local viewpoint (*2 miles there and back)*.

★ **Selworthy** – The white-walled thatched cottages and ancient stone tithe barn make a perfect setting for the small, embattled Church of All Saints.

The 15C-16C **church**★, white-walled with dark stone trims, is entered through a two-storey porch set between finely traceried windows. The door is linenfold panelled. The interior is light, with slender piers. The **south aisle** (1538) is known for its original wagon roof embellished with carved **bosses** and **angel wall plates**. Note the slender turned balusters of the **communion rail** (*c*1700).

Outside, there is a splendid **view★★** of Dunkery Beacon to the southwest across Exmoor.

Allerford – The village of a few houses and a pub, nearly all built of local red sandstone, is known for its ancient **packhorse bridge**.

★ **Porlock** – Porlock is an attractive village. It is surrounded on three sides by the Exmoor hills and has a narrow winding main street marked by a church with a lopped spire, and thatched and creeper-covered houses. **Porlock Hill** to the west with a superb **view★★** remains as notorious as ever with a 1:4 gradient; "the man from Porlock", who interrupted Coleridge as he was writing *Kubla Khan*, remains as unknown a character as ever.

The local **Visitor Centre** provides information on cycle routes, bridleways, guided walks and maps. Look out for **Exmoor Glass** ⓥ where glass blowers demonstrate their skill.

★ **St Dubricius Church** – The church has a truncated, octagonal **spire** covered in oak shingles set on a solid 13C stone tower. It is not known whether the tower was ever completed and subsequently destroyed in a storm or whether it was abandoned halfway – one story has it that the workmen left to follow the hunt as it passed through the village and never returned from the moor.

Inside, the **Early English arcade**, the **east window** of three tall lancets under one arch, the double piscina and arch at the west end of the nave are all 13C; the Perpendicular windows were inserted during the 15C reconstruction. Note the remarkable **canopied tomb** with alabaster effigies of John, 4th Lord Harington and his wife (dd 1417, 1461).

The dedication and tradition of foundation by St Dubricius or Dyffrig is a reminder of the work in the southwest of Celtic missionaries from Wales in the 5C-6C; Dubricius, a legendary figure who died aged 120 in *c*612, is said to have been a friend of King Arthur and present at the Battle of Bladon Hill in 517.

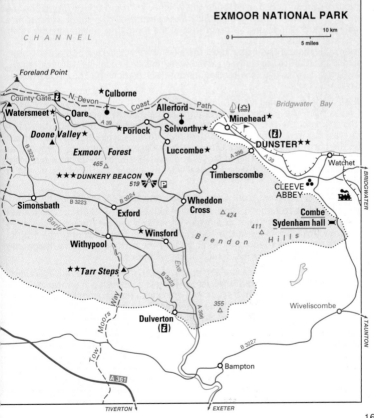

Alabaster effigies of John, 4th Lord Harington and his wife

Porlock Weir – *Take the by-road on the right at the end of the village.*
The small harbour filled with pleasure-craft is overlooked by white-washed cottages and old inns.

★ **St Beuno, Culbone** – *2 miles along the Ashley Combe Toll Road; park at the old farm toll gate; 3 miles steeply uphill on foot there and back: go armed with insect repellent or a fly whisk in high summer (40min from Porlock Weir).*

The irregular path is through broad-leafed woods which extend back from 400ft cliffs towards the Exmoor hills – but always within sound of the sea.
Suddenly, in a dell with a rushing stream, there is the 12C-13C church of St Beuno, the smallest complete church in England (12ft 4in across by 35ft long). The walls of rubble stone are intended to be rendered and whitewashed; the roof is of slate, as is the spirelet added *c*1810 (allegedly removed from Porlock Church by the Devil). On the north side, the possibly **Saxon window** of two lights, cut out of a single block of sandstone, is decorated at the top of the mullion with a relief of a cat-like face.
Inside, the chancel has had a too-large east window inserted and a neo-Gothic reredos but the **rood screen** was carved with foils and cusps by 14C craftsmen. The family pew is 17C, the **benches** are pre-Reformation and the circular **font** is possibly Saxon.

Oare – Oare, mentioned in the Domesday Book, lies in a green valley only a couple of miles from the sea and owes its fame entirely to the novel *Lorna Doone* by R D Blackmore. The 14C-15C **church**, with a tower rebuilt in the mid-19C when much else was restored, is the one in which John Ridd and Lorna Doone were married and the north window the one through which Carver is reputed to have shot at Lorna. Note the 18C painting of Moses and the 18C-19C **box pews, pulpit** and desk. Blackmore's grandfather was a typical, mostly absent, rector of the village in the 19C.

★ **Doone Valley** – *Access from Oare: 6 miles return on foot, 90min.*

The valley came to fame in 1869 with the publication of R D Blackmore's novel *Lorna Doone*, based on tales of a group of outlaws and cut-throats who settled in the Badgworthy Valley in the 1620s and were not expelled until the 1690s. The path from Oare to the two contenders for the fictitious valley via **Badgworthy Water** and **John Ridd's Waterfall** attracts many visitors each year.

★ **Watersmeet** – *1.5 miles east of Lynmouth by A39, then 200yds along a footpath.*
The spot is where the waters of the East Lyn River and Hoaroak Water meet in a deep, wooded valley, dappled with sunlight and green with ferns; the river bed is strewn with great boulders around which the water swirls and falls in an unending cascade. A fishing lodge of 1832 stands on the far bank across a footbridge.

★ **Lynmouth and Lynton** – The complementary small towns nestle in a hollow at the top and at the foot of 500ft North Devon-Exmoor cliffs, rejoicing in glorious **views**★ across the Bristol Channel to the distant Welsh coast, in sweeping moorland, cliff walks and wooded valley walks beside rushing torrents and waterfalls and, since 1890, in a **Cliff Railway** that links them together. This was also one of the first settlements in Britain to be powered by electricity, provided by the hydro-electric power station (now destroyed), from 1890.

The architecture in **Lynton** is predominantly Victorian-Edwardian, the larger houses in their own gardens now largely converted into hotels (the Valley of the Rocks Hotel having accommodated the likes of Bertrand and Dora Russell in 1924).

Lynmouth remains a traditional fishing village with small stone cottages and houses, a few still thatched, to which have been added seaside villas and more recent buildings following the flood disaster of 1952 when the River Lyn burst its banks, broke bridges and swept through the village, bringing down mud and 40 000 tons of boulders and broken tree trunks in its storm waters. In the 18C the isolated port traded coal and limestone for oysters, farm and woodland produce with Wales.

The Rhenish Tower which stands in the harbour is thought to have dispensed private showers of salt water – built at a time when bathing was permitted in segregated areas.

Literary associations

The 14C thatched pub, the **Rising Sun Inn** on Mars Hill, is said to have sheltered R D Blackmore while he wrote his novel *Lorna Doone*. From here it is a steep climb up the Lyn valley to Watersmeet.

In 1797 the poets Wordsworth and Coleridge arrived here on foot having walked 30 miles from Nether Stowey in the Quantock Hills. While staying at Culbone nearby (now called Ash Farm), Coleridge began his poem *Kubla Khan* before being rudely awakened from an opium-induced reverie by the "person from Porlock".

Years later in 1812, the disowned young poet Shelley came to Lynmouth accompanied by his 16-year old "bride" Harriet Westbrook, her sister Eliza, a former governess and an Irish servant. During his stay, Shelley distributed his revolutionary pamphlet the *Declaration of Rights* he'd had printed in Ireland: some he sealed inside bottles which were wrapped in oiled cloth and packed into crates equipped with a sail before being launched from the beach; others he despatched in miniature hot-air balloons from Countisbury Hill.

Cliff Railway ⊙ – The funicular railway rises almost 500ft at a gradient of 1:1.75 to connect the two resorts. The last working water-powered Victorian cliff railway in Europe comprises two cars which operate by gravity, the top car taking on 700 gallons of water as ballast to hoist the lower one and discharging as it reaches the bottom.

★ **Valley of Rocks** – *1 mile west of Lynton along the Coastal Road*. The rocks, swathed in bracken, rise from the wide, grass-covered valley floor to crests of bare shale, spectacularly carved by the wind into fancifully named outlines...

Heddon's Mouth – *5 miles east by the Coastal Road to Hunter's Inn then 3 miles on foot there and back through the woods*. The road skirts three bays from above before coming to the village of Martinhoe and, just beyond, Hunter's Inn. The rift followed by the Heddon is spectacular with rock walls rising 700ft in places before it opens out into a small, sheltered, pebble bay.

Combe Martin – *16 miles west by A39 and A399*.
The village, between Exmoor and Ilfracombe, straggles the length of the combe, marked by an 18C folly, the **Pack of Cards Inn** and a pink sandstone **church** with a west tower 99ft tall, decorated with gargoyles. Lead and silver mines were worked locally from the 13C to the 19C.

The **Combe Martin Motorcycle Collection** ⊙ (*Cross Street*) has motorbikes and motorised invalid carriages, archaic petrol pumps and garage paraphernalia, including a Brough Superior said to be that on which **T E Lawrence** met his death.

★★ Dunster

Dunster is an exceptional small town in a beautiful setting on the northern edge of Exmoor. Its name derives from *dun* or *dune*, a ridge of hills, and *torre*, a fortified tower; its landmark is the Conygar Tower, an 18C embattled folly high on a hilltop, and its symbol the dormered Yarn Market in the centre of the High Street.

By 1197 Dunster had developed into a chartered borough with a flourishing coastal and continental trade exchanging beans and barley for Welsh wool and Bordeaux, Spanish and Italian wine; by the 15C-16C the sea had retreated – it is now a mile distant – and the town had become a wool market and weaving centre. Today, in season, the town is a popular tourist destination.

★★ Dunster Castle ⊘ – *45min*. The red sandstone castle high on its tor dominates the town, its rugged appearance of towers and battlements belying its age but not its history: in Saxon times the hilltop probably served as a frontier fortress against the Celts and Northmen. The present castle, however, is largely 19C.

The de Mohuns and the Luttrells – Two families only have owned the castle throughout the centuries: William de Mohun (d 1155), who accompanied the Conqueror and was rewarded with the office of Sheriff of Somerset, built a Norman-style fortress upon the tor and a priory in the town. By 1374, however, the de Mohun line was dying out and the castle, three manors and a Hundred were sold for 5 000 marks (£3 333) to Lady Elizabeth Luttrell. After possession by successive Luttrells who preferred action on the field and in politics to husbandry in Somerset, the castle came in the late 16C to George Luttrell who reconstructed the residential quarters within the medieval walls; in the town he rebuilt the Yarn Market and remodelled the Luttrell Arms.

17C to 19C – The castle defences were put to the test in the Civil War: first Thomas Luttrell, a Parliamentary sympathiser, capitulated, paid a fine and allowed the Royalists to occupy the stronghold; then, in 1645 Robert Blake laid siege to it until, after 160 days, peace was negotiated. Parliament gave orders that Dunster was to be slighted: the curtain walls fell but destruction of the house and gateways was stayed – the owner paid a hefty fine and swore allegiance to Cromwell.

A new phase opened in the late 17C when **Col Francis Luttrell** and his rich bride, Mary Tregonwell of Milton Abbas, inherited the castle. They spent extravagantly on clothes and on the decoration of the house but in 1690 the colonel died and all work ceased.

Apart from construction of the **Conygar Tower** folly in 1765, little was done until 1867 when **George Fownes Luttrell** inherited the 15 374-acre property. He promptly called in the architect **Anthony Salvin** to enlarge and reconstruct the castle to its present appearance of a fortified Jacobean mansion.

Buildings – A 13C gatehouse, which was part of the medieval castle, leads into the forecourt, formerly the castle lower ward. The various periods of construction are evident throughout the castle.

The first **Hall** was created in the 19C; the portrait of Oliver Cromwell is contemporary but the wooden overmantel is a Jacobean pastiche.

The second, **Inner Hall**, is a 16C-17C adaptation of the medieval castle's great hall, complete with the original Jacobean spider-web plaster ceiling and overmantel, decorated with the Luttrell arms. On the wall between the hall archways hangs an allegorical portrait (1550) by Hans Eworth of *Sir John Luttrell*, in which, like a triton, he dominates the Scottish storm or forces who had opposed Henry VIII.

The panelled **Dining Room** displays one of the most beautiful moulded plaster ceilings in southwest England. It was installed in 1681 by Col Francis and Mary Luttrell *(see above)* whose portraits hang over the fireplace and whose arms are displayed in the frieze. Adjoining is a small panelled **serving room** with another remarkable ceiling. The black lacquer long-case clock has a 1730 movement.

The **Grand Staircase**, which is graced with another great ceiling forms the climax of Francis and Mary Luttrell's alterations: the stairs rise in three shallow flights around a square well; a carved flower-filled vase stands on each newel post, a handrail frames the 4in-thick elm balustrade, carved and pierced to illustrate a swirling pattern of acanthus leaves and flowers, inhabited by cherubs and hounds at the chase; a pile of Charles II silver shillings dates the carving as 1683-84. The portrait of an unknown *Young Cavalier* is by Edward Bower. *Continue up stairs.*

After the stair-hall, the upper rooms are an anti-climax except for the **views★** from the windows. Among the furnishings, nevertheless, are late 18C mahogany seat furniture reputed to be by Thomas Chippendale (**Morning Room**), hand tooled and coloured leather wall hangings depicting the meeting of Antony and Cleopatra, the former moustachioed and both ringleted and costumed in 17C fashion (**Gallery**), a 1620 overmantel illustrating the *Judgement of Paris* (**King Charles' Room**), a great arched fireplace in the Billiard Room and late 18C satinwood tables and painted seat furniture (**Drawing Room**).

Circle the castle and walk down through the gardens beside the River Avill or, if the castle is closed, along Church Street, West Street and Mill Lane to the mill.

★ Dunster Water Mill ⊘ – The mill stands in an idyllic setting beside the River Avill; its machinery runs throughout the open hours. The integral museum displays traditional agricultural machinery and tools.

The mill, rebuilt and improved at intervals since Domesday, ground corn until the late 19C when it was abandoned. In 1939-45 it came back into temporary wartime use; in 1979-80 the present tenants rebuilt and restored it – a task involving re-roofing with 20 000 random Delabole slates, copper nails and roof lead, re-making the overshot water-wheels, rebalancing the phosphor-bronze bearings, re-dressing the stones...

Water power – The diagram is applicable to all water-wheels and to windmills with the obvious difference that in the latter the main vertical shaft is powered from above. At Dunster the two overshot water-wheels, both fed

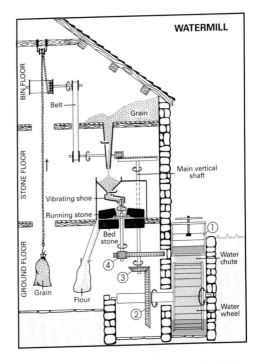

by the one chute controlled by a sluice gate (1), are 12ft in diameter by 3ft 6in wide, with oak spokes and shrouds and 40 elm-wood buckets each holding about 10 gallons of water (100lb approximately); 16 buckets are full at any one time so each wheel carries just under 1 ton of water; both wheels turn 4-6 times a minute.

The **pit wheel** (2) turns the wallower (3) and main vertical shaft 4 times to the water-wheel's once; the **spur wheel** (4) with applewood cogs, drives the stones' gear 7 times faster – the running stone, therefore, turns 4 x 4 x 7 or 112 times a minute to produce 1cwt of flour in 15-20 min or 1.5 tons a day per pair. Mills often used one pair of stones for flour, a second for animal feed. The **stones**, 4ft across, each have an "eye" and one also a "swallow", to receive the grain from the runner; both are "dressed" or "feathered" and "furrowed" – a highly skilled incising to reduce, grind and finally expel the flour. These incisions could take up to a week to do.

Mill-stones were made of one piece or of many lumps or burrs of particularly hard rock, principally from quarries in Derbyshire. The burrs would be fitted together and bound with a number of white-hot iron hoops. As the hoops cooled they cinched the rock into a solid mass; as the stones wore down the hoops would be removed – old mill-stones, sometimes seen in farmyards, are often quite thin. Note how quietly the mill runs.

Before returning to the town, turn left off Mill Lane to go through the car park.

The twin arched **packhorse bridge** over the River Avill leads to the open Exmoor countryside.

Dunster High Street – The long, very wide street, characterized by the unique 17C octagonal, dormered **yarn market**, is bordered on either side by 17C-19C houses with shops at ground level. At one end is the **Luttrell Arms** (*c*1500), the interior of which still centres on the Great Hall with its hammerbeam roof, twelve-light window and huge fireplace with 17C overmantel.

In the Memorial Hall is housed the **Dunster Dolls Museum** ⓥ, which boasts some 600 dolls collected for Mollie Hardwick between 1957 and 1970, old (17C) and new, many in traditional dress (Japanese, Eskimo, West Indian, Russian, Indian sub-continent).

Church Street – The street is marked by buildings related to the priory founded in 1090 and dissolved in 1539. The **Nunnery**, slate roofed with slate-hung floors above a stone ground floor, dates in part from the 14C when it was built as the priory guest-house. The half-timbered **Priest's House** of the same date was over-restored in the 19C.

171

Market Cross, Dunster (1929)

The **Dovecote**★ ⊙, which stands beyond the gate in the end wall of the Priory Garden behind the church, is a 20ft high, early medieval round pigeon house with a conical slate roof.

Inside are over 500 L-shaped **nest holes** set in 4ft-thick stone walls accessible up a **ladder** attached to two arms fixed to a central, 400 year old **pole** made of ash. A 3in-long, solid metal cone has been lodged at the pole base enabling it to revolve upon a 7in, dome-headed pin set in the oak floor beam. At the top a pin protrudes from the pole to revolve in a replaceable oak shoe fastened to the exact centre of the cross-beam.

Pigeons pair for life and have a breeding life of 7 years; for most of the year, the breed kept for food laid and hatched two eggs every 6 weeks; the squabs were removed at 6 weeks when they weighed 16oz. Meat production, in a good year, could have amounted to 3 tons.

★ **St George's Church** – The red sandstone parish church, which was built by the Normans in 1120 on an early Christian site, was rebuilt by the monks in the Early English style (1333-55) and extensively remodelled (1842-76) by the Luttrell family. The **tower** (110ft) was erected in accordance with a contract (1443) which stipulated that it should have a "batylment and pynacles... three french botras (buttresses) and gargoyles". It contains a clock (1876) and a separate carillon which plays a different tune each day of the week at 9am, 1pm, 5pm and 9pm.

Interior – Beneath the **wagon roof** the nave and aisles are divided from the chancel by a wide **screen** (54ft), an example of local carving with blank panels below cusped and traceried openings separated by slender columns which lead the eye up to a strongly sinewed fan vault and richly carved friezes. It survived both the Parliamentarians and the Puritans as it was built not as a rood screen, although it carried the three figures of the Holy Rood until 1548, but on the orders of the Bishop of Bath in 1498 to settle a long running dispute between the priory and the parish.

Note also the 16C Perpendicular **font** with quatrefoils carved with Christ's wounds and the instruments of the Passion; two iron-bound chests (12C-13C) and one in the form of a desk (15C) *(south aisle, east end)*; Charles II's coat of arms *(nave north wall)*; the 19C bench-ends; the 20C ambo. Among the **funerary monuments** are a lady of *c*1300 in a wimple beneath a canopy *(chancel)*, the gravestone, bearing a foliated cross, of Adam de Cheddar, Prior of Dunster (c1345-55) (south transept), a brass of John Wyther (d 1497) and his wife (nave, west end), a Jacobean tomb of 1621, the Luttrell tombs, including one dated 1428, and a selection of Luttrell hatchments (17C-18C) hanging on the walls.

Timberscombe to Challacombe

Timberscombe – The village of reddish stone houses with slate roofs, straddling the A396 just south of Dunster, has a Perpendicular church★ with an early 18C castellated west tower which was crowned in the 19C with a pyramid roof. Inside, beneath the wagon roofs, note the **rood-screen** with carved dado, coving and cornice.

Wheddon Cross – The crossroads and minute village which stand at 1 200ft, are a good **vantage point**★ from which to view Dunkery Beacon (3 miles west), the Brendon Hills and deep, wooded valleys.

★★ **Dunkery Beacon** – Access from A396: turn west into B3224 at Wheddon Cross; take the second turn right to Dunkery Gate, then follow the path, 3 miles return on foot.
The 1 706ft beacon, the highest point on the moor, is visible for miles around and from its summit commands **views**★★★ of sixteen counties, so it is said.

Exford – The central green is the heart of the village, with the occasional farmstead and cottage on surrounding hillsides. Exford is the home of the Devon and Somerset Staghounds and at the centre of the hunting country.
The **church**★, to which the blacksmith in 1532 left £3 towards "the makying of an yled" – now the only ancient part of the building – contains a 14C octagonal **font** with quatrefoils and a 15C oak **rood screen** with panelled coving and a cornice of richly carved friezes.
The choirstalls were presented by Queens' College, Cambridge.

Simonsbath – The village, the centre of John Knight's and his son's operations in the 19C, stands on the River Barle where the Lynton road meets the main east-west road across the moor. The church, with its slate-hung west wall, the school, many of the houses, even the east windbreak of mature beech trees, owe much of their form to the Knights. The **hotel** was built as a royal hunting lodge. The historic water-powered sawmill set amongst 24 acres of water meadows, has recently been acquired by the Exmoor National Park Authority with the intention of restoring it to working order.

Combe Sydenham Hall ⊙

The house, beyond the gatehouse which incorporates a stone arch believed to be of c1450, was built to a typical Elizabethan E shape by Sir George Sydenham, father of Elizabeth (d 1598), whom Sir Francis Drake married as his second wife in 1585. Expansion, demolition, rebuilding and further neglect sum up the history of the hall until its rescue by the present owners who have been restoring the house, gardens and grounds, the mill, trout stream, fishponds, nature trails...
Among the rooms completed are the **Great Hall**, the 18C staircase and panelled sitting room and the Restoration banqueting room. On the stone flags in the Great Hall is **Drake's cannon-ball** weighing over 100lbs, others claim it to be a meteorite: legend has it that, although Drake had wooed her before going to sea, Elizabeth Sydenham was at the church door when the ball hurtled through the air to fall between the would-be bride and stranger groom. Drake sailed into Plymouth on the next tide...
The cornmill is again in working condition and new trails have also been marked out.

Dulverton to Withypool

★ **Dulverton** – Sited 450ft above sea level amid beautiful scenery, the "capital" village of the area is characterised by a solid **church** with a plain 13C west **tower** (rest of the church rebuilt in the 19C) on a hillock at one end and by an old stone bridge with five arches between cutwater piers above the River Barle at the other.
Between, the **main street** and **market square** are appointed with shops, a 19C market-house, stone terrace houses and colour-washed cottages, some thatched, others with broad chimneys built up from ground level. Along a back path to the church is a terrace of small Georgian houses.

Tarr Steps

★★ Tarr Steps – *Access from B3223; parking in car park only, then 6 minute walk down steep path – car turning point only at the bottom or continue through the ford.*

The finest **clapper bridge** in the country crosses the River Barle at the centre of an open, wooded valley. The 180ft causeway of 17 "arches", built of flat stones laid upon uprights in the stream bed with many of the stones weighing 2 tons or more, dates certainly from the early Middle Ages and probably centuries earlier. It has often been swept away by floodwaters and as often been rebuilt.

★ Winsford – Streams run on all sides through the village with the result that within yards there are **seven bridges**, the oldest being the **packhorse bridge** over the River Exe *(by the vicarage)*. The **green**, shaded by huge trees, is marked by old thatched houses and cottages and the Royal Oak which has a thatched roof which folds and turns as it tucks up the corners of the rambling old inn.

Withypool – The village, which stands beside one of the only two commons on the moor, boasts an ancient Norman font in the church (largely rebuilt 1901) and a 19C **bridge**.

EXMOUTH

Devon – Population 30 386
Michelin Atlas p 4 and Map 403 – J 32

Exmouth was a port in pre-Roman times; in the Middle Ages it was subject to North African and other pirate raids and was supplying ships and men for English return ventures.

In the 18C it went with the fashion and determined to become Devon's first watering place: Georgian terraces were built such as those in Bicton Place and on the **Beacon**, where among the early tenants were the sad wives of Lords Nelson (no 6) and Byron (no 19).

The **beach** of fine sand is two miles long.

Littleham Church – *1 mile east along Maer Lane (Sandy Bay Road).*
The church, which stands on an older site and serves as Exmouth parish church, was begun in 1234; Drake's aisle (north) was added in 1528.

The **hammerbeam roof** was rebuilt in the 19C using the original 15C carved oak **bosses** and **angels**. The piers with unusually carved **capitals** are of Beer stone. The lectern (13C) was made from an old oak beam. The **rood screen** is early 16C. The late 15C **glass** *(north aisle, 3rd window)* depicts Christ with a reed and crown of thorns.

Lady Nelson, who is buried in the churchyard, is commemorated on a memorial in the chantry chapel.

St John in the Wilderness – *1.5 miles northeast; north off A376, Budleigh Salterton Road.*
The church with its unique **boss** has had a chequered history. After rebuilding in the 15C it was first abandoned then demolished except for the tower and north aisle. In 1936, as restoration work was nearing completion, King George V died and, in anticipation of the coronation of the new king, a boss with the cypher **ER VIII** – the only one ever to be carved – was set in the chancel roof.
In the churchyard *(southeast corner)* is the grave of the Romantic artist, **Francis Danby**.

EXCURSIONS

★**A la Ronde** *2 miles north by Exeter Road, A376 and Summer Lane*

The unique 16-sided house with sweeping views of the Exe estuary was built in 1798 by two unmarried cousins, Jane and Mary Parminter, to designs inspired by San Vitale (in Ravenna) said to have been by Jane herself. The original thatch roof was replaced with tiles in the Victorian era when dormer windows were added.
Jane Parminter was the daughter of a Barnstaple wine merchant with interests in Portugal, where Jane was born; she spent her early years in London where, under the influence of Mrs Delany, she learnt many of the genteel arts of the period including the use of shells, feathers, paper, paint and needlework for decorative effect. In 1784 she set out with her sister Elizabeth and her cousin Mary on a Grand Tour of Europe which was to last 10 years. On their return, they decided to retire to the then fashionable seaside town of Exmouth and set about designing their own unique sixteen-sided house with a thatched roof.

House ⊙ – The **interior** comprises eight rooms radiating from a central octagon 35ft in height, with the shell gallery above. Each essentially rectangular room is connected by wedge-shaped anterooms.The tour goes anticlockwise through the study, a former bedroom, into the music room and library, before progressing upstairs to a suite of five rooms with splendid views inserted by Reverend Oswald Reichel in the late 1880s when the house was considerably modernised.
The main feature upstairs is the central **shell gallery** *(no access)* which, together with a pair of staircases, is encrusted with shells and recessed feather tableaux depicting various birds. This truly unique Rococo decoration, painstakingly completed by the two ladies, is a typical example of fashionable "Ladies' Amusements" practised in the late-18C.
The varied furnishings date from the various owner-occupiers of the house and most of the decor has been preserved where possible or recreated faithfully according to designs uncovered during restoration. The eclectic interests and somewhat eccentric spirit of the spinsters is perhaps best found in the Octagon

A La Ronde

R. Truman/The National Trust

and Drawing Room downstairs. The Octagon is hung with Parminter ancestral portraits and furnished with hinged shelves and seats sunk into the door jambs, and unusual tailor-made triangular-backed chairs; the rather cluttered Drawing Room retains its ornate pelmets, inlaid longcase clock, occasional tables and painted chairs, Parminter watercolours and silhouettes, shell-work and quill-work. Elsewhere, among the highly skilful pictures created out of sand, seaweeds, shells and paper collages hang Piranesi prints capturing views glimpsed on the Grand Tour, while Chinese porcelain figures and Wedgwood creamware reflect an appreciation of very different artistic tastes.

Point in View - *300 yards up the lane.* The delightful Congregational (now United Reformed) Chapel up the hill was also built by Jane Parminter, in 1811 for private use. It was conceived originally as a tiny chapel flanked by four small single-storey almshouses and a schoolroom: these have now been knocked into one, and surrounded by modern purpose-built bungalows run by a trust as envisaged by its benefactor.

Exmouth to Sidmouth

Budleigh Salterton – The small town maintains to some degree the atmosphere of a mid-19C watering place. An old sea wall lines the short parade above the beach of steeply shelving shingle – Sir John Millais was living in the town in the 1860s and used both wall and shingle as the setting for his famous painting *The Boyhood of Raleigh.* Several large late-19C houses betray the strong influence of the Arts and Crafts movement.

An unusual geological feature, the liver-coloured quartzite pebble bed between Triassic and Permian beds of new red sandstone, was formed by an ancient river that once flowed northwards from France. Salt pans in the marshes beside the River Otter gave Budleigh Salterton its name.

East Budleigh - *2 miles north on A376.* The small, one-time wool town near to the birthplace of Sir Walter Raleigh (the long, thatched farmhouse at Hayes Barton) has a 12C **church**★ where Raleigh's father was churchwarden. Note especially the carved and coloured **bosses** and 16C **bench-ends**, carved with a sailing ship, craftsmen's tools, dolphins and portrait heads.

★ **Bicton** - *3 miles north by A376.* The grounds and gardens of Bicton House, remodelled by James Wyatt in 1800 and now an Agricultural College, have been progressively designed and planted with specimen trees over the last 200 years.

★ **Gardens** ⊙ – In the 1730s Baron Rolle, the first in a line of keen horticulturalists, rebuilt the house and had the formal **Italian Gardens** laid out after a design by the 17C French landscape gardener, André Le Nôtre. The most substantial changes, however, were implemented by John, Lord Rolle, who is commemorated in a mausoleum designed by Pugin on the edge of the gardens.

To these gardens he added the lake (dug by French prisoners of war in 1812), arboretum and monkey-puzzle avenue(1830-42), the glorious curved Palm House (*c*1820-30), conservatories, an **American Garden** (started in the 1830s), a secluded **Hermitage Garden** with its small summerhouse and lake, heather and dwarf conifer plantations, a pinetum and acres of close-mown lawns banked by rhododendrons, azaleas and magnolias.

Woodland Railway – The 18in gauge railway, originally from the Royal Arsenal, Woolwich, extends over 1.25 miles through the grounds, running close beside the lake and through the woodlands and plantations.

James Countryside Collection – A museum displays the tools and implements that were in use on the land almost unaltered for centuries, and the revolution in the same equipment over the last 50 years: there are horse-drawn harrows and a blacksmith's forge, a regal gipsy caravan (1902), a steam traction engine (1894), a Fordson tractor (1917), a cider press (1800).

Otterton Mill ⊙ – *2.5 miles by A376 and right at main crossroads beyond East Budleigh.*

The early 19C mill *(tour)* produces stoneground wholewheat flour which is baked on the premises. There are also craft workshops: pottery, quilting, tie-dyeing, knitwear, wood-turning and table mats. The stream running the length of the village street is spanned by individual **stone bridges** to the houses.

For SIDMOUTH *and* LYME REGIS: *turn to relevant chapter or consult the index.*

FALMOUTH★

Cornwall – Population 19 217

Michelin Atlas p 2 or Map 403 – E 33

From Pendennis Castle on the point a low ridge runs inland dividing the town in two; the hotel-residential district looks south over Falmouth Bay while the old town with its waterfront faces north up the Fal Estuary, which is always known by its Cornish name of the **Carrick Roads**. It is in fact a drowned river mouth which drains the waters of the Fal and its two tributaries the Tresillian and the Truro.

In the early 1600s, Falmouth comprised some eight houses; in 1665, the number had risen to 200. The hotels and tourism began with the arrival of the railway in 1863; the harbour town, by contrast, evolved over centuries, the quay being built in 1670.

In 1688 Falmouth was appointed the most westerly **Mail Packet Station**. The designation brought prosperity: ships called making regular passage to the Mediterranean, the West Indies, North America; docks and boat-building yards were established; a mail coach service to London was instituted; ships required provisioning.

It was to Falmouth that HMS *Pickle* brought Collingwood's despatch on **Trafalgar** for it to be taken by mail coach to London.

For 150 years Falmouth prospered; then ships turned to steam and the port waned. Today the town's economy relies largely on tourism, cargo handling and **yachting** – Falmouth is a major sailing centre and plays host to important annual summer regattas.

OLD TOWN

High Street – The street, lined by the older shops and buildings in the town, leads up to the former Town Hall (now an antiques market) where the last case of cannibalism in England was tried.

The Moor – The main "square" occupies the site of a former creek; the large, cream coloured building at the bottom of the square *(northeast side)* was built on wooden piles and straw.

Packet Memorial – The monument commemorates the long-standing importance of the Packet Service to the town: the first of the Falmouth Packets sailed in 1689.

Municipal Art Gallery ⊙ – The town gallery, housed in the **Municipal Buildings** above the Library, has an interesting collection of maritime, Victorian and early 20C paintings (Dame Laura Knight, Henry Scott Tuke, Alfred Munnings, J W Waterhouse's study for *The Lady of Shallot*) and a painting of the *Reconstruction of the Killigrew Monument, Arwenack* (c1830).

The Waterfront – The frontage which extends for over half a mile from Greenbank Quay to the pier is paralleled inland by the shop-lined Market and High Streets. There is no continuous path along the waterfront; access to different quays and slips is through the alleys and opes descending from the main street.

Greenbank Quay – The quay and 19C hotel stand on Penny-come-Quick or more properly Pen y Cwn Gwic, the Cornish for Headland in the Valley of the Creek.

Prince of Wales Pier – *The embarkation point for river cruises.* The river, between Greenbank Quay and the pier, is overlooked by 18C houses and warehouses standing on the 17C harbour wall which was built after the Dutch fashion with large stone slabs set endways on to the sea and piled without mortar to allow slight play.

North and Custom House Quays – The quays, which enclose the inner basin, date back to c1670. At the landward end of the Custom House Quay stands a strange, square brick chimney, known as the King's Pipe, which was built to burn contraband tobacco.

Cornwall Maritime Museum ⊙ – *2 Bell's Court, uphill off Market Street opposite Marks and Spencer*. The small regional museum installed in the former Packet Service Office documents the importance of Falmouth's coastal defences; the emergence of smuggling as a result of salt taxes imposed on the local pilchard and mackerel curing industry; the myths and superstitions associated with mermaids capable of luring fishermen to their death; the emergence of the telegraph and packet service during the 18C and 19C.

Historical displays *(upstairs)* chart the ship-building industry that supplied luggers and schooners for use in coastal waters and trade with the continent (a full database of Cornish-built ships is being compiled). Fine collection of ship models.

King Charles the Martyr – Falmouth's Parish Church is dedicated to King Charles I, an honour bestowed upon the monarch by his most loyal subjects in Cornwall. For it was shortly after Charles I escaped to the Scillies from Falmouth that Sir Ralph Hopton surrendered Cornwall to the Parliamentarians, thereby bringing the Civil War to a virtual end. At the Restoration, King Charles II granted Falmouth its charter (1661) and sponsored the building of a church in memory of his martyred father, entrusting the project to Sir Peter Killigrew who lived at Arwenack Manor. The style was intended to be "the last expression of Gothic combined with Renaissance Cornwall... an effort to combine Pointed Medieval with Classical details, joining the two styles".

Inside the pulpit is made up of 16C English panels carved with grapes and vines, and 17C German figures; the credence table, bearing the Killigrew arms, and the font cover are dated 1759. The portrait of Charles I on the south wall is attributed to Lely; it was presented to the church by the Royalist Society in 1913. The Royal Arms hanging from the organ loft are a rare example of those used by Queen Anne after the passing of the Act of Union of England with Scotland in 1707: the union is heraldically represented by England impaling Scotland in the first and fourth quarters between France and Ireland, and the Scottish thistle flowering from the same stem as the English rose.

Arwenack Manor – *Grove Place*. Though redeveloped, Arwenack Manor incorporates the remains of Falmouth's oldest building: the 16C wall of the old Banqueting Hall is still visible *(left)* from the street, together with the manor's 16C possible gatehouse *(left wing)* and northwest corner *(right wing)*. First records of Arwenack date back to the 14C when Jane, daughter of Robert of Arwenack, married a member of the Killigrew family. In 1544 John Killigrew became the first governor of Pendennis Castle *(see below)* and the house began to be enlarged. Sir Walter Raleigh was a guest at Arwenack.

Killigrew Monument – Although the **pyramid** *(opposite the house)*, erected by a member of the Killigrew family, bears no inscription it is believed to be dedicated to the memory of the Killigrews.

Port Pendennis – *Behind Grove Place and Bar Road.* Beyond the smart development of colour-washed houses surrounding a modern marina stretches Falmouth's shipyard.

Shipyard, Falmouth

★**PENDENNIS CASTLE** ⊘ *1 mile southeast of Falmouth*

In the face of "pretensed invasion" in 1539-43, Henry VIII began to fortify the coastline, erecting two forts at Falmouth and St Mawes to safeguard the mile-wide entrance to the Carrick Roads and one of Britain's finest deep water anchorages. The effective range of Tudor guns being 800m, crossfire overlapped and, as Carew put it, "St Mawes lieth lower and better to annoy shipping, but Pendennis standeth higher and stronger to defend itself". Elizabeth increased the defences against surprise Spanish raids. The challenge finally came in the Civil War: St Mawes yielded without a shot being fired but Pendennis withstood a 23 week siege before starvation brought submission in August 1546.

A hundred years later, first Queen Henrietta Maria sought refuge at Pendennis before fleeing to France in the wake of Exeter's fall to Cromwell's army; then Prince Charles (later Charles II) stopped here on his way to France via the Scillies.

In 1795, the site was further fortified with a cannon platform below the south curtain wall; this later served as a coast guard station.

Passing through the main gate *(ticket office on right)*, on the left stands the guardhouse, arranged as it might have been during World War I. The main building, a barracks block for the Royal Garrison Artillery dated 1901, is now a Youth Hostel.

Across the parade ground, Henry VIII's three-storey octagonal stone **keep** commands a superb **view**★★ of the coastline beyond St Mawes to St Anthony's Lighthouse. The entrance, complete with wooden portcullis, is emblazoned with the royal arms framed between Tudor lion and Welsh dragon supporters: inside the gatehouse were the governor's lodgings. Inside, the main chamber is plainly furnished; above, the same space is arranged with working replica 17C sakers firing from a ship's carriage out to sea. A twisting staircase provides access to the ramparts.

Additional guns ranging in date from the 1540s to 1956 adorn the various bastions around the site: a leaflet provided by English Heritage provides additional information about these.

EXCURSIONS

Glendurgan and Mawnan

★★ **Glendurgan Garden** ⊘ – *4 miles southwest of Falmouth; half a mile southwest of Mawnan Smith.*

Dropping down to Durgan, a hamlet of stone cottages on the Helford River, is the great sub-tropical Glendurgan Garden. The valley garden was planted in the 1820s by the Fox family with English broad-leaved trees, conifers and ornamental foliage trees from all over the world (everything is unobtrusively labelled), including two impressive tulip trees (Liriodendron), a weeping swamp cypress and weeping Mexican cypress, Japanese loquat, cedars, pines, firs and bamboo. In spring and early summer the garden is a brilliant profusion of flowers: wild daffodils, bluebells, Lent lilies, primroses; rhododendrons, camellias, flowering cherries, azaleas, magnolias, mimosa. Later come hydrangeas and later still, a blaze of autumn colour.

The garden also contains a **Giant's Stride** (maypole) and a famous laurel **Maze** (ideal for children, although tiring as it is on a slope!) complete with viewing platform; all mazes, it is said, have the same solution, but it is nonetheless best to allow one hour to complete it...

★ **Trebah Garden** ⊘ – *500 yards beyond Glendurgan; 2hours.*

Set in a steep valley, this wooded garden tumbles some 200ft down to a beach on the Helford River from where the 29th US Infantry Division set out for the D-Day landings on Omaha Beach in Normandy (1944) – this is perfect for a picnic and safe bathing. In Domesday, the 25 acre ravine is listed as the property of the Bishop of Exeter; in 1826 it was acquired by the Fox family, a branch of which also lived at Glendurgan, who were responsible for planting the shelter belt of pine trees.

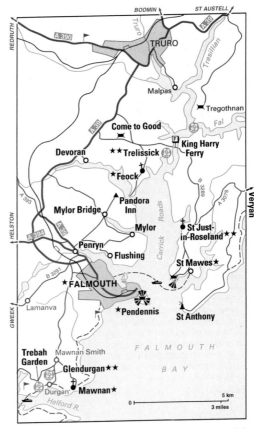

The estate was broken up in 1939 and the Fox's mansion was destroyed by fire in 1948.

Highlights of the garden include two acres of blue and white **hydrangeas**, sub-tropical tree ferns and **Chusan palms** variegate a thick canopy of mature rhododendrons (including the hybrid Trebah Gem).

For children, there are garden trails, a Tarzan Camp, paraglide and adventure playground enclosed within a giant tree canopy.

★ **Mawnan Parish Church** – *Half a mile east.* The 15C granite church stands on a spur at the mouth of the Helford River – walk round to see the view★★.

The church incorporates part of an Early English sanctuary and has massive granite piers; it is noted for its impressive modern needlework which gives colour and warmth to the interior.

Brazilian rhubarb *(Gunnera manicata)*

★ **Cruises up the Helford River** – The scenery is predominantly pastoral. There are no stops, few houses, two landmarks: Durgan hamlet and Gweek Seal Sanctuary (*see* LIZARD PENINSULA).

Penryn to Feock

Penryn – The ancient, still-working quarry village lies far up the creek, marked by the tower of its town hall (1839).

Flushing – The village was founded in the 17C by Dutch settlers.

Mylor – The 16C-17C church **(St Melorus)** has two Norman doorways, a gable turret, detached belltower and weather-boarded upper storey. Inside there is an Elizabethan pulpit and a painted, carved roodscreen. A tall Celtic cross stands guard in the churchyard.

The village, now a yacht and pleasure craft centre, is a short distance further up the inlet which is straddled at its end by Mylor Bridge: look out for the excellent village shop **Mylor Stores**.

Devoran – On the same creek, Devoran was once a tin and copper port.

Come-to-Good – Come-to-Good, which appears the from outside to be just a whitewashed, thatched cottage with stables for the churchgoers' horses on one side under the same roof, is a Quaker Meeting House. Built in 1710, it measures 27ft long by 20ft wide, cost £68 18*s* 3*d* to construct and is still in use.

★★ **Trelissick** ⊙ – *4 miles south of Truro on B3289 to St Mawes.*

The house and grounds occupy a promontory where the Fal widens out into the Carrick Roads, partly enclosed within a skirt of old oak and beech woodland.

The Classical, giant-porticoed, house (built 1750, remodelled 1825) stands on a high promontory, superbly overlooking, and clearly visible from, the Carrick Roads. In the Stables are displayed a fine range of tack and saddlery; another farm-building houses a gallery for temporary exhibitions organised in association with the Cornwall Craft Association.

Beyond the house *(private)*, the gardens offer superb **views**★★ over the lush, undulating park, Falmouth and the open sea. The woodland, which drops down towards the Fal (both sides of the road) consists of tall trees underplanted with dense shrubs, exotics (magnolias, tree ferns, banana), bulbs, wood anemones and primulas; it is threaded with a maze of paths that meander through the sea-spray and wind-resistant eucalyptus, maples, oxydendrums and cypress to open areas of spacious lawn displaying a Japanese cedar or belt of summer-flowering shrubs to best effect: highlights of the collection include the **hydrangeas** (a particular speciality with over 130 varieties), azaleas and rhododendrons. Through summer, crinums, agapanthus, fuchsias, acanthus, cannas and other wonderful perennials give a show of colour.

The Cornish Apple Orchard has been created to preserve as many traditional varieties of apple as possible.

King Harry Ferry ⊘ – How the ferry, which has an 18ft tide rise and fall and is now a chain ferry, got its name and how long it has been operating across the picturesque valley no one knows, though the old **Ferry Boat Inn** on the bank is clearly several centuries old.

Feock – The **church**★, standing above the village which overlooks the Carrick Roads, is distinguished by having a separate west **tower belfry** with a pyramid roof dating from the 13C. The church is 15C, restored in the 19C. Note the carved Catacleuse **font**.

Roseland Peninsula

★★ **St Just-in-Roseland Church** – *23 miles south of Falmouth by A39 east, then by A3078.*
The church stands in the most perfect setting imaginable. The path leads steeply down from the lichgate, through the churchyard garden of rhododendrons, brooms, fuchsias, hydrangeas and a strawberry tree, to the church which stands so close to the creek that at high tide its mirror image is reflected in the water. The sanctuary, on a 6C Celtic site, is partly 13C (consecrated 1261), largely 15C but suffered a fierce restoration in the 19C.

★ **St Mawes** – The small low-lying stone houses, thatched, pink-washed or ivy-covered – one dated 1760, another with a Sun Life Insurance firemark – the hotels, pubs and small shops along the curving line of the waterfront continue up the steep road and tributary alleys behind the square. Flowers everywhere confirm that St Mawes is blessed with the mildest, sunniest of climates.

★ **St Mawes Castle** ⊘ – The clover-shaped Tudor castle with motte-and-bailey (1540-43), constructed as a pair to Pendennis, commands a **view**★ up the Carrick Roads and across to Falmouth. Unlike Pendennis which withstood many weeks of siege in 1646, St Mawes capitulated to the Parliamentarians; neither fort, in the event, defended the Roads, the purpose for which they were originally constructed with their overlapping gunfire. What is of particular interest here is the use of the lobed shape: round bastions appeared in Italian Renaissance contexts in the early 1500s and they were recommended by Dürer in his book on fortifications in 1525: by the time St Mawes was being built the Italians had long since adapted their designs into angular bastions which proved far more effective. The decoration, meanwhile, shows a keen appreciation of Renaissance motifs.

Cruises to Truro

The banks are densely wooded with oak trees down to the water's edge where the birds include herons, cormorants and waders. Villages with a church, an old pub and half a dozen moored craft line the inlets: boathouses, slipways, laid-up ships of up to 30 000 tons and ships on the move mark the course; above are open fields, more woods, a church or two, houses in their own parkland.

St Anthony-in-Roseland – The forked peninsula between the Carrick Roads and the open sea is known as Roseland, meaning promontory. The headland points are marked respectively by St Mawes Castle and the lighthouse on St Anthony Head, from which the **view★★** extends up the Carrick Roads and, on a clear day, northeast towards Dartmoor.

The **church**, according to Pevsner, "can still be regarded as the best example in the county of what a parish church was like in the 12C and 13C": the simplicity of its form, crossing tower and Norman doorway intact.

★ **Veryan** – The small village is guarded by four curious little white-walled **round houses** with Gothick windows and a conical thatched roof surmounted by a cross – built, it is alleged, so that the devil could not linger in the corners.

FOWEY★★

Cornwall – Population 2 123
Michelin Atlas p 3 or Map 403 – G 32

The attraction of Fowey (pronounced "Foye") lies in the exploration of its quay, houses, yards, church and museum; in the prospect of walks out towards Gribbin Head, or of boat trips round the harbour and the coast – where the cliffs rise dark and sheer from the water – or upriver between slopes densely wooded with oak, past small creeks and the china-clay quays with long tails of loaded railway wagons. Another pastime is just to watch the **river** while ships of up to 10 000 tons – British, French, Belgian, Swedish, Danish, Norwegian, Spanish, Italian, German – come in to load the clay; fishing boats set out in the evening; small yachts moored at Polruan swing with the tide; launches and rowing boats manoeuvre the waters; the pilot vessel comes and goes; the dredger keeps the channel clear; the ferries ply; fearsome rocks appear and disappear as the tide turns...

Town Quay – Bordering the square, which marks the centre of the town and the waterfront, is an old inn, the **King of Prussia**, named after an 18C smuggler who also gave his name to the cove by Cudden Point. The adjoining building was the fish or butter market with the counting house on the floor above.

Trafalgar Square and Lostwithiel Street – The second square is overlooked by the 18C granite ashlar **town hall** (*museum* ⊙), built over a 14C building, once the local prison – note the grilled window. **Toll Bar House** which dates back to the 14C, 15C and 18C and the **Ship Inn** opposite, built by the Rashleighs *(see below)* as a town house in the 15C, were linked by a bridge-room. Inside the inn are a carved ceiling and, above a fireplace, a marriage inscription: John Rashleigh – Ales Rashleigh 1570.

St Nicholas – *South Street.* The 14C-15C church with a tall, pinnacled tower rising above the trees, a two-storey Decorated **porch**, a long south aisle and clerestory, is the last in a line of churches. The site was first occupied in the 7C by a chapel to St Goran which was succeeded by a wooden chapel to St Finn Barr or **St Fimbarrus**; the Norman church was destroyed by a pirate raid in 1150. The new church, dedicated in 1336, was set alight by French seamen in 1456 in retaliation for raids by the **Fowey Gallants**, those "rich, proud and mischievous

Fowey

men", part traders, part privateers, part pure pirates; even today the carved pulpit, formerly a doubledecker, is Gallants' booty, made from panelling from the captain's cabin of a Spanish galleon taken in 1601.

Inside, beneath the early **wagon roof**, note the octagonal **piers** without capitals and the Norman **font** of dark Catacleuse stone; at the east end are portrait tombs, memorials, aged brasses and slates to two local families, the Rashleighs of Menabilly House (built 1600s, rebuilt 19C), which was used as the setting for *Rebecca* and *The King's General* by Daphne du Maurier , and the Treffrys of Place, a 19C house in the town centre enclosed by high walls with two thin, dissimilar castellated towers.

In the church tower is an 18C **ringer's rhyme.**

The almshouses west of the church are 17C.

Fore Street – The narrow shopping street is lined by old houses with jettied gables or houses angled into corners as are the **Lugger Inn** (1633) and Globe Posting House.

Post Office– The handsome Georgian house facing down Fore Street is entered through a shell-hooded doorway; adjoining is the Customs House of the same date.

Car Ferry – The vehicle ferry, known for the last 700 years as **The Passage**, links North and Passage Streets *(the continuation of Fore Street)* to Bodinnick. Lining the street are houses built by prosperous 17C-19C townsmen overlooking their wharves and the river; the smaller houses with windows and balconies overhanging the water were built later on the former slips. At the ferry end, note **Captain's Row** (1816), a modest range complete with Captain Bates' own brass knocker.

★★ On foot to Gribbin Head *6 miles.*

Follow the Esplanade to its end (car park); then join the Cornwall South Coast Path.

Fortifications at the water's edge – The blockhouse and its pair opposite were built following a raid in 1457 by the French, an incident which resolved the locals to build defences across the harbour; it also serves as an anchor point for the chain that extends across the river mouth (note the marks on the rocks) to control traffic; **St Catherine's Castle**, now a ruin, was built slightly later: one of several fortifications ordered by Henry VIII.

Readymoney Cove – The small cove serves as the town beach; a stretch of sand is revealed at low tide. The Coast Path comes out on the cliff top and makes a gradual climb to the headland.

★★ Gribbin Head – The head, extending half a mile out to sea, 242ft high and topped by an 82ft waymark, affords **views**★★ for miles in all directions.

★ Across the water to Lanteglos Church and Polruan *5 miles.*

Bodinnick – The ferry lands at the foot of the steep main street. To the right is a former boatbuilders' yard, long since converted into a private house, and to the left, the medieval **Old Ferry Inn**; stone and slate houses with minute, flower filled gardens support each other up the hill.

Take Hall Walk (right) downstream past the 1939-45 War Memorial.

From the monolithic memorial to "Q" (Sir Arthur Quiller Couch) there is a **view**★★ across to Fowey. Further on there is a shelter bearing a **plaque** which records that on 17 August 1644 **Charles I** narrowly escaped death from a sniper's bullet while surveying the Parliamentary forces occupying Fowey.

The path turns inland by Pont Pill creek and descends to the road bridge at Pont; start down south bank and where the road turns inland (beyond Carne), take the footpath (350yds) across the fields.

★ Lanteglos Church – The large 14C-15C parish church (St Willow) stands isolated on a wooded valley slope. A large proportion of the fabric is 14C with Norman elements such as the south doorway which incorporates a 7C-8C **Chi-Rho stone**. The interior, divided by unequally tall arcades of plain octagonal columns, is covered by the original carved **wagon roof**. The **font** of Pentewan stone carved with stiff-leaf decoration is early 13C; many of the carved bench ends are *c*1500. At the east end are **tombs** of the Grenvilles and the Mohuns; Thomas Mohun supervised the building of his own tomb (in a canopied recess) but, being still alive when the brass was finished, left the date of death incomplete.

The road leads west to Polruan.

Polruan – Before the descent to the old town at the water's edge, bear left to the coastguard station from which there is a **view**★★ west to Gribbin Head, Dodman Point and the Lizard and east to Rame and Bolt Heads. Drop down to the harbour past the cliff and waterside houses, the pubs and boatyards to the passenger ferry.

EXCURSIONS

Up-river to Golant

Tristan Stone – *1.25 miles from town centre, before Four Turnings, on right side of the road.* The stone, a relic of the Tristan legend, stands 8ft tall and was transferred from a nearby site where it was said to have been erected in AD 550.

Castle Dore – *3 miles by A3082 and B3269, 200yds north of the crossroads, 15yds inside a field with a broken gate.*

The second Tristan-Arthurian relic is an Iron Age lookout point which is said to have been one of King Mark's wooden halls of residence in the 6C AD *(now densely over-grown).*

Return to the cross-roads and take the left by-road (east) down to the river.

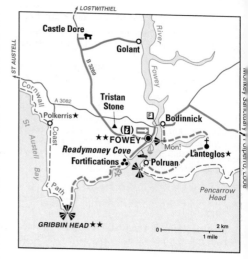

Golant – *5 miles north of Fowey on A3082 Lost-withiel Road.* The river-side village has a 15C-16C landmark parish church, **St Sampson**, with a low, embattled tower. Inside, a single arcade divides the nave and aisle beneath fine original wagon and cradle roofs respectively; **bosses** and wall plates are beautifully carved as are the **pulpit** and **stalls** made from medieval bench-ends (Apostles, St Sampson, a jester). The **sculpture** of Christ's head is believed to be Spanish, possibly taken from one of the Armada ships.

For Restormel Castle, see BODMIN MOOR.

The coast east to Polperro and Looe

★ **Polperro** – *9 miles east by Bodinnick.*
The oldest cottages in this attractive and popular, vehicle-free, fishing village are at the bottom of the steep road which follows the stream down to the inner and outer harbour by the creek.

Twisting and stepped alleys are close-packed with cottages, millhouses, shops, forges and boat-houses; from the head-lands, views extend far out to sea.

> ### Crumplehorn Inn
>
> Housed in the ancient Old Mill, this charm-ing inn is reputedly haunted: definitely worth the detour! ☎ 01503 277 2348

A converted pilchard factory on the waterfront, once under Italian ownership, presently accommodates a small **museum** ⊙ for its collection of photographs taken by Lewis Harding (1806-93) and 18C memorabilia acknowledging the area's prosperity that was long dependent on fishing and smuggling contraband tea, tobacco, brandy and gin from Guernsey at a time when the government imposed taxes on such luxury commodities to finance the wars with France. Other exhibits include a model of the *Lady Beatrice*, a typical large gaff-rigged Polperro fishing boat.

★ **Looe** – The picturesque town, renowned for its safe, fine sand beaches, lies in the open valley on either side of the River Looe which divides almost immediately upstream into two tributaries. East and West Looe are linked by a 19C bridge.

Continue east by B3253.

★ **Monkey Sanctuary** ⊙ – *2 hours.* In a 19C seaside villa and in an enclosure occupying much of the garden, dozens of Amazon woolly monkeys live and breed, perform effortless acrobatics and, when inclined, come out to meet their visitors.

Bear west, A387, to Sandplace Station then right by the B3254 to St Keyne Station.

Paul Corin Magnificent Music Machines, St Keyne Station ⓥ – The rare assemblage of automatic instruments and mechanical music-makers performing to paper rolls and punch cards includes pianolas, an orchestrion, a Dutch street organ, and a 1929 Wurlitzer Theatre Pipe organ from Brighton. Full Victorian Era animation and Music Hall entertainment is also provided!

Traditional Cornish dishes include Muggety Pie (sheep's offal), the re-nowned Cornish pasty, Kiddley Broth (the staple fare of poor tin-mining families: bread soaked in boiling water) and Stargazy Pie (so-named because of the pilchard heads poking through the crust).
For details of other regional specialities, consult the Introduction.

FROME

Somerset – Population 23 159
Michelin Atlas p 17 or Map 403 – M, N 30

The town, founded by the Abbot Malmesbury St Aldhelm at a crossing on the river of the same name, was from AD 685 until the 19C an important market and wool cloth town. After the Dissolution (1539), the church lands passed to the Thynne family, who later bought more before building their manor house at Longleat. Today it ranks the fourth largest in Somerset and still holds the largest one-day agricultural show in the south west (third Wednesday in September).
Market days: Wednesday (cattle: at Standerwick Street) and though smaller, Saturday in Market Yard and Market Place.

Streets – Market Place and Bath Street, which lead up steeply from the shop-lined **bridge** (1667), are lined with shops beneath older 17C-19C upper floors and skylines punctuated by gables. The chief interest, however, lies in the side streets: 18C houses and two and three house terraces; a **Blue Coat School** and **almshouses** of 1726; the picturesque **Cheap Street** with 16C-17C shops, lamp standards, bay windows, oversailing upper floors, swinging iron signs lining either side of the cobbled pathway divided at the centre by a swift-running stream; the paved and winding Gentle Street with larger 17C-18C houses and a gabled 17C inn...
In Bath Street stands a remarkable building, the **Rook Lane Congregational Church** (or Chapel), built in 1707: the interior is much altered but the front is especially gracious. At the far end of Rook Lane is **Sheppard's Barton**, another well preserved street of 18C clothworker cottages, and Valentine Lamp, the working gas lamp dedicated to the memory of St Valentine.

St John's – The church, overlooking Cheap Street and standing on a Saxon site, is largely 14C-15C, restored in the 19C. The north and south round-headed doorways are 12C of a type found at Bristol and Malmesbury; the castellated tower and recessed octagonal spire were initiated in the early 1300s, completed in the 15C and rebuilt in 1830; the five-arched screen is by Jeffry Wyatt (Wyattville) and dates from when the designer was engaged at Longleat in 1814 *(3 miles east of Frome).*

EXCURSION

A36 to Farleigh Hungerford Castle

Rode Bird Gardens ⓥ – *5 miles north.* The 17-acre park which includes ornamental trees, flower gardens and a clematis collection, lakes, a stream and a waterfall, provides the setting for strutting ornamental pheasants, free-flying macaws, penguins, flamingos and large aviaries containing more than 220 different species: eagles, owls and other birds of prey; finches and canaries; parrots, parakeets and cockatoos; endangered birds from jungle and island habitats like pink crested touracos and red tailed Amazons, and breeding ground hornbills... Throughout the summer the narrow-gauge **Woodland Steam Railway** runs through the grounds.

Norton St Philip – *8 miles from Frome.* The village, off the main road to Bath, was known for centuries to wool and cloth merchants who came twice a year to what were among the biggest cloth fairs of the West Country.
Charters to hold the fairs were obtained, originally, in the 13C by the Carthusian monks who had built a monastery nearby at Hinton, on land given them by Ela, Countess of Salisbury, the founder of Lacock Abbey. The charterhouse which

was called *Atrium Dei* was dedicated to the memory of her husband, William Longespée (d 1226), natural son of Henry II and half-brother to Richard Lionheart. By the 18C the local speciality, in Defoe's words, was "fine medley, or mixed cloths such as are usually worn in England by the better sort of people and are exported in great quantities to Holland, Hamburg, Sweden, Denmark, Spain, Italy etc".

At the centre of the main street, lined by old stone houses, stands the famous George Inn.

★ **George Inn** – The building was erected *c*1223 as the monks' hostel while they were constructing Hinton Charterhouse. When the priory was complete the hostel became the priory guesthouse and inn and eventually a storehouse for wool from sheep raised on the priory lands.

It was initially a single-storey building of local stone with a wide **central archway**; in the 15C two half-timbered, oversailing storeys were added, with three attractive **oriel windows**.

George Inn, Norton St Philip

At the Dissolution, while the priory lands passed to the crown and the priory itself was encouraged to fall into ruin, the inn continued to provide hospitality to wool merchants and clothiers since Norton had become a weaving centre. Despite the decline of the industry in the early 18C, the village remained a welcome halt for travellers. Samuel Pepys, who stopped by with his wife on 12 June 1668, commented "dined very well, 10*s*".

Ten days before the Battle of Sedgemoor, **Monmouth's** men fought a running battle with the king's force in the fields outside the town. The duke, who had a price on his head, was surveying the scene from the inn, when a sniper fired but missed, at which, according to a local ballad, he "gaily turned him round and said: My man you've missed your mark and lost your thousand pound".

The arch leads to the old beamed rooms and the flowered **courtyard** at the back with a long **medieval gallery** along one side.

★ **Farleigh Hungerford** – *6 miles east of Frome.* The **castle ruin** ⊘ stands guard on the Wiltshire-Somerset border.

In 1369-70 Sir Thomas de Hungerford, a Wiltshire squire and onetime Speaker of the House of Commons, bought Farleigh manor house; he subsequently fortified it, transforming it into a rectangular walled castle with five-storey angle towers with conical roofs.

In 1420-30, Sir Thomas' son increased the castle to the south by the addition of an Outer Court enclosed by a new wall, towers and the two-storey East Gate which is still the entrance. Also enclosed by the new perimeter was the 14C St Leonard's Chapel, formerly the parish church.

★ **St Leonard's Chapel** – From the 16C west porch, steps lead down into the nave (1350) which contains a chaplain's funerary stone (*c*1480), a 12C font and a giant **wall painting** *(right of the east window)* of St George killing a now invisible dragon.

Under the wide semicircular arch in the chantry chapel, added by Sir Thomas in 1380-90, are the remarkable **Hungerford funeral monuments** of Sir Thomas (d 1398) in chain mail and his wife (d 1412) in cloak and mantle; beyond, beautifully carved in white marble, are the Parliamentarian, Sir Edward Hungerford (d 1648) and his wife.

A36 to Shepton Mallet

★ **Nunney** – *3 miles west*. The village of 17C-18C stone houses and cottages, with an inn sign spanning the main street, surrounds a moated castle and small church. Dating back to 1393, **Nunney Castle**, which was slighted in 1645, remains as a picturesque ruin, its tall towers reflected in the waters of the moat.
The **church**, vigorously restored in the 19C, is 13C-16C. Note the spirally fluted Norman **font** with a Jacobean cover, 14C arcades with no capitals between the piers and arches.
Among the **tomb effigies** are Sir John Delamere (d 1390) who built the castle, Richard Prater and his wife who bought it in 1577 and their Cavalier grandson who lost it to the Parliamentarians. Note the castle model.

Cranmore – *8 miles west*. The **East Somerset Railway Station** ⊘ has been restored to a modest Victorian appearance; the signal box converted into an exhibition gallery.
The depot, built in the tradition of Victorian train sheds, is a repair workshop for stock which includes, as jewels of the collection, the locomotives Bluebell (P/0-6-0T/1910), Green Knight (4MT/4-6-0/1954), Black Prince (9F/2-10-0/1959) and Lord Fisher.
The broad gauge East Somerset Railway opened in 1858, became part of the Great Western Railway and ultimately of British Rail, and was closed in 1967. The private line, reopened by the wildlife artist and passionate steam-engine enthusiast David Shepherd, now extends 2 miles.

★ **Shepton Mallet** – Sceapton, meaning sheep fold, is listed as a Saxon village in the Domesday Book. Shepton Mallet, with Wells and Glastonbury, was a stocking knitting town in the 17C-18C, and a wool town producing pure wool cloth, serges, sailcloth and silk in the 18C-19C with as many as 4 000 people employed in the giant mills. Another important industry is brewing: the Anglo Bavarian Brewery (*c*1860) was the first in England to brew lager; one at Charlton has been transformed into a business park, while the one at Kilver Street produced Babycham and Gaymers Cider.

> The development of "henge" architecture in England was probably due to the Bronze Age invaders from the Rhineland area: the Beaker Folk.
> These physically strong, warlike people were well-equipped archers and had shapely stone battle axes. The beakers and mugs found buried with them, and from which they derive their name, suggest that they were great drinkers of beer.

The town, which is situated in the valley of the River Sheppy, at the foot of the Mendip Hills, has always been and remains a livestock centre and market close to main highways including the Roman Fosse Way and the roads to Bristol, Frome and Ilchester. Evidence of an important Bronze Age settlement has come to light on the south side of the town near Cannards Grave.

Market Place – Market day is Friday. The Market Place is bordered by 17C inns, 18C houses, shops and a modern public library. The Market cross, a tall pinnacle (1500), is encircled by an 18C hexagonal arcade and by the Shamble.

Market Shamble – First built in Shepton in 1450, it is an obvious development from a little shed – the Anglo-Saxon meaning of the word. The shed developed into a permanent line of roofed stalls, which, in time, became a street of open fronted shops – mostly butchers', sometimes fishmongers' – from the disorder of whose backyards, slaughterhouses etc, the modern meaning evolved.

Walk through the modern buildings to the parish church.

★ **St Peter and St Paul** – The **west tower** with its stump of a spire is evidence of a change in architectural fashion. It was constructed on a Norman base in *c*1380 of local Doulting stone and, as it was intended to support a spire, it is a solid structure. It is also the earliest tower in the Somerset style: it is strengthened by pairs of set-back buttresses at the angles as it rises from the west door through stages marked by a big six-light window, statuary niches, a clock bay and a bell tier of three paired openings, to reach the pierced balustrade and solid buttress pinnacles at the crest.
An eight-sided **spire** was begun, halted and capped; it was never completed, for what reason is unknown. The numbers of skilled masons and craftsmen had been seriously depleted by the Black Death (1348) and people may have grown used

to the sight of a tower without a spire; some maintain that Shepton Mallet tower was so beautiful as to need no enhancement. It may also have been realised that a spire was a hazardous structure owing to human error and natural causes; countless Norman spires collapsed and all were at risk from lightning.

The interior reveals the church's Saxon origins, the Norman rebuilding, the 13C-17C enlargement, the Puritan depredations and the ardent Victorian remodelling. Note the circular **Saxon font**, the knights in chain mail and the **pulpit** of Doulting stone, richly carved in 1550 with niches, Renaissance cornucopias and flowers. The finest feature is the "richly wrought" **barrel vault** (1450); "the most glorious of all **wagon roofs** in England" consisting of 350 carved panels and 1 400 leaves caught into nearly 400 bosses and half bosses.

Town Houses – It is worth strolling round the town to admire the pedimented doorways and well-proportioned windows of the **Georgian houses** and the **Strode Almshouses** of 1699 *(south of the church)*; to explore the narrow, stone-walled lanes leading to **Legg Square** and the 18C clothiers' houses, **Eden Grove** and **The Hollies** with their columned doorways.

Perpendicular Somerset church towers

The one at **Evercreech** dominates the village square and medieval market cross, rising between shafted and pinnacled buttresses to immensely tall, twice-transomed bell-lights – the lower bays blind, those above tracery-filled. Pinnacles and sub-pinnacles continue the vertical lines ever higher above the crest. Inside is a tie-beam roof of angels and bosses richly gilt and coloured.

Batcombe Church west tower of 87ft is a complete contrast to other church towers in the county, the profusion of pinnacles being all below the skyline.

Inside, the church lost most of its original features to 19C restoration, save a 15C font, 17C brass and altar rail, George III coat of arms over the south door.

The half-timbered **King's Arms**, locally known as the Dusthole because it was regularly frequented by quarrymen from the Quarr quarry nearby, supplied ale to the prison opposite: HM Prison, Gaol Lane, is presumed to be the oldest operational prison in the country; during World War II precious documents from the Public Record Office (Domesday Book, Magna Carta) were stored here, while still in use by the American Services.

Peter Street is lined with Georgian houses. In the lane to the left stands the old **Grammar School**, which was founded in 1627; the uncompromising Latin tag on the wall of the Georgian annexe reads *Disce aut discede* which means Learn or Leave *(north side of the church).*

On the far side of the Market Place and Town Street is **Great Ostry**, bordered by a 17C three-storey terrace of seven identical houses with mullioned windows. Further exploration of the lanes provides views of the old mills, the 17C gabled weavers' cottages and their handkerchief-sized gardens.

★ **Downside Abbey** *5 miles north of Shepton Mallet off A37 and A367 at Stratton-on-the-Fosse*

Downside is the senior Benedictine monastery in England.

The Community of St Gregory the Great was founded in 1605-07 at Douai in northern France by English and Welsh Benedictine monks who had been trained abroad since the Reformation. Among their number were priests who travelled to England on missionary work.

In 1793 Douai University was suppressed by the French Revolution, the Benedictines were put under guard and the monastery was ransacked. Although Catholicism was still officially proscribed in England, the penal laws were not being enforced and in 1794 the Community crossed the Channel and, after a brief interval, settled at Stratton-on-the-Fosse in 1814.

The community today numbers 45 members; the school about 500 boys. The buildings *(private)*, which include a 17C-18C mansion known as Old House, have multiplied in every architectural style current in the last 150 years.

★ **Abbey Church** ⊙ – *30min*. The abbey church was built in the neo-Gothic style between 1870 and 1938; only the tower (166ft) acknowledges the Somerset tower tradition; the rib vaulting is in the 13C French style. The internal proportions are cathedral-like (330ft long and 74ft high). Colour is provided by the windows, pictures and statuary.

Nave – The austere nave – very tall, narrow and of white stone – is by Giles Gilbert Scott.

North Transept – The transept contains the altar and shrine (a gilt oak casket) of **St Oliver Plunkett**, hanged in 1681, the last Roman Catholic to die at Tyburn. Note the windows with St Aldhelm and St Dunstan.

In the **Holy Angels Chapel** sits a 16C Flemish School triptych of the *Adoration of the Magi.*

In **St Placid Chapel**, note the old oak **statue** of the Madonna, a Spanish 16C **reliquary** and a very old oak **statue**, a copy of Notre Dame de Foy near Dinant, Belgium.

St Sebastian Chapel has a 15C Italian painting of a bishop by Sir Ninian Comper (1864-1960).

St Sylvia's Chapel and Sacred Heart Chapel: one contains a modern relief of the Crucifixion, the other has modern ceramic panels.

The all-gold **Lady Chapel** was decorated by Sir Ninian Comper.

The **bosses** in **St Benedict's Chapel** depict the arms of the 54 Benedictine abbeys and priories dissolved by Henry VIII.

South Aisle – Both the **Virgin and Child**, from the Upper Rhineland, and the statue of **St Peter** *(west end)* are believed to date from the 15C.

GLASTONBURY★★

Somerset – Population 7 747

Michelin Atlas p 8 and Map 403 – L 30

Glastonbury Tor and the Polden Hills were once islands rising out of the marshes which were connected by tidal channels to the open sea; by the Iron Age (450 BC) the hilltops were occupied by forts – the name Glastonbury means hillfort of the Glastings people – hut settlements being built above the waterline. Archeological surveys indicate that the Iron Age Glastonbury Lake village was an important Celtic centre of industry from where manufactured goods have found their way into south Wales, Gloucestershire, Devon and Cornwall. It has been suggested that it even provided sanctuary to continental craftsmen fleeing France during Caesar's conquest in 56BC. Access across the flooded Levels was provided by timber trackways.

The town, which grew up round the abbey, has become an important centre of spiritualism and alternative lifestyle which finds expression in the hugely successful open-air **Glastonbury Festival** for contemporary music.

Market day: Tuesday all day.

★★ ABBEY ⊘ 30min

Although there has only been a ruin on the site for the past four and a half centuries, the name immediately conjures up the great abbey, its existence for centuries as one of the richest houses owning vast amounts of land *(see* SHAFTESBURY*)* and as a centre of learning.

Legend and history – The abbey foundation appears most likely to have been as a 4C-5C Celtic monastery and church – a supposition which by the 12C had developed into a tale that it had been founded by St Patrick in person. Other legends developed: that Christ's disciples established the monastery and, most famous of all, that **Joseph of Arimathea** landed in Somerset one Christmas morning (some said returned, having come originally with the boy Jesus), bearing the Holy Grail. Joseph, according to the legend, set foot on a hill known as Avalon and later rested on a second hill, Wearyall, where he stood his staff upright in the ground; it promptly sprouted and flowered and has been known ever since as the **Glastonbury Thorn** – *Crataegus praecox.* The original tree was cut down by the Puritans but descendants still bloom twice a year in December and May in the abbey grounds and in St John's churchyard *(see below)*. Joseph was given land by the local ruler, Arviragus, and constructed a wattle and daub church on the site of the abbey Lady Chapel.

Another legend concerned **King Arthur** *(see* TINTAGEL*)*, who, it was claimed, after being mortally wounded at the Battle of Camlann in 537, sailed away to the island of Avalon or Glastonbury, where his and Guinevere's bodies were "discovered" in the abbey cemetery in 1191 and re-interred in the chancel in 1278. The tomb survived until the Dissolution; the site is now marked by a plaque.

"Disputable matter", as **William of Malmesbury** termed the various theories of the abbey's foundation when he began to write its history in 1120, is replaced by "solid fact" from the 7C. In 688 **Ine**, King of the West Saxons – who had by then driven the Celts from Somerset – in consultation with **Aldhelm**, built an additional church to that already on the site; in 943 Dunstan was appointed abbot. **Dunstan**, the son of a West Saxon noble, was born *c*910 near Glastonbury where he was educated before he entered the household of his kinsman, Athelstan (925-39), whose policy, in the tradition of Alfred, was the supremacy of Wessex against the Danes. When Dunstan lost favour at court, he went to Winchester where he became a Benedictine.

Glastonbury Abbey ruins

Successive kings recalled him to court; appointed him abbot of Glastonbury which he enlarged and rebuilt both spiritually and physically and which during his abbacy (943-59) became famous as a centre of learning. He was recalled as a political administrator, suffered royal displeasure and outlawry before Edgar appointed him Bishop of Worcester and London and, in 961, Archbishop of Canterbury in which capacity he crowned **Edgar** first King of all England in Bath Abbey (973). Edgar died two years later and was buried at Glastonbury.

The abbot appointed to Glastonbury after the Conquest considered the church inadequate for the richest abbey in the land (after Westminster) and, in the manner of Norman prelates of the time, began to rebuild it. The task was completed by his successors only to be destroyed entirely in a fire in 1184. Rebuilding began immediately with the St Mary's or Lady Chapel, which was completed within two years, and then proceeded slowly over the next two centuries. It was at this period and immediately following that the abbacy was taken over by the ambitious Bishop Savaric (d 1205) of Bath and Wells and the abbey church declared to be a cathedral; it was also at this time that the abbey began to acquire vast manorial holdings and great riches and that **Abbot Richard Bere** (1493-1524), who was a great populariser as well as a great churchman and builder, developed the cult of Joseph of Arimathea.

The Dissolution in 1539 brought annihilation: the abbot, Richard Whiting refused to surrender forcing Thomas Cromwell to seek evidence to charge him of treason; despite having taken the Oath of Supremacy, Whiting was brutally hanged, drawn and quartered with two brothers on Glastonbury Tor, the other forty-five monks and 120-130 lay servants were dispersed, the manors were confiscated and the buildings allowed to fall into ruin.

Early in 1552, the Duke of Somerset offered the abandoned monastery to a large group of Flemish Protestant refugees that consisted of some forty families and six widows. Unable to practise their clothmaking skills for lack of equipment, seconded by Queen Mary's accession to the throne which brought their stay in Glastonbury to an end and keen to flee from possible further religious persecution, they moved to Frankfurt.

Abbey complex – The ruins, extending far across the lawns, stand tall amid majestic trees. The tower piers, arches, south nave wall, even the relatively complete shell of the Lady Chapel, give no idea of what the abbey church must have looked like during the short years of its prime – the remains in their glorious setting are, nevertheless, unforgettable.

Visitor Centre – A spacious display area is used to present the history of the abbey, reinforced with artefacts retrieved from archeological digs.

St Mary or Lady Chapel – The chapel, in Doulting stone, has a **corner turret** and walls decorated with blind arcading and a modillioned cornice; the west end has three stepped lancets. The **doorways** are rounded, that to the north being enriched, possibly later, with **carved figures** of the Annunciation, the Magi and Herod.
The chapel stands on the site of the first wattle and daub church; all subsequent churches, including King Ine's (which measured 42ft), have been built to its east. Within the chapel are embrasures with zigzag decoration and arcading, the St Joseph Crypt (c1500) and a view east through the arch in the chapel wall *(see below)*.

Nave – The distant chancel walls rise east of the transept piers, which supported the crossing tower, with the site of the Edgar Chapel beyond – the nave, chancel and retrochoir together measured 375ft, the full length of the abbey was 555ft – longer than Salisbury or Wells Cathedrals, shorter than Winchester.
Bishop Bere's rebuilding was completed in the early 15C with the construction of the **Galilee** which joined the main church to the Lady Chapel through the arch in the chapel wall.
The **Edgar Chapel**, a rebuilding of a mausoleum for the Saxon Kings, whom the abbey also claimed as founders, was undertaken early in the 16C.
Throughout, the style was Gothic which became slightly more ornamented with time. Each area would have been painted, directly on the stone, shortly after it was completed (a scale model in the museum gives an idea of the completed church).

★ **Abbot's Kitchen** – The 14C kitchen, the sole building to survive intact, is square with an eight-sided roof rising to superimposed lanterns which served to draw the smoke from the corner fires in the kitchen up the flues in the roof.

Glastonbury Thorn Tree – The large thorn tree *(labelled)* stands north of the abbey.

St Patrick's – The church was built in 1512 to serve no longer extant almshouses.

TOWN

The two principal streets, High Street and Magdalene Street, intersect at the Victorian-Gothic Market Cross.

Magdalene Street – The street contains a number of attractive small 17C-19C town houses. South of the abbey entrance are the pedimented town hall (c1814), the 1754 Pumphouse *(private)* from the days when Glastonbury aspired to be a spa (1751-1830s) and **St Margaret's Almshouses** (built in 1251, altered in the 16C) which includes a 13C chapel grouped attractively around a garden.

St Benedict's – The pinnacled tower, glimpsed *(west)* at the top end of the street just before the market cross, belongs to a Perpendicular church of c1520. It was built on an older site by Bishop Bere, whose mitre and initials may be seen outside the north porch and whose rebus is carved on one of the roof corbels in the north aisle.

High Street – The street is overlooked by two buildings formerly connected with the abbey, the tribunal or old courthouse and a hotel, founded in the 14C and nobly rebuilt in the 15C by an abbot to ensure that there was suitable accommodation for the pilgrims, lawyers and other respected visitors to the abbey.

George and Pilgrims Hotel – Interesting features of the Abbot Selwood's 15C inn's front include its actual height below the embattled roofline, the heavy string courses to emphasise the width of the building, the intricate, panel-style decoration and asymmetrically placed entrance decorated with the abbey arms, those of Edward IV and one blank. Inside are the original oak panelling, beams, doorways, an early fireplace and old Dutch tiles.

Tribunal – The building dates from the 14C when it was timber fronted; the fine ashlar stone face, the canted bay, stone mullions and doorway were added by Bishop Bere in 1500; the latest additions were made in Elizabethan times when it ceased to be abbey property; later serving as a prosperous merchant's house and shop.

Today it houses the Tourist Information Centre and a **museum** ⊙ of excavated antiquities from an Iron Age **Lake Village** ⊙ located northwest of Glastonbury in the Somerset Levels: well-preserved artefacts including decorated ware pottery is largely due to the stable conditions provided by the peat bog in which they were found.

The **Peat Moor Visitor Centre** ⊙ *(Shapwick Road, Westhay)* nearby provides additional insight into the conditions of life 150BC-50BC with demonstrations from a flint knapper and a traditional turf cutter on Living History Days; the nature reserve alongside preserves marshland habitat for wildlife.

★★ **St John the Baptist** – The 134.5ft church **tower** is one of the finest in Somerset with its "crown" of crocketed pinnacles which rise through buttresses and shafts from the lower stages to stand high above the battlements of two tiers of pierced arcading.

The church was rebuilt in the 15C in part because of the collapse of the earlier, Norman, crossing tower; only parts of the northern chapel dedicated to St Katherine survive from the 12C. The **nave** of seven bays has a clerestory, making the interior "lightsome", as Leland declared, beneath its 15C Somerset oak **roof** on angel corbels.

Note especially the finely carved Charles II **royal arms**, the **chest** bought secondhand in 1421, the **domestic cupboard** of 1500, the **15C glass** *(chancel north window)*, the 15C **tomb chests** of the wealthy cloth merchant Richard Atwell and his wife *(transepts)* and another with an alabaster effigy with angels and camels round the base.

In the churchyard is the **Glastonbury Thorn Tree** *(Crataegus praecox)* from which the Queen is sent a sprig in bloom each Christmas.

At the end of the High Street turn right down A361 Shepton Mallet Road Lambrook-Chilkwell Street; turn off right into Bere Lane; 550yds in all.

★ **Somerset Rural Life Museum** ⊙ – The 14C "home" barn of Glastonbury Abbey is the outstanding exhibit of the museum, which illustrates 19C daily life on a Somerset farm, at work outside and in the home, and is appropriately housed in a 19C farmhouse and the adjoining farm buildings. Practical demonstrations of local country crafts are also regularly held.

The **farmhouse** (1896) illustrates domestic life: the original kitchen with its range, rag rugs, lead pump and sink; *(cellar)* cheese production – copper vat, presses, awards; *(upstairs)* history of John Hodges who spent his life in the village of Butleigh working for the local squire.

The **cowsheds** are used to illustrate the cycle of activities in the farming year – including cider making and peat digging – complete with hand tools and early machinery.

The modestly sized **barn** (93ft x 33ft) has an exceptional **roof** and **stonework**. Cruciform in plan, it has buttressed walls and two porches framing the massive double doors; the four gable ends are decorated with animal finials and roundels containing the symbols of the four Evan-

> Tithe means "tenth" and tithe barns date from the Middle Ages when farmers had to give a tenth of all crops grown to the Church. The grain was kept in the tithe barns, which are noticeable now for being sturdy, handsome buildings which are much larger than ordinary farm barns.

gelists; a carved head surmounts each corner buttress. During restoration in 1978 the original local roofing stone was replaced with shingles from the Cotswolds (80 tons). The dominant internal feature is the timber **roof**, composed mainly of oak with some elm and chestnut; the exceptional width is spanned by a skilful two-tier cruck structure.

The barn and the adjoining courtyard display the wagons, ploughs and other machinery which after centuries of slow development are now historic farm relics.

Return to Chilkwell Street; turn right (250yds).

Chalice Well and Gardens ⊙ – The chalybeate spring, a natural spring pouring out 25 000 gallons of water a day at a constant temperature of 52°F – 11°C, has long been associated with the abbey legend of Joseph of Arimathea who is said to have hidden the Grail or Chalice in the well, whereupon the water flowed red: a more scientific explanation for the water's colour, betrayed by its metallic taste, is its large iron content.

In the 12C a stone wellhouse was built and conduits were laid to take water to the abbey; it was also used to supply a Pilgrim's Bath with alleged healing properties. Today, the complex is managed by a trust which highlights the spiritual qualities of the place; water may be sampled at the Lion's Head.

Wellhouse Lane, which provides an outlet for the clearer, sweeter water just beyond the well, leads to the Tor. Park at the bottom and walk up the steep path or continue 250yds along the lane to a gentler path.

★ **Glastonbury Tor** – The Tor (521ft high) is a landmark visible for miles around and worth the climb. The tower at the summit is the last remnant of a Church to St Michael, built in the 14C on a hillfort and Saxon church site, destroyed by an earthquake in c1275. Excavation undertaken in the 1960s revealed traces of a Dark Age settlement (5C-7C) and fragments of pottery imported from the Mediterranean region, possibly used for olive oil, fish paste or wine; further study has revealed a complete spiral maze.

Today, regarded as a junction point for the earth's spiritual and cosmic forces by followers of the New Age culture, the tor attracts large numbers of visitors intent on contemplating the ley lines radiating from there, connected to the Glastonbury Zodiac, a mystical representation of astrological figures in the surrounding countryside. The ridges in fact may be the result of natural geological formations and early farming practices.

On a fine day, the view★★★ includes the Quantocks and Bristol Channel *(northwest)*; the Mendips – Wells Cathedral, *(northeast)*; the Marlborough Downs and possibly Salisbury *(east)*; the Polden Hills *(southwest)*.

EXCURSIONS

Street *2 miles southwest on A39*

The town takes its name from an ancient causeway which ran north across the River Brue to Glastonbury; the hamlet's prosperity long depended upon its blue lias quarries and on agriculture. In the 19C it became a centre for tanning sheepskin for rugs and shoes, and, as mechanisation transformed the shoe-making industry from an out-worker's craft to a factory skill, Street became transformed. In 1825 **C & J Clark** founded their shoe factory here assuring the town's future; these premises in a setting of lawns, trees, a clock tower and a Henry Moore bronze sculpture near the centre of the town continue to provide the business's corporate headquarters.

Nearby is located **Millfield** School.

Clark's Village – Off the High Street, stands a factory shopping complex, the first in Britain to offer branded goods at discount prices. In the **Shoe Museum**★ ⊙ are displayed hand-tools for making shoes, 19C machinery, fashion plates and showcards, tally books and a collection of shoes from Roman times to the present: button boots, dancing slippers, postilions' boots, children's shoes...

In the town *(between the shopping centre and car park)* is a modern stone mosaic-mural of familiar heights, towers and the landscape of central Somerset.

Somerset Levels

Traces of the oldest man-made road in the form of a wooden causeway known as **Sweet Track** *(no access)* still exist near Westhay. For this wide, flat area south of the Mendip hills and east of the Quantocks has been used since the most ancient times during the summer months as lush pasture for grazing and fertile arable land when the banks of the water-filled rhines are a haven for a variety of wild flowers (marsh marigold, lady's smock, frogbit, flowering rush, arrowbit). In winter, much of the same area is waterlogged: useless to man, the meadows then provide a rich feeding ground for golden plovers, lapwings (peewits), snipe, redwings, fieldfares and, in parts, wigeon, teal, shovelers and Bewick swans. The busiest bird season (April and early May) attracts passing flocks of whimbrel and breeding heron, lapwing, curlew, snipe, redshank, yellow wagtails, whinchats...

Among the best places to birdwatch are **Shapwick Heath** (south of Westhay), Tealham and Tadham Moors, (off B3151 between Westhay and Wedmore), West Sedgemoor RSPB reserve (off A378 between Fivehead and Langport). For further information consult the Willows and Wetland Visitor Centre, Meare Green *(see* BRIDGWATER).

Meare – The 14C Abbot's Fish House was used for drying, salting and storing fish for Glastonbury Abbey. *To view the interior, apply at the house next door.*

Wedmore – The village, with its lantern-headed market cross, is historic as the signing place of the treaty between King Alfred and the Danes in AD 878.

The crossing **tower** of the Perpendicular **Church of St Mary Magdalene** was inspired by that of Wells Cathedral. Inside, the tower **roof** is fan vaulted, the pulpit Jacobean, the **wall painting** of St Christopher 16C and the **chandelier** 18C.

Burnham-on-Sea

Two associations spring to mind at the mention of the seaside resort of Burnham on Sea on the Bristol Channel: the lighthouses on stilts and the Grinling Gibbons carvings.

Lighthouses – In the shallows on the seven mile beach, beyond the sunbathers, sand-castle builders and donkeys, there stands a lighthouse on stilts – a pair with one behind on the sand dunes; in line, they serve as a navigation bearing for ships in the channel; both are vertically striped red and white, the upper one shows a light.

Parish Church – St Andrew's stands just back from the beach, its 14C-15C **tower** noticeably "leaning" out of the vertical. Inside are a delightful gathering of **cherubs** and two expressive **angels** carved by **Grinling Gibbons** (1648-1700) and Arnold Quellin for the Whitehall Palace chapel. After the palace fire of 1698, the altarpiece found its way to Westminster Abbey before being transferred, in part, to Burnham in 1820.

HONITON

Devon – Population 9 008
Michelin Atlas p 7 or Map 403 – K 31

The **pottery** and **lace** which have for so long made Honiton a household name are both still made in the town. A new jabot made in 1983 for the Speaker of the House of Commons took 500 hours to complete.

Despite its 17C-18C Georgian appearance – the result of numerous fires which swept the wide main street from the Middle Ages to the 18C – the town dates back to the 12C when it was founded as a village settlement on either side of the London-Exeter road (A30 – now by-passed). By 1257 a pannier market and the annual July fair were in being; by Tudor times fine glove-making, a cottage industry, was complementing the important local sheep and wool industry, and by the early 17C pillow lacemaking had also been established. In the 18C Honiton became a staging town with coaching inns flanking the wide High Street.

Market day: Tuesday and Saturday.

★ **All Hallows Museum** ⊙ – *High Street, next to the 19C parish church.*

This local museum's major displays concentrate on lace: a fine wedding veil, a matronly overskirt with a 40in waist, handkerchiefs, flounces, a lacemaker's sampler with prices...

Other exhibits include Honiton pottery, Victorian scent and smelling bottles, bead purses, card and table games, a 19C kitchen-laundry with tub and washing line.

Honiton Lace

Reference to a distinctive style of bobbin lace associated with Honiton appears in the 17C at the same time as the art was developing in Flanders, France and Italy. At that time the area already had an established textile industry using locally produced wool and flax – the art of lacemaking probably developed as demand for fashionable cuffs, collars, christening robes and wedding veils grew. Items were made to commission by women at home and sold by wealthy merchants; their choice of Honiton as a distribution centre was based on its geographical situation within easy reach of Exeter, Taunton, Yeovil and Dorchester. Honiton lace which often comprises flowers and butterflies, differs from the tape lace made at Beer or Branscombe which consists of ribbons of lace that are then stitched into motifs.

EXCURSIONS

★ **Ottery St Mary** *7 miles southwest by A30 and B3177.*

Ottery, standing on the River Otter, surrounded on all sides by lush green slopes and well away from the main road, avoided the arterial plan and developed gradually on a hillside site as a network of winding streets, small squares and hidden corners, each lined by 17C and Georgian houses. At the top of the hill is the twin-towered parish church, reminiscent, in miniature, of Exeter Cathedral.

★ **St Mary's** – The manor was given in 1061 by Edward the Confessor to a church foundation in Rouen and bought back in 1336 by **Bishop John de Grandisson** of Exeter in order that he might found a college or sanctuary for poetry and learning here, in this village only twelve miles from the cathedral. The college endured for 200 years before being dissolved in 1545 by Henry VIII: who took "all the plate jewells ornaments goods and cattalles apperteigninge to the late surrendered College"; the medieval college houses and choir school (the Kynges Newe Grammer Scole of Seynt Marie Oterey) were allowed to remain. The manor was presented to Edward Seymour, future Duke of Somerset, but on his attainder reverted to the crown and was finally resold by Charles I.

The church in which the villagers had always worshipped became the property of the parish under the supervision of first four, then twelve, local residents or "Governors", a system which continues to this day.

The **towers** (64ft high) were built in the 14C when the existing church was remodelled in the Decorated style by Bishop Grandisson. The lead-covered **spire** (31ft), which was re-structured in 1908 using the old lead, resembles one which crowned the north tower of Exeter cathedral until 1752; the **weather vane**, one of the oldest in the country, is a **Whistling Cock**, so-called on account of the two tubes which run through its body and make it moan in the wind: it was used as target practice by Cromwellian soldiers billeted there during the Civil War.

Inside, the high rib and panel vaulted nave contains the canopied tombs of Sir Otho de Grandisson, the bishop's younger brother, in full armour (d 1359) and his wife; at the **crossing** the bishop himself is portrayed on the centre boss.

Against the wooden gallery in the south transept is **Grandisson's clock**, dating from the collegiate period, cared for in 1437-38 at a cost of 3s 4d and more recently totally rebuilt so that, like its fellows at Exeter, Wells and Wimborne Minster, it still tells the time.

Note the 19C mosaic **wall tiling** and monuments to the Coleridge family (see INTRODUCTION: Literary associations).

The carved altarscreen is 19C-20C; the **sedilia** is pure 14C Decorated Gothic. The tomb is that of John Haydon (d 1587), sometime "governor" of the church and builder of Cadhay.

In the ambulatory note the Elizabethan **brasses** (south side) and the stone minstrels' gallery. The **Lady Chapel** beyond contains the church's gilded wooden **eagle lectern** dating from Grandisson's time, one of the oldest in England, also medieval **choirstalls** and a **corbel portrait head** (at the opening, south wall) of Bishop Grandisson in a mitre.

The **Outer or Dorset aisle**, added in 1520, is notable for its **fan vaulting** with large pendent bosses terminating in Tudor roses, its **corbels**, its owls on the piers at the west end and, on the second pier from the west end, an elephant's head (1520).

Cadhay ⊘ – 1 mile northwest of Ottery St Mary. 30min. "John Haydon esquire, sometime bencher of Lincoln's Inn, builded at Cadhay a fair new house and enlarged his demesne". Haydon was a successful Exeter lawyer who had married Joan Cadhay in 1527 and become rich as one of the local commissioners responsible for selling the dissolved priories in and around Exeter.

Construction – The house, incorporating the earlier Great Hall, was built round three sides of an oblong courtyard, probably in the early 1540s. John Haydon's heir, Robert Haydon, installed massive Tudor fireplaces with ornamental emblazoned tracery inside and, in a second building phase, enclosed the open side of the courtyard known as the **Court of Sovereigns**. The 18C owner included among his alterations the horizontal division of the Great Hall and the "Georgianising" of several rooms.

The furniture includes a 16C oak refectory table, 18C mahogany tables and chairs, chests, a secretaire... The owners' taste is reflected everywhere: in the collection in the Long Gallery and Roof Chamber and in the garden, enclosed by tall hedges and white clematis-draped walls, which slopes down to the 15C canons' fish-ponds.

Interior – The **Court of Sovereigns**, the house's unique feature, was enclosed at the end of the 16C and further transformed by the refacing of the **walls** with dark knapped flints and small sandstone blocks in an irregular chequered pattern, and the setting of four elaborate Renaissance-style **niches** above the doors at the centre of each range. In the niches, in full robes of state, stand Henry VIII, Edward VI, Mary Tudor and Elizabeth I – hence the court's name; it was completed in 1617.

The **Dining Hall**, part of the original Great Hall, has a high coved ceiling, an arcade – formerly open at one end – and one of the giant Tudor fireplaces. The **Drawing Room** is one of those Georgianised in the 18C.

The **Roof Chamber** is the upper part of the Great Hall and, although the timbers have been much cut about, many are the original 15C beams.

The **Long Gallery** runs the length of the Court of Sovereigns.

Farway Countryside Park ⊘ – 6 miles south by A375 and B3174.

The **views★** from the 189-acre hilltop park extend over the fertile east Devon landscape of fields, woodland and the Col River valley. Among the penned animals are rare breed sheep, a Brahman bull, Bagot and Pygmy goats, spotted pigs and small hogs bred back to resemble those of the Iron Age. In the paddocks are deer, ponies and Long Horned cattle.

Donkey cart rides, pony rides and pony trekking are available.

Axminster

The **carpet weaving** which was to make the 2 000 year old town's name a household word in Britain was introduced in 1755 by the Axminster clothier Thomas Whitty. During a visit to London he had seen a very large (36ft x 24ft) and beautiful Turkey carpet. He promptly erected an upright loom in his own factory, which still stands in Silver Street (now the Conservative Club), trained his five young daughters, charged his sister as overseer and on midsummer's day began weaving his first large carpet. In 1835 the factory faced bankruptcy and the looms were sold to the works at Wilton. The modern carpet works *(closed to the public)* are located off King Edward Road, by the station.
Market day: Thursday (livestock in South Street).

Minster Church ⊘ - By the Middle Ages Axminster was a community of sufficient prosperity to rebuild its Saxon Church in the 12C Norman style, and to add a tower in the 13C (recased in the 19C); it was again rebuilt in the 14C and 15C in the Decorated and Perpendicular styles. The tower was repaired after being damaged in an affray against the Parliamentarians in 1644 and the church was enlarged and remodelled in the 18C-20C.

Inside, note the cut-down Jacobean **pulpit, reading desk** and altar table, the charity boards, the royal arms painted in 1767 at a cost of £9 14*s* and, in the chancel, the tomb with the lovely recumbent **effigy** with steepled hands of Lady Alicia de Mohun (d *c*1257).

Streets and Squares - The two squares, Trinity and Victoria Place, and the streets between are marked by occasional Georgian houses, rounded shop-fronts and a coaching inn with a Venetian window above the wide yard entrance.

For Seaton, Beer, Branscombe and Axmouth, see SIDMOUTH. LYME REGIS is listed separately.

ILFRACOMBE

Devon – Population 10 941
Michelin Atlas p 6 or Map 403 – H30

The town, long the most popular resort on the North Devon coast, achieved success in the 19C with the development of steamship day outings from South Wales and the arrival of the railway bringing visitors in their thousands from the Midlands and the North Country.

Holy Trinity - The parish church overlooks the sea and the town. According to legend it was founded on land given by three maiden ladies, although little else is known about who they were. The tower is considered to be the oldest extant part dating from Saxon times. The church was greatly enlarged in 1324.
Inside, a remarkable **wagon roof**★★ is decorated with carved and painted bosses. Set along the nave are a series of 28 stone corbels, each carved with a mythical beast and bearing a black figure - thought to symbolise the triumph of good over evil. The stone coffin lid by the north porch is 14C. Note also the fine carved Jacobean (early 17C, restored and remodelled in 1901) oak pulpit, altar and altar table.

★ **Capstone Hill** - From the "summit" of the 156ft high hill there is a good bird's-eye **view**★ of the town, the harbour mouth, the rock-enclosed bays and beaches on either side.

Hillsborough - The hill on the town's eastern edge, at the centre of the pleasure ground, rises to 447ft and affords an even more extensive **view**★★ along the coast - an ideal situation for a Stone Age fort.

St Nicholas' Chapel ⊘ - In the early 14C a beacon on Lantern Hill served as a marker for ships at sea in the Bristol Channel; this was replaced by the mariners' "Little Chapel" (1300-25) which, though much altered through time, still shines a red bearing light at night. It may also have served as a place of refuge to pilgrims on their way to Hartland and to women and children from marauding pirates.
From the rock platform on which the chapel, dedicated to the patron saint of sailors, stands there is a good **view**★ out to sea and of the almost land-locked harbour. A promenade (starting from the quay) half circles the headland a few feet above sea-level.

Tunnels Beaches ⊘ - *Granville Rd.* The pools were an early 19C enterprise in which the hill between the road and the sea was tunnelled by Welsh miners and the rock cove, on the far side, made accessible. The cove was then equipped with a sea wall to prevent the tide running out and so provide all day bathing. In the 19C water was pumped to the baths at the entrance and heated in winter. The pools, now surrounded by amenities, are still very popular today.

EXCURSIONS

Hele Corn Mill ⊙ – *1 mile east by A399*. Deep in the valley stands a restored 16C watermill producing stone-ground flour. The machinery turns very quietly, driven by an overshot waterwheel (18ft): detailed explanations of the mill and milling.

Chambercombe Manor ⊙ – *1 mile southeast by A399*. The white-painted stone house (15C-17C) lying in a wooded dell is slate-roofed where it was once thatched. Inside, features include 200-300 year old polished **lime ash floors**, hard as granite and said to be made of wood ash and scrumpy laid like cement; a 13C Peter's Pence **almschest; barrel vaulting**, a Tudor plaster frieze and the arms of Lady Jane Grey in the principal room. Upstairs, the robustly carved Elizabethan four-poster bed is made from Spanish oak timbers. A Cromwellian oak **cradle**, Jacobean chest of drawers, William and Mary yew **tallboy** and a Victorian room are also of note.

In the gardens is set a bird sanctuary and arboretum.

★★ Mortehoe

The point marks the western end of the spectacular Somerset-North Devon coast and offers good **views** over the coastline and the impressive landscape inland.

★ **St Mary's Church** – The late 13C **tower**, which was added to the original 12C Norman church, was saved from ruin in 1988 when a banker's draft for £25 000 was stuffed into the offertory box by an anonymous benefactor. In the 13C a chantry to St Catherine was added to the south side of the church by the then rector, Sir William Tracey; tradition claims, probably falsely, that it contains the bones of Sir William de Tracey, who fled to Devon after murdering Thomas Becket in 1170.

The **font** is Norman or Early English; the finely carved 16C **bench-ends** show the Instruments of the Passion; the **angel mosaic** adorning the early chancel arch dates from 1903.

Morte Point – *Half a mile there and back on foot*. From Mortehoe a walk over the close-cropped turf on the gently rising headland leads to the 200ft **vantage point**★ that is Morte Point, from which the coast and other headlands may be surveyed.

To the south lie Devon's best known sand beaches, providing a contrast to the rocks and cliffs which characterize the rest of the north coast.

Woolacombe – *1 mile south by B3343*. The holiday village overlooking Morte Bay is known for its miles of yellow sands.

Croyde – *6 miles south by B3343 and B3231*. The small village lies in a bay between Baggy Point and a lesser headland.

★ **Braunton** *8 miles south along A361 to Barnstaple*

The older, prettier part of Braunton lies at its northeast end, by the church which overlooks thatched cob-walled cottages and houses with elegant balconies. The River Caen gently splashes beside the churchyard and through the village to the marshes and estuary at Velator. At the Conquest, the Braunton Hundred included Barnstaple and Ilfracombe. In the 1850s a channel and quay were built at Velator, to allow ketches of up to 100 tons to come up the estuary; 100 vessels at a time were using the area up until the First World War. Imports of coal, bricks, salt, flour, grain, fertilizer and limestone were traded for exports of potatoes, apples and cider. The importance of the quay declined with the arrival of the railway in 1874.

★ **St Brannock's Church** – The largely 13C building with its solid Norman **tower**, surmounted by a 15C lead covered **spire**, was originally cruciform in shape. Inside, the **bosses** on the wagon roof (restored 1850) include a litter of piglets, an angel, a pelican... The **font** is 13C or earlier, with later carvings; the faces at the corners are probably the Evangelists. Note the 16C carved chestnut **bench ends** and the pews themselves, great uneven timbers worn smooth and glossy over the centuries.

The Lady Chapel *(right of chancel)*, a later addition, contains a late 16C Portuguese **chest** which was probably made for the wedding of the couple on its front. Note, on the south wall, the copies of a **palimpsest** (two-sided brass): the knight's head side is said to be the oldest brass in Devon. The original is fixed to a tombstone.

The small **chapel** with tiny windows under the tower is the oldest part of the church; the slab of pale carved stone above a window dates from before the Norman Conquest and was probably a tombstone.

Great Field ⊘ – To the southwest of the village lies the Great Field, one of the very few examples remaining in Britain of **open field cultivation**. Within the 'Great Hedge' that separates this fertile stretch of land from Braunton Marsh, are some 360 acres which are divided into 16 furlongs and subdivided into strips shared by five farmers.

★ **Braunton Burrows** ⊘ – *Access by a toll road through the Braunton Marsh.* In 1815 the bank was built to enclose the tidal salt marsh and drainage channels were dug to transform the **Braunton Marsh** into rich grazing pasture.

The burrows comprise one of the largest **sand dune systems** in Britain, covering an area of *c*2 400 acres (over 3.5 miles north to south and about 1.5 miles wide); two-thirds of the area is now a **National Nature Reserve** (some of it leased to the Ministry of Defence – red flags and sentries during training exercises) supporting a wide variety of plant and animal life.

The dunes are made of windblown sand largely formed by crushed shells. They form because marram – a grass which grows more quickly when stimulated by moving sand – traps the sand until it stabilises; the grass then grows less vigorously, allowing other plants to colonise the area. The dunes are never entirely stable, however, and the sands are constantly shifting. As the wind cannot dislodge wet sand from below the water level, ponds have been dug; these add to the wildlife as many of the low-lying areas which flood in the winter dry out in the summer.

Animal life ranges from lizards, frogs and newts, shrews, hedgehogs, weasels and foxes, to beetles, butterflies and moths. The occasional buzzard, more common peregrine falcons and ravens may be seen as well as kestrels, magpies and the many waders (curlews, ringed plovers) which congregate on the adjacent estuary, and the migratory birds which stop at the reserve to rest and feed. Prickly saltwort, sea-holly, biting stonecrop, rest-harrow, wild thyme, marsh orchids and the rarer sand toadflax are among the 400 different species of flowering plants which have been recorded here.

On the coastal side the burrows are bordered by the 3 miles of fine beach known as **Saunton Sands**.

Early communal farming practices

At one time, every village in England was surrounded by three large fields, two of them cultivated while the third lay fallow, being grazed and manured by cattle. The sections were then subdivided into strips based on the amount of land which a man with two oxen could plough in a day.

Each landowner had several strips which were scattered over the field so that fertile and infertile land was allocated fairly. The villagers shared implements and common land was set aside for grazing (here it was mainly on the tidal salt marshes). The division between the land of different owners was formed by one furrow being left unploughed so that it showed as a line of grass and weeds (many strips have now been amalgamated and ploughed as one); these strip divisions are known locally as landsherds. Bondstones – usually large smooth stones from the beach – at the end of the landsherds serve as boundary markers; today few remain.

LACOCK ★★

Wiltshire – Population 1 068
Michelin Atlas p 17 or Map 403 – N 29

The calm, picturesquely attractive, stone and brick-built village, located on the main route from London to Bath, has always been under special patronage: first of the Augustinian canonesses resident in the abbey, then the Talbots and now the National Trust. Its name is derived from the Saxon word for stream *(lacuc)*. Picturesque in the extreme, the village provides an ideal film set for period dramas (*Pride and Prejudice, Moll Flanders* and such like).

The village comprises four streets which form a hollow square.

West Street – The broad street at right angles marked the old village's perimeter.

The **George Inn** is the oldest inn in the village, hence the reason it became simply known as "The Inn". Inside, set by the fireplace is the original three foot tread-wheel, powered at one time by a dog, which turned the roasting spit. Cribbage, shove-ha'penny provides period entertainments.

The Brash, a high, up-raised **pavement** which turns the street corner, is named after the loose broken rock used in its foundation.

★ **High Street** – The wide thoroughfare, often blocked in medieval times by the weekly wool and produce market and the three-day fair, leads to the abbey. On either side mellow roofs of tile and stone cover cottage-shops and houses of various heights, sizes and designs. The gabled, black and white half-timbered **Porch House** is 16C. The **Red Lion** was refaced with red brick in the 18C and is furnished, inside with a selection of old farming implements. The **Tithe Barn** with its timber roof, on the street corner, dates from the 14C.

East Street – The fourth of the village's four streets is narrowly enclosed by 16C and 18C houses and onetime shops.

Church Street – The street runs parallel to the High Street up to the church. To the left, **Cruck House** derives its name from the exposed beam which, following a 14C building method, supports both roof and wall. Beyond is the 15C **Sign of the Angel Inn**, named after the gold coin of the time (1480) bearing the figure of the Archangel Michael. The horse passage leads to the old coaching yard and provides access to the beamed interior.

To the right, the street leads into **Market Place**, the village's original market place; Lacock's first market charter was obtained by Ela, Countess of Salisbury and abbess, in 1241. **King John's Hunting Lodge**, or so-called lodge, dates from the 16C.

Beyond, the **Tanyard** (now a pottery) was built to have a drying loft for skins above a gaunt 19C work-house.

★ **St Cyriac** ⊘ – The Perpendicular church is a "wool church" from the time of Lacock's prosperity from the 14C-17C as a wool and cloth market. Much of its present appearance, however, is the result of restoration undertaken in 1861. Distinctive exterior features include the large embattled and pinnacled **porch**

Eating, drinking and sleeping...

Lacock boasts a range of hostelries, Bed and Breakfast accommodation and teashops to make a weekend stay especially comfortable. At night once the daytrippers have left, the village returns to its sleepy self. Tip-top fare from the **Sign of the Angel** (☎ 01249 730 230); choice of real ales from the 16C **Carpenter's Arms** (☎ 01249 730 203); Sunday roast at the **Red Lion** (☎ 01249 730 456); antique interiors at the **George Inn** dating from 1361 (☎ 01249 730 263).

fronting an older **tower** which was crowned, in the early 18C, with a recessed, octagonal spire; the Perpendicular tracery of the north aisle west window; and, on the south side, which is decorated with amused gargoyles, a mullion-windowed **cottage**, added c1615.

Inside is the **Talbot** or **Lady Chapel** which has 15C lierne vaulting with rib encircled pendants and arches decorated with carved masks and small animals, all of rare craftsmanship. The **tombchest** in the chapel is also remarkable: dating from 1566 and set up for Sir William Sharington (see below), it is ornamented with carved strapwork, cartouches, panels, vases of flowers, cherubs and a shell crest.

In the south transept is a brass to Robert Raynard (d 1501) in armour and heraldic tabard, his wife in a kennel headdress, and their 13 sons and 5 daughters.

Ela, Countess of Salisbury (1186-1261)

Brought up as the ward of Henry II (1154-89) Ela was betrothed to William Longespée when still a child: Longespée was the half-brother of Richard I and John and was probably present at the signing of the Magna Carta at Runnymede. Her involvement in ambitious building projects may have begun with the laying of a foundation stone (the fifth) for Salisbury Cathedral where both her husband and eldest son killed in the crusades are entombed. In memory of her husband, Ela founded two religious houses 16 miles apart: Lacock for women and Hinton Charterhouse for men; she laid the foundation stones for both institutions on 16 April 1232. Dedicated to St Bernard and the Virgin Mary, Lacock began with a community of 15 nuns; Ela joined them in 1238 and became the first abbess (rather than prioress) in 1241. By that time it had evolved into a kind of boarding school accommodating 15-25 young women from well-to-do families who lived according to a rule of obedience and celibacy, without the obligation to take religious vows and free to visit family as they pleased. This retreat also welcomed lodgers in times of need, when their husbands were away at war perhaps and provided shelter to local inhabitants during times of epidemic.

Of Ela's other seven children, the youngest son Nicholas became Bishop of Salisbury in 1291 and requested that his heart be buried at Lacock where the heart stone survives.

Lacock Abbey

★ **Fox Talbot Museum of Photography** ⊘ – The museum is housed in the 16C barn at the abbey gate. The ground floor is devoted to **William Henry Fox Talbot** (1800-77), the pioneer of modern photography having found a way of capturing impressions of fern leaves, lace and similar flat objects on paper which he had treated with sodium chloride and silver nitrate. He then evolved what he termed photogenic drawing (1834) to capturing three dimensional images with the aid of a camera obscura: a technique suggested by his use of the camera lucida for drawing topographical views of landscape. Further experimentation led to calotype or Talbotype and eventually to photoglyphic engraving or photo-gravure. Displayed are his notes and letters, equipment, early cameras and collotypes and awards from all over the world. The upper floor (note the splendid roof timbers) celebrates the work of present-day photographers.

★ **Lacock Abbey** ⊘ *45min*

"A grand sacrifice to Bacchus" was held by **John Ivory Talbot** to celebrate the opening in 1755 of the new entrance hall to the abbey, constructed in the Gothick style recently made fashionable by Horace Walpole at Strawberry Hill, Twickenham. The house had been in the family for two centuries having been purchased at the Dissolution in 1539 from Henry VIII by Talbot's ancestor, **William Sharington** for £783 and repurchased by him from the crown for £8 000 in the 1550s, after unsuccessful political intrigues and coin-clipping at the Bristol mint had put him in the Tower. On Sharington's return to Lacock he built the tower on the south front and the Stable Court which includes domestic quarters, a bakehouse, dairy, brewhouse and hay lofts, beneath large dormered roofs, decorative chimneys and heraldic beasts.

As Talbot followed Talbot (Sharington's niece married the first), alterations followed in the style of the day: Ivory Talbot continued to add his Gothick embellishments, three oriels were added to the south front in 1827-30 by **William Henry Fox Talbot** whose first successful photograph was of the centre window. It was this same Talbot, a well-respected botanist, mathematician, astronomer, Egyptologist, MP for Chippenham and Fellow of the Royal Society, who was responsible for planting the grounds with exotic trees (American black walnut, Judas tree, tulip tree, swamp cypress, nettle trees).

House – Of particular interest inside is the Gothick entrance hall which was designed by Sanderson Miller, an amateur architect renowned for his ready-made Picturesque ruins; it was later ornamented with "not expensive terra-cotta performances" made by an Austrian and the vault was emblazoned with the coats of arms of Talbot's friends; the windows date from the earlier building. The Brown Gallery was adapted from the former refectory: note the medieval carvings at the west end, a massive bronze **pestle and mortar** engraved with Sharington's name and scorpion crest, *View of the Abbey* painted by John Piper.

The Stone Gallery has an exquisitely carved stone fireplace, its hearthstone inlaid with lead. In the Short Lobby is displayed a modern copy of *Magna Carta* which was re-issued by Henry III in its final format in 1225 (the original Lacock Abbey Magna Carta having been presented to the British Museum by Matilda Theresa Talbot in 1946), probably sent to William Longespée as Sheriff of Wiltshire and kept by his wife when she succeeded him in the office – the only woman sheriff in the county's history.

Sharington's Tower – The main room, an eight-sided chamber 9ft in diameter, which was designed to serve both as a strong room and belvedere, is furnished with a fine continental style **stone table** (*c*1550); its octagonal top is supported on the shoulders of four grinning satyrs carved by John Chapman, who also worked at the court of Henry VIII. Along the walls windows alternate with recessed cupboards. The ceiling is elegantly vaulted and ornamented with pendants. Note the fine 16C doors with their original iron fixtures at first floor level.

In the South Gallery or Drawing Room note the prints from Fox Talbot's **original negatives** (now in the Science Museum in London) of the centre oriel taken in 1835, making it the oldest negative in existence and one of the shelves of china.

Furnishings – Examples of early 18C and 19C English and Continental furniture set off the many portraits including one by Van Dyck of Charles I's children, Aubusson and Wilton carpets.

Walk round to the south front to visit the cloisters.

Cloisters – The surviving conventual buildings date from the foundation of the abbey; they include *(see plan beside south door)*: the sacristy, flanked by two chapels; the chapter-house, entered through double arches; the warming room with a bell-metal cauldron made in Malines (1500); much of the original fabric of these buildings, however, was destroyed in the 18C.

The Countess' tomb was originally housed in the church which was demolished in 1540, shortly after Henry VIII suppressed the nunnery.

The **15C cloisters** are decorated with carved bosses of angels and animals, the pelican and lamb, a mermaid and a jester.

In the 16C the north gallery was converted by Sharington into offices and lodgings with decorated chimneys and dormer windows.

Brewhouse – The 16C building contains a mash tun and boiler, lead-lined cooler and fermenting vessel.

EXCURSION

★ **Bowood House**

The house was still under construction in 1757 when **Lancelot Brown** was summoned to Bowood and, for a fee of 30 guineas, gave his opinion of the "capability" of the park; during the period 1762-68 he returned to execute his plans which centred on the creation of the idiosyncratic lake and woodlands and the planting of specimen trees including the cedar of Lebanon (now 140ft tall). As the park matured, the house evolved under a succession of famous architects; it was begun in 1725 and sold, still incomplete, in 1754 to the first Earl of Shelburne, father of the future Marquess of Lansdowne.

This marquisate was created in 1784 for negotiating peace with America at the end of the War of Independence: subsequent marquesses have been political men holding high office in government at home and appointed as governors, viceroys and diplomats abroad. Although Bowood was their principal residence in England, they were often away, sometimes at Lansdowne House in London. In 1955 the "big house" at Bowood was demolished; the Orangery and its attendant pavilions were retained as a residence and sculpture gallery.

Grounds ⊙ – Three paths radiate from Temple Gate *(50yds from the car park)*: ahead to the front of the house; left, through glades of trees, across lawns characterized by specimen beeches, cedars, elms, to the timber-built adventure play area; and right, to the far end of the lake (cascade, 18C Doric temple, caves and grotto), circling through woods and coppices in a 2 mile arc.

The 100yd long Italianate **terraces**, enclosed by low balustrades and punctuated by clipped yews and box hedging, are bright throughout the summer with roses and bedding plants.

The **woodland garden** (*entrance off A432, nearer Sandy Lane*) is at its most picturesque in May and June when the acres of bluebells, rhododendrons and azaleas are in full bloom.

House ⊙ – 45min. Entrance to the house is now through the Orangery, classically designed by **Robert Adam** in 1769 with an important pedimented and giant-columned centre doorway. Inside, the briefest Ionic colonnade leads across the gallery to the chapel.

The small room on the right is the **laboratory** where **Joseph Priestley** discovered oxygen in 1774 and Jan Ingenhouse (d 1799) the process of plant photosynthesis.

The end **library** was designed by C R Cockerell after Robert Adam; the warm decor includes a gilded, coved and coffered ceiling and portrait medallions of Greek writers; it is furnished with Etruscan vases by Josiah Wedgwood, a white marble fireplace (1755) from the old house, handsome bookcases and shield-back chairs. From the windows there is a **view**★ of the park.

The **sculpture gallery**, which extends the length of the Orangery, is the setting for chosen pictures, statuary and tapestries from Lansdowne collections past and still in the making – the head of Hermes, the Florentine sleeping cupid, the Diskobolos, portraits by Reynolds, a Gainsborough landscape, gilded, marble-topped console tables, porcelain, a gilded French clock with a blue face framed by a mirror and torchères.

Surprises in the upper galleries range from the **Albanian costume** in which **Byron** was painted in 1814 (given by the poet to the mother of the 4th marchioness as fancy dress), 18C-19C furniture and small possessions, an immensely rich and colourful assembly of objects collected by 5th Lord Lansdowne when Viceroy of India (1888-94) and a glittering display of family honours, orders, swords, insignia, fabulous jewels...

This guide, which is revised regularly,
incorporates tourist information provided at the time of going to press.
Changes are however inevitable owing to improved facilities and
fluctuations in the cost of living.

LAND'S END★

see PENWITH

LANGPORT

Somerset – Population 997
Michelin Atlas p 8 or Map 403 – L 30

The town, at the tidal limit of the River Parrett, was for centuries a small but important centre for traffic sailing upstream into the heart of Somerset and down to Bridgwater and even overseas. Its main street, Bow Street which crosses the River Parrett by an iron bridge, follows the ancient course of a Roman causeway. The town's architectural heyday was in the 18C-19C, the late Georgian period, when Palladian-styled, Tuscan-pillared houses were erected in Bow Street and Cheapside.

All Saints – The church was rebuilt in the late 15C; the **stone relief** *(over south door)* of a lamb and cross supported by twin angels and saints, carved c1200, was retained from the Norman church previously on the site.

The **tower**, buttressed, battlemented and pinnacled, with a taller stair turret, rises from the door and west window, through transomed windows with Somerset tracery and flanking niches, and a bell stage of three windows abreast, the outer ones blind, the centre traceried. Embattling marks the rooflines; pinnacles add to the height of the chancel which is enriched with tall windows and handsome tracery.

The **east window** contains largely medieval glass.

Buried in the churchyard is Langport's famous son, **Walter Bagehot** (1826-77), economist, banker and author of *The English Constitution*.

The Hill (A372) continues east, the road bridged at the town boundary by the **Hanging Chapel**, a 16C guild or corporation chapel, constructed over a vaulted gateway which effectively frames the view of the one mile distant Huish Episcopi *(see below)*.

EXCURSIONS

Huish Episcopi, Muchelney and Midelney Manor

Huish Episcopi – St Mary's church **tower**★★ is one of the great jewels in the Somerset crown.

Built in the 15C of local blue lias and mellow Ham stone, it rises, supported by stepped and pinnacled buttresses, to pierced battlements and fountains of crocketed pinnacles.

Each stage is underlined by panel tracery or a quatrefoil frieze: the Somerset traceried and transomed three-light window is flanked by niches, the paired bell lights are divided and framed by shafted pinnacles... The height to the very top is 99ft.

The Norman **west doorway** (1150-1200) with zigzag decoration was "fired" to a dark rust-gold in a disaster in the early 1300s when much of the church perished.

The parish is said to have served Trollope as the model for Plumpstead Episcopi in *The Warden*.

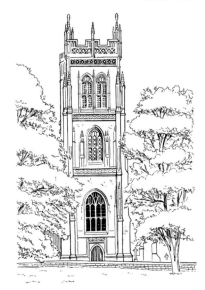

St Mary's, Huish Episcopi

★★ **Muchelney** – The abbey ruins, the 15C parish church, the medieval priest's house and the village of attractive 17C-18C cottages – many obviously incorporating dressed stones from the abbey – make an attractive group.

Abbey ⊘ – Part of the abbot's lodging is all that remains of the Benedictine monastery which was founded in AD 693 on what was then an island at the centre of the frequently flooded Somerset Levels (*see* GLASTONBURY*). The abbey was destroyed by the Danes in the 870s, refounded *c*950 and finally dissolved in 1538.

The abbey's annual income, recorded in Domesday as being £51 16*s*, had risen by the 16C to £447, an increase which contributed, at the expense of the spirit, to the brothers' temporal well-being: after a visitation in 1335 they were charged with living too well, leaving the church in disrepair, riding about the country and keeping unfit company, dining in private, owning costly utensils and ornate beds. Whether the house reformed or not, the abbot's lodgings were rebuilt in the Tudor Gothic manner and remain as testimony to the grandeur of monastic life in the 15C-16C.

After the Dissolution, the domestic quarters were occupied as farmhouses for some 200 years while the church, which measured 247ft, and conventual buildings were ruined and looted for their fabric. Backing onto the south cloister walk, which remains, would have been the refectory and, in the corner, the abbot's lodging.

Abbey precincts – The gabled and battlemented south front leads into the **Kitchen**, a long, lofty room with a massive, double-sided **fireplace**, 17ft wide by 7ft deep. *Walk up the stairs at the far end.*

A fine **door** *(right)* leads into the large **Guestroom** which has a coffered oak ceiling, mullioned windows and a stone fireplace. *Return to the ground floor and walk up the wide stone staircase.*

The **Abbot's Staircase** leads through a decorated **archway** to the **Parlour**. This room, which served as a waiting and meeting room, is lined with linenfold panelling and equipped with a large settle set before stone mullioned and transomed windows. It also contains an impressive stone fireplace, ornamented with quatrefoils, friezes of fruit and foliage and, high on the framing shafts, a pair of couched lions.

★★ **Parish Church** ⊘ – The early 15C Perpendicular church on an older Norman or even Saxon site stands within three feet of the north transept of the former abbey church.

The massive **tower** rises through three stages from the west door and window to a window flanked by canopied niches, a belfry stage of two bays framed by shafts springing from lower buttresses and continuing like those at the centre through the battlemented crest to end as secondary pinnacles to those at the angles.

Inside, the wagon roof was transformed in 1600-25 by a local man into a full colour, **painted ceiling** of smiling, bare bosomed angels in Tudor costume enjoying the heavenly life.

Note also the panelled arch to the west tower, the 15C octagonal font with carvings of the Crucifixion, the 19C **barrel organ** still capable of playing 25 hymns and 3 double chants, the 17C Netherlandish **stained-glass** roundels *(chancel windows)* and, in the chancel and around the font, 13C **tiles** from the abbey Lady Chapel.

Priest's House ⊙ – The thatched house dating from 1308 has a medieval two-storey hall and a 16C cinquefoil Gothic window; the interior is well preserved with much original masonry and timbers.

Muchelney Pottery ⊙ – *1 mile south of the village.* At the pottery John Leach, son of David, grandson of Bernard (*see* INTRODUCTION: Glass and ceramics), produces the hand-thrown, Noborigama-kiln wood-fired wholesome, tawny utilitarian stoneware to be seen in shops and exhibitions in many parts of the country.

Behind the pottery, a 9-acre conservation area has been allowed to develop with broad-leafed trees and wildlife pond providing a perfect Somerset Level habitat for birds and plants.

★ **Midelney Manor** ⊙ – The manor dates back to King Ine's charter of 693 under which he granted Muchelney, Midelney and Thorney – Great, Middle and Thorn Islands which rose above the surrounding marshlands – to the Benedictines. The abbot built a hunting lodge on Midelney which, by the 16C, was let to a John Trevilian whose sons built the present house which is still occupied by the family. The classic H plan of the grey stone house was disrupted by the brothers' quarrelling when it was under construction: no central porch but two separate entrances in opposite corners of the forecourt were built and, inside, a massive partition wall which was not pierced until 1926. Trevilians in the east wing enlarged and improved their range, notably in the 18C when the interior was remodelled in the Queen Anne style.

Inside are Georgian and Louis XV **furniture**, porcelain and **armorial china**, paintings and family portraits and **mementoes** including high sheriffs' banners and city freemen's presentation caskets – one of which, in silver, is a model of the house. The intertwined histories of the manor and the family are also explained. In the flower-filled garden is an early 18C **falcons' mews.**

Curry Rivel – The Perpendicular **church** which incorporates earlier features within its walls has strangely banded **buttresses** and a tall tower with a taller stair turret built of blue lias with Ham stone dressings. Note the quatrefoil frieze and transomed, Somerset traceried bell openings.

The urn-crowned column, in the vicinity, is the **Burton Pynsent Monument.** Built of blue lias faced in Portland stone, it was designed by Capability Brown and erected in 1765 by William Pitt the Elder to Sir William Pynsent, who left the statesman his Elizabethan manor.

LIZARD PENINSULA★

Cornwall

Michelin Atlas p 2 or Map 403 – E 33, 34

The Lizard, England's most southerly point and the source of **Serpentine rock**, is known for the telecommunications dishes on windswept Goonhilly Downs and the coves and fishing villages strung like a necklace around its high-cliffed shore.

Helston Pop 8 505

Helston is one of Cornwall's busier little towns, having long served as a stannary or tin assay town (recalled in the name Coinagehall Street). Local government reorganisation in 1974 stripped Helston of its borough status and authority, yet it remains the market town for the Lizard Peninsula and the principle provider of major schooling to the area; for the present, it has escaped mass tourism. It is also the home town of the famous Furry Dance.

Guildhall – The Classical building, complete with sculpted pediment fitted with a striking clock, stands at the heart of the town at the junction of the major thoroughfares, Coinagehall, Wendron and Meneage Streets.

Folk Museum ⊙ – *Church Street.* In the old market halls, at the foot of the wide granite steps below the Guildhall, the local museum of trades and domestic bygones has well laid out exhibits on fishing (flat "maglans" for scooping fish from the sea), agriculture, mining and housekeeping.

Two Helston men are given pride of place: Bob Fitzsimmons (1863-1917), prize-fighter, who was born in a 17C thatched cottage (61 Wendron Street), and Henry Trengrouse (1771-1854), inventor of the ship-to-shore rocket life-saving apparatus, whose tomb is in the churchyard.

St Michael's – The 18C church with Furry Dance angels in the east window is lit by a 24 branch 18C chandelier.

Cross Street – Characterizing the street are the late Georgian **Great Office** with a columned porch, top floor bay window and iron balcony, the 18C vicarage with an oriel window, neat doorway (no 10) and small-paned **bow windows.** Leading off the street to the parallel Coinagehall Street are a number of "opes".

Flora Day Furry Dance★★

The origins of this Spring Festival are lost in time and, unlike the maypole dances elsewhere in Britain, this pagan celebration is held on 8 May so as to coincide with the Feast of the Apparition of St Michael the Archangel, the patron saint of Helston and also of Cornwall – if 8 May date falls on a Sunday or Monday, the dance is held on the previous Saturday.

Five processional dances are performed, at 7am, 8.30am, 10am, 12noon and 5pm, all except the Hal-an-Tow (8.30am) accompanied by the band. The 3-4mile route has minor variations but all dances begin and end at the Guildhall and go up Meneage Street; all pass through houses, shops and banks as if to chase out the darkness of winter and herald in the light of spring; doors and lower windows along the route are decorated with bluebells and greenery.

The most charming dance begins at 9.50am when hundreds of school children, dressed all in white process around town; this pre-empts the principal dance of the day at midday at the first stroke of the Guildhall clock when some 150 couples start circling in the Invitation Dance – the men in top hats and suits, the women in big hats and garden party dresses.

Coinagehall Street – The wide street is drained by ancient gutters, known as "kennels". Set among the shops stands the 16C **Angel Inn**, with its own well, once an Excise Office (see the string course above the porticoed entrance), the pre-17C thatched **Blue Anchor Inn** with 18C horizontal sash windows – built as a boarding house for monks, possibly the oldest brew pub in England – and **Chymder House** (early 19C), square and stuccoed. At the bottom of the hill, the street is punctuated by a great granite archway and the town's bowling green beyond.

★ **Flambards Village Theme Park, Culdrose** ⊘ – *3 miles southeast off A3083.*
To the constant whirr of the Royal Navy helicopters stationed at Culdrose, the headquarters of the land and sea rescue operations *(no public access, but viewing area outside the perimeter fence)*, comes the pleasure world of Flambards Village. Here, a Concorde flight deck may be explored, a gallery of World War II mementoes may be studied and other attractions may be enjoyed: space quest laser show complete with eclipse 1999 special, safari parrot show, in Britain in the Blitz, gardens and "hornet" roller coaster, live shows, buskers and clowns...

By contrast the lamplit, cobbled street of houses in the **Victorian Village** reveals crowded rooms, an inn and 19C shops with wooden counters and racks of jars, drawers, boxes and barrels: an apothecary's, milliner's, butcher's, baker's, chemist's...

Places of interest

A tour of all the villages (100 miles – about 5.5 hours) is possible but indigestible.

★ **Seal Sanctuary, Gweek** ⊘ – *5 miles east off A394.*
The sanctuary, a good walk along a woodland trail from the visitor centre (alternative transport provided) enjoys a beautiful **setting**★ overlooking the Helford River. Set up to care for young pups separated from their mothers or found injured in a special "hospital", the young seals go on to larger pools where they disport themselves before being restored to the ocean. Permanent residents include seals of different species and, in the field above, donkeys to provide rides.

Mawgan-in-Meneage – The village and its granite **church**★ stand by a creek on the Helford River – Daphne du Maurier's inspiration for Frenchman's Creek in her novel of the same name.
The 15C **tower** rises through three stages to ribbed pinnacles on **angel corbels**. Coats of arms flank the door; angel capitals adorn the tower arch.
Note the **squint**, and the **sword** and **helmet** of the Royalist, Sir Richard Vyvyan.

★ **St Anthony-in-Meneage** – St Anthony and Gillan lie on either side of a small creek. The church, to which Gillan parishioners come by boat at high tide, is 12C-15C.

Manaccan – The Norman church, altered in the 13C-15C and restored in the 19C, is known locally for the fig-tree growing out of the 14C, slate tower wall. Note the Norman door with three orders of columns and ribbed *voussoirs*, also the **squint** inside.

St Keverne – The original octagonal ribbed church **spire** had become so important as a landmark to shipping avoiding **The Manacles** underwater reefs that it was immediately rebuilt when struck by lightning in 1770.

Lizard coastline

The **church**★ was built in the 14C-15C by Cistercian monks but the **arcade** in green-grey-white-rose stone probably came from Brittany in the 13C.
Note the three sets of **rood-screen stairs**, carved **bench-ends**, a faded St Christopher **wall-painting**, the 15C font and Jacobean pulpit.

★**Coverack** – A 1:6 descent leads to the old **fishing village** of thatched and slate-roofed cottages overlooking the harbour and wide cove. The village was famous for smuggling – even the name means "hideaway" in Cornish. In 1840, it is said, officers seized some 125 casks of spirits from a band who then undertook a "second wrecking" or raid to recapture the kegs so as not to disappoint their customers – spirits were usually bespoken. Three casks were left for the officers as consolation…

Goonhilly Satellite Earth Station ⊘ – *7 miles southeast of Helston by B3293.* The largest operational satellite station on earth, one of the first three, opened in 1962; today it has 25 dishes named after gods and characters from Cornish legends (Tristan, Isolde, Uther, Guenevere, Merlin) which focus radio energy to orbiting satellites for transmission around the globe. British Telecom Visitors' Centre explains the history and development of telecommunications through a short film, comparison to Arthur C Clarke's sci-fi vision of the future, working models of telephone exchanges and fax machines, audio-visual and interactive displays; terminal access for the internet; a bus tour of the site includes a visit to the first aerial, the old Observation Tower, and the Operation Control Area.
The surrounding downland, acquired by English Nature in 1976, became Cornwall's first nature reserve with established colonies of rare plants and standing stones, erected, it is said, to help Neolithic people communicate with the gods in the heavens.

Ruan Minor – The **church**★, once a Norman chapel, built of granite and the local dark green serpentine stone, gained its serpentine tower (25ft) in the 14C. At **Poltesco** there is the ruins of a serpentine factory (1855-1893). The circular building is a former capstan house for hauling fishing boats up the beach.

★ **Cadgwith** – The delightful **fishing village** of thatched and slate-roofed cottages with whitewashed walls overlooks the shingle beach of a minute cove.

Grade – The village's present church (1862) incorporates all that survived the ravages of wind and rain over the years: the early 14C two-storey **tower** of square blocks of serpentine and granite with tall pinnacles, the **font** and 16C brass.

★ **Landewednack** – **Serpentine** is the hallmark of the pretty, old thatch-roofed village where the **church**★ and its tower are made of the glossy green and black-velvet stone, the Norman **door** in the battlemented porch is framed with black serpentine columns and zig-zag and circle decorated *voussoirs,* and the pulpit and lectern entirely carved out of the stone. Today village craftsmen turn and polish the stone into ornaments.

The Lizard – The lighthouse is the only feature of interest on the point: the foundations for a permanent light were laid in 1619 but its survival was brief: shipmasters claimed that it was a wrecker's decoy and refused to pay the tolls. In 1752 a second lighthouse was built which had four towers each burning a coal fire; in 1812 the building was altered to its present outline; first an oil lamp and then an electric light were installed. In 1903 a 12 000 000 candela light was installed; this was reduced to 4 000 000 candela in 1926 following local fishermen's complaints that its brightness affected their pilchard catches.

★★ **Kynance Cove** – The high cliffs, sand beach uncovered at low tide and pinnacle rocks emerging from the brilliant blue-green sea on a clear day are a memorable sight. It is advisable to visit out of hours as up to 10 000 visitors have been counted on a fine summer's day.

★★ **Mullion Cove** – The cove, which lies back from the line of cliffs, is framed by a white sand beach, small harbour, a natural **rock arch**, pinnacles and an offshore island.
Nearly a mile inland in Mullion village stands the 15C-16C **church**★, dedicated to the Breton saint, Malo or Mellane of Rennes; it has a granite and serpentine tower, polished lime ash floor, the royal arms of Charles II, early 16C carved **bench-ends** and a 13C font decorated with a serpent. Sheep-dogs attending church with their masters could leave by the "dog-door" in the nailed south door when nature called.

Poldhu Point – The **Marconi Memorial**, a granite obelisk at the cliff edge 200yds south of the point, marks the site of the radio station from which signals were first sent out by Marconi and successfully received in Newfoundland on 12 December 1901.

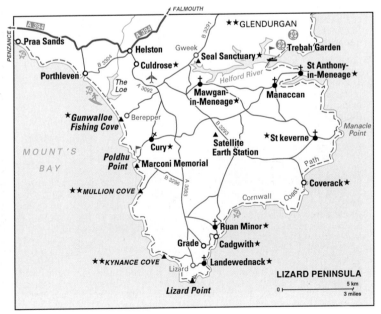

* **Cury** – The 14C **church**★ of St Corentin of Brittany is distinguished by a **Celtic cross** (9ft), a Norman **south door** framed by columns and a decorated tympanum, a rosette-carved font and a transept-chancel squint with an octagonal column.

* **Gunwalloe Fishing Cove** – The thatch roofs of Berepper mark the descent to the even smaller village of fishermen's cottages crowded behind the minute **cove**. Pieces of eight (gold coins) have been washed up on the beach from a galleon lost off the point.

The Loe – The freshwater **lagoon** known as The Loe (no bathing or fishing) is a drowned valley, dammed at its mouth by the shingle bar swept up by the Atlantic.
Along the foreshore the sand extends from Gunwalloe Cove to **Porthleven**, a resort, active fishing port and boat-building harbour, distinguished by a 19C clock tower.

Praa Sands – Praa Sands, just west of the Lizard peninsula, is known for its three-mile beach.

For Marazion, see ST MICHAEL'S MOUNT.

LONGLEAT★★★

Wiltshire

Michelin Atlas p 8 or Map 403 – N 30

Approaching the house from the signposted entrance, the drive passes through a gentle landscape of rhododendrons and azaleas before emerging from the woods; suddenly the splendour of Longleat, nestling down in the valley below, is revealed as the magnificent Elizabethan house of pale golden stone rises from a glorious lakeside setting.
The square building comprises three tiers of large mullioned and transomed windows surmounted by an animated skyline of balustrading, ornamental chimney-stacks, turrets and gesticulating statues. Arranged around the house stands a stable block, the orangery surrounded by walled gardens, safari park, several mazes (including the longest in the world), a butterfly house, a narrow-gauge railway (15in), a two-acre adventure playground and numerous other attractions.

House ⊙ *90min*

The house and its many contents – portraits, furniture, porcelain, books, embroideries, silver – span a period of six centuries, reflecting the diverse interests of the unbroken line of Thynnes from Sir John – who purchased the site of a 13C Augustinian priory from Henry VIII for £53 in 1541 – to the present Marquess of Bath who continues to reside at Longleat in private apartments. The family tree dating back to 1215 is displayed within the house.

Longleat House

Exterior – The house, completed in 1580, was intended to reflect the status of its owner Sir John Thynne, "an ingenious man and a traveller", who acted as his own architect in collaboration with Robert Smythson. Many ideas Thynne would have gleaned during a life at court as brother-in-law to the financier Sir Thomas Gresham, founder of the Royal Exchange in London and builder of Osterley Park, and as adjutant and steward to the Duke of Somerset in whose service he travelled abroad, served on the battlefield and observed the remodelling of Syon House and the construction of the original Somerset House in London, a building in the Renaissance style.

The result is a harmonious expression of a new "unmistakable Elizabethan" style drawn from the indigenous Perpendicular tradition as well as from abroad: the Early Italian Renaissance, the French taste flourishing in the Loire region and the geometric simplicity of Flanders. Pevsner celebrates the effect as being an expression of "one England, of one spirit and one style in building, vigorous, prolific, somewhat boastful of a healthy and hearty soundness which, it is true, is sometimes coarse and sometimes dull – but never effeminate and never hysterical" (*An Outline of European Architecture*).

Interior – It was Sir John's idea that the rooms at Longleat should look not on to inner courts, as was 16C custom, but out over the park. In the 19C nine rooms along the east and south fronts were radically remodelled in the Italianate style at the behest of the 4th Marquess, a traveller and connoisseur who returned from Venice, Florence and Rome with ideas, craftsmen and artefacts that included painted panels, marble chimney pieces, plaster work, wall hangings and furnishings. Against this sumptuous background are set family portraits, master paintings, English, French, Italian furniture, 16C and 17C tapestries, ceramics from Europe and the Orient, silver centrepieces...

Ground floor – The late-16C **Great Hall** contains a splendid **fireplace** pillared by fluted columns supporting an elaborate combination of five terms, 18C clock and wind direction indicator. The hammerbeam ceiling and elaborate screen are decorated with the arms of Sir John Thynne and his patron, the Duke of Somerset: note the Gresham golden **grasshopper crest**. The walls are hung with prehistoric giant fallow deer antlers retrieved from Irish bogs, arms and armour, and a large series of hunting scenes by the 18C painter John Wootton. The gallery opposite the ornate 16C screen was added in 1663, it is said, following the visit to the house of Charles II and his retinue. Note the *View of Longleat* by Jan Siberechts (1675) which shows the house before its outbuildings were transformed by Wyatville; the 30ft 16C **shuffle-board** table, 17C armchairs with elaborate legs, and the rare astronomical clock of 1706...

The **Ante-Library** is one of seven rooms accommodating Longleat's exceptional private library. The interior decoration is the work of John Dibblee Crace: the furniture, tailor-made marble door frames, inlaid walnut doors are Italian, as are the ceiling panels showing the attributes of Art, Science, History and Poetry. The contemporary portraits are of the present Lord and Lady Bath.

Leather-bound books with gold lettering in the **Red Library** echo the red and gold embossed wall covering and the coffered ceiling set with trompe l'oeil panels painted on black linen: one of several in the house modelled on those adorning Renaissance palazzi in Rome and Venice. Fine furnishings include a bureau Mazarin by Boulle, a fine portrait by Sargent and another (above the bookcases) depicting Thomas Ken, the onetime Bishop of Bath and Wells who, when deprived of his see by William and Mary in 1691, was lodged at Longleat by the 1st Viscount; at his death in 1711, the Bishop bequeathed his library to his host.

In the **Breakfast Room**, yellow damask offsets Chippendale-style chairs and fine japanned gaming tables; the walls are hung with family portraits: 1 Marquess by Lawrence, 5th Marquess by William Orpen *(over the fireplace)*, 4th Marquess, who Italianised the house, his wife by G F Watts (full length in a dress to be seen in the collection displayed in the corridor on an upper floor). The ceiling panel depicts *Peace and Justice dispelling Discord.*

The gilded, coffered ceiling of the **Lower Dining Room** is modelled on one in the Doge's Palace in Venice; the fine 17C peer glasses and silver wall sconces are from Garrards (1853); the pair of ebony chairs are Indian (*c*1670-80) the William IV dining chairs are ebonised beechwood. The walls, panelled by Wyatville in the 19C are hung with portraits of Sir John Thynne, the builder of Longleat *(left)* and Thomas Thynne *(window alcove)*, a friend of the Duke of Monmouth, known for his riches as Tom o' Ten Thousand and assassinated in Pall Mall in 1682.

Six windows in the **passages** along the back of the house are inset with panels of 16C-17C continental stained glass. Modern works of art from Lord Bath's Wessex Collection are also hung here – the murals in the private apartments by Lord Bath, a painter in his own right, are also open to the public: ask for details.

Upstairs – The lead-lined, cooper-built bath was the first of its type to be installed at Longleat by the 3rd Marchioness (1840), and continued to be used well after it was plumbed with running water until 1946. The cold **bedroom** next door is furnished with Victorian baby cots: the painting over the mantel is after a portrait of Charles I's children by Van Dyck.

In the **State Dining Room**, the first of the state rooms, the table displays a Meissen porcelain **centrepiece** (c1760) representing the Temple of Minerva. The ornate Crace ceiling is set with a panel from the School of Titian; the walls are covered with tooled Cordoba leather (1620) which was included by the Venetian dealers in a shipment of paintings – damaged sections date from the World War I when Longleat served as a hospital and "protective" pieces of linoleum were applied to protect the leather from scuffing. The marble fireplaces are 19C; the pair of ebony document cabinets are Franco-Flemish. View from the windows over the Lunar Labyrinth and the Solar Maze.

The 90ft 17C Long Gallery or **Saloon**, with a wall of windows facing on to the park has a massive **marble fireplace** copied from one in the Doge's Palace in Venice; the overmantel is pure Crace. The ceiling is inspired by one in the Palazzo Massimo in Rome. The 17C Flemish tapestries depict the Life of Cyrus, King of Persia. The furniture includes a tulipwood and coromandel lacquer commode, Boulle-style desks – one the mirror image in tortoise-shell and brass marquetry of another, Regency chairs and ebonised "gout" stool, Louis XV parquetry games table; Sicilian clock.

The **State Drawing Room** overlooks the Great Hall through an embrasure. The ceiling, set with panels after Titian and Veronese, is inspired by that in St Mark's Library in Venice; the continuous frieze depicting the *Life of Circe* is attributed to Pietro Liberi and 17C Genoese velvet from which the gold thread allegedly disappeared on the journey from Italy. The **paintings** are mostly Italian (*Persephone* by Tintoretto), exceptions being the portraits by Hans Eworth of the son and daughter of Sir John the builder. Note among the furniture the French Régence Boulle **table**, a **bureau** made for Louis XVI and acquired by Talleyrand, and an 18C writing table with exquisite marquetry *(centre)*. The fireplace is Italian, whereas the Agra work door frames were designed by Crace. The vivid green carpet was dyed to complement the grass outside by an impulsive marchioness much to the fury of her husband.

Apartments – The **Dress Collection** and 1953 Coronation robes are displayed with cabinets filled with English (Wedgwood, Chelsea and Derby) and Continental (Sèvres) porcelain in the corridor on the first floor.

The original **Grand Staircase** designed by Wren was lost during Wyatville's transformations; its replacement is hung with yet more portraits of figures associated with the Thynne family including Sir Walter Raleigh.

The **Royal Bedrooms** comprise an elegant dressing room hung with hand-painted Chinese wallpaper which is furnished with a tin bath and a theatrical bed; a Music Room-cum-sitting room with a gold Crace ceiling and furnished with a 17C Italian virginal, George III barrel organ and Boulle commode: Reynolds portrait of the actress Kitty Hunter of Croydon. The ceilings in this section of the house, still by Crace, are influenced by a visit the designer made to the Middle East.

The **Prince of Wales Bedroom** takes its name from the portrait over the fireplace of Henry; note the Italian silk bed hangings and Chinese embroidered cover; the bureau cabinet, inlaid with ivory and mother-of-pearl is Milanese.

The way out is down the stairs and through the Victorian kitchens decked with copper pans and cabinets of food moulds.

Outbuildings – A model of the house occupies most of the butchery.

The stable block has been converted to accommodate an eclectic collection of ephemera under the title **Lord Bath's Bygones**: horse shoes for mowing the lawn, archaic tennis rackets and presses, an early children's side-saddle, old fashioned ice-skates and rollerblades; the tack room and blacksmith's forge.

A second exhibition area is dedicated to the present Lord Bath's father, **Henry Frederick Thynne**, 6th Marquess, who witnessed both World Wars and the man who first opened his home to the public: portrait by **Graham Sutherland** (1903-80), personal effects and memorabilia reinforcing his loyalty to Edward VIII (video and broadcast of the abdication speech) and distrust of Hitler. On the way out are displayed the Longleat Dolls Houses. Another stables block houses a limited collection of **historic vehicles** (c1820 State chariot, George VI's 2.5 litre Daimler).

Park and gardens ⊘

The park was landscaped (1757-62) by **Capability Brown**, who planted specimen trees in the foreground and dense woods on the hillside; he also created the present tree-fringed Half Mile Pond out of the late 17C "canal" which had been contrived by combining and diverting the original ponds (long leat) in the valley. Boat trips *(15min)* circumnavigate Gorilla Island and offer a view of the Californian sea-lions and resident hippos.

The flower gardens, containing roses, hydrangeas and flowering trees graced by free-roaming peacocks have been developed since Brown's day. They are enclosed by high yew hedges and wisteria-covered walls. An orangery houses exotics.

Tucked away behind the house are the **Maze**, planted in 1975 and consisting of over 1.5 miles of pathways bordered by yew hedges, a huge children's playground, a heated greenhouse-butterfly house, the narrow-gauge railway which runs through the woods and beside the lake (coarse fishing available)...

Safari Park ⊙ *40min. Follow the road that leads from the car park away from the house.*

The "drive-in zoo" is most famous for its lions; it also has enclosures for wallabies; giraffes, zebras, llamas, dromedaries, camels, white rhinos, long horned cattle, eland; fallow deer; rhesus monkeys (which may climb over the car); fallow deer; Indian elephants; Canadian timber wolves; white, golden tabby and Siberian tigers...

For STOURHEAD *see separate chapter.*

LUNDY ISLAND★★

Devon – Population 20
Michelin Atlas p 6 or Map 403 – F, G 30

Visiting Lundy ⊙ is a carefree adventure, starting with the boat trip from the mainland: there are no cars – except for a Landrover and a tractor – no telephones, no newspapers; there is a shop selling necessities and the island's own **puffin stamps**, a tea-house, a pub and a farm. The attraction of the island is its fascinating bird, marine and wild life, and the simple pleasure of a place undisturbed by modern attractions.

The island derives its name from the Icelandic word for puffin, *Lunde*, but there are reportedly only thirty breeding pairs on the island (May to July); other sea birds nesting in large colonies include razorbill, guillemot, fulmar, Manx shearwater, shag, kittiwake, different species of gull (and ravens). Animals on Lundy include Devonshire cattle, wild **Soay sheep**, mountain goats, **Sika deer** and the free-roaming, handsome dun-coloured **Lundy ponies** (a New Forest-Welsh Mountain cross established in the 1930s). In 1986 Lundy was established as a Marine Nature Reserve with grey seals, basking shark and porpoise as regular visitors. The clear waters and numerous wrecked ships in the area offer excellent diving, notably around Rat Island and **South Light** where a number of ships have foundered.

Geography – The island is a triangular granite rock mass, three miles long, less than a mile wide, rising 400ft out of the Atlantic-Bristol Channel breakers. The west face mounts sheer from the sea, the cliffs advancing and retreating behind sharp offshore rocks and coves; to the north, the line of the cliffs appears to extend to the horizon. The east coast is less precipitous, descending in steps and by way of hanging valleys to wide bays and shingle beaches all covered by the sea at high tide.

A. Taverner

Puffins

The undulating land is clothed with turf, close-cropped at the south end by the farm stock and to the north by the wild goats, the dark Soay sheep brought over from St Kilda's in 1920 and now naturalised, and rabbits in whose burrows puffins sometimes nest in the spring. Gorse, bracken and peat bogs are to be found in the hanging valleys; sycamore in the sheltered hollow at the southeast end of the island. In the spring pink thrift covers the upland grass, rhododendron groves enliven the east cliff lower path.

History – The Mariscos, a Norman-Somerset family, came to Lundy in the 12C; they were a lawless, violent group who built a stronghold where Bronze and Iron Age man and Celts had previously settled. In the 13C, a Marisco plotted against Henry III who had him hanged, drawn and quartered before seizing the island, destroying his stronghold and appointing a royal constable who in 1243 completed the castle still confusingly known as **Marisco's Castle**.

The island's position in the Channel made it the perfect hideout for pirates throughout the centuries of Bristol's trade with Europe, America and the West Indies: a 17C captain is noted as stating in a letter to the Lord Treasurer "Egypt was never more infested with caterpillars than the Channel with pirates". In 1750 Thomas Benson, MP and High Sheriff of Devon, leased the island and became the biggest pirate of all, diverting prisoners he had undertaken to transport to America to work the quarries, preying on cargo ships and swindling insurance companies. The modern era dates from the 19C when the quarries were worked industrially, the road built up from the beach and the church erected. The last private owners introduced the Lundy ponies, the rarely-seen deer, the Soay sheep, also the puffin stamps.

Lundy is now the property of the National Trust; it is financed and managed, however, by the Landmark Trust (see PRACTICAL INFORMATION).

The island is three miles long and half a mile wide: a complete circuit is 11 miles, for which four hours should be allowed. Flat shoes and outdoor clothing are advised.

Tour of the Island – Landing Beach is overlooked by **Marisco Castle**, a 12C-13C castle. The track leads steeply up hill (350ft) to the village of Lundy, past **Millcombe House**, a Classical-style granite house built in the 1830s as the home of the island's then owners. The village comprises a **St Helena's**, a large, strangely urban looking church erected in 1896 (exhibition about life on the island), the shop and the Marisco Tavern (food and drink). A footpath continues west to the Old Light.

Old Light – The original lighthouse of 1819 was erected on the island's highest point where, shining at 567ft into the mist and clouds, it was invisible from the sea.

Battery – *West coast*. The battery was built by Trinity House as a fog signal station in 1863 *(path down just south of Quarter Wall)*, blank rounds being fired in bad weather every 10 minutes from the George III cannon.

Earthquake – The major landslip takes its name from a suspected earthquake in the 19C. From here the path traces its way north past **Jenny's Cove**, from where views extend across the fractured cliffs, pounded by the Atlantic: this is also a strategic point from which to watch the breeding gulls and auks (including puffins).

Devil's Slide – The steep slip, far up the northwest coast, is a proving ground for rock climbers.

North Light – The now automatic lighthouse was built, with its pair, in 1896 to replace the Old Light. The stones in the fields are from Bronze and Iron Age hut circles.

From here a path continues back along the eastern coast; however, the more popular route returns along the centre of the island.

Northwest Point Walk – The path, which runs along the island's spine, is lined by 2.5-ton stones set by Trinity House as markers for the lighthousemen who had to find their way in fog and darkness to the northern light, crossing the 18C **Quarter, Halfway** and **Threequarter Walls** which divide the island.

Tibbetts Point and Cottage – *East coast*. The Admiralty look-out and granite building were constructed in 1909 on the second highest point on the island.

Quarries – *East coast*. Past the old hospital are the quarries, which were worked in the 18C by Benson and industrially in the 19C. The Quarry Pool is inhabited by great orfe (fish).

East Cliff Lower Path – The path, noted for its rhododendrons, extends from Quarter Wall to Castle Hill, and Marisco Castle.

Colonies of sea birds – cormorants, fulmars, gannets, guillemots, gulls, puffins, shags – nest on inaccessible cliffs, stacks and rocky islands: Isle of Purbeck, Lundy, Scilly Isles...

LYME REGIS *

Dorset – Population 3 566

Michelin Atlas p 5 or Map 403 – L 31

"The remarkable situation of the town, the principal street almost hurrying into the water, the walk to the Cobb skirting round the pleasant little bay... the Cobb itself, the very beautiful line of cliffs stretching out to the east of the town, are what the stranger's eye will seek", wrote Jane Austen in *Persuasion* (1818), following her two visits to Lyme in 1803 and 1804.

The town was given its royal charter in 1285 and acquired its name in the 14C when Edward I gave the manor to his second queen.

Broad Street – The main street is lined along its steep sides by late Georgian houses with shops below, and inns of earlier date including the Royal Lion, bay windowed above a pillared porch.

Bridge Street – The street, bearing left, crosses the outlet of the Lyme and before it turns uphill, overlooks a ledge known as the **Gun Cliff** from the days when the town was besieged by the Royalists (1644).

Philpot Museum ⊙ – Several eminent personalities are associated with Lyme, namely Sir George Somers (1554-1610), the discoverer and coloniser of Bermuda; Thomas Coram (1668-1751), a benevolent man who amassed his fortune while trading with the American colonies and instigator of the London Foundling Hospital at the heart of Bloomsbury; John Gould (1804-81), renowned ornithologist and taxidermist. Perhaps the most famous, however, is **Mary Anning** (1799-1846), the fossil hunter extraordinaire who found the first complete fossil of an **ichthyosaurus** from the Jurassic era, a **plesiosaurus** (in 1824) and a **pterodactyl** (in 1828).

The museum, endowed by and named after the family of keen amateur fossilists who first settled in Lyme in 1805, collects together a variety of things ranging from fossils (note the fine Coade pavement apparently set with swirling ammonites at the entrance), 18C **lace** - particularly point lace sold to merchants in Honiton and Colyton, to topographical pictures and a miscellany of items relating to Lyme's maritime history

The best areas for **Fossil hunting** are west of the Cobb, **Monmouth Beach** (where the Duke landed in 1685), round the point and in Pinhay Bay, east *(2 miles)* of the town, below the 450ft high **Blue Venn Cliffs** (Charmouth), **Stonebarrow** and **Golden Cap**.

It is dangerous to set out, however, without checking for the times of high tide, when the sea is quick to cut off access. It is also worth noting that after rain, mudslides are liable to collapse down the cliff; so be vigilant and take care.

A. Taverner

St Michael the Archangel – The church, truncated at its west end by the road and ever in danger at its east end of sea erosion and landslip, has nevertheless survived since Norman times - one of the bells is inscribed "O Sea spare me". The 58ft west **tower** was the crossing tower of the Norman church, the present porch that church's nave.

When the larger, Perpendicular church came to be built, the Norman chancel was demolished and replaced by a wide nave and aisles.

Note the difference in level from west to east, the **piers** with their shield and foliate carving in place of capitals, the plain, testered **Jacobean pulpit** presented by a Mercer and Merchant Adventurer in 1613, the **gallery** of 1611 with the borough arms and the **window** to Mary Anning *(see above)*.

Dinosaurland ⊙ – *Coombe Street.* The Jurassic rocks around Lyme Regis continue to yield large numbers of fossils ranging from the large marine reptiles (plesiosaurs) to the more common ammonites, belemnites and crinoids. This museum, set up by an enthusiastic paleontologist, provides an introduction to the world of fossils with particular emphasis on those found locally; he also organises fossil-hunting expeditions that nurture further interest.

A small display provides a history of the United Reform church building.

Marine Parade – The houses lining the parade, pink washed, pantiled and many with upper observation window bays, date back to the 18C and early 19C; note, on the house between the hotel and Library Cottage, the huge **ammonite fossils** embedded in the walls.

★ **The Cobb** – The Cobb is a breakwater, a curving 600ft long stone jetty, with its back braced against the Atlantic swell and a small harbour on its lee side. It lies half a mile west of the town, built of boulders and rocks at the end of the Marine Parade. Neither the origin of the name nor the date of the first wall of rocks, in which fossils can still be seen embedded, are known although it is recorded that repairs were being carried out in the 14C. It is Lyme's focal point and the dramatic setting used by novelists from Jane Austen (*Persuasion*) to John Fowles (*The French Lieutenant's Woman*, filmed in 1981).

For Beer, Branscombe, Seaton and Landslip, see SIDMOUTH.

MALMESBURY ★

Wiltshire – Population 4 218
Michelin Atlas p 17 or Map 403 – N 29

One most striking feature of the small town is its attractive terraces of irregular stone tiled roofs, many of which were refaced in the 18C with stone ashlar. The network of older streets and alleys is interconnected by a rare number of footbridges crossing tributaries of the Avon and Ingleburn Rivers which almost encircle the town. The centre of Malmesbury boasts one of England's finest market crosses, overlooked by the abbey which stands outlined against the sky, crowning a spur.

The town's name is a combination-corruption of Maidulf and Aldhelm: Maelhelmsbury.

Other men associated with Malmesbury include Elmer, the **Flying Monk**, who launched himself from the old abbey tower in 1010 and "flew" 250yds before crashing but remained convinced that it was only lack of a tail which had brought him down; **William of Malmesbury** (1095-1143), monk, abbey librarian and great early historian, and the philosopher **Thomas Hobbes**, born in the town (1588-1679).

Three historic American families also have associations with the area: the **Washingtons** who in the 17C lived in Garadon *(3 miles east);* the Penns who originated in Minety *(6 miles northeast);* and **Abraham Lincoln's mother**, Nancy Hanks, who was a member of an old Malmesbury family.

St Aldhelm (639-709)

The man (later canonised) who by his preaching, it is said, completed the conquest of Wessex, was a pupil at the school which was part of the religious community established in the town in the 7C by the Irish teacher, Maidulf: uniquely for the time, he went on to Canterbury, so becoming the first English scholar to combine the learning of Ireland and Europe. In 676 he returned to Malmesbury as teacher, abbot, builder of churches in the town at Bruton and Wareham, founder of monasteries at Frome and Bradford-on-Avon, and counsellor to his kinsman, the West Saxon King, Ine (r 688-726). In 705, when the See of Sherborne was founded, Aldhelm was appointed its first bishop. He is buried at Malmesbury.

★★ **Market Cross** – The cross was built of local stone in 1490 when the town was known for its tanning and felt making, silk weaving, lace making, spinning and of course its woollen weaving; it had a twice weekly market. More than a mere shelter, the cross rises 40ft high in a paean of buttresses, crocketed pinnacles, castellations and flying arches to a spirelet, supreme pinnacle and cross. Note the carving and small, grinning masks – 'a right faire costly peace of worke' as John Leland declared.

★ **Abbey** ⓥ – *15min.* The present church, an amazing conjuncture of gaunt ruin and living architecture, was begun in the 12C. At its zenith, in the 14C, it extended 320ft from east to west, had a clerestory and vaulted roof, possessed a central crossing tower with a spire, and a west tower. It was surrounded by Benedictine conventual buildings.

In 1479 a fierce storm brought down the spire and tower, which in their fall destroyed the east end, transepts and crossing; one hundred years later the west tower fell, destroying three west bays of the nave. A majestic six bays remain. Between these cataclysmic events the monastery was suppressed by Henry VIII on 15 December 1539 and sold for £1 516 15s 2 1/2d to William Stumpe, a local clothier, who used the stone to construct Abbey House. At first he set up looms in the nave of the old abbey church but in 1541 he presented the building to the people as their parish church.

M. Stevens

South porch, Malmesbury Abbey

Porch – The unique feature of the abbey is the south **porch**: mid-12C Romanesque carving with trail and geometrical patterns on the eight orders, allegorical figurative medallions (defaced), continuous banding and, in the **tympanum**, two angels supporting a mandorla with Christ in Glory at the centre – the figures of Christ and the Apostles are elongated like those in the lunettes on either side above the blind arcading which have often been compared to similar sculpture in southwest France, notably Souillac and Moissac, churches on the pilgrimage route to Santiago di Compostella in northern Spain.

Interior – The massive Norman pillars with scalloped capitals support just-pointed arches and a **triforium** of great rounded bays, crisply collared with zig-zag carving. On the south side note the **watching loft** from where the abbot or a monk could follow the service beyond the chancel screen. Note the large, crisply carved bosses in the fine lierne vault and the unusual grotesque animals terminating hood mouldings and the masks at the apex of the nave arcade arches.
The medieval stone screen at the end of the south aisle marks the chapel of St Aldhelm who was buried in an earlier abbey destroyed by fire in 1050; also buried in this earlier church (medieval tomb: *north aisle*) was **King Athelstan** (r 925-39), like his grandfather Alfred, a great admirer of Aldhelm.
A tombstone in the churchyard *(left of the path)* commemorates Hannah Twynnoy, mauled to death by a tiger from a travelling circus in 1703.

Bell Hotel – The hotel was built in the 16C to replace the guesthouse of the suppressed monastery using stone and timber from the conventual buildings.

St John's Bridge – The bridge *(on A429 towards Devizes)* got its name from the hospital built by the Order of St John of Jerusalem on the town outskirts in the 13C. The hospital was dissolved, the knights banished; in 1694 the aged buildings were re-founded as almshouses and later still as a silk factory. Through an archway is the Old Courthouse.

EXCURSION

Badminton *5 miles southeast by A46 and B4040.*

Badminton is well known on three counts: the original court dimensions and rules of the game of badminton were established from the size of the hall at Badminton House when bad weather compelled the younger members of the household to play battledore and shuttlecock indoors; the Three Day Event Horse Trials are held in the park in April; the Beaufort hounds are kennelled near the house.
The house *(private)* is a palatial mansion in biscuit coloured stone, set on the edge of the Cotswolds in a park landscaped by Capability Brown. It was built in the 1670s and 1740s. There was already a "fair stone house" on the estate but in the eyes of its young owner it proved inadequate for entertaining Charles II when he came on a visit in 1663. By 1682, therefore, when the king created the man reputed to be his richest subject the first Duke of Beaufort, the house had been rebuilt and taken on much of its present appearance. The second phase came after the third duke had returned from the Grand Tour with a great enthusiasm for the Palladian style and commissioned William Kent to enlarge the house accordingly.

MARLBOROUGH★

Wiltshire – Population 6 788

Michelin Atlas p 17 or Map 403 – O 29

The town, strategically placed on the London-Bath road *(A4)*, has been known since the 19C for its school and in earlier centuries was famous as a market town; it was named by John Aubrey as "one of the greatest markets for cheese in the West of England". The main street, parallel to the River Kennet, developed westwards from a Saxon settlement (now The Green) to where the Normans, soon after the Conquest, took over a prehistoric mound (60ft) as the site for a motte and bailey castle. By 1068, a mint that had been moved from Great Bedwyn was issuing silver pennies in Marlborough where a sophisticated wooden stronghold, second only to another in Bristol, was completed in 1100.

By the time the castle had fallen into ruin in the 1360s, Marlborough had developed into an important market town: the long street was filled weekly with downland sheep and cattle and stalls of wool, meat, fresh produce and cheese. Room was needed to herd the animals; the cottages of the period were small and insubstantial and they were pushed further and further back until the street attained the extraordinary width which even permitted open stalls, or shambles, to be pitched in a double line down the centre as they are still on market days.

The Civil War left scars but they were as nothing compared to the fire of 1653 when, it is recorded, "in the space of three or foure houres, there was burnt down to the ground about two hundred twentie foure dwelling Houses, besides many out-houses and stables, and most of the Household goods and Wares in the shops of many of the Inhabitants... The whole losse arising unto four score thousand pounds likewise there was burnt downe to the ground one of the Churches (St Mary's), and the Market House."

Marlborough Downs – The Downs, which extend in a wide semicircle north of the town, are traversed by the ages-old **Ridgeway Path** *(see AVEBURY)*. The chalk slopes once grazed by the vast flocks of sheep, which make every town in Wiltshire a wool town in origin, are now scattered with small towns and villages, to the west especially, and threaded by local roads running between high hedges; to the east, the land folds in a quilt of large arable fields outlined by straggling files of trees, hedges and ditches, and, on the skyline, stalwart clumps of dark green deciduous broad-leaves.

The Green

The Green, beyond the east end of the High Street, was the site of the Saxon settlement; the nearby Silverless and Kingsbury Streets are bordered by a variety of handsome 17C-19C houses: timber-framed, Classical 18C with pillared porches, ashlar-faced and weatherboarded and with windows from lattice to sash, oriel to Venetian.

High Street

The wide High Street leads from The Green at the far east end of the town to the College at the west end. It is not the architecture which makes the street attractive but the up and down rooflines, the individuality of the houses with their ground-floor shopfronts, and at the east end "the pent houses", as Pepys called them when he stayed in the town in 1653, "supported on pillars which makes a good walk". In the same range are several shops which were "improved" in Georgian times by the insertion of first floor Venetian windows.

St Mary's – The church, also at the east end of the High Street in a network of small streets (Perrin's Lane, Patten Alley), was rebuilt after the fire during the Commonwealth, hence its Puritan austerity. The chancel is 19C.

Town Hall – The hall in brick and stone, overlooking the High Street along its full length from the east end, was built to a Classical 17C-18C design on an island site by late Victorian craftsmen.

Coaching inns – The **Castle and Ball**, built in the 17C, was refronted after the fire and turned into a coaching inn in 1745. The house next door, which was pantiled in the 18C, was once an inn where Shakespeare is said to have played. Just north of the Church of St Peter and St Paul stands the **Sun Inn** which dates from the early 17C.

St Peter and St Paul – The redundant church on the green island site at the west end of the High Street is, like St Mary's, Norman in origin. It was largely rebuilt in the mid 15C and graced with a vaulted nave (unusual for a parish church at that time). It underwent substantial restoration in the early 1860s under the auspices of Thomas Wyatt: it was at this time that the Minton tiles in the chancel were laid and the east wall was adorned with stencil decoration and further tiling. Note the painted monument on the north wall by the altar rail dated 1626. It was here that Thomas Wolsey, the future Cardinal, Archbishop of York and Chancellor of the Kingdom in the reign of Henry VIII was ordained a priest in 1498. Today it extends a warm welcome to all visitors as a centre for local artists and craftsmen.

Marlborough College ⊘ – *Private.* The mound-site of the Norman castle was acquired in 1550 by Protector Somerset; in the 17C-18C both his grandson and the 6th Duke built separate mansions in the grounds, 1.5 million bricks being required before the second was completed (*c*1725). In 1750 the house was let as a coaching inn, which flourished until the advent of the railway, when it was sold to become a school. At its foundation in 1843 the College numbered 200 boys; in the century and a half since, buildings have proliferated and pupils (now including girls) have increased in number to *c*900.

Marlborough White Horse – The small and elongated **white horse** (62ft long, 47ft high), perky with a docked tail and round eye, is cut into a low escarpment on the south side of the Bath road (A4) just west of the College. It was designed and cut in 1804 by boys from the local town school run by Mr Greasley. Access along the banks of the Kennet along the footpath to Preshute Church.

EXCURSIONS

★★ **Savernake Forest** *2 miles southeast.*

Entrances off A346 Andover and A4 London roads; parking and picnic places; hearths for open fires – otherwise NO FIRE; modestly equipped camping sites (c/o Forestry Commission).

Savernake was a royal forest, hunted by Norman and Tudor kings alike, its woodland yielding boar and deer. In the 18C Capability Brown replanted the 4 000 acres, which it now comprises, with oak, ash, larch and thousands upon thousands of beech trees. Despite being Crown property, managed by the Forestry Commission, the forest is a wonderful place for exploring on foot or bicycle.

Crossing the forest in a northwest-southeast line, passing halfway along its 3-mile course through the compass point intersection known as the Eight Walks, is the **Grand Avenue**★★★, palisaded with the superb grey-green trunks of beeches.

Savernake Forest

★ **Littlecote** ⊘

Signposted off the B4192 to Swindon about 2 miles northwest of Hungerford.

History – "The Knight was brought to his tryall, and to be short this judge had this whole house, parks and manor, and (I thinke) more, for a bribe to save his life": the knight was Sir John Darell; the crime, the murder of his newborn bastard baby; the judge, the future Lord Chief Justice, Sir John Popham; the house, Littlecote; the date, 1587.

In those dark days a handmaid was delivered of a son by Darell by a local midwife; when she took the newborn baby to the father waiting by the fireplace in the corridor outside he put it on the fire; the mother remained masked throughout her travail. The midwife, after two years, told a justice of the crime and Darell was brought to trial before Sir John Popham.

House – The brick mansion, which in part predates Queen Elizabeth I, nestles elegantly alongside the River Kennet, surrounded by lush farmland. The main part of the house was extended eastwards during the 16C to almost the full length of the present north (garden) front; it was built of flint relieved by brick courses, stone tiles and had a fine oriel window providing a good view of the gardens from the gallery. The south (park) front, in deep rose brick with stone dressings outlining the large windows and centre gables, was added by Sir John in 1590.

Over the years Littlecote has received seven royal visits: Henry VIII in 1520 and 1536, Elizabeth I in 1601 (commemorated in a plaster overmantel), Charles II in 1663, William of Orange in 1688, Queen Mary in 1928, George VI and Princess, later Queen, Elizabeth in 1941. In 1996 the estate was acquired by the Warner Group and has been converted into a hotel.

The austere Cromwellian **Chapel**, with a central pulpit and no altar, has survived unaltered since that period. The rich **panelling** in the Brick Hall contrasts with the most unusual early 18C **wall paintings** in the Dutch Parlour. The **Great Hall** (1590) has magnificent panelling and plasterwork ceiling. The long 17C table (30ft) was built in situ and is netted at one end for the game of shuffle-board.

Roman Mosaic – Beside the river *(west of the house)* are the remains of an extensive Roman settlement that included grain stores, a brewery and bakery; later a baths complex was added; eventually the barns were adapted for residential use and the Orpheus chamber was added; in 360-362 AD seven buildings and gatehouse were converted to cult usage. Intermittent occupation of the site ceased in the 15C when the area was incorporated into the manor's hunting grounds; a lodge was unknowingly built over the mosaic (1650-1715) which was discovered by accident in 1727 by an estate steward. An archeological survey was completed in 1730 before the excavations were infilled and lost until 1977. Excavation and restoration in keeping with George Vertue's coloured engraving (1730) were completed in 1980.

The main panel of the **mosaic floor**, "the finest pavement that the sun ever shone upon in England", shows Orpheus surrounded by female representations of the four seasons associated with the Orphic cycle of rebirth and dates from a campaign launched by Emperor Julian to encourage the restoration of old cults; its shape conforms with a triconch structure of a type later used for Byzantine churches.

Round tour

14 miles; leave Marlborough south by A346, bear left into A338.

★ **Wilton Windmill** ⊙ – The five-storey brick tower mill (visible from A338 beyond East Grafton) was built in 1821 on top of the down behind the small village of Wilton, grouped around its duckpond.

The sweeps, two rigged with canvas sails, two with louvres, turn when corn is being ground but cannot be allowed to operate when visitors are in the mill owing to insufficient room in the cap. Inside the cap, the grinding machinery, similar to that of a watermill, can be seen together with the way in which the fantail, which never stops whirring, turns the sweeps into the wind.

Great Bedwyn – The old church dedicated to St Mary the Virgin (1092) is built of flint in the transitional Norman-Early English style with a square tower dating from the late 12C. The interior features arcades with dogtooth decoration supported on round columns with deeply undercut, all-different capitals, corbels carved with crowned heads and Seymour memorials: the tomb of Sir John (d 1536), father of Edward Seymour (Protector Somerset) and of Jane Seymour, a brass to John Seymour (d 1510) and a bust and gay cherubs on the tomb of a 17C duchess.

Most of the buildings post date a devastating fire that swept through the village in 1716.

The unusual **stone museum** ⊙ presents a static display of worked stone and artefacts set in a working stonemason's yard.

★ **Crofton Beam Engines** ⊙ – *20min.* This pumping station was built in 1809, installed near the highest point on the Kennet and Avon Canal to supply water from underground sources and that collected in Wilton Water, 40ft below the level of the canal, to the leat which feeds water into the canal and its locks descending in either direction. There are two engines designed to pump up to a ton of water at each stroke, 12 strokes a minute: the 1812 **Boulton and Watt** with 42in piston and cast-iron beam – the oldest beam engine regularly in steam in the world, and an 1846 Harvey of a type engineered in Cornwall to pump water from the tin mines (*see* CAMBORNE and REDRUTH). On entering the building, proceed up the stairs to the Beam Gallery at the top before descending through the various levels back down to the two coal-fired Lancashire boilers, taking note of the valves, levers, catches and rods of oiled cast iron and polished brass. Telephone for details of Steam Weekends throughout the summer months. The pumping station occupies a fine site overlooking Wilton Water – a haven for ducks and wild water fowl, lock 60 of the Kennet and Avon Canal (*see* DEVIZES) and the Great Western railway line to Great Bedwyn, via Newbury, which is regularly used by express trains and more occasionally by privately-run steam locomotives. The other side of the canal running straight up Wilton Hill to the windmill beyond is an old Roman road.

Rejoin the A346 to Marlborough.

Pewsey – *7 miles south on A3455.* The village of Pewsey, the chief feature of which, since 1911, has been a statue of King Alfred, gives its name to the **Vale of Pewsey★**, a beautiful stretch of country between Salisbury Plain and the Marlborough Downs.

Pewsey Vale White Horses – The **Pewsey Horse**, 45ft high x 66ft long, strides easily across the hillside; it is the second figure on this site having replaced one cut in 1785. It was commissioned by the town council to celebrate the coronation of King George VI in 1937; after being pegged out by its designer, it was excavated and chalk-filled by the local fire brigade. It is best glimpsed from the A345 Marlborough to Upavon road, beyond Pewsey.

2.5 miles further on towards North Newton, at the Woodbridge Inn take the A342 to Devizes, continue 1 mile to the village of Rushall and turn right for Devizes.

The **Alton Barnes Horse**, 166ft by 160ft long looking south over the Vale of Pewsey from Old Adam Hill, was cut on a gradual slope in 1812 by a local farmer; its general outline follows that of the Cherhill horse. Its dominant feature, probably due to weathering and scouring, is its enormous eye which is 11ft long by 8ft deep. Access on foot from the Ridgeway, Wansdyke and Tan Hill Way.

MINEHEAD★

Somerset – Population 9 904

Michelin Atlas p 7 or Map 403 – J 30

Minehead was the chief port in the area from the 14C to the 17C, trading with Ireland (in wool), Virginia and the West Indies. In the 19C with the arrival of the railway the town became a "seaside watering place"; today Minehead's economy revolves around local light industry and the large summer holiday camp east of the town.

The town was the birthplace, in 1917, of the science and space writer **Arthur C Clarke**, author of *2001: A Space Odyssey.*

Market day: Tuesday and Thursday all day (summer only).

Esplanade and Quay Street – The wide roads follow the curving line of the sea wall round to the harbour jetty and the small harbour filled with pleasure-craft and rowing boats. Lining the side of the road, at the foot of the wooded slopes of North Hill, is a thread of colour-washed and stone seamen's cottages (17C-19C).

Higher Town – The community of houses on North Hill, many thatched and with round-cornered cob walls, is linked by steeply rising and turning roads, winding lanes and stepped alleys.

★ **Church Steps** – *Access: on foot, by Church Path, an opening off Quay Street; by car, up Quay Lane, at the junction of the Esplanade and Quay Street. In both cases keep bearing right to lead into St Michael's Road.* Church Steps are best explored from the top downwards.

★ **St Michael's** – The church of light grey sandstone with a buttressed and battlemented **tower** (87ft high) has stood on the hill since the 14C-15C when it replaced a Norman building in turn probably successor to a Saxon church.

Inside is a 16C coved **rood screen** with a foliated crest which remained intact throughout the Commonwealth because, fortunately, the churchwardens were Parliamentarians.

The octagonal font with a kneeling figure, possibly the donor, dates from *c*1400; the brass of a young woman and effigy of a priest *(both east end)* are late 15C; the pulpit is 17C as is **Jack Hammer**, the clock jack; the **chandelier** is 18C.

The **royal arms** on the north wall and over the south door are of Queen Anne, George II and Charles II, at whose coronation the churchwardens, at a time when beer was less than 1*d* a pint, provided 16*s* for beer for the refreshment of the bellringers.

Outside, on the tower, note the figure of God holding a Crucifix *(north face)* and St Michael weighing souls with the Virgin tipping the scales in our favour *(east).*

West Somerset Railway ⊙ - The WSR, which owns the longest private line in Britain, operates diesel business and shopping services and, in the holiday season, **steam trains** from the Quantock Hills along the Bristol Channel coast. The line, which opened in 1862, was extended to Minehead in 1874; the track, originally the Great Western Broad Gauge of 7ft 0.25in, was converted within ten years to standard size. In 1922 the West Somerset became part of the Great Western Railway, in 1948 of British Rail and in 1971 the line was closed. This was not the end, however, for in March 1976, under "new management" the West Somerset Railway Company re-opened for business, successfully recapturing the atmosphere of a Great Western Railway branch line. Ten restored stations punctuate the line complete with signal boxes, engine sheds, engines, rolling stock.

West Somerset Railway, Minehead

★ **Minehead Station** - The 20 mile journey by train to Bishop's Lydeard *(75min)* begins from the platform which is long enough to take a 16-coach train; note the signal box from Dunster and water tower from Pwllheli, North Wales. Past the restoration depot, the line follows the shore round the bay - view of Hinkley Point Power Station and the Welsh coast on a clear day.

For Luccombe, Selworthy, Conygar Tower and Dunster Castle (20min on foot), see EXMOOR.

Blue Anchor - Signal box; railway museum; seaside village with caravan site; sand and pebble beach.

Washford Bank - 1:65 gradient; Washford; restoration depot with rolling stock on display; the **Somerset and Dorset Railway Museum** ⊙ commemorates the amalgamation of the Somerset Central and Dorset Central Railways. *10min walk to ruins of Cleeve Abbey; 1hr along former West Somerset Mineral Railway to Watchet.*

Watchet - On the hilltop the 15C tower of St Decuman Church, below a large papermill at the entrance to the town. Watchet, home port of Coleridge's *Ancient Mariner*, is the oldest commercial harbour along this part of the coast still in active trade. The line approaches to within feet of the cliff. Helwell Bay is popular with fossil-hunters.

Williton - Brick-built signal box, second water tower from Pwllheli (steam trains often take on water - halfway point), restored 1860s booking office, goods shed and siding; diesel locomotive depot. Views of the Quantocks *(east)* and Brendons *(west)*.

Stogumber - Charming country station, 20min walk to village with red sandstone church with 14C tower *(1 mile)*.

Crowcombe Heathfield - Small museum and trackwork display. Village *(1.75 miles)* 400ft above sea-level, the topmost point of the line, beautiful countryside, walking centre for the Quantocks.

★ **Bishop's Lydeard** - Signal box, goods shed, renovation depot, model railway; short walk to village: see TAUNTON DEANE.

EXCURSION

★★ Cleeve Abbey *90min.*

The red sandstone **abbey ruins** ⏰ in a pretty setting are particularly interesting since they comprise the buildings most often destroyed, the monks' quarters. Cleeve was colonised by an abbot and 12 monks in 1198 when building began on the church. Construction was in two main phases: 1198-1297 and 1455-1537. In the first phase the community increased to nearly 30 monks, a pilgrimage chapel was built at Blue Anchor and land in the area was brought under cultivation; the second phase was a period of renewal and improvement verging on the luxurious, with the provision of sets of rooms decorated with wall paintings for the monks. All was abrogated at the Dissolution.

A two-storeyed gatehouse leads into a 3-acre outer court and to what was the west end of the priory church (now only footings); walk up the nave and through the arch just before the south transept.

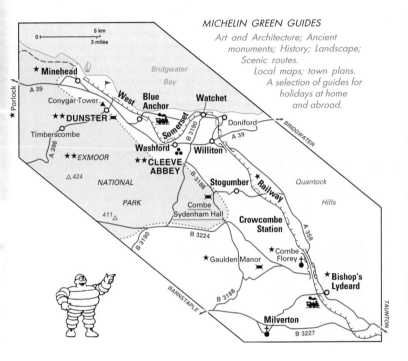

MICHELIN GREEN GUIDES
Art and Architecture; Ancient monuments; History; Landscape; Scenic routes.
Local maps; town plans.
A selection of guides for holidays at home and abroad.

Cloister – Despite the destruction of all but one arcaded wall along part of the west gallery, the enclosed feel of the cloister remains, with the church occupying one side and the high dorter and frater ranges still standing on the east and south sides. Note the **collation seat** in the centre of the church wall, from where the abbot presided over the reading before Compline.

Dorter range – The doorways led, respectively, to the **library**, the **chapter-house**, the parlour and the slype or passageway to the commonroom *(sharp right)*. Climb the stairs to the vast dormitory or **dorter** (25ft by 137ft), built to accommodate 36 monks. It had a lime and mortar floor supported on the vaulting of the ground-floor rooms and was lit by lancets. Note the night stair into the church *(left of the two doorways in north wall)*.

Frater range – The range is a 15C rebuilding of an earlier construction.
The original refectory, of which the splendid **tiled pavement** remains, lay on the far side of the range *(through the barrel vaulted passage at the corner)*. The tiles, which from their heraldry date from 1272-1300, show in still-bright red, yellow, black and white the **three leopards** of England borne by Henry III (1216-72), the **lion** of Poitou and **border** of Cornwall of Richard, Earl of Cornwall (1209-72, second son of King John) and his son, Edmund – both abbey benefactors – the **double-headed** eagle of Richard who also held the title King of the Romans, the central **diamond** of Cornwall flanked by those of England...

Return to the cloister.

The later **frater**, through the wide 13C doorway and up the stairs, is a hall (51ft by 22ft) lit by 9 transomed windows with traceried heads – note how the north windows are blank below, where the cloister roof once abutted the wall.

The outstanding feature of the hall is the **roof**, a great timber construction supported on stone corbels, with archbraced collars, trusses, purlins, richly moulded and further decorated with 50 deeply undercut, foliated bosses and crowned angels. The roof is unfinished, being intended as a boarded-in barrel; also it was never painted.

The lobby at the top of the stairs opens on to an office while the gallery alongside the cloister wall leads to small rooms decorated with still visible wall paintings.

NEWQUAY

Cornwall – Population 17 390
Michelin Atlas p 2 or Map 403 – E 32

Newquay has long been a popular sea-side resort with golden sands backed by cliffs which advance into headlands and points – East Pentire, Towan and Porth Island – once settled by prehistoric man. The "new quay" dates back to 1439 when the villagers set about protecting the inlet. During the 18C and 19C Newquay was a pilchard port, exporting salted fish to Italy and Spain; the **Huar's House** still stands on the clifftop where the huar sounded his long horn to summon the fishermen when a shoal of pilchards entered the bay. When the railway arrived in the 1870s the town became a china-clay and mineral port and then a resort. Today, Newquay enjoys a revival among surfers off Tolcarne, Towar, Great Western and Watergate beaches.

Animal World ⊘ – *Trenance Park.* As animal conservation becomes an ever more important preoccupation, Newquay zoo is an informal sanctuary for domesticated pets (guinea pigs, rabbits), old favourites (lions, pumas, zebras, ducks and swans) and endangered species (Humboldt's penguins) where children, in particular, can learn and interact with animals, birds and insects. Popular attractions include the free-range pheasants, the meerkat and capybara enclosures, feeding time accompanied by informal talk, the tropical house, Dragon maze and walk-through aviary.

Tunnels Through Time ⊘ – *St Michael's Road.* A series of static tableaux recreate various legends and stories about Cornwall: Bolster the Giant; King Arthur and Merlin; pirates, smugglers and treasure trove seekers; undersea world of Lyonesse; Morvena the mermaid. An optional, more gruesome section illustrates the vile and cruel punishments of former ages.

Newquay Sea Life Centre ⊘ – *Towan Promenade.* Octopus, sea horses, sting rays and sharks are just some of the varied marine life on display here.

EXCURSIONS

★ **Trerice** ⊘ *3 miles southeast by A392 and A3058. 45min.*

The small, silver-grey, stone **manor house** stands in a wooded valley, framed by the walls and yew hedges of its flower gardens, orchard of West Country fruit trees and parade ground , where the Home Guard trained during World War II. The house was rebuilt in 1572-73 to an E shaped plan with, on the east front, highly decorative scrolled gables and a hall with a beautiful window, stone mullioned and transomed with twenty-four lights and 576 small panes of 16C glass.

The interior is particularly notable for 16C **plasterwork**: the fine ceiling of the **Great Hall** is ribbed and pendented, the scrolled overmantel and the miniature arcade which fronts the musicians' gallery demonstrate the plasterers' skill. Note also, from inside, the great window and, among the furniture, a 20ft table made of oak from the estate in the 19C, the mid-16C chest, late 17C travelling desk and 18C oak travelling case beneath an Aubusson tapestry.

The **Library**, with a faded green 19C Donegal carpet, is furnished with 18C-19C mahogany and walnut pieces among which are a domed coffer and a chiming, long-case clock.

The **Drawing Room**, the former solar, is also decorated with outstanding plasterwork, notably a barrel roof, with the family arms high on the wall at one end, and a decorated overmantel on telamons, dated with hybridised numerals. A **Musicians' Gallery** offers an overview of the hall and a closer look at the plasterwork ceiling.

The **Court Chamber** is furnished with 17C-18C walnut furniture, notably a double dome **secretaire-bookcase** and a long-case clock by Thomas Tompion (*c*1680) – another stands in the lobby.

The Georgian mahogany furniture in the **North Chamber** is highlighted by a four-poster with clustered columns and a painted cornice. The ebonised bracket clock is by Joseph Knibb (1650-1711).

Mower Museum – In the barn is a large collection of mowers tracing developments since 1893.

Coast south to Hell's Mouth *26 miles south*

★ **Penhale Point and Kelsey Head** – From each of the headlands there is a **view**★★ north to Towan Head and Trevose Head, south to Godrevy Lighthouse and St Ives and, inland, from the St Austell china-clay pyramids to Camborne and Carn Brea.
The Coast Path turns away before the end of Penthale Point East but follows the cliff line of Penthale Point West and Kelsey Head. Roads lead out to both Penthale Points stopping short about half a mile from the cliff edges.

Perranporth – Three miles of beach provided the setting, and the coming of the railway the opportunity, for Perranporth to turn itself, early this century, into the resort which it has been ever since. The time also was ripe: the pilchard, after 100 years, had vanished, smuggling had ended and the mines were ceasing to be profitable.

St Piran's Oratory – *1 mile on foot across the sand dunes.* St Piran's stood like a rock, appearing and disappearing in the tide of sand which surrounded it from its construction in the 6C-7C on the burial site of the saint who, according to legend, crossed the sea from Ireland on a millstone. In 1835 the sands, always shifting, blew away from the 7C oratory, revealing a building 29.5ft long, 16.5ft wide and 19ft high, of granite, porphyry, slate, quartz and rubble. In 1980 the ruins were reburied *(site marked by a plaque).*

★★ **St Agnes Beacon** – The beacon *(last 500yds up a field footpath)* at 628ft, between the village and the headland, affords a **panorama**★★ from Trevose Head to St Michael's Mount. In the foreground, between 300ft high Cligga Head, where the granite begins, and the beacon, there extends the typical north Cornwall landscape, short-turfed, undulating, windswept, speared by old mine stacks.

Porthtowan – The attractive small cove is known for its surfing.

★ **Portreath** – A 1:6 road descends the valley on either side to lead to the cove, the harbour with its stalwart breakwater and the small village resort.
Follow the coast road, B3301.

★ **Hell's Mouth** – *Car park beside the road.* From the cliff edge the blue-green-black sea breaks ceaselessly against the sheer, 200ft encircling **cliff-face**; the only sounds are the screaming of the sea-birds and the endless wash of the waves.

PADSTOW★

Cornwall – Population 2 855
Michelin Atlas p 2 or Map 403 – F 32

Padstow was for centuries a major port, being the only safe harbour on the north Cornwall coast, once the rocks, cross winds and currents at the mouth of the Camel Estuary had been negotiated. In the 6C St Petroc, landing from Wales, founded a Celtic minster here before journeying on to Bodmin; in 981 minster and town were destroyed by the Vikings. During the Middle Ages Padstow was granted the Right of Sanctuary by King Athelstan, enabling criminals to seek refuge there: this privilege was forfeited at the Reformation when ownership of the land around Padstow transferred to the Prideaux family who continue to live at Prideaux Place to this day.

The town thereafter developed over the centuries into a fishing harbour complete with shipyard, a port handling china-clay and copper ore destined for the refineries outside Bristol as well as wheat, barley, oats, cheese. During the 19C many trans-Atlantic emigrants set out

---

Padstow 'Obby 'Oss

The May Day celebrations, their origin lost in the mists of antiquity, begin at midnight in the square or Broad Street with the singing of the Morning Song – "let us all unite for summer is acome unto day". In the morning a children's horse, a **blue 'oss** and the original **red 'oss** make their appearance and prance throughout the day to accordion and drum bands.

At Christmas Padstow rings with the sound of carols that are unique to the town, dating back to the 18C.

---

in craft as small as 10 tons. As boats became bigger however, fewer could make port owing to the sand or **Doom Bar** at the estuary mouth, formed, according to legend, at the curse of a dying mermaid shot by a local man.

Today, Padstow's popularity cannot be divorced from the name Rick Stein, a successful restaurateur who extols the fresh flavours of locally-caught seafood.

Harbour – The harbour which resists falls in tide levels with a sluice gate is often filled with fishing boats, yachts and launches: surrounded on three sides by quays each backed by old houses, boathouses and pubs, it provides the focal point of this colourful little town.

South Quay – Opposite the Harbour Master's Office is a group of 16C, two-storey granite houses with slate roofs, comprising the **Old Court House** with a shell hood over the door, **Raleigh Cottage**, where Sir Walter Raleigh as Warden of Cornwall collected dues, and the minute **Harbour Cottage**.

North Quay – The 15C **Abbey House**, once a nunnery and now privately owned, has a dripstone carved with a nun's head.

A network of narrow streets runs back behind the quay, the alleys darkened by tall houses, many with exposed beams and oversailing upper floors above small shop-fronts.

Boat Trips ⓥ – Despite what the boatmen say, to a landsman it is frequently quite choppy. The cruises head beyond the Camel Estuary to view **Stepper Point**, **Pentire Point**, the **Rumps** and, in Portquin Bay, the spectacular **cliffs**, caves and rocks, and possibly a modern wreck, caught on the rocks, her back broken by the waves. The **Camel Estuary**, guarded by the cliffs of Pentire and Stepper Points, is a beautiful haven for waders: curlews, ringed plovers and redshanks which are often put to flight by peregrine falcons.

St Petroc Major – *Up the hill.* The church with its embattled west tower begun between 1420-1450 contains an octagonal **font** of Catacleuse stone carved by the **Master of St Endellion**.

The cross-shaft in the churchyard is Celtic, the wrought-iron gates are 18C.

Forth an Syns

The Saints Way begins at the door of Padstow Parish Church where in 520 St Petroc established his first monastic settlement – intending perhaps to cross Cornwall on foot before setting sail for Brittany.

It climbs Dennis Hill before snaking its way across what would have been treacherous forest land to No Man's Land (junction with A39 Padstow to Wadebridge road). Up to St Breock Downs (216m above sea level) past the prehistoric longstone known as Men Gurta (the Stone of Waiting) and a wind farm... Halfway point is Lanivet and then the path rises again to Helman Tor, a granite outcrop from where views extend some 50 miles on a clear day.

Legend has it that he sailed the seas on a plantain leaf – alluding perhaps to the practice of lining coracle boats with leaves to waterproof them.

St Petroc was the son of a Welsh chieftain who has been likened to St Francis of Assisi, a protector of animals, having saved a stag from a hunting party, drawn a splinter from a dragon's eye and released a trapped sea-monster from a lake.

★ **Prideaux Place** ⓥ – The Elizabethan house is set in gardens and parkland, one of the oldest deer parks in England, which have been landscaped in the 18C, in the manner of Capability Brown with a Classical temple, obelisk, grotto and stone arbour sheltering a series of Roman urns.

Built by Sir Nicholas Prideaux in 1592 on the site of the former Barton of the Monks of Bodmin, the E-shaped granite building has undergone some remodelling, but the 16C plaster ceiling in the Great Chamber, preserved by a false ceiling inserted in Georgian times, survives intact. The house was occupied by the American Army during the Second World War and, more recently, has featured in a number of feature films (some sets are displayed in the stables).

The former Great Hall (**Dining Room**) is panelled with both Elizabethan and Georgian stained oak set with an inlaid frieze and Jacobean-style geometric designs: note the carved female figure standing on a boar to the left of the fireplace – this is alleged to be an allegory of Elizabeth I stamping out ignorance or vice; the portrait above the fireplace is of Sir Nicholas Prideaux.

The **Morning Room**, a family sitting room, is hung with fine portraits by John Opie (1761-1807) who grew up on the estate before aspiring to court circles. A pastel of Humphrey Prideaux by the Venetian artist Rosalba Carriera was executed in Italy when he was on the Grand Tour; when the frame was subsequently dismantled for cleaning, a love letter from the artist was discovered, but the recipient to whom it was addressed had long since died. Note the fine silver Art Nouveau switch plate.

Added in 1799, this wing is decorated in Strawberry Hill Gothick; the **Drawing Room** is suitably furnished with satinwood furniture and fine porcelain.

The Dining Room (**Grenville Room**) built by the first Earl of Bath was removed to Prideaux Place in the 18C: it is a powerful expression of Restoration taste complete with gloriously gilded carvings by **Grinling Gibbons**, Italian paintings by Antonio Verrio, Royalist Caroline portraits and a handsome wine cooler.

Ornamenting the **stairway** up to the library are two cases displaying rare 18C Chinese Nankin porcelain - made of Cornish china clay - its underglaze blue decorated with delicate gilding; the second case holds pieces from the Wedgwood, Spode and Worcester factories.

Regency Gothick furniture complements the **Library**, a comfortable vaulted room, lined with leather backed books: pull-down maps suggest that it was from here that decisions about the family's estates were made.

Upstairs is the **Great Chamber** with its fine plaster ceiling, one of several to survive in the West Country made by the Abbott family of Frithelstock (*see also* BODMIN MOOR: Lanhydrock). This one illustrates the story of Susannah and the Elders among ornamental animals. From the windows the view stretches out to sea.

EXCURSIONS

Cornish coast west

Trevone - *3 miles west by A3276.*

The village and chapel with a slate spire stand in a small sandy cove, guarded by fierce offshore rocks. The spectacular approach to the village from Padstow is by way of the **Cornwall Coast Path**★★ *(5 miles on foot)* which circles 242ft **Stepper Point** with its white waymark and passes the natural rock arches of **Porthmissen Bridge**.

★ **Trevose Head** - *6 miles west by B3276 and by-roads; last half mile on foot.*

The 243ft head stands halfway between Hartland Point, 40 miles to the northeast, and West Penwith - four light-houses are visible at night. By day the **view**★★ is of bay following bay, offshore rock islands, small sandy coves palisaded to seaward by towering rocks.

Portcothnan - The tiny village lies at the back of a deep square cove.

★ **Bedruthan Steps** ⓥ - *8 miles southwest of Padstow by B3276.*

The 1.5 mile arc of sand spectacularly scattered with giant rocks worn to the same angle by waves and wind is visible over the cliff edge - the rocks were the stepping stones, legend has it, of the giant Bedruthan.

Inland to St Issey and Wadebridge

Little Petherick - *3.5 miles south by B3274. Turn left into A389.* The remodelled medieval church lies at the bottom of a steep-sided valley, its tower just visible in the trees; from the hilltops on either side there are **views** far across the Camel River.

St Issey - The medieval church tower collapsed in the 19C, necessitating a total rebuilding and meticulous repiecing of the Catacleuse stone altarpiece by the Master of St Endellion; a second carving is on the south altar.

Wadebridge - The most remarkable feature of this sleepy little town is the magnificent bridge, at 320ft the longest in Cornwall, built in *c*1468.

Penwith, the western tip of Cornwall, the most westerly headland in England with Land's End at its edge, has a windswept beauty all its own deriving from its granite foundation, restless blue ocean, the silent monuments of myth and ancient time, small granite churches with their individual landmark towers, and Celtic Christian wayside crosses.

The area has been settled for over 4 000 years and many of the ancient stone field boundaries may date from that time. Spiking the undulating hillsides along the north coast are the chimneys and derelict engine-houses of old mines; older still are the prehistoric villages and ancient hillforts which crown the hill tops. It is an area of legend which combines wide open space prickled with gorse and thorn bushes, with lush leafy vales.

Hayle – Penzance

Hayle – The estuary town is flanked by Porth Kidney Sands *(west)* to Carbis Bay, and the three mile stretch of Hayle Towans Beach *(north)* to Godrevy Point – *towan* being Cornish for sand dune. Its prosperity in the 19C was largely based on Harvey's foundry at Hayle which subsequently manufactured the largest steam engines to be used for pumping with a 144 inch cylinder, and a foundry at Copperhouse built on the site of an 18C copper smelting works. Each works had a harbour.

Paradise Park ⊘ – *Off the B3302.* Paradise Park is the headquarters of the World Parrot Trust. The bird collection is nurtured so as to encourage breeding and conservation. Various shaded aviaries provide homes notably to brightly coloured macaws, parrots and cockatoos; owls, eagles (flying demonstrations), flamingos, penguins, kookaburra and the near-extinct **Cornish chough**. The otter breeding sanctuary (baby Asian otters sometimes on view), red squirrels, chipmunks, goats and pigs, Fun Farm, play area and Victorian walled garden provide added interest for the full range of ages.

★ **Ludgvan** – The village, straggling along one of the old main roads, opens out on a corner with a small green bordered by the churchyard. The main landmark, the 14C **church**★ has a 15C granite **tower** complete with its gargoyles, battlements and pinnacles. Christianity is said to have been brought to the area by Ludewon, a 6C Irish missionary; a contemporary **Celtic Cross shaft** has been built into the tower steps while inside is a small wedge-shaped, **granite slab** with two incised crosses, believed to be a 7C Christian grave marker *(on a window sill)*. The scalloped **font** is Norman.

★ **Gulval** – The village centre is marked by a vivid triangular flowerbed and by the parish **church**★ of 1440 with its three stage granite tower. Inside the church are a 14C-15C **font** with an angel on one corner, angel-capitalled **pillars** stained where iron rings were attached by the Parliamentarians to tie up their horses when using the nave as stables, a **cross** *(south aisle window sill)* of mother-of-pearl inlaid in dark, ancient wood, said to be from a tree from the submerged Forest of **Lyonesse**, located, according to some, in Mount's Bay.

Carn Euny

★ **Madron Church** ⊙ – **St Maddern** was constructed between the 14C and the 16C, the third church on the site overlooking Mount's Bay.

Its 250 **bosses**, carved to 16 different patterns, and the **cornice angels** (retained when the roof was renewed) date from the 15C. The furnishings and monuments include an **inscribed stone** *(southwest wall)* thought to be 8C Celtic; an Early English sedilia *(Lady Chapel)*; five pre-14C animal **bench-ends**; a 17C brass; several 17C slate memorials; a 14C English **alabaster panel** of ten angels, probably from a reredos or shrine. The wooden panel bearing the Tudor rose and the royal arms of Henry VII was carved in earnest of the loyalty of the vicar and the congregation after a lapse in support of Perkin Warbeck.

The **rood-screen**, with faintly coloured original wainscot panels and crocketed gables, dates from 1450. The bell from the local **Ding Dong Tin Mine** (closed 1878) hangs by the south door; opposite is a panel of **tin marks**, in local use from 1189. The **Nelson banner** *(north wall)* was made in haste in 1805 to be carried before the major and burgesses of Penzance processing to Madron for the first Trafalgar Service; the procession and service are held annually on the Sunday nearest 21 October.

Well and Baptistery – *1 mile north (sign: Wishing Well); park; 10 mins on foot.* A track leads though moss-covered trees and May-flowering hawthorn to a tree decked in ribbons and rags; these tokens of a wish made by the well are evidence of a continued trust in its water's healing properties. Slightly further on, in the ruins of St Maddern's Baptistery (6C) is a circular basin and altar stone, often strewn with flowers.

Penzance – Land's End

For Penzance and Trengwainton Gardens, see PENZANCE.

Sancreed – The **church**★★ was rebuilt in the 15C when the population of the village numbered less than 100 – it reached its maximum of 1 398 in 1851 when the local tin mines were in peak production.

The two stage granite **tower** of alternate deep and shallow courses is crowned by battlements and corner pinnacles. Inside, the arcade of five bays on solid granite columns, transept arching, a traceried window *(west end, south aisle)*, 14C Norman **font** with crowned angels at the bowl corners remain from earlier sanctuaries. The **rood-screen** shows typical medieval human and animal figures half-hidden in the foliage on the lower panels.

Outside in the churchyard are 5 **Celtic Crosses**★★ – two of them (8C-11C) are outstanding, with carved shafts and, on the heads, Christ in a tunic with expanded sleeves.

> ### Celtic crosses
>
> There are some 300 crosses scattered in Cornwall marking sacred sites and rights of way: they are to be found in churchyards *(usually east of the south porch)*, by the wayside or in fields indicating the route followed by pall bearers bringing a corpse for burial. They are usually incised on the shaft with typical Celtic-Irish interlacings and knots, and carved with signs of the Cross, the Chi-Rho (XP) monogram, the figure of Christ, sometimes in a tunic.

★ **Carn Euny** ⊙ – *5min walk across the fields from the road between Sancreed and St Just.* The outstanding feature of this Iron Age and Romano-British village, inhabited from the 7C BC to mid-Roman times, is the **fougou** (Cornish for cave). This comprises a creep and 40ft long passage, dry stone-walled and roofed with large granite slabs, which leads to the unique round chamber, some 10ft across, stone walled, corbel roofed and once domed.

Carn Brea – *East of B3306.* The ground rises to 200ft in a rounded hillock, the most westerly in Cornwall from where, on a clear day, may be seen the Isles of Scilly some 30 miles away. Its name Chapel Carn Brea is derived from a medieval chapel (now gone) built on top of a large Bronze Age burial cairn.

★ **Newlyn** – Newlyn has always been, and remains, the major fishing harbour in Mount's Bay and the west, noted for its catches of mackerel and whitefish, lobster and crab. The heart of the village is made up of whitewashed cottages which cluster round the harbour and rise up the hillside: full of the same charm that attracted painters who founded the **Newlyn School** in the 1880s.

Harbour – The working fleet comprises various types of fishing vessel: beam trawlers (Dover sole, lemon sole, megrim and monkfish), side trawlers (whiting, cod, ling, John Dory, red mullet), gill netters (hake, dogfish, ling, cod, tuna),

Fishing fleet, Newlyn

long liners (ray, skate, turbot, cod, ling, conger eel), crabbers (lobster, spider crab, brown crab, crawfish) as well as smaller boats for hand-line fishing (mackerel).

The small building alongside the lighthouse is the **Newlyn Tidal Observatory**, which in 1915 was established as the Ordnance Survey datum point from which the mean sea level is calculated and therefore from which all altitudes are set throughout Britain.

★ **Pilchard Works** ⊘ – The now dwindling pilchards trade was once a mainstay in Cornwall: as pilchards were caught returning from the Brittany coast to British waters to spawn, huge catches would be landed and cured for the home and continental markets. This salt pilchard factory has exported its hand-packed *salache inglese* to the same Genoese family since 1905, a reminder of times when it was traditional in Catholic countries to eat fish on Fridays and where it was impossible to supply distant mountain hamlets with freshly caught fish during the summer months.

An interesting introduction to traditional fishing practices with seine nets prefaces access to the actual curing works where the fish, landed during the winter months, are loaded into large concrete bins (1826) with coarse salt. After several weeks, they are packed and pressed into wooden barrels or pine "coffins" into six layers of 14 fish. These are then marked up with copper stencils ready for export. Additional information boards complete the tour, highlighting colourful stories of such characters like May Kelynack, a jowster (or fish seller) who walked from Newlyn to London to see Queen Victoria.

Newlyn Art Gallery ⊘ – Founded as a venue for displaying paintings by local artists, the **Passmore Edwards Art Gallery** runs exhibitions of traditional Newlyn School works in alternation with shows of international contemporary art. The four repoussé copper panels ornamenting the building were designed by J D Mackenzie and executed by Phillip Hodder (*see* INTRODUCTION: Silver and copper): they represent the four elements: earth, air, water and fire.

Continue along the coast road.

Penlee Point – The old lifeboat house, from which the *Solomon Browne* set out on a heroic rescue attempt and perished with all on board in December 1981, now shelters an auxiliary boat, RNLI memorabilia and "honour boards" of boats manned by Mousehole men.

Adjoining is a memorial garden to the men of the *Solomon Browne*.

★ **Mousehole** – Mousehole (pronounced Mowzell) is an attractive – and often crowded – small village. The **harbour** is protected by a quay of Lamorna granite and a **breakwater** dating from 1393. Standing back from the fishermen's low granite cottages at the water's edge is the half-timbered Keigwin Arms, the only house left standing after being raided by the Spanish in the 16C.

Beyond the harbour stretches the beach; **Merlyn**, an offshore rock; the Battery Rocks, which until the 19C was the site of a gun emplacement; the Mousehole, an old smugglers' cave, and **Spaniards' Point**, where the raiders landed in 1595 before marching inland to pillage the countryside, burn **Paul Church** – of which the 15C pinnacled tower, a major seamark, survives – and sack Mousehole, Newlyn and Penzance; they were eventually driven off.

Lamorna and Lamorna Cove – Half a mile separates the village from the cove below the Carn-du headland which marks the boundary of Land's End granite: this favourite spot frequented by several Newlyn School painters at the turn of the century, has a picturesque "harbour" which was once used by ships for loading locally-quarried granite for export.

★ **The Merry Maidens and The Pipers Standing Stones** – Two Pipers stand hauntingly in the field 100 yards apart just north of the road *(B3315)*; the Merry Maidens (4ft tall), 19 in number, squat and still, form a circle in the field to the south. The story goes that the Bronze Age maidens and pipers were turned to stone for dancing and making music on a Sunday.
A little further is the early Bronze Age **Tregiffian entrance grave**, a kerbed cairn with a chamber roofed with slabs.

★★ **St Buryan** – The village and surrounding landscape are dominated by the 14C granite **church tower**★★ (92ft) square and pinnacled, from which, it is claimed, the towers of 16 other Cornish churches can be seen. The ring of six bells is the second heaviest in Britain.
King Athelstan built the first St Buryan Church in AD 931, following his conquest of the Scilly Isles. The major features today are the striking granite porch; 15C font bearing three angels and a Latin cross; 17C slate tombstone, finely carved (*west wall;* other beautifully lettered 18C stones outside); 13C coffin-shaped tombstone *(northwest corner of the tower);* 15C rood screen. Standing guard outside are the Celtic crosses.

Penwith coastline

★ **Porthcurno** – The road, which drops through the trees to the village, ends at the cove where the Atlantic laps the shelving shell-sand beach, protected on either side by bluff headlands.

★ **Museum of Submarine Telegraphy** ⊙ – Since 1870 Porthcurno beach has been the landing point for submarine cables – the largest international cable station in the world – linking Britain first to Bombay, then Australia and thereby to her Empire and the intercontinental telegraph network. In 1934 the British Government pressed for a merger in the two most effective communications systems by merging the Eastern Telegraph Company's cable services with the operating side of Marconi Company (who pioneered the transmission of signals via radio waves across the Atlantic from Poldhu Cove on the Lizard) to create Cable and Wireless. Porthcurno became a major centre for research and development, notably in refining techniques for detecting faults on submarine cables. During the Second World War, reinforced tunnels were built to house this highly secret operation complete with power station. Modern satellite technology having made all the extant equipment obsolete, the training station was closed in 1993: the collection was given by Cable and Wireless to the Porthcurno Trust and the beach and cliffs to the National Trust; it is now managed by the Trevithick Trust which is caring for aspects of Cornwall's industrial archeology. The bay is still the landing point for fibre optic cabling from the Continent.

On display are the early telegraph systems and vintage wireless technology used to transmit Morse signals, then cable-code as electric pulses and finally as the binary code that is effective in the digital computers: many of the brass and mahogany instruments, including some from the 1870s, are kept in working order.

Minack Open-Air Theatre ⊙ – *Access by road from the beach car park; also by a stairway and steep path from the beach (20min).* The history of the cliffside theatre which was created in 1929 by Miss Cade, with its stunning ocean back-drop, is told through photographs, models and audiovisual techniques in the **Rowena Cade Exhibition Centre** ⊙. The box office is adapted from a World War II "pill-box" defence position of the type that were built to safeguard the cable station.

Logan Rock – *Access on foot from the Coastal Path.* The "logan", a 70-ton boulder which moved at the touch of a finger, was displaced by a Royal Navy party as a prank last century; although repositioned it has never been as keenly balanced.

★ **Land's End** – Access for vehicle-borne visitors to the famous stretch of coast is now via the **Land's End Visitor Centre** ⊙, though the Cornwall Coastal Path provides an impressive alternative approach for ramblers and walkers. The attraction of Land's End itself is less its physical beauty than its position on the western tip of the mainland overlooking some of the finest local **cliff scenery**★★★ perpetually assailed by the surging swell of the Atlantic: inshore rocks, the **Armed Knight** and the holed **Enys Dodnan**, may be the mountain peaks of the lost land of **Lyonesse** submerged beneath the waves. Offshore stands the Longships Lighthouse *(1.5 miles)* among swirling currents and submerged reefs; further west lie the Isles of Scilly *(27 miles)*.

The sense of magnificent isolation has been diminished somewhat by the complex which comprises a host of popular exhibitions, attractions and entertainments: the *Legendary Last Labyrinth (20min audio visual)* retells the maritime and legendary history of Cornwall; *Deep Sea Quest* is a submarine quest for Lyonesse; others include *Land of Greeb* (rare breeds of animals, craftsmen at work), Dollar Cove suspension bridge, land trains, a model village, the Lobster Pot Maze, the Shipwreck Play Area... but the coastline itself remains largely unaltered and just a short walk (RSPB warden tours available) leads away from the crowds.

Early morning always provides a quiet, solitary view while sunset and nightfall, when the lighthouses come into their own, offer a more memorable experience.

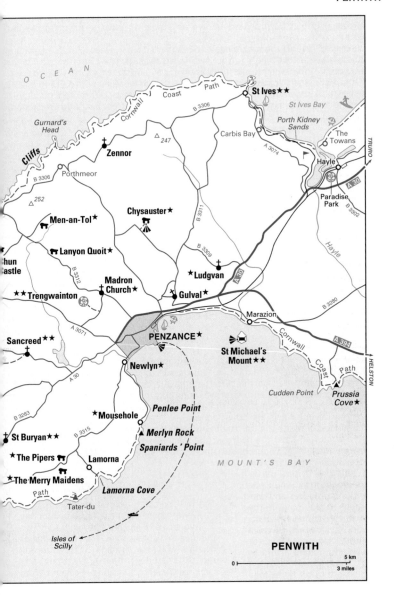

OCEAN

Gurnard's
Head

Coast   Path

Cornwall

St Ives★★

St Ives Bay

B 3306

Porth Kidney
Sands

Carbis Bay

The
Towans

Cliffs

△ 247

A 3074

Hayle

Zennor

Porthmeor

B 3306

Paradise
Park

B 3302

△ 252

Men-an-Tol★

Chysauster★

B 3311

B 3309

Lanyon Quoit★

hun
astle

B 3312

Madron
Church★

Ludgvan★

A 30

★★Trengwainton

Gulval★

Marazion

B 3280

A 3071

Cornwall

A 394

HELSTON

Sancreed★★

PENZANCE★

St Michael's
Mount★★

Coast

TRURO

Hayle

Newlyn★

Cudden Point

Path

Prussia
Cove★

A 30

Penlee Point

Mousehole★

B 3283

Merlyn Rock

St Buryan★★

B 3315

Spaniards' Point

MOUNT'S BAY

★The Pipers

Lamorna

★The Merry Maidens

Lamorna Cove

Path

Tater-du

Isles of
Scilly

PENWITH

0 _____ 5 km

3 miles

Land's End – St Ives

Sennen – St Sennen on the cliff-top, the most westerly **church** in England, its three stage, pinnacled, granite **tower** a marker for ships at sea, is an enlargement of a 13C chapel of which the chancel, transept and north wall remain. The south aisle, granite arcade and the tower were completed by 1430 when a petition was sent to the pope requesting a licence for a local burial ground, since experience showed that attendance at funeral services in St Buryan three miles away left the village open to local pirate raids. By the tower is a 7ft **wayside cross★**. *Walk down to the cove along the road or footpath (20min there and back). The footpath skirts a number of small standing stones in a field.*

★ **Sennen Cove** – The cove, with the massive Pedn-men-du headland at its back, the breakwater, fishermen's hard and small harbour, the surfing beach, RNLI station and slip, houses and pub, offers a wide **view★** over Whitesand Bay, the Brisons Rocks and Cape Cornwall.

Land's End Aerodrome ⊘ – *Signposted from the A30.* Short coastal flights and day excursions to the Isles of Scilly; public viewing terrace.

St Just-in-Penwith – The prosperity enjoyed by this 19C mining town is reflected in the substantial buildings lining the triangular square, the fine terraces of cottages and the very large Methodist Chapel in Chapel Street.

Adjacent to the square is a grassy arena intended for performing Cornish miracle plays; in Cornish it is known as a *plen an gwarry*, meaning playing place.

The **church**★ just off the square has a 15C pinnacled **tower**, walls of dressed granite and an elaborate 16C porch. Note two faded **paintings**; the *Christ of the Trades* is especially interesting for its illustration of 15C craftsmen's tools. Dating from the mid-5C, when St Just himself was alive, is a gravestone with a Chi-Rho (XP) monogram, known from its inscription as the **Selus Stone** *(before north door)*. In the churchyard are part of a wayside cross and a market cross bearing a Crucifixion.

★ **Cape Cornwall** – *1.5 miles from St Just, last 400yds on foot – 30min there and back*. The **view**★★ opens out as the path climbs to the "summit", distinctively marked by a ruined mine chimney. During the walk, even on a fine day, all may be momentarily obscured as a wisp of cloud tangles with the 230ft hillock. From the vantage-point by the stack may be seen the **Brisons Rocks**, Whitesand Bay, **Land's End** and the Longships Lighthouse, sometimes even the Scillies.

Not far to the northeast is the ruined, now legendary **Botallack Mine**, marked by two engine houses perched precariously on the cliff, a calciner and chimney (for recovering arsenic), extensive workings, ruins of processing works and the mine offices, now a National Trust information point.

Levant and Geevor Tin Mines ⊘ – *Northwest of Pendeen on B3306, 5 miles from Land's End*. **Levant**, one of Cornwall's major copper and tin mines, finally closed in 1930: it earned notoriety in 1919 when the beam on which miners were travelling up the shaft sheared off and plunged to the bottom killing 31 men. Today, painstakingly restored by the Trevithick Society in association with the National Trust, the oldest steam-driven beam engine in Cornwall (1840) is back in working order.

Prospecting at Wheal Carne and the Old North Levant mine began modestly in the early 20C when a group of St Just miners were forced to return to Cornwall by the war in South Africa. By the 1920s, wooden headgear had been constructed over the Victory Shaft workings.

Geevor was one of Cornwall's last working mines; it was closed in 1990 after the collapse of the tin market in 1984 made tin-mining in Cornwall unviable. A vertical shaft sited on the cliffs here gave access to workings over 2 000ft below sea level and when Levant was incorporated in the 1960s extended over 4sq miles including horizontal tunnels (drifts) and inclines beneath the ocean bed. All these tunnels are now flooded.

The **surface tour** visits the tin treatment plant where tin, copper, iron and arsenic were separated from the bedrock; the magnetic separator produced high (70% tin) and medium (25% tin) grade concentrates. Access to **underground workings** are possible in the adit levels.

A video provides background information on the working practices and conditions at the mine. In the small museum next door, working models, archive photographs, specimens of rock and mining artefacts are assembled. Guided tours are given by ex-miners with an intimate knowledge of the works and the processes involved: an intricate skeleton of coloured rods recreates in 3D the extent of the interrelated shafts radiating down and below the sea.

---

11 August 1999

The first complete eclipse of the sun since 1927 will reach totality at 11am on Monday 11 August 1999 and last approximately two minutes and six seconds. The central line of totality will pass through St Just to Falmouth (Cherbourg, Reims, Stuttgart, Munich, Bucharest...), hitting Geevor before any other land mass elsewhere. Thousands of fascinated spectators are expected to witness this rare phenomenon. Other events planned to coincide with the eclipse include the revival after two centuries of three medieval Passion plays including the *Passio Domini* written in Cornish in 1388.

Pendeen Lighthouse ⊘ –
Signposted from the road from St Just to St Ives (B3306) Since the automation of all lighthouses by Trinity House, Pendeen is now open for conducted tours of the light and engine house (complete with generators) that provides power for the largest fog signal in Britain. At low tide, it is possible to glimpse Trevose Light.

Morvah – The tiny village with a **church tower** which long served as a seamen's beacon is a place from which to make for the North Cornwall Coast Path (200yds) for a spectacular **view**★★ of the 300ft granite cliffs which drop vertically into the Atlantic.

Chun Castle – *From the farm at the end of the road, walk half a mile up the marked hill track; 45min*. The Iron Age stone hillfort, 100yds across, with gateway uprights and scattered stone walls, can only be seen before the bracken grows. A little to the west is a Neolithic chamber tomb topped by a massive capstone.

★ **Men-an-Tol** – *On the moor, to the right of the lane.* The Early Bronze Age stone, once known as the Devil's Eye, stands between two upright boulders, a 5ft disc with a large hole at the centre, through which, "to bracken" disease (rickets) and infertility, one had to crawl nine times against the sun.

★ **Lanyon Quoit** – The quoit of three upright stones supporting a massive capstone is immediately recognisable from the road *(climb the stile for a close view).* Dating from the Neolithic Age and therefore over 4 000 years old, quoits (also known as cromlechs or dolmens) were burial chambers inside barrows or mounds of earth and stones.

Zennor – Zennor sits half a mile inland, in a dip in the rock-strewn, windswept countryside. Its charming **Wayside Folk Museum** ⊘ accommodated in an old miller's house, mill and outbuildings, shows the evolution of implements from stone to iron used in a kitchen, by a wheelwright, a blacksmith, for quarrying, mining... Inside Zennor's 12C-13C granite **church★**, built on a 6C site, enlarged in the 15C and restored in the 19C, are a **tithe measure** now serving as a holy water stoup, two **fonts** of Hayle limestone and the legendary **mermaid** – a small 16C seductress on a bench-end-chair, neatly carved with floating hair, a tiny waist and a long scaly tail. Outside the church, note the 1737 sundial and three Cornish Crosses.

Chysauster

★ **Chysauster** ⊘ – *100yds from the road uphill across fields.* This, the best preserved **prehistoric Cornish village**, never fortified, inhabited probably from 100 BC to AD 250, consists of at least eight houses in two lines of four, built below the crest across a hillside. The roughly circular houses are constructed of stone – the massive thick walls are up to 6ft high – with entrance passages to inner courtyards. Each round or oval house, complete with hearth stone, was thatched – stone post supports being visible. A stream flowed from the hilltop to the marsh below where thatching reeds grew. A model of the agrarian community is displayed in the Royal Cornwall Museum in Truro. Off to one side is a *fougou (see Carn Euny, above).*

The **view** extends over towards Penzance and Mount's Bay.

If continuing on to ST IVES, *turn to the relevant chapter.*

PENZANCE★

Cornwall – Population 20 284
Michelin Atlas p 2 or Map 403 – D 33

Penzance with its wonderful **outlook★★★** on Mount's Bay and St Michael's Mount, has been a holiday resort since the arrival of the Great Western Railway. Progress in communications brought about each successive stage in the town's development: from mineral and passenger port to spring vegetable and flower despatch point, fish market within easy reach by train of London and the Midlands, and now holiday resort accessible by train, coach, car, aeroplane; Penzance Heliport also provides regular services to the Isles of Scilly (weather permitting).

The town, which suffered badly in the Spanish raid of 1595, extends for a couple of miles in each direction around the bay. Within the overall area it divides into three distinct districts: the Harbour and Quay, east of the Battery Rocks; the town centre located around Market Jew and Chapel Streets; and the Western Promenade.

Harbour – The MV **Scillonian III** ⊘, the boat to the Isles of Scilly, berths daily throughout the summer in the harbour which is crowded with pleasure craft, small cargo vessels, fishing boats and the pilot's launch.

★ **National Lighthouse Centre** ⊘ – *Wharf Road.* The museum is arranged in the old Trinity House buoy store and centres on a fascinating assortment of lighthouse artefacts, including the beautiful and ingenious lights themselves and a reconstructed lighthouse room with original curved furniture. The collection traces the development from the early days of lighted chandeliers through cut-glass prisms to a massive optic rotating in a bath of mercury. Displays of ship's lights and fog horns, model ships and the reconstruction of a room inside a lighthouse are among the exhibits. A short video tells of the dramatic construction of the surprisingly decorative Eddystone lighthouse.

Quay – At the end of the quay, on the corner between the dock and the Battery Rocks, behind the typical massive Cornish sea wall and the large, turn-of-the-century open-air swimming pool, stands the **Barbican**, a mid-18C granite "cellar" or fish store now housing a craft centre *(upstairs)* and aquarium.
Behind the quay, a maze of alleys leads back to the main streets.

Town centre – The heart of the town is 18C-19C, older buildings having perished in the Spanish raid of 1595.
Market Jew Street rises from the station and harbour to a statue of **Humphry Davy** (1778-1829), the chemist responsible for isolating the elements sodium, potassium, calcium and magnesium, pioneer in the use of nitrous oxide before the invention of anaesthetic, physicist, inventor of the miner's safety lamp. The distinct granite building (1837) with a green copper dome is known as the **Market House**.

Cornwall Geology Museum ⊘ – *West wing of St John's Hall.* The Royal Geological Society of Cornwall was founded in 1814, making it the second oldest, by a number of important scientists associated with the mining industry. During its long history, the Society accumulated an ever more extensive collection of minerals and samples from Cornwall; as members of the Society travelled abroad, reference material continued to be added. Pride of place goes to the earliest surviving geological map of Britain drawn by William Smith, a land surveyor employed by large land-owners interested in the prospect of finding coal; printed in Italy (1815), the map charts the distribution of granite, coal, chalk and limestone.
The Earth Science exhibition comprises a video about the formation of the earth; the display of the extensive collection of minerals complete with identification and provenance (in glass cases and drawers below); a section about china clay mining; the collection of fossils found by a former coast-guard, Charles William Peach (1800-84).

★ **Penlee House Gallery and Museum** ⊘ – *Penlee House, west of the Market House.* The fine Victorian house, built in 1865, has recently been refurbished to provide West Cornwall with a centre for art and heritage that is equipped with multi-media technology and inter-active computers. The ground floor spaciously displays changing selections from the museum's fine collection of art from 1750 to the present day, including a premier collection of works by the **Newlyn School**. Temporary shows may comprise works by Richard Pentreath (fl 1844-61) and Henry Martin (fl 1870-1894); Walter Langley, Stanhope and Elizabeth Forbes, Harris, Todd, Garstin, Benjamin A Bateman, Percy Craft and examples of contemporary copper and enamel by the Newlyn Industrial Class; block-printed textiles designed by Alec Walker from the 1920s.

Breadwinners by Walter Langley

Upstairs, the history of the area is presented in a gallery dedicated to **Human History**. This includes a range of artefacts that span the region's evolution from its megalithic culture (tools and pottery) whose tombs and monuments still litter the Penwith peninsula, to the age when fishing and mining were the people's mainstay, until the 20C when tourism is generating new forms of employment and industry.

★ **Chapel Street** – The street cuts down from the side of the Market Hall to a goose's foot of four lanes leading to the Battery Rocks, the Quay, the Dock and the Promenade; its distinctive character includes something of both the old harbour and the spacious 18C-19C days. Among notable landmarks is the amazingly decorated **Egyptian House** from *c*1835, the sole survivor of several designed in the style at the time.

The **Union Hotel**, refronted in 1810, was built twenty years before as the Town Assembly Rooms; from the minstrels' gallery in the ballroom (now the dining room), the news was first announced in England of the victory at Trafalgar and the death of Nelson. The master of a Penzance fishing boat crossed the course of HMS *Pickle* as she was making for Falmouth with Collingwood's despatch, heard the news and broke it to the mayor before their lordships received it in London.

In **Abbey Street**, a 17C group of buildings, including no 44 and **Abbey House**, is said to have been associated with St Michael's Mount when it was a priory. Probably the oldest building in the town is the 13C inn, the **Turk's Head**, which was refronted after the Spanish raid of 1595.

The **Admiral Benbow** long served smugglers in times past as a regular meeting place: its name commemorates an incident during a raid, when the second in command of an 18C band, the Benbow Brandy Men, clambered on the roof and fired his pistols to create a diversion; the revenue men rushed out and shot him down but the inn and the band were saved and he recovered, to be raffishly commemorated in the figure lying along the roof ridge. The 15C-16C inn has been restored with ships' timbers and decorated with vividly coloured coats of arms, figureheads and the gilded carving of a cherub's head from the *Colossus*, the man o' war from Nelson's fleet wrecked off the Isles of Scilly when bringing back Sir William Hamilton's collection from Sicily in 1798.

At no 19 is the local **Maritime Museum** ⊙, which displays shipwrights' tools, sailor-made models and half-models, hanging church ships, a model of a dockyard with two wooden-walled battleships under construction, a full size, walk through section of a four-decker, 95-gun, man o' war of *c*1750... There are cannon, an ancient handgun and telescope, flintlock pistols, silver and pewter forks and spoons, keepsakes and medicine chests, treasure, objects from the *Association* which, with three other men o' war, *Romney*, *Eagle* and *Firebrand*, foundered in October 1707 off the Isles of Scilly.

Western Promenade – The wide promenade and the Queen's Hotel, built in 1861, epitomise the confidence Penzance so rightly had that it would become a prime resort. Half a mile long and extended by the road to Newlyn, it affords a **view**★★★ of St Michael's Mount and the headlands round to the Lizard.

Behind the wide road, inland at the town end, the network of short streets includes **Regent Terrace**, **Voundervour Lane** and **Regent Square**, lined by small, 18C-19C town houses. Further inland, the streets lead to **Morrab Gardens**, the public gardens planted with tropical species and graced with a 19C bandstand.

EXCURSION

★★ **Trengwainton Garden** ⊙ *2 miles northwest of Penzance.*

The garden lies along the half mile drive to the house which is covered in wistaria and the New Zealand scarlet lobster claw plant. Beyond is a second garden of island beds of azaleas and rhododendrons, from which there is a **view**★★ of Mount's Bay.

An early owner, Sir Rose Price, who was a great tree planter, built the walled gardens to the right of the drive with beds banked up to face the sun, to produce early fruit and vegetables.

In the early 20C, with the owners of Trewithen and Hidcote in Gloucestershire, Sir Edward Bolitho financed Kingdon Ward's plant collecting expeditions of 1927-28 to bring back specimens from Burma, Assam and China from which the rhododendron and azalea collections have since been built up and hybridised. All the important and unusual plantings are fully labelled for easy identification.

Garden – A mass of rhododendron bushes, with blooms ranging from magenta to pale yellow to pure white, line the drive; overtopping them are the first of many tree ferns from Australia.

Two paths branch off the drive. The left-hand one makes for a stream and glades of rhododendrons beneath the trees, which include a maidenhair and the beautiful white ladies' handkerchief or *Davidia involucrata*. The right-hand path enters the series of five walled gardens, now particularly rich in tender magnolias – pink flushed, dark purple, narrow white, saucer-large and fragrant – besides a host of other flowering trees such as a Tasmanian cider gum, the small white flowered New Zealand tea, the Canary bird, the scarlet lobster claw, the passion flower, acacias, rhododendrons, camellias, fuchsias...

Beside the drive, the gurgling stream garden includes primulas, astilbes and wax-white arum lilies in front of a magnolia stellata, a tulip tree...

For St Michael's Mount and Marazion (5 miles east by A30, A394) see ST MICHAEL'S MOUNT; *for Newlyn and Land's End (10 miles west by A30) see* PENWITH.

PLYMOUTH★

Devon – Population 243 373
Michelin Atlas p 3 or Map 403 – H 32

The name Plymouth conjures up many famous names and events: the Hoe, Drake, Hawkins, Frobisher, Raleigh, Cooke, the Pilgrim Fathers, the Sound and, since the early 18C when William III laid down Devonport Dockyard, Royal Naval ships of the line.

The city developed from the amalgamation of three towns: Sutton, at the mouth of the Plym, Dock (renamed Devonport) on the Hamoaze and Stonehouse on the coast in between. In earlier times Sutton was "a mene thing, an inhabitation of fishars" (Leland) but trade with France under the Plantagenets and worldwide under the Tudors, particularly Elizabeth I, brought prosperity, so that for a time Plymouth was the fourth largest town in England after London, Bristol and York. In the early part of the 20C, various international liners bound for Europe from the USA called at Plymouth, landing many passengers eager to continue their onward journeys before the ships docked at Southampton. Rivalry between the Great Western and the London and South Western services was partially resolved by allocating mail to the GWR and passengers to the LSWR. Between 1900-05 sleeping-cars were built to cater for ocean liner passengers delayed by fog or bad weather; between the two World Wars, GWR further improved their service with the superbly attired Ocean Specials in their finest chocolate and cream livery, this time to attract eastbound Cunard and White Star passengers sailing to New York. Today, Plymouth, which has a spacious, airy feel to it, is arranged in three distinct areas: the Hoe and its environs, adorned with the splendour of Victorian and Edwardian buildings; the older, bustling Barbican region by the harbour with its fish market and narrow streets; the modern commercial centre, rebuilt after the Second World War, providing wide, shop-lined avenues.

Plymouth Hoe – The hoe (the word meant hill) evokes the vision of Drake looking out to sea across the Sound in 1588 towards the approaching Armada and stooping to finish his game of bowls while he waited for the tide to turn so that

Plymouth Hoe

his ships could leave harbour. Visitors still gaze out over the water, spotting the naval vessels, the pilot cutters, the daily ferries to Roscoff, the twice-weekly ships to Spain from Millbay Docks, the fishing and pleasure boats leaving or returning to their moorings.

The east side of the headland is occupied by the Royal Citadel overlooking the Barbican and across the mouth of Sutton Harbour to **Mount Batten**, now an RAF weather, rescue and marine craft repair station; facing The Sound are Millbay Docks (continental ferries); on the west side are Cremyll and Torpoint ferries, the Royal Naval Base in Devonport and the Tamar bridges: Brunel's Royal Albert Bridge and the impressive suspension bridge.

3 Elliot Terrace (Z G) – The house was the home of Lord and Lady Astor who were both MPs for Plymouth, one after the other: Waldorf between 1910 and 1919, Nancy until 1945.

Monuments – The bronze **Drake Statue (Z A)** by Boehm was erected in the 19C, west of centre, on the inland side of the wide east-west Promenade. The **Armada Memorial (Z B)** stands as a pendant on the east side of the Hoe. The pillar **Naval War Memorial (Z D)**, surrounded by rose gardens, bears the names of 22 443 men. The anchor in Anchor Way is from the last Ark Royal.

The **Royal Air Force Memorial**, a bronze figure of a pilot, pays tribute to the heroism of over 2 000 men of the Commonwealth and Allied air forces.

Smeaton's Tower ⊙ **(Z)** – The white and red painted lighthouse replaced a beacon obelisk when it was re-erected on the Hoe in 1884 after its 123 storm-battered years on the Eddystone Rocks (*see* INTRODUCTION: Lighthouses).

Climb up the steps and ladders (*93 steps*) in the ever narrowing cylinder – note how the two bunks are fitted round the walls – to the gallery and splendid **view★★**.

★ **Plymouth Dome** ⊙ **(Z)** – The large, modern centre tells the rich history of the city through tableaux, surprising guides in period costume and audio-visual shows, abetted by high technology (computers, radar). It follows the glory days of the Elizabethan era, through the Age of Piracy and the troubles of the Civil War to the town's rebirth as a seaside resort in the 19C and the devastation of the Blitz.

Royal Citadel ⊙ **(Z)** – The Royal Citadel, now garrisoned by the Royal Artillery, was built in the reign of Charles II between 1666 and 1671 to incorporate the Elizabethan fort, begun in 1590 by Sir Francis Drake but never completed, designed to protect Plymouth from sea-borne attack. The cannon on the 17C fort could be trained not only on enemy ships entering the Sound, at that time the Dutch, but also on the town, since Plymouth had supported the Parliamentarian cause during the Civil War.

The **rampart** walls, which have a circumference of about three quarters of a mile and present a sheer face of 60ft in places (now used as a commando scaling exercise) command **views★★** of the Barbican, the Sound and the mouth of the Tamar.

The **main gate** of Portland stone (1670) originally contained a bust of Charles II in the niche to complement the royal arms and inscription. It was, however, considered politic to remove the head and substitute four cannon balls when the citadel was surrendered personally to William III in 1688. Inside, most of the buildings have been subject to 19C and 20C alterations.

Chapel of St Katherine ⊙ – The small chapel was rebuilt with walls 2ft 9in thick in 1688 and enlarged to twice its size in the 19C. The frescoes on the east wall were painted by an NCO in the Royal Engineers who died in the First World War.

Barbican – Old, historic Plymouth survives in the Barbican, an area extending over a quarter of a mile inland from the harbourside. The district combines modern interests and amenities – shops, restaurants, ships' chandlers, pubs, craft studios – with medieval houses, Jacobean doorways, cobbled alleys, the harbour...

Begin at the waterfront.

Mayflower Stone (Z) – *West Pier*. The pier, adorned with stones and plaques, was the embarkation and alighting point for many famous voyages, including the sailing of the **Pilgrim Fathers** on 6 September 1620 in their 90ft ship, *The Mayflower* (17C pavement stone); the *Tory* sailing to colonise **New Zealand** in May 1839; the *Sea Venture* voyaging to **Bermuda** in 1609; the return of the **Tolpuddle Martyrs** in 1838; the safe arrival of the American seaplane, *NC4*, on completion of the first **Transatlantic Flight** in 1919; the sailing of Sir Humphrey Gilbert to Newfoundland in 1583.

On the far side of the road (*left, high on the wall by the flight of steps*) a plaque commemorates "10 Squadron **Royal Australian Air Force** stationed at Mt Batten 1939-45".

Turn north.

Island House (Z K) – The late 16C house (restored) is where the **Pilgrim Fathers** (the names are listed on a board on the wall) may have spent their last night before setting sail.

Turn right behind the house into New Street.

Elizabethan House ⓥ (**Z**) – *32 New Street.* The timber-framed and limestone house and its neighbour *(opposite),* distinguished by **windows** which extend across the full width of the fronts on the ground and first floors, were built in the late 16C as part of a development of thirty houses for small merchants and ships' captains, prosperous from the trade in wine, Newfoundland cod, tobacco and sugar and in booty captured at sea.

Inside, the house remains largely unadulterated: there is no electricity, no lights or fittings, just exposed **beams** and large **fireplaces**. The layout of the rooms is familiar, however, with kitchen and "living" area at ground level, bedrooms upstairs. The rooms are sparsely furnished with beautiful pieces of stout 16C-17C **oak furniture**, carved and patinaed with age – note the snug box bed on the top floor – and give an idea of the comforts of the time for a modestly wealthy household.

Note the **pole staircase** round a ship's mast; the worn wooden treads were mended by putting another on top until there were as many as four boards to a tread.

Elizabethan Gardens ⓥ – *Further up New Street, left and down a narrow passage between houses.* Aspects of a typical period garden of a ship's captain's house have been recreated: herbs and a knot garden.

Return to New Street and take the first street opposite through to Southside Street.

PLYMOUTH

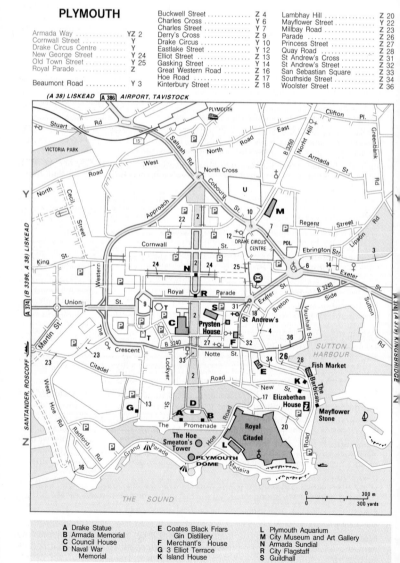

A Drake Statue
B Armada Memorial
C Council House
D Naval War Memorial
E Coates Black Friars Gin Distillery
F Merchant's House
G 3 Elliot Terrace
K Island House
L Plymouth Aquarium
M City Museum and Art Gallery
N Armada Sundial
R City Flagstaff
S Guildhall

Coates Black Friars Gin Distillery ⓒ (z **E**) – A low, wide granite doorway leads into a chamber containing the onion shaped, glass lined, steel vats in which today's Plymouth gin is prepared – a secret process by which 100% raw barley spirit produced in Scotland is transformed by distillation, flavouring and dilution with pure Dartmoor water.

The **Refectory Room** (now a restaurant) dates from 1425 when a Dominican (black friars) monastery stood on the site – note the plaque on the façade, above the low stone archway. Enter the main gateway to peer through the glass partition up at the **roof** built on arch braces and resembling an upturned keel, and to see prints of old Plymouth.

Cut through one of the "opes" on the opposite side of the street.

Parade (z **26**) – The quayside, lined by houses, warehouses and inns, takes its name from the days when the Royal Marines, established in Plymouth by the Board of Admiralty in 1755, used to parade on the cobbled pavement. Note the imposing Custom House.

City Centre – Following the devastation of the Second World War, much of the city was rebuilt following designs by Sir Patrick Abercrombie (1879-1957), a pioneer of post-war urban planning. The result is wide streets and pedestrian areas, enlivened with sculptures and carvings (note the figure of Drake on the corner of Armada Way and Notte Street, for instance).

The **Civic Centre** (1961) in Royal Parade has been described as "a disturbingly prominent lopsided imposition" but blends into the skyline if seen from the east: a deliberate modern statement in the otherwise rather indifferent post-war buildings. The other successful 20C civic designs include the **Magistrates Court** which is sandwiched among some of the oldest houses in Plymouth and the polygonal **Theatre Royal** (1977-82) with its especially spacious interior.

Council House ⓒ (z **C**) – Inside, **engraved glass panels** adorn the doors and the staircase by John Hulton. It is here that the **corporation plate** is housed.

City Flagstaff (z **R**) – The mast at the juncture of Armada Way and Royal Parade is mounted on a replica of Drake's drum (the original is in Buckland Abbey).

Armada Sundial (y **N**) – The impressive monument stands proudly at the crossing of Armada Way and New George Street.

Guildhall ⓒ (z **S**) – The building with a campanile-style tower dates from 1873, the last in a line going back to the 15C; on the Hoe side the city's coat of arms is visible, transferred from the 17C poorhouse.

In St Catherine Street stands the oldest **Ashkenazi synagogue** in England (1762): its unassuming exterior shielding a well-preserved 18C interior, fine brass candlesticks.

St Andrew's ⓒ (z) – *Royal Parade.* The church, which was founded in 1050, was rebuilt in the 15C in the Perpendicular style. In 1941 a fire bomb exploded in the church; only the outer walls, fluted granite piers, chancel arch and tower (136ft) survived. The church was rebuilt and reconsecrated in 1957.

The six distinctive windows were designed by **John Piper** (1904-92) in the 1950s. The tower window depicts the instruments of the Passion; note how the ladder, the lance and the reed are arranged to form St Andrew's Cross. The vivid colours of the glass contrast with the patina of the floor, surfaced in Delabole slate. Below each window is a complementary altar.

On a window ledge *(first window west of the south door)* is the so-called **Drake crest scratching** which shows the *Golden Hinde* with a cord from her bow partly encircling a globe; the rough engraving is believed to have been made by a mason working in the church at the time of Drake's return on 3 November 1580 from his circumnavigation of the world.

Among the **memorials** are a 12C-13C Purbeck marble effigy and a tablet to **Frobisher** and **Drake** *(north transept)* and a tablet to William Cookworthy *(south wall; see below)*. Note the royal arms of Charles I, George III and George IV.

Door of Unity – The door facing the church commemorates two US naval officers killed in action in 1813 and buried in St Andrew's churchyard.

Prysten House ⓒ (z) – The stone-built three storeyed house arranged round an inner courtyard, dates from 1490 and as such is thought to be the oldest house in Plymouth; it may have lodged Augustinian canons from Plympton Priory who came to officiate at St Andrew's. The courtyard probably served as a courtroom for cases tried before the prior, who held civil as well as ecclesiastical authority in the town.

Note the **window frames** and stone mullions, stone **fireplaces** and the beams – smoke-blackened from the time when, after the Dissolution, the house was briefly used for bacon-curing.

Merchant's House Museum ⓒ (z **F**) – *33 St Andrew's Street.* The Museum of Old Plymouth is accommodated in the 16C Merchant's House. The three-storey timber building has limestone walls and jettied upper floors supported on stone corbels; the windows extend almost the full width and height of the front.

The **pole staircase** is built round a shaft (35ft). Each floor consisted of a principal front room and a back room; there were small bedrooms on the upper floors. Although built in the 16C the house was probably given much of its present style in the 17C when it was bought by William Parker, mayor of Plymouth in 1601-02. Parker was a sea-captain, merchant and typical adventurer and privateer, who had amassed enough gold to buy and improve the house through buccaneering on the Spanish Main and possibly also as master of the victualling ship to Drake's fleet at the time of the Armada.

Among the exhibits is the reconstruction of one of Plymouth's old pharmacies.

★ **City Museum and Art Gallery** ⊘ (Y M) – *Drake Circus*. The spacious Victorian building displays a mere fraction of its rich and splendid collections relating to the city's **maritime history** in terms of its mercantile associations and naval dockyard (ship models, marine paintings, royal charters, documents, naval memorabilia, navigation equipment), local industries, regional natural history and contemporary arts scene.

On permanent display upstairs is a selection from the **Cottonian Collection** which comprises paintings, old master drawings, prints and engravings (Leonardo, Dürer, Raphael, Michelangelo, Rembrandt, Rubens), books, manuscripts furniture and various *objets d'art* accumulated by several generations of collectors: notable pieces include those amassed by the connoisseur Charles Rogers (1711-84) who was Head of the Certificate Office of the Customs House in London, a post which allowed him to meet the likes of Horace Walpole, Charles Townley, Sir Joshua Reynolds, Paul Sandby and Angelica Kauffmann. Particularly strong representations of **Reynolds**, who was born in Plympton St Maurice. Other fine art is displayed from reserve collections in rotating temporary exhibitions (Burne-Jones, Girardet, Newlyn School – Garstin, Harvey, Elizabeth and Stanhope Forbes, Tuke – *see* INTRODUCTION: Painting).

Plymouth became the home of **William Cookworthy**, discoverer of the Cornish kaolin which made the production of **hard paste porcelain** a reality in this country from 1768: an excellent display relates how the new material rapidly developed, how it related to the highly-prized contemporary Chinese wares that were being imported in large quantities, how patterns were moulded to shapes prevalent in domestic silverware (tea, coffee and chocolate pots) or on decorative pieces being made by the Continental factories of Sèvres and Meissen, and how English marks evolved to denote particular styles and types of objects typical of each factory. A separate series of glass cabinets enclose pieces of highly collectable 19C-20C decorative studio pottery.

Sir Joshua Reynolds (1723-92)

Undoubtedly, Reynolds was the most important English painter of the 18C. Not only was he accomplished, intelligent and versatile as a painter of Society portraits, he compounded a body of ideas on art, which he delivered through a series of 15 *Discourses on Art* (1769-90), against which critics, commentators and artists could measure their opinions for generations to come. As the founding President of the **Royal Academy**, Reynolds combined the philosophical ideals of the Age of Reason with the aesthetics and sensitivity of the emerging Romantic Movement to establish a truly English School of painting. He confirmed portraiture, appreciated by the growing ranks of military leaders, successful businessmen, and leading intellectuals (like Dr Johnson, Horace Walpole) as the most highly regarded art-form after History painting; landscape and sporting pictures, preferred by the country gentry, he respected as a medium worthy of merit in their own right.

Reynolds was the son of a Devon clergyman-schoolmaster; he served his apprenticeship in London (1740-43) under the fashionable portraitist **Thomas Hudson**, before travelling to Italy to assimilate the examples of Renaissance and Baroque art, notably in Rome. There he came to appreciate the value of History painting whereby the artist must study Nature and then improve on it so as to formulate an expression of drama and poignancy in the grand style. Despite his theories, Reynolds' most enduring work are his portraits, a genre at which he excelled. As a person, he was astute enough to appreciate the powerful image that portraiture might project for his patron: by representing his sitters in a pose borrowed from Classical sculpture (like the Apollo Belvedere), and surrounding him with allegorical attributes in the manner of Rubens and Van Dyck, Reynolds could impart some of the spirit of History painting in the grand manner to his portraits. His success as an artist largely rested in his resourceful ability to vary gesture, texture and detail so as to best flatter his sitter, and capture the spirit of individuality of each personality.

Plymouth Aquarium ⊘ (Z L) – *Madeira Road.* The fish, eels and flatfish and mackerel, the sea anemones, starfish, dog-fish, crabs and other crustacea swimming in the sea-water tanks around the gallery are almost all from local waters. The 50 kinds of fish and many hundred invertebrates are there primarily, in fact, for observation by the **Marine Biological Association of the UK** as part of their research on increasing the supply of food from the sea.

Devonport, Stonehouse, Keyham – The **Royal Naval Base** was developed as a dockyard and arsenal in the late 17C and extended to meet the changing needs of the Board of Ordnance, Admiralty and ever larger warships. Although badly hit in 1941, considerable numbers of buildings range from the 18C (slipway, hemphouse and roperies; avant-garde RN Hospital), 19C (Royal William Yard, 1825-33) and 20C (Frigate Complex, 1971-80, with fleet maintenance base and submarine refit complex). In 1824 the name was changed from Dock to Devonport and in 1914 the town was merged with Plymouth.
The memorial that crowns **Mount Wise** is to **Scott of the Antarctic.**

Cremyll Ferry – The old Cremyll Ferry was a rich source of revenue.

Boat Trips ⊘

Dockyards and Warships – *1 hour.* From Phoenix Wharf past the Mayflower Steps round under the Hoe to Devonport Docks on the Tamar.

River Yealm – *2 hours.* From Phoenix Wharf past the Breakwater at the entrance to the Sound and east along the coast to Newton Ferrers at the mouth of the Yealm.

River Tamar – *4-5 hours; optional return by train from Calstock.*
From Phoenix Wharf up the Tamar to Calstock, Morwellham and Weir Head (Gunnislake). *See Tamar River.*

EXCURSION

Crownhill Fort ⊘ *North of Plymouth, beyond the A38 Cornwall to Exeter road, signposted left off the A386 to Tavistock.*

The stone complex (1868-72) was built as the largest of ten land defences around Plymouth endorsed by the then Prime Minister Lord Palmerston in 1859 (history and purpose explained inside). Its main interest is its completeness having served the army from its completion until sold to The Landmark Trust in 1987. During World War I the fort operated as a centre for recruitment and a transit depot for troops destined for the Turkish and African fronts; during World War II it was deployed as an anti-aircraft battery, then as a demobilisation depot. In 1982 it was used to rally troops and assemble equipment for action in the defence of the Falkland Islands.
The 1949 Ordnance Survey pillar mark 1 on top of the Haxo of No 16 gun position is one of the original points used for the Plymouth Baseline in the triangulation of the United Kingdom.

The complex – *1.5 hours.* Within the 16-acre site there are four levels of underground tunnels, hidden gun towers, secret passageways, ammunition stores and 32 gun emplacements furnished occasionally with cannon or breech loading guns. Above ground, the grass-covered ramparts provide extensive **views** over the surrounding landscape to Dartmoor, the open parade ground and stone-built barracks. A walk along the Covered Way, which encircles the site, provides an understanding of how the 30ft ditch, excavated from rock, assured the fort's impregnability and of the complex's sophisticated design.
Individual rooms such as the Guard Room at the entrance, house displays of uniforms, weaponry and other associated regimental paraphernalia related to life in the fort from its completion and occupation by the Royal Engineers.

★★ Buckland Abbey *9 miles north on A386 to Yelverton.*

Yelverton Paperweight Centre ⊘ – *200yds along a loop road just off the roundabout.* A dazzling array of *c*800 paperweights, ranging from deep, resonant colours to misty pastel, reveal the rich variety of designs – marbled, floral, swirling – made in the 19C and 20C by English, Scottish, French, German and Chinese craftsmen.

★★ **Buckland Abbey** ⊘ – *2 miles from Yelverton; signposted from Crapstone. 1 hour.* Buckland was founded in 1278, the last Cistercian monastery built in England and Wales, by the widowed Countess of Devon who endowed it with a considerable estate. At the Dissolution the abbot and twelve remaining monks were expelled and the property was sold to Sir Richard Grenville, Marshal of Calais.

First he, then his son Roger who later perished when the *Mary Rose* capsized off Portsmouth, set about converting the buildings; however the most radical transformation was completed by the next heir, the second Richard Grenville, in 1576. Although knighted in 1577, royal endorsement of his intended privateering in the South Seas continued to elude the ambitious naval commander (who was to die off the Azores aboard the *Revenge* in 1591); he eventually may have been forced by debt to mortgage, then sell the abbey through nominees, for £3 400 to his cousin Sir Francis Drake in 1581. At that time, Drake was forty; he had sailed to West Africa and the Spanish Main, and in 1577-80, having secured the queen's financial backing, had circumnavigated the globe. He was famous, newly knighted and rich: the house was intended to provide a suitable setting should he retire from the sea – but of course he didn't. In the next few years he made expeditions to Vigo (1585) and Cadiz (1587), where he "singed the King of Spain's beard", captured a Spanish vessel off the Azores with cargo worth £114 000 and confronted the Armada.

The property subsequently passed through the generations. The garden is largely 20C; the herb garden, it has been suggested, was established following a visit to Buckland from Vita Sackville-West.

Great Barn – The barn, buttressed and gabled, dates back to the 14C, built to store the dues from the surrounding woodland, moorland, mills and fisheries paid by the neighbouring manors (Buckland, Bickleigh, Walkhampton, Cullompton), and corn tithes from their churches. Its dimensions reflect the huge prosperity enjoyed by the Cistercians at that time, largely as a result of their promotion of good husbandry and efficient working practices. By the west porch stand a pair of millstones, while at the north end sits an 18C cider press.

Abbey – The house is approached from the south; to the left is Grenville's kitchen wing which incorporates the retaining arches of the chapels arranged along the east wall of the former abbey's south transept. Note, above the entrance, the carved keystone head which may be a portrait of the founder, Amicia, Dowager Countess of Devon. Inside, the over-riding impression is of a Georgian family house: a panelled corridor leads to the main staircase, hung with topographical prints and, at the top, a formal portrait of John Carteret, 2nd Earl Granville in his garter robes (1744). The **Four Lives Gallery**, which extends the length of the former abbey nave, outlines four phases in the history of the abbey from 1278 to 1988. Displays show how the medieval abbey was transformed into a Tudor mansion, a Georgian home and finally, restored after a devastating fire (1938), it came to be assigned to the National Trust (1946) and used by Plymouth City Council as a branch of the City Museum and Art Gallery. Note the Drake coat of arms set into the plaster overmantel in the north crossing arch, bearing his motto which in translation reads "Great achievements from small beginnings".

The south wing was added in the 1790s to accommodate a practical entrance; a three-light window on the stairs contains four panels of glass engraved by Simon Whistler to commemorate the 400th anniversary of Drake's defeat of the Spanish Armada.

The **Drake Gallery**, which dominates the first floor, was added in the 1570s. It presently houses an exhibition on the life of Sir Francis Drake: this includes several **portraits**, notably of Queen Elizabeth I, Sir Francis Drake, and Lady Drake – his second wife Elizabeth Sydenham of Combe Sydenham, *see* EXMOOR – wearing the Drake Jewel which incorporates the portrait miniature of Queen Elizabeth I by Nicholas Hilliard, given to Drake by the queen herself; two 16C Royal Standards flown when the queen knighted Drake at Deptford in 1581 and two 16C regimental banners used by Drake's personal band of soldiers; the **Drake Cup** engraved with a version of Mercator's world map of 1587; the letters of patent bearing the royal seal endorsing plans for the Cadiz raid; the Armada Medals – the first medals to be struck in England in celebration of a historical event; and, a late 16C side drum, possibly the oldest surviving in Europe, known as **Drake's Drum**.

The panelled **Drake Chamber** is furnished with a series of 16C-17C portraits (notably Marcus Gheeraerts the Younger's painting of *Sir Henry Palmer*); the furniture, English and Continental is of the same period. The west window provides a fine view out over the Tavy valley.

At the opposite end of the Drake Gallery is the **Georgian Room** fashioned in a completely different taste: dignified portraits by John Opie, James Northcote are hung alongside marine pictures by Nicholas Pocock and Thomas Butterworth; the dining room furniture is 18C-19C and reflects the age of Chippendale and Sheraton. Further contemporary family possessions are displayed in the Georgian corridor. The **Pym Gallery** is dedicated to the four murals commissioned by Lord and Lady Astor for the Festival of Britain celebrations of 1951 and to the legends associated with Drake. The **Great Hall**, located at the heart of the old abbey, below the tower, is paved in pink and white (possibly Dutch) tiles and lined with oak panelling relieved by fluted pilasters. A delicate frieze of holly and boxwood inlay is punctuated by a series of animal masks and figures. The room's most striking feature, however, is the fine plasterwork, much of which is original. The moulded ceiling is further ornamented with pendants; an allegorical scene at the west end alludes to Grenville's retirement from a military career, while a second frieze along the east wall is more straightforwardly decorative. Unlike these, the shields and personifications of the four cardinal virtues ornamenting the overmantel seem at one time to have been coloured. The furniture is predominantly 16C-17C. The **Chapel**, initially recreated in 1917 on the site of the abbey church high altar, includes several empty graves; the three painted panels are attributed to Cornelis Engelbrechtsz (1468-1533), a follower of Quentin Matsys.

The kitchen, added in the 17C, has brick charcoal ovens of a type that was invented in France. It is equipped with a broad range of utensils from a bygone age.

Sparkwell *9 miles east on Plymouth-Cornwood by-road.*

Dartmoor Wild Life Park ⓥ – The collection, in large paddocks, aviaries and shelters on the edge of Dartmoor, ranges from timber-wolves, lions and tigers, to chickens, from monkeys to owls and red deer.

★★ Saltram House ⓥ
3.5 miles east of Plymouth, just south of A38, before Plympton.

"The place is so gay, so riant, so comfortable and so everything that it ought to be" wrote the bride of 1809 of her new home. The house today looks much as it did then; however, as the curators continue to research so as to restore objects to their original positions, pictures, furniture and bibelots may be moved from where they are listed below.

In 1712, when Saltram House was purchased by the local Parker family, it was a Tudor mansion. In 1743 when John Parker inherited it his wife, **Lady Catherine Parker**, "a proud and wilful woman", set about aggrandising it. The extensions were largely conceived in the Neo-Classical style, with the exception of the Rococo interior plasterwork. Lady Catherine died in 1758.

In 1768 the house passed to her son, John Parker II, who was an MP and man about town. He was a lifelong friend of **Joshua Reynolds**, who was by then President of the Royal Academy. At Westminster he became acquainted with Lord Shelburne, statesman, patron of the arts and owner of Bowood House *(see LACOCK)* who introduced him to the architect **Robert Adam**, who was working with **Thomas Chippendale**, the cabinet maker. Between 1768 and 1772 and again from 1779 to 1782, following a fire, Adam, Chippendale, Reynolds and Angelica Kauffmann all worked at Saltram.

Since the 18C there have been only two major alterations made in 1818 and 1820, by the local architect, John Foulston. The library was extended by the addition of the music room; the entrance front was remodelled by the addition of a balustraded porch with Doric columns and the addition to the pediment of the coat of arms (1812) of John Parker III, and coronet (added in 1816) when newly invested with the title Earl of Morley.

Porcelain and china were bought in the fashion of the day but not "collected", the pictures, almost all family portraits, are closely hung as in a family album. The parkland and gardens surrounding the house include an octagonal summer-house, an orangery (now used for exhibitions of contemporary fine craftwork), a temple and 18C stables.

House – *1 hour.* Dominant in the **Entrance Hall** decorated with plasterwork from the 1740s and a great painted limestone fireplace are the portraits of *Lady Catherine Parker* and *John Parker II, Lord Boringdon* (by Thomas Hudson). Note also the serpentine side-tables and Chinese-style Dutch delftware, the Louis XIV Boulle clock on its original bracket.

In the **Morning Room**, hung with Genoa silk velvet, are family portraits painted by Reynolds of *John Parker II, Lord Boringdon*, leaning against a gate, *Theresa Robinson, Lady Boringdon* – with her son, John Parker III the future Lord Morley, and the boy with his sister.

The mahogany cabinets on stands are Chippendale, the black basalt vases are Wedgwood (*c*1780), the Chinese-style cabinet is English.

The deep red and gold **Velvet Drawing Room** with its original stucco ceiling is furnished with Adam giltwood side-tables and pier glasses. The Rococo giltwood mirror is mid-18C.

The **Saloon**, a double cube of 50 x 25 x 25ft, was designed almost entirely by Adam, from the ceiling to the complementary carpet (£126), the giltwood furniture upholstered in pale blue silk damask like the walls, the pier glasses, the *torchères* which support ormolu-mounted tortoise-shell and blue-john "candle vases" by Matthew Boulton; the chandeliers are 19C; the portrait of *Lady Boringdon* is by Reynolds.

Following the fire, the **Eating Room** and library were transposed and both entirely redesigned. Robert Adam helped redesign the **Dining Room**: note again the ceiling and complementary carpet, the picture frames, the marble-topped table and mirror between the windows, the curved serving table in the end bay.

The **Hall** with its cantilevered staircase is a return to the pre-Adam house. The large Boulle writing table of tortoise-shell and brass is said to have been given by Louis XIV to Sarah, Duchess of Marlborough and by her daughter to Lady Catherine Parker. Note also the 18C bracket clock in an ormolu-mounted Boulle case; five 18C mahogany armchairs with their original needlepoint; *The Fall of Phaeton* by Stubbs, the portrait of Joshua Reynolds and set of history paintings by Angelica Kauffmann; fine *famille rose* punchbowl.

Chinese mirror painting, Saltram House

Upper Rooms – Two rooms follow the fashion for 17C-18C Chinese painted wall hangings, figured, exotic, often formally comic and perfectly complemented by the slender posted 18C bed with acanthus cresting, the Chinese-Chippendale chairs, the painted mirrors.

The olive-green and gold **Boudoir** became Lady Morley's sanctum on the death of her husband (John Parker III) in 1840. It is graced with a Regency marble-topped table, an 18C mahogany table, an 18C mahogany secretaire bookcase and a series of excellent watercolours by Lady Morley herself. In **Lord Morley's Room**, note the picture by Gardner of the *1st Lord Morley as a Boy*.

Downstairs – The **Library** presents a gallery of portraits: by the American artist Gilbert Stuart (1755-1828), Reynolds *(Lord Boringdon* and *Sir John Chichester of Arlington)*, Northcote and Angelica Kauffmann *(Self-Portrait)*. The tables are functional as well as beautiful: the circular drum is a rent table with alphabetically labelled drawers, another is a writing table, another a games table; one of the Pembroke tables opens into library steps.

The **Great Kitchen**, built in 1779, was modernised a century later. It presently displays a glorious *batterie de cuisine* comprising some 600 copper moulds and utensils.

Yealmpton *9 miles southeast off A379.*

Kitley Caves ⊙ – *650yards along a gravel track with a stile: for access by road, telephone for directions.* The caves, in a wooded setting beside the River Yealm, were discovered in the early 1800s by quarrymen blasting for limestone – a couple of ruined kilns stand near the entrance. The caves contain stalactites and stalagmites and a number of rock pools; a small museum displays artefacts found on site, a brief description.

National Shire Horse Centre ⊙ – *1 mile beyond Yealmpton turn right.* Though the large centre specialises mainly in shire horses, the complex also includes a falconry centre (flying displays) and other animals from butterflies to pigs. The 40 Shire stallions, geldings, mares and foals, mostly black with blazes, white socks, characteristic feathered legs, and curved Roman noses, weigh up to one ton each. They work and dominate the 60-acre farm.

The old stone farm buildings date back to 1772 with the long main stable, its hayloft above, turning the corner opposite the house. The porch leads into the harness room, gleaming with brass and leather, and stable, where those horses not at work may be viewed.

There are daily parades of horses, mares and foals, and special pageants.

PLYMOUTH SOUND – RIVER TAMAR★★

Michelin Atlas pp 3, 6 or Map 403 - G 31, H 32

Traditionally and physically, despite its many bridges, the **Tamar** marks the boundary between Devon and Cornwall – between Cornwall and the rest of the world, perhaps, since in conversation places are described as in the county or "beyond the Tamar".

Although traders from the Mediterranean came to Cornwall by sea in the earliest times, the Roman legions never crossed the river; despite bridges and modern transport, it is still a dividing line. It takes its name, according to legend, from the goddess who was transformed by her father into a river for refusing all her suitors.

Geographically the Tamar rises away up in the far northeast corner of Cornwall, 60 miles from where it flows with the **River Lynher** from Bodmin Moor into their broad estuary, known as the **Hamoaze** and Plymouth Sound. It is still navigable at high water as far as Calstock and even Morwellham and Gunnis-

lake. A thoroughfare in the Middle Ages and more importantly in the 19C for ships bringing down ore from the mines, the river is now peaceful with woods, undulating fields and market gardens on either bank and beautiful along almost its entire length.

Birds in residence – Plymouth Sound and Tamar estuary provide a range of feeding grounds and habitats for a broad variety of birds: **St John's Lake** shelters Brent geese, shelducks, wigeon, redshanks, greenshanks and godwits; little stints, curlew sandpipers and terns in autumn. **Warleigh Point Nature Reserve**, situated at the confluence of the Tamar and Tavy, has woodland stretching down to the water's edge: home to waders on the mudflats at low tide.

Weir Quay is renowned for its wintering flocks of pie-bald **avocets** with their striking black and white plumage, blue-grey legs and delicate upturned black bill especially adapted to filtering for tiny shrimp and insect larvae in the brackish waters.

Plymouth Sound – The Sound forms a natural harbour at the mouth of two rivers, the Plym *(east)* which gave its name to the growing port in the 14C and the Tamar *(west)* which flows into the Sound round **Drake's Island.**

Breakwater – The breakwater (1811-41), which marks the southern limit of the Sound two miles offshore, was constructed against the heavy sea swell which rolls in from the southwest. It is 5 100ft in length and a feat of engineering by **John Rennie**, taking, it is said, 4.5 million tons of local limestone to build.

Beside it, on an island rock, stands the round **Breakwater Fort** (c1860).

At either end are beacon lights and, at the east end, a large iron lobster-pot refuge at the top of a 24ft pole, into which anyone wrecked can climb and await rescue, now by helicopter.

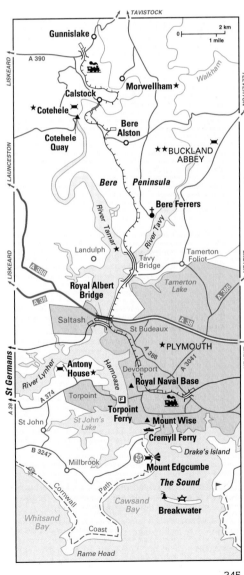

245

On the skyline 14 miles offshore sits the **Eddystone Lighthouse** (*see* INTRODUCTION: Lighthouses).

Torpoint Ferry – Until the road bridge was built the chain ferry was the only vehicle link between Plymouth and Cornwall.

Mount Edgcumbe ⊙ *9 miles west of Plymouth by Torpoint car ferry, A374 and B3247 to Cremyll or 2 miles by Cremyll passenger ferry from Admiral's Hard, Stonehouse.*

Walks through the 800-acre park and gardens and along 10 miles of coastline paths afford extensive **views**★ across the Sound. Birds to look out for: the busy grey-blue cloaked nuthatch and nut-dappled treecreeper in the woods, linnets perched on gorse.

In 1353 William Edgcumbe of Edgcumbe, Milton Abbot, Devon married Hilaria de Cotele whose dowry was Cotehele House; in 1493 their descendant Piers Edgcumbe married Jean Durnford, heiress to considerable estates on both sides of the Tamar and the important **Cremyll Ferry**; in 1539, just before he died, Piers received a royal licence to enclose grounds for the park in which his son, Sir Richard, built Mount Edgcumbe House in 1547-54.

> ### The Rising Sun
>
> Overlooking Kingsland green, a village of narrow streets, stands this useful watering hole: the elegant old Customs House has been converted into an atmospheric pub serving excellent meals and good (guest) beer. A favourite stop for those walking the coastal path. ☎ 01752 822 840.

Richard Carew in his *Survey* (*see above*) described Mount Edgcumbe as "buildid square, with a round turret at each end, garretted on the top, and the hall rising in the mids above the rest, which yealdeth a stately sound as you enter the same (and) the parlour and dining chamber (which) give you a large and diversified prospect of land and sea". This house with later additions was gutted by incendiary bombs in 1941. It was rebuilt to the original square plan and the additional 18C octagonal corner towers so that it now looks much as in Carew's description.

The interior includes a family **portrait** by Reynolds, a **longcase clock** of 1610 (John Matchett, Covent Garden), 17C and 18C furniture (two fine Boulle desks) and a pair of **Bronze Age hunting horns**.

The **higher gardens**, near the house, feature a wooded amphitheatre, formal Italian and French gardens, a New Zealand garden and an English garden with specimen shrubs and trees.

★ Antony House ⊙ *45min.*

Visitors cross the park and turn into the forecourt to face the Classical grey stone house, extended through short colonnades to red brick wings. The building was completed in 1721 and houses a collection of portraits and mementoes.

Interior – The halls are dominated by one of the four memorable portraits by Edward Bower of **Charles I** at his trial. In addition there hang on the walls the likenesses of Sir William Carew, ardent Jacobite and builder of the house, and **Richard Carew** (*by the staircase*), high sheriff, colonel of the troops guarding the estuary at the time of the Armada and author of the fascinating *Survey of Cornwall* of 1602. In the **staircase**, note the three turned balusters to each tread and the original bubble lights.

Set outside the **Dining Room** is a series of chairs covered with still-bright 17C-18C Soho tapestry; those set against the panelled walls hung with early sporting paintings and a lovely Queen Anne pier-glass, are by Chippendale.

The panelled **Saloon** contains three portraits by Reynolds; its Queen Anne furniture includes a pair of mirrors set over gesso tables as originally intended. The George I period chandelier is Waterford glass; the porcelain collection includes Chelsea and Worcester (by Dr Wall *c*1752-76) vases and late 18C Staffordshire cockerels.

The **Tapestry Room** takes its name from the 18C Soho Diogenes tapestries: it is furnished with a carved gilt-wood, eight branch William and Mary chandelier and tables with seaweed marquetry, George I with satyrs' masks and Queen Anne with carved Red Indians' heads; the armchairs are by Chippendale; the overmantel mirror is original (1721).

The **Library**, which contains a copy of the *Survey of Cornwall*, is hung with Carew family portraits and a likeness of Sarah Jennings, Duchess of Marlborough.

Upstairs – The sporting paintings on the west staircase walls are by Francis Sartorius (1734-1804); the bedrooms have four-posters or rare 18C single beds.

Norman doorway, St German's

B. Kaufmann

St Germans *9 miles northwest on A374; after 7 miles turn right.*

At the centre of the old village stand the attractive and practically-designed Sir William Moyle **Almshouses** of 1583 (restored 1967), surrounded by neatly kept stone cottages set in gardens of roses and clematis.

★ **St Germans Church** ⊘ – *Half a mile east.* The church possesses a majestic **west front** of dissimilar towers framing a Norman doorway, encircled by seven decorated orders carved in the local, dark blue-grey-green, Elvan stone. It stands on the site of Cornwall's Saxon Cathedral.
The doorway was begun before 1185, the towers *c*1200 but abandoned until the 13C and 15C when the north tower was completed to an octagonal plan with Early English lancet windows and the 72ft south tower in the Perpendicular style. Simultaneously work progressed on the attached monastery, for St Germans was a priory church. In 930 Athelstan appointed its abbot Bishop of Cornwall; in 1043 the see passed to Crediton.
Inside, note the Norman capitals, the East window with glass by William Morris, the battered Purbeck stone font and the 15C porch with a groined moorstone roof.

River Tamar

Since before the Norman Conquest, Tavistock boasted one of the wealthiest abbeys west of Gloucester: from the Dissolution, the Earls of Bedford increased their land-holdings to rank among the most significant landlords in Britain.
Between 1848-58, the Tamar Valley became Europe's chief source of copper: so all in all the area has enjoyed considerable prosperity through the ages.

Tamar Bridges – The bridges, one rail, one road, connect Devonport with Saltash. The **Royal Albert** was built by Brunel in 1857-59 as part of the extension of the GWR into Cornwall. A combined suspension and arched bridge, supported by towering granite piers, it is an engineering feat even greater with its day-in day-out rail traffic than the more spectacular and graceful Clifton Bridge.
The **Tamar Road Bridge**, opened in 1962, replacing the centuries-old Saltash ferry, was the model for the Forth and Severn Bridges, and the Salazar Bridge in Lisbon.

Landulph – *Cornwall.* **Parson's Quay** is one of several landing stages along the river: this one was once used to embark locally mined lead, silver, tin, copper and arsenic; today it is used by pleasure-craft moorings. Parson's Quay was, in addition, an embarkation point in the 15C for pilgrims setting out on the venturous journey to Santiago de Compostela in northern Spain.

Bere Peninsula – The tongue of land between the Tamar and the Tavy – which rises on Dartmoor, with **Bere Alston** as its principal town and Bere Ferrers' 13C **church** overlooking the Tavy as a local landmark, was an important silver and lead mining centre from the 13C-16C and again in the 19C, until the river burst its banks and flooded the workings in 1856.

On the double bend look out for avocets and other birds.

★ Cotehele ⊘

This old fortified manor house (built 1485-1627) overlooks the Tamar from a wooded hillside. The formal gardens boast yew hedges, a golden ash and large tulip tree, camellias, rhododendrons, magnolias (in bloom at the end of March); a tunnel provides access to an informal valley garden containing a medieval dovecote and a fish stewpond. Ferns, moss, lichens, gunnera, palms and hostas thrive here providing wonderful variations in leaf shape, colour and texture. The gateway, tower **(views)** and great barn are late 15C.

The 16C **Great Hall** has a timbered roof, Tudor fireplace, 18C campaign chairs and crested pewter. The **Old Dining Room** is hung with tapestries and contains a restored 16C centre table and 17C-18C furniture.

The late 16C **Chapel** features the original barrel ceiling, 16C Flemish triptych and Crucifixion panel, a rare faceless pre-pendulum clock, unaltered since *c*1489. Bacchic Soho tapestries adorn the **Punch Room**. Upstairs, note the late 17C four-posters with original hangings.

Cotehele Mill and Quay ⊘ – Estate workshops by the river include a wheelwright's, a blacksmith's, a saddlery, cider house and mill. Cottages, a small maritime **museum** ⊘ and the *Shamrock*, a restored Tamar barge, give an idea of 18C-19C activity on the river.

Calstock – *Cornwall. Landing stage for most of the Tamar boat cruises.*
The small, once important river port was killed in 1908 when the spectacular, 12-span railway viaduct was opened 120ft above the river.

Upstream, on the Devon side is **Morwellham Quay** (*see* TAVISTOCK*),* the highest point on the tidal Tamar to which vessels of any bulk could reach and from where horse-drawn barges operated upstream to Gunnislake.

Gunnislake – The minute village below rock heights tunnelled by old tin mines on the Cornish side, famous for centuries as the most southerly bridge across the Tamar. The 182ft long New Bridge, built in 1520 of large regular granite blocks, has seven arches divided by cutwaters and refuges.

For Launceston see BODMIN MOOR.

The picturesque way to travel

Besides the boat trips from Plymouth, it is also possible to go up the Tamar Valley from Plymouth to Gunnislake by train and return from Calstock by boat. The train passes through Devonport, St Budeaux, under the Tamar bridges, over Tamerton Lake and the Tavy Bridge.

POOLE★

Dorset – Population 133 050
Michelin Atlas p 9 or Map 403 – O 31

Poole overlooks one of the largest natural harbours in the world. The port, with ships sailing to foreign parts, appears to have been well established by the 12C-13C when it took the ascendancy over Wareham (to the west) where the channel was silting up. Warehouses such as the Town Cellars were built, especially after Henry VI granted the town the status of a **Custom Port** and **Port of the Staple** in 1433, thereby licensing it to export wool and woollen cloth, at that time Dorset's and England's most valuable product brought by road (A350) from Wiltshire and beyond. In 1483 the Channel Islands were declared neutral for the purposes of trade, thereby allowing tin, lead, beer, leather and horses to be sold indirectly to Spain and Portugal, from where olive oil, wine and cloth was imported. The city obviously prospered; in 1568 Elizabeth I made Poole County Corporate making it independent of Canford Manor under which it was listed in Domesday. During the Civil War, the levy of ship money by the king gave the city merchants reason to side with Parliament.

As trade increased during the 16C-18C, particularly with Newfoundland, the town found even greater prosperity which resulted in the refacing or rebuilding of many houses in the Georgian style still evident in parts. It is at this period that a house *(private)* of Tudor origin in Market Street was divided: the owners were presumably of different fortunes as in the one case the frontage was kept unaltered with exposed beams; in the other the more prosperous owners had the frontage Classically refaced. But trading dwindled after the industrial revolution and trains were built only as far as Bournemouth, some two miles down the coast.

Unfortunately, much of old Poole was bulldozed in the 1960s to make way for modern office blocks; these, in turn, have attracted the national and multinational enterprises which underpin a new age of prosperity.

Shipping – Since the Iron Age, the coastline has provided the region with a sheltered harbour and the area known as Hamworthy as a convenient site for ship-building. This area also was once equipped with great salt pans (like at Lyme Regis); in the 15C salt was exported from Poole to France. At the same time, hops were imported from the Netherland to supply Dorset's many breweries: beer was then shipped to the Channel Islands, malt from locally grown barley, meanwhile, went to Portsmouth and London.

The **Poole fleet**, carrying cod and salt fish, oil, seal skins and fur, to Spain and Portugal, continued to expand until by 1802 it had 80 ships on the Newfoundland run and more than 200 engaged elsewhere; in 1815 there were some 350 ships and 2 000 mariners. In the mid-19C trade shifted to Scandinavia (timber, coal and clay) and Poole saw the introduction of packet boats to the Channel Islands. Today, in addition to bulk traffic in grain, fertilizer, timber and clay, it has developed into a major lorry and heavy vehicle **roll-on-roll-off port** with transporter parks, entrepôt sheds and as many as three ferry sailings daily for the Continent (Cherbourg) and the Channel Islands. **Yachting** and **powerboat racing** have also become popular.

Old Town and Quayside

The district extends inland to the church and Old Guildhall. On the quay stand the handsome late 18C **Customs House** *(now a public house)* of red brick with a gilded crest above the doorway at the top of twin stairways.

Guildhall – *Market Street.* The high cost of the building, £2 260 14*s* in 1761, is justified by its **perfect proportions** and the contrasting curved and straight lines; the circular clock-face in the triangular pediment, the round-headed door beneath the square porch, the round and flat-topped windows, the **horseshoe staircase** with plain iron railings. It was used by the corporation for meetings, as a quarter sessions courtroom and by the court of admiralty, which determined prize money and salvage dues.

Waterfront Museum ⊘ – *High Street.* The 18C warehouse has been carefully converted to provide displays – 19C room sets and obsolete artefacts – to illustrate the history of Poole's maritime community: archeological finds from the Iron Age and Roman occupation; charters and documents; a smuggler's den provides additional local colour of a different type. On the second floor, a large collection of ship models, together with a series of tableaux illustrate the trades and skills behind the port's success; this is complemented by a special section dedicated to 20C marine archeology: the Studland Bay wreck of a Tudor (pre-*Mary Rose*) ship and the Poole log boat found off Brownsea Island. The exhibition on the first Scout Camp on Brownsea Island is situated on the top floor.

In the lower ground floor, the **Town Cellars**, part of a 15C wool warehouse with a fine timber **roof**, is devoted to temporary exhibitions.

Scaplen's Court, beside the museum, is a Tudor house built around a central courtyard and was discovered this century beneath years of accretions; it is now used for temporary exhibitions and children's workshops and cooking demonstrations in its Victorian kitchen.

Northwest of Poole, at **Upton Park**, is the Romano-British Farmstead which has been created by the Museum Services to provide children with a programme of activities and events related to the Roman occupation of Britain.

Poole Quay – The quayside is forever a hub of activity – lined with inns and restaurants, attractions for day trippers and booths selling excursions to Brownsea Island.

The giant, dark blue steel sculpture entitled *Sea Music* (1992), by Sir Anthony Caro, is a landmark for ships entering the port. Viewing platforms around it provide a panorama of the town, the harbour and out to sea.

Aquarium Complex – *1hr.* The warm rooms of this combined **aquarium and serpentarium** ⊘ contain tanks of sharks, exotic and local fish, frogs, iguanas, spiders, snakes, crocodiles and any number of other creepy, fascinating or usually dangerous reptiles, arachnids, insects, fish and amphibians.

Upstairs, a **model railway display** ⊘ runs up to 10 trains over 3 000ft of track, through 12 scenes.

Poole Pottery ⊘ – The Isle of Purbeck has supplied white clay to potters for generations; it is a darker clay, however, found to the north of Poole, traditionally used for making building bricks, tiles and architectural ornaments, which supplies this pottery (at one time 100 brickworks encircled the area of Poole and Bournemouth). The move into decorative lustreware was initiated by Owen Carter, an admirer of the Arts and Crafts potter, William de Morgan. He began experimenting with large tile tableaux and producing hand-painted blue and white delftware. During the 1920s the pottery started making figures, during the 1930s, under John Adams' management, it produced the stylish Art Deco tableware which has become so collectable today. The making of mass-produced utilitarian pieces came after the war, although designs continued to reflect fashion (Robert Jefferson Compact tableware, the Delphis Range) and to attract young art-school trained ceramicists: a precedent continued today.

The tour of the pottery and shopping centre which incorporates Dartington Crystal, passes through a display of pieces with historical interest, a video presentation *(12min)* of the enterprise before threading its way past the various areas of activity: platemaking, fettling and finishing, drying, firing, glazing, decorating, checking...

The factory also accommodates a glassblower, who may be seen blowing, moulding and fashioning his distinctive products.

RNLI Lifeboat Museum ⊙ – Large models show developments in the design of lifeboats and the heroic deeds of the crews since the Institution's foundation in 1824.

Poole Harbour from Studland Heath

SANDBANKS *2 miles southeast by B3369.*

The promontory runs like a mile-long, built-up breakwater to enclose Poole Harbour. This prized residential area also has Poole's best beaches. At the point is a drive-on-drive-off chain ferry to Studland *(see SWANAGE).*

★BROWNSEA ISLAND ⊙

The island (1.5 miles long, 0.5 mile wide) is covered with heath and woodland and fringed by inviting beaches along its south shore. Its 500 acres might be considered as two nature reserves, one on either side of **Middle Street**, the island's central spine.

The **north reserve** is a sanctuary for waterfowl and other birds and supports a heronry, blackheaded gullery and a colony of common tern.

In the open reserve south of Middle Street, visitors may wander at will (and picnic) by the church built by Colonel Waugh incorporating several wooden features from Crosby Hall in Chelsea (1853) with its painted angels and memorial tablets, in the **Peacock Field**, habitat of an enormous number of birds, in the **Daffodil Field** *(steps to the beach from paths at the east and west ends of the field),* westwards to the **Baden-Powell Stone**, commemorating the first experimental Boy Scout Camp in 1907. The stone is also the island's principal viewpoint, affording a **panorama**★★ from Poole Bay to the Purbeck Hills with Corfe Castle just visible in the Gap.

When walking or sitting still, look out for **red squirrels.**

The island's "castle" was built in the 18C on the site of one of Henry VIII's forts.

★★COMPTON ACRES *3 miles southeast of Poole by B3369.*

Gardens ⊙ – The 15-acre garden, or series of gardens, set in a rift or *chine* in the sandstone cliffs, is famous for having flowers brilliantly in bloom in all seasons.

The **Italian Garden** is graced with a Classical canal and fountain, statues and vases, which are highlighted by quantities of flowers, carpets of bedding plants, roses, rhododendrons, clematis...

The **Rock and Water Garden and Woodland Glen** are informally landscaped to include cascades and pools, planted with iris, agapanthus, eucalyptus, mimosa, palms, jacarandas, a Judas tree.

The **English Garden** lies open to sunsets and a westerly **view**★★★ of Poole Harbour, Brownsea Island and the Purbeck Hills.

The **Heather Dell** presents a mottled carpet of purple shades.

A. Taverner

The very big **Japanese Garden** is lavishly endowed with garden ornaments, animal and bird statuary, and brilliant with flowers and ornamental trees reflected in the waterfall and pools traversed by stepping stones and bridges.

For Kingston Lacy and Cranborne Manor Gardens, see WIMBORNE.

Admission times and charges for the sights described
are listed at the end of the guide.
Every sight for which there are times and charges is identified by the symbol ⊙
in the middle section of the guide.

ST AUSTELL

Cornwall – Population 21 622
Michelin Atlas p 3 or Map 403 – F 32

The old market town of St Austell rose to importance in the mid-18C with the discovery in the area by **William Cookworthy** of **china-clay** which has been mined at the top of the town ever since.

The sprawling town is built around a maze of steep one-way streets, especially around the 17C **Market House**, the White Hart, once a posting inn and, on an island site, the parish church.

★ Holy Trinity Church – The exterior is remarkable for its tall, late 15C **tower**, embattled, corner pinnacled and profusely decorated on all four sides with masks, angels and niches containing statues and groups of the Annunciation, the risen Christ and the Trinity.

Inside, separated by a 15C arcade, the nave and aisles have wagon roofs. Note how the **nave** is out of line with the tower and the older 13C chancel. Several of the early Tudor pews nearest the crossing are carved with instruments of the Passion (hammer, nails, sponge, pincers..). The granite **font** (c1200), at the west end, one of the most impressive in Cornwall, is carved with "gorgons, hydras and chimeras dire" the late 19C pulpit is of Derbyshire alabaster.

> ### Carlyon Arms
>
> A mile east of St Austell along the Bethel Road is this friendly local pub: good beer and home-cooked food. ☎ 01726 721 29

EXCURSIONS

A391 to Carthew and Roche

★★ **Wheal Martyn China Clay Heritage Centre, Carthew** ⊘ – *2 miles north.* China clay (feldspar or kaolin) is a constituent of many manufactured products as well as porcelain. The English China Clays Group, which works 26 pits, has the greatest production in the world at nearly 3 000 000 tons a year. Of this 15% goes into fine china, earthenware, tiles and sanitary ware, 75% into papermaking and the rest into plastics, rubber and synthetic rubber, paints, pharmaceuticals, cosmetics, fertilizers, textiles, leather goods… More than 70% (2 100 000 tons) is exported annually (this may be seen at Fowey). A short film explains the original extraction process involving the now obsolete drags, settling tanks, waterwheels, drying kiln, horse wagons and steam engines visible outside. Today, modern pressure jet extraction and high tech refining continues with operations in two modern clay pits surveyed from the high point of a Nature Trail. Disused pits have been planted with rhododendrons and other acid soil-loving plants, providing an undulating area for nature trails and well-designed assault courses for children.

Roche Rock – *6 miles north on A391 and B3274.* Above the man-made landscape of fields and distant china-clay pyramids there rises an age-old elemental outcrop of grey-green-black schorl on which an early 15C anchorite built a granite chapel.

★★ St Austell Bay

The wide bay circles west from **Gribbin Head**★★ to the line of cliffs terminating in **Dodman Point** (373ft) to the south.

★ **Polkerris** – The small village with a sand beach is sheltered to landward by steep cliffs, to seaward by a curving sea wall.

Par – The onetime pilchard harbour and processing town, tin port and smelting works is now powdered white from the clay loaded into ships in the dock.

Biscovey – In an old Victorian school *(north side of A390 by Par crossroads)* the **Mid-Cornwall Galleries** ⊘ present a brimming display of pottery, modern brasswork (fenders), textiles and knitting, painting and sculpture in wood and stone.

★ **Charlestown** – From 1792-98 Charles Rashleigh (after whom the village was subsequently renamed) began to turn the fishing village of West Polmear into a busy port, flanked on either side with beaches and small coves. The long,

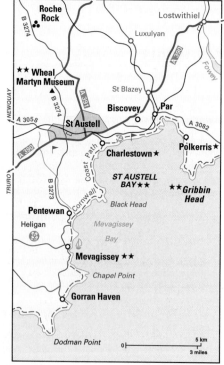

unspoilt main street, designed to take six horses and carts abreast, runs between rows of stone cottages down to the pier (1792) and outer basin (1794) from which emigrants, later, sailed to America. The dock (1798), designed by Charles Smeaton, was where china clay was once loaded: today the privately-owned dock features regularly in period films filled with tall-masted schooners.

Shipwreck and Heritage Museum ⊘ – Tunnels of an old china-clay works are now lined with tableaux of 19C life in Charlestown including the necessary trades practised locally such as coopering and pilchard processing. The main displays, however, consist of varied exhibits giving a comprehensive survey of shipwrecks, their causes, sea rescue, laws of salvage, diving on wrecks (fascinating reconstruction of a 17C barrel diver), items recovered from famous ships (gold, leather, porcelain, pewter, gun flints and ammunition, cloth, spices from the East India Companies…).

Across the open space sits the old **weighbridge** where a "tally-clerk" would have monitored the weight of each tram carrying clay before loading onto the ships.

Pentewan – Stone for many of Cornwall's churches and large houses was quarried nearby for centuries and shipped from the harbour, which lies sheltered between the promontories.

★★ **Mevagissey** – Facilities. A popular fishing port with houses irregularly terraced up the hillsides, colour-washed, half-timbered or weather-boarded with over-sailing upper floors; an inner harbour with 1770s pier, old quayside boathouses and sail lofts (now shops and restaurants); a maze of twisting back streets and steps; nets drying on walls; slate everywhere, on roofs, as front doorsteps and window sills; a fisherman's loft with nets of every variety of mesh size, weight and colour – such is Mevagissey. The town is crowded with visitors all summer long but a few minutes' walk leads to one of the headlands for a gull's eye view.

★ **Lost Gardens of Heligan** ⊘ – *90min to 3hrs*. The name Heligan comes from the Cornish word for "willows", of which there are few in evidence. The main attraction of these 57-acre "lost" gardens is the remarkable story behind their recovery from dereliction, against all odds in 1991.

In the 16C, the estate was acquired by the Tremayne family in whose hands it remained until 1970. Over the years subsequent generations nurtured the self-contained complex of farmland, quarries, wood, the earliest brickworks in Cornwall (1680), flourmill, sawmill, brewery, bee hives and extensive kitchen garden until 1916,when the war in Flanders had already culled most of the workers and the house was requisitioned by the War Department. In 1943, American forces came to practise exercises for landing in Normandy on Pentewan Beach and officers were billeted in the house.

The form of the gardens was shaped and ordered by Thomas Gray in the 18C; in the 20C, abandoned, soon overgrown with ivy, brambles and ferns, the garden had disappeared into confused jungle. Cleared, painstakingly researched, repaired,replanted and eventually hyped by a television series (and therefore likely to be busy), the gardens comprise **Flora's Garden** which is populated by enormous rhododendrons (including those introduced to Britain by Hooker) and camellias – best between late March and mid April; an immaculate 1.4 acre **walled vegetable garden** with adjacent orangeries housing passion-fruit, bananas and

Lost Gardens of Heligan

E. Light

peaches, manure-heated pineapple-pits, vinery and melon house; **fruit orchards** comprising medlars, plums and apples; a miscellany of ride, ravine (rockery), grotto, Italian garden, sundial garden and summerhouse flanked by ornamental exotics. Stretching down into the valley is "The Jungle" **woodland** which was planted during the late 19C with giant-leaved gunnera, tree-palms, chusan palms, gingkos and Japanese black pine. This soon merges with the **Lost Valley** where indigenous species like holly, sycamore, ash and beech harbour a number of modern batboxes, shade carpets of wood anemones, primroses, bluebells and ragged robin, and shelter a water-meadow planted with bullrushes and frequented by wildlife.

Gorran Haven – The oldest **houses** are to be found in Church Street, Fox Lane and Rattle Alley. The tiny **church** of St Just was built as a seamen's chapel and lantern; the distinctive pentagonal **tower** is 15C.

ST IVES★★

Cornwall – Population 10 964
Michelin Atlas p 2 or Map 403 – D 33

St Ives, the picturesque fishing harbour and former mining town, has attracted artists since the 1880s when Whistler and Sickert followed in the footsteps of Turner; later, as sail lofts were adapted to painting studios, the town was adopted by a growing number of painters, who like the French Impressionists in Brittany were keen to paint seascapes out of doors.

Today, St Ives is animated by a thriving community of artists (resident or part-time) and curious visitors largely attracted by the Tate Gallery. Areas of interest include the small headland known as the **Island**, a network of stepped and winding cobbled alleys, hillside terraces, archways, "back doubles", all lined by colour-washed fishermen's houses with narrow doorways, crowded shoulder to shoulder. The curving quayside and main street are known as **The Wharf** and **Fore Street**.

★ **Parish Church** – The church with its pinnacled 85ft **tower** of golden Zennor granite, clearly visible from the harbour, dates – except for the 20C baptistery – from the 15C when it was built in a single phase. It is dedicated to the fishermen-Apostles St Peter and St Andrew, and St Ia, the early missionary who arrived in the area from across the sea on a leaf, after whom the town is named. Inside, the **wagon roof** is ornamented with painted figures of angels. Note the carved **bench-ends**, a number of which have been used to furnish the pulpit, and the altar reredos set with alabaster panels. The **Lady Chapel** has a tender *Mother and Child* by **Barbara Hepworth** (1953), given by the sculptress in memory of her son who was killed over Thailand while serving in the RAF; the stainless steel Christmas rose candle holders were presented by the artist in 1972.

In the north aisle sits the stone **font** carved with four fantastical demons at its foot.

★★ **Tate Gallery St Ives** ⊘ – This splendid building (1973), erected on the site of a gas works, enjoys a **view**★★ over the sands of Porthmeor Beach. Designed by Eldred Evans and David Shalev, the asymmetrical gallery consists of swirling forms spiralling upwards: shallow steps lead up to the entrance as a wheelchair ramp turns elegantly down between high walls.

Inside, stairways climb through airy space for access to the changing exhibitions of post-war modern works from the London Tate collection. These concentrate particularly on artists associated with St Ives including Alfred Wallis, Ben Nicholson, Barbara Hepworth, John Wells, Terry Frost, Patrick Heron (who has a studio nearby and who designed the stained glass window on the ground floor). A number of works by Bernard Leach are also on display.

★★ **Barbara Hepworth Museum** ⊘ – Barbara Hepworth (1903-75) came to St Ives during the Second World War (1939) with her husband Ben Nicholson. She settled into Trewyn Studio in 1949 having separated from Nicholson, and later died there on 20 May 1975 following a fire.

The **St Ives Society of Artists** was founded by John Park and Borlase Smart, students of Julius Olsson, in 1926/7. During the following decade, the sculptors Ben Nicholson, **Barbara Hepworth** and Naum Gabo moved there from London; they befriended the local self-taught artist **Alfred Wallis** who painted naive marine pictures that have as much charisma as those of Theodore Rousseau. Typical subjects include the sea, the coastal landscape and boats, although later the figurative element dissolved into abstraction. The 1950s witnessed the arrival of a new generation of painters inspired by the local landscape but influenced by trends from New York. Since then, new generations of painters have continued to come to St Ives to capture the light and the movement of the sea including **Patrick Heron**, Terry Frost and Peter Lanyon.

Tate Gallery, St Ives

Barbara Hepworth Museum

The small house is simply arranged: the ground floor displays archive material and a selection of unfinished wood carvings. Upstairs, the simply furnished, airy studio is filled with sleek polished wooden and stone **sculptures** spanning a life's work. The white-walled garden, planted with trees and bamboo, provides a serene setting for some twenty abstract compositions in bronze and stone. The meandering path leads to three additional workshops left much as they were at the sculptor's death: tools, smooth plaster shapes, unfinished blocks of stone and plaster maquettes for cast bronzes abandoned for all time.
Barbara Hepworth is buried at St Ives, in the Longstone cemetery. Several of her works are on view in the town (before the Guildhall, in Malakoff Gardens by the bus station, in the church, at the Tate...).

Commercial Galleries – Several galleries operate in St Ives selling traditional (post-1880) and contemporary paintings, sculpture and pottery; these include those set up by the **St Ives Society** and the **Penwith Society**, the latter in a converted pilchard factory. Maintaining the tradition set by the Leach Pottery, founded by Bernard and continued by his widow Janet, St Ives has an active community of potters; while Trevor Corser remains at The Stennack, the main retail outlet for pottery is John Bedding's **St Ives Pottery** in Fish Street.

St Nicholas Chapel – The chapel on the "Island" is the traditional seamen's chapel built as a beacon. It commands a wide **view**★★ including Godrevy Lighthouse across the bay, the inspiration for Virginia Woolf's *To the Lighthouse*.

St Ives Museum ⊘ – The local museum is filled with everything to do with historic St Ives: shipwrecks, lifeboats, mining, fishing and other such trades associated with the town (wheelwrights, coopers, a blacksmith's shop); extensive collection of archive photographs of St Ives and Polperro in the 1860s; room dedicated to Hain Steamship Company of St Ives; paintings by old School of St Ives (Parks, Titcomb, Clare White, Leonard Fuller, Nance).
Reconstructed Cornish kitchen, children's section and area dedicated to the Great Western Railway.

Smeaton Pier – The pier was constructed in 1767-70 by the builder of the then Eddystone lighthouse. At its shore end is the small St Leonard's sailors' chapel.

For the coast between St Ives and Land's End see PENWITH.

The West Country provides ideal conditions for a short breack away,
Areas suited to enjoying the outdoors are identified by a
Special map entitled Activities: sea, sand, birds and rambling.

ST MICHAEL'S MOUNT★★

Cornwall – Population 36
Michelin Atlas p 2 or Map 403 – D 33

St Michael's Mount is the focal point of every **view** across the bay and itself commands **views**★★ towards the Lizard and Land's End.
The castle is approached up a steep zig-zag path through the trees *(25min)*.

Legend, foundation, Dissolution – In the 4C BC ships came from the Mediterranean to the **Island of Ictis**, as they named it, to trade in tin, copper and gold; in AD 495, according to Cornish legend, fishermen saw St Michael standing on a westerly ledge of the granite rock which rises high out of the sea, whereupon the island became a place of pilgrimage. By the 8C, it is said, a Celtic monastery had been founded upon it which endured until the 11C. At the same time, in 708 in France, St Michael appeared three times in a vision to Bishop Aubert of Avranches, who then built an oratory to the saint on the island from then known as Mont-St-Michel. By the time of the Battle of Hastings, the oratory in France had developed into an important Benedictine community to which St Michael's Mount passed as a dependency. The English house, always modest by comparison with the French monastery, was ultimately appropriated during the course of the Hundred Years War by Henry V as alien property and was finally suppressed in 1425.

Strongpoint – Even while it attracted foreign pilgrims, the Mount suffered attack from French and Spanish raiders. In the Middle Ages it became a strongpoint from which Perkin Warbeck set out in 1497, and the men of the **Cornish Rebellion** tried to resist the imposition by Edward IV in 1549 of the Book of Common Prayer in English which they claimed not to understand.
In 1588 it was from the church on the summit that a beacon signalled the approach up the Channel of the 130 galleons of the Spanish Armada.
In the 17C the Mount became involved in the Civil War: through the harbour were imported arms for the Royalist cause, purchased with Cornish tin from the French; in April 1646 the island surrendered to the Parliamentary forces and a year later received its last military commander, Col John St Aubyn, who subsequently purchased the castle as a family residence. In times of war the island is still garrisoned.

The Mount's owners – Col John St Aubyn, who died in 1684, according to tradition by being swept off his horse by a mighty wave when riding along the causeway, began repairs to the fabric and positioned his arms over the entrance when he was still governor. His great-grandson (d 1744), the third baronet, became famous when in an age of corruption Sir Robert Walpole, as Prime Minister, declared in the House, "All

these men have their price except the **little Cornish Baronet**". He rebuilt the harbour and the causeway (1727) and altered and embellished the castle interior in the 18C style. A third phase of alterations occurred in 1873-78 when Piers St Aubyn, architect and cousin of the then Sir John St Aubyn, first Lord St Levan, added a Victorian domestic wing to the southeast which descends by as many as five storeys down the rock face to preserve the familiar medieval skyline.

Jack the Giant Killer - Giants once abounded in Cornwall, according to an old map still in the house. They sat on the hilltops, dressed in loose tunics and floppy hats. St Michael's Mount was even built by a giant, a black-beard named Cormoran who would wade ashore to capture sheep and cattle and then return to the rock to sleep. Jack, a local boy, decided to kill the giant. One night he rowed to the island and halfway up the path he dug a very deep pit; as dawn was breaking, Jack sounded his horn; Cormoran woke, came rushing down the path with the sun in his eyes, fell into the pit and died - the **pit** into which he fell is halfway up the hill.

Castle ⊘ - *90min.* Beyond the Tudor doorway emblazoned with the St Aubyn arms come the hall, guardroom and garrison room, the **oldest part of the house** (14C) and still much as they were in the priory-fortress period.

The **armoury**, altered in the 19C, displays, among the trophies, sporting weapons, coat of arms and a silken banner, the oak chest of the first Col John St Aubyn and 1944 paratrooper beret of another member of the family. Note the first of many paintings of the Mount throughout the centuries; in the rooms which follow there are family portraits in oil, in silhouette and in miniature.

The **library**, in the oldest part of the castle, was transformed in the 18C. Note the watercolours of Mont-St-Michel and views from the lancet windows.

The **Chevy Chase Room**, the former monks' refectory, was given the lively 17C plaster frieze of scenes depicting bull-baiting, hare and hounds, stag-hunting and ostrich hunting. The main roof timbers date from the 15C, the royal arms from 1660 (the 1641 date is a mystery). The dado and doors are 18C Gothick. The great oak table dates from the 1620s; the chairs were made by the estate carpenter in 1800 after the pre-Dissolution Glastonbury model still in the room; the triangular chair is Elizabethan; the court cupboard 17C.

Church - The church at the island summit, dedicated in 1125, was rebuilt in the 14C following an earthquake. In the 15C the windows were enlarged to include the two roses. Note the banners, the alabaster panels in the altarpiece - the smaller ones are 16C Flemish, the larger rare 15C work from Nottingham - also the late 15C Flemish gilt brass chandelier (similar to that in Bristol Cathedral) with figures of the Virgin and Child and of St Michael killing the dragon.

H. Phillips/The National Trust

257

At the church entrance is a restored Gothic Lantern Cross carved with the Crucifixion, the Virgin and Child and the heads of an unknown king and pilgrim. The **Anteroom** and **Blue Drawing Rooms**, converted from the Lady Chapel (1463-1500) into three rooms, was the idea of the "little Cornish Baronet" in the 18C. Blue walls, deeper blue furnishings, paintings by Zoffany, Opie and Gainsborough, Chippendale chairs and settee, a highly ornate Louis XVI clock on a marble-topped commode, two alabaster and jasper vases stand beneath the glorious pre-Strawberry Hill Rococo-Gothick plasterwork. On the walls are choice family portraits by Gainsborough and Opie, and an 18C conversation piece by Arthur Devis with two Misses St Aubyn before a distant outline of the Mount. The chairs in the anteroom are Strawberry Hill Gothick.

Battery – The battery *(below the entrance on leaving)* is armed with guns from a French frigate driven aground by fire from the Mount during the Napoleonic Wars.

Dairy – The octagonal walled dairy, built in the 1870s, accommodated the 9 cows stationed on the island.

Mainland coast

Marazion – Pilgrims, waiting for the ferry or for the tide to fall so that they could cross the sands to St Michael's Mount, gave Marazion an increased importance throughout the Middle Ages. Pillage by local raiders, the Dissolution of St Michael's Priory and finally the Spanish raid of 1595 on Mousehole (*see* PENWITH) and other towns around the bay so reduced the town that it never recovered.

★ **Prussia Cove** – *9 miles east by A30 and A394.* The cove inside Cudden Point is renowned for tales about its smugglers. The hero of the most famous is John Carter, known like his inn as the **King of Prussia.**

SALCOMBE

Devon – Population 2 189

Michelin Atlas p 4 or Map 403 – I 33

Devon's most southerly resort lies at the mouth of the Kingsbridge Estuary between Prawle Point to the east and Bolt Head to the west. The town, a onetime fishing village overlooking the estuary, has small sand beaches and coves (North Sands, South Sands, Batson Creek) within minutes of the main street which is lined with more ships' chandlers than grocers. Old houses, boat-yards, the custom house and its quay, ships and a pontoon-pier line the waterside; larger Victorian houses sprawl back up the wooded hillside. The town's fortune in the 1860s and 1870s hinged around the local shipwrights who specialised in building Salcombe yawls and swift schooners suited to the transport of salt from Cadiz to Newfoundland, salted cod back to the Mediterranean and fruit home to Salcombe. The estuary harbour, which extends from the sand bar in line with Sharpitor Rocks and after which Tennyson is said to have written *Crossing the Bar*, teems all summer with small yachts.

Salcombe's defensive castle, **Fort Charles**, was built at the entrance to the harbour in 1544, rebuilt in 1643 and besieged by the Parliamentary troops from 15 January to 9 May 1646 (cannon balls on display at the Overbeck's Museum) when it surrendered. It is now a picturesque ruin.

Ferries ⊙ – Ferries ply the harbour estuary: across to **East Portlemouth** (sand beaches and paths to Prawle Point), seawards to **South Sands** and inland to **Kingsbridge**.

Bolt Head

3.5 miles on foot, joining up with the South Devon Coast Path: follow the Cliff Road, North Sands, The Moult, South Sands, left by hotel, over 400ft Sharp Tor or Sharpitor Rocks to round Starhole Bay and on to the downland head. This is a particularly beautiful road along the coast rising steeply up to Sharpitor – signposted all the way.

★ **Overbecks Museum and Garden, Sharpitor** ⊙ – *2 hours.* Sharpitor enjoys a spectacular **view**★★ over the estuary from different levels of the terraced garden laid out by Edric Hopkins, the builder of the house in 1901.

Sheltered by cliffs and blessed by a mild microclimate, mature trees protect a Mediterranean-style **garden** so fashionable in Edwardian times and a broad variety of sub-tropical plants (camphor tree, chusan palms, watsonia, agapanthus, ginger plants, banana, datura and echiums) and trees from New Zealand and Australia introduced by subsequent owners. A formal garden comprising herbaceous borders planted with brightly coloured flowering perennials and annuals surrounds a bronze figure entitled *First Flight* (full plant list available).

House – In 1913 the cramped Victorian house was sold to Captain G M Vereker (1860-1924) who set about rebuilding the house as an Edwardian-style villa. In 1928 it was purchased by **Otto Overbeck**, a research chemist, inventor, accomplished linguist and artist (FRSA); having no heirs, Overbeck left the property to serve as a youth hostel (72 beds), and the contents to the National Trust. The house contents include early photographs of Salcombe, a large collection of ship models, ship portraits and artefacts relating to Salcombe's maritime past, Mr Overbeck's personal belongings that relate his broad range of interests in natural history, scientific inventions (notably his patented electrical rejuvenator and German made Polyphon), commemorative china and 19C dolls, and Mr Norris' collection of lead soldiers.

Of especial interest to children is the "Secret Room" and the delights it contains. *For Prawle Point, accessible via the Coastal Path – see* DARTMOUTH.

EXCURSIONS

★ **Kingsbridge** *5 miles north by A381*

The old market town at the head of the estuary is the capital of the area known as South Hams. Fore Street descends very steeply to the quay where a weekly market, first allowed by the Abbot of Buckfast in 1219 for his monks to sell their surplus produce, is still going strong (Tuesday livestock and street traders). The busy little town continues to proffer regional delicacies: home-baked cakes and full-cream icecreams, smoked fish.

Quay – The Quay stands on land reclaimed from the once important harbour.

Fore Street – The street is bordered by slate-hung houses dating from the 15C-19C, between which run narrow passages leading to small, medieval courtyards. The **Town Hall** (local cinema and craft market on Tuesdays and Fridays in summer) has a tower with three clock faces – the fourth face would have faced the workhouse and was therefore deemed inappropriate. The colonnaded walk known as the **Shambles**, once the site of the town's substantial meat market, is fronted by eight Elizabethan granite pillars which support the 18C upper floor.

Making the most of the estuary

★★ **Boat Trip** ⊘ – A trip into the estuary between the open downland, past the mouths of the six wooded creeks and additional inlets headed by small waterside villages, watching the terns and buzzards overhead and, if the tide is falling, waders including heron in the shallows, can be a very enjoyable experience.

Otherwise – For enthusiastic bird-watchers, **Slapton Ley** *(located off A379 between Dartmouth and Kingsbridge)*, a large fresh-water lagoon enclosed by a shingle beach, may provide the opportunity of seeing great crested grebes which nest there, wintering wildfowl such as goldeneye and red-breasted mergansers. The reed marsh section is home to bearded tits, sedge and Cetti's warblers; it attracts firecrests in spring and autumn, and chiffchaffs in winter. Details of guided walks, nature trails and summer residential courses are available from the Field Centre and Information Unit in Slapton village; Slapton Ley is owned by the Witley Wildlife Trust, *see* TORQUAY: Paignton Zoo.

St Edmund, King and Martyr – The tower and spire are 13C but the church was rebuilt in the 15C when the town was prosperous, and restored in the 19C. Inside, note the variation in the chancel arches, the two squints and the 13C font.

King's Arms – The coaching inn (1775) near the top of the street *(on the right)* became a stage in 1775 for the Exeter-Plymouth coaches, a day's ride from Exeter and the 170 mile journey to London.

Cookworthy Museum of Rural Life ⊘ – The long stone building on two floors was erected by Thomas Crispin, a fuller, as a grammar school in 1670. Its name honours **William Cookworthy** (1705-80), the Quaker apothecary who was born nearby and who went on to discover how kaolin (china clay) and petunze (china-stone) from near St Austell could be used to make porcelain in 1756. The **panelled schoolroom** with a **master's seat** surmounted by the royal arms of Charles II contains a display on local trades (clotted cream, fullers, basket-makers, tuckers, dyers and weavers) and business concerns. Elsewhere, there is a costume room for children, a turn of the century pharmacy complete with bedpans, bottles and drug-jars, a special exhibitions room for grammar school memorabilia. Small selection of Plymouth and Champions Bristol 18C porcelain. Downstairs, the one-time school kitchen which produced food for 60 boarders, holds a variety of Victorian equipment (iron skillet, stoneware store jars, mincers); the farm gallery at the rear is for old tools and agricultural implements.

SALISBURY★★

Wiltshire – Population 39 268

Michelin map fold 28 – O 30

The magnificent cathedral, with its spectacular great spire, is a building planned and executed in a single style; the town, equally, was planned and did not just grow – such order was the result of both town and church having been brought specifically to the site in the 13C.

The earlier city of **Old Sarum** was two miles away, an Iron Age hillfort, a Roman, Saxon and, finally, a Norman strongpoint where two successive cathedrals were built in the outer bailey: the first by Bishop, later **St Osmund**, nephew of the Conqueror, which was struck by lightning and largely destroyed only five days after its consecration; the second, a much larger, richer building, was designed by **Bishop Roger**. The bishop also converted the existing keep into an Episcopal castle-palace which, on his fall from power in 1139, was garrisoned by the king's men. His immediate successor, Bishop Joscelin, built a new Episcopal palace beside the cathedral but friction between the king's garrison and the clergy, want of water, the bleakness of the hilltop and the lack of fear of attack finally combined in the 13C to make the citizens and clergy of Old Sarum seek pastures new and undertake the construction of a third Cathedral Church to the Blessed Virgin.

Market days: Tuesday and Saturday all day.

★★★ CATHEDRAL

For many people Salisbury epitomises the Early English style at its best, medieval Gothic in its purest, most ascetic form. It is unique among England's older cathedrals as it is built in a single style, with the slimmest Purbeck marble columns and the tallest spire, conceived largely by Elias de Derham. It was built in two phases: foundation stone to consecration and completion of the west screen (1220-58-65); heightening of the tower and construction of the spire (1334-80).

The materials used were silver-grey limestone from Chilmark *(12 miles west)*, Purbeck marble, cement (the vaulting is painted cast concrete), lead for the roofs, masses of timber for scaffolding, shuttering and supports for the spire.

Exterior – The **west screen** extends from the gabled portals through lines of statue-filled niches, lancet windows and arcading to the pointed gable and corner towers with their miniature angel pinnacles and ribbed spires. The upper stages of the **tower**, built a century later than the base, are complemented by the proportions of the lancets and two friezes of crested decoration; at the top of the corner, pinnacles and sub-pinnacles rise like fountains but fall just short of the first of the three carved bands encircling the spire itself. From the heightened tower the **spire** (180ft) rises on walls 2ft thick at the base to its summit (404ft above ground level).

A. Taverner

Salisbury Cathedral spire

Interior ⓥ – *45min excluding roof tour.* The interior of the west screen exemplifies the beauty of pure line; nothing remains of the medieval colour – black, red and gold. The **nave** extends (229.5ft) over half the length of the total building (449ft), its vault towering to a height of 84ft. Along the arcade, piers of Purbeck marble reach up to quatrefoils of grey, unpolished stone, canted by polished black shafts capped with moulded capitals, then up again through galleries marked by clusters of black colonnettes, to the tall lancets of the clerestories.

Between the arcade pillars, tomb chests with recumbent figures recall the great of Old Sarum, Salisbury and the West Country: on the south side, **Bishops Roger** (d 1139) and **Joscelin** (d 1184), the shrine of **St Osmund** (d 1099) and the chain-mailed **William Longespée** (d 1226), half-brother of King John, husband of Ela, the founder of Lacock Abbey; opposite are Longespée the Younger (d 1250), warrior and crusader, Montacute (d 1390) and Hungerford (d 1449).

Marking the **crossing** are giant piers of clustered black marble columns, intended to support the original low tower but, since the 14C, required to bear the extra 6 500 tons of the heightened tower and spire. Reinforcing internal and external buttresses and, since the 15C, massive tie-beam arches across the transepts and a Decorated stone vault over the crossing have relieved the strain in part but the piers have buckled by a clearly noticeable 3.5in. At the centre of the crossing pavement, an octagon reflects the outline of the spire 45ft below its apex; in 1668 Sir Christopher Wren, when surveying the cathedral, dropped a plumb-line from the spire point (brass plate) which shows that it has settled with a declination of 29.5in to the southwest.

In the north aisle sits a **medieval clock** (*c*1386), the oldest working clock in England – its counterpart at Wells dating from *c*1390; in 1931 it was restored to its original condition with a verge and foliot balance instead of the later pendulum escapement; the modern parts are painted green to differentiate them from the original. It was originally housed in the Bell Tower (demolished 1790) in the Close. In the **north transept** is a fine statue to Sir Richard Colt Hoare and a 13C cope chest. In the **south transept**, the Mothers' Union Chapel has an altar-frontal and hangings made from material from the 1953 Coronation.

The **south chancel aisle** accommodates the coloured tomb is of Sir Richard Mompesson (d 1627) and his wife, ancestors of the builder of the house in the Close *(see below);* the window behind them is by Burne-Jones. Note the inverted, 14C scissor arches in the sub-transepts.

Chantry chapels flank each side of the choir filled with monumental tombs, including the ledger stone or plain lid of the coffin of **St Osmund** *(southeast corner).*

The blue window dedicated to *Prisoners of Conscience* (1980) in the **Trinity Chapel**, is by Gabriel Loire, a stained-glass maker from Chartres. See how it compares to the great **west window** containing six medieval shields (once in the chapterhouse) and 15C-16C figures. (The other glass is almost all monochrome or grisaille.) Most beautiful of all in the chapel are the slimmest of slim, black Purbeck marble shafts rising as ringed pilasters, columns and clustered piers to the groined vaulting.

Roof Tour ⓥ – *1 hour.* The tour ascends by spiral staircases *(120 steps)* to the Parvis Room (original medieval wooden roof and lead covering) and the triforium (full length **view** of the nave from the west end); it continues *(restoration work*

Salisbury Cathedral cloisters

permitting) up the tower through the clock and bell chambers to the external gallery at the base of the spire; otherwise to the gutters of the nave roof. **View** of the Close and Old Sarum.

Cloisters and Chapter-House – Work began on building the chapter-house and the cloisters in *c*1263, making the latter the earliest in any English cathedral; they are also among the longest (181ft). Both are in the Decorated Gothic style. The octagonal chapter-house (58ft across) rises from a single central column surrounded by eight ringed Purbeck shafts which ascend from the foliated capital as ribs to ceiling bosses, before dropping to clusters of slim columns which frame the eight giant windows. Below these a frieze of stories from the Old Testament (restored in the 19C) fills the spandrels between the niches which circumscribe the canon's seats. The main floor display is dedicated to one of the four original copies of the Magna Carta.

★ CATHEDRAL CLOSE

The spacious and mellow Close with 16C-18C houses of ancient stone and terracotta brick was enclosed in the 1330s against the "riotous citizenry", using stone from the cathedral and castle of Old Sarum.

St Ann's and Bishop's Gates – The northern gate in the east wall (opening into St John's Street) abuts Malmesbury House where Charles II took refuge in 1651; originally built in the 13C, the house has been remodelled several times; its west front was designed by Sir Christopher Wren.
The southern gate *(private)* gives access to the Old Bishop's Palace, now the Cathedral School.

Harnham or South Gate – The distant south gate leads to the suppressed De Vaux College and St Nicholas Hospital, the latter the source of Trollope's *The Warden*. Beyond, runs the River Avon which was bridged in 1244 by Bishop Bingham, to ensure easy access and ensure prosperous trading; it was from these water meadows that John Constable painted his most endearing views of Salisbury.

★ **Salisbury and South Wiltshire Museum** ⊘ – *West side of the Close.* The medieval house of stone, to which brick additions have been made throughout the centuries, has been known as the **King's House** ever since James I lodged there on a visit to the city.
The museum contains fascinating displays about Stonehenge, complete with artefacts retrieved from the site before it was made into a World Heritage Monument; the 19C archeologist General Pitt-Rivers, a pioneer of scientific excavation who worked at Cranborne Chase; on local history including the Salisbury Giant and Hob-Nob, 15C processional guild figures, local paintings and prints. Upstairs, rooms are reserved for lace, embroidery and costumes from the 1750s; several hundred pieces by Wedgwood; English glass and china enlivened by Bow and Chelsea figures, and a collection of tea-pots.
The **Medieval Hall** adjacent is all that is left of the 13C Deanery.

★ **Royal Gloucestershire, Berkshire and Wiltshire Regiment (Salisbury) Museum** ⊘ – *West side of the Close.* The county infantry regiment was formed in 1959 when the Royal Berkshire and Wiltshire Regiments were amalgamated. The museum is housed in the **Wardrobe**, one of the first houses to be erected in the Close (1254) as the Bishop's document storehouse and wardrobe; it was altered in the 15C and later converted into a dwelling.
Against the lime-yellow *papier mâché* wall decoration in the hall, in the decorated 18C reception rooms and in the ancient cellar, epic moments in the regiments' histories are illustrated through displays of combat dress, weapons of the day, despatches, items of enemy uniform, maps, campaigns and medals, regimental silver, the overseas postings; William and Mary tankards (1691), snuffboxes, chased Indian silver claret jugs (1875) and centrepieces, including a long and scaly Chinese dragon.

★ **Mompesson House** ⊘ – *Choristers' Close.* An 18C wrought-iron gate leads to the Queen Anne House, built in 1701 by Sir Charles Mompesson: note his initials in the cartouche over the door.
Inside, an oak staircase, which was inserted in the 1740s beyond the wide arch at the back of the marble-paved hall, rises by shallow flights with three crisply turned banisters to each tread. The staircase walls and ceiling are covered with a generous outpouring of **Baroque plasterwork** swags, scrolls and cartouches; additional fine plasterwork decorates the Drawing Room, Dining Room and Green Room *(upstairs)*. The furniture is mostly from the 18C. At the back is a secluded wall garden.
The **Turnbull collection of 18C English drinking glasses** comprises some 370 different types of glass displayed in period cabinets in the Dining and Little Drawing Rooms. The early examples of 1700-45 are characterised by thick glass and knobbed stems, the later glasses – after an excise tax of 1745 placed a levy on glass by weight – by lighter bowls and slender stems. Decoration as well as

---

Inns of note

Salisbury is a thriving centre of trade and commerce for the region. In times past itinerant workers, craftsmen, pilgrims and merchants would have relied on the many hostels and coaching inns for board and lodgings. Most have traditional names like the New Inn, the Pheasant, the Red Lion and the King's Arms (associated with the escape of Charles II after the Battle of Worcester). The medieval-looking **Haunch of Venison** which overlooks the Market Cross, was built as the church house for St Thomas's in 1320; inside, it has a cosy, smoke-darkened wood-panel snug warmed by a log fire; in an alcove sits a preserved severed hand holding a set of 18C playing-cards; the bar is pewter topped; a rare set of antique taps dispense allotted measures of spirits (including 150 different malt whiskies) and brandies. Good food, ranges of wine and real ale.

---

shape took all forms including air and opaque twist stems, enamelling and engraving, which was often commemorative or had a hidden or symbolic meaning as in Jacobite toasting glasses.

North or High Street Gate – North of the cathedral an engaging bronze *Walking Madonna* by **Elisabeth Frink** (1981) strides across the grass. The asphalted path leads to the gate with a statue of Edward VII. This opens from the **Choristers' Close** into the town by way of an alley bordered by old houses and the **College of Matrons**, built in 1682 as almshouses for 12 widows of the clergy, possibly to designs by Wren.

The High Street Gate portcullis was lowered during times of unrest; today the gates close at 11pm.

BEYOND THE CATHEDRAL PRECINCT

Medieval streets – Between the cathedral and the 19C **Market Square** to the north lies a network of medieval streets and cut-throughs, lined by half-timbered houses with high oversailing upper floors and tall gables, dating from the 14C-17C with a few later insertions; the shops and stalls which once flourished along their length are recalled in the names: Fish Row, Butcher Row, Silver Street, Blue Boar Row, Ox Row, Oatmeal Row.

At the centre in a small square is the **Poultry Cross**, a 15C hexagonal structure decorated with buttresses, pinnacles and a spirelet.

★ **Sarum St Thomas Church** – *Northeast end of the High Street, overlooking St Thomas Square and the medieval streets west of Market Square.* The low, castellated, square tower (1390) with its Tudor Quarter Clock Jacques and the light and spacious Perpendicular church are a rebuilding on the site of a wooden chapel of ease erected c1219 to provide a place of worship for the cathedral craftsmen; it was dedicated to St Thomas a Becket in c1220.

The nave is enclosed by a particularly fine, carved **angel roof**. The chancel arch bears the largest **doom painting** (c1475) in England painted in gratitude for the safe return of a pilgrim: its rare state of preservation is largely due to having been whitewashed at the Reformation. At the apex, Christ in Majesty in the New Jerusalem: in attendance are St James (patron saint of pilgrims) and St Osmund (first Bishop of Salisbury).

The **choir** (1470, "modernised" by G E Street in the 19C) has angel musician roof supports: the north side was subsidised by the Dean and Chapter, the south side by merchants and citizens whose names are listed on the south pillar; note the brass commemorating a 16C wool merchant and mayor John Webbe, and his wife and six children. The **Lady Chapel**, which was built by a wealthy wool merchant, master of the Tailors' Guild and mayor, is decorated with very small 15C frescoes (*Annunciation, Visitation, Nativity*, interspersed with the badge of the Order of the Garter and flowering lilies) and, since 1725, by splendid wrought-iron railings and finely carved woodwork endowed by the Eyre family whose fortune was based on trade with the Indies; fine Georgian mayoral mace stands, fragments of early glass. Among the other furnishings, note the carved oak panel of 1671 on south nave wall, "his own worke", by Humphrey Backham, the painted royal arms of Queen Elizabeth with the Welsh dragon supporter which preceded the Scots unicorn. Most of the funeral hatchments are 17C-18C. In the north aisle is a fragment of 15C-16C *opus anglicanum* needlework.

Creasy Collection of Contemporary Art ⊙ – *Salisbury Library, Market Square.* In memory and celebration of the work of John Creasy, this collection of modern works by distinguished artists (Hodgkin, Joe Tilson, Kossof) with a Wiltshire connection continues to acquire contemporary pieces by Art College students.

Fisherton Mill ⊙ – *108 Fisherton Street.* A former grain mill plays host to broad ranging displays of contemporary art, craft and design on several floors of gallery space.

EXCURSIONS

★ Old Sarum

2 miles north on A345 (west side – signposted; car park through East Gate)

Standing on the rubble walls of the castle's Norman inner bailey ⊙, visitors may view Salisbury Plain as did the guards of old. Two miles away to the south is the cathedral spire.

From the walls, which are those of Bishop Roger's 12C castle in the inner bailey – the first castle-keep on the site – can also be seen in the foreground, in the northwest corner of the outer bailey, the footings of Bishop St Osmund's 11C cathedral and, superimposed, Bishop Roger's larger 12C church. Models in Salisbury Museum provide an insight as to how it may have been.

Woodford

★ **Heale House Garden** ⊙ – *4 miles north of Salisbury by A360 and by-road to Lower, Middle and Upper Woodford; Heale House is between Middle and Upper Woodford.*

The 17C house of old rose brick with stone dressings, tall windows, pediments and a pitched roof, where Charles II sheltered after the Battle of Worcester in 1651, stands in a wooded valley at the end of a long tree-lined drive, surrounded with grazing sheep.

The informal garden of eight acres, secluded by clipped yew hedges, opens on to the River Avon; it is scented by a border-hedge of musk and sweet-smelling, old-fashioned roses and coloured by a long, wide and richly planted herbaceous border. A walled garden, part flowers, part vegetables, is quartered by a pergola of pleached apple trees; a wild water garden, planted with magnolia, cherry, mulberry, medlar, walnut and acer surrounds a Japanese thatched tea-house approached over a red painted Nikko Bridge.

Delicate colour is provided in this charming, inspirational English garden by a broad range of roses, wisteria and clematis; textures are contrasted by varieties of early iris, cyclamen, tulips, exquisite fritillaries, peonies, bluebells, scilla, primulas, delphinium, achillea, campanula and autumn crocus.

Salisbury Plain

The Plain (10 x 20 miles) lies north of Salisbury extending from the Wylye Valley in the south to the Vale of Pewsey in the north. Although known as a plain it is, in fact, gently undulating, clay-chalk downland with many of its knolls marked by prehistoric monuments – burial barrows, hillforts (Battlesbury and Scratchbury) and Stonehenge. Prehistoric forts were succeeded by defended towns such as Old Sarum and Wilton and, eventually, by peaceful settlement.

Today, most of the area is managed by the British Army who tenant out some of the open pasture and arable farmland on condition it may be used for military training exercises; other downland, reserved for manoeuvres (**beware of road warning panels; red flags denote areas where access is suspended during exercises**), provides habitats for downland plants and wildlife (especially small mammals, hawks). The army, which arrived in the 19C, garrisons its principal fighting troops around Tidworth and Bulford; the spiritless barracks at Larkhill now serve the Royal School of Artillery; while Warminster provides the combined forces with a school for tactical warfare and arms training centre.

Army manœuvres, Salisbury Plain

On the Plain itself, the village of Imber was evacuated by decree in 1943, and a town was built on Copehill Down (visible from B390 between Shrewton and Chitterne) for use exclusively as a training ground for fighting in built-up areas: tactical exercises that proved especially important during the British intervention in Bosnia.

For the Fovant Badges, see SHAFTESBURY; *for other regimental badges and the Wylye Valley, see* WILTON.

Redlynch *9 miles south by A338 and B3080*

Newhouse ⊘ – The three-storeyed Jacobean house of *c*1619, built of red brick to a Y or "Trinity" plan, has pitched roofs giving gables at the end of each wing and, in addition, three gables at the front. In the 18C the house was enlarged by flat-roofed, single-storey extensions to the two front wings.

In the 17C it was bought by the Eyres in whose family it has remained ever since; in the 19C a daughter of the house married Horatio Nelson's nephew, which explains the presence of various documents relating to Nelson, and period costumes.

Isles of SCILLY★

Cornwall – Population 2 048

Michelin Atlas p 2 or Map 403 – inset – 28 miles southwest of Land's End
For access, see PRACTICAL INFORMATION section

Scilly is designated as an Area of Outstanding Natural Beauty, its coast as a Heritage Coast and its waters a Marine Park managed by the Isles of Scilly Environmental Trust in collaboration with the Duchy of Cornwall; additional sites are further protected under English Nature's conservation scheme for Sites of Special Scientific Interest. The Fortunate Islands, an archipelago of granite islands and outcrops – once a single land mass – have been variously identified as the mountain peaks of Atlantis, the lost land of **Lyonesse**, the westerly tin islands of the Phoenicians, known to Herodotus as the Cassiterides, or the Islands of the Blest where dead heroes were buried and from where Olaf, King of Norway introduced Christianity to his realm. The approach by sea or by air provides a partial **view★★★** of the five inhabited, 40 uninhabited islands and 150 or so named rocks set in a close group in the clear, blue-green ocean. Headlands, reefs and saw-toothed needles stand ruffed in white spume, the larger islands lush and green. An almost constant wind blows in from the Atlantic bearing clouds low over the ocean, which, when they hit the rocks, drop their moisture in short, soaking showers – windproof and waterproof clothing and shoes are, therefore, essential. On all the islands' leeward sides are long white sand beaches, coves, walks or flower-filled gardens. The water, clear, safe (except over the sandbars) and tempting, is icy.

History – Archeological surveys confirm that the islands were Bronze and Iron Age settlements long before the Romans knew them as outposts of Sylicancis, named after the Viking Syllanger and that from AD 400-1 000 Christian hermits were living there while Benedictine monks settled on Tresco. Other records show that Athelstan ejected the Danes from the islands in AD 930 and that Tresco, St Sampson, St Elidius and St Theona were given to Tavistock Abbey during the reign of Edward the Confessor (1042-66), while the other islands were entrusted to the Earls of Cornwall: this was reiterated as so by Henry I (1114).

At the Dissolution, the properties of the larger religious houses were requisitioned by the Crown. Defences were initiated on Tresco and St Mary by Thomas Seymour, Lord Protector of the boy King Edward VI, who had married Henry VIII's widow Catherine Parr, and who was subsequently executed for consorting with pirates and for other such misdeeds. Fearing that the Spaniards should attempt to muster the Armada in the islands prior to attacking the mainland, Elizabeth I entrusted the Godolphins with the task of supervising the islands. In 1831, the Duke of Leeds failed to renew the lease and the islands reverted to the Duchy of Cornwall.

Economy – As **Squire Augustus Smith** became Lord Proprietor in 1834, so began a 40 year period of prosperity: houses, churches and schools were built, five shipbuilding yards were established on St Mary's, the **flower industry** was established (1868) giving islanders an income through the winter to complement their harvesting of **kelp** *(see below St Martin's – White Island)*. Most of the flowers are of the narcissi family including paper whites, golden dawn, soleil d'or and Scilly whites (watercolours of the complete range are displayed in the museum on St Mary's); bulbs are lifted in June, treated for eelworm and replanted; about 30 million blooms are harvested from October to March.

Once the railway was extended to Penzance (1859), these cottage industries were slowly superseded by tourism. The building of additional housing, however, is rigorously controlled; although national grid electricity is now available on the outlying islands, further development of facilities is severely restricted, especially since such a large proportion of hitherto unexploited land is now protected. Without sophisticated "modernisation" these islands preserve their genuine "old fashioned" charm and air of informal friendliness; visitors are offered an ecological brand of tourism which allows for locally caught flat-fish (megrim, plaice, John Dory) and craw-fish (lobster, crab) to be accompanied in season by home-grown fresh vegetables (especially early potatoes) to be listed on restaurant menus.

Constitution – The islands, owned by the Duchy of Cornwall since 1337, were reclaimed in 1920 when the leases to all but Tresco were relinquished; in 1987 the Duchy leased all the uninhabited islands and untenanted land to the Isles of Scilly Environmental Trust for a peppercorn rent. The rest of the islands fall within the jurisdiction of Cornwall: locally, they are administered by a council of 21 comprising 13 members elected from St Mary's, two from each of the off-islands: Tresco remains independent while continuing to be leased to the Smith family.

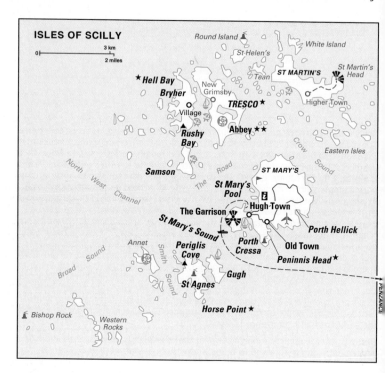

ST MARY'S

St Mary's is the largest island with nine miles of coastline, where the majority of Scillonians live. At the Old Quay lie the excursion launches which provide access to the neighbouring off islands of Tresco, Bryher, Samson, St Martin's (and Eastern Islands), St Agnes, Annet and the Western Rocks: see St Mary's Boatmen Association blackboards on the quay, outside the Atlantic Hotel and by the Steamship Company offices in Hugh Street for details.

Hugh Town – The main settlement so named from the Cornish word *hugh* meaning promontory, runs the length of the sand bar between the main part of the island and a hill to the west crowned by the **Garrison** which overlooks the sea on two sides: south across the silver **Porth Cressa Beach**; north over the harbour, **St Mary's Pool**. Being closest to the harbour where the *Scillonian III* from Penzance downloads its cargo, Hugh Town provides the main amenities (post office, bank, "super market", chemists, pubs and restaurants, Tourist Information Centre).

★ **Museum** ⊙ – The local museum was built to house prehistoric and Roman objects found during excavations on the offshore island of Nonours (Neolithic tools and funerary urns, coins and pottery sherds); additional finds from the areas around Ennor and Star Castles have revealed material from the Middle Ages and 16C. These, together with a broad collection of objects retrieved from the sea (treasures from ship wrecks include several cannon and pieces of eight from the *Association*, flotsam and jetsam, stones illustrating local geology) and from the past (early maps and charts, children's school books, Victorian toys, Edwardian clothes, watercolour studies of bulbs once grown commercially) illustrate different aspects of life in the Scillies.

The lower ground floor is dedicated to a substantial natural history section: the 19C Tresco collection of birds (native and migrant), cases of shells, framed pressed specimens of ferns and sea-weed, and, during the summer months, a flower table with samples of local plants. The cluttered kitchen setting evocatively suggests subsistence on the islands in 1900.

★ **Garrison Walk** – *2 hours, best enjoyed at dusk.* The moulded granite **Garrison Gate**, was built in the mid-18C during the Spanish Wars (1715-50); defences were further reinforced with 18 batteries. This provides access to **Star Castle** (now a hotel), which takes its name from the eight-pointed keep, curtain wall and dry moat on the brow of the hill. The fort, erected speedily between June 1593 and December 1594, dates from the time of Queen Elizabeth's feud with Spain; during the Civil War, the castle first harboured Cavaliers on their flight to France (1646), surrendered and became the last Royalist stronghold (1648), which was finally defeated in 1651. Outside the castle sits a seat given by Richard Branson (1986) in thanks for hospitality bestowed following his successful Atlantic crossing challenge in *Virgin Atlantic Challenger II*.

The **gunpowder store**, just inside the gate, has also doubled as a prison cell.

The popular mid-18C promenade inside the rampart wall leads to a succession of batteries which circle the headland, providing extensive **views★★**; these are complete with gun emplacements, a series of 12 cast-iron 18C-19C cannon and sunken ammunition stores.

Behind the Duke of Leeds or Garden Battery is a range of houses: the one with a crest, **Hugh House**, accommodate the offices of the Duchy of Cornwall.

Old Town and the eastern end – Roads and paths make it possible to follow the coastline, to cut across in any direction or even to start out on or, halfway round, to pick up the bus which makes regular circular tours. Features of interest include :

Porth Mellon – *West shore, just beyond the lifeboat.* The remains of a Henry VIII square fort are known as **Harry's Walls**.

Telegraph Tower – Past the island's golf course stands Telegraph Tower watch point (German binoculars in situ), at 158ft the island's highest point, and within easy reach on foot of **Bants Carn**, a burial chamber of stones and capstones (*c*1800 BC) and the walls of an Iron Age village (200-300 AD).

Porth Hellick – The large inlet is marked by a rough monument where Sir Cloudesley Shovel was washed ashore from the wreck of the *Association* in 1707. A gate close by opens the way to the top of the Down and ancient passage grave.

Old Town Church – The church, founded in the 12C and rebuilt in the 19C, is surmounted on its east gable by a 10C stone cross; in the churchyard are the graves of local Scillonians, ship-wreck victims (notably from the *Schiller* which went down in 1875), and Lord Harold Wilson (d1995), Lord of Rievaulx who loved to retreat to St Mary's on holiday.

Round the bay, the main road leads to Old Town where the medieval Castle Ennor once stood. Excellent sheltered beach, especially for young children.

★ **Peninnis Head** – The spectacular head has eroded granite rocks of majestic size with such names as Monk's Cowl, Tooth Rock, Kettle and Pans, Big Jolly Rock, Izzicumpucca, Tuskless Elephant, Sleeping Bear and Laughing Old Man.

★ TRESCO

Depending on the state of the tide which can reach up to 19ft, boats from St Mary land at one of two points: New Grimsby on the western shore and Carn Near Landing at the southern tip of the island. From New Grimsby (shop and public conveniences) a path leads north through the low gorse to **Cromwell's Castle**, a single round, 60ft tall, tower built in 1651 in case of attack by the Dutch;

Gig racing★★ ⓥ

The gigs of elm planking 0.25in thick, 28-30ft long with 5ft beam and less than 2ft draught, were built as rival pilot launches and smuggling craft – they were banned from having more than six oars so as not to have an advantage over the excise cutters. On Wednesday and Friday evenings throughout the summer the six-oared island gigs race in the St Mary's roadstead, starting from Nut Rock off Samson at 8pm sharp, and finishing at the Quay. Traditional favourites built by perhaps the most eminent Peters boatyard at St Mawes include *Bonnet* (built 1830) and *Golden Eagle* (1870) which are manned by St Mary's crews, and St Agnes' *Shah* (1873); the *Islander* (1989), built in Scilly from Cornish elm, is arguably the fastest and most beautiful.

- Latterly, the sport has enjoyed such a revival as to warrant a World Championships event held in May.

across the sheltered cove is Hangman's Island (from the Cornish *An Mair,* meaning The Rock). The path continues to the ruin of **King Charles' Castle** which dates from 1550-54 when the islands served as a base where Royalists could arm their frigates ready to harass Parliamentarian forces operating in the English, Irish and Bristol Channels: it was badly placed, however, and reinforcing earthworks had to be laid in case of attack. Beyond, towards the Round Island lighthouse and past a number of tin workings, is **Piper's Hole**: a secret, deep chamber with a fresh-water pool, associated with smugglers and mermaids. A second track leads over the hill to Old Grimsby on the east coast. The most direct route to the gardens is provided by a concreted path (1.25 miles from New Grimsby, 0.5 mile from Carn Near: bicycles, tractors and electric buggies only).

★★ **Abbey Gardens** ⊘ – The destruction of the priory dedicated to St Nicholas, patron saint of sailors, was due to fire rather than to the Dissolution, a vulnerable target at the hands of pirates and marauders.

Augustus Smith chose to settle on Tresco on being appointed Lord Proprietor in 1834. There he built a Victorian-medieval castle mansion using island stone and wrecked ships' timbers. Below the house, in a sheltered hollow around the old abbey ruins, he created the soon famous, subtropical gardens from seeds and plants (succulents and hard-leaved salt-resistant plants from the Mediterranean and Canary Islands) brought back by Scillonian sailors and professional plant collectors. Smith's nephew, T A Dorrien-Smith, inherited the estate in 1872 and besides introducing a series of Monterey pines and cypresses as wind-breaks to subdue the force of the salt-bearing gales, developed the islands' potential for growing early-flowering bulbs. His successor, Major Arthur Dorrien-Smith, having seen active service in South Africa, Australia and New Zealand, further extended the range of exotic plantings at Tresco. It has befallen the subsequent generations to maintain and sustain the gardens that continue to enthrall horticulturalists and amateur gardeners alike.

The south-facing terraces are enclosed and punctuated by mature trees (lily of the valley tree, eucalyptus, Mauri pine, New Zealand tree ferns, Australian proteaceae, South African silver tree from Table Mountain, rhododendron, holm oaks, palms, magnolia). Elsewhere proliferate a coloured profusion of abutilon, agapanthus, agave, bananas, bougainvillea, citrus trees, clematis, convolvulus, datura, echiums, fuchsia (and so on through the alphabet to wisteria and yucca); in 1987 severe weather conditions damaged large numbers of plants, allowing for some remodelling of the gardens which continue to evolve.

Gravel tracks provide access to the terraces; high points, marked by a bench or a piece of sculpture offer fine **views**★★ over the garden, its pond and ingenious fountain, Valhalla and the other islands beyond.

Valhalla – Some fifty ships' figureheads, trailer and name boards, fiddles and carved ornaments from the thousand ships wrecked off the islands in the past two centuries stand gilded and boldly coloured, facing into the wind.

Beyond the garden fence is the island's **heliport** which provides regular flights to Penzance.

Tresco Abbey gardens

BRYHER

From the landing on the east shore (public conveniences) a road snakes up past the 18C church to a junction: left fork and straight on for the **Great Pool** (good for migrating birds) and Hell Bay Hotel; right to The Town (post office and stores). **Watch Hill** provides a perfect high point with a most splendid **view★★**, from where in days of yore locals would look out for ships in distress. From here, paths *(white-painted marker stones)* lead north to Bad Place Hill (colonies of nesting birds between March and July) and Shipman Head beyond; the track then doubles back southwards along the western coast to **Hell Bay★** where the waves can thunder onto the beach scattering spray and spume, all the way around to the sheltered beach at **Rushy Bay**.

A tour of the **Norrard Rocks** *(90min circular trip from St Mary's)* may also take in landings at Bryher or Tresco.

ST AGNES

St Agnes and the islet of **Gugh** *(accessible across a sandbar at low water: beware of dangerous currents during rising tides)* are separated from the other main islands by **St Mary's Sound**, a deep water channel flushed by strong currents followed by the *Scillonian* at low tide: the channel is said to have made the islanders the most independent, the men the finest pilots, and the fiercest smugglers and wreckers. Landings are made across Porth Conger, overlooked by the Turk's Head public house (public conveniences). The left track at the fork leads to The Cove and **The Old Man of Gugh**, an upright stone (9ft) from which radiate some 14 ley lines; dotted over Kittern Hill are a number of ancient burial sites.

Follow the main narrow concrete track up to the brow of the hill.

Before the Post Office Store, a track leads left down Love Lane between fields planted with flowers, towards the grandiose rock scenery of **Horse Point★** and Beady Pool, so called because 17C Dutch beads continue to be washed up there.

The track otherwise continues towards the lighthouse.

Beyond the cottages and Post Office Store the track forks again: to the right it leads down to Lower Town and the **Big Pool**, a favourite transit point for migrating birds. Walk back round **Periglis Cove** (long lifeboat launching slip) to the small **church** (1838) whose roof is largely built using timbers salvaged from a foreign frigate wrecked in 1781; the colourful **east window** dates from 1960. From here, the main track climbs up towards the lighthouse *(private)* and forks right past a row of former coastguard cottages; the footpath continues towards open down, past the strangely weathered **Nag's Head** rock, and down to Troy Town Maze *(marked)*, a miniature pebble stone maze laid by a lighthouse keeper in 1729.

ST MARTIN'S

The two mile long granite spine which is St Martin's presents a rugged shore to the northeast and stretches of the finest sand beaches on all other fronts. Little Arthur Farm (inland from Higher Town Bay) is the island's main organic food producer; elsewhere minute flower fields shelter in the hollows enclosed by high hedges; tumuli or burial mounds crown the more exposed sites; the rest is covered with rhododendrons, purple heather and golden gorse.

Landings are made either at Higher Town Quay or at Lower Town (luxury hotel); these are linked by a track via Middle Town.

A path from **Higher Town** (post office, tea-shops, sailing centre) leads to the prominent red and white shipping marker known as Day Mark erected in 1683 on St Martin's Head: this 160ft high **viewpoint★★** provides a broad prospect towards the **Sevenstones Reef** *(7 miles northeast)*, grave of the *Torrey Canyon* in 1967, and, two miles further off, the **Lightship**, on station since 1841. On a clear day the mainland coast is clearly visible; closer to hand northwestwards, lies **White Island** (accessible at low tide) where kelp was once burnt to extract soda, which was then exported to Bristol and Gloucester for making alum, soap and glass.

UNINHABITED ISLANDS

Samson – The uninhabited island consists of two hills joined by a narrow isthmus of sand – a desert isle with megalithic remains, the ruins of cottages emptied of their elderly tenants in 1855 and abandoned stone walls; those on the eastern side appear only at low tide, and once served the handful of inhabitants as fish traps.

St Helen's – An annual pilgrimage takes place in early August to the ruins of a 10C oratory. The main granite and brick building, however, is all that remains of an 18C pest-house where people suspected of carrying the plague were off loaded from passing ships.

The neighbouring island of **Teän** was once inhabited by the descendants of a family from Falmouth who earned their living from kelping.

Excursions to both these islands are included in a tour *(90min from St Mary's,* that also takes in **Round Island** and Men-a-Vaur; landing at Bryher, St Martin's or Tresco depending on tide and weather.

Eastern Isles – A circular trip *(90min)* from St Mary's taking in St Martin's consists of a leisurely meander through the rocky outcrops to view the sea birds (shags, cormorants, gulls) and snoozing Atlantic grey seals.

At times it is also possible to land at **Great Ganilly** and **Little Arthur** (access to Middle Arthur and Great Arthur) to explore ancient burial sites including, it is alleged, the grave of King Arthur who may have been conveyed to Scilly after the Battle of Camlan (*c* AD 537).

Annet, Western and Bishop Rocks – *2 hours round trip*. Weather and season permitting, this excursion includes the sea-thrift covered bird sanctuary of Annet (extensive colonies of puffins and shearwaters which are decimated by the resident rapacious great black-backed gulls), the rocks which have seen the demise of countless ships now harbouring a thriving colony of seals, and the most southwesterly point in Britain, marked by the Bishop Rock Lighthouse. This is Britain's tallest pillar light standing to a height of 175ft; the top of the tower is still calculated to swing through an arc of up to six feet in gale-force winds; it was electrified in 1973 and automated in 1992.

Landing on the uninhabited islands

Scilly is famous for its birdlife as the more remote islands attract rare and unusual species at migration times, especially in autumn when hoopoes, golden orioles and bee-eaters may be spotted; in October, North American rarities such as the blackpoll warbler and gray-cheeked thrush have been known to transit here. The rocky outcrops also shelter breeding colonies of guillemots, razorbills, puffins, kittiwakes, fulmars, lesser and great black-backed gulls, storm petrels and Manx shearwaters, common terns... Special bird-watching trips are run on Sundays.

Rosevean, White Island off Samson, Gweal, Samson, the Eastern Islands, St Helen's, Puffin Island, White Island off St Martin's and Northwethal are **open all year.**

Annet, the Western Rocks, Crebewethan, Corregan, Melledgan, Rosevear, Norrard Rocks, Castle Bryher, Illiswillgig, Teän, Maiden Bower, Mincarlo and Scilly Rock, Stony Island, Green Island off Samson, Menavour off St Helen's, however, are **closed through the breeding season**, between mid-March and end August.

For reference, see INTRODUCTION: Birding in the West Country.

SHAFTESBURY

Dorset – Population 6 203
Michelin Atlas p 8 or Map 403 – N 30, 31

The town is built on the crest (700ft) of a spur which King Alfred fortified in his struggle against the Danes; little remains of his or earlier hillforts. During the 17C and 18C, Shaftesbury was a convenient halt on the road south (now the A350) from Cirencester, Chippenham and Warminster to Blandford Forum, Dorchester and the coast (Weymouth and Poole). One particular trade to flourish at this time was button-making – although a machine exhibited at the Great Exhibition of 1851 soon proved to be more viable.

There is an extensive **view★** south from Gold Hill and Park Walk across the Blackmore Vale, west into Somerset where Glastonbury Tor is visible on a clear day and north towards Salisbury Plain.

Market day: Thursday all day in the High Street, also local cattle market.

★ **Gold Hill** – Behind the Town Hall the road descends in a steep cobbled curve into the valley below. It is bordered on the east side by small **16C, 17C and 18C houses**, thatched, tiled, built of stone or brick, each sitting on the shoulders of the one below; opposite stands a massive buttressed 13C ochre-coloured **wall**. At one time stalls would have been set up along the west side: today this only happens once a year when the Gold Hill Fair takes place in July.

Gold Hill Shaftesbury

★ **Local History Museum** ⊙ – A garden path leads to the house which in the 19C was a barber's shop and before that a doss house. Today it shelters a large collection of interesting and amusing miscellany of bygones: highlights include 18C trade tokens, medals and Anglo-Saxon coins (three moneyers were licensed to issue coinage in Shaftesbury in Domesday); the town's hand-pulled wooden 1744 fire-engine with leather buckets; a broad range of traditional farm and domestic implements; horse brasses; municipal standard corn-measures and town-crier's outfit; cards of Dorset buttons for which Shaftesbury was particularly renowned rare copper plate for a map of Shaftesbury made in 1799.

Abbey and Museum ⊙ – The Benedictine house of 100-140 nuns stood within a 4-acre precinct; today a walled garden not quite the extent of the great abbey church, which measured 240ft from east to west, encloses the excavated footings. Most of the stonework has been pillaged through the ages for re-use elsewhere. In the **museum** are a number of fragments and medieval floor tiles. From its foundation in 888 the abbey was rich, as King Alfred endowed it with "100 hides of land" (9 000 acres). In 948 it was given the hinterland and the "right of wreck" along the coast west of St Aldhelm's Head; thirty years later it

> ### The Shaftesbury Byzant
>
> A curious gold object decorated with beads, ribbons and feathers, likened by some to a pineapple, this 18C Byzant was ritually processed on 1 May out of the town in a ceremony to secure the town's water-supply for the ensuing year. The practice (c1522-1830) also included the symbolic gift of a calf's head, a penny loaf , a new pair of gloves, a leather pouch of coins and a gallon of ale – most of which was returned to the town.

became the centre of the cult of St Edward, the boy-king and martyr, murdered at Corfe Castle by his step-mother. In 1368 the abbess was granted a licence to crenellate the church and belltower; in the same period she took the rank of baron, keeping seven knights in fealty to protect the monarch and sending a representative to parliament.

Among the abbesses was **Marie de France**, the 12C Anglo-Norman lyric poet who was half-sister to Henry II, Plantagenet; among visitors was **Canute**, who died in the abbey in 1035.

It was said in the 15C-16C that if the Abbess of Shaston (Shaftesbury) were to marry the Abbot of Glaston (Glastonbury) their heirs would own more land than the king. In 1539 Henry VIII dissolved both abbeys.

EXCURSIONS

A30 to Wilton

★ Old Wardour Castle – The old castle stands on a spur, sheltered on three sides by wooded hills looking out west across an 18C man-made lake known as the Fish Pond. In May-June the lawns, where once the inner bailey was, are vividly outlined by rhododendrons.

The tower house, rock-like in its mass, hexagonal in form with corbel turrets marking the angles and a front advanced squarely as twin bastions to guard the entrance, has been falling into Romantic ruin since the Civil War – its heroic hour. The castle, a royal manor in King Alfred's reign, a Benedictine property from Domesday to the Dissolution, was purchased in 1547 by Sir Thomas Arundell as part of the Wilton estate; the land around Tisbury meanwhile had already been acquired from the sale of the Shaftesbury estate.

In the Civil War the castle's defences were put to the test: in 1643, when Lord Arundell was at Oxford with the king, a Parliamentary force of 1 300 men laid siege to the castle which had a garrison of 25. On its surrender the house was looted, the contents sold, the park plundered. In 1644 the 3rd Lord Arundell besieged the place in his turn and again, after mining had wreaked further damage, the garrison surrendered.

Ruined Castle ⊙ – The ruins are those of a 14C-16C bailey or fortified tower house, built with accommodation for domestic living and lavish around a hexagonal courtyard. The Great Hall above the gateway (like at Nunney in Somerset) had the chapel, solar and lord's chambers on one side and the screens passage, service rooms and kitchens on the other. The remaining rooms were guests' lodgings which were approached by spiral staircases built into the walls.

The 16C Renaissance entrance is decorated with the Arundell arms and a bust of Christ in a niche. Just inside the courtyard *(left)* are the stone stairs to the Great Hall, beautifully framed by a **Grand Entrance**, lion decorated, Tuscan pillared and with a contrasting, plain entablature.

Nestling in the gardens is a grotto (1792) and a Late Georgian Gothick summer house.

Across the lake may be seen **New Wardour Castle** *(private)*. In 1769-77 the 8th Lord Arundell commissioned the architect James Paine to build what turned out to be the largest Georgian mansion in the county. The stone house has a circular, marble-floored hall, from which twin cantilevered staircases rise round the walls to a gallery ringed by Corinthian columns. The large chapel was extended by Sir John Soane. In 1960 it was taken over by Cranborne Chase School.

Tisbury Parish Church – Dedicated to **St John the Baptist**, this is the largest church in the vicinity: records confirm that it was an important centre of worship and burial from Saxon times. The earliest fabric of the extant building is Norman (crossing and transepts); the Decorated nave and chancel date from the late 13C – when the large and ancient yew tree outside may also have been planted.

The tower rises in two tiers: the lower section housing the bells is Norman Transitional (1180-1200); the upper part replaces the original spire which was hit by lightning in 1762, collapsing into the north transept.

In the north porch note the early trumpet and stiff-leaf capitals. The tall nave (1450) is lit by a clerestory of square-headed windows with two lights; its 15C wagon roof consists of three pairs of hammerbeams decorated with carved angels; the aisle roofs are later (16C), possibly endowed by Lord Arundell.

The chancel (St Andrew's Chapel) was largely remodelled in the 19C, the roof and altar rail are Victorian; the main window is alleged to have been designed by Christopher Wren, who was born nearby at East Knoyle; below, sits a pre-Reformation stone altar inscribed with five crosses representing the wounds of Christ; before it are a series of 16C and 17C monuments (Lawrence Hyde brass and Arundell family tablets including one for Ann who married the second Lord Baltimore who colonised parts of Virginia: the connection between these lords of the manor is related in the church guide book).

In the eastern churchyard lie the parents of Rudyard Kipling.

Fovant Regimental Badges – The frieze of military crests was cut into the escarpment by successive companies of soldiers encamped on Fovant Down in 1916. As a sign of changing times, they and all other hill figures were covered over in 1939 to prevent their use as navigational bearings.

Among the figures, from east to west, are: a map of Australia, and about 4 along, a rising sun and a kangaroo (all Australian), RAMC badge, YMCA triangle, 6th City of London Rifles, London Rifle Brigade, the Rifle Brigade, Devonshire Regiment (towered castle), 7th Royal Fusiliers, Royal Warwickshire Regiment (a deer).

For Fiddleford Manor and Sturminster Newton, see BLANDFORD FORUM.

The town, in triumph, bought back the abbey as its parish church at the Dissolution, paying 100 marks for the fabric and 400 for the roof timbers, lead and bells, or £327 in all. It was a goodly sum but represented victory in the feud with the Benedictine community, and Sherborne, a prosperous market in a wool and sheep area, was about to become one of the principal cloth towns of the West Country. Market days: Thursday and Saturday all day.

★★ SHERBORNE ABBEY ⊘ 30min

The abbey began as a **Saxon stone church**, which grew to greatest importance in 705 when Ine, King of Wessex, appointed as first bishop **St Aldhelm** (see MALMESBURY), of whom it was said that "by his preaching he completed the conquest of the West". Gradually the church was rebuilt by Aldhelm's 26 successors until by the Conquest a large Saxon cathedral stood on the site. In 998 a Benedictine community had replaced the earlier, secular canons and in 1121, 50 years after the see had removed to Old Sarum (see SALISBURY), the church had become an independent abbey with the east end reserved for the monks, the west for the laity. During the 12C the church was rebuilt in the Norman style but west of the nave St Aldhelm's original church probably survived until it was replaced in the 15C by a chapel of ease, All Hallows.

In the century before the Dissolution, 1420-1504, the monastic church was again rebuilt, this time in the Perpendicular style but the Early English Lady Chapel and Norman porch, both of which survive in part, were left intact. As the chancel was nearing completion in 1437, a quarrel arose between the townsfolk and the monks over the narrowing of the doorway between All Hallows and the abbey. The townsfolk rioted and "a priest of All Hallows", according to Leland, "shott a shaft with fire into the top of that part that the monks used (the chancel) from that which the townsmen used (the nave); and the partition, chancing at the time to be thatched in the roof (while the rebuilding was going on), was set afire and consequently the whole church, the lead and the bells melted, was defaced". The chancel limestone walls remain to this day reddened by the heat of the fire. All Hallows was demolished after the Dissolution.

Exterior – The abbey is built of Ham Hill stone: deep honey-gold in sunlight, dark ochre on a grey day, old gold by floodlight. The Perpendicular windows rise in two tiers along the south front, divided midway by the great eight-light transept window. The **crossing tower**, on massive Saxon-Norman piers and walls, lifts to a final stage on thinner, recessed, 15C walls with bell openings in pairs below a parapet and twelve crocketed pinnacles. A parapet outlines the roofs; flying buttresses support the chancel.

The main porch shelters a rounded **Norman doorway** with zig-zag decoration.

Interior – The most striking feature on entering is the magnificent fan vaulting. The beautiful late 15C **nave** vault is slightly arched and so stands proud after 550 years. Indeed, the nave builders' problem was not the vault but a shortage of funds. The Norman aisle walls, Saxon west wall and arcade piers were, therefore, all retained; the piers were, however, neither opposite one another nor evenly spaced, the north file being 14ins to the west, making impossible a facsimile of the chancel fan vault with shafts rising from the ground to meet at the crest. Instead, a well-marked string course was inserted emphasised by angel corbels, a regular clerestory built above – the windows are out of line with the arcades – and the shafts sent from on high on their upward sweep to a cobweb of ribs in which only the bosses are coloured.

In the **north aisle** the Saxon doorway to the original Saxon church can still be seen. Besides the several early tombs with effigies, in an open coffin (at the east end), is the skeleton of one of the **Saxon Kings**, Ethelbald or Ethelbert (850-60 or 860-66), elder brother of King Alfred.

A splendid, unadorned Norman tower arch divides the chancel from the nave (the keystone mask reminiscent of others at Malmesbury and Christchurch Priory).

The vault of the 15C **choir** is the earliest large-scale fan vault in the country. In the early 15C choir the overall linearity of design would have been emphasised by being brightly painted: mouldings framing the arcade arches are echoed above to contain clerestory windows while vertical shafts shoot unhindered from the floor to the roofline before breaking out into a series of concave fans articulated by a network of slender ribs. When it was ascertained that the ridge across the almost flat ceiling had dropped some seven inches over 400 years despite the flying buttresses, the vault and buttresses were rebuilt exactly in 1856.

The **choir** stalls are modern with humorous medieval misericords and arm-rests.

The **Lady Chapel**, with its engraved glass reredos by **Laurence Whistler** and its flanking chapels (baptistry and vestry), was converted into a house for the Master of the School *(see below)* in 1560 and occupied as such for 300 years, hence the arms of Edward VI, the school's founder, on what is now the outside south wall of the abbey. Among the various tombs in the **south transept** is that by John Nost of John Digby, 3rd Earl of Bristol (d 1698), a man, according to the epitaph, "naturally inclined to avoid the hurry of public life, yet careful to keep up the port of his quality". The great west window (1998) is by John Hayward.

Sherborne School – The school was granted a royal charter as a Free Grammar School by Edward VI in 1550 *(see above)*. The buildings, including the Gatehouse and Great Court, are predominantly 19C-20C but follow the Jacobean style and are in the same Ham Stone where they abut such areas as the **Jacobean Schoolroom** (Old School Room) of *c*1625 and the **Library** (*c*1470).

St John's Almshouses – *Across the green from the abbey*. The foundation (1437-48), blessed by Royal Charter, comprises a **chapel** (medieval glass), a **hall**, several two-storey houses and a cloister surrounding a low-walled courtyard for use by the elderly residents. To the rear is the Abbey Close, ringed by modest 16C-18C houses.

Museum ⊘ – *Abbey Gate*. The museum's miscellany of exhibits relate to the town and district: a 15C wall painting downstairs, Victoriana and items on the local 17C-18C silk (as illustrated in Diderot's *Encyclopaedia* of 1772) and present glass fibre industries upstairs. The extension holds a number of tools, implements and signs, displays relating to local flora and fauna and a model of the 12C castle which makes the ruins comprehensible.

Sherborne Silk to Marglass

Westbury Mill was a grist mill before being converted to silk throwing by John Sharrer of Whitechapel in 1753; in 1769 William Willmott was appointed manager, and subsequently introduced Italian and Spanish silk winding machines. Later, the business switched to weaving, manufacturing the fabric until 1955.

The bales of silk were imported via London and the East India Company from Italy, Bengal, China and Asia Minor to "Throwing Mills" to be mechanically wound onto bobbins, before being ridded of dirt and waste; the weight of the silk and its waste were then compared to the original gross weight. Records relate that Sharrer declared himself in 1765 a silk throwster employing 500 hands in London, 200 in Gloucestershire, 400 in Dorset and 400 in Cheshire: a man, therefore of considerable wealth.

The transition to synthetic textiles came about indirectly when before the outbreak of war, the owners decided to switch to making parachute silk for the Ministry of Aircraft Production; the move into producing insulation silk for aircraft, submarines and electrical motors followed, hitherto a Japanese monopoly – a timely decision because soon after perfecting the technique, Japan attacked Pearl Harbor (December 1941). Contracts with the Ministry were consolidated to include the supply of rayon uniform attire. In August 1942, Frederick Marsden pitched for a bid to weave glass insulating fabric using technology that had been developed in America in 1939. In 1962 Marglass was sold to Courtaulds and United Merchants and Manufactures Inc.

Town centre – The abbey lies at the centre of the town west of the main, Cheap Street. This is marked at its start by an open square in which stands the six-sided **Conduit** *(left side)*, the transposed lavatorium from the abbey cloister. On the same side *(corner of Abbey Road)* are 17C **stone houses** and a combined wood-framed and stone house with three advanced, half-timbered gables. **Newland** curves southeast to join up with Long Street. It and the two streets before it are lined by 18C and early 19C **houses** built in irregular terraces in stone with period doors and windows. **Long Street** leads off right to Sherborne Castle.

★ SHERBORNE CASTLE

Raleigh and Elizabeth – The Old Castle *(half a mile east)* is a **ruin** ⊘ standing proudly, if somewhat indecipherably erect *(see Museum above)*. At the outbreak of the Civil War the Digbys, Earls of Bristol, moved into the old castle but in 1645, after being pounded by artillery fire and mined while under siege, it was ordered by Parliament to be slighted.

It was constructed in 1107-35 by Bishop Roger of Salisbury. At the end of the 16C **Sir Walter Raleigh** saw it from the London-Plymouth road and, to persuade Elizabeth to buy it for him from the church, gave the queen a jewel of the estimated value of the castle, namely £260. The jewel, or more probably a slightly smaller sum of money, was passed to the bishop, and the queen obtained the castle which she first leased and finally gave to her favourite. The favourite, however, had committed the cardinal sin only a few weeks before of marrying one of the queen's ladies-in-waiting, Bess Throckmorton. On discovering the marriage Elizabeth, in a jealous rage, banned them from her court for ever – although Raleigh returned after five years – and threw them, separately, into the Tower. They were released after five weeks and journeyed to Sherborne.

By 1594 Raleigh had decided, after spending lavish sums, that the castle could not be made into the type of house he wished to live in and he built Sherborne Lodge, the nucleus of the present castle, on the far bank of the River Yeo.

The Procession of Queen Elizabeth I

Courtesy of Mr Simon Wingfield Digby, Sherborne Castle

James I and the Digbys – James I, who repossessed Sherborne Castle in 1608 when he imprisoned Raleigh, gave it to Prince Henry, then to his favourite, Robert Carr, who, however, soon fell from grace; the king next offered it for £10 000 to **Sir John Digby**, long employed in trying to arrange a marriage between the future Charles I and the Spanish Infanta. Digby, created Earl of Bristol, purchased the house, which had an intrinsic attraction and the sentimental link of Digby's grandmother and Raleigh's wife both being Throckmortons. It has remained in the family ever since.

Castle Builders – When he came to build the new castle, **Sir Walter Raleigh** created a four-storey house beneath a Dutch-style gable and balustrade; each angle was marked by a hexagonal turret and each turret angle alternately by a tall, plain, square chimney or heraldic beast. The fabric was Ham stone with rendered walls.

In 1620-30, between missions abroad, **Sir John Digby** enlarged the castle to the typical H-plan mansion of the time and its present appearance, using the same style and materials. The interior, by contrast, has rooms decorated in the styles and furniture of every period from the 16C-19C. "I imagined it to be one of those fine old seats... but this is so peculiar," wrote Alexander Pope in 1722, "and its situation of so uncommon kind, that it merits a more particular description."

Grounds ⊘ – The drive through the deer park to the house passes a 50-acre **lake**, inspired by a flash flood in 1757 which made the river overflow; the then Lord Digby determined to make the effect permanent and called upon **Capability Brown**. The Adam-style stables and **dairy** constructed in stone from the Old Castle are also 18C.

Raleigh's Seat, a stone bench under the trees on the far side of the lake, is said to be where Sir Walter was enjoying a quiet pipe when his servant, bringing him a drink, grew alarmed at seeing him apparently on fire and doused him with ale. Among the trees are giant Virginia cedars grown from seed brought back from the colony.

House ⊘ – *45min*. The first three rooms epitomise the house's kaleidoscope of styles.

The **Library** gallery was redecorated in the 18C in Strawberry Hill Gothick (as at Lacock Abbey); the furniture is Georgian. Note Raleigh's *History of the World* (1614) and the portrait of *Sir Kenelm Digby* (1603-65), traveller, founder member of the Royal Society.

The **Solarium** or Raleigh parlour was converted in the 19C into a Victorian dining room. The heraldic chimneypiece, installed at the time of the conversion, includes the ubiquitous family ostrich, adopted some 350 years ago for reasons unknown but present everywhere even on the weather-vanes in Sherborne town. The monkey supporters, sometimes to be seen with the arms, originate from the time when monkeys, kept as pets in the house, alerted a nursemaid of a fire in the children's rooms.

The plaster ceiling of the **Red Drawing Room** is 17C, the furniture Georgian. Among the pictures are a portrait by Cornelius Jansens of *Sir John Digby*, first owner of the present house, another of *Sir Kenelm Digby* with his wife and children, and a historic painting (1600) of Queen Elizabeth.

The **Sporting and Porcelain Rooms**, filled with prints, trophies, Meissen and Chinese figurines show the family's interest in the chase and as founders of the Blackmore Vale Hunt. In adjoining rooms pieces of 17C Chinese Transitional and 17C-18C K'ang-hsi periods make a proud display.

In the **Green Drawing Room**, Raleigh and Digby arms appear in the decoration: Raleigh's five lozenges in shields on the ceiling; the Digby fleur-de-lis over the fireplace. The walnut despatch box is said to have held the would-be English-Spanish marriage contract *(see above)*. Note the French kingwood writing-table, the late Georgian commodes and a portrait of Col Stephen Digby, "Mr Fairly" in Fanny Burney's diary.

The **Blue Drawing Room**, so-called from the original colour of the wallpaper, is crowded with fine English and French 18C furniture, Chinese and Japanese lacquer and porcelain. Among those portrayed are *Sir Jeffrey Hudson;* Henrietta Maria's Dwarf; Henry, 1st Earl of Digby, by Gainsborough; John Digby, 3rd Earl of Bristol, who received the future William III on the latter's journey from Brixham to London in 1688.

The **Hall**, in the 16C part of the house, still has the studded door and lattice windows from when the end wall was the outer wall of Raleigh's house.

Tudor and Stuart oak furniture are seen through the Elizabethan doorway of the **Small Dining Room.**

The **Oak Room** with 1620 panelling contains two remarkable, draught proof Jacobean inner porches, decorated with fluted pilasters, pierced parapets and heraldic beasts (note the wooden spring on one of the door latches). The prehistoric antlers above the wide fireplace were found in Ireland; the medieval helmet is a tilting helm; the portrait is believed to be of Sir Walter Raleigh.

EXCURSIONS

★ **Sandford Orcas Manor House** ⊘ – *4 miles north by B3148. 45min.*

The story of the house is as straightforward as the house is attractive in its setting amid the gently undulating countryside and a terraced garden with long, flowered borders (especially attractive in May and June when roses, lilac and laburnum are in bloom). It was bought two and a half centuries ago by the Medlycotts, the present owner's family, as a farming property and leased to careful tenants. Since the 1870s the family has lived in it and returned it to life.

Exterior – The long and rambling house in brownish Ham Hill ashlar, rebuilt on medieval foundations in the 1550s, is many gabled with every point the perch of a heraldic monkey, lion or other beast. The **windows** are hoodmoulded, stone mullioned and transomed, those to the Hall and Great Chamber above wide-bayed to let the light flood in through plain and armorial glass. Slim square **chimneys** crown the stone roofs.

The **entrance porch**, off-centre and advanced under its own small gable, is framed by slim octagonal shafts topped by minute obelisks.

Hall – The chamber is single storeyed with oak panelling, a **fireplace** with a Ham stone lintel and an overmantel displaying the full range of Jacobean carved fantasy. On the walls are **Gainsborough** family portraits; among the furniture, examples of the periods represented in the house include Tudor, Jacobean, William and Mary and Queen Anne.

Upper rooms – At the top of a **spiral stone staircase**, the Great Chamber, closets, landings, bedrooms are furnished with English and Dutch **marquetry chests** opening to reveal ever-smaller decorated drawers, cupboards and hidden recesses.

The **testered beds** range in date from Elizabethan to slender 18C; note the two **embroidered covers**: one in natural silk on silk *appliqué*, the other a William and Mary work, all glistening greens and brown.

★ **Purse Caundle Manor** ⊙ – *5 miles east by A30.*
The silver-grey stone house, approached through courtyard gates, was L-shaped in the 15C-16C and extended to an Elizabethan E in the 17C. Its gables are crowned with the slim square chimneys known to be the hallmark of a group of local Dorset builders who flourished between 1600 and 1630.
Inside, the **Great Hall** boasts an arch-braced roof reinforced with tie-beams and built up with struts and king posts; there are massive 16C fireplaces and 17C panelling and gallery balustrading. The first floor **Great Chamber** has a barrel roof and is decorated with a Chinese painted wallpaper. Off the east end is the small, late 15C **oriel** seen from the lane.

Worldlife, Over Compton ⊙ – *3 miles west off north carriageway, Sherborne-Yeovil Road, A30.*
The setting for this modern enterprise designed to promote awareness of conservation issues is the part-19C, part-16C Tudor-style mansion **Compton House**, built on the foundations of houses dating back to pre-Domesday.
In the garden are tall cedars of Lebanon and a small 12C **church** with a high, pinnacled and embattled tower. Its several periods were "beautified" in 1882 by Robert Goodden, ancestor and namesake of the present owner, who had his **statue** sculpted from life and set inside the church three years before he died.
In the grounds roam pheasants, peacocks, squirrels and badgers. In the Tropical houses butterflies in brilliant velvet colours with wingspans of 6-9ins fly freely amid jungle plants growing in glass enclosures which each fill a whole room in the ancestral house; in high summer, in the Palm House, visitors walk among them. On the first floor are the silk-worms which, maintaining the tradition of the **Lullingstone Silk Farm** founded in 1932 and now at Compton, has supplied silk for several famous royal occasions.

For Sturminster Newton see BLANDFORD FORUM; *for Montacute House see* YEOVIL.

SIDMOUTH

Devon – Population 12 982
Michelin Atlas p 5 or Map 403 – K31

The town lies at the foot of wooded hills which descend to the sea where they sheer off exposing rock which is pinky-cream to the east (Salcombe Hill Cliff) and dark red to the west (Peak Hill, 500ft). The ebbing tide uncovers a beach of golden sand and, to the west, the **Chit Rocks** and further west still **Jacob's Ladder** or Western Beach – Jacob's Ladder itself comprises three flights of wooden steps to a fort-like building on the cliff top.
The **Esplanade** and several streets and terraces are lined by attractive Georgian and Regency houses from the time when Sidmouth had dreams of being a fashionable watering-place.

Sidmouth to Lyme Regis

Ladram Bay – *2 miles west along South Devon Coast Path. Start from Peak Hill Road.*
From Peak Hill Cottage (thatched) the path goes through a glade of beeches to follow the line of the cliff edge before eventually dropping down to the small Ladram Bay (crowded in summer) with its spectacular eroded red cliffs and offshore stacks.

Donkey Sanctuary, Salcombe Regis ⊙ – *3 miles northeast by A3052; turn at signpost Dunscombe, Weston, Branscombe; entrance 300yds.*
The fields and stables of Slade House Farm accommodate rescued donkeys, gazing out of every corner, alert, inquisitive and enjoying life. In the **Slade Centre**, an indoor riding school, donkeys give rides each week to hundreds of handicapped children drawn from a wide area.

★ **Branscombe** – The small village straggles in clusters of thatched cottages within small flowered gardens, along either side of a steep and winding road which at the end of two miles arrives at the beach and a group of old coastguard cottages. The village itself, which has a recorded history dating back to King Alfred, includes old and historic houses, a **forge** of 1580, an **inn** – the Mason's Arms – of 1360 and, on the valley side, the Norman church, **St Winifred**, built on a Saxon site in the 12C. Inside, the oak-beamed roof and **Elizabethan gallery** with access from the outside staircase, the late 18C **three-decker pulpit** and box pews, the late 17C altar rail with twisted balusters, and a macabre monument of 1606 are all of particular interest.

Beer – Despite its huge popularity, Beer remains essentially a fishing village where the spring continues to tumble down the length of the main street into the sea, with boats hauled up the shingle bank of the small cove between gleaming white rock headlands. In times past it was also famous for its lace which rivalled that of Honiton and its stone quarries, although its prosperity probably depended rather more upon smuggling.

The rock is the **Beer stone** used by the Romans and since the 15C as a contrasting trim for cathedrals, churches and houses; the quality of the stone is such that it can be cut with a saw when newly quarried and hardens when exposed to wind and weather. The quarries *(1 mile along the coast)* are open for guided tours ⊙ underground.

Seaton – The small seaside resort at the mouth of the River Axe close to the Devon-Dorset border lies behind a mile-long pebble beach between two headlands **(views★★)**: to westward are the dramatically white 400ft cliffs of Beer Head, to the east those of Lyme Regis spike.

Seaton Tramway ⊙ – *Harbour Road.* The swaying ride on the top of the 2ft 9in gauge, electric tram with a great iron arm reaching back to the overhead wire, the hard seats, open guard-rail and sounding bell, is fun in itself. Open toppers operate in good weather; closed saloons at other times. The track, originally laid from Seaton to Seaton Junction by the Seaton and Beer Railway Company in 1868, follows the Axe Valley to Colyton *(see below).* It was remodelled by Claude Lane, a builder of battery-powered vehicles, in the 1970s. The ride from the Victorian-style terminus affords a good view of the countryside and the birds (notably waders) on the river.

Seaton Hole – At the west end of the beach is Seaton Hole (sand and rock pools at low water) and above, a semi-wooded headland from which there are wide views out to sea – this area of coastland consisting of cliff, open scrubland and woodland provides a rich habitat for gulls and fulmars; stonechats, linnets and yellow-hammers; spotted flycatchers, warblers and nightingales.

Landslip – *Access: from the east side of the river make for the Axmouth Golf Course or Steppes Lane in Axmouth, then follow the cliff path down the face and into the slip.*

The signposted path is rough and can be slippery; it is NOT for those unaccustomed to rough walking; there are no intermediary exits and it is 5 miles to Underhill Farm on the outskirts of Lyme Regis.

Minor slips occur almost annually along the length of cliff but on Christmas Day 1839, between Bindon and Dowlands Cliffs, there opened a chasm three-quarters of a mile long, 400ft across and 150ft deep, which has been known ever since as The Landslip. About 8 million tons of rock are estimated to have foundered in the one night. The area is now a woodland nature reserve.

★ **Colyton** – *3.5 miles north of Seaton by B3172, A3052 and B3161 or by the electric tram (see above; 8min walk up from the station).*

The village is dominated by its **church**★ with pointed pyramid roof and lantern. It was built on a Saxon site when the Courtenays, Earls of Devon, were lords of the manor; it was enlarged during the 14C-18C. The pinnacled, octagonal **lantern** surmounting the roof was added in the 15C by a rich wool merchant, partly to serve as a beacon for his ships sailing up the then navigable River Axe. Inside, note the carved capitals at the east end, which was enlarged in the 14C; the great, Perpendicular west window (15C); the transept **screens** – one Perpendicular (16C) with lacelike stone tracery surrounding a canopied tomb, the other Jacobean (17C) with strapwork and surmounting obelisks.

Axmouth – *2 miles east along the Harbour Road (B3172) or the Esplanade to the Old Harbour, over the river bridge* **(views★)** *then left upstream.*

Once a bustling riverport, the village is now a tranquil place with a winding main street overlooked by small houses, some still thatched, occasional 15C-16C larger houses on the hillside and two old thatched pubs, one half-timbered and 800 years old.

The **church** was rebuilt *c*1140 on what may have been a Saxon site and again in 1330 so that now it appears with Norman round columns marking the south aisle and a Norman north doorway, a Decorated chantry chapel and a Perpendicular tower. Note the Italian-style medieval paintings of an unknown saint and a Christ of Pity on the Norman pillars, also the 1667 Charles II hatchment.

For Otterton, East Budley, Budleigh Salterton and Bicton Gardens, see EXMOUTH.

The Romans first introduced wine into Britain over 2 000 years ago, though it remains a mystery when exactly the first vines were planted. Since the Second World War there has been a great revival in wine-making and many areas now offer local vineyard trails.

SOMERTON★

Somerset – Population 4 489
Michelin Atlas p 8 or Map 403 – L 30

The small town with an arcaded market cross alleges to have been the capital town of Wessex in the 10C and the county town in the 13C-14C; now it is blissfully off all main routes and closely surrounded by rolling, wooded farmland. Its name is a corruption of "the summer settlement", which is thought to reflect the practice of pasturing cattle on the Levels before the water rose. A number of important Roman villas have been found in the vicinity.

The houses and inns along the two main streets, which together form an L, are of the local blue lias or limestone with Ham stone trims, mullioned windows and stone tile roofs.

Houses and Inns – Around the **Market Place★** there stand the unique arcaded **cross★** (1673, much restored), the Town Hall of the same date but much altered, and the White Hart on the site of the town's early castle. East of the church are several **17C-18C houses**, a **16C house** with symmetrical oriels and dormers in the tiled roof, a **round-cornered house** with a Tuscan porch (now a bank), and, closing the street, the **Red Lion**, a 17C coaching inn with a rounded archway entrance surmounted by a pedimented Venetian window. In contrast the tree-shaded **Broad Street** is lined by substantial 18C houses.

Market Cross, Somerton

★ **St Michael's Church** – The octagonal south **tower**, which dates from the 13C, is the oldest part of the church. The interior was transformed c1450 by the addition of a clerestory and a magnificent **tie-beam roof** (1510) with king posts and castellations, tracery, foliage, carved wall plates, 640 identical quatrefoil panels, dragons and angels, all now highlighted in gold. Local beer and cider making are said to be celebrated in the **barrel** (1ft long) which is shown bunghole downwards *(north side of centre beam, 3rd oblong from west end)*.

The bench ends are c1500, the painted **pulpit** is dated 1615, the **panelling** behind the altar and the **altar** itself, which has symbols of mankind's fall and salvation carved on its legs, are all Jacobean; the **bishop's chair** is said to be from Glastonbury; the brass **candelabra** are 18C.

EXCURSIONS

★ **Lytes Cary** ⊙ *Charlton Mackrell. 45min.*

Two 16C oriels in Ham Hill stone beneath swan and gryphon finialled gables and an attached chapel distinguish the manor house which was occupied by fourteen generations of the Lyte family from the time when William Le Lyte, Sergeant-at-Law under Edward I, built the first house on the site in 1286, until they were forced by debt to sell in 1755.

The Lytes of the 16C-17C were interested in botany and genealogy: Henry made a garden at Lytes Cary and published (1578), as an enlarged translation from the Dutch, a work which became widely known as *Lyte's Herbal;* his son traced the genealogy of James I from Brutus, which earned him the king's pleasure and award of the Nicholas Hilliard miniature of the king set in gold and diamonds (now in the British Museum).

In the 18C the house was sold and fell into decay. In 1907 it was rescued by Sir Walter Jenner, son of the physician, who restored the fabric, furnished the interior with 17C-19C pieces and textiles in character, and laid out Elizabethan topiary gardens in the original forecourt, a parterre garden, a yew alley...

House – The **Hall**, which was added to the original house c1453 has a typical Somerset roof of arch braces, cusped wind braces and an ornate cornice marked by supporting half-angels holding shields bearing the Lyte arms.

The 15C fireplace is original, the landscape above it is by Jan Wyck (17C). Of especial note among the furniture and furnishings are two oak refectory tables, one with the massive turned legs of c1600, the second with the fluted frieze of the mid-17C, the pair of late 17C delft tulip vases and the late 18C mahogany cheese coaster.

The **Oriel Room**, which served as the family dining room, was heated by a miniature version of the hall fireplace. The oak bird cage dates from the 18C; note the copies of pages from the *Herbal*.

The **Great Parlour**, with the bay and other windows overlooking the garden almost filling one side, is notable for its original 17C panelling with fluted Ionic pilasters and pillared chimneypiece. Among the wealth of beautiful 17C-18C oak and walnut furniture, note the laburnum oyster parquetry side-table on six legs, a red tortoise-shell bracket clock (London, 1700) and, in contrast, a Chinese lacquer bureau cabinet (*c*1700).

The smaller "**Little Parlour**", a carpenter's shop until restored by Sir Walter Jenner whose portrait hangs on the wall, was probably the study of the antiquarian-botanist Lytes of the 16C-17C. Among the furnishings are a pair of 18C jardinières, 17C brass lantern clock (Taunton), 18C-19C glass and a semicircular mahogany drinking table with a wheeled decanter trolley, which enabled both wine and imbibers to be warmed by the fire.

The **Great Chamber** at the top of the stone newel staircase is embellished by the upper part of the parlour bay window and a plaster ceiling, coved and ribbed; on the end wall are the arms of Henry VIII.

Chapel – The detached chapel, dating from 1343, is the oldest feature of the house. The frieze of coats of arms was added by the genealogist member of the family in James I's reign.

South to Martock

★ **Long Sutton** – The parish church★★ at the village centre dates from 1490. The **tower**, with a taller stair turret, rises through three stages from the spandrelled door and west window with tangential arcs instead of transoms, to a window with framing niches, three belfry windows, the outer ones blank, the centre filled with Somerset tracery and, finally, an embattled crest with every feature ending in a pinnacle.

Inside are an outstanding **roof** of tie-beams, king posts and angel figures, a coloured **rood screen** with slender tracery between the mullions and a contemporary 16-sided, coloured **pulpit** with small 19C figures filling the original canopied niches.

★ **Martock** – The glory of Martock, a village built entirely in its older parts of Ham Hill stone, is the 15C-16C church and the glory of the church is its **angel roof**.

★★ **All Saints** – The west **tower** marked the completion of the church's reconstruction in the 15C-16C. It rises from a shafted door and five-light window, which starts below the string course and fills the second stage, and the elevation then continues through a bay and paired, transomed bell openings, all tracery-filled, to a typically pinnacled crest.

Inside, the **roof** presents an ordered arrangement of embattled tie-beams, purlins, king posts and braces, of carved pendants, tracery and pierced coffering – 768 panels in six different patterns. The 67 **life-size angels** in wood and stone were added in 1513.

The paintings of the Apostles, in the niches above the arcades of Ham Hill stone, date from the early 17C; St James the Less is portrayed as James I and St Simon Zelotes as William Cecil, Lord Burghley (W on his cuff).

The clerestory was originally glazed with heraldic glass: ten shields to each window, "about 120 coats" a 17C diarist calculated; in July 1645 the Parliamentarians came to Martock, held a thanksgiving service for the capture of Bridgwater and smashed the lot.

The five stepped windows at the east end are relics of the Early English church on the site.

Main street – Among the houses lining the main street close to the church are the **Treasurer's House** ⊘ (1290), so-named because the rector of Martock was treasurer of Wells Cathedral; the 17C gabled manor house, much rebuilt after a fire in the 19C, and **Church House**, a long low building of two storeys with mullioned windows in which the door is surmounted by the date, 1661, and a composite inscription in English, Latin, Greek and Hebrew from the time when it was the local grammar school.

The main road also borders the **Market House**, a small Georgian building with a Venetian window, upraised upon arcades which once sheltered market stalls, and a market cross in the form of a Doric column.

★ East Lambrook Manor ⊘

The visit is primarily to the **garden** – a garden of "cottage mixtures", of exotic, old-fashioned, foliage and simple plants, lacking vistas but showing the close-up beauty of plants in separate gardens which extend round two sides of the rambling, stone and brick malthouse, once thatched and now Somerset-tiled. Today it accommodates an archive that charts the painstaking evolution of the site.

When it was built *c*1470 the house probably belonged to a minor squire, a merchant or a prosperous yeoman; in 1938, when discovered by Margery Fish and her husband, it was derelict and rat-infested; the garden, of course, was a wilderness. Before she died, Mrs Fish converted it into the **plantsman's** garden for endangered plants which it has remained. It is attractive throughout the year, modest in size (about 2.5 acres) and contains a mass of different species: hydrangeas, salvias, achilleas, alyssum, primulas, lavender, ivies, vines, double daisies... The most important collection, however, is that of the geranium or cranesbill family and its cultivars.

★ **Barrington Court** ⊘

Gardens – Nothing certain is known about the origins of this beautiful 16C house of golden Ham Hill stone, surrounded by delightful gardens. It was constructed (1550-60) to the usual Elizabethan E-plan with a porch flanked by two projecting wings enclosing a south facing forecourt; the **roofline** is embellished with gables, finials and spiral chimney stacks. The **Strode block** (1674), originally open on the north side, was built as stabling.

The property changed hands several times, eventually being leased as a farm. It was restored from a mere shell in the 1920s by Col A A Lyle, whose hobby was collecting oak panelling and interior fittings.

The charming gardens bear the imprint of **Gertrude Jekyll** (1843-1932) who advised on the planting.

Kitchen Garden – High brick walls provide shelter for the vegetables and fruit trees *(plants and produce for sale)*; the lead water tanks are dated 1782.

Maple Garden – Fine autumn colour is provided by the maples in the tennis court garden which is enclosed by a great hedge of Lawson's cypress.

Walled Flower Gardens – The old cattleyards now enclose the **Iris Garden**, a harmony of purples, pinks and blues; the **White Garden**, consisting of geometric beds round a central statue; the lovely brick **Beef Stalls**, built in the 16C for rearing oxen but now planted with climbers and roses; the **Lily Garden**, a display of vivid colours.

Arboretum – The pleached lime walk, east of the south lawn and the sundial, is flanked by an orchard and an arboretum of unusual trees and shrubs – pines, conifers and wych hazels – planted in the 1930s.

House – Several features of the original building have survived. Over the library door are the **arms** of William Strode, who owned the house in the 17C. The door to the **garde-robe** of the best bedchamber is visible in the north wall of the stair hall. West of the south door in the screens passage is a **lavabo** where people washed their hands before entering the Great Hall. The huge kitchen **fireplace** in the west wing is disguised by blind windows on the exterior; the lintel is composed of two massive pieces of Ham Hill stone. Beneath the window sill *(left)* are the original charcoal **braziers**. Two **overmantels** (1625), originally brightly painted, survive on the upper floor; they show *(east wing)* the Strode family arms and *(west wing)* the Judgement of Solomon. The **Great Hall** is furnished with a specially designed Ham stone fireplace, Italianate beams and English screens, doors and 16C linenfold panelling. An inner wall of early **16C latticed lights** divides the Dining Room, which has a wooden ceiling composed of a deep honeycomb of star patterns, from the Buttery, which is panelled with **Jacobean wainscotting**. The staircase, of which only the lowest newel post is original (early 17C), rises under a **15C timber ceiling**. There is more Jacobean wainscotting in the dressing room where the radiators are covered by **wooden lattices** from the ventilator shafts of old sailing ships.

For Ilminster, see CHARD; *for Midelney Manor see* LANGPORT; *for Street see* GLASTONBURY; *for Montacute see* YEOVIL *or consult the index.*

STONEHENGE★★★

Wiltshire

Michelin Atlas p 9 or Map 403 – O30

Stonehenge ⊘ is one of the world's classic sights – and a perpetual enigma. It is perfectly oriented so that on Midsummer Day the sun, rising in its most northerly position, appears exactly over the Heel Stone to anyone standing at the centre. It can be assumed only that Stonehenge was considered a sacred place; little else is certain about it.

Radiocarbon dating indicates that the construction of Stonehenge began in about 2950BC and was largely completed by 2300BC; mystery, however, still surrounds the reasons why it was built and why the site was abandoned in 1600BC. In context with other comparable feats of civil engineering, it is several centuries later than the Great Pyramid in Egypt, contemporary with the Minoan culture in Crete, a millennium earlier than the first Great Wall of China, 2 000 years earlier than the Aztec constructions (and carved stone calendars) of Mexico and 3 500 years older than the figures on Easter Island.

STONEHENGE

The Druids, a Celtic priesthood, are a "modern" appendage: they arrived from Europe in 250 BC. Their legendary association with Stonehenge probably dates from the 12C when Geoffrey of Monmouth suggested that Stonehenge was built by giants in Ireland before being transported to Salisbury Plain by Merlin as a memorial to the nobles of Britain's army killed in war against the Saxons. In the 17C and 18C, John Aubrey and William Stukeley suggested that Stonehenge might have served as a Druid temple – an assertion that fired the imagination of such Romantic writers as William Blake. Archeological surveys carried out in 1901, during the 1920's and between 1950-64 have not substantiated the claim; artefacts recovered are on display in the museums at Salisbury and Devizes.

The Stones – There are two types of stone at Stonehenge: **bluestones** from the Preseli Mountains and the shores of Milford Haven in western South Wales, and **sarsens** from the Marlborough Downs, 20 miles away.
The bluestones, so-called from their colour when first cleaved and weighing up to 4 tons each, were transported, it is believed, along the South Wales coast to the Bristol Avon, along the River Frome, overland to the Wylye and Salisbury Avon and, finally, overland from West Amesbury to the site – a total distance of 240 miles on log rollers, sledges, rafts and lashed alongside small boats. Most were collected together in around 2600BC, although the larger upright stones were installed some 300 years later.
The sarsens weigh up to 50 tons each; the journey was shorter but partly uphill. Motive power was human muscle.
The stones, blue and sarsen, were shaped on arrival with football-sized sarsen hammers: the **standing stones** were tapered at one end and tenoned at the top to secure the curving, morticed **lintels** which were linked to each other by tongues and grooves. To position the stones, holes were dug (with red deer antler picks and cattle shoulder-blade spades) into which the stones were levered until they toppled upright and could be made fast with rammed stones and earth. The trilithon lintels were next positioned at the base and either gradually levered up on ever-rising log platforms, or perhaps levered up by means of ropes along greased and debarked oak beams angled against the uprights.

The period – Stonehenge was built in **three phases** between 2950 and 1600 BC, when its purpose in the life of the people of Wessex, of Britain as a whole and probably nearby areas of Western Europe, must have been self-evident.
When work began the area was inhabited by nomadic hunters and their families and by early farming settlers who had made the hazardous crossing of the Channel and North Sea in skin boats.
By 2000 BC the **Beaker Folk**, who had spread into Wessex along the chalk upland tracks, had grown into a community of perhaps 12-15 000 people, ruled by the powerful cattle barons of the Salisbury Plain who also controlled the metal industry.
There was a growing priesthood, which at peak periods in the construction of Stonehenge would call on the population to provide as many as 600 men at one time to pull the heaviest sarsen stones up the south slope of the Vale of Pewsey, or 200 to erect a sarsen upright...

The building design – In the **first phase** (2950-2900BC) an outer ditch, an inner, chalk rubble bank 6ft high, and a ring of holes, known as the Aubrey Holes after a 17C antiquary, were dug to enclose an area 1.5 acres in extent, 300ft in diameter. To the northeast the ditch and bank were cut to afford an entrance marked inside by two upright stones and, outside *(near the road)*, by the **Heel Stone** (and a timber gateway). Inside the enclosure, four **Station Sarsens** were set up at the cardinal points of the compass.
In the **second phase**, *c*2100 BC, a double ring of bluestones began to be set up at the centre and the **Avenue** was begun towards the River Avon at West Amesbury.
In around 2000 BC, during the **third phase**, the structure was transformed: the incomplete bluestone rings were replaced by a circle of tall sarsen trilithons, the lintels forming an upraised stone hoop; inside, five separate, giant trilithons rose in a horseshoe opening towards the Heel Stone. The entrance was marked by new uprights, one of which, the Slaughter Stone, now fallen, remains (names, now irrelevant, were given to many stones in the 18C); the bluestones were re-introduced to form an inner horseshoe. At the end of this phase, *c*1550 BC, Stonehenge appeared, it is believed, as illustrated.
Gradually the population and prosperity declined; Stonehenge, in use in 1100 BC, fell into ruin as stones tumbled and were removed. While it is certain that the axis of the sarsen stones points to where an observer at the centre would see the sunrise on midsummer's day, other original sightlines to the horizon have been largely destroyed and are less easy to verify. Lines joining the Station

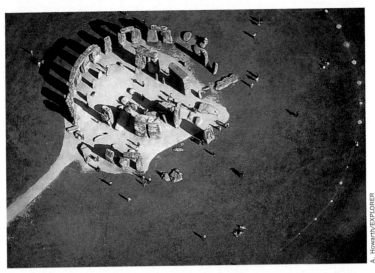

Aerial view of Stonehenge

Stones may have marked the most northerly and southerly points on the horizon of sun and moon settings; the Aubrey Holes may represent a means of calculating the eclipses of the moon. It seems that Stonehenge may have been constructed as an observatory by a people who had a considerable knowledge of astronomy and were capable of erecting a monument the equal of the Seven Wonders of the Ancient World.

EXCURSIONS

Amesbury

The town and its church, which stand at a major road crossing beside the Avon, are descendants of a centuries-old market and an abbey. According to legend it was to a nunnery at Amesbury that, in the 5C-6C, **Guinevere** (*see* GLASTON-BURY) fled from the court of King Arthur and remained until she died.

In 979 **Queen Aelfryth**, in expiation of the murder of Edward the Martyr, founded a Benedictine abbey in Amesbury dedicated to St Mary and St Melor, the Breton boy saint murdered by his uncle. In 1501 the abbey lodged Catherine of Aragon on her way to London but, like the queen, the abbey suffered Henry's displeasure and in 1539 it was suppressed and the church presented to the parish. Today it is used as a private nursing home.

St Mary's Church – The main fabric of the flint parish church is Early English, with traces of Norman and Perpendicular work: a low tower sits squarely over the crossing. Inside, there is an unusual two-tier piscina *(to the right on entering, south aisle)* by the Norman font; a second Saxon lavatorium sits by the western-most pier. The wood work is also worthy of note: the plain oak rood screen separating the chancel; the nave's 16C oak roof beams resting on stone corbels contrast with the stone-vaulted Early English Jesus Chapel, built as a chantry chapel by Henry III. In the north transept sits the rare 15C clock mechanism which predates the invention of the pendulum.

Woodhenge ⊙ – *2 miles north east just off the A345.*
Concrete markers now replace the original oval timber post structure aligned with the summer solstice sun, a complex intended, it is believed, for ceremonial use, and contemporary with the first phase of Stonehenge.

Bulford Kiwi – *4 miles east by A303: on Beacon Hill, above Bulford Barracks.*
Viewpoint:the kiwi faces northwest from the escarpment and is best viewed from the Bulford-Tidworth side road off A303 (Amesbury-Andover road).
The bird is vast, being 420ft long and covering 1.5 acres of ground; the letters NZ below the bill are 65ft high and the bill itself 130ft long. It was designed by a New Zealand engineer to commemorate the troops' stay in the barracks and was cut in 1918. Note especially the brilliant foreshortening which makes the bird instantly recognisable from a great distance and many angles.

STOURHEAD★★★

Wiltshire

Michelin Atlas p 8 or Map 403 – N30 – 3 miles northwest of Mere

The garden or "pleasure ground" is an example of an 18C "designed" English garden at its supreme best. In early spring the trees in bud present infinite shades of tender green, summer enriches the tones until in autumn the leaves turn to gold, scarlet, russet, brown, before abandoning the brown-black branches to winter; against this canvas are set changing flashes of bright colour provided by daffodils, bluebells, rhododendrons, azaleas, foxgloves through the seasons. The creator and first architect of these "pleasure grounds", which occupy some 400 acres, was Henry Hoare II (1705-85).

Autumn colours at Stourhead

Gardens ⓥ – Henry Hoare II, nicknamed The Magnificent, was influenced in his garden design by the landscapes he encountered on his travels in Italy and by the paintings of Claude, Nicolas Poussin and Gaspard Dughet in which landscape is presented in luminous shades, distance is suggested by a serpentine watercourse or lane, punctuated by statuary, some ruin or Classical building. In the same way as one viewed a picture, therefore, and in contrast to the preceding fashion of overlooking a formal parterre garden from the house, the grounds were laid out to be viewed from specific vantage points (*see* INTRODUCTION: Landscape garden design).

The first phase to be implemented formed the great triangular **lake** there followed the plantings of beeches, ashes, alders, sycamores, oaks, Spanish chestnuts, maples and conifers, "ranged in large masses as the shades in a painting". The buildings, often associated with water deities, were designed with the architect Henry Flitcroft, to act as **focal points** of interests which, circling the lake in an anticlockwise direction may be pinpointed from across the water as the Temple of Flora (1744-46) and the Grotto (both with inscriptions taken from Virgil's *Aenead*), the Gothic Cottage, the Pantheon (1753-54) – originally known as the Temple of Hercules for which the statue was commissioned from Rysbrack in 1747, not to mention the temple of Apollo and the Palladian Bridge.

In 1765 Hoare acquired the Civic High **Cross** from Bristol which enabled him to create an entirely English vista of the lake, the Turf Bridge, the Cross and, in the background, Stourton church and village. The short path, at the water's edge, is 1.25 miles easy going with benches at several vantage points.

Colt Hoare laid the continuous paths, added new trees to increase the range of colour and introduced the first rhododendron in 1791.

At the far extent of the "outer circuit" stands **Alfred's Tower** ⓥ, a triangular brick folly (1772) set in the woodland but visible across the rolling landscape from afar. It was built there (2.5 miles north west of the house) on the spot where, it is alleged, Alfred raised his standard when resisting the Danes; more likely, it commemorates the succession of George III and the peace with France (1762). With 206 steps up a narrow tower to the viewing balcony, this is not for the faint hearted!

House ⊙ – *1hour*. Henry Hoare I (1677-1725), son of the founder of Hoare's Bank (*c*1673) in the City of London, acquired old Stourton House in 1717 and had it demolished. The design for a new house was entrusted to Colen Campbell, pioneer of English Palladianism and future author of *Vitruvius Britannicus*. The house of 1721 consisted of the central block; the flanking pavilions containing the library and picture gallery were added by Henry Hoare II's heir, Sir Richard Colt Hoare (1758-1838), antiquary, county historian and, like his grandfather, a traveller and collector.

The house suffered a grim sale of much of its contents in 1883 and a fire in 1902 which destroyed the early 18C interiors although nearly all the contents of the ground-floor staterooms were saved.

Hall – The 30ft cube-entrance hall, severely damaged in the fire, is hung with family portraits (Sir Richard Hoare, founder of the bank, Henry Hoare I holding plans of the house, Henry Hoare II, Colt Hoare and his son); it is furnished with 18C **console tables** with fox supports, wheelback chairs, and a fine gilded bronze **bust of Charles I** by Le Sueur.

Instead of the single stairway destroyed by fire, twin flights were installed in the **Inner Hall** by Doran Webb: the large Rococo pierglasses are attributed to John Linnell.

Library pavilion – The **Music Room and Library Ante-Room** are hung with contemporary "fancy" pictures acquired by Colt Hoare. The furniture was supplied by Chippendale and reflects the influence of French Empire taste following a visit he made to Paris during the Peace of Amiens (1802-03).

Considered as one of the finest Regency interiors, the long barrel-vaulted **Library** is sober in its decoration: the Wilton carpet apes a Roman pavement design, the lunettes at either end are modelled on Raphael's *School of Athens* and *Parnassus* in the Vatican. The ornate gesso chimneypiece and overmantel (1720s) were installed in 1913, transferred to Stourhead from the family seat at Wavenden; the early 18C central panel illustrating *Tobit lending money to Gabael* is Pierre Legros's preliminary model for a marble relief intended for the Monte di Pietà in Rome. The furniture (1795-1820) by **Thomas Chippendale the Younger**, is particularly fine: note the detail of the mahogany library table ornamented with heads of Egyptians and philosophers. The two busts of Milton are by **Rysbrack**, as is the terracotta modello of Hercules; the pen and wash drawings of Venice are by **Canaletto**.

South wing – The shellback **chairs** in the **Little Dining Room** date from 1740; the 17C **silver-gilt centrepiece**, made in Germany, incorporates the double-headed eagle of the Hapsburgs, adopted by the Hoares as their bank emblem. On the walls hang a series of pastel portraits.

The **South Apartment** is arranged as a private sitting-room.

The walls of the Edwardian style **Saloon** are hung with portraits of Harry Hoare, who was tragically killed in 1917 and his mother Alda, Lady Hoare, the great admirer of Thomas Hardy.

In the **Column Room** Colt Hoare assembled a large part of his collection of topographical views in watercolour – the best works, including those by Turner, were sold in 1883.

The **Italian Room** was intended by Henry Hoare II as the state bedroom reserved for visiting royalty; furnished subsequently as a sitting room, it was used by Sir Henry, 6Bt, for taking his regular siesta. The central card table, equipped with an ingenious extension mechanism, is by William Linnell (1740).

The **Cabinet Room** is named after the mid-17C "Pope's **cabinet**" of ebony and gilt bronze with stone inlay made in Florentine; the 18C blue-john vase comes from Derbyshire; the landscape pictures include works by Richard Wilson and Zuccarelli. The Picture Gallery Ante-room is particularly splendid, as if to exaggerate the impact of the Picture Gallery completed in 1802.

Picture Gallery – Colt Hoare specially designed this room to face east, thereby catching the natural light that best flattered the delicate landscape views painted by Claude and Poussin. The Picture Gallery was strictly reserved for admiring his own pictures and the Old Masters acquired by his father Henry Hoare II, who used them in planning the gardens outside. The sober yet exquisite furniture was supplied by Chippendale, set off to full effect by the original black and yellow carpet, curtains and covers: note particularly the English commode inlaid with satinwood and harewood.

The Red Lion at Kilmington

Tucked inside the Stourhead Estate on the B3092 is this friendly free house serving excellent Wiltshire ham in sandwiches or as part of a ploughman's lunch. Standard ales from Bass, Butcombe and Wadworths; tasty farm ciders and a changing selection of house wines; also darts, dominos, shoveha'penny and cribbage to while away the hours by the log fires.

SWANAGE ★

Dorset – Population 9 037
Michelin Atlas p 9 or Map 403 – O32

The quarry town and harbour, from which stone and marble were shipped to build Westminster Abbey and the cathedrals of Exeter, Lincoln and Salisbury, was transformed by the arrival of the railway into a "pleasant little watering place with a good beach".

Some years before, **John Mowlem**, a native of Swanage, had begun to beautify the town. He had started as a local quarry boy before setting out for London where he founded a construction firm for which he imported stone from Purbeck and granite from Cornwall, Aberdeen, Guernsey and Leicestershire, to accomplish the massive Victorian rebuilding of the City and the resurfacing of roads and bridges with granite sets. The sailing ketches which brought the stone to London returned to Swanage with unwanted **street furniture**, dressed and carved stone, even **monuments**.

Mowlem Institute – *The Parade.* The modern complex on the front stands on the site of the institute presented to the town by John Mowlem in 1863.

Pier – The small pier was built in 1896; the landmark-like tower stood at the south end of London Bridge until 1863 when it was pronounced an "unwarrantable obstruction". Mowlem offered to remove it and shipped it home. It never included a statue of the duke. Additional London street furniture, in this instance City of London **bollards**, ornament **Queen's Street**, further up the High Street.

Old Millpond – *Church Hill. Right off High Street.* The old millpond with a couple of ducks is surrounded by pretty 18C-19C cottages and houses with flowering creepers.

St Mary the Virgin – The church, rebuilt for the third time in 1859, has a **tower** which dates, in its lower half, from the 12C-13C when it served as a refuge for local townsfolk from marauding pirates – note the arrow slit windows. Originally there was no door at ground level, entry being by means of a ladder to the first floor.

Town Hall – The ornate **17C stone front** of the hall originally stood in Cheapside in the City of London as the façade of the Mercers' Company; when Cheapside was widened, it was decided that it would be less costly to reproduce the stone front than to clean it of its "London black" and re-erect it. London, therefore, has a 19C replica and Swanage Town Hall has the original 17C stone which Mowlem shipped home and which, for good measure, the sea air has gradually cleaned.

Our Lady of Mercy Convent – The Scottish baronial-style building, built by Mowlem's nephew George Burt *(see below)*, incorporates columns from London's old Billingsgate Market, statues from the Royal Exchange, tiles from the Houses of Parliament...

Durlston Country Park – *1 mile south by Lighthouse Road.*
The headland, from which there is a panoramic **view ★★**, the castle-folly-restaurant, Great Globe, London bollards and the lighthouse today make up the country park George Burt had in mind when he purchased 80 acres (now 260 acres) in 1862.

Castle – The folly is built of Purbeck stone with a full complement of towers, turrets, battlements and bastions; the stalwart granite bollards at the entrance are prototypes of those in Trafalgar Square. The interior is designed as a winter garden.

★ **Great Globe** – *Take the path down towards the head.* Mowlem had the globe made in his yard at Greenwich. It is 10ft in diameter, 40 tons in weight and is made up of 15 segments of Portland stone held in position by granite dowels.

Anvil Point Lighthouse – *40min circular walk.* The path to the all-white lighthouse passes the **Tilly Whim Caves**, a former cliffside quarry. The **view ★★** extends from St Aldhelm's Head to Portland Bill *(west)* and from Hengistbury Head and The Needles *(east)*; inland are the Purbeck Hills.

Swanage Railway ⊙ – The railway linking Swanage with Wareham opened in 1885, collecting farm produce for despatch to London. It closed in 1972. Painstakingly restored, the track has been relayed as far as Norden with stations at Herston, Harman's Cross and Corfe Castle; there are hopes of extending the line to join the national rail system at Furzebrook (for Wareham).

EXCURSIONS

Studland *5 miles north by Victoria Avenue and Northbrook Road to B3351, bear right.*

Studland is the promontory closing Poole Harbour from the south. A **chain ferry** ⊙ runs from Shell Bay at the north end to Sandbanks *(see POOLE)*.

Studland Beach – The two mile arc of sand below a narrow band of shingle is crowded in summer; the bay is wide and shallow; the **view ★** vast across Poole Bay.

Studland Village – The village is small and scattered with houses half-hidden in gardens, and, not far from the water's edge, **St Nicholas Church★**, early Norman and fortress-solid with a low tower. Note the **corbel table** with grimacing heads, the lancets, the **leper squint** peering through the south chancel wall (glazed 1881). Inside are a **groined vault** and plain Norman arches on **cushion capitals**.

★★ **Old Harry Rocks** – The two stacks of gleaming chalk were once part of a continuous shoreline from The Needles but are now separated from the mainland and even from each other; Old Harry is the larger and three-legged, his wife the slimmer.

Isle of Purbeck and Lulworth Cove

Worth Matravers – *4.5 miles southwest by B3069.*
This small village of stone houses round a duck pond once produced the finest-quality local marble; the slender shafts in Salisbury Cathedral were quarried here. In 1506 Swanage took precedence.

And did those feet in ancient times...

In one local disused quarry a trail of 52 dinosaur footprints has been discovered. 44 inches wide, they are thought to have been made by a family group of four-footed vegetarian sauropods (diplodocus or brachiosaurus) that would have stood 26ft tall, in the cretaceous or Upper Jurassic period some 145 to 140 million years ago. The site is owned by the National Trust.

St Nicholas – The church of rubble stone with ashlar dressings and 19C pyramid roof over its ancient square **tower** has several Norman features including, outside, the decorated south doorway (worn tympanum carved with the *Coronation of the Virgin*) and the **corbel table** which runs the length of the eaves, carved with grotesque heads of birds and beasts.
Inside, the nave and chancel are Norman – the **arch** with its chevron moulding above round columns being *c*1130; the plain **tower arch** at the west end is earlier still.

Continue through the village 1.5 miles southwest along surfaced roads and farm tracks.

St Aldhelm's Chapel – The chapel, dedicated to the local saint Aldhelm, stands squat and square on the windswept clifftop; the shallow, pyramid roof is surmounted by a turret which must once have held a fire cresset, or basket, as a sailors' lantern. It was built between 1150 and 1200. The rounded, Norman doorway leads into a 30sq ft chamber reminiscent of an undercroft with a square pillar supporting rib vaulting.

★★ **St Aldhelm's Head (or St Alban's Head)** – The headland (352ft), one of the highest in the area, affords a grandiose **view★★★** north to the Purbeck Hills, east to the Old Harry Rocks, Hengistbury Head and The Needles, and west to Portland Bill. West along Kimmeridge Cliffs *(2.5 miles on foot)* is **Chapman's Pool**, a dark circular pool eroded by the sea.

★ **Corfe Castle** ⊙ – Corfe Castle has dominated the landscape since the 11C, for its first 500 years as a towering stronghold and since 1646 as a gaunt but enthralling ruin. It stands on a high mound in the single break in the line of the Purbeck Hills, the **Corfe Gap**. The **views★★** are spectacular.

History – In 978 the 17 year old King Edward, the son of Edgar, went to visit his half-brother at the castle. Still mounted, he stopped at the inner gate-house to greet his stepmother, **Queen Aelfryth** who handed him a cup of wine. As he drank the poisoned wine, the boy king was stabbed to death. The body was removed to Wareham and, in 980, to Shaftesbury; in 1001 the king was canonised as **St Edward, King and Martyr**. Aethelred the Unready, Queen Aelfryth's son, took his place as monarch.
In 1635 the castle was purchased by **Sir John Bankes** whose wife was alone in residence when it was twice besieged by the Parliamentarians. Lady Mary resisted the first siege but in 1646 she surrendered; the castle was slighted. At the Restoration, Lady Bankes recovered the family estates; in 1663-65, her son, Sir Ralph Bankes, built a new house at Kingston Lacy.
Today archeological finds from the castle and a tapestry, housed in the **visitor centre** ⊙, recall its rich history.

★ **Blue Pool** ⊙ – The heavenly blue-green lake (3 acres) is fringed by silver birch and pine woods, gorse and heather through which a circuit of sandy paths meander, providing views over the Purbeck Hills. The colour comes from the diffraction of light on minute particles of clay suspended in the water (36ft deep) which flooded in when the open-cast mine ceased production in 1880.

The **museum** explains the history of the Furzebrook Estate and the extraction of clay for use in the making of tobacco pipes and porcelain. Also on display is a collection of Chinese porcelain retrieved from the wreck of the Dutch East Indiaman, *The Geldermalsen*, which was lost in the South China Seas in 1752.

View from Purbeck across to Lyme Bay

★ **Lulworth Cove** – The cove, which is circular, is almost enclosed by the downland cliffs.

From here the Dorset Coast Path leads to **Durdle Door** which lies to the west, beyond Dungy Head, at the far end of St Oswald's Bay. The whole area of headlands and scalloped bays has been likened to a "crash course in geology" with Durdle the dramatic climax, for whereas elsewhere the geological material is mostly lias (at Lyme Regis), oolite, Purbeck stone, Portland limestone and chalk (Old Harry Rocks), at the Door impermeable folded strata were forced up on end to produce a striking **cliff archway.** *For access, it is 2.5 miles from Lulworth Cove and back on foot, or continue on B3070 through West Lulworth to Toll Gate/Newlands Farm.*

SWINDON

Wiltshire – Population 145 236
Michelin Atlas p 17 or Map 403 – O 29

In the early 19C Old Swindon was a typical hilltop market town of some 1 700 inhabitants; by 1900 the new combined borough of Swindon, which included the market hill-top town with the extensive railway works below, numbered nearly 45 000 of whom 10 000 were directly employed by the GWR; others concentrated on growing and selling food, providing houses and lodgings... The demise of the GWR came when the railways were taken into the public sector with the advent of World War II: large engineering works were commandeered for building submarines and gun bases. In 1948 the Labour government nationalised the entire railway network under the flag of British Railways. In 1960 the *Evening Star*, the last locomotive to be built at Swindon, left the works which were finally closed in 1986. Today the town's prosperity depends upon car manufacture, corporate headquarters and computer services engaged in the high tech age.

"New Swindon" – Swindon was the Mecca of the Great Western Railway from 1831, when it was chosen as the line's main junction and site for its maintenance depot, and, later in 1845, its locomotive and carriage workshops, until 1948 brought about the demise of individual lines under nationalisation. Brunel meticulously planned his GWR village around an open green; this was fronted with lines of shops and parallel terraces of cottages; Emlyn Square was later built over when the Mechanics' Institution (1854-55), a market hall and an armoury for the GWR rifle corps were constructed.

Joseph Armstrong's Locomotive Works (1864-76) doubled in size again under George Churchward.

Designer Outlet Village – Restored and converted, the fabric of the former GWR brass and iron foundries, assembly halls and painting shops, complete with mighty hoists, winches and locomotives, now accommodate a series of retail units; the Food Hall collects together various eateries, some modelled on the original refreshment rooms at Swindon Station.

National Monuments Record Centre ⊙ – The **Royal Commission on the Historical Monuments of England** (RCHME) was established in 1908 to prepare inventories of monuments and buildings "connected with or illustrative of the contemporary culture, civilisation and conditions of life of the people in England". A precedent for the **National Monuments Record** (NMR) was instigated in the 12 months that followed the declaration of World War II in September 1939, as frantic plans were implemented to protect and preserve Britain's national art treasures; the threat to immovable buildings, however, could not be averted, especially as Hitler began mounting his offences with doodle-bugs and long-range rockets in 1944.

Reformed and amalgamated, the organisation has evolved into "the national body of archeological and architectural survey and record". As such it has expanded its activities to provide and maintain a comprehensive database of information about England's heritage in the form of a public picture library (this includes a broad range of pictures from the earliest days of photography to the very latest aerial surveys), a log of man-made sites (which is used for compiling Ordnance Survey maps) and of underwater wrecks in English territorial waters. It also publishes the results of exacting surveys and studies on English buildings and archeology.

The RCHME and NMR are now housed in the refurbished GWR drawing office set up by Daniel Gooch, the Locomotive Superintendent and the man who recommended Swindon to Brunel when a site for the railway works was sought. A "window on the riches of the NMR" is provided by a small **gallery** which continually displays changing selections of images, old and new from the extensive archive of some 7 million photographs and 200 000 drawings.

A foot-tunnel leads from the railway works to Swindon town centre.

★ **Great Western Railway Museum** ⊙ – *Faringdon Road.* The museum is housed in the onetime "model lodging house", a hostel for single men, built by the company workers who came from all parts of England, particularly the North, Wales and Ireland. The house was not popular and was remodelled as a Wesleyan Chapel – an appearance it maintains outside.

The collection includes a full-size replica of the *North Star* (which hauled the first GW passenger train from Paddington to Maidenhead), the original *Lode Star*, a "Dean Goods", the 1903 *City of Truro*, the *King George V* – built in the town in 1927 – and an 0-6-0 1947 tank engine. Carriage doorlocks, signals, working models, the prized gold disc railway pass, silver table centres and coffee urns modelled on famous locomotives, rattles, truncheons, lights, headboards... give some indication of the array of equipment needed to run the line which, in its heyday, extended over 9 000 miles of track between London, Bristol, Penzance, Fishguard and Liverpool, maintained 3 600 locomotives, 9 000 passenger coaches, 82 000 freight wagons and employed more than 100 000 men.

Lining the corridor walls are posters, commands for royal trains and, in one gallery, Brunel's signed drawings for the Clifton Suspension Bridge competition at Bristol after which he was appointed, in his own words, "Engineer to the finest work in England". Upstairs, conditions in GWR works and offices are carefully recreated with period furniture, tools, time clocks, information boards etc.

Note: the museum is presently transferring a number of its larger locomotives to the Great Western Designer Outlet Village nearby where a GWR Heritage Centre will be created for the millennium.

★ **Railway Village Museum** ⊙ – *34 Faringdon Road.* To house its workers, the company built not only the lodging house but also 300 one, two, three-up and three-down houses. The building material used was the limestone excavated from the nearby 3 212yd long Box Tunnel (1837-41).

In 1969-80 the cottages were cleaned of soot and grime; all were modernised save one, no 34, a three-bedroomed house which was left with gas and oil lighting, a range, washing dolly, copper, mangle, brown-glazed sink and tin bath in the kitchen and outside lavatory. It is furnished for the 1900s and, although now connected to the national gas network, still smells of the past: an evocation that is further emphasised by details such as the carefully preserved samples of coal-tar soap, washing powder, fly papers and the bowler hat on the peg in the hall (the unmistakable mark of a foreman's rank to those in the know).

King George V locomotive (1927)

Civic Centre and Brunel Shopping Centre – The Civic Centre (late 1950s-1980s), comprising administrative offices, the law courts, the Wyvern Theatre, the College and monolithic commercial buildings, is constructed of diverse materials including black brick and white marble, and remains strangely rudimentary. By comparison the **Brunel Centre** (mid-1970s), which adjoins an earlier shopping centre, is closely knit; the overhead arching above the mosaic pavement and the peripheral arcading are airily reminiscent of the iron-work and glass of the great 19C railway termini. In one avenue stands a larger-than-life statue of Brunel.

Museum and Art Gallery ⊙ – *Bath Road.* The museum, installed in a 19C house in Swindon Old Town, has displays of fossils and local history. It also boasts a remarkable collection of **Studio pottery** and **20C British graphic artworks** by the likes of Sickert, Steer, Augustus and Gwen John, the Bloomsbury painters, Ivon Hitchens, David Bomberg, Paul Nash, Graham Sutherland, John Piper, Michael Ayrton, Leon Kossoff, Howard Hodgkin: display space, however, is strictly limited and so items are regularly changed around.

Richard Jefferies Museum ⊙ – *Marlborough Road, Coate. A345 before the roundabout, opposite a large garage and hotel.* In the farmhouse in which the naturalist and writer Jefferies was born in 1848 are early editions of his works and personal mementoes, also writings of Alfred Williams, the Hammerman or Railway Poet.

Renault Distribution Centre – *Follow signs for West Swindon, past Link Centre, turn right at next roundabout opposite road to Sainsbury's.* Sir Norman Foster's modular structure, four bays wide and eleven long, combines high tech modern materials (glass, steel, pvc) with precise carefully engineered detailing. For those familiar with Foster Associates' design for Stansted Airport, this structure (1983) provides a clear precedent in the treatment of a unified, flexible space. Access to the interior is limited, but a tour of the exterior is encouraged.

EXCURSION

Lydiard Park ⊙ *3 miles west, signposted from Junction 16 of M4.*

The elegant stone house, two storeys high, eleven bays wide with pyramid-roofed pavilions, overlooks an extensive park with spreading cedars and distant avenues. Largely remodelled by Lord John St John (1743-79), the house was subsequently abandoned in favour of the family's London seat (Old Battersea House): in 1943 when the place was acquired by the Swindon Corporation, the contents of the house had been auctioned, lighting relied on oil lamps and candles, water was drawn by hand from the well...

The rooms are notable for their comfortable proportions, moulded plaster ceilings and white-painted woodwork. A considerable number of the original family portraits, 18C furniture, beautiful pier glasses, silver and porcelain have been reassembled in the ground floor state rooms. The end boudoir chamber, with its Neo-Classical decoration and unusual 17C Dutch painted window, is further ornamented with works by Lady Diana Spencer, 2nd Viscountess Bolingbroke, a talented 18C amateur artist.

★ **St Mary's** - Traces of medieval wall paintings, early stained glass and the Jacobean pulpit all predate the Dissolution. The most unusual features, however, are 17C: the Stuart coat of arms, the east window documenting the manor's changes in ownership, Charles I chairs, late 17C italianate wrought-iron **communion rail** and the famous family **memorials**.

Indeed, the minute 13C-15C parish church is now so full of **monuments** to St Johns that, in the words of John Aubrey, the antiquary, it "exceeds all the churches of this countie". Twenty nine figures are represented – two kneeling in prayer (south aisle), ten painted in a remarkable triptych (1615), three recumbent surrounded by their 13 children in alabaster below a Renaissance canopy with the figures of Hope, Faith, Charity and Immortality (1634), and one standing in gilded armour between parted curtains (1645 commemorating Edward who died in the Civil War).

Wroughton

Science Museum ⊘ - *3 miles south off A361 towards Avebury and Devizes.* In order to alleviate storage problems the Science Museum acquired the Wroughton Airfield and its six hangars in the hope that it might continue to acquire large civil aircraft for its aeronautical collection founded in 1912, expand its collections of road transport and agricultural machinery and house objects from its space technology, civil engineering and marine engineering departments. Over 17 000 objects are now stored here, although not all are on regular display on event days (phone for details). Aeroplanes include a Boeing 247D; Douglas DC-3; Hawker Siddeley Trident 3; Lockheed Constellation and Electra; De Havilland Dragon, Dragon Rapide, Dove 6; Piaggio P166.

Occupying a most wonderful site high above Swindon, the airfield provides spectacular **views**★★ across the Wiltshire Downs and beyond. It was built as a maintenance unit for the RAF in 1940 and used as a Royal Naval Aircraft Yard between 1972-78.

TAUNTON★

Somerset – Population 38 545
Michelin Atlas p 7 or Map 403 – K 30

Taunton's recognition as the county town in the 1850s was marked with the building of the Shire Hall. From humble beginnings as the battlefield where King Ine of Wessex won a victory against the English (710), Taunton has grown into the most important agricultural and livestock market at the heart of one of the nation's most fertile regions, the Vale of Taunton. For more than six centuries it had also been an important cloth weaving town: it was the first to introduce the fulling mill to this country in 1218 and so start the shift from cottage industry to company mills. It is said that the Black Death so decimated the population in the 14C as to cripple any intent to build churches; as the tide eventually turned in the late 15C, initiatives were once more stunted by the Dissolution. In 1702 Defoe described Taunton as a "large, wealthy, and exceedingly populous town (that had) so good a trade that they had 1 100 looms going for the weaving of sagathies and duroys" (fine wool and silk, and coarse woollen cloths).

Another important part of Taunton is the Somerset County Cricket Ground *(Priory Avenue)*, complete with cricket museum ⊘.

Market day: Saturday all day; cattle: Saturday and Tuesday (morning only).

Castle - In 1497 **Perkin Warbeck** passed through Taunton on his rebellious expedition against Henry VII and was brought back to stand trial in the Great Hall of the castle: almost two centuries later the **Duke of Monmouth**, another rebel, passed through the town, and in 1685 after the Battle of Sedgemoor (*see* BRIDGWATER) many of his followers were brought before **Judge Jeffreys** at the **Bloody Assizes** in the same hall. Jeffreys condemned 508 to death but how many actually died is not known; estimates range from 300-500 with between 800 and 1000 transported to the West Indies; there was a brisk trade in pardons. The Bloody Assizes remain a raw memory in the southwest.

During the Civil War Taunton and the castle in particular were under siege three times, most notably in 1645 when the town, under **Robert Blake**, resisted the Royalist forces for three months. In 1648 Parliament ordered the castle and manor to be sold; the sum realised was £9 210 17*s* 1/2*d.* In 1662 the Royalist government ordered the castle to be slighted.

After the slighting the 11C-12C castle remained a ruin until it was rescued in the 18C. The east gatehouse is now incorporated into a hotel; the 15C **gateway**, which leads through the south range into the inner ward, serves as the entrance to the museum *(below)*.

★ **Somerset County Museum** ⊘ – A contemporary portrait of **Judge Jeffreys** by Kneller hangs in the **Great Hall**.

Displays in the section on early history include the **wooden trackways** laid in 2900 BC across the marshlands of the **Somerset Levels**; the prehistoric dugout canoe and other finds from the **Lake Villages** around Glastonbury; the Roman mosaic of Dido and Aeneas. The **ceramics collection** contains pieces of Eltonware, local Donyatt and 19C Martinware. There is a collection of Nailsea glass. The highlights of the Chinese pottery bequest are the Han dynasty vases (206 BC-AD 220) and a robust T'ang tomb figure (AD 618-906).

The **17C silver collection** displays a set of apostle and seal top spoons and beakers. A separate gallery recalls the Somerset Light Infantry with battle honours, uniforms and mementoes including a Stars and Stripes captured in 1813.

★ **St Mary Magdalene** ⊘ – The church with its soaring tower closes perfectly the vista along Hammett Street.

The **tower**, which was completed in 1514 after 26 years of building, was the joy and climax to the 15C reconstruction of the parish church on its ancient Saxon site. At a period when the county was the third or fourth most densely populated in England and amongst the wealthiest, it represented the final flowering of what has remained Somerset's great contribution to church architecture. Built of Ham Hill stone, it is marked at every stage by crocketed pinnacles on set-back buttresses. From the door and a transomed west window it mounts to a frieze surmounted by the first of three similar sets of paired openings each of three lights with transoms, tracery and Somerset tracery, divided and framed by pinnacled shafts; the top pair, the bell openings, are taller, the pinnacles set diagonally, the walling above, panelled; higher still are a fourth frieze, spouting gargoyles, another frieze and the great **crown** of pierced battlements, pinnacles and, at the angles, four tiers of arcading and pierced, crocketed pinnacles flaunting iron wind-vanes – 163ft in all, the top pinnacles 32ft and pierced to minimise wind resistance. The vanes were added, as their 3.5in numerals indicate, in 1682.

Inside, the church is almost square with a narrow nave and double aisles; the outer aisle and arcade on the north side only were not rebuilt in the 15C and are Early English. The roof is typical of Tudor Somerset with crested tie-beams, king posts, moulded arch braces, panelling, small oak-leaf bosses and **angels**, recently gilded and painted for the first time. Angels reappear in the arcade capitals, while amusing **medieval masks** decorate bosses above the light brackets, the inner aisles and the chancel arch *(north side possibly Henry VII)*; otherwise the statues are 19C replacements of those destroyed by the Puritans.

★ **St James'** – All of the church, except for the north arcade and aisle, is 14C-15C. The 120ft **tower** of Quantock red sandstone with Ham stone decoration, which many believe to be the forerunner in design to St Mary's, rises from the doorway and six-light west window in stages marked by pinnacled buttresses and diagonally set pinnacles to a bell stage with transomed openings filled with Somerset tracery. Above are a **crest** of gargoyles, a pierced parapet, pinnacles and an overtopping **staircase tower** with a pyramid roof.

Nearby is **Vivary Park**, like St James', in the former priory grounds. Named after the monks' fishpond or vivarium, it has a striking Victorian fountain.

Public buildings and streets – Among the more notable buildings are the **Shire Hall** of 1855-58 in early Tudor style which brought county town status to Taunton *(see above)*; the **Tudor House** of 1578 (Fore Street) with its carved timbers and oversailing gable with multi-light oriel windows; the red-brick Market House of the 1770s with a pediment spanning its full width which stands at the centre crossroads.

The Bristol Road leads to two charitable institutions. **Gray's Almshouses** *(south side of East Street)*, two storeys built of brick with nine chimney stacks each comprising two diagonally set chimneys, date from 1635. St Margaret's Leper Hospital, founded in the 12C, rebuilt early in the 16C and converted into almshouses in 1612 has been largely destroyed by fire. In 1977 the **Brewhouse Theatre** opened in a converted 19C warehouse by the river.

The most appealing streets are **Hammett Street★** of 1788 with twin lines of dark brick **terrace houses** with attractive pillared and pedimented porches making the perfect frame for St Mary's at the street's end; The **Crescent★** of 1807 *(westerly parallel to the High Street)*, designed as a single undertaking; **Bath Alley★** *(between the High Street and the end of Corporation Street)*, in which every house, cottage and shop was built in the 17C-18C to a different design; the wide High Street *(pedestrian precinct)*, leisurely with late Georgian-early Victorian houses, shops and pubs...

EXCURSIONS

Trull – *3 miles south.* Pop 4 122. The **church**★, which is Perpendicular with a 13C tower, is known for its wooden pulpit which is carved all round with figures of saints and guardian angels wearing clothes in the style of the 1530s.

Hatch Court ⊙ *6 miles southeast off A358.*

The square Georgian house of Bath stone, graced by a tall arcade of columns at the top of a shallow flight of steps, small end pavilions with pyramid roofs and a pierced balustrade, dates from 1755. It was designed by Thomas Prowse, MP, a substantial landowner and amateur architect.

House – The **Hall** is planned with great style to lead through a screen of fluted Ionic columns to the cantilevered staircase, which rises to a half-landing where it divides and returns; the landing above, columned, triple-arched and with a groined vault, sweeps round behind a curved balustrade. In the hall stand rare 17C walnut benches and an oak table of *c*1630 (9ft 6in).
The **Drawing Room** has its original plasterwork ceiling; the Japanese silk embroidery of peacocks is 19C.
The bookcases in the **Library** follow the line of the walls in a graceful arc while the **Orangery** gallery is curved to enhance the house's exterior appearance.
The **China Room** displays a fine selection of English porcelain and glass including a dark green set of Minton dessert plates with birds in white relief; the adjoining room collects together mementoes of the Empire's last privately raised regiment **Princess Pat's Regiment** (Princess Patricia's Canadian Light Infantry) and its founder Brigadier Hamilton Gault, MP for Taunton.

Gardens – The house, surrounded by an immaculate walled kitchen garden, herbaceous borders, trees and shrubs, overlooks a small park populated with fallow deer, an embryonic arboretum and the Somerset countryside beyond.

St John the Baptist – The church behind the house was rebuilt on an older site in the 15C-16C when it was given its embattled tower of blue lias which is overtopped by its stair turret and the surrounding trees.

TAUNTON DEANE

Somerset

Michelin Atlas p 7 or Map 403 – K 30

Taunton Deane or the Vale of Taunton lies west of the town, a beautiful diamond of fertile agricultural and cider apple country, watered by the River Tone and ringed by the moorlands and hills which characterise the county: the Quantocks to the northeast, the Brendons to the northwest and the Blackdowns to the south. At the foot of the hills are a number of small market towns, an old manor house and, on the Blackdowns, a monument.

Towns and country houses in the Vale

★ **Bishop's Lydeard** – The **houses**, some still thatched, the **almshouses** of 1616, with mullioned windows and curved doorway arches, and the church all in local **red sandstone** reflect the village's situation below the Quantock Hills.
The **church**★ in true Somerset tradition is notable for its west **tower** of *c*1470 which rises from a transomed west window to the bell stage where the flourish begins with a three-light opening – transomed and traceried – flanked by buttress pinnacles; above are a collar of gargoyles, a pierced parapet and countless more pinnacles.
Inside is an early 16C **rood screen** in which the elaborate tracery complements the fan vaulting and has a unique decoration of **lead stars**; note the finely carved **cornice.** The carved **bench-ends** of the same date are coloured the better to show the windmill and flying birds, the ships and symbols of the Passion. The pulpit is Jacobean.
In a wall cabinet *(light switch)* is the town's **market charter** of 1291 sealed by Edward I.

★ **Combe Florey** – The picturesque small village in a valley at the foot of the Brendon Hills is romantically named after a 12C knight, Hugh de Flori.
Almost every building is in the local pink-red, Quantock sandstone, most noticeably the **church** where a particularly deep-coloured stone has been employed for the embattled and pinnacled tower and for the trims and window tracery. Inside, note the **angels** at capital height *(tower arch and north arcade)* and the early 14C **tomb** with a lifesize effigy of a cross-legged knight and, presumably, successive wives.

★ **Gaulden Manor, Tolland** ◷ – *9 miles northwest of Taunton: 30min.*
Gaulden Manor, a two-storey 16C red sandstone manor house with exceptional 1642 **plasterwork** inside, stands between the Brendon and the Quantock Hills. It is surrounded by tall trees, an immense old monastic fishpond bordered by poplars and by individual small gardens – quiet, secret, shaded, flower-filled or scented with herbs.

In the 1560s the house was chosen by **James Turberville**, Bishop of Exeter (d 1571), as the place to end his days after he had refused to take the oath of supremacy to Queen Elizabeth I and suffered a spell in the Tower of London.

In 1618 the house and farm were bought by a mercer from Wellington whose son, **Henry Wolcott**, emigrated to America in 1630 and founded a family which has since become so extensive that the members have formed a descendants' society. In 1639 the bishop's great-nephew **John Turberville** repurchased the manor; although at first there was "scarce a chamber yet ready to lodge myselfe or my friends", he soon had it entirely refurbished and his arms implanted on the overmantels.

Interior – Throughout the house choice pieces of **furniture** of all periods are on display, from 17C refectory tables to early ladder-back and Hepplewhite-style chairs, 16C-17C and late 18C oak chests, English and Meissen **porcelain**, modern **needlework**... The porch and iron-studded oak door lead into the screens passage.

The former kitchen, now the **Dining Room**, has a huge fireplace complete with a bread oven and salt niche.

The **Great Hall** has a splendid **plaster ceiling** of three garlanded roundels, the centre one descending in a solid ribbed pendant, the others showing reliefs of King David with his harp and an angel blowing the last trump. Round the room, a deep **frieze** continues the Biblical theme and, possibly in reference to Bishop Turberville's misfortunes, includes the scales of justice and a tower, from which it has been surmised that the ceiling and frieze and the considerable decoration over the Tudor fireplace date from the 16C; the decoration on the overmantel itself, however, showing the arms of John Turberville impaling those of his wife, must be 17C; possibly all the plasterwork is 17C, some of it achieved using older moulds. At the far end of the room, 17C panelling and a line of lesser pendants screen a smaller room with its own 16C fireplace, known as the Chapel.

The stairs have their original **oak treads**; the old crooked **window** with bottle green glass dates back to the 17C. Upstairs, the **Turberville Bedroom** records the house's 17C associations through the **Turberville arms** over the fireplace and a **Wolcott window** and brass plate. The mirror is by Chippendale.

Gardens – Roses, scented and bog plants are a few of the features of the attractive gardens which largely date from this century, laid out by the present family.

Milverton – The town, with the Brendon Hills to the northwest, surrounds a hillock crowned by the parish **church**, a 14C-15C building in the local red sandstone. The Perpendicular tower with a square stair turret rises to bell openings filled with Somerset tracery and a crest of battlements and pinnacles. Inside, the **north arcade** is 14C, the **font** with cable moulding and a frieze of crosses is Norman, the **rood screen**, as can be seen from the date, was made in 1540. The **stalls** and **benches** (15C-16C) are attractively carved with poppyheads, the twelve Apostles, local characters, the arms of Henry VIII...

The **village** itself is a mixture of Georgian houses (North and Fore Streets and south Sand Street), small cottages and 19C houses, spiced with the occasional 17C house and, east of the church, the 15C-16C parsonage.

Wellington – The town had become a market and cloth centre by the 15C. In the 19C its communications were revolutionised by the construction of the Bridgwater-Tiverton Canal and in the 1840s by that of the Bristol-Exeter railway. The houses, the town hall of 1833, the Baptist Chapel, even the Friends' Meeting House, reflect the late Georgian–early 19C prosperity.

The 15C **church**★ has a fortress-like **tower** of red sandstone which rises through three stages from a west door and four-light window to bell openings with Somerset tracery and a final flourish of gargoyles, battlements and pinnacles, of which there are three to each angle and nine on the stair turret.

Inside are an Early English **east window** of three stepped lancets below encircled quatrefoils, a **lily crucifix** carved into the centre mullion of the east window of the south aisle, and the **funerary monument** of Chief Justice, Sir John Popham (d 1607), who presided at the trials of Guy Fawkes, Sir John Dayrell of Littlecote and Sir Walter Raleigh, and is shown recumbent on a chest beneath a canopy ornate with achievements and obelisks.

Wellington Monument – *2 miles south via by-roads.* The Duke of Wellington took the town's name for his title as it closely resembled his family name of Wellesley. Although he had no other connection with Wellington, the townspeople erected a grey stone monument in the form of a bayonet (175ft tall) in his honour on the Blackdown Hills; it is visible for several miles.

From its base there are **views**★★ across Taunton Deane to the Polden Hills, the Quantocks, the Brendons and Exmoor and into Devon *(viewing table).*

TAVISTOCK

Devon – Population 10 222
Michelin Atlas p 4 or Map 403 – H 32

The modern market town constructed in the local volcanic, grey-green stone, retains many traces of its 19C days as a copper mining town and also of the monastic borough which it was from 980-1539. A bronze statue of **Sir Francis Drake** is a reminder that he was christened in the parish c1541.

The Benedictine Tavistock Abbey (f 874) was the most resplendent house west of Glastonbury. The abbot obtained a charter for a weekly market in 1105, also an annual **Goose Fair; tin mining** in the area so developed that in 1281 Tavistock was named a stannary town; by the 1290s silver and lead were also being exploited locally. Wool and cloth meanwhile provided the main wealth both to the abbey and to the lay community, resulting in the parish church, already rebuilt in the 14C, being again rebuilt during 1425-50.

In 1539 the abbey was dissolved and the town was given by Henry VIII to **John Russell**, courtier, ambassador, counsellor and future Earl of Bedford.

With the start of the Napoleonic wars in the 1790s, **mining** became the most important local industry and when in 1844 one of the richest ever **copper lodes** or veins in Europe was discovered near the surface in a pheasant covert, Tavistock became a boom town. Five separate mines in an area of 167 acres were grouped into a company known as **Devon Great Consols** whose £1 shares, three years after being launched, were quoted on the Stock Exchange at £800. Production was at its peak from 1848-58 then slackened as the mines became exhausted (1901); in the half century 730 000 tons of copper ore and 72 000 tons of refined arsenic – used then in dyes, paints, glass-making, ink and insecticides – had been produced at a sale price of £4 000 000.

Bonuses from the new wealth were an increase in the population of the town to one and a half times its present size; the construction from 1803 to 1817, with French prisoners-of-war as navvies, of the 4 mile long **canal**, including 1.5 mile tunnel, connecting Tavistock with the Tamar at Morwellham; the remodelling in neo-Gothic style of the **guildhall** and the Bedford Hotel (then a private house), and the construction of the **pannier market** and houses for the miners and townspeople.

St Eustachius Church – The embattled **tower** (106ft) was built in the 14C as one of the abbey gateways with doorways facing north and south. In the interior note: *(west end)* a 14C octagonal font, medieval chests, a brass **ophicleide** (an obsolete wind instrument from the 18C church band), carved organ case; *(northeast chapel)* early 17C **pewter flagons**, 15C bench-ends, window designed by William Morris (1876); *(south aisle)* **Clothworkers' Aisle**, bosses in the wagon roof.

★ **Morwellham** *4 miles southwest of Tavistock, off A390 to Liskeard.*

The success of the woollen trade in the 13C led to Morwellham Quay being leased from the abbey as a separate concern; at the Dissolution, the property passed to the Russells in whose hands it remained until 1956.

Morwellham's heyday was the brief period between the Devonshire Great Consolidated Mining Company (Devon Great Consols) copper strike of 1844 and the coming of the Great Western Railway to Tavistock in 1859. In those few years it became "the Greatest Copper Port in Queen Victoria's Empire": some 450 000 tons of mineral ore were shipped the 20 miles downstream to Plymouth in boats which, in most cases, carried only 50-100 tons a time. The industry and traffic were prodigious: copper ore and arsenic were brought from Tavistock by canal barge to a point 237ft above the river from where it descended by an inclined railway powered initially by a waterwheel and later supplemented by a second railway powered by steam. The quays, which had developed slowly since the river port came into existence before the Conquest, had to be modified beyond recognition to provide tiled wharves to keep the ore and arsenic clean and a dock large enough to take six 300-ton schooners at any one time. The number of villagers increased to 200; model cottages, houses, a shop, school, two chapels, a butcher's shop, pub a hostelry (the Ship Inn), workshops and warehouses were built.

As rapidly as it had boomed Morwellham died: the canal was superseded by the railway; the richest copper deposits in the country became exhausted; Devon Great Consols declined; the population fell to 50. In 1969 the Morwellham and Tamar Valley Trust took over the area around the old port, which had remained virtually untouched since the last century, as part of a conservation project encompassing the region. Nature trails, picnic areas and bird-watching hides in the **wildlife reserve** ⊘ provide the means to explore this rural idyll, while Morwellham Quay is a bustling re-creation of its former self, populated with figures dressed in period costume apparently going about their daily business.

Morwellham Quay ⓥ – The electric **Riverside tramway** runs along above the river before entering the George and Charlotte copper mine, which was last worked in 1868; here, 19C working conditions are dramatically evoked.

The **lime kilns** are a reminder of an era when lime was produced to counteract the local acid soil by burning limestone.

The **Mining Museum** and **Port Museum** describe the operation of the two enterprises. In the workshops which include a smithy, cooper's shop and assayer's laboratory, different skills are demonstrated by staff dressed in 19C costume. Quay Cottage recreates the domestic life of a 19C workman.

Water power pumped drinking water for the villagers, drove the mill which ground manganese ore to powder, flushed silt from the docks and operated the first inclined plane railways, of which few traces remain.

The **Great Dock** was built in 1858 to handle the rising output of the copper mines; the quays were covered with tiles which are visible in places.

Victorian farm buildings contain a water-powered threshing machine, typical 19C farm animals and the stables of the shire horses which draw the carriage for rides along the Duke of Bedford's drive.

Canal Tunnel – Above the village (250ft) is the entrance to the tunnel (1.5 miles), built by John Taylor from 1803 to 1817, which carried the canal (4.5 miles) under Morwell Down to Tavistock; in 1880 it ceased ferrying cargo and in 1933 the water was diverted to the electricity generating station.

For Gunnislake and Cotehele (6 miles southwest via Gulworthy, A390 west and by-roads) see PLYMOUTH SOUND-RIVER TAMAR.

TEIGNMOUTH

Devon – Population 13 403

Michelin Atlas p 4 or Map 403 – J 32

The dark red cliffs and offshore rocks, which characterise Devon for so many holiday-makers, appear in an almost unbroken line between the Exe and Teign estuaries, the second distinguished by a huge red sandstone headland known as **The Ness**. *(Passenger ferries across both estuaries, also a bridge in the town across the Teign.)*

The **railway**, given pride of place as it travelled west in the mid-19C, runs at the foot of the cliffs, skirting the waterline, tunnelling through the headlands and rumbling in each resort, between the flower-decked esplanades and the beaches.

Fishing for cod off the Newfoundland Grand Banks, shipbuilding and the export of dried fish brought prosperity to Teignmouth centuries ago; today its industries are offshore fishing and marketing, the handling of ball clay, and tourism.

EXCURSIONS

North to Powderham Castle

Dawlish – *3 miles northeast by A379.*
With the arrival in the 19C of the railway along the coast, the village at the mouth of Dawlish Water developed into a fashionable resort. **Dawlish Warren**, a long spit of sand dunes obstructing the mouth of the Exe, is now a nature reserve.

Powderham Castle ⓥ – *8 miles northeast by A379.*
The home of the Courtenay family, Earls of Devon, stands in its own deer park overlooking the Exe estuary. The rooms are hung with family portraits, many by Cosway (1742-1821), and a series of **coats of arms** tracing the family descent decorates the 19C dining hall, designed by the Devon-born architect Charles Fowler. The medieval ante-room contains a pair of rosewood **bookcases** (1740) and an unusual window, screened at night by a mirror, inserted over the fireplace. The library bookcases were made in Dawlish in the 1820s. James Wyatt designed the handsome **domed Music Room** (1794-96) which has a Carrara marble fireplace; Corinthian pilasters alternate with alcoves containing alabaster vases on marble stands; the gilt furniture incorporating the dolphin – the Courtenay family crest – and the Axminster carpet were made to order. The original great hall was converted into the staircase hall, which is decorated with magnificent **18C Rococo plasterwork.** The Marble Hall contains two 17C Brussels tapestries and a clock (1740) which plays tunes. The family **porcelain**, which is mostly French and was in daily use until 1935, is displayed in one of the medieval towers. The chapel is now housed in a 15C barn with a timber roof.

Newton Abbot *6 miles west by A379.*

The busy market town, comprising two separate districts until the 20C, was originally founded around a ford at the tidal limit of the River Teign which linked two medieval manors. Wolborough Manor was given by William Brewer to the monastery he founded at Torre Abbey (see TORBAY: Torquay) in the 12C, hence the name corrupted from New Town of the Abbot.

The second, originally known as Teignwick, was renamed Newton Bushel after Robert Bushel who built the earliest manor house at Bradley: it is now known as Highweek. In 1633 the two markets were combined and held on the Newton Abbot side; the town's fortunes, however, were assured in 1846 when Newton Abbot became the main junction connecting the Great Western with the South Devon Railway. Here the engines were changed and the pace of onward journeys was slowed down as the line snaked through the hills and undulations of south Devon to Cornwall: only after the demise of the broad gauge in 1892, was a continuous service possible when a regiment of powerful locomotives, known as the Duke of Cornwall class, was introduced (1895-99).

The main landmark of Newton Tower is the free-standing 14C **St Leonard's Tower**, devoid of its adjacent chapel which was demolished in 1836: it was here that William of Orange first proclaimed his intention to be king in 1688.

Market day: Wednesday (pannier and livestock); Antiques: Tuesday.

Forde House – *No general access.* In the late 17C the Courtenays of Powderham Castle arrived through marriage and, in the 19C, set about rebuilding the town centre and developing an elegant suburb eastwards towards the new railway junction. The E-shaped house in its present form, however, mostly dates from the tenure of Sir Richard Reynell who is known to have entertained Charles I there in 1625. The most remarkable feature is the period plasterwork ceilings which in design may be considered alongside Montacute in Somerset. It is now owned by Teignbridge District and is flanked by additional offices (1985-87) with 17C-inspired detailing.

Bradley Manor ⊘ – The house which replaced Highweek Castle, was largely rebuilt in the early 1400s on earlier foundations (*c*1250). It lies low in the wooded Lemon valley at the end of a long driveway over the mill leat. The gabled east front is rough-cast and limewashed, set with Perpendicular oriel windows. Now leased by the National Trust to the former owner, there is restricted access to the great hall (emblazoned with the arms of Elizabeth I), chapel, buttery and kitchen.

Chudleigh

8 miles northwest of Teignmouth via Ideford by B3192 and by-roads.

Much of the market town, now by-passed by the Exeter to Plymouth road, had to be rebuilt following a fire in 1807. It therefore has a homogenous elegant Regency air about it, despite the medieval-looking church (St Martin and St Mary) and the rather less attractive 20C library and health centre.

Ugbrooke House ⊘ – *0.5 mile east of Chudleigh. 75min.*

Before the Dissolution, the estate belonged to Exeter Cathedral, from which it passed to the Courtenay family, then by marriage to the Cliffords. In 1763 the 4th Lord Clifford of Chudleigh employed Robert Adam to redesign the E-shaped Tudor manor house, and "Capability" Brown to design the park through which flowed the brook that gave the house its name.

Adam promptly demolished one wing of the house and used the material to connect the other two around a courtyard; he then added the solid, castellated towers at the angles. The house has an almost square ground-plan consisting of 10 by 11 bays.

Interior – The entrance is reached through an archway into the courtyard. The small **entrance hall** with an Adam cornice contains fine Brussels **tapestries** of *Romulus and Remus* – a present from Cosimo III of Tuscany to the 1st Lord Clifford in 1669 – and a tapestry by Francis Poyntz of Hatton Garden, London. The domed **staircase hall** has the christening present given by Charles II to his godson the 2nd Lord Clifford in 1671: a magnificent **silver gilt ewer and salver**. Family portraits adorn the walls and an Epstein bronze bust of Lord Fisher of Kiverstone (grandfather of the present Lady Clifford) sits at the top.

The **morning room** replaces the original Tudor entrance hall: it now contains family portraits, a fine William and Mary walnut **writing desk** (*c*1700), an 18C **breakfront bookcase** made (by Gillows of Lancaster) to a design by Chippendale. The Adam cornice includes a dragon and a lion (family crests). The Wilton carpet was made to a Persian design for the American magnate William Hearst and later bought by Lord Clifford.

The **drawing room** contains a notable collection of **portraits by Lely** and a portrait of Catherine of Braganza, by Huysman, in which the sitter is shown wearing the diamond earrings she later gave to her goddaughter Catherine Clifford. The very fine **Elizabethan tapestry** (now in three sections) with its rich colouring and vivid detail was rediscovered after centuries in store. The furniture includes a Georgian games table, a French Boulle table, a William and Mary cabinet (1685), a pair of Adam semicircular tables and a Victorian centre table with marquetry flowers. The Adam **dining room** was originally hung with gold and silk damask.

The Chinese armorial **porcelain dinner service** (c1740) on the mahogany Georgian **dining table** was a coming of age present for the 4th Lord Clifford. Other items include a fine George III mahogany spirit box (c1790) with its original bottles and glasses, and pieces of Worcester ware on the mantelpiece. Thomas Weld was a widower with one daughter when he decided to enter the Church; he subsequently became a bishop and then a cardinal. The **Cardinal's room** has various vestments, a patchwork bedspread (c1820) stitched by his daughter who married the 7th Lord Clifford, and an early 18C travelling medicine chest in laburnum veneer.

Adorning the walls of the **tapestry room** are two Francis Poyntz **tapestries** (1670-71) after Raphael cartoons in the Victoria and Albert Museum; they were probably made for the chapel. The **George III bed** is hung with silk **embroidered hangings** from c1720. The tepoy is one of only six made commemorating the death of Lord Nelson.

Additional rooms – Beyond the passages (coronation robes, 18C clothes etc) is the Victorian conservatory which leads to the oldest part of the house. Here the library and anterooms contain military uniforms, and matter relating to the **Secret Treaty of Dover** (c1670) which gave rise to the word "cabal" from the ministers who were in league with Charles II to unite with the French against the Austrians: Clifford, Arlington, Buckingham, Ashley and Lauderdale.

Chapel – The older chapel (consecrated 1671) is ornately decorated in an Italian Renaissance style with coloured marbles – installed when the building was remodelled into a Greek cross plan (1840s); the Lady Chapel and Baptistery were added in 1866.

Gardens – Devoid of Classical monuments, Gothick ruins and Picturesque follies, Capability Brown has created a particularly successful composition within the contours of the rolling landscape. Parkland and woodland are easily offset against strategically designed formal beds, herbaceous borders and informal plantings; only the two lakes, created by damming the Ug, might appear in the least bit contrived. A **Pets Corner** includes sheep, rabbits and goats, and elsewhere beautiful species of pheasant (Golden, Silver, Lady Amherst) scratch in large pens.

TINTAGEL

Cornwall – Population 1 721

Michelin Atlas p 3 or Map 403 – F 32

Tintagel especially and the West Country in general are associated with the elusive legend of Arthur, 'the once and future King'. The tale has existed in the telling since the 8C and in written form since the 12C, retold in the spirit of the time, with locations shifted, in the 12C by William of Malmesbury, Geoffrey of Monmouth, the 12C chronicler **Wace** who added the Round Table, by Sir Thomas Malory, Spenser, Tennyson, Swinburne and T H White. Today the spirit lives on, perpetuated by tourism and followers of the New Age movement.

Tintagel is also known for having disclosed the largest find of 5C-6C eastern Mediterranean pottery sherds (more than in the rest of the British Isles put together) suggesting a buoyant trade in olive oil and wine.

Situating the King Arthur story

Arthur, son of Uther Pendragon, was either born or washed ashore at Tintagel; there he had his castle and lived with his queen, **Guinevere** and the **Knights of the Round Table** which included **Tristan**, the nephew or son of King Mark whose fort was Castle Dore. **Merlin**, the magician, lived in a cave beneath Tintagel Castle and on a rock off Mousehole. The sword **Excalibur**, forged in Avalon, was withdrawn by Arthur from the stone and finally thrown into **Dozmary Pool. Camelot** is believed by some to be Cadbury Castle (see YEOVIL).

The Battle of Mount Bladon (c520), when Arthur defeated the pagan Saxons, was possibly fought at Liddington Castle near Swindon or Badbury Rings, Dorset; the **Battle of Camlan**, the last struggle against Mordred, the king's usurping stepson or bastard son, took place on the banks of the River Camel on Bodmin Moor. Mortally wounded, Arthur sailed into the sunset, to the Islands of the Blest (the Isles of Scilly), or to Avalon, held by some to be close to Glastonbury where his tomb was 'discovered' with that of Guinevere in the 12C.

This legend has inspired a number of poets and authors through the ages: Malory's *Le Morte D'Arthur*, Tennyson's *Idylls of the King*, TH White's *The Once and Future King*...

Arthur's Castle ⊙ – *Access by a steep road from the main street; 30min on foot there and back, or by Landrover.* The **site★★★** overlooking the sea from precipitous rocks is more dramatic than the fragmentary **castle ruin**, which includes walls from the 1145 chapel and great hall, built on the site of a 6C Celtic monastery, and other walls dating from the 13C – all centuries later than Arthur's time...

★ **St Materiana** – *Signposted down the hill.* Small and low-lying on the cliff, with its rough, early 15C granite **tower** standing four square against the wind, Tintagel Parish Church has long been a sailors' landmark. Saxon elements are apparent in the north wall pierced by tiny side windows (*c*1080); most of the rest of the building is Norman (*c*1150) including the south porch sculpted decoration, as is the **font** with its rudely carved heads and serpents. At the crossing note the 13C **memorial stone** with a carved foliated cross; in the south transept a medieval slate-topped **stone bench** predates the use of pews; set in the wall is a memorial **brass** of 1430. The main chancel window is a recent addition (1991). St Materiana has been identified as St Madryn, a princess from Gwent whose relics disappeared from Minster (near Boscastle) and were lost at the Reformation.

★ **Old Post Office** ⊙ – The small, rambling manor house, built with 3ft thick stone walls and undulating slate roofs at the centre of the village, dates from the 14C.
Inside are a small, two storey, stone-paved medieval hall, with an ancient fireplace beneath exposed roof timbers, the postmistress' office and, up the narrow wooden staircase, two bedrooms beneath a maze of beams and collar braces. This atmospheric, compact little house is simply furnished with country furniture.

King Arthur's Great Hall of Chivalry ⊙ – The interior of the first hall is darkened: then Merlin begins to narrate the story of Arthur *(15 min)* as a spotlight illuminates different panels painted by a follower of the Pre-Raphaelite Brotherhood William Hatherall. The second, larger building is lit with stained glass windows illustrating the ideal attributes of the Knights of the Round Table and is furnished with a granite throne worthy of a legendary court; the outer corridor has 59 smaller windows bearing the heraldic devices of Arthur's valiant supporters.

EXCURSIONS

★ **Boscastle** *3 miles northeast off B3263*

The village straggles downhill from the road to a long tongue of sea which pours in at high tide between 300ft headlands. The picturesque inlet is the only **natural harbour** between Hartland Point and Padstow. The inner jetty dates from 1584, the breakwater from the 19C; the onetime coaching inn is 15C; the cottage gardens are bright with flowers.

Delabole, Port Isaac and Trebetherick

Delabole – *4 miles southeast by B3263 and by-roads.* The village is built of slate – church, houses, walls, steps, sills, gates and posts...

Quarry ⊙ – Delabole, a name synonymous with slate in Cornwall and once much further afield, is the oldest continuously worked slate quarry in Europe; Beaker Folk on Bodmin Moor in 2000 BC used slate as baking shelves. The quarry, one of the largest **man-made holes** in the world, has a perimeter of 1.75 miles and is 500ft deep – *viewing terrace.*
Demonstrations of slate splitting are occasionally held; old tools once used in quarrying may also be on display with roofing slates sized down from queens and duchesses to mere ladies.

Wind Farm ⊙ – *1 mile beyond the village on the B3314 towards Camelford.* Britain's first commercial wind farm was prompted by Cornish opposition to a nuclear power station: the result is a privately-owned enterprise. The ten Danish-built Vesta WD turbines are placed approximately 270m apart; each measures 105ft – 32m tall and weigh 32tonnes; the glass-fibre blades are 16.8m long and run at a constant speed of 35rpm; maximum power generated is 690volts, which is converted to 11 000volts before being cabled into the local electric grid. Total annual power is calculated as 12million kilowatt hours.
Other private substations are located at the junction of the A30 / A39 and on the Lizard.

Pixie House ⊙ – Located at Penpethy on the B3263 Tintagel to Camelford road is a small stone house (1870) built of blue, rustic and grey slate as a show house for the local quarries. Today it provides a picturesque setting for a large collection of pixies with pointed ears in green hats and elderly gnomes in red hats, ageless elves and wood sprites: the little people long associated with Cornwall.

For Camelford (6 miles southeast by B3263 and B3266), see BODMIN.

Port Isaac – *9 miles southwest by B3263, B3314 and by-roads.*
The ancient fishing village with narrow streets and alleys and a small, protected harbour, from which Delabole slate was once shipped, stands in a designated area of outstanding natural beauty: cliffs drop to the sea in an almost unbroken line, any break being occupied by minute hamlets like **Port Gaverne** and **Portquin**.

Trebetherick – In the churchyard of St Enodoc overlooking Padstow Bay lies the poet **Sir John Betjeman** – as indeed his parents, lost apparently in 'the wideness which larksong gives the sky'. The church is reached across the golfcourse.

Walkers, campers, smokers... please be careful!
Fire is the worst threat to woodland.

TIVERTON

Devon – Population 17 213
Michelin map fold 25 – J 31

The town between Dartmoor and Exmoor, at the confluence of the Rivers Lowman and Exe, grew up around its castle and accumulated its wealth in the 13C-17C with **wool**. In Tudor times merchants settled in the town, added an aisle and chapel to the church, endowed schools and almshouses.

By the 18C, in Defoe's words, Tiverton had become 'Next to Excester, the greatest manufactoring town in the county and, of all the inland towns, next to it in wealth and in the numbers of people', supported by some 55 fulling mills and 700 woolcombers. In the 19C the population reached 10 500; **lacemaking**, brought by **John Heathcoat** from the Midlands, became the major industry, as it remains today although modern techniques have also brought diversification into net-making.

Tiverton Castle ⊙ – *North Hill; just north of the church.* In the 12C Henry I created the Norman, Richard de Redvers, Earl of Devon and presented him with a great swathe of land on which to build a ring of defensive forts: Tiverton, Exeter, Plympton, Christchurch and Carisbrooke. The present building was largely constructed by Hugh Courtenay (d 1340) who also built the castle at Okehampton (*see* DARTMOOR). In the Civil War Tiverton castle was first besieged and then slighted; at the Restoration it was purchased by a rich wool merchant, Peter West.

The massive 14C red sandstone **gatehouse** (under restoration), vaulted in white Caen stone, gives access to a large grassed courtyard bounded by the curtain walls and towers above the River Exe (60ft below). Several rooms in the gatehouse and round tower now contain Civil War arms and armoury, items relating to the history of the castle, a panel from the New World Tapestry and a collection of historic clocks.

★ **St Peter's Church** – 'A gorgeously ostentatious display of civic pride' is how Pevsner describes this church. The 99ft **tower** in pink sandstone with corner pinnacles dates from c1400, striking a major contrast with the whitewashed body of the church which is embattled with ships denoting the origins of the town's wealth. In 1517, after the nave and aisles had long been completed, the merchant **John Greenway** enlarged the south aisle and added the south **porch** (reconstructed and reinforced in the 19C) and **chapel★★** in the fashionable late Perpendicular style with larger windows, ornamented castellations, crocketed pinnacles, heraldic panels and a frieze of scenes depicting the *Passion of Christ*. The additions were in contrasting white stone and the chapel decorated with reliefs including a line of **armed merchantmen** such as shipped their woollen cloth from Devon and brought home wine and raw wool.
Also of note are the 18C paintings, organ of 1696, Victorian and Edwardian stained glass.

St George's – *Fore Street*. Tiverton's second major church dates from 1714-33, designed by the London architect John James who was responsible for St George's, Hanover Square. The overall appearance is rational and elegant, complete with rusticated quoins and round-headed windows.

Museum ⊙ – *National Schools, St Andrew Street*. The local museum, a former school, harbours a great variety of artefacts from Roman times, including the Roman Fort at Knightshayes, to more recent archive material: agricultural implements and an important collection of horse-drawn wagons; domestic utensils; the steam locomotive GWR 0-4-2T 1442 known as the Tivvy Bumper and associated railway equipment; toys, dolls, clocks, model aircraft, musical instruments and medical paraphernalia... Perhaps the most distinctive exhibit is the original lace-making machine designed by John Heathcoat.

Grand Western Canal – *Canal Hill. Continuation of Gold Street-Station Road*. The system was intended to connect the Bristol and English Channels by way of a 30-mile canal from Taunton to Topsham on the River Exe, with a spur coming off the mainstream to Tiverton. Although the Taunton-Tiverton reach was opened in 1814, no further building was undertaken and, when the Bristol-Exeter railway opened in the 1830s, the canal traffic decreased until only locally quarried stone and limestone were carried in the horse-drawn narrowboats. In the 1960s 11.5 miles of the canal course were reclaimed and repaired, wide boats and horses were found. Now it is possible to walk along or fish from the towpath or glide in the brightly painted *Tivertonian* drawn by amiable shires.

Old Blundells School – *Station Road*. The school *(private)*, which stands back from the road, can be seen through a gateway above which is a tablet announcing its name and foundation in 1604 by the local clothier, Peter Blundell. The building, intended for the education of local boys, is a long single-storey range in dark gold stone with a slate covered, pitched roof on the crest of which rides a small, colonnaded clock turret. Twin gables, each with a rounded doorway arch, divide the range.
The drive from the gate in the outer wall divides to approach each doorway creating before the house a grass triangle, the scene of the fight between John Ridd and Robin Snell in *Lorna Doone*: Blackmore himself was a pupil at the school.

EXCURSIONS

★ **Knightshayes Court** *2 miles north on A396, turn right at Bolham.*

The house, which is a fine example of Victorian Gothic architecture, is situated on the east bank of the Exe Valley facing south overlooking parkland and the town of Tiverton in the distance. It was at Tiverton that **John Heathcoat**, a prosperous lace-mill owner, born in Derbyshire in 1793, built a new mill in 1816 after his Midlands works (where he had installed his own bobbin net (1808) and other machines) had been wrecked by Luddites. Philanthropist and man of liberal ideas, as well as an inventor, Heathcoat represented Tiverton in parliament (1832-59). His grandson, **John Heathcoat-Amory**, inherited the business, took over the parliamentary seat and, in the late 1860s, commissioned an architect to build him a new house out of town.
William Burges was a skilled and inventive architect – there is a brilliantly balanced or compensating asymmetry about the house exterior which gives it life – but he was expensive and so in 1874 Heathcoat-Amory sacked him, employing in his stead **J D Crace** (1838-1919), who also worked at Longleat. The result is a country house, complete with conservatory, which is a true period piece.

Knightshayes Court

House ⊙ – *30min.* The furniture is 18C and 19C English with some 18C Dutch marquetry pieces; what is most intriguing, however, is to make out the contribution of each designer-architect through the ages.

In the **hall** the corbels of men and animals are by Burges, the other decoration by Crace; the walls of the **bedroom corridor** are covered by Crace's original stencilled designs. In the **boudoir**, the teak panelling, chimneypiece and repainted ceiling are all by Crace. The decoration of the downstairs **dining room** is by both architects; the walnut chairs were made in Wales in the early 19C.

The ceiling in the **morning room** is by Crace; the brass chandelier is after Pugin's Gothic style. Note the collection of 17C Italian majolica and a *Madonna and Child* by Matteo di Giovanni (1435-95).

Beneath Burges' elaborate ceiling in the **library sitting room** is hung a Flemish **Annunciation** of *c*1400. The mahogany drum table is 18C; the bracket clock is French with an English movement.

In the **drawing room**, the ceiling and chimneypiece are by Burges; among the pictures are a Constable *(Field Flowers and Poppies)*, a Bonington, a Turner and a Rembrandt self-portrait.

Recommended pit-stops

One mile along the Tiverton road out of Bampton, is the **Exeter Inn**, a 15C Devon longhouse, which prepares good food and offers a selection of beers (Exmoor Ale, Marston's Pedigree). ☎ 01398 331 345.
The **Drewe Arms** at Broadhembury may be a bit of a detour, but is nevertheless picturesquely located among whitewashed thatched cottages.
☎ 01404 841 267.

Gardens ⊘ – The renowned gardens are not old – the transformation and expansion to the present 25 acres began in the 1950s when the then Sir John and Lady Amory began improving the elaborate scheme of regular, stepped parterres, designed by Burges and Kemp, into **terraced gardens** (tree peonies, roses, herbaceous plants).

They next incorporated the yew hedges, planted east of the house in the 1880s, into pool and formal gardens with a brilliant alpine terrace below. Note the **topiary fox and hounds** of the 1930s. Finally, extending the cultivated area yet once more, they created the interesting **Garden in the Wood** (magnolias, azaleas, cornus, hydrangeas, conifers, beeches, oaks and limes underplanted with foxgloves, cyclamen, blue omphalodes and pink erythroniums) and the **Willow Garden.**

Bampton – *7 miles north on A396.* The small town, with Georgian stone houses bedecked with flowers lining the main street, is the gateway to Exmoor and famous for its annual October **Pony Fair.**

Uffculme, Cullompton and Bickleigh

★★ **Coldharbour Mill** ⊘ – *11 miles east by A373; after passing over M5 turn right at the T-junction and left to Uffculme; the mill is at the entrance to the village.*
The working wool and worsted mill museum stands between a fast-flowing stream and leat which have provided power for paper, grist and woollen mills on the site since possibly as long ago as Domesday. The last, a wool mill, which had run for nearly 200 years, flourishing at a time when the industry was moving north, closed in 1981.
The mill produces cloth and knitting yarn on sample machines, enabling the visitor to watch each process of combing, drawing, spinning, reducing, twisting, warp and weft winding and weaving. Also on show is the **New World Tapestry**, a 264ft panorama of scenes relating the history of the English colonisation of America (1583-1641).

★ **Cullompton** – The market town comprises a long main street punctuated by shops, a Tudor manor house (now a hotel), the Walronds of the same date, small courts and alleys and the occasional Georgian house.
Over-riding all is the 120ft red sandstone tower of **St Andrew's Church★**, vast and Perpendicular throughout on a much older site. Inside are a richly painted and gilded barrel roof, an equally magnificent rood screen, aisles with diamond-patterned roofs and the 1528 Lane aisle with pendented fan vaulting. At the west end note the Jacobean oak gallery on wooden Ionic columns and the medieval Calvary or Golgotha carved from a single oak trunk. The external carvings depict 16C cloth machinery.

★★ **Bickleigh** – Bickleigh looks as a Devon village should: from the old stone bridge over the Exe there is a view across to thatched houses and cottages with whitened cob walls and gardens running down to the water's edge, against a backdrop of rising fields and trees.

★★ **Devonshire's Centre, Bickleigh Mill** ⊘ – *South side of the bridge.* The mill with its water-wheel and machinery has been restored to working order. Craftworkers – potters, painters, spinners – can be seen at work in individual log cabins. There is also a fish farm where trout and carp may be fed or fished...

★ **Bickleigh Castle** ⊘ – *Turn right (A3072) before the bridge, then follow the signs.* Pink and white water lilies and irises transform the moat; wistaria decks the 14C tufa-stone gatehouse walls; thatched buildings add to the overall charm; 17C Italian and 18C English wrought-iron gates grace the approaches.
The thatched **Norman Chapel** was built between 1090 and 1110. The nave and chancel masonry and the doorway arch are original; so also are two windows, the others being 15C when the chancel was barrel roofed.
Note the **sanctuary ring**, the Early English font, the medieval glass, the 15C poppy-head **benches** and the hour-long sand-glass sermon **timer**.
Only the **gatehouse** remains of the castle itself, Fairfax having ordered all to be slighted so that the Royalist Sir Henry Carew was compelled to construct an adjoining farmhouse of cob and thatch. Beside the vaulted gatehouse **sits** an **armoury** displaying Cromwellian arms and armour and an explanation on the siege of the castle in 1646, and the former **guard room** which now contains Tudor furniture.
The early Tudor wooden staircase leads up to the 50ft long **Great Hall**, which extends across the full width of the gateway and contains two stone fireplaces; the panelled minstrels' gallery is Tudor, the furniture Carolean-Queen Anne.
The rooms in the **Farmhouse Wing** are notable for their inglenook fireplaces: the first has a 1588 fireplate and a bread oven to one side, the second a large vaulted oven and an aperture to control the smoke in the adjoining bacon-curing store;

the third, in the Garden Chamber, a 17C carved overmantel which depicts crowded, possibly historic, scenes from the lives of the 14C-17C castle owners. Note the wooden Ionic pillars in the first room which are believed to have furnished the stateroom of a Spanish man o' war, and the French ceramics in the Garden Room.

The thatched barn houses the most complete collection in existence of Second World War **spy** and **escape gadgets** and an exhibition about the **Titanic** and the **Mary Rose**, which was commanded by Vice-Admiral Sir George Carew when she sank in 1545.

TORBAY★

Devon – Population 119 674
Michelin Atlas p 4 or Map 403 – J 32

Torquay, Paignton and Brixham all began as fishing villages. In the 17C and 18C the Fleet would lie up in the bay, and wives, the first tourists, would come to visit their sailor husbands. By the early 19C the population of Torquay had grown to 2 000 and when the railway came to the town in 1842, the town resolved to profit from the natural advantages of a mild climate, exotic palm-tree vegetation, sea views and wide sand beaches. Hotels, a promenade, a pier and a pavilion were built, public gardens were laid out to make the town the 'Queen of English watering-places'. By the turn of the century Torquay was famous and the resident population, working largely for the tourists, had increased to 25 000. Fifty years later Paignton followed Torquay's example.

In Torquay and Paignton – which market themselves as '**The English Riviera**' – the houses extend up the hill behind the shore; large pale Victorian and Edwardian hotels and villas set in lush gardens are now being replaced by modern apartment blocks and high-rise hotels, white by day, a spangle of lights by night. Following his visit, Dickens described Torquay as 'a compound of Hastings and Tunbridge Wells and bits of the hills about Naples'.

TORQUAY

Torre Abbey ⊙ – *King's Drive, next to the Riviera Centre.* Set back from the sea front, the haunted 'Abbey' is adapted from a Premonstratensian **abbey** founded in 1196, in fulfilment of a vow made for the safe return of his son by William de Brewer, the lord of the manor and a justiciar in Richard Lionheart's absence on the Third Crusade. On the king's capture, de Briwer set out to raise the 150 000 marks demanded in ransom; he found 70 000, which were sent to Austria together with 67 hostages of whom one was his son. In the event the Austrian captor was fatally injured and, on his deathbed, released his royal prisoner without benefit of the ransom. The community became unusually prosperous when it was suppressed in 1539 and the church was razed. In 1598 the complex was refurbished by the Ridgeway family; the 'big house' was remodelled between 1741-43 in the Georgian style by the Cary family.

During World War II, Torre Abbey was used by the RAF as a training school.

Interior – In 1930, the property was acquired by Torquay Borough Council and converted for use as a museum containing a broad range of furniture, silver, Torquay and Watcombe terracotta and souvenir ceramics, a rich art collection including a rare set of proof copies of **William Blake's** illustrations for the *Book of Job*, marine and topographical pictures, Victorian oils (Holman Hunt), watercolours (T Miles Richardson, J Sell Cotman, David Roberts...), etchings and drawings by the Arts and Crafts designer **Burne-Jones**. Many items among the house's original contents were returned in 1995 and are being restored for display. Upstairs in the **abbot's tower**, beyond the Adam-styled formal dining room, is a memorial to the life of **Agatha Christie**; the small study contains the novelist's typewriter, several manuscripts, personal possessions and early photographs.

Dame Agatha Christie (1890-1976)

Agatha Miller was born and brought up in Torquay. At the outbreak of World War I she enrolled in the Volunteer Aid Detachment, working at the Town Hall while it doubled as a Red Cross Hospital: this experience provided the novelist with inspiration for Hercule Poirot who was distilled from the many Belgian refugees stranded in Torquay at that time. From nursing, Agatha rose to dispenser and trained thereafter in a pharmacy for the Society of Apothecaries – a perfect source of inside information for concocting her detective stories. Her first marriage ended in divorce; her second husband, Max Mallowan, was an archeologist with whom she travelled extensively to the Middle East. Agatha Christie published several other novels under the pseudonym Mary Westmacott.

Note in the family chapel (1789) that was installed in the shell of the monastery's great hall, the medieval painted ceiling bosses. The 14C **Mohun Gatehouse**, in stark contrast with the rest of the house, has been carefully arranged with dark oak furniture and displays of early pewter.

Grounds – Round the cloister garth are the ruins of the medieval **church** (168ft long) excavated 1986-89 to reveal a series of tombs; the impressive east **wall** pierced by the entrance to the sacristy and chapter-house *(see also Cockington below)*. The turreted gatehouse is better preserved because it was not slighted. West of the house, set among colourful gardens laid out in the 1930s, is an elegant Victorian-style Palm House, rebuilt in 1969.

The **tithe barn★** or 'Spanish Barn', its great length (124ft) massively buttressed, dates from 1196; the 12 ribs of its original oak roof were increased to 17 during restoration in the 15C. Its name dates from 1588 when the flagship of the Andalusian squadron of the Spanish Armada, *Nuestra Señora del Rosario*, was captured by Drake in Torbay and the 397 crew were imprisoned in the barn.

Torquay Museum ⊙ – *Babbacombe Road.* Founded by the learned **Torquay Natural History Society**, the museum has built its most informative displays around a substantial collection of geological and archeological samples from the surrounding area of Devon ranging from fossilised coral formations to granite from Dartmoor. This leads into an explanation of the region's natural history and provides a pertinent introduction to the remains recovered from Kent's Cavern – the discovery and analytical study of which proved vital in establishing man as being considerably older than Biblical estimates and fuelled Darwin's famous theories in *The Origin of Species*.

Other exhibits, other than those on temporary display, are drawn from **Hester Forbes-Julian's** bequest of letters, annotated albums and autographs from the Victorian and Edwardian eras (Keats, Darwin, Jane Austen, the Brontes, Abraham Lincoln, Verdi and Dr Livingstone); an archive of photographs and views of old Torquay; fine examples of Torquay pottery and terracotta sculpture; Agatha Christie and her fiction; an assortment of ethnological specimens; furniture and ephemera from the past. Upstairs is a gallery dedicated to the Devon Regiments (uniforms, weapons and memorabilia).

★ Kents Cavern Showcaves ⊙ – *Wellswood, Ilsham Road (right off Babbacombe Road, B3199).* The limestone caves run back 180yds into the hill. Excavations in the last two centuries have shown the caves were inhabited by large prehistoric animals, by animals (bears and hyenas) and by humans for long periods from the Paleolithic era to Roman times.

The **tour** (half a mile) leads through galleries with rugged roofs and walls and contrasting chambers with beautiful crystal white, red-brown and green frozen water, pagoda and organ pipe **formations**, past **stalactites** and **stalagmites** – one 54ins tall is estimated to have been growing for over 50 000 years.

Babbacombe Model Village ⊙ – *Signposted off Babbacombe Road; 75min.* Minutely manicured gardens planted with bright flowers, dwarf conifers and bonsai trees form the backdrop to numerous miniature re-creations of scenes from English life: weddings, bank robberies and car breakdowns complete with appropriate sound effects. Villages with thatched cottages, mineral oil drilling, waterskiing on the lake, a typical High Street, Stonehenge, a windfarm, race track, telecommunication station are all set among immaculate lawns...

Bygones ⊙ – *Situated around the corner from the Babbacombe Model Village; 1 hour.* A darkened Victoria Street is lined with old-fashioned shops: through the windows may be glimpsed a vast array of goods and chattels, outdated tools of various trades and services, precious possessions and sentimental memorabilia. Through the pub, and upstairs, a further selection of interiors is recreated around a display of scale models representing foreign cities interconnected by a working model railway. The Station Tea Rooms are decked in fixtures dating back to the times when the railways made Torquay a fashionable holiday destination.

PAIGNTON

★★ Paignton Zoo ⊙ – *Half a mile west along A385 Totnes Road. 2 hours.* A comprehensive collection of **wild animals** linked into a far reaching conservation programme and a luxuriant **botanical garden** extend over 75 acres, making Paignton one of the largest zoos in Britain. Opened in 1923 as Primley Zoo, the project was conceived by Herbert Whitley as a place for children to learn about wild animals; in 1955 the Whitley Wildlife and Conservation Trust was formed as a scientific and educational charity. Today it owns the zoo and the Slapton Ley National Nature Reserve (*east of Kingsbridge, see* SALCOMBE).

In line with other associated members of the National Federation of Zoos (in Jersey, Bristol, Newquay), Paignton promotes awareness of animal welfare, sustainable conservation of habitats and research into ecological issues associated therewith. Enclosures rather than cages provide spacious environmentally-controlled conditions of different habitats: wetlands, desert, tropical forest, savannah, islands and indigenous woodland. These, in turn, shelter a variety of animals and birds including scarlet ibis and flamingoes, Mandarin ducks; laughing doves, cockatoos, baboons, Barbary sheep; tortoises, stone curlews, parakeets, monitor lizards; macaws, Asiatic lions, Sumatran tigers, elephants, hornbills, cassowaries; red lechwe, cheetah, ostrichs; lemurs, fruit bats, macaque; silverback gorillas, Bornean orang utangs; woodcocks, squirrels, woodmice, voles, weasels and bats, to mention but a few! A **miniature railway** (10.25in gauge) provides rides round the lake.

Among the species that have been successfully bred for release into the wild are the golden lion tamarins, Barberry carpet moths and Bali starlings; Paignton Zoo also manages the stud book (monitoring genetic information for captive breeding of endangered species) for spider monkeys, lechwe and mandrills. A range of activities and residential courses is provided by the Education Centre and animal adoption schemes are in operation. Substantial funds are being invested in the zoo to provide ever-better enclosures and improved data-collection, monitoring and information diffusion.

Oldway Mansion and Gardens ⊙ - *Torquay Road.* The vast, Classical mansion (now council offices) with a giant portico, tall Georgian-style windows and balustraded terraces overlooking formal parterre **gardens** was built by the American sewing-machine magnate **Isaac Singer** (1811-75) when he retired to Torquay in 1854. Inside, beyond displays on the mansion's history, is the imposing **hall** with its staircase rising to a gallery, heavily decorated with marble and *faux* marble, an Italianate painted ceiling, and squat brass balusters, oddly angled up the stairs.

Paignton Parish Church ⊙ - *Church Street. Opposite Hyde Road.* The Perpendicular church (1450-1500) of dark red sandstone, with a very tall landmark-style tower with pinnacles, stands amid houses all of the same colour. Inside, the Kirkham Chantry Chapel, with 15C-17C family tombs, is separated from the nave by a fine stone screen (mutilated at the Reformation). Note the Norman sandstone font with honeysuckle decoration, the mutilated pre-Reformation stone pulpit and the dog door complete with latch *(north door).*

Paignton and Dartmouth Steam Railway ⊙ - *Queen's Park Station.* Steam locomotives provide a service on the former British Rail line (standard gauge) via Goodrington and Churston, along the Dart Estuary to Kingswear *(6.75 miles – passenger ferry to Dartmouth).* It is both an efficient and nostalgic ride with the old Victorian cast-iron furniture on the platforms, and the drivers and porters in period uniform.

BRIXHAM

Brixham has remained a fishing village at heart, its fishing fleet of trawlers – second to Newlyn – providing the main industry of the little town and the main source of interest to the restless gulls that perpetually call across the bay. The new fish quay was completed in 1990 equipped with a fish market, ice-plant and refrigeration unit: it processes catches of flat fish (plaice, megrim, sole), sprats, squid, mackerel, crab and lobster from the various boats – crabbers, beam and inshore trawlers.

On the Strand Quay stands a wide-eyed statue of William of Orange who landed here in 1688 on his way to take the crown from James II. Additional colour is provided by a replica of the *Golden Hinde* adapted from a 70ft steel barge. From the harbour spreads a network of steep narrow streets lined with brightly coloured fishermen's cottages and small houses, some dating back to the late 17C.

Battery Gardens - *Access from Freshwater Quarry or on foot from the coastal footpath.* This favourite spot from which to follow the Brixham trawler races was at one time heavily fortified with several cannon: the gun emplacements visible today date from World War II.

★ **Berry Head** - *Car park on the south side of the headland.* An extensive **view**★★★ is visible from the headland. A **viewing table** announces 'from this point 190ft above sea-level about 800 sq miles of sea are visible' and identifies every landmark round the sweep of Lyme Bay to Portland Bill *(42 miles east).* The headland attracts many seabirds – guillemots (largest breeding colony along Channel coast), razorbills, kittiwakes, fulmars, shags and herring gulls *(listed on notice board in car park).*

Brixham Harbour

For obvious reasons, there have been lookouts and fortifications on the headland since the Iron Age: the most in evidence are the forts built in 1803 which Napoleon never put to the test, although he did put in to Tor Bay on board the *Bellerophon* on his way into exile on St Helena (1815). The strange-looking modern construction is an aircraft navigational beacon.

EXCURSIONS

★ **Cockington** – *1 mile west from Torbay Road along Cockington Lane.* The village is pure picture-postcard with all the **cottages** thatched above red sandstone or white-washed walls, an ancient (now modernised) **forge**, a mill pond, the Drum Inn – a period pub by Sir Edwin Lutyens – and horse-drawn, open carriages plying between the village and the sea front.

Cockington Court ⊘ – The Classical 19C house, surrounded by 270 acres of wooded parkland and gardens full of rhododendrons, azaleas and camellias, accommodates the **Devon Rural Skills Centre** where traditional rural skills are kept alive and demonstrated to visitors: wood turning, wheelwrighting, rush and cane seating, hurdlemaking, drystone walling, stained glass, patchwork...
The **parish church**, which dates from 1196, was given a tower when it was acquired by Torre Abbey *(see above)* in 1236. Note the 15C rood-screen, the old wicket door with its sanctuary ring, the 15C font and the pulpit from Torre Abbey.

Compton Castle ⊘ – *2-3 miles west of Torbay.* The massively fortified manor house stands on land granted in the 12C to the de Comptons who married into the Gilbert family which, except between 1800 and 1930, has held the manor ever since.
Among the family were **Sir Humphrey Gilbert** (1539-83), navigator, founder of the colony of Newfoundland (1583), his brother **Adrian**, navigator, colonist and seeker after the North West Passage (both half-brothers of Sir Walter Raleigh) and **Raleigh Gilbert**, founder of Sagadahoc Colony in the State of Maine (1607).

Castle – The castle was built in three phases. In the 1320s the **Great Hall** (42ft x 21ft x 33ft) rose on its east-west axis; in 1450 a west range, including the north-south oriented chapel, was rebuilt on a larger scale; in 1520 a similar structure was raised on the east side as well as the **fortifications** – the curtain wall and gateway with its machicolations and portcullis, the towers, once six in number, and the massive surrounding wall. These defences were required as protection against raids by French and, since the Armada, more especially Spanish marauders and pirates. A high wall at the back encloses a small garden.

Berry Pomeroy Castle ⊙ – *5 miles west via by-roads; turn before Berry Pomeroy village.*
The Pomeroy family settled in Devon at the time of the Norman Conquest, attracted to this area by the lush landscape and the good hunting it provided. In 1547 the castle was acquired by Edward Seymour, 1ˢ Duke of Somerset, uncle and governor of Edward VI and Protector of England. Major alterations were implemented by his eldest son Edward who transformed the castle into a four-storeyed Elizabethan mansion; this was extended by his heir, also Edward, *c*1600 with a wing looking outwards from the walled deer park, across the glorious countryside, as far as Dartmoor in the distance. Abandoned some time between 1688 and 1701 when the family moved to Maiden Bradley (near Warminster), the castle was stripped of precious building material and soon clad in ivy: the perfect Picturesque ruin reputed to be the most haunted castle in Britain – details of the White Lady, Blue Lady, disquieting experiences and jinxed cameras are given in the guide book.
Archealogical excavation by English Heritage has revealed fragments of a (late 15C Flemish) fresco depicting *The Adoration of the Magi* in the Gatehouse chamber, fragments of Chinese porcelain and early tobacco clay pipes. A path runs from the car park (a former slate quarry) down through the woods to the Gatcombe Brook.

The charms of the area

Torquay has the air of a faded seaside resort; its shops are full of souvenir pottery, its waterfront lined with fish-and-chip bars. Brixham smells of the sea and rings with the screech of circling seagulls. Totnes, meanwhile is set back from the coast, set amongst lush countryside threaded with hawthorn hedgerows; the shops here harvest all the pleasures of the region: a vast range of locally-produced cheeses, cream and ice-cream; West Country wines, cider, scrumpy, brandy and beer; bakers offer coloured fairycakes and butter-rich pastries; craftshops retail hand-turned ceramics, delicate etchings and inlaid wooden boxes; not to mention acupuncturists, natural medicines and wholefoods... This is where the successful novelists the likes of Agatha Christie, Mary Wesley and Desmond Bagley have resided.

TOTNES★

Devon – Population 7 018
Michelin Atlas p 4 or Map 403 – I, J 32

Totnes is described in Pevsner's series *The Buildings of England: Devon* as 'one of the most rewarding small towns in England': its narrow main street acting as an axis to the town as it rises steeply between two and three-storey buildings, half-timbered, 16C-17C wealthy merchants' houses, built of brick or stone, slatehung in the 18C-19C, or colour-washed. In Neolithic times, tracks converged at this point as it was the highest navigable point and the lowest bridging point on the River Dart: Totnes's most prosperous period (1550-1650), however, dates from the time it controlled the ships that shuttled from Dartmouth to Spain and France with cargoes of cloth and Dartmoor tin traded against linen and manufactured goods. Decline in business led to houses being remodelled rather than rebuilt, hence the extent of preservation of the old town. From the river, Fore Street leads into High Street before climbing beyond **East Gate**, also known as the Arch, a much-altered gateway dating back to Tudor times when Totnes was a walled town; the gate gives access to the old ramparts.
Market day: Friday morning. *Public car parks are situated both at the bottom and top of town.*

Bridge - The bridge at the bottom of the town, rebuilt in 1828, marks the tidal and navigable limit of the Dart. The quay below is still active as the departure point for excursions down river to Dartmouth; the Riverside Walk extends to Dartington (see excursions below).

The Plains - *Sharp left on the town side.* A stone **obelisk** in the market square honours **William John Wills**, a member of the first party to cross the Australian continent in 1860, who was born in the nearby coaching inn, the Royal Seven Stars, built in 1660.

J. Allan Cash/VLOO

Totnes Arch

Fore Street - The houses which line the street include **The Mansion** *(left)* in dark red brick, refronted in the 18C, which was originally the **King Edward VI Grammar School**, founded under royal charter in 1153 and now used for community education; a late 18C Gothick house *(left in Bank Lane);* a 17C house (no 48), a 16C house with an oversailing upper floor (no 52) and, close by, the grandest Tudor house in the town, now the local museum.

★ **Totnes Elizabethan Museum** ⊘ - *70 Fore Street.* The museum displays items of local life from flint weapons to Great Western Railway bygones, 15C, Elizabethan and Jacobean furniture, Victoriana and a turn-of-the-century grocer's shop. One room is devoted to **Charles Babbage**, a mathematical genius, who was educated at the Grammar School; he designed the first computer, a cypher-breaking machine and an analytical machine using punched cards.

The most remarkable exhibit is the house itself, a rich Tudor **merchant's house** built *c*1575 when Totnes was enjoying the prosperity derived from the wool and cloth trade which had developed since the Middle Ages. The house has four floors with a half-timbered, jettied first floor, broad windows and a full-width gable pierced by the windows of the topmost small bedrooms. Inside, note the height and lightness of the main rooms, the timbering, the unevenly-wide floorboards, 16C fireplaces and simple country furniture; a number of small **closets** and corners are now used for exhibits. One room is devoted to local history, including explanations of the **Brutus Stone** and its alleged association with Brutus the Trojan; the courtyard would have delayed fire spreading to the main block from the kitchens; the garden is planted with herbs appropriate to the period; a study centre *(by appointment)* houses an archive for local and family history research.

Continue up Fore Street; just beyond the Arch turn right up a flight of steps.

Rampart Walk - The cobbled path of the old ramparts leads past cottages fronted with magnificent displays of flowers in tubs, troughs and pots.

Charles Babbage (1791-1871)

Babbage's interest in mathematical computation was aroused when he was still at Trinity College, Cambridge on realising the significant discrepancies in the calculation and tabulation of logarithms so necessary to navigation, surveying and astronomy. In 1822 he began developing his Difference Engine capable of the four mathematical functions and calculations, by successive addition, to 20 decimal places; in 1842 funding was exhausted and the project was abandoned. The next project, the Analytical Engine, was based on mechanical weaving technology pioneered by Jacquard using punched cards: the truly modern concept in this invention was the contraption's arithmetic unit or memory store which could be programmed to fulfil pre-set functions – a prerequisite in modern computer technology. Alas, Babbage lacked the wherewithal to build his machine and he died leaving most of his ideas unmaterialised. Projects which did see fruition include the 'cowcatcher' attached to the front of trains; a black-box recorder monitoring progress in case of accident (on the lines of those used in modern aircraft); the introduction of colour theatre lighting to replace the prevalent glaring gas footlights of the day; the ophthalmoscope. A co-founder of the Analytical Society, Babbage collaborated with such figures as Michael Faraday, I K Brunel and the noted astronomer John Herschel (*see* BATH).

Guildhall ⓥ - The original guildhall was situated at no 8 High Street when King John granted a charter to Totnes in 1206; this site belonged then to the Benedictine Priory which was dissolved in 1536. The present building, largely dating from 1553 when Edward VI granted permission for the extant parts to be re-used (note his coat of arms above the mayor's canopy), was acquired by a wealthy Elizabethan merchant who bequeathed it to the town for use as a guildhall with a council chamber, courtroom and mayor's parlour at the peak of the town's prosperity. During the Civil War, members of Cromwell's army were billeted here. The building continued to be used as a magistrates court until 1974; now it is used for town council meetings.

The open loggia was added in the 19C using granite columns from the former Fruit Market House of 1611, built south of the church. Inside, the purpose-built furnishings of the council chamber remain intact. Among the exhibits relating to the town's history are Saxon coins pressed in the town mint in the reign of Edgar (958-75) and the segregated cells of the 17C town gaol (mantraps, stocks) accommodated in what was originally the priory kitchen.

★ **St Mary's** - The 15C parish and priory church has a massive red tower adorned with gruesome gargoyles, modelled on the tower of Ashburton. Inside, the most outstanding feature is the once coloured Beer stone **rood screen** of 1459 which, with paired lights, carved mullions, arched panels below, cusped tracery and fan coving above, extends across the full width of the church.

The other furnishings of note include the elegant brass chandelier (1701), the pale stone pulpit (1460) which was for centuries enclosed in mahogany cladding, hence its near-pristine condition and, halfway down the aisle, the 1636 corporation pews. In St George's chapel lies the tomb of Walter Smythe (d 1555), founder of Totnes Grammar School; against the north nave wall, the **memorial** to Christopher Blackhall (d 1633), seen kneeling at prayer above his four wives; against the back wall of the 19C north aisle, the large **terracotta plaque** to Walter Venning, born in Totnes in 1781, who became a London merchant and was the founder of the Prison Society of Russia where he himself died of gaol fever in 1821.

High Street - The house at no 16, now a bank, was built in 1585 by a salted-pilchard merchant, Nicholas Ball (note the initials on the front). After his death in 1586 his widow married a second wealthy man, **Thomas Bodley** of Exeter, scholar, diplomat and founder of the Bodleian Library, Oxford.

The modern **Civic Hall** has a large open forecourt on which, in summer, a pannier market is held, when Tudor fare is offered by sellers in Elizabethan costume. Beyond, the granite pillared **Butterwalk★** has protected shoppers from the rain since the 17C.

Devonshire Collection of Period Costume ⓥ - *Bogan House, 43 High Street.* The old Tudor merchant's house, which has features from the Elizabethan to Georgian periods, makes a complementary setting for changing displays of costume from the years 1740 to 1970, selected for their meticulous detailing, with pressed pin tucks, matching accessories and underclothes.

Castle ⓥ - Little remains of the motte and bailey within the medieval castle walls, although the site commands excellent **views★★★** of the Dart River Valley, upstream towards Dartmoor where the high tors rise one behind the other and downstream along the estuary towards Dartmouth. The castle's strategic situation made it an obvious place for a settlement since earliest times. Records confirm that William the Conqueror awarded Totnes and 107 manors in Devon to his loyal follower Judhael in c1069. It was he who first built a castle straddling the town's defences and then in 1088 founded the Benedictine Priory of St Mary on the site now occupied by the parish church. The ramparts which encircle the central mound are 14C, a rebuilding and strengthening in stone of the motte and bailey earthwork raised in the late-11C.

EXCURSIONS

★ **British Photographic Museum, Bowden House** ⓥ - *Half a mile southwest by A381; turn left (signposted).*

Bowden House dates back to the 9C when it served as the residence of the De Broase family, builders of the 13C Totnes Castle... The Tudor mansion dates from the times of John Giles (1510).

The purpose-built museum with small cinema (films shown) stands beyond a house with a handsome Queen Anne exterior, on the site of the old stableblock. It includes period reconstructions (Victorian studio, Edwardian darkroom) though the bulk is the enormous collection of cameras; the Exhibition Room alone contains over 400 Kodak cameras beneath changing photographic displays. Upstairs, every showcase is crammed with cameras and relevant paraphernalia ranging from the very earliest to the most modern, and features the big names in photographic equipment: Gandolfi, Leica, Ensign, Zeiss Ikon, Ilford, Agfa and many others.

The development of photography and cinematography is traced from the early ether, petrol or gas powered projectors and driers, mahogany plate cameras with brass fittings (1880s and '90s), box Brownies, a camera gun, coloured cameras (1930s), Bakelite models... There are press cameras, flash guns, miniature cameras, single and twin lens reflex cameras, more modest magic lanterns, cartoons and early hand-tinted photographs.

For South Devon Railway see Buckfastleigh under DARTMOOR.

Dartington *2 miles northwest by A385 and A384.*

Seventy five years after its foundation, Dartington flourishes, ever expanding the concepts of the founders: **Leonard** (1893-1974) and **Dorothy** (1887-1968) **Elmhirst** who believed in the encouragement of personal talent and responsibility through progressive education and rural regeneration. This, in practical terms, meant the establishment of a working community where people would find scope for their personal development and a sense of fulfilment while earning a living. Initially, the first school was set up to cater for the children on the estate, classes were then held for the adult employees, and before long workshops were organised offering a different spectrum of disciplines including music (Imogen Holst), pottery (Bernard Leach), painting (Cecil Collins and Mark Tobey) and weaving. The estate, meanwhile, also provided hospitality to artists fleeing Nazi Germany and war-torn Russia. Within relatively few years of the Elmhirsts' purchase of the long-desolate house and 800 acres of land around it, the name Dartington had become a synonym for 'advanced' co-education, summer schools, art courses, exhibitions and concerts...
Today, the **Dartington Hall Trust** continues to provide a conference centre, educational facilities and a varied educational programme; also accommodated on the estate is the Schumacher College, an international Centre for Ecological Studies.

Dartington Hall ⊘ – The estate and fine gardens have been carefully tended to provide the perfect landscape setting for the Great Hall initiated in 1388-1400 by John Holand, the soldier half-brother of Richard II. Home to Holand, Duke of Exeter, the complex passed to the Crown, Margaret Beaufort (mother of Henry VII), Henry Courtenay, Earl of Devon and the Champernowne family before being purchased, derelict, by the Elmhirsts in 1925. Its rebuilding was entrusted to the then most eminent exponent of 'conservative restoration', **William Weir**.
The buildings are grouped around an unusually large courtyard given its date. The Hall *(through arch beneath clock tower)* has been described as being 'on the grandest scale and among the finest of its date in the whole of England', complete with 17ft fireplace and roof, rebuilt as 'an experimental interpretation of hammer-beam construction'.
The late medieval or 16C low barn on the eastern side of the courtyard was converted for use as a theatre by **Walter Gropius** and Robert Hening in 1933-8. Most of the other apartments are closed to the public, as is much of the organically-farmed 750-acre farming estate.

Gardens – The park and gardens, meanwhile, were remodelled in three phases by different designers, notably the American landscaper **Beatrix Farrand**, under the strict supervision of Dorothy Elmhirst who insisted on saving the ancient trees (the churchyard yew, Spanish chestnuts, London planes and Irish yews known as the Twelve Apostles) and tiltyard or tournament ground to be used as an open-air theatre: the carefully positioned sculptures include a *Reclining Woman* by **Henry Moore** (1945-46) and two compositions (*Swans Fountain* 1950, *Bronze Donkey* 1935) by **Willi Soukop**.

★ **High Cross House** ⊘ – In stark contrast with the older buildings is High Cross House (1931-32), William Lescaze's International Modernist style building painted in blue and white, intended as the residence for the headmaster of Dartington school (closed 1987), WB Curry.

Dartington International Summer School

The great music festival which is held annually has its roots in the dynamic interaction of such figures as Imogen Holst, Artur Schnabel, Elizabeth Lutyens, Igor Stravinski (1957), Benjamin Britten (who wrote his *Rape of Lucretia* for Dartington), the Amadeus String Quartet (who formed the quartet at Dartington), Peter Maxwell Davies, Mark Elder, Harrison Birtwhistle, Michael Flanders and Donald Swann (who perfected their evening cabarets entitled *At The Drop Of A Hat* there)...

The interior is painted in vivid primary colours that complement the overall asymmetrical space, in-built cupboards and well-crafted, practical furniture: the overall effect being one of informally stylish, modern comfort.

Besides being renovated and converted for use as a home for the Trust archive and study centre, the house acts as a showcase for temporary exhibitions including material selected from the large collections of 20C art, documents, film and fine craft accumulated by the Elmhirsts. The archive holds written works by Martha Graham, Julian Huxley, Bertrand Russell, Rabindranath Tagore; artists represented in the collection include Jacob Epstein, Roger Fry, Eric Gill, Nina Hammett, Ben and Winifred Nicholson, John Nash, John Piper, Alfred Wallis, Bernard Leach, Shoji Hamada, Lucie Rie, Michael Cardew, Michael Casson, Marianne de Trey...

Cider Press Centre ⊘ – *Shinners Bridge*. The visitor centre, housed partly in the 16C and 17C stone buildings of an old cider house, provides a permanent exhibition and sales centre for goods produced by the Trust's local enterprises and by other craft workers in the southwest. Products include designed and handmade ceramics, textiles and woodwork; wines and farm foods, plants, kitchenware, crystal, stationery... During the summer months street entertainers, exhibitions and demonstrations provide further interest.

For boat trips up the River Dart, see DARTMOUTH, *for Berry Pomeroy Castle see* TORBAY.

TROWBRIDGE

Wiltshire – Population 25 279
Michelin Atlas p 17 or Map 403 – N 30

Trowbridge, long established as a major wool and cloth town, became the county town only when the 1888 Local Government Act required councillors to be elected and it was found that Trowbridge, being on the railway, was accessible and convenient. Since the decline of the cloth trade it has turned to brewing and the manufacture of dairy products, bacon, pies, sausages and yogurt, in some cases, in the old mills. The earlier prosperity funded the multitude of 19C Nonconformist chapels and schools, the workers' terraced houses and Georgian houses. The history of the town and its prosperity from the woollen industry are recorded in the **Trowbridge Museum** ⊘ located in The Shires shopping centre.

EXCURSIONS

★ **Steeple Ashton** *7 miles east of Trowbridge.*

Steeple Ashton gives the lie to the saying that lightning never strikes twice in the same place: the church possessed a 'Famous and Lofty Steeple, Containing a height above the Tower 93 Foot' – it was breached on 25 July 1670 and had almost been rebuilt when 'another terrible Storm of Thunder and Lightning happened October 15 the same year, which threw (it) down'. The church, but not the steeple, was restored.

A local church had been in existence since 1252 and a weekly market and annual fair established since 1266. In the two centuries which followed, wool merchants and clothiers prospered, work people were attracted to the village, and many of the houses, forges and inns surrounding the green and lining the main street were built. Two clothiers and their wives added new north and south aisles to the church, the rest of the parish a new nave and the ill-fated steeple.

Decline came in the 16C-17C when a series of fires damaged and destroyed many houses and fulling was invented, a process in the manufacture of woollen cloth requiring running water which the village lacks. The people turned to agriculture and in the 19C many emigrated to America, Australia and New Zealand.

★ **The Green** – The **market cross** dates from 1714; the octagonal stone lock-up or **blind house** with a domed roof and no windows dates from 1773. Of the houses on the Green, the two black and white half-timbered houses, one known as the **Old Wool Market**, are 16C and 17C; the timber-framed house with brick herringbone infilling on the upper floor, variously known as the Old Merchant's Hall and **Judge Jeffreys' House**, is 16C; **Ashton House** is early 16C with additions, extensions and a 1724 refronting; The Longs Arms is 17C. Blackburn Farmhouse *(by the telephone box)* was begun *c*1500; the cottage with three big brick chimneys, at the end of the High Street, is built on cruck beams; **The Sanctuary**, off Dark Lane, according to the records, was enlarged in 1500...

St Mary's – Gargoyles as opposed to a steeple decorate the Perpendicular exterior. Inside, it is the **roofs** which are chiefly of interest: the nave, even before the steeple fell upon it (possibly because an earlier stone roof had cracked), is covered with a lofty fan vault of oak and plaster; the aisles have intricate lierne vaulting in stone, the ribs descending to canopied niches supported on boldly carved half-figures. The chancel was added when the building was restored in the 19C.

Edington

Edington is where, in 879, **King Alfred** finally defeated the Danes. It is also where William of Edington, Bishop of Winchester (1345-66), Treasurer and Chancellor to Edward III, was born and decided in 1351 to rebuild the existing church as a chantry, soon afterwards enlarged into an Augustinian monastery. The monastery was later dissolved, the church given to the village.

★ **St Mary, St Katherine and All Saints** – The church (150ft long) was built in the transitional period between the Decorated (reticulated tracery) and Perpendicular Gothic phases (upright, straight-sided panel tracery).

A massive, low, crossing **tower**, a three-storey porch and a twin turreted west gable, framing a wide Perpendicular window over a processional door, are the striking exterior features.

Inside are great clustered columns in golden stone, 17C and 18C pink-and-white and all-white plaster **ceilings**, and a double **chancel screen** or monastic pulpitum of c1500 with seats between the trellises and a gallery above. The **chancel**, the Decorated part of the church, has a combined Decorated-Perpendicular window and 14C canopied niches with lively figures. In the north transept, the Crucifixion window is 14C.

The furnishings are principally Jacobean: the testered pulpit (with 18C stairs), the font cover, the **communion rail** with alternating flat and turned balusters and a row of points possibly following Archbishop Laud's injunction to keep 'dogs and cows' away from the altar. The monuments are older: three early 14C-15C knights, one with his lady, and a partly coloured tomb *(south transept)* of a blue-robed monk; the barrel or tun at his feet and the sprigs of bay suggest a rebus of his name – Bayton.

Westbury and Warminster

Westbury – *8 miles north on A350.*

The small town, its busy main street lined with 18C-20C shops and houses, has an old **market square** at one end overlooked by a Tuscan-pillared 19C town hall, a few houses, a few shops, three inns – one now Georgian, said to date back as an inn to the 14C. Nearby in its churchyard, surrounded by **Georgian houses**, is the 19C renewed Perpendicular Church of All Saints with a rare, oblong crossing tower and a lierne vaulted porch.

Westbury White Horse

A. Taverner

White Horse – *Bratton Down: best viewed from 1.5 miles along B3098 from Westbury (continue along B3098 almost to Bratton village, signposted right up a steep track to Bratton Castle and the horse).*

The horse, near the end of the steep west-facing chalk down, measures 166ft x 163ft high and is Wiltshire's oldest, having been cut in 1778 by a connoisseur of horseflesh who had been irritated for many years by an earlier figure on the same site. The earlier animal, smaller, dachshundlike in form and facing the other way, might possibly have been Saxon and carved in celebration of King Alfred's victory over the Danes at Ethandun in 878. This figure, now secured by stones and concrete, has sired a long line. From the escarpment extends a glorious **view★** over west Wiltshire.

Warminster – The former wool and cloth town boasts several Elizabethan and Georgian hostelries, some with galleried courtyards; off the main street, the tributary roads, with end-on views of the countryside, are marked by small Classical 18C houses. The history of the town, together with local archeological finds and the Victor Manley collection of geology are displayed in the local **Dewey museum** ⊙ within the public library.

The small church of **St Lawrence** in the High Street was founded as a chapel of ease in the early 13C; since the 15C it has housed the town bell which rang the daily curfew at 4am and sounded feast and holy days. Closed by Edward VI, it was bought back by the townspeople for £38 6s 8d in 1675 and committed, uniquely, to the temporal care of local feoffees or trustees.

Bratton Castle – *3.5 miles east off B3098.*
A side road leads up to Bratton Castle and the horse's back and head (the view of the white horse is too distorted to be comprehensible).

Bratton Castle, an Iron Age hillfort with earth mound ramparts enclosing some 25 acres, commands far-reaching **views★★** from its 300ft down.

Mead, which was drunk in pre-Roman times in Britain, is made by fermenting honey with hops or yeast; it was sometimes flavoured with spices or wild flowers. Metheglin, a speciality of the West of England, was a type of mead flavoured with herbs and spices which was said to have aphrodisiac properties.

TRURO

Cornwall – Population 16 522
Michelin Atlas p 2 or Map 403 – E 33

In 1859 Truro seized the opportunity, rejected by Bodmin, of bringing the railway into the centre of the town.

By the 18C-19C Truro, once a river port, mining centre and stannary town *(see* INTRODUCTION: Tin Mining*)*, was known as the county 'metropolis' with a theatre, assembly rooms, county library (1792), horticultural society, the Royal Institution of Cornwall and the cathedral (1850); it had developed into the most notable Georgian town west of Bath with 18C houses in Boscawen, Lemon and other streets. In 1980 the new County Court, designed by Evans and Shalev, was declared Building of the Year by the *Architects' Journal*.

South of the city, on the headland between the Truro and Tresillian Rivers, sits **Malpas.** Further south on the next headland sits **Tregothnan**, a large 19C Georgian mansion which was built from the proceeds of privateers; it has a cluster of slim octagonal turrets and chimneys and can be seen on the point where the River Truro joins the Fal.

Truro Cathedral – Requests made over the centuries for Cornwall once more to become an independent see were finally acceded to and in 1850 the cathedral foundation stone was laid. Bishop Benson sought a church 'exceeding magnifi-cal', rural parishioners wanted 'a proper job', the architect J-L Pearson, steeped in the last of Gothic Revivalism, proposed a 'house of prayer' in the 13C Early English style. The approved design, an admixture of Normandy Gothic with up-swept vaulting, space and vistas through tall arcades and, outside, three steeple towers which give the cathedral its characteristic outline, was completed by 1910.

★★ Royal Cornwall Museum ⊙ – *River Street.* The museum is the learned and vibrant showplace of the **Royal Institution of**

Gold collar or lunula

Cornwall (f 1818) and the repository for a varied collection of artefacts relating to the geology, archeology and social history of Cornwall as well as a fine collection of fine and decorative arts. Early evidence of human presence in Cornwall is provided by a Paleolithic stone axe found at St Buryan; items from the ensuing Mesolithic, Neolithic eras chart settlements on the Lizard, at Dozmary Pool (on Bodmin Moor) and at Carn Brea. Early Bronze Age collars of beaten gold (found near Padstow and Tintagel), unique in England, seem to indicate sophisticated trade links with Ireland and Brittany; other rarities include metal moulds for casting bronze and copper axe-heads and early ceramic burial urns. Models of Chysauster recreate the Iron Age village. A miscellany of domestic items, trade tokens and church fragments date from the pre-industrial age; fishing, an economic mainstay, is represented as is the development of mining at the end of the 18C (model of Trevithick's Pennydarren steam-driven locomotive, mining safety lamps designed by Humphry Davy).

One area is wholly dedicated to the fabulous **minerals** collected largely by Philip Rashleigh (1729-1811), landowner and mining entrepreneur, who lived at Menabilly: the particular strength of this study collection is the predominance of Cornish specimens, notably copper ore and its affiliated minerals (rare liroconite or copper ore crystal sample), and a large gold nugget found while tin-streaming in the Carnon Valley. On the far side of the central hall is the Bonython Gallery which displays material illustrating the diverse **natural history** of Cornwall (birds, plants, insects, sea-shells).

Upstairs, a small but excellent selection of **antiquities** is displayed: items from ancient Egypt (painted sarcophagus and burial ornaments), Greece (red figure vases) Rome (glass vessels from Palestine), Japan (metalwork, ivories, lacquer). Rows of glass cases along the balcony harbour a small selection from the larger, comprehensive collection of British, European, Oriental and South American **ceramics**: porcelain notably from Plymouth, Bristol, Worcester, and pottery from Staffordshire, by Bernard Leach, Shoji Hamada and associated members of the Leach Pottery. In the upper galleries are displayed **Newlyn School** paintings; Newlyn copperwork and enamels from the permanent collections (*see* INTRODUCTION: Fine and Applied Arts). In addition to these, the museum holds an excellent collection of Old Master and English School paintings, drawings, engravings and prints (the Alfred de Pass Collection) by Lucas Cranach, Rembrandt; Tiepolo; Claude, Watteau, Boucher, Gericault; Lely, Hogarth, Van Dyck, Gainsborough, Romney, Opie, Rowlandson, Blake, Constable, Turner, Augustus John, Sargeant...

A separate spacious gallery space is reserved for changing temporary exhibitions.

Courtney Library ⊙ – The library holds manuscripts, books and documentation relating to Cornwall's social history (emigration posters, bills for wanted criminals, photographs from the 1850s onwards); it also has an extensive archive of records on microfilm, parish registers and other reference material on Cornish families, genealogy and land ownership.

EXCURSIONS

A39 to St Austell

★ **Probus** – *9 miles northeast by A39 and A390.*
The granite church **tower★** (125ft 10in) is the tallest in Cornwall. Dating from 1523, it rises through three stages of niches, fenestration, carved string courses and gargoyles to a castellated crest complete with pinnacles. In the lofty interior, note the **tower screen** with its alphabet from the time when the room was used as a school, the royal arms of 1685, the two-figures **brass** of 1514 *(aisle, under the red carpet).*
The **Probus Garden★** ⊙ is full of ideas and information for well-established and new gardens. Within its 54 different sections it displays shrubs, annuals, herbaceous perennials, plants for shady and exposed positions, ornamental trees, herbs, hydrangeas in acid and alkaline soils, garden design for small spaces, fruit and vegetable growing...

★★★ **Trewithen** – *3 miles northeast by A39, A390.* Trewithen, literally meaning 'house of the trees', is famous for the beautiful landscaped 28-acre garden.

Garden ⊙ – *2 hours.* Already in 1730 the ancestor of the present owners was reported as having 'much improved the seat, new built a great part of the house, made good gardens'. His successor Thomas Hawkins planted large numbers of trees before the estate became more or less abandoned; the vegetation therefore grew to such good effect that, by 1904, a descendant decided 'it was necessary to take an axe and claim air and light from amongst the trees, first for the house and those that should live in it and then for the plants'. In 1905 there arrived direct from Tibet, China and Nepal the seeds of some 100 hybrids of *Rhododendron arboretum* collected in the wild – precursors of the present 50 or more different varieties of **rhododendron**, azalea, 30 of **camellia**, 40 of **magnolia**, maples and birches which give the garden its especial beauty. The opportunity to landscape the gardens came when the government ordered 300 beech trees be felled during World War I: this allowed George Johnstone (1882-1960) to shape the **great glade** that runs south from the house, providing a fine perspective across the lawn between serpentine lines of beds set against a back-drop of trees. Beyond, in alleys and dips, these dark shiny-leaved exotics contrast with the dark red feathered leaves of *Acer palmatum atropurpureum:* from early March, they present overlapping splashes of delicate colour. Ground

Rhododendron

cover is provided by primroses, bluebells, cyclamen and wood anemones. Of specialist interest are the **house hybrids**: rhododendron Trewithen Orange, Alison Johnstone, Jack Skilton, Elizabeth, camellia Trewithen pink, Glenn's Orbit and Donation (most plants are labelled).

The walled garden harbours the most vulnerable immigrant plants from New Zealand (the Lobster claw – *Clianthus puniceus*), China (*Clematis armandii*) and the clone of a Californian native (*Caenothus arboreus*) called Trewithen Blue.

House ⓥ – *30min*. The privately owned country house (1715-55) has all the classic features and proportions of a comfortable Georgian country house, furnished with period panelling (library), painted stucco work and furniture (Chippendale and Hepplewhite). In addition to portraits and paintings there are Bristol glass, Chinese small bronzes and porcelain – notably blue and white ware – a collection of Japanese great plates and a collection of clocks. Visits, accompanied by guides, are limited to the ground floor.

Grampound – The town, which boasts a high cross (12ft) in the market place, was once a parliamentary borough. In 1620 it returned John Hampden as its MP. In the 18C-19C it was a by-word for corruption: bribery was so rife that in 1821, eleven years before the Reform Act, Grampound was disenfranchised by special act of parliament.

For St Mawes, the Roseland peninsula and Trelissick see FALMOUTH.

WAREHAM★

Dorset – Population 5 644
Michelin Atlas p 8 or Map 403 – N 31

The attractive town is distinguished by its long main street which runs north-south from the River Piddle to the Frome and is lined by tightly packed Georgian and Victorian houses, most with shops below. Most earlier buildings were destroyed in 1762 when fire engulfed 133 houses in the town centre. In the 9C and 10C Wareham was often fired by the **Danes** as they retreated after making incursions inland from the port; **Canute**, who mounted his invasion of southern England in 1015 through Wareham, also fired the town. From the 10C Wareham was enclosed, except on the south side, by an earth rampart, pierced by three gates and later surmounted by a stone wall which was demolished by the Parliamentarians; these Saxon defences make an interesting **walk** *(30min)*.

The town's prosperity, based on trade in wine, fruit, olive oil, wool and woollen cloth, cereals and foodstuffs, which developed in the Norman period, was marred in the 17C first by the Civil War, when the town changed hands a number of times, and then by the arrival of Judge Jeffreys to scourge those who had supported Monmouth in his Rebellion. By the 18C, when the fire occurred, trade was in decline as Poole Harbour and the River Frome had silted up, making Wareham inaccessible to shipping.

Market day: Thursday morning.

★★ **St Martin's** – The church at the north end of the High Street appears as the epitome of an Anglo-Saxon church. It dates from c1030, the Danes having destroyed an earlier church which, if legend is to be believed, was built by St Aldhelm in AD 678.

Traces of **Anglo-Saxon building** remain in the 'long and short' work in the external angles at the east end of the nave and chancel, the nucleus of the 11C church. The **chancel arch** was rebuilt, the **north aisle** added by the Normans, the arcade rebuilt in the 13C, the south wall pierced and the elegant **window** inserted in the 14C; finally, in the 16C, although some hold that it dates from the 11C-12C, the **tower** was erected with its saddleback roof and round doorway. Decorating the walls are 11C-18C **paintings** *(timer switch)*, faint, faded, clear and indistinct by turns, of St Martin dividing his cloak, the arms of Queen Anne superimposed over those of Charles II, the Commandments... In the north aisle lies the posthumous marble effigy by **Eric Kennington** of Lawrence of Arabia in his desert robes, his hand on his dagger.

High Street – Three buildings in particular mark the street: the square **Red Lion Hotel** at the crossroads, typical of the rebuilding in brick after the 1762 fire; the **Manor House** (1712) in Purbeck stone which escaped the fire; and the **Black Bear** (c1800) with bow windows and a columned porch supporting its emblematic black bear.

Quay – The quay, where pleasure-craft now tie up, is lined to the east by an ancient russet-red brick **granary**, three storeys high (restaurant), and an adjoining **18C house** also of brick with tablet stones above the windows. The **Local History Museum** ☉ houses a number of cuttings and photographs on T E Lawrence and his motor-cycles, notably the Broughs.

Lady St Mary Church – Rising behind the buildings at the east end of the quay is the battlemented tower of the parish church.

Adjoining it was one of England's oldest priories: a Benedictine nunnery reformed by St Aldhelm in the late 7C, destroyed by the Danes in 876; rebuilt by one of King Alfred's sisters in 915 it was sacked by Canute in 1015; rebuilt, it was dissolved in the 16C; it is now a hotel.

The foundation of the church went back equally far, the first being built before AD 700. The erection of the second on the churchyard of the first resulted in the unearthing of the uniquely engraved stones of 6C-7C pre-Saxon, British chieftains and landholders *(north aisle)*.

This second church, unlike the priory, was not sacked by the Danes and survived as one of the largest and most magnificent **Saxon churches** in the land until 1842 when it was substantially rebuilt 'on the grounds that the oratorical qualities of the then rector deserved a better setting'...

In the nave on a 13C Purbeck marble pedestal stands a very fine, late 12C lead font, one of only 29 surviving in England and unique in being hexagonal; in the aisle is the stone coffin traditionally associated with the murdered King Edward. In the chancel there are examples of bar tracery (12C-13C) to the north, reticulated (13C-14C) to the east. Among the memorials are brasses *(south wall)* and two 13C knights in chain mail and surcoats with crossed legs.

EXCURSIONS

Isle of Arne – *4 miles east by by-roads.* This secret place on the peninsula at the mouth of the River Frome offers large amounts of peace and quiet: over 1 000 acres of the peninsula are a **nature reserve** owned by the RSPB. The woodland, heathland and saltmarshes teem with birdlife, wildlife and plantlife (nature trail, hide).

In the village, the one-room **Toy Museum** ☉ is crammed full of endearing old favourites: china dolls, teddy bears, a particularly fine collection of Victorian musical boxes, automata and wind-up toys; tin trains, boats, aeroplanes, steam engines and lead soldiers...

The Early English **church** (c1220) consists of nave and chancel under one roof with a porch and buttress on the south side; note the triplet east window hewn out of a single stone, and the remains of an early fresco above the door.

For Corfe Castle (5 miles southeast by A351), see SWANAGE.

Bovington – *7 miles west on A352.* The all-weather driving circuit was created in 1993 to provide facilities for cross-country and tactical driving training, although tanks have been tested here since 1916. The Royal Armoured Corps Centre was established in 1947; today it also accommodates the Cavalry and Royal Tank Regiments who may be watched on exercise from the barrier.

★★ **Tank Museum** ⊘ – *7 miles west on A352.* Conceived in 1923 by Rudyard Kipling, the tank museum has expanded its collection from 26 to some 350 vehicles from around the world, several of which are unique prototypes. Displays, enhanced by dioramas, audio-visual presentations, interactive exhibits and simulators, are arranged chronologically through six huge halls-cum-hangars covering the Great War, mechanisation between the wars, the Second World War, the Desert War, to modern battle tanks used in the Gulf War. Background information is provided alongside collections of associated artefacts and memorabilia, a section dedicated to Lawrence of Arabia, to the Home Front and modern weaponry.

Firepower and mobility display

Early vehicles chart evolution from a 1909 Hornsby Chain Track Layer: pride of place is given to **Little Willie** (1915) – the first tank to be designed and developed at Winston Churchill's instigation by his specialist Landship Committee as a result of a 'vague idea ... in the form of a power-driven, bullet-proof, armed engine capable of destroying machine-guns, of crossing country and trenches, of breaking through entanglements, and of climbing earthworks'.

The ranks of tanks on display, many of which are maintained in running order, include British (HMLS *Centipede* or Mother, Medium A or Whippet, Matilda IIA), French (Renault FT17 or Mosquito, Citroen-Kegresse P10 Half Track), American (Boarhound Armoured Car T18E2),German (Hanomag, Jagdpanther, Panther), Japanese (Type 95 Ha-Go), Canadian, Australian, Italian (Carro-M13/40), Swedish and Russian/Soviet (Klementi Voroshilov) machines – including some repatriated after the Iraqi action during the Gulf War (1991). Besides these, there are a valuable assortment of armoured cars, airborne light tanks and guided missiles and in odd corners and on the walls, souvenirs from the field, maps and field orders, models, insignia and battle honours, a T E Lawrence room.

Throughout the summer, the museum puts on a series of **Firepower and Mobility Displays** involving battle re-enactments and manoeuvres in full uniform, demonstrations of tanks and armoured vehicles to the sound of pyrotechnic gunfire. Rides in armoured vehicles also on offer.

Monkey World ⊘ – This popular attraction was established in 1987 as a rehabilitation centre for chim-

The Bovington Tiger

During the inter-war years, German designers concentrated upon conceiving a more manoeuvrable and faster machine than anything that the British had used in the First World War: this was to be a close support infantry tank, 30-33 tons, equipped with a long-range Howitzer. The Tiger was delivered to the 1 SS Panzer Division.

panzees rescued from abuse or smuggled illegally from the wild. Other species of primate to be seen here include orang utans, lemurs, macaques, racoons, capuchins and vervets. Facilities for young children include an adventure playground, jet ski boats and motor bikes.

Return to the T-junction; turn right and right again.

Woolbridge Manor★ *(private)*, a three-storeyed house with a brick front and projecting porch, dates from the 17C when it was owned by the Turbervilles. As **Wellbridge Manor** it appears in *Tess of the d'Urbervilles* by Thomas Hardy as the setting for the ill-fated wedding night of Tess and Angel Clare. Beyond it the road crosses a medieval **packhorse bridge** with pointed cutwaters which rise to the parapet as pedestrian refuges.

WELLS★★

Somerset – Population 9 763
Michelin Atlas p 16 or Map 403 – M30

While the streets of England's smallest cathedral city bustle with shoppers, especially on Wednesday and Saturday when the twice-weekly market occupies the main square, within the precinct gates calm reigns. The prosperity of Wells, together with that of Frome, Glastonbury, Shepton Mallet and Street – the five Mendip towns, was secured in the Middle Ages, as a centre of the wool trade.
Market days: Wednesday and Saturday all day; antiques: Thursday.

Medieval Gates – Three 15C gates lead through from the city streets to the calm of the Green: **Brown's Gate**, a tall gatehouse (now a hotel) from the narrow Sadler Street, **Penniless Porch**, the towered gatehouse built by Bishop Bekynton in the 15C which affords access from the Square *(northeast corner)* and got its name from the medieval beggars who used to crowd it, and the **Bishop's Eye**, a polygonal towered archway from the centre of the east side of the Square.

Cathedral Green – The north side of the cathedral precinct is flanked by the Liberty, an area containing several 17C-18C houses; the Old Deanery, buttressed, battlemented and turreted in the 15C, was remodelled in the late 17C; the Chancellor's House, remodelled in the 18C, is now the home of the **Wells Museum** ⊘ which provides an insight into the social history of Wells and the Mendip area: Iron Age artefacts from Wookey Hole, including relics attributed to the legendary witch retrieved by Balch; samples of lead, iron, copper and zinc which was mined from Roman times to the 19C, together with a description of the local geology; 13C statuary from the west front of the cathedral, 18C stitched samplers.

★★★ CATHEDRAL ⊘

The Cathedral Green acts as a perfect foil to the galleries of Apostles and saints, kings of the Bible and this land, queens, holy women, bishops, hermits and knights in armour aligned in the west front, that panoply of the church displayed through the famous of all ages, from Christ in Majesty.

History and construction – The cathedral is 12C, the bishopric of Bath and Wells 10C, the foundation by Ine, King of Wessex 8C and the site as one of Christian worship possibly 4C, being Roman or even Celtic. Of the early churches nothing remains above ground. In 1091 Bishop John de Villula (d 1122), having purchased the city and abbey of Bath, removed the throne; a successor, Bishop Savaric (d 1205), equally power-hungry, seized Glastonbury and omitted Wells from his title. Glastonbury, in time, regained its autonomy; the title of Bath and Wells was re-adopted and the throne returned to Wells.
The cathedral took more than three centuries to plan and build, from *c*1175 to 1508.

*c*1175	Building began – Wells was the first cathedral church in the Early English style. Three bays of the choir and most of the transepts were completed under Bishop Reginald de Bohun (d 1191).
1239	Cathedral consecrated. Nave completed, west front partly built and many statues carved under Bishop Jocelyn.
Pre-1250-1306	Chapter-house built in successive stages as finance allowed.
1315-22	Central crossing tower (182ft) constructed and separate Lady Chapel built beyond the east end.
1338-48	Scissor arches inserted to counteract tower subsidence on the west side.
*c*1320-40	Choir completed; retrochoir built to link east end and Lady Chapel, making the cathedral 415ft long from west to east. East, Golden Window glazed *c*1340.

The west towers (125ft) were added in 1384-94 and c1430; the cloisters rebuilt in stages c1420-1508.

Exterior – Long ago the **west front** would have been blazingly dramatic, the figures coloured and gilded; it would have resembled an illuminated manuscript or a magnificent tapestry. Today it is more monochrome though tinted at sunset and gilded by floodlight. Despite much destruction by the Puritans, it is England's richest display of 13C sculpture.

The screen front is nearly 150ft across, twice as wide as it is tall, extending round the bases of the west towers – strange constructions which continue the gabled lines of the screen in slim and soaring pinnacled buttresses and tall paired lancets, only to stop abruptly. It may have been felt that elaborate cresting would detract from the screen with its near-300 statues, half of them life-size, which rises to a climax in the centre gable with a frieze of Apostles and Our Lord. The figure of "Christ in Majesty" was sculpted by David Wynne as part of the 20C restoration.

Continue round to the north side of the cathedral.

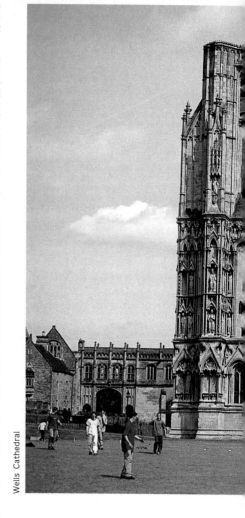

Wells Cathedral

The **North Porch** leads to a twin doorway with a central pier of ringed shafts, flanked on either side by a display of 13C delight in pure line, in the form of shallow tiers of subtly varied blind arcading.

The **Chain Gate**, known simply as the "gate" (1459) is an opening in the two-storey covered way which links the orielled Vicars' Hall *(see below)* to the chapter-house and the north transept of the cathedral. Set into the west wall of the north transept is the **Quarter-Jack**: 15C knights strike the bells with their pikes at the quarters.

Cathedral roofs, crossing tower, chapter-house – A good view of the pinnacled and balustraded roofs of the east end, of the crossing tower with paired lights; shafted buttresses, a pierced balustrade and fountains of pinnacles may be seen at this point, and of the octagonal chapter-house again buttressed, pinnacled, arcaded and balustraded above wide, foil-traceried windows. (Another beautiful view of the east end is from the Bishop's Palace garden - *see below*.)

Interior – *1 hour*. Straight ahead is one of the **scissor arches** inserted to west, north and south when the west piers of the crossing tower sank; whether considered graceful or gaunt, they were an outstanding and successful solution to a nightmare problem and have become a hallmark of the cathedral.

The constant features, the **roof vaulting** and the **pier shafting**, are subtly varied in design in each cathedral sector – the vaulting reaches its climax in the star in the Lady Chapel, and the piers in the slender clustered column in the chapter-house...

Nave – The **piers** are topped by stiff leaf **capitals**, crisply carved and deeply undercut at the west end. At the east end, the stone **pulpit** dates from c1547 and the adjoining **Sugar Chantry** from 1489 - a pair in hexagonal plan with that opposite

A. Taverner

of Bishop Bubwith of 1424, but enriched with fan vaulting, angel figures in the frieze and an ogee-arched doorway. Beyond the scissor arch, the crossing **fan vaulting** is from 1480.

South Transept and Chancel Aisle – The **capitals**, less sharply carved, have men's heads and animal masks hidden among the leaves or digress to show a man with toothache or tell the tale of two caught in the act of robbing an orchard *(southwest pillar)*.

The **corbels** also portray figures including an angel. The circular **font**, with a Jacobean cover, is the only relic of an earlier cathedral on an adjacent site. Among the **tombs** note that of Bishop William de Marcia (d 1302), possibly a true portrait effigy, on a low chest encircled by a frieze of heads.

In **St Calixtus Chapel** stands the beautiful **tomb chest** of Thomas Boleyn (d 1472), faced with several panels of Nottingham **alabaster** carved to represent God the Father and the Annunciation.

The south chancel aisles are the resting place for **tombs** convincingly carved in 1220-30 to resemble seven early **Saxon bishops**. *Continue up the aisle to enter the choir.*

Chancel – Immediately striking are the **vista** east through the three pointed arches behind the high altar to the retro-choir and Lady Chapel, and on high, of the Jesse or **Golden Window** of medieval glass. Note the **bishop's throne** made of stone, the tapestry bishops' banners and stall coverings of 1937-48 workmanship and the **Bekynton Chantry** of 1450, with the bishop, Keeper of the Privy Seal to Henry VI, both in full vestments and as a cadaver.

Retro-Choir – The **piers**, few in number with shafts almost separated, produce a forest of ribs to support an intricate **tierceron vaulting**. Note a 13C cope chest and three of the cathedral's **misericords** which show respectively, a left-handed man killing a wyvern or dragon, Alexander the Great being lifted to heaven by two griffins, both medieval carvings, and a 17C illustration of a boy pulling a thorn from his foot.

Lady Chapel – The **star vault** meets in a finely **painted boss** above the unequal octagon which enters spatially into the retro-choir; most of the glass, smashed at the Reformation, has been replaced in its fragmentary state.

North Transept – The **life-size carving** (1955) shows Christ rising from the tomb on Easter morning. The **astronomical clock** with the sun and a star revolving round the 24-hour dial dates from c1390 – commissioned by Bishop Erghum from the same craftsmen who made a similar clock for Salisbury; above is a **knights' tournament** which revolves eight times every quarter hour, one knight

Scissor arch, Wells Cathedral

A. Taverner

being struck down each time; also at the quarters, **Jack Blandiver**, the seated figure at gallery level, kicks his two quarter bells and, on the hour, strikes the bell in front of him (the mechanism is silent during services).

Chapter-House – A broad and graceful flight of worn **steps**, laid c1290, sweeps up to the **chapter-house**: an octagonal structure supported by a clustered **central pier** from which 32 tierceron ribs radiate to meet others springing from each angle of the encircling octagon. Below traceried windows, whose glass was smashed by Roundhead supporters, are the stalls, separated by Portland stone shafts, capped by crocketed and cusped gables resting on **figured corbels**, carved as portrait heads by medieval masons.

Vicars' Hall – The chapter-house steps were modified in the 15C when the Chain Gate was built; an exhibition on the building of the cathedral is housed in the covered way leading to the Vicars' Hall (1348).

Cathedral precinct

★ **Vicars' Close** – East of the Chain Gate *(see above)* beneath the Vicars' Hall a gateway opens into the Vicars' Close, a long street (150yds) of **identical stone cottages** with tall chimneys built in 1348 by Bishop Ralph for members of the cathedral choristers and singers in minor orders. The houses, to which the walled front gardens were added c1415, have been continuously occupied and altered except for **no 22**, which has retained its original outward appearance. At the far end – the street tapers for the sake of perspective – is a 15C chapel.

★ **Bishop's Palace** ⊘ – The palace, on the south side of the Green, stands stoutly walled and encircled by a moat visited by wildfowl and swans. The approach is through the Bishop's Eye *(see above)* and an inner, 14C gatehouse, square, castellated and formerly preceded by a drawbridge.
Inside are walled gardens, the springs or **wells** from which the town gets its name – 3 400 000 gallons a day or 40 gallons a second – the mellow ruin of the Great Hall, the present palace and a beautiful **view**★★ of the east end of the cathedral. The **palace** itself dates in part from the 13C: the walls with bastions and angle towers (rampart walk) and the moat were constructed in the 14C as a status symbol. The oldest part is the centre block with its undercroft of 1230-40, re-ordered and re-decorated inside in the 19C when a top storey was also added. The chapel dates from c1280.

At the end of the 13C, as a final embellishment, the **Great Hall** (115ft x 60ft) was built of red sandstone with corner turrets and great traceried windows. In 1552 the roof was stripped of its lead (the proceeds going to the king) whereupon the roof timbers rotted and fell in. Part of the remaining walls were removed in the 19C to make "a picturesque ruin".

ADDITIONAL SIGHTS

Market Place – The bustling town centre has been equipped since the Middle Ages with a **conduit** bringing water from the springs in the palace garden *(see above)*; the Gothick fountain is a late 18C replacement of earlier fountainheads. Along the square's north side is a range of houses erected in 1453 by Bishop Bekynton and still known as the **New Works** (Nova Opera). There have been repairs but the range appears still much as described in a document of 1480. Marked on the pavement is Mary Rand's record long jump of over 22ft achieved at the 1964 Olympic Games.

High Street – The short High Street is lined above 20C shopfronts by houses with uneven rooflines which date from the 15C-17C; the King's Arms still has its 14C roof; the **City Arms**, a low, half-timbered building surrounding a small courtyard served as the city gaol from the 16C-19C.

★ **St Cuthbert** ⊙ – This magnificent Perpendicular parish church, overshadowed by the cathedral at the other end of town, succeeds an Early English church (transept chapel window), a Norman predecessor built on the site of a wooden Saxon building of which only the dedication remains; Cuthbert was an English monk and Bishop of Lindisfarne in 685-87. The **tower** (122ft) is distinguished by its slender stepped buttresses framing enormously tall bell openings, a crest of blind arcading between corner buttresses and pinnacled turrets; its elegance is transferred to the homogenous treatment of aisle windows (the clerestory was inserted later).

Inside, the typical 16C Somerset-style wooden **roof**, with tie-beams, cresting, coffering and a chorale of demi-angels, rosettes and heraldic shields, was vividly restored to its true medieval colouring in 1963. Note the **piers**, elongated to take the clerestory and with differently carved capitals, the **royal arms** of Charles I and Charles II *(north aisle and north transept chapel)*, the superb late-Jacobean **pulpit** (1636), exceptionally carved with scenes from the Old Testament (Jonah and the Whale, David and Goliath), two much mutilated early **altarpieces** (transept chapels), also the **contract** for the altarpieces' erection in 1470; the main altar reredos is 19C; several 17C memorials. The numerous side chapels suggest the need to accommodate visiting pilgrims attracted to the parish by the cathedral; in one there is a memorial to a 19-year old German student who had come to Wells to learn English.

Outside, at the east end, stands **Priest Row**, a line of Victorian cottages on the site of former priests' lodgings, with neat porches and flowered gardens.

EXCURSION

★ **Wookey Hole**

"Just under the hills, is the famous and so much talked of Wokey Hole" wrote Defoe in 1686. Since his day many more caves have been discovered but the stalactites he saw have grown only one inch apiece since then.

The approach is through a wooded valley at the foot of the Mendip plateau. Mill buildings in a wooded glen screen the hole in the cliffs (200ft) from which the River Axe gushes in a torrent at the rate of 12 million gallons a day. The river has no visible source: two miles away up on the plateau the soil composition alters from impervious shale to permeable carboniferous limestone through which rainwater percolates, collects in rock faults and wears a course which forms the passages and caves which comprise the Hole.

★ **Caves** ⊙ – *90min.* The river is always present in the caves, in echoing, although mostly unseen, cascades and in deep green-blue-black pools, mirroring the walls which vary in colour from iron rust-red to leaden-grey and green-white. The caverns and narrow fissures of the tour (about 350yds) represent less than one tenth of the explored passages.

Stalactites, stalagmites, frozen falls, translucent pools, cliff faces of different-coloured rock, the stone outline of the witch – who one legend even claims was killed by King Arthur – ferns growing beside the arc lights, present an immutable world. During their 500 million year lifecycle the caves have been inhabited by Iron Age man in 300 BC and later by Romano-British and Celtic peoples.

The **Witch's Magic Cavern** concludes the tour with the unfurling of history and legend in times past, present and future...

★ **Papermill** – Handmade rag paper with body, texture and a watermark has a unique quality of simple luxury; it looks deceptively easy to scoop exactly the right amount of raw material from the vat and distribute it evenly in the mould. Paper was first made at Wookey Hole *c*1600; the mill supplied paper for the Confederate banknotes issued at Richmond, Virginia.

Other attractions include the **Mirror-maze**, which refracts a kaleidoscope of images all the way to the dancing fountain within, and the **Old Penny Arcade** which offers the chance to play on Edwardian slot machines or the possibility of dressing up in period costume for a sepia print photograph.

Museum – The display traces the geological formation of the caves, the source of the River Axe, the exploratory diving expeditions and the construction of the link tunnel in 1974. Note the **waterwheel** at the entrance.

WESTON-SUPER-MARE

North Somerset – Population 640 935
Michelin Atlas p 16 or Map 403 – L29, 30

The town is in the classic tradition of a large, popular English seaside resort: donkeys, miles of dark gold sand scoured twice daily by the tide, hotels, restaurants, shops and stalls fringing the arc of the bay, public gardens, a **museum** of local history, the Tropicana Pleasure Beach with two water chutes and other attractions... The popularity of Weston-super-Mare has developed since the turn of the century, since when its population has quadrupled.

Besides the Worlebury Camp, an Iron Age fortress located on the prominent headland, Weston is entirely 19C.

★★ **The view** – Across the bay lie the islands of **Flat Holm** (lighthouse) and **Steep Holm** (bird sanctuary); to the south is the square-towered **Uphill Church** (19C on an ancient site), further over, the long finger of Brean Down Point (Somerset) and, on the horizon, the Welsh hills.

EXCURSIONS

★ **Clevedon**

The Victorian resort, which grew out of a fishing village, retains its wide 19C roads bordered by substantial villas, Tuscan, Gothic or Italianate in style, rows of cottages built in local stone and unhurried shops.

The promenade is bordered by gardens with flowers, closely mown lawns, and trees, especially windbent pines. Characteristic of the time also are the **bandstand** (Green Beach Gardens), the **Clock Tower** and the pagoda-roofed **pier** (1869). From the park benches the **view**★★ extends across the mouth of the Severn to the Welsh hills.

★ **Clevedon Court** ⊘ – 1.5 miles. *45min*. The mellow stone house, begun in the 14C, had achieved its present appearance by 1570; the interior, which reflects every period, has all the attraction and comfort of an Edwardian country house. The 14C **Great Hall** with Tudor windows and fireplace is hung with family portraits; among them is Abraham Elton, purchaser of the house in 1709, Master of the Bristol Merchant Venturers, mayor and MP. The chairs are Stuart, the drawer table late 16C, the Dutch chandelier 17C.

The **State Bedroom**, 14C solar with an inserted Elizabethan window, reflects the family taste through ten generations. Among the contents are a portrait of the merchant Nicholas Elton, a Hepplewhite tester bed, Queen Anne spoonback chairs, Cromwellian chairs and chests, late Georgian and Regency pieces and small 18C-19C children's chairs.

The **Hanging Chapel** has unique reticulated window tracery; the prayer desks are 17C, the Biblical carvings 15C and 16C, the glass 19C.

Note in the smaller bedrooms portraits of and drawings by Thackeray including Jane Octavia Brookfield, model for Lady Castlewood in *Henry Esmond*, and of Arthur Hallam, nephew of the then owner of Clevedon Court, in whose memory **Tennyson** wrote *In Memoriam*.

The small **Justice Room** and walls of an adjoining staircase display a fascinating collection of the local Nailsea glass made between 1788 and 1873. There are bottles and jars and "friggers" or craftsmen's spare-time mouldings including green glass hats, trailed, blotched and colour-striped perfume bellows, rolling pins and a unique set of brilliantly coloured walking sticks.

The **Old Kitchen** contains a rare collection of Eltonware, the remarkable experimental pottery of Sir Edmund Elton, man of many parts, designer of Clevedon Clock Tower *(see above)*, who essayed new shapes, decoration on coloured slips and metal lustrework.

Garden – The outlook is over Clevedon Moor to the Bristol Channel and Wales; immediately behind, the hillside rises sharply, covered in dense woods. Between is a long, steeply terraced garden on three levels comprising wide borders at the feet of precipitous stone walls.

WEYMOUTH* – PORTLAND*

Dorset – Population 61 233
Michelin Atlas p 8 or Map 403 – M32

Weymouth has long provided sheltered berths for boats: it was through Weymouth that the Black Death is claimed to have been brought by a trading vessel in 1348. Its heyday, however, came in the 18C when trade with France and the Americas began to gain momentum: it is a Georgian town associated with **George III** who was the first monarch to stay in a seaside resort and chose Weymouth for the experiment: "The preparations of festive loyalty were universal," Fanny Burney wrote in her diary in July 1789, "think but of the surprise of his Majesty when, the first time of his bathing, he had no sooner popped his royal head under water, than a band of music, concealed in a neighbouring machine, struck up God save great George our King". The sovereign returned many times; in 1810, "the grateful inhabitants" erected the statue on the Esplanade which remains the town's major landmark.

Modern Weymouth is still proud of its pale sand beaches and popular seaside attractions (Punch and Judy, donkey rides, merry-go-rounds), served by a mainline railway station and numerous waterfront hotels.

Market day: Thursday.

Esplanade – The Esplanade beyond King George's statue, punctuated with blue and white-painted Victorian shelters and, some 200yds further along, by Queen Victoria's Jubilee Clock, follows the enormous sweep of the bay. Facing the sea are terrace houses of the late 18C–early 19C with first-floor iron balconies, sash windows (some with slender glazing bars), canopies, copings and fine proportions, notably at the harbour end.

A **land train** runs the length of the Esplanade from the Tourist Information Centre to the **Lodmoor Nature Reserve** (nature trails and bird observatories) and **Sea Life Park** ⊘, equipped with a hi-tech Shark Academy (PCC-controlled video, animatronics and under-water simulated sound) and displays of native varieties of sharks, fish, octopus and crabs to be found off the Dorset coast. At the southern end of the beach is located the **Weymouth Pavilion Complex** and ferry terminal.

Weymouth Harbour

Harbour and Old Town

The lively old harbour has been extended to provide additional moorings upstream from the ferry terminal; here the traditional fishing fleet lands its catches and private boats berth. Beyond, on the **North Quay** is the heart of the old town, which as the town grew, spread to the mainland from the promontory on which Sandsfoot Castle had been erected in the 16C and Nothe Fort *(see below)* in the early 19C.

Old Melcombe Regis – Set back behind Alexandra Gardens – the town's rubbish tip in medieval times – survive a number of early houses including elegant Georgian establishments and Milton House, in St Alban Street, a one-time hostel for pilgrims bound for Compostella and rare survival from Elizabethan times.

St Mary's (1817) was designed by James Hamilton, its reredos is by James Thornhill (painter of the dome in St Paul's in London and the Greenwich Hospital, also father-in-law of William Hogarth).

Custom House Quay – The quayside (extending upstream from behind the Alexandra Gardens Amusement pavilions) is lined with ship chandlers, inns and houses overlooking the town bridge and the old harbour; many of the buildings are 18C-19C. The **Ship Inn**, on the corner, is housed in a block from the 17C.

The first **Town Bridge** was erected in 1534 to provide easy access between Weymouth and the hamlet of Melcombe: these were combined into a single borough in 1571. The present bridge dates from 1930. *Cross the bridge and walk downstream along Trinity Road, past the fishing and ferry excursions (to Portland Castle and Fleet) departure points to Cove Street.*

Tudor House ⊘ – The house (1570-1603) at 3 Trinity Street, belonging to the Weymouth Civic Society, is marked by a twin gable. Inside, it has been furnished as for a wealthy merchant: at that time the house would have fronted onto The Ope, an inlet off the harbour for berthing trade vessels, in-filled in the 18C. The furniture is largely 17C English. In the living room, one fireplace is equipped with a spit and andirons, the other (inserted when the house was split into two cottages long before being saved from dereliction and painstakingly restored in the 1950s) with a fine 18C kitchen crane decorated with a Tree of Life design, cauldron and Georgian fire basket. Upstairs there are three bedrooms.

Guided tours provide explanations of the house's interior and an insight into life in 17C Weymouth.

Brewers Quay – *Hope Square.* This redevelopment of the large Victorian Devenish Brewery (1869-1904) and other old buildings provides small and interesting shops, stalls and attractions.

★ **Timewalk Journey** ⊘ – The **museum** displays panels and showcases highlighting aspects of the town's history. The Timewalk comprises a series of animated tableaux and special effects providing a tour of the town over the centuries: the grim horror of the plague, the looting of a Spanish galleon, the Civil War, King George III taking the waters, smugglers... The tour concludes with the Devenish Story, explaining the traditional brewing process using the original copper-lined vats and other dependent craftsmen such as coopers and farriers.

Discovery ⊘ – This friendly hands-on gallery explores the laws and processes of science and technology (lasers, mirrors, water, sound, gravity) in an interesting and approachable way, appealing to all ages.

Nothe Fort ⊘ – The semicircular fort, built between 1860-72 by the Royal Engineers to accommodate a 12-gun battery of cannon, played an active part in the defences of Portland Harbour until 1956. Sold in 1961, it now houses the **Museum of Coastal Defence**, dedicated to all the fighting services and civil defence since the arrival of Roman ships in 43AD. Perched on the edge of Weymouth's promontory, it offers panoramic **views**★ over Portland Harbour and Weymouth Bay. The numerous items on display range from 19C cannons and 20C guns, trucks, medals, models, military uniforms, photographs and Second World War newspapers; tableaux represent scenes depicting life in the fort, from gun drill to ablutions: a quartermaster's store, an engineer's workshop, a barrack room, cells, signals office and guardroom...

Besides the exhibition rooms, the fort's magazines, ramparts and tunnels may be explored; the gardens, ideal for a picnic, extend downhill from the fort to the shore.

★ **Boat Trip** ⊘ – Weymouth Bay and Portland Harbour.

RSPB nature reserves – **Radipole Lake** attracts large numbers of visitors intrigued by the arrival (1960s) and subsequent breeding of the Cetti warbler among the resident reed, sedge and grasshopper warblers and bearded tits: the tidal lagoon and reed beds are overlooked by a hide which provides shelter in bad weather, when many of the birds are grounded; listening posts help to recognise distinctive calls. The waterbirds (teal, shoveler, cormorant and great crested grebe), now accustomed to visitors, can be uncannily tame and therefore a good way to kindle interest in children; at other times, rare migrants draw the specialists.

Nearby, **Lodmoor** offers a similar habitat of grazing marsh and pools lined with ample reed beds for nesting warblers, reed buntings, bearded tits; lapwings, redshanks, yellow wagtails. Plenty of wildfowl in winter when the area is waterlogged, and numerous gulls attracted by the neighbouring rubbish tips away from the turbulent sea. Migration periods see the passing presence of waders (ruff, avocets, Temminck's and little stints).

Warblers

Cetti's warbler *(Cettia cetti)*, named after an Italian 18C Jesuit, is the only European passerine with ten – rather than twelve – tail feathers. Easily confused with a nightingale, this secretive little bird has a most striking song which starts suddenly, explosively, fast and loud. Unlike the other warblers, this one, which was first found to have bred in England in 1972, appears to be happy to winter here.

The **Grasshopper warbler** *(Locustella naevia)* is another mysterious bird: it takes its name from its striking reeling, insect-like, song delivered at a high pitch that is inaudible to many. This call, often lasting a minute or so, has also been compared to "a distant, small, tinny, muffled alarm clock or the rapid ticking of a free-wheeling bicycle" (RSPB *The Complete Book of British Birds*).

Sedge warblers *(Acrocephalus schoenobaeus)* arrive in England in April or early May, having crossed the Sahara Desert, Mediterranean and Europe in one single flight. Their call is a loud 'tuc' and their warbling song has grating trills and sparrow-like chirrups.

Reed warblers *(Acrocephalus scirpaceus)* choose to make their nests in dense reedbeds where they breed in colonies. Alas, their efforts to escape from ground predators seems to have made them vulnerable to predation from cuckoos – the reason these little birds seem to accept the fat-cat intruder may be due to the warblers incubating their eggs before the clutch is complete (a practice known as asynchronous hatching), thereby ensuring that in times of food shortage only the eldest survive.

★ Isle of Portland

The peninsula is some 4.5 miles long, attached to the mainland by a narrow strip of land edged by Chesil Beach: in winter it stands defiant amid the Channel storms, its name ever associated with gale warnings around the **Bill** in shipping forecasts; in summer it attracts those sunseekers happy to enjoy the springy turf and idly watch the horizon, sportsmen (anglers, rock climbers, sailors, scuba divers, windsurfers), nature lovers and bird watchers.

Portland stone has been quarried all over the island since the Middle Ages and the landscape is pockmarked with worked-out quarries. Everything on Portland is built of local stone: either the pure white limestone which is durable yet soft enough to carve (chosen by Wren for St Paul's Cathedral) or the cheaper, coarser shelly stone.

During 1944 some 520 000 US soldiers and 115 000 vehicles passed through Portland in preparation for the D-Day landings in Normandy: an event commemorated by a monument in Victoria Gardens.

Ferrybridge – At the eastern end of the Fleet Lagoon is the **Chesil Beach Centre** ⊙, designed to reinforce the importance of the nature reserve as a conservation area: displays relate to the delicate balance of sea-loving and fresh-water marine life.

For Chesil Beach, see Abbotsbury, *below.*

On the far side of the lagoon is the **Abbotsbury Oyster Farm** ⊙.

Tout Quarry – Now disused, this quarry has evolved into an informal sculpture park where artists have carved their work into the natural rock.

Portland Bill – The southern tip which extends six miles into the English Channel, in addition to being a splendid **vantage point**★★, is distinguished by three markers: **Portland Bill Lighthouse** ⊙ (built 1903-06), the **Bird Observatory and Field Centre** and the **Obelisk** of Portland stone, erected as a way-mark in 1844. This often bleak, windswept promontory is a popular migration landfall site for a wide range of birds: warblers, chats, swallows, martins, hoopoes, golden orioles, gannets, kittiwakes, even arctic and pomarine skuas.

Pulpit Rock may be climbed to provide a perch high above the waves.

Portland Museum ⊙ – *217 Wakeham.* Two thatched cottages house the museum, Avice's House in Thomas Hardy's *The Well-Beloved.* Artefacts relate to smuggling and shipwrecks, Portland's natural history and geology (fossils); local history is related with exhibits from 19C days when convicts worked the quarries, and built the prison (1848) and St Peter's Church.

Portland Castle ⊙ – *Accessible by road or ferry from Brewer's Quay and Ferry Bridge.* The compact castle was built in 1539-40 at the water's edge on a Saxon site as one of **Henry VIII's forts** along the south coast, paired for defensive purposes with Sandsfoot Castle on the mainland opposite. The fabric is Portland stone, the cost was a colossal £4 964 19*s* 10 1/4*d*, it being the finest of all the castles erected. Additions were made in Elizabeth's reign, in the 17C and early in the 19C; having been re-commissioned to stop piracy, the castle was actively used until 1954.

Alongside is **HMS Osprey Air Station**, a Royal Naval helicopter base which implements highly effective air-rescue missions: although the air station is being run down, the rescue service will continue to operate. Beyond is the old naval base, now Portland Port,

Portland Bill

The patent for the lighthouse overlooking the Portland Race, the meeting of tides between the Bill and the Shambles sand-bank, was delayed nearly 50 years before finally, in 1720, two lighthouses with enclosed coal fire lanterns were constructed. In 1789 a new building was erected which nine years later was fortified against possible Napoleonic invasion by the installation of two 18lb cannon. The lighthouse has since been twice replaced, the present 133ft tower dating from 1906.

under private management with working shipyard and, since 1997, provides anchorage on a temporary basis to the controversial prison ship HMP *Weare*. This, in turn is overlooked by **Verne Citadel** which was built in the 19C to consolidate the defences of Weymouth and Portland harbours which also included forts at the Nothe *(see above)* and on the breakwaters; it is now used as a high-security prison.

Portland Harbour – The harbour Henry VIII's castle was designed to defend was protected on three sides but wide open to the east. In the mid-19C work began on the system of breakwaters and channels which, after 20 years' construction by convicts, was to provide one of the largest and safest harbours in the world. It is here that many of the national and international dinghy-sailing and windsurfer championships are held.

★★ Abbotsbury *9 miles west along B3157 coastal road to Bridport.*

Abbotsbury, which takes its name from St Peter's Abbey, a Benedictine community established here in 1040, lies at the western end of the Fleet, the lagoon formed by Chesil Beach. In the Domesday Book records show eight villages to depend on the community; at the Dissolution there were 22. The abbey was demolished by Henry's agent Giles Strangways who later paid £1096 for a 20 year lease and settled in one of the few remaining abbey buildings which were all subsequently destroyed during the Civil War.

In 1765, Elizabeth, 1 Countess of Ilchester built a summer residence there; little remains of the castle which was burnt down in 1913.

The village street is lined with immaculate slate or reed-thatched stone cottages.

Abbey ruins – In 1541, after the Dissolution, the abbey lands were leased on condition that all "edifices being within the site and precinct of the late Monastry.... be hereafter thrown down and removed"; the church was reduced to mere footings, the monastic buildings converted into a private residence (burned down in 1644).

Tithe Barn and Children's Farm ⊙ – The magnificent thatched barn dates from the early 15C and was one of the largest of its kind in England comprising 23 bays, measuring 272ft by 31ft. The present building, 170ft long, has close standing buttresses, a west gable and wide porch.

Surrounding outbuildings include a 17C dovecote built to accommodate 3000 birds, and modern stables housing a variety of farm animals (cows, horses, pigs, rabbits, goats...).

St Nicholas' Church – The parish church, in local buff stone with Portland stone dressings, was built between the late 14C and the 17C. Note the plaster vault of 1638 above the two east bays; the 18C pedimented and Corinthian-columned **altarpiece** with a vineleaf frieze; the 15C-16C **stained-glass panel** of the Virgin; the 18C **chandelier** and the plain Jacobean testered **pulpit** with a back panel punctured by two musket balls from a skirmish in 1644, after which the Royalist Sir John Strangways, owner of the abbey lands, was imprisoned in the Tower.

A 14C stone figure of a monk stands in the porch.

★ St Catherine's Chapel ⊙ – *Half a mile uphill; 30min there and back on foot.*

The small chapel, rugged and windblown on its 250ft downland crest, is the only 14C monastic building to remain. It has thick walls, an octagonal stair turret with lancet windows, and flat-topped buttresses which are surprisingly stout for such a small building: they support the stone tunnel vault. The Perpendicular windows were added later.

The church probably served as a seamen's lantern.

★★ Chesil Beach – This strange geological bank of **shingle** forms a unique, eight mile beach between Abbotsbury and the Isle of Portland to the southeast, joining the isle to Weymouth. The pea-gravel at Abbotsbury increases to cannonball-sized

stones at Portland, an illogical grading given the prevailing south-westerly winds. In the lee lies the **Fleet Lagoon**, a shallow tidal waterway draining into the sea at the Portland end where conditions have been harnessed for farming oysters. This shallow, predominantly freshwater canal provides an ideal habitat for fish fry (mullet, flounders, bass, eel) which attract grebes, herons and cormorants, and a sheltered sanctuary for wintering migrant waterfowl (mallard, teal, wigeon, pochard, shoveler, pintail and tufted duck, ringed plover, little tern). Parts of the beach, a nature reserve, are closed during the nesting season.

★ **Swannery** ⊙ – A natural colony of swans seems to have existed here long before records relate of the monks' swanherd (1393), when they were protected and nurtured as a source of game. Unlike other mute swans in Britain which belong to the Crown (tagged with yellow rings), this colony comprising some 800 birds, has been the property of the Fox-Strangways family since the 1540s. The swans are ringed (rather than pinioned) from which it has been discovered that they live in excess of 10 years, do not necessarily keep a mate for life, but do return regularly to the same nesting sites on the two-acre meadow, where they are prepared to do battle against upstarts.

The Decoy House – the original together with much of the village of Fleet was destroyed by a violent storm and tidal wave in 1824 – provides an audio-visual display outlining the work undertaken by the Swanherd through the nesting season (March to early April), the hatching of the cygnets (mid-May to end June), their learning to fly (September to October) and their release (third Sunday in October); allied to this is the maintenance of the traditional reed beds used for thatch.The **Reedbed Walk** passes the rearing pens and the **duck decoy**. This would traditionally have comprised 5 "pipes" or netted tunnels where wild ducks are lured; today the sanctuary operate three pipes to trap wild birds for ringing and monitoring. Sheltered hides provide additional details of salt-marsh plants, birdlife and the ongoing maintenance of the reed beds.

Bearded Tit (*Panurus biarmicus*)

This long tailed reed bed dweller is not in fact a member of the tit family but a parrotbill. It is the male which grows a black set of hanging "whiskers" in stark contrast with its grey head and brownish body; the female is plainer in appearance.

★ **Sub-Tropical Gardens** ⊙ – The woodland gardens lie in a hollow, a geological fault, protected from the salt-laden winds by bands of holm-oak. The original garden was laid out by Elizabeth, 1st Countess of Ilchester as a walled kitchen garden; subsequent owners gradually wooded over the open fields, introduced exotic species from Chile, the Canary Islands and the Orient, the Mediterranean basin, and finally, species from the Far East, Australia and New Zealand (1990s). The tour begins with a Caucasian wingnut tree which shelters the rare holly-like shrub from Chile (*Citronella mucronata*); a collection of mature Chusan palms and low altitude rhododendrons, Japanese maples, bamboo, yuccas, agaves, agapanthus, aloes are punctuated by a large Azorean bay tree (*Laurus azorica*), loquat (*Eriobotrya japonica*), Kashmir cypress (*Cupressus cashmeriana*), female maidenhair tree (*Ginkgo biloba*), false olive (*Picconia exelsa*), Persian Ironwood trees (*Parrotia persica*) – to name but a few. Colour through the seasons is provided by bluebells, azaleas, camellias, rhododendrons, hydrangeas, bog plants and countless perennials. Focus points are provided by a summer house, lily ponds, aviary, sunken lawn and Gardener's Bothy.

Hardy Monument ⊙

4 miles northeast of Weymouth on B3157 and a by-road.

The strange 70ft tall stone tower visible for miles around, perched high on Blackdown, commemorates **Admiral Hardy** (1769-1839), Nelson's flag-captain, who spent his boyhood in the village of Portesham. It was erected in 1844. There are panoramic **views** from the foot of the tower *(not open)*.

For additional sites in the area turn to BRIDPORT, DORCHESTER, SWANAGE, WAREHAM.

Osmington White Horse

This white horse *(6 miles east along A353)*, which, with Uffington, is the only animal facing right, is unique in having a rider. The figure is popularly supposed to be George III, patron of Weymouth from 1789; an alternative version credits engineers, stationed at Weymouth in case of invasion in 1815, with the carving, whereupon the rider would be Wellington; Hardy, in *The Trumpet Major*, described it as a memorial to Trafalgar... The figure is the largest of all, being 323ft high by 280ft long.

Wiltshire – Population 3 717
Michelin Atlas p 9 or Map 403 – O30

Wilton became the local fortified capital in the 7C-8C in the reign of Ine, King of Wessex, when "hundreds" were being grouped into "shires" which then, in many cases, took the name of their appointed centres – thus Wiltshire. In the 9C Alfred founded a Benedictine convent in the town; in 1033 Wilton was sacked by invading Danes and hardly had it recovered before it was devastated by the Black Death. Although nominally it remained the county town, it was eventually outstripped by Salisbury.

Market Place – At the centre, trees shade the ruined Perpendicular arcade and west window of what was originally a **Saxon church** dedicated to St Mary. The Cross, nearby, is a composite of artefacts from an early Crucifixion to an 18C urn.

Italian Church – Set back from the wide Cotswold-style shopping street of 17C houses with later shopfronts is the **Basilica of St Mary and St Nicholas** (1841-45), a feat of Italianate Romanesque designed by Thomas Wyatt at the behest of the Hon Sidney Herbert and his Russian mother Catherine, Dowager Countess of Pembroke and Montgomery. Inspired by the Italian churches of San Pietro and Santa Maria near Viterbo, it is aligned on a north-south axis (allegedly because this was the traditional orientation of churches built in Russia); it has a freestanding 110ft high campanile and ornately decorated, gabled, west front. The lions are of carved stone from the Isle of Man.

Inside, it is embellished with ornament imported physically from Italy or modelled on Italian prototypes: the columns at the end of the aisles come from the Temple of Venus at Porto Venere in the Gulf of La Spezia, which was built by the Roman Consul Lucius Porcius Licinius in 151BC; the four 12C twisted Cosmati work columns incorporated into the pulpit come from the shrine of Santa Maria Maggiore in Rome, which had been acquired in 1768 by Sir William Hamilton and given to Sir Horace Walpole; at his death, many ornaments from the Strawberry Hill estate were dispersed by John Webb of Bond Street onto the open market. Within the altar rails are monuments to both patrons, inlaid with malachite, mosaic and carving. The apse is decorated with mosaic completed by Gertrude Martin. Precious panels of **stained glass** (1144-17C) survive having been removed and buried during the Second World War.

★ **Wilton Carpet Factory** ⊙ – *King Street*. Carpet weaving in England began as a cottage industry but by the 17C had declined to so poor a standard that the much-travelled 8th Earl of Pembroke arranged for two skilled French Huguenot weavers, who were banned from leaving France on pain of death, to be smuggled over in wine barrels to set up a carpet factory. The Wilton works began weaving Brussels carpet in the 1740s and soon developed the Wilton Carpet technique for which it became famous: Wilton beam looms produced a worsted-face carpet with a dense, thick pile cut from loops. In 1835 upright hand looms (some with a 40ft warp) were acquired from the bankrupt factory at Axminster (*see* HONITON) providing Wilton with additional capacity for hand-knotted carpet-making (maintained until 1959) alongside the mechanically woven Chenille Axminster which was pioneered in 1839. During 1939-45 the works were employed to supply army blankets and camouflage nets for the war effort. Today, having manufactured designs to suit a diverse range of interiors to suit Adam and Morris buildings, contemporary demands for bespoke hard-wearing replacements (notably for National Trust houses) and modern pieces (private apartments of Wilton House) continue to underpin the factory's survival.

The museum and factory are housed in the purpose-built 18C-20C weaving sheds, the oldest arranged around a courtyard, the more modern mill across the River Wylye and River Nadder. The **tour** *(80min)* comprises an introduction to the different carpet weaving methods: visitors are shown old looms, how they are threaded-up, the different techniques and materials used through the ages, the various textures of the finished products (ranging from 16 to 100 knots per square inch). All is then put into context with a visit to the clattering mill where a number of modern Wilton and Axminster power looms may be seen noisily at work and manned, in the main, by long-serving weavers with nimble fingers.

★★ WILTON HOUSE

William Herbert, the quick-witted favourite of Henry VIII, received from his sovereign – to whom he was related – the property of the dissolved Wilton Benedictine Convent in 1544. Within ten years he had been created Lord Herbert of Cardiff and Earl of Pembroke, and had constructed a house on the old convent site worthy of receiving the new king, Edward VI.

The idiosyncratic contributions of successive generations can still be clearly distinguished as they meld into the whole: 2nd Earl married "the greatest patronesse of wit and learning of any lady of her time", the sister of **Sir Philip**

Sidney who, while staying at Wilton, composed his poem *Arcadia* (paintings in the Single Cube Room); 4th Earl, munificent patron commissioned **Inigo Jones** to design the house anew and incorporate within the plan a stateroom in which to hang his collection of royal and family portraits by **Van Dyck** (the task was completed by his nephew John Webb following a fire in 1647 which destroyed the internal decorations on the south and east fronts); 8th Earl, founder of the carpet factory, traveller, connoisseur, collector, notably of the Wilton Diptych (since 1929 in the National Gallery, London), appointed agents to find new pictures, and marbles to replace those sold to pay the debts of the spendthrift 7th Earl; 9th Earl, soldier, architect and friend of Lord Burlington and William Kent, built the **Palladian Bridge** and redesigned the **garden**; 10th Earl, also a soldier and an authority on disciplined horse-riding, commissioned the **equestrian portraits** and 55 **Spanish Riding School gouaches** which hang in the Large Smoking Room; 11th Earl employed **James Wyatt** in 1801 to recast the house, demolish the old great hall, rebuild two fronts and build the two-tier Gothic cloister in the original inner court to provide galleries for statuary and historic mementoes such as Napoleon's despatch box, a lock of Queen Elizabeth's hair, verses by Sir Philip Sidney in his own hand...

In more recent times, the house has featured in the films the *Madness of King George* (1994) and *Sense and Sensibility* (1995).

Palladian bridge, Wilton House

Tour ⊘ *1 hour*

Old Riding School – In the Visitor's Centre, a short video provides an atmospheric introduction to the house before visitors are ushered through the Victorian kitchens and laundry.

Cloisters – The raised entrance hall and cloisters, which are a remodelling of the former inner courtyard, are furnished with a number of Classical marble sculptures, paintings (*Rape of the Sabine Women* by Pietro da Cortona; landscapes by Richard Wilson), fine furniture and oriental porcelain; two cabinets display medals and mementoes of famous people (lock of Elizabeth I's hair, sash worn by Florence Nightingale).

Smoking Rooms – A staircase, inserted by James Wyatt, leads down to the ground floor; note the terracotta busts by Roubillac and Ribera's *Democritus*. The 19C **Gothic hall** includes portrait busts of **Sidney Herbert** and **Florence Nightingale** (Lord Herbert of Lea was Secretary of State for War in 1852 when Florence Nightingale went to the Crimea).

The two smoking rooms are hung with the oil equestrian portraits and the Spanish Riding School gouaches. Note the typical Inigo Jones moulded detail in cornices, doorways and chimneypieces and the beautiful **furniture** including a late 17C walnut table, a mirror and stands with ivory marquetry, three Chippendale tailor-made Spanish mahogany bookcases (1750) and music cabinet, the walnut and leather Regency chairs.

State Apartments – The suite of formal apartments by **Inigo Jones** is characterised by a wealth of Classical enrichment, including large ceiling paintings, marble chimneypieces, heavily carved cornices, covings, doorways, overmantels, columns, escutcheons at the centre of broken pediments and such like... all picked out in gold leaf. The **furniture** includes massive marble and gilt tables and red velvet and gilt sofas by William Kent and pieces by the younger Chippendale, 18C French commodes and Boulle-style tables inlaid with tortoiseshell and brass.

The **Little Ante Room** is hung mainly with small Dutch and Flemish scenes (Van Goyen, Van der Goes, Mabuse). The **Corner Room**, overlooking a great stretch of lawn planted with Lebanese cedars on the east side and the Palladian Bridge to the south, is decorated with pictures by Andrea del Sarto, Parmigiano, Rubens, Frans Hals; the striking portrait of the young *Prince Rupert of the Rhine* over the elegant marble fireplace is by Honthorst (1590-1656). The ceiling of the **Colonnade Room**, intended as the State Bedroom, is painted with fantastical *singerie* decoration borrowed from 17C contemporary pattern books and textile designs; the walls are decked with family portraits by fashionable English painters (Reynolds, Lawrence); over the fireplace is a rare painting by two Italian painters – Sassoferato and Nuzzi – the first responsible for the pious Madonna, the second for the garland of flowers that enclose her.

In the **Great Ante Room** is displayed a portrait of Rembrandt's mother reading (*c*1629), two portraits by Van Dyck and a double portrait of Francis II with Charles X of France by Clouet (1517-1572), note also the fine marine pictures by Van der Velde; the two cabinets are filled with a service of Vienna porcelain made for the 11h Earl.

The **Double Cube Room**, measuring 60ft x 30ft x 30ft, was especially designed by Inigo Jones as the sumptuously rich gold and white setting for the 4th Earl's unique collection of splendid **Van Dyck portraits** of the Herbert family and of Charles I, his Queen and their children (1635-36). It was completed by Webb (1653). The bulky furniture is largely by Thomas Chippendale and William Kent (save the 19C divan covered in fabric woven at the Wilton Carpet Factory).

It was in this room that many strategic plans were made by the likes of Eisenhower and Churchill (a frequent visitor anyway) during the Second World War when Wilton House served as the headquarters of Southern Command.

The 30ft x 30ft x 30ft **Cube Room** is decorated in white and gold, the ornament delicate in keeping with the size of the room. The generations of portraits include Henriette de Querouaille, sister of Charles II's mistress and wife of the 7th Earl by Lely, and a portrait of Van Dyck by Charles Jervas.

Garden – The house sits full square on the flat lawn which stretches southwards across to the river, marked by a Palladian Bridge and a few trees, before becoming grazing pasture beyond. The eastern front recalls the original Tudor mansion with angle pavilions and a central door beneath tall oriel windows: from here, the gardens extend along the river to a water garden complete with Japanese bridge, a west-facing stone whispering seat that catches the last rays of the setting sun, and finally, a woodland walk.

Tucked behind the tea rooms and shop is a complex of wooden climbing frames, slides and swings for children of various ages.

EXCURSIONS

Wylye Valley *Follow the A36 northwest towards Warminster.*

In Wilton the road turns north into the Wylye Valley and follows the course of the river upstream along the southern edge of Salisbury Plain.

Attractive villages, usually comprising a church, a "big" 17C or 18C house, two or three lesser houses and several cottages, nearly all stone-built, mark the route every few miles.

Stapleford – The village is notable for its castle earthworks and a **church** with a square north tower, pinnacled, demi-pinnacled and balustraded, which makes it a landmark. Inside, the pillared arcade and font are both Norman.

Steeple Langford – The village is named after the small lead-covered **broach spire** crowning its Early English church.

Regimental Badge – *1 mile before Codford St Mary (right).* The emblem of the Australian Army, the Rising Sun behind a Crown, was cut into the chalk by Australian troops during the First World War.

Anzac War Graves – *On entering Codford St Mary, turn right by the church.* The tiny cemetery is maintained by the Imperial War Graves Commission.

Heytesbury – Note the 17C style **almshouses** of brick with a pedimented centre and lantern, the Hospital of St John and St Katherine *(left side of the road).* For Warminster, see TROWBRIDGE.

*Use the **Index** to find more information about a subject mentioned in the guide – people, towns, places of interest, isolated sites, historical events or natural features...*

WIMBORNE★

Dorset – Population 6 292

Michelin Atlas p 8, 9 or Map 403 – N31

Wimborne Minster, glimpsed across the water meadows, arouses curiosity about its size, its disparate towers, its extraordinary, chequered stonework.

The town is compact and still lies largely within the bounds of its three bridges: the **Canford** on the Poole road (A341), constructed of Portland stone with three bold arches in 1813, the **Juliana**, to the west (A31), over the River Stour with eight pointed arches and refuges in the brick parapet, which dates from 1636 (widened 1844), and the **Walford** to the north (B3078) which was originally a medieval packhorse bridge over the River Allen (widened in 1802).

On Fridays, Saturdays and Sundays large bric-a-brac markets draw substantial numbers of visitors.

★ **Minster** – *45min.* The foundation dates from 1043, when Edward the Confessor established a college of secular canons on a site occupied by a Benedictine nunnery until it was sacked by the Danes in 1013. In 1318 Edward II declared the church a **royal peculiar**; in 1537, as a collegiate church, the community was suppressed by Henry VIII and the church given to the parish.

The stone is local and varies in colour from grey to pinky-brown and cream; the towers are Norman (*c*1120-80) at the crossing, ornamented with blind arcading, round-headed and lancet windows, and Perpendicular at the west end, the latter being built in 1448-64, to take a peal of bells. The church had by then taken on its present appearance and size, there having been extensions in the 13C-14C. The **quarter-jack** on the south wall of the west tower, installed in 1612, was originally a monk but since the Napoleonic wars, a grenadier, who strikes the two bells every quarter of an hour.

Interior – The Decorated outer walls of 1307-77 fit like a glove round the 12C Norman church which forms the core of the present 190ft long minster.

In the nave, the **arcades** march west from the crossing, the first bays with rounded arches, the keystones of which are decorated by a gargoyle mask (as at Malmesbury) or a pair of heads; above run the small round windows of the Norman clerestory although the actual **clerestory** is Perpendicular. In the north aisle are an **almsbox** set into the nearest pillar to the door, and a small tablet to a certain **Snodgrass**, who, with **Wardle** (in the tower), furnished Dickens with two famous names.

At the crossing, the round columns with plainly **scalloped capitals** are Norman, as is the triforium with small rounded arches and Purbeck marble columns. The **eagle lectern** is 17C.

Tower – The octagonal black Purbeck **marble font** on marble shafts is late Norman (all decoration was stripped from it during the Commonwealth); the **astronomical clock** dates from 1320, pre-Copernican times when the earth was shown as the still centre of the universe with the sun (the hour hand) revolving round the outside of the dial face, and the moon also revolving to show the lunar phases. The present works are of 1792 – the model is modern. The **royal arms** on the wall are of Charles II – a relimning at the Restoration of those of Charles I which had been painted out.

East End – The east window of three tall lights surmounted by foiled circles dates from the *c*1220 extension of the church, the *Tree of Jesse* is 15C Flemish glass. In the **sanctuary**, adjoining **chapels** and the cusp-arched **crypt** are a **brass** of King Ethelred (d 871), elder brother of King Alfred, and a number of **tombs** including Sir Edmund Uvedale (d 1606) – a coloured Renaissance figure, restored to have two left feet; the **Bankes** of Corfe Castle and Kingston Lacy; **John de Beaufort**, Duke of Somerset and his duchess – the grandparents of Henry VII; Anthony Ettricke, 17C eccentric, who is buried in a recess so that he is neither within nor without the church and who had a final date of 1693 carved ready on his coffin but lived on, as the altered numbers show, to 1703. There are also old **chests**, one Saxon with a recess in the solid oak for relics...

Chained Library ⊙ – The library, one of the earliest in England, was established in 1686; the story goes that once sufficient funds were raised, several boys from the local orphanage were apprenticed to the blacksmith and set making lengths of chain, modelled on those designed by Michelangelo for the Laurentian Library in Florence. Unusual for the times, the 240 books, bound with oak and parchment covers, besides those on theology include works on civil law, medicine, etiquette, viniculture, gardening, building and good husbandry, Eusebius' *Histories*, writings by Bede, Camden, Plato, Pliny and Plutarch. The most precious volumes are Walton's "mighty" Polyglot bible (1653-57) with sections in Hebrew, Greek, Latin, Arabic, Syriac, Persian, Gheez (Ethiopian): the first book ever sold on subscription.

High Street – The approach to the minster is one of the town's earliest streets. The early 16C **Priest's House Museum**★ ⊙ is Wimborne's most complete medieval dwelling; additions were made in the 17C and 18C. The "front" room (an 18C addition) has mid 18C panelling and contains original stock from the onetime Victorian stationer's shop here. The rear parlour with a Tudor moulded plaster ceiling and c1700 panelling reveals its older wall treatment and carved stone fireplace. The cloth-hung hall, the main room originally, has its timbering still intact. Upstairs, note the dry storage space set into the chimney breast.

The **Victorian kitchen** and the Rural Life Gallery (wattle hurdle making, thatching) provide additional interest. The long, narrow and peaceful **walled garden**, richly planted and boasting a very ancient mulberry tree, leads to a shallow mill stream. It offers a lovely view of the house's original Tudor gables.

At No 77 is the East Dorset Heritage Trust's **Heritage Centre** ⊙, which provides a recorded "guided" tour of Wimborne retold by the infamous smuggler Isaac Gulliver, and one for the Iron Age hill-fort of Badbury Rings; it also provides information on local walks, flora and fauna.

Off the High Street is the **Cornmarket and Square**, an old street and former market square overlooked by 17C-19C houses. **West Borough**, the wide street leading north out of the Square, was in the 18C the principal area of expansion and is therefore distinguished by Georgian houses.

Wimborne Minster Model Town and Gardens ⊙ – A scale model of the town in the 1950s, complete with lighting and miniature furnishings is laid out among a well-planted garden. Wendy houses for toddlers, a model electric train circuit and baskets of Lego under cover provide worthy family amusement.

Walford Mill Craft Centre ⊙ – Down by the river, a converted mill houses a number of workshops making jewellery, ceramics, weaving... Changing exhibitions organised by the Dorset Craft Guild.

EXCURSIONS

★★ **Kingston Lacy** *3 miles southeast.*

Once a royal estate, Kingston Lacy was purchased between 1632-36 by Sir John Bankes (1589-1644); he also bought the Corfe Castle estate in 1635. The house was built by his son, Sir Ralph Bankes (c1631-1677), to designs drawn by Roger Pratt in 1663 and considerably altered by Robert Brettingham for Henry Bankes after the latter's marriage in 1784.

Carlton House inlaid writing desk, Kingston Lacy

A major transformation was undertaken by his son, the eccentric William Bankes (1786-1855), who travelled extensively on the continent and in the Middle East; although he lived in exile in Italy after 1841, following a scandal, he continued to direct the work by letter. His architect was Charles Barry, who encased the compact red-brick mansion in Chilmark stone, installed a grand staircase and added a *porte cochère* to the new entrance at ground level on the north front. The family collection of paintings, one of the earliest made by a member of the gentry to survive, was enriched by William. He himself was responsible for much of the interior decoration, commissioning many ornamental features, particularly those in *biancone*, a hard stone-coloured marble from Bassano in Italy, so suitable for crisp high relief carving.

Further alterations were made at the turn of the century; in 1981 the whole estate was left to the National Trust which has carried out extensive restoration work.

House ⏱ – *1 hour*. The **entrance hall**, created at basement level by William Bankes, is supported on Doric columns with a decorated ceiling: the carved marble tables are Italian, the bronze cranes 19C Japanese. Beyond the screen is a chimneypiece bearing the Bankes coat of arms, flanked by two Carrara marble radiator covers, with bronze insets: the one on the right shows the original Kingston Hall above the coat of arms.

Barry was delighted with the Carrara **marble staircase** which turned out "far beyond" what he had expected. Half way up is the **loggia**, from where the view extends over "Dutch" parterre planted with golden yews to the great tall Lebanese cedars beyond. The **bronze figures** by Marochetti (1853) represent Sir John Bankes, Lady Mary Bankes and Charles I; below the king the siege of Corfe Castle is shown in relief.

The **library** was designed after 1784 by Brettingham for Henry Bankes, whose portrait by Batoni, who painted many an Englishman on the Grand Tour in Rome, hangs on the window wall; Sir John Bankes is portrayed in his judge's robes. Above the shelves hangs a series of portraits of his children by **Sir Peter Lely**. Over the fireplace are the keys of Corfe Castle granted to Lady Mary Bankes in recognition of her courageous defence of the castle when it was besieged by the Parliamentary forces in the Civil War. The "Persian design" carpet (1819) is from Axminster.

The **drawing room**, typically Edwardian in character, was refurnished by the late Mr Bankes' mother on her marriage in 1897; the walls were hung with rose damask. Some features are older: the 18C chimneypiece and doors; the stencil for the Bankes motto on the frieze came from Venice in 1846. There are several family portraits by **Van Dyck**, **Romney** and **Lawrence**. Among the **enamel miniatures** painted on copper by Henry Bone (1755-1834) are portraits of Elizabeth I and several members of the Bankes family circle.

Owing to a fire in 1910 little has remained of Barry's work in the **dining room**: the ceiling, the crests above the windows, the walnut shutters and the boxwood doors which were carved in Venice (1849-1853) from original models selected and arranged by William Bankes. The room was repanelled in oak and cedar from the home park. The dominant feature is the painting of *The Judgement of Solomon* attributed to Sebastiano del Piombo, although William purchased it as by Giorgione. Below it stands a late 16C Italian cedarwood coffer. To the right of the organ, moved here from its original position in the saloon over the doors to the drawing room, hangs an 18C English tapestry, probably made in Soho; the Bankes family silver is displayed on a sideboard bought in Soho in 1786. The William IV dining chairs are made of mahogany and covered in giraffe hide. The four tapestry runners are after Carraci; the deeply carved *nature morte* panels by Grinling Gibbons, dark oak chests Continental.

The original flat ceiling and gallery in the **saloon** were removed in Henry Bankes' time when the painted barrel vault, cornice and frieze, then in fashion locally, were introduced. The walls are hung with the family collection of paintings: *The Holy Family with St John* by **Giulio Romano**, once in Charles I's collection and bearing the royal cipher on the back, in a frame designed by William portraying the four previous owners; **Rubens'** portraits of two Grimaldi sisters; *The Four Elements* by **Jan Bruegel the Elder**; portrait of Francesco Savorgnan delle Torre by **Titian**: portrait of the First Earl of Portland after Van Dyck; an Italianate landscape by Berchem, owned by Sir Ralph Bankes; (his uncle) *Mr Altham as a Hermit* is attributed to Salvator Rosa. The oil sketch of William Bankes on the table in the north window is by Sir George Hayter. The lustre, the pelmets and the Savonnerie carpet were supplied by Henry Bankes; William provided most of the furniture: Anglo-Indian ebony seats covered with Berlin floral embroidery, four 18C colonial Dutch "burgomeister" chairs of ebony or satinwood, a pair of Louis XIV Boulle pedestals, a pair of Italian giltwood candelabra set in marble niches designed by William, the centre tables made in the 19C from 17C walnut cabinet doors; a Charles II marquetry box mounted in the 19C.

Spanish Room: William Bankes spent 17 years creating his "Golden Room" as a setting for the Spanish paintings he had collected during the Peninsular War: **Velasquez'** portrait of Cardinal Massimi (and *Las Meninas*). Although the paintings are uneven in quality, Bankes was ahead of fashion in his taste and devoted much thought to their framing and hanging. The **ceiling** (*c*1609) came from a Venetian palazzo, as did the **gilded tooled leather** covering the walls; the Cosmati-style fireplace is also Italian. The pearwood doors, painted with Seasons, are Bankes' own design. The carpet is an Axminster bought in 1820.

Both the Venetian bed, carved in holly, and the ceiling in the **state bedroom** were incomplete when William died. Note the Dutch walnut seawood marquetry cabinet.

Additional rooms on the floor above include the nursery and spare bedrooms: more family portraits and miscellaneous furniture.

Billiard Room – The important collection of ancient Egyptian artefacts amassed by William Bankes during his two expeditions to the Nile in 1815 and 1818 (the second with the seasoned tomb-robber Giovanni Belzoni) are largely housed here.

Gardens ⊘ – The terrace with its furnishings, which was introduced by William Bankes, leads down to smooth lawns and the pink granite **obelisk** discovered by William at Philae in Egypt in 1815. It was finally erected in 1829, the Duke of Wellington laying the foundation stone. The Greek inscription, which helped in the deciphering of the hieroglyphs, commemorates a decree exempting priests from taxation. The great **cedars** were planted by the Duke of Wellington, Edward VIII and the Kaiser. The landscaped park with a "wilderness", now the Fernery, was created in the 18C to replace the original 17C formal gardens.

Stapehill ⊘

Signposted off the B3073 Wimborne to Ferndown Road.

The Cistercian abbey, founded in the early 1800s to provide shelter for a number of Trappist nuns fleeing the terror of the French Revolution, now provides workshop premises for a number of craftsmen (candlemakers, jewellers, toymakers, blacksmith). Outbuildings have been adapted to accommodate an extensive collection of superseded farm equipment and a broad range of farm animals for children to feed, ride and pat. Newly landscaped gardens and a temperate house appeal to gardeners and plant lovers.

Cranborne Manor Gardens ⊘

18 miles north on B3078. Note: limited opening times.

The tall house, a former royal hunting lodge in Cranborne Chase, took on something of its present appearance in the early 17C when Robert Cecil, first Earl of Salisbury and Chief Minister to Elizabeth I, received the manor from James I whose accession he had helped to secure. Today, the house *(closed to the public)* continues to be lived in by Viscount Cranborne, elder son of the Marquis of Salisbury.

The garden, including avenues of fine trees, was laid out by Mounten Jennings and **John Tradescant** (1570-1638), designer and plantsman. Among the several areas enclosed by old walls and high hedges are an Elizabethan **knot garden** and a rare Jacobean **Mount Garden** where three low, circular grass tiers surround a central mound while outer beds with old-fashioned roses, peonies and foxgloves fill the spandrels. 20C additions continue the theme of enclosed gardens.

YEOVIL

Somerset – Population 28 317
Michelin Atlas p 8 or Map 403 – M31

The bustling town, the base of Westland Aircraft, takes its name from the River Yeo which marks the boundary of Somerset and Dorset. Antique remains, including a middle Bronze Age torc and a substantial Roman villa indicate the area has enjoyed continued settlement since earliest times. At the centre of the dairy farming industry, Yeovil was an important glove and leather centre from the 14C when gloving was a cottage industry, the skins then coming from sheep on the Polden and Quantock Hills – there is still a Glovers' Walk in the town. Later, it became known for its flax which was turned into webbing (Crewkerne) and canvas sails (Coker), notably during the Napoleonic Wars.

Big increases in the population came after 1853, when the railway link with Taunton was opened. The **buildings**, therefore, are principally 19C-20C with a few scattered 18C-19C Georgian houses and older inns, most notably in **Princess Street**, the **High Street** (two old inns), **Silver Street** (inn sign on a fine wrought-iron bracket). The brick **Church House**, west of the church, is also Georgian.

Market days: Fridays; cattle: Monday and Friday (in designated area); craft: Tuesday.

★ **St John the Baptist** ⊙ – The parish church stands tall upon the central hillock around which the town grew up, the 90ft **tower** a dominant landmark since it was erected in the late 14C. Severe and stoutly buttressed, it rises from a plain doorway and five-light window through an opening and a belfry bay to a high, pierced parapet.

The church itself, an early Perpendicular, much pinnacled structure, was entirely constructed of grey lias, with Ham Hill stone dressings, between 1380 and 1400. All the **windows** – there are 18 – have five lights and measure 9ft wide by 20ft high, from which the church has come to be known as the "lantern of the west". Note also the dragon and other savage gargoyles.

The **roofs**, above the tall, slim, clustered arcades have retained their original **bosses**, a strange collection of human faces and animal masks, many of the men, in the aisles especially, apparently in full African tribal warpaint, possibly inspired by the travellers' tales of returned crusaders.

Below the chancel is a **crypt** with rib vaulting resting on a central **octagonal pier**; it was once used as a charnel house and is approached from the chancel through an ogee-arched doorway decorated with a wreathed skull.

The **lectern** and **font** are both 15C, the former one of only four to remain from 1450. It stands 6ft 6in high, has lion feet and a triangular-section reading desk engraved with the figure of a friar, whose face was obliterated by the Puritans in 1565.

Museum of South Somerset ⊙ – The museum is housed in an 18C coach house of mellow brick with Ham stone angle quoins and Venetian upper windows.

On the ground floor are arranged a series of tableaux about the local industries: leather and gloving, flax and hemp production, engineering and stone working, newspaper printing, and a **Petter oil engine**, the invention of a local man in 1895. Informative display boards relate the importance of these activities to the local economy through the ages.

Upstairs are displayed a miscellany of objects ranging from antiquities recovered from the Roman site at Westland, discovered in 1823, Lufton and Ilchester; a bequest of 18C-19C **glassware**, **costume** and **firearms**.

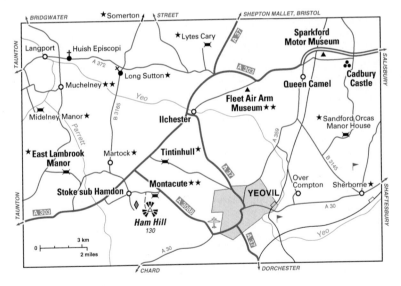

EXCURSIONS

A303 Ilchester to Cadbury Castle

Ilchester – The triangular **green** with its Tuscan column and ball finial erected in the 18C, the **square** overlooked by Georgian houses – among which is the **town hall** – and by the **parish church** with a 13C fortress-like octagonal tower, hint at the town's long and varied fortunes.

Its importance began with the Romans who made it a cantonal capital, called Lendinis, at the junction of the Fosse Way and the road from Dorchester; the Saxons maintained it as a centre and by 950 it had become a royal burgh. In the 11C-12C it possessed a flourishing market and a mint; by 1327 it had taken over from Somerton as the county town, a position it maintained until the 19C when Taunton took its place.

★★ Fleet Air Arm Museum, Yeovilton ⊘ *Signposted off the B3151*.

Immediately adjacent to the active Royal Naval Air Station where Sea Harriers and Sea King helicopters are put through their daily paces, the museum is dedicated to aviation in the Royal Navy from its earliest beginnings to the present day, with over 40 aircraft, paintings and photographs, medals, uniforms, models, artefacts and memorabilia on display. Recommended routes, lasting up to four hours, are indicated at the entrance to assist visitors in making their way through the four halls. **World War I** and the interwar years (1920s-1930s) features such historic planes as the Sopwith Pup and Camel in a Western Front diorama; supporting galleries outline some of the Royal Navy Air Service activities at home and overseas during the Great War. The Fleet Air Arm **World War II** campaign is related in association with the biplane torpedo bomber and the Fairey Swordfish

> **Roger Bacon** (c1214-94), born in Ilchester, grew to become a leading philosopher and scientist: inventor of spectacles, Bacon foretold the advent of telescopes, aeroplanes, submarines and ocean liners.

which, incredibly, flew throughout the war. Here too are the naval version of the Spitfire, Seafire and the four important American Lent-lease aircraft: Wildcat, Hellcat, Corsair and Avenger which the FAA flew from its armoured aircraft carriers in the **Pacific War**. An original **Japanese Kamikaze** aircraft hangs above a display dedicated to this particular brutal aspect of war. A broad range of artists' impressions are provided by paintings and drawings.

The Royal Navy created the **aircraft carrier**, and this story introduces a vivid and atmospheric recreation of life on a major warship in the 1970s: animation is provided by high tec special effects as 11 aircraft (including the first actual Sea Vampire to make a jet landing on such a flight deck and the supersonic Phantom fleet fighter of the 1970s) await instructions.

The West Country has made major contributions to aeronautical technology, among which the production of **Concorde** and the **Harrier jump-jet**: the development of both is retold in the last exhibition hall where the original British-built Concorde 002 may be boarded to view its decks of test equipment and instrument gauges, and where early prototypes of the Harrier may be compared to the Flying Bedstead.

The evolution of the Harrier jet and the British prototype of **Concorde 002** fitted with test equipment, a Super X Flight Simulator *(additional charge)* provides an insight into the technical demands on pilots.

Peripheral displays of models, interactive panels, memorabilia and photographs; about the Wrens and the auxiliary services; training, reconnaissance and rescue illustrate the ongoing role of the Royal Navy's airborne section.

For details of flying displays - routine and training most days, acrobatic and breathtaking on special occasions: call on number given in Practical Information section or check notices advertised locally.

Queen Camel - The small village possesses a parish church with a severe 14C west tower which rises to battlements and pinnacles, overtopped by the stair turret.

Continue along A359 to Sparkford.

Haynes Motor Museum, Sparkford ⊘ - Almost 300 vintage, veteran and classic cars and motorcycles, racing cars, military vehicles, children's pedal cars, (Sinclair C5) and bikes are exhibited here; a theatre shows old motoring films. The international collection ranges from the more modest (Mini, Messerschmitt) to the most extravagant (Model J Duesenberg Derham Tourster Rolls Royce, Lanchester) by way of Italian sportscars (Lamborghini Countach, Ferrari Boxer), American models (Chevrolet Corvette), British favourites (Jaguar E Type, Aston Martin DB4)... Also displayed are memorable cartoons, illustrations, signs, insignia and paraphernalia. Children's adventure playground.

Take the by-road east towards Chapel Cross and Cadbury Castle.

Cadbury Castle - The castle with commanding views★★ crowned a hilltop 500ft above sea-level. Nothing remains on the 18-acre site, which was excavated in 1966-70.

Cadbury, which began as a prehistoric settlement, was converted in the Iron Age into a hillfort. It was still occupied at the time of the Roman invasion in AD 43 and was re-fortified in the late 5C.

The names of the River Cam to the west and Queen Camel have given rise to a belief that the Battle of Camlan was fought nearby, that the builder could only have been King Arthur, that Cadbury was, therefore, the fabled **Camelot**.

East Coker

St Michael's – The main building to grace this picturesque Somerset village is the church: a late 18C tower replaces the original 14C Perpendicular one which, unusually, sits at the east end.

Inside, the chancel is misaligned with the nave and the stained glass windows, smashed by the Puritans, replaced by plain ones.

In the northwest corner rest the ashes of the poet TS Eliot (1888-65) who chose to be commemorated at East Coker because it had been where his ancestors had come from before emigrating to America in the mid 17C. The author of *The Waste Land*, *Old Possum's Book of Practical Cats*, *Murder in the Cathedral* and *The Cocktail Party* attained the Order of Merit and Nobel Prize for Literature.

Montacute

Montacute House, the village and its Perpendicular parish church were all built of Ham Hill stone; the tawny-ochre and grey-brown colour casts a warm glow upon the houses, large and small, and the inns and small bay-windowed shops which surround the Borough, or large village square.

Montacute House

Rupert Truman/The National Trust Photo Library

★★ **Montacute House** ⊙ – *75min*. The Elizabethan H shaped mansion of three storeys was built in 1597-1601 for Sir Edward Phelips, a successful lawyer, Speaker of the House of Commons (1604) and Master of the Rolls (1611), probably by William Arnold, the designer of Cranborne Manor and Dunster Castle. Nearly two centuries later, in 1786, Sir Edward's namesake and his wife attended a "Sale of the Materials of Clifton House then Pulling Down" and bought "The Porch, Arms, Pillars and all the Ornamental Stone of the Front to be Transferred to the Intended West Front of Montacute".

The **early house**, true to the Elizabethan style, rose majestically and symmetrically on either side of a porched entrance front, through tiers of transomed windows to an open balustrade, obelisks and small, rounded gables. Flanking either side were taller, shaped gables and columnar chimneys; bay windows gave subtle relief to the lower walls. In deference to Renaissance fashion, there were a modest entablature and niches filled with nine roughly carved worthies in Roman armour. The rear, west face, between advanced wings, was plain with pointed gables and square chimney stacks.

The "Intended West Front" – The front was a key part of 18C Edward Phelips' plan to reverse the house: he determined that instead of entering from the east through the balustraded forecourt with its twin pavilions with ogee roofs crowned by open stone spheres, a new approach should be made from the west, which, however, needed to be dignified for the role – hence his attendance at the Clifton House sale.

The Ham stone from Clifton matched perfectly. Phelips used his purchase as a shallow infilling between the advanced wings to produce a new west front. On the new **porch** at the centre he implanted his own arms, on either side fluted and spiral shafting, pierced balustrading, a Noah's ark of heraldic animal finials... Land, farms, furniture and possessions were accumulated and sold as the Phelips family fortunes rose or declined. From 1911 Montacute was let – the most famous of the tenants being **Lord Curzon** (1915-25) who entrusted the redecoration to the novelist Elinor Glyn. In 1931, in a sad state of dereliction, the house was purchased by the National Trust.

Ground floor – The original east doorway opens into the screens passage. On the left is the **Dining Room** which was created by Lord Curzon out of the old buttery from which dishes were once carried in ritualistic procession through the Great Hall and up the stairs to the formal dining room *(see Library below)*. The Elizabethan-style chimneypiece bears the **Phelips arms** of 1599; the tapestry of a knight against a *millefleurs* background is Flemish (Tournai); the walnut refectory table, 16C Italian. Among the portraits are Mary, Queen of Scots, and Robert Dudley, Earl of Leicester.

The **Great Hall**, the communal living room until after the Restoration, retains from the 16C its panelling, the stone screen with rusticated archways and pillars with ram's head and acanthus leaf capitals and a roughly carved crest, and the heraldic glass in the window which includes the arms of Queen Elizabeth and Sir Edward Phelips. The **Skimmington frieze**, a 17C plaster relief at the far end of the hall, shows a hen-pecked husband taking a drink while minding the baby and later being paraded around the village astride a pole.

The **Parlour** retains its original Ham stone fireplace, Elizabethan panelling and frieze of nursery animals. Among the 18C furniture are a Gobelins tapestry of 1788, *The Hunter*, a settee and chairs with needlework covers, a giltwood table, Gothick long-case clock and a centre table of beautiful simplicity by Thomas Chippendale the Younger.

The **Drawing Room** contains chairs covered in red damask made in 1753 by Walter Linnell for Sir Richard Hoare *(see STOURHEAD)*, giltwood side-tables with eagle supports, a George I walnut card-table, a Boulle brass and tortoise-shell chest, and Chinese porcelain lion dogs and birds.

The **staircase**, of which each tread is a single 7ft block of stone, rises by straight flights around a stone core – the intermediary stage between spiral stairs and Jacobean wooden staircases built around open wells. The tapestries are 15C-16C.

First floor – **Lord Curzon's Room** contains besides his lordship's bath neatly stowed in a "Jacobean" cupboard, a 17C overmantel of *King David at Prayer*, an 18C bed, a Dutch oak drop-leaf table and an 18C japanned skeleton mirror.

The **Crimson Room**, so-called since the 19C when red flock wallpaper replaced the tapestries which once hung below the plaster frieze, is furnished with a sumptuous oak four-poster carved with the arms of James I.

The **Library**, formerly the dining room and the destination of the dishes brought in procession from the distant kitchens, is chiefly remarkable for its brilliant heraldic glass – a tourney of 42 shields displaying the Phelips arms, those of the sovereign and, by way of a compliment, those of Phelips' Somerset neighbours and friends at court. Other features from the time when this was a stateroom are the monumental Portland stone mantelpiece and plaster frieze, the Jacobean inner porch, the 19C moulded plaster ceiling and bookcases. The library steps date from 1770.

Top floor – The 172ft **Long Gallery** lit with oriels at either end, occupies the entire floor: it is the longest in existence. Today it provides a perfect setting, through 90 **portraits** (on loan from the National Portrait Gallery), for a panoply of **Tudor England** and the early Jacobean Age.

In the main gallery contemporaries, friends and rivals stand together, kings and queens *(centre bay)* and full-length portraits of Lord Burghley, James I as a boy with a falcon, Prince Henry, Charles I as a boy, Francis Bacon, and Philip Herbert,

4th Earl of Pembroke, who was responsible for so much at Wilton House. Five dependent rooms are filled with the personalities of the Reign of Henry VIII, Elizabeth and her Court, The Elizabethan Age, The Early Stuart Court and The Jacobean Age.

Gardens – The formal layout of the gardens is designed to enhance that of the house: lush green lawns and yew hedges provide a fine foreground to the warm hues of the Ham stone. Colour is provided by changing borders and the rose garden.

Ham Hill

The hill (425ft) is a notable landmark and commands **views**★★ of the rolling countryside for miles around. It was once crowned by a prehistoric hillfort but its fame is due to the **quarry** from which limestone has been cut to build churches, beautiful houses and small cottages throughout Somerset and the southwest. The stone varies in colour from creamy white and grey to yellow, gold and brown ochre depending on the ferrous deposits in the ground. After more than a thousand years the quarries are exhausted and stone is now found only for repairs.

Continue half a mile along A3088; turn left and then right.

Stoke sub Hamdon – The village, which is in two parts and built almost entirely of Ham Hill stone, has an attractive collection of 17C-18C houses and cottages. The **parish church**★ stands amidst trees near a stream at the bottom of the hill. A mixed building, it dates from the 12C-16C: the **tower**, on the north side, is 13C at the base, 15C above, with battlements, a cornice and gargoyles; the chancel and nave in Ham stone, comprising the Norman church, were erected *c*1100 – note the corbel tables along the chancel walls; the north transept was added *c*1225, the south in 1300; the two-storey, north porch is *c*1325 though the doorway is Norman.

Inside, the **chancel arch** in dark Ham stone is carved with three orders of zigzag and lozenge decoration above small columns. Note the Norman **font** with cable mouldings and frieze, Jacobean pulpit and **hour-glass** and 17C **communion rail balusters**.

★ Tintinhull House Garden

The **house**, comprising the present east front with a cross wing at the south end and only one room deep, was built as a farmhouse *c*1600. In 1630 Thomas Napper rebuilt the south wing, completing the gable with an **initialled datestone**; nearly a century later his grandson increased and reversed the house to its present appearance with a new **west front** and a **walled forecourt** which he intended to be the formal entrance.

This 18C pedimented front in Bath stone, dignified by giant pilasters and with a corresponding pedimented doorway, nevertheless retains such 17C touches as stone mullions and transoms in some of the windows.

The two-acre **garden** ⊙ is so planned that borders, flowering and foliage trees, and shrubs and colour schemes can be viewed from a number of angles and so planted that there is something to enjoy in all seasons.

The individually enclosed, formal gardens are laid out in line with the west front: the **Eagle Court** (named after the birds on the piers marking the 18C forecourt), the **Azalea Garden**, and the **Fountain Garden** where white flowers stand star-like against outlining yew hedges.

Off the view line are a Cedar Lawn, Pool and Kitchen Gardens.

The planting is arranged so that colours contrast, are massed or shade from the darkest to the palest tone, texture is varied with flowers and foliage, outlines with climbers, trees and shrubs, the exotic and the everyday...

For Martock, East Lambrook Manor and Barrington Court Gardens, see CHARD.

Jersey : Mont Orgueil Castle, Gorey

Channel Islands

The bailiwicks

For many people the name of the Channel Islands conjures up a northern mini paradise providing a low-duty haven for the very rich or sun and sand for the care-free holiday-maker. To frequent visitors and residents alike, the pervading air encourages a care-free, easy-going existence and an enhanced feel good factor. The islands enjoy a mild climate that nurtures spring flowers and semi-tropical plants, long sandy beaches alternate with wild cliffs, quiet country lanes meander between traditional granite houses.

Although the Channel Islands have been attached to the English crown since 1066, they lie much nearer to the French coast and were largely French-speaking until this century. Under their apparent Englishness lie a thousand years of Norman tradition and sturdy independence.

Threats of invasion – Early invaders left impressive Neolithic remains: **menhirs** and **dolmens**. In 933 the islands were annexed by the Normans and attached to the English Crown by William the Conqueror. When King John had to cede Normandy in 1204 to the French, the Channel Islanders chose to remain loyal to the English Crown in exchange for special privileges: one outcome was an independent parliament – although in matters of defence and international relations the islands are subject to decisions made by the Home Office in London. Despite this, the French made repeated attempts over the centuries to regain the islands. In 1483 a Papal Bull of Neutrality was issued which remained in force until 1689.

During the English Civil War Jersey upheld the Royalist cause while Guernsey sided with Cromwell; this is supposed to be the basis of the traditional rivalry between the two major islands. Later, the rise of Napoleon brought the threat of invasion

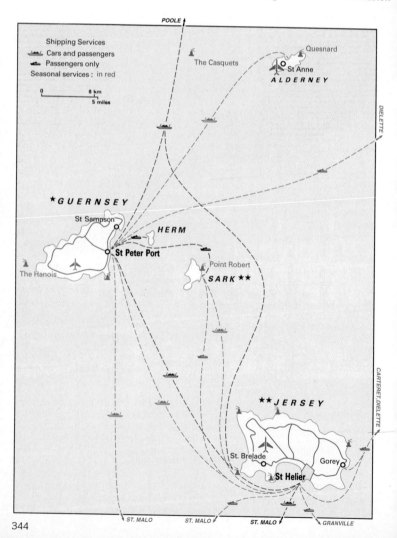

and so defensive towers, similar to the later Martello towers, were built along the coasts. In the mid 19C fresh fears of French invasion brought more fortifications, particularly in Alderney.

German Occupation – The Channel Islands were finally invaded in 1940 and occupied by the Germans for five years: the only British territory to fall to the enemy. This was regarded by islanders who had long pledged their loyalty to the Crown as a symbolic act by Hitler. The occupation brought hardship: the people were completely isolated save for news picked up by clandestine radios, there were deportations to Germany, shortages of food and clothing throughout the winter of 1944 brought occupier and islanders close to starvation for even after the Allies had taken hold of the Normandy coast and St Malo, the port used by the Germans to support the Channel Islands, had been surrendered, it was not until 9 May 1945 that British Liberation Task Force 135 arrived. Meanwhile, massive concrete fortifications, built by the slave labour of the Todt Organisation as part of Hitler's impregnable Atlantic Wall, were constructed; these can still be seen in places. Fortunately, they were never tested, simply by-passed by the Normandy landings.

Constitution – The Channel Islands are divided into the **Bailiwick of Jersey**, which includes two rocky islets – the Minquiers and the Ecrehous – and the **Bailiwick of Guernsey**, which includes Alderney, Sark and Brecqhou, Herm and Jethou. The original Norman laws and systems enshrined in the first charters granted by King John in the 13C have been renewed by subsequent monarchs, although modifications were introduced this century to separate the judiciary from the legislature.

> ### Clameur de Haro
> The ancient legal remedy which is still in force is thought to invoke Rollo, a 10C Norse chieftain. A victim of wrongdoing must kneel down in the presence of two witnesses and say "*Haro, haro, haro, à l'aide, mon Prince, on me fait tort*" (Help, my Prince, someone is doing me wrong). This must be followed by the recital of the Lord's Prayer in French. The wrong-doer must then desist until a court ruling has been obtained.

Religion – Christianity seems to have been introduced in the 6C by Celtic saints from Brittany, Cornwall and Wales. Originally the parishes were attached to the diocese of Coutances in Normandy and remained so until Elizabeth I transferred them to the See of Winchester in 1568.

At the Reformation, **Calvinism** (Reformed Protestantism) took hold, a natural choice given the linguistic links with France, boosted by the influx of Huguenot refugees fleeing persecution on the Continent. **Anglicanism** was eventually introduced at the Restoration in 1660 but the English language was not used for church services until this century. **Methodism** was preached in the islands by John Wesley himself and has always had a strong following, particularly in Guernsey.

Language – English is now the universal language of the islands, as the native tongue, a dialect of Norman-French the language of William the Conqueror slowly dies out. In Jersey and Guernsey, societies for its preservation exist which trace the regional variations in vocabulary and pronunciation.

Livelihood – The Channel Islands (76 sq miles), which are composed of fertile granite plateaux sloping to open sand dunes, lie west of the Cherbourg peninsula and south of the main shipping lanes in the English Channel. The Gulf Stream and the southerly latitude ensure a mild climate.

Until the 18C fishing and agriculture were the main activities. In the Middle Ages large quantities of cod and conger eel were exported to England and Normandy to be eaten on the many days in the medieval church calendar when meat was forbidden. The fish were split and dried on small sticks (*perches*) in remote places: the smell was reported as being most unpleasant. The trade died when the Newfoundland fisheries were established in the 16C but the practice is recalled in *eperquerie*, a common place name in the Channel Islands. Following heavy storms, seaweed (*vraic* – pronounced "rack") was collected from the beaches to be used as fertiliser and fuel. On the higher exposed ground were kept large flocks of sheep; indeed the words Jersey and Guernsey have entered the English language to mean woollen cloth or garment, reminiscent of times (17C) when people engaged in knitting often neglected the harvest.

In the 18C huge fortunes were made from privateering under Letters of Marque (*see* INTRODUCTION: The Sea), and ship-building flourished. In the 19C granite was exported in vast quantities for road-making and construction work. Cattle too, usually known on the mainland as "Alderneys" – probably because this was the last port of call for ships returning to Poole or Southampton – came to be in great demand for the high butter fat content of their milk; now only Jerseys and Guernseys are pure bred.

20C local economy – Being self-governed, the Channel Islanders benefit from a VAT exempt economy and lower rates of income tax; coins, bank-notes and postage stamps are issued locally but are not legal tender elsewhere. The islands have therefore become a tax haven for British citizens and developed a buoyant industry in financial services including offshore banking, trust management and insurance. Additional income, although small, is generated by international collectors of coinage and the highly decorative special issues of stamps.

Tourism – Blessed by better weather than mainland Britain, the Channel Islands have developed facilities to attract sailors to their marinas, surfers and swimmers to their beaches, bird-watchers, walkers and cyclists to the unspoilt rural countryside. Trade in imported luxury items is also boosted by the minimal duty levied on such merchandise.

Agriculture – Farming still plays an important part in the local economy, reducing, where possible, the needs for importing basic foodstuffs and maintaining a supply to mainland Britain of early vegetables (potatoes, tomatoes, grapes) and cut flowers. A characteristic feature of the islands are the "honesty boxes" along the road advertising fresh, home-grown produce.

Wrecks and lighthouses – The Channel Islands are surrounded by extensive offshore reefs and rocky islets. The coast, together with strong tides, treacherous currents and fog, make these seas some of the most hazardous in Britain claiming many ships through the ages. Among those documented are a Roman galley which sank off St Peter Port; the *White Ship* carrying the heir to the English throne which foundered on the Casquets in 1119; HMS *Victory*, which went down on the Casquets in 1774 with the loss of 1 000 men; the *Liverpool*, the largest sailing ship wrecked in the Channel Islands, which ran aground off Corblets Bay in a fog in 1902; the *Briseis*, which struck a reef off Vazon Bay in 1937 with 7 000 casks of wine on board; the *Orion*, an oil rig mounted on an ocean-going barge, which ran aground off Grand Rocques in Guernsey in 1978. There are now four lighthouses owned by Trinity House in the Channel Islands.

The earliest to be built was the one signalling the **Casquets** (1723); then followed the three towers, known as St Peter, St Thomas and Donjon, which stood 30ft high and were lit by coal fires. In 1770 oil lamps were introduced, and in 1818 revolving lights which had to be wound every two hours. Today, the main light is placed 120ft above sea-level with a range of 17 miles in clear weather. The story of the lightkeeper's daughter, who found life on Alderney too noisy, is beautifully told by Swinburne in his poem *Les Casquettes*.

The **Hanois Lighthouse** was built in 1862 on the treacherous Hanois Reef. The first approaches for a light were made to Trinity House in 1816 but 43 years passed before the decision to build was taken. The tower of Cornish granite is 32ft in diameter at the base, rising to 117ft above sea-level.

Quesnard Light (1912) on Alderney and **Point Robert** (1913) on Sark are sited on land rather than offshore and can be visited. Point Robert is most unusual in that the light is mounted above the buildings for stores and accommodation which cling to the cliff face like a Greek monastery.

Channel Island Cattle

The distinctive pale biscuit coloured, petite, long-lashed doe-eyed, black nosed Jersey cow *(illustrated)* is largely the result of a careful breeding programme undertaken by Colonel John Le Couteur in the 1830s after the importation of foreign stock was banned in 1789. In 1866 a herd book was started listing

by name the animals which were selected on the basis of their looks and high milk yield, so rich in butterfat. In winter Jersey cattle are often protected from the cold by special woollen coats.

The Guernsey cow is heftier than the Jersey: her colouring varies from a dark red to a pale honey colour, her face distinguished by a pink nose and, occasionally, by a white scar. Her milk is a distinctive yellow colour during the summer when she is put out to pasture. Cross-breeding with imported strains ensures faster production for beef stock only; the true Guernsey bloodstock has been contained since 1819. Still today, cattle may be seen in fields tethered to a post with a chain around the horns – this is a more economical way of controlling grazing although far more labour-intensive as the animals have to be watered regularly.

D. Mar/EXPLORER

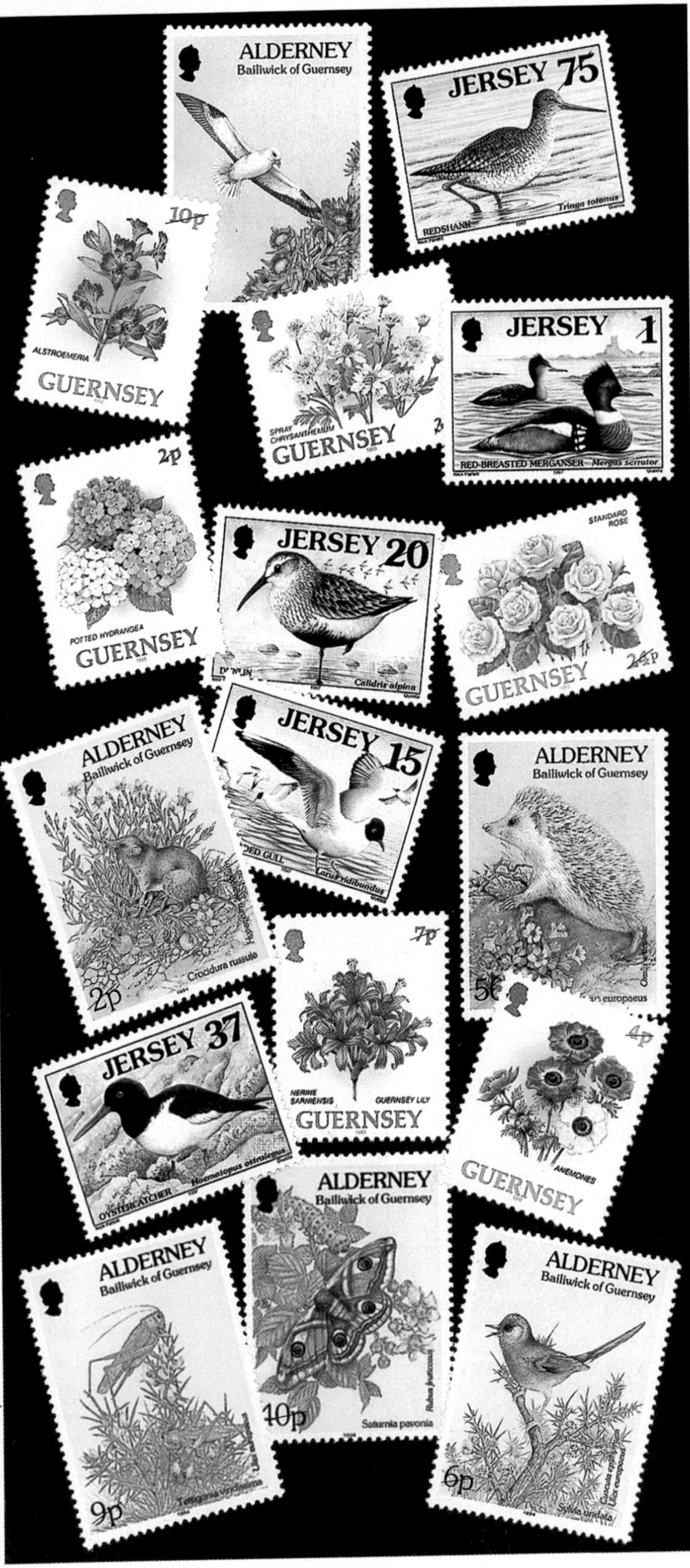

ALDERNEY
Baillwick of Guernsey

JERSEY 75
REDSHANK · Tringa totanus

10p
ALSTROEMERIA
GUERNSEY

SPRAY
CHRYSANTHEMUM
GUERNSEY

JERSEY 1
RED-BREASTED MERGANSER — Mergus serrator

2p
POTTED HYDRANGEA
GUERNSEY

JERSEY 20
DUNLIN · Calidris alpina

STANDARD
ROSE
GUERNSEY

ALDERNEY
Baillwick of Guernsey
Crocidura russula
2p

JERSEY 15
BLACK-HEADED GULL · Larus ridibundus

ALDERNEY
Baillwick of Guernsey
Erinaceus europaeus
5p

JERSEY 37
OYSTERCATCHER · Haematopus ostralegus

7p
NERINE
SARNIENSIS · Guernsey Lily
GUERNSEY

4p
ANEMONES
GUERNSEY

ALDERNEY
Baillwick of Guernsey
9p

10p
Saturnia pavonia

ALDERNEY
Baillwick of Guernsey
6p

JERSEY★★

Population 85 150
Michelin Atlas p 5 or Map 403

Jersey is the largest of the islands (45sq miles-116sqkm); it measures 9 by 5 miles and lies only 12 miles from the coast of France. The visitor is greeted by a charming combination of Englishness tinged with Norman French tradition. Local features echo not only Normandy but also Cornwall.

Owing to Jersey's proximity to the Gulf Stream, it enjoys a mild climate and is thick with flowers in spring and summer. **Victor Hugo**, who spent 3 years in Jersey (1852-55) before moving to Guernsey, was enchanted: "It possesses a unique and exquisite beauty. It is a garden of flowers cradled by the sea. Woods, meadows and gardens seem to mingle with the rocks and reefs in the sea".

The island is ringed by several circular defensive towers, built in the 18C and 19C and similar to the Martello towers on the south coast of England.

Local economy – Jersey is roughly rectangular in shape. The sparsely populated north coast is formed of steep pink granite cliffs opening here and there into a sandy bay; along the rest of the shoreline the retreating tide reveals great sandy bays (St Aubin, St Brelade, St Ouen, St Catherine, Grouville, St Clement).

Historically, agriculture has long sustained the islanders: wheat, and rye, turnips and parsnips, four-horned sheep supplying wool for the famous Jersey stockings and knitwear (17C), apples for cider (18C) eating grapes grown under glass and famous Doyenne de Comice pears. Today, the mild climate continues to favour the cultivation of flowers (daffodils, freesias, carnations and lavender) and vegetables for export (potatoes including the famous Jersey Royal, cabbages, broccoli and tomatoes which became more lucrative than apples). Some crops are grown in the open fields, others under glass. Unique to Jersey is the giant cabbage (Brassica oleracae longata) which grows up to 10ft tall.

As traditional industries such as boat building, knitting and fishing have dwindled, more lucrative businesses have developed in financial services and tourism: industries which sustain the highly competitive young residents who have benefited from an excellent local primary and secondary education.

Recreation – The island offers a broad range of outdoor activities: besides walking and cycling, the most popular are swimming, fishing, botanising and bird-watching.

The **southwest coast** is good for fishing (garfish, grey mullet, pollack, wrasse, conger, bass and mackerel) and blessed with beaches that are less prone to heavy swell from the Atlantic; in sheltered spots, the cliffs provide a haven for oxeye daisies, thrift, sea campion, sheepsbit scabious, spotted rock roses and for such birds as gulls, shags, oystercatchers and ravens. The **west coast** consists of a long stretch of firm beach flanked by rocky outcrops: fish are swept in from the open sea with the tides and currents, notably bass and wrasse. The landward side of the coastal road is a conservation area where green lizards bask among hundreds of different plants, watched by kestrels and skylarks. The **northern coastline** is probably the most dramatic with 300 to 400ft cliffs plunging into the sea: the deep water is good for wrasse, bass, garfish, black bream and conger and the cliff paths are littered with wild flowers which attract a profusion of butterflies. These areas are also frequented by different sea birds: fulmar petrel, shag, lesser and greater black-backed gulls, herring gulls

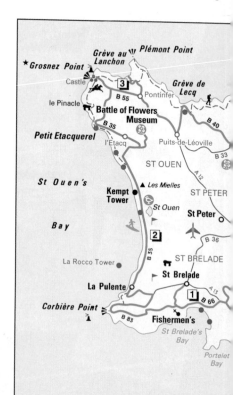

and the occasional puffin. The continental shelf along the **eastern coast** is shallow so that at low tide, the sands and rocks are warmed by the sun and attract feeding bass and mullet as the water returns.

Beware of the Spring water, however, which involves some of the biggest tidal variations. Tide tables are published daily in the local newspapers and lists are available at tackle shops and newsagents.

Historical notes – The tombs and prehistoric monuments found on the island indicate human habitation between 7500 and 2500 BC. The Roman presence was brief, and in the 6C St Helier arrived and established Christianity. The dominant influence is that of the Normans who invaded the islands in the 10C and who left a rich heritage of customs and traditions that survive even today.

Ever since 1204 when King John was forced to cede Normandy to the French, they have made repeated attempts to recover the Channel Islands: the last attempt occurred in 1781 when Baron de Rullecourt, a soldier of fortune, landed by night in St Clement's Bay in the southeast corner of Jersey. Taken by surprise the Lt Governor surrendered but under Major Peirson, a young man of 24, the militia and British forces engaged the enemy and defeated them in the main square in what came to be known as the **Battle of Jersey**; both leaders were mortally wounded.

Constitution – Jersey is divided into 12 Parishes, which together with two groups of islets, the Minquiers to the east and the Ecréhous to the north east, make up the Bailiwick of Jersey. The parliament, known as the States of Jersey, is headed by five officers: the Lt Governor, a high ranking military man who represents the Queen; the Bailiff, a senior judge who acts as President of the States; the Attorney-General and the Solicitor-General who contribute to debates in Parliament in a consultative capacity only – these four officers are appointed by the Crown and are elected to serve for a period of three to six years – the fifth officer is the Dean of Jersey, an Anglican clergyman. Together, they preside over 12 Senators, 12 Constables and 29 Deputies – all of whom assume different functions on the different committees.

ST HELIER

St Helier is named after one of the first Christian missionaries to land in Jersey and who was murdered by pirates after living as a hermit there for 15 years (*c*555AD). The area would already have been exploited in the Bronze Age because of its sheltered position on the south side of the island, but by medieval times the place was a marsh.

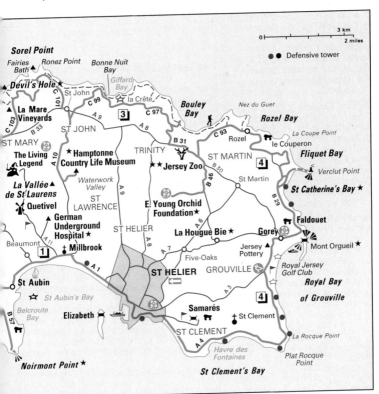

Later the scant local population was swelled by two waves of French refugees fleeing from repercussions of the St Bartholomew Massacre (1572) and the Revolution (1789). Today, St Helier is a lively town, the main commercial centre on the island and the seat of government.

Although the first market was established by 1299, the town was largely developed in the 19C when new houses were built and the harbour was extended. Many of the evocative Norman street names have English translations: Church Street was formerly called Rue Trousse Cotillon where women had to tuck up their skirts out of the mire. The shops in the pedestrian precinct formed by **King and Queen Streets** are a popular attraction for visitors to the island.

Famous sons and daughters

The most famous name connected with Jersey is **Lillie Langtry** (1853-1929) – the "Jersey Lily" who became an actress and captivated British high society with her beauty and a close friend of Edward VII – she is buried in St Saviour's churchyard.

The fashionable 19C painter, **Sir John Everett Millais** (1829-96) who won acclaim with his painting entitled *Bubbles*, grew up in Jersey and belonged to an old island family. So too did **Elinor Glyn** (1864-1943), who became a novelist and Hollywood scriptwriter.

The well-known French firm which makes Martell brandy was started by **Jean Martell** from St Brelade.

St Helier Parish Church (Z B) – The foundation of the present pink granite church with its square tower pre-dates the Conquest. It was here that Parish business was decided up until 1830 and where the militia cannon was kept until 1844. It continues to be the seat of the Dean of Jersey – hence the epithet "Cathedral of Jersey". In the south transept hangs a plan of the seating in 1868 showing the names of the pew-holders: the higher the rent the nearer the altar. The altar cross and candlesticks were a gift from Queen Elizabeth, the Queen Mother.

Royal Square (Z 20) – The gilded lead statue of George II, dressed as a Roman emperor, looks down on this charming small square with its spreading chestnut trees; from this point are measured the distances to all the milestones on the island. It was here in the Market Place that malefactors were once exposed in the pillory during market hours and where the Battle of Jersey erupted. Bordering the south side are the granite buildings of the **Royal Court House** (ZJ) ⊙. The public entrance bears the arms of George II, the Bailiff's entrance the arms of George VI. A plaque records the birth of the Norman poet, **Wace** (1135-1174).

At the east end of the range of buildings are the **States Chambers** *(entrance round the corner)* where the Jersey parliament sits in session.

Vega Memorial – Ten yards from the entrance to the States Building is a monument erected to commemorate the arrival of the Red Cross ship on 30 December 1944 bringing urgent supplies for the islanders, some of whom boldly incised a 'V for Victory' into the granite pavement under German gaze.

Central Market (Z E) – The granite building (1882) is furnished with cast-iron grilles at the windows and entrances, and covered with a glass (perspex) roof on iron columns. Inside, open stall holders proffer local produce to the sound of the fountain making this a lively and colourful scene. The **fish market** is around the corner in Beresford Street.

★ **Jersey Museum** ⊙ (Z M²) – Housed in a former merchant's house and adjoining warehouse belonging to Philippe Nicolle (1769-1835) is the local museum which prides itself in telling the story of the island, its traditions and its industries. The **ground floor** area is shared by temporary exhibitions and a room screening films about Jersey. The treadmill, which was turned by 12 men and operated a pepper mill, was used in St Helier prison during the 19C. By the stairs is displayed a number of silver toilet articles from the set which accompanied Lillie Langtry on her travels.

On the **first floor**, the history of the island from the Stone Age to the present is unfurled as a series of tableaux: artefacts excavated at La Cotte; archive photographs and interactive screens complement historic tools and implements in relating the traditional farming and fishing practices; the development of Jersey as a Victorian resort; Jersey's interests in offering off-shore banking and other financial services.

The **second floor** displays the Barreau-Le Maistre collection of fine art with paintings, drawings and water-colours by local artists or of topographical interest: Sir John Everett Millais PRA (1829-1896), P J Ouless (1817-1885),

"the Jersey Turner" J Le Capelain (1812-1848) and the illustrator Edmond Blampied (1886-1966). Works by **Sir Francis Cook** (1907-1978) bequeathed to the Jersey Heritage Trust are on permanent display in their own gallery, a converted Methodist Chapel, in Augrès (located on the La Route de Trinité [A8]).
The **third floor** rooms recreate domestic interiors (1861) typical of a middle class Jersey family.

New North Quay (z) – The most prominent landmark is the world's largest **steam clock** (36ft tall), modelled on a traditional paddle steamer of a type that once shuttled between the islands and Southampton. Inaugurated in August 1997, this marks a landmark in the ongoing development of the St Helier waterfront with a fabulous 600-birth marina and leisure pool complex well under way.

Maritime Museum and Jersey Occupation Tapestry ⊘ (**M³**) – Installed in converted 19C warehouses, Jersey's **Maritime Museum** is dedicated to celebrating the importance of the sea with changing displays relating to the fishing, ship building, trading industries and piracy.

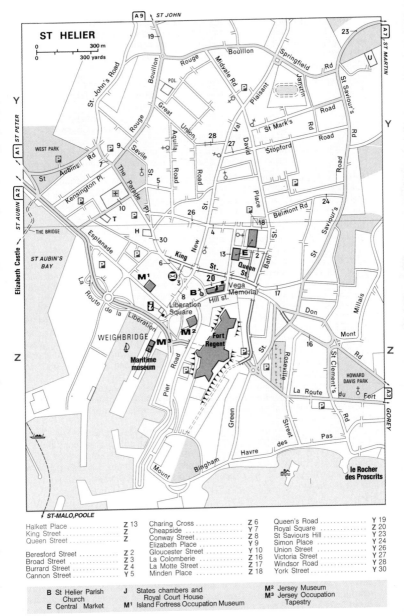

St Clements: Liberation, Jersey Occupation Tapestry

The **Jersey Occupation Tapestry** comprises twelve panels, 6ft x 3ft, illustrating the story of the Occupation of Jersey from the outbreak of war to the Liberation: each scene, based on archive photographs and contemporary film footage, has been embroidered by a separate Parish. An audio-visual presentation provides additional background information.

Fort Regent ⊘ (Z) – *Access by cable car or bus in Hill Street (summer only) or by escalators in Pier Road.* The massive fortifications of Fort Regent were built to protect Jersey from invasion by Napoleon. Within, topped by a shallow white dome, is a modern leisure centre providing a variety of sports facilities and entertainment: swimming pool, badminton, squash, table-tennis, snooker, play-area for children, puppet theatre, exhibitions, aquarium and audio-visual shows on the history and culture of the island. It is also home to the Jersey Signal Station. The rampart walk provides splendid **views**★ of the town and St Aubin's Bay *(west)*.

Island Fortress Occupation Museum ⊘ (Z M¹)– A limited collection of military uniforms, flak sheds, weaponry and equipment evoke this five-year period in the island's history. A video tells of the anguish endured through the occupation and relief of the eventual liberation (1940-45).

Elizabeth Castle ⊘ (Z) – *Access on foot across a causeway at low tide (30min); otherwise by amphibious vehicle from West Park Slipway.*
In the 12C William Fitz-Hamon, one of Henry II's courtiers, founded an abbey on St Helier's Isle in St Aubin's Bay. The castle buildings were completed shortly before Sir Walter Raleigh was appointed Governor (1600) and called Fort Isabella Bellissima in honour of Queen Elizabeth I. It was considerably reinforced during the Civil War while occupied by Royalists resisting the repeated assaults from Parliamentary forces on the island; after a 50 day siege the Royalists surrendered. Contemporary documents confirm that the young Prince of Wales stayed here when fleeing from England in 1646, and again three years later when returning to be proclaimed King Charles II. During the Second World War the Germans added to the fortifications by installing a roving search-light, bunkers and gun batteries. In 1996 Queen Elizabeth II handed the castle with Mont Orgueil, to the islanders.
Inside, the various stages in the construction of the castle are shown in the guard room. The **Militia Museum** contains mementoes of the Royal Jersey Regiment: uniforms, weapons, flags and silver including an unusual snuff box in the shape of a ram's head.
The Upper Ward encloses the keep, known as the Mount, where the Germans built a concrete fire control tower surmounted by an anti-aircraft position. There is a fine **view**★ of the castle itself and also of St Aubin's Fort across the bay. South of the castle a breakwater extends past the chapel on the rock where, according to legend, St Helier lived as a hermit *(procession on or about 16 July, St Helier's Day).*

EXCURSIONS INLAND

Trinity

Leave St Helier by the main road north Le Mont de la Trinité [A8] and turn right at la Rue Asplet [B31] towards Trinity Church. This road soon becomes La Rue des Picots and passes before the zoo on the right.

★★ **Jersey Zoo** ⊘ – *2-3 hours.* The Jersey Wildlife Preservation Trust, with its headquarters at Jersey Zoo (Les Augrès Manor), was founded by the naturalist **Gerald Durrell** in 1963 as a unique centre for research and breeding of rare and endangered species. The high rate of success in this prime objective has led to exchanges with other zoos (Bristol, Newquay, Paignton) and the reintroduction of a number of threatened species into native habitats. The symbol of the Trust is the dodo, the great non-flying bird of Mauritius which was first identified in 1599 and was extinct by 1693.

Ten acres of undulating park are dedicated to providing compatible environments to some thousand animals in cages, temperate housing, landscaped enclosures or open garden and woodland. Exotic species of plants are grown to provide the animals with both food and natural cover – their controlled diets being otherwise supplemented with locally produced organic meat, fruit and vegetables. Residents include babirusas from Indonesia; spectacled bears from the forest uplands of Bolivia and Peru (the only bear indigenous to South America); snow leopards and cheetahs; a long list of birds ranges from the St Lucia parrot, the Mexican thick-billed parrot, white eared pheasants from China, pink pigeons from Mauritius, white-naped crane native of Japan and Korea, Rothschild mynah birds, Chilean flamingos to Waldrapp Ibis.

Perhaps the most popular animals, however, are the primates: a dynasty of lowland gorillas descended from the silverback "Jambo" (1961-1992); orang-utans from Sumatra and the less extrovert lemurs from Madagascar, marmosets and tamarins from Brazil, some of which roam freely in the thick shrubbery. Tortoises, terrapins, snakes, frogs, toads and lizards happy to lounge in their warmed enclosures among sprigs of flowering orchids, thrive in the **Gaherty Reptile Breeding Centre**. A special unit enables visitors to observe the activities of rare fruit bats and the intriguingly named aye-aye by subdued artificial light.

Ring-tailed Lemur

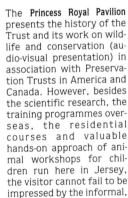

The **Princess Royal Pavilion** presents the history of the Trust and its work on wildlife and conservation (audio-visual presentation) in association with Preservation Trusts in America and Canada. However, besides the scientific research, the training programmes overseas, the residential courses and valuable hands-on approach of animal workshops for children run here in Jersey, the visitor cannot fail to be impressed by the informal, happy atmosphere of the place which has been so congenial to successfully breeding endangered species in captivity.

★ **Eric Young Orchid Foundation** ⊘ – *Victoria Village, Trinity. 1 hour. The Orchid Foundation is remarkably difficult to find: it may be easiest therefore to ask for directions to Victoria Village and then look out for signs.*

A fabulous show of prize plants appealing to both amateur and professional growers of orchids is presented here in a Display House. The mission of the Foundation is to "promote orchid improvement for all" – it therefore collaborates on a conservation and research basis with the Royal Horticultural Society and the Royal Botanic Gardens at Kew, and other passionate growers ever fascinated by variations in colour and form achieved by hybridisation. Displays are regularly re-organised to ensure constant shows of species, each group arranged to allow close study of their distinctive blooms. The five adjacent growing houses *(open but roped off)* are dedicated to the genera Cymbidium, Paphiopedilium or slipper orchids, Cattleya, Phalaenopsis or moth orchids, Odontoglossum or butterfly orchids (including Miltonias or pansy orchids).

Grouville

Leave St Helier by either of the main roads running north-eastwards: La route Bagatelle [A6] or St Saviour's Hill [A7] to Five Oaks. Follow Princes Tower Road [A7] and look out for the entrance to La Hougue Bie on the left.

★ **La Hougue Bie** ⊙ – *1 hour.* The tiny park, encircled by trees, is dominated by a high circular mound. Its name may be derived from the Old Norse word *haugr* (meaning barrow) and *bie*, a shorthand for Hambye, a Norman lord who in the Middle Ages came to rid Jersey of a dragon that stalked St Lawrence marsh. During the occupation, the site was heavily fortified, providing, as it does, an excellent **view** over outlying countryside.

Archeology and Geology Museum – Artefacts displayed were brought to light by local excavations – notably from La Cotte de St Brelade, a sea cave in the Ouaisné headland and the Belle Hougue caves on the north coast: remains of mammoths, polished stone axes, flint tools, stone querns for grinding corn (belonging to Neolithic settlers who were farmers), pottery, ornaments; Bronze Age metal objects found in St Lawrence etc. The geology section presents samples of the various rocks and minerals found on the island: shales (south of island), volcanic lavas (north), pink and grey granites and diorites (NW and SW), Rozel conglomerates or puddingstone.

★ **Neolithic Tomb** – The cruciform passage burial chamber, long suspected by archeologists but only excavated in 1924, dates from 3500 BC. Similar tombs have been discovered in England and Brittany. The grave would originally have been built above ground with upright stones and roofed with granite slabs before being covered by a 40ft mound of earth and rubble. A passage, 33ft long, leads to the funeral chamber which measures 10ft by 30ft, covered with huge capstones (the heaviest weighing 25 tonnes); this central space opens into three smaller chambers. Note that the central granite pillar is a modern addition providing support when the large capstones were found to be cracked.

Chapels – The mound is surmounted by two medieval chapels: the **Chapel of Our Lady of the Dawn** (Notre Dame de la Clarté) dates from the 12C; the altar (late Medieval) came from Mont Orgueil Castle. The abutting **Jerusalem Chapel** was built in 1520 by Dean Richard Mabon after a pilgrimage to Jerusalem. The interior bears traces of frescoes of two archangels.

German Occupation Museum – A German bunker, built in 1942 as a communications centre, houses radio equipment, weapons, medals, original documents (orders and propaganda) and photographs of the period.

Waterworks Valley

Leave St Helier by the main road La Route St Aubin [A1], turn right up Le Mont Felard [A10] and continue through St Lawrence.

La Vallée de St Laurens, set between St Peter's Valley and Waterworks Valley, boasts a number of important traditional Norman-style stone (granite) farmhouses and remnants of water-powered mills. Several of the most typical houses now belong to the National Trust of Jersey, including La Ferme Morel, Le Colombier, and the 17C cottage locally named Le Rat. Of the six mills which operated in the valley, one is in working order although some were reactivated during the occupation; the streams now supply Jersey's mains water supply.

Fork right along La Rue des Corvées which joins La Rue de la Patente and Le Chemin des Moulins [C119].

★ **Hamptonne Country Life Museum** ⊙ – Hamptonne House was built by Vicomte (Sheriff of the Court) Laurens Hamptonne – the same man who proclaimed Charles II King in the market place in St Helier in February 1649. The land was acquired in 1633, the house is presumed to have been completed in 1637. Aligned along the northern yard are a series of restored 19C **farm outbuildings**, arranged as a labourer's cottage, coach house, bake-house, wash-house and stables. A gateway leads to the orchard and open meadow beyond, and to the south facing walled garden overlooked by the square pigeon-house or colombier (one of two on Jersey).

The **Langlois Building**, on the south side, is an upper hall house of a type found in medieval Brittany, accommodating animals at ground level and quartering humans above. The interior is thoughtfully recreated to suggest life in the 18C with hand-made country-style oak furniture.

Hamptonne House, partly thatched and partly slate-roofed is particularly atmospheric: museum staff, dressed in period costume are on hand to provide a more complete insight into the family and its life style during the 17C and early 18C.

The Syvret Building provides space for thematic exhibitions relating to rural practices. The northern section shelters a cider barn complete with apple crusher and twin-screw press (activated in October). Home-made produce including bread baked in cabbage and cider are available from the café.

Sadie with visitors, Hamptonne Country Life Museum

St Peter's Valley

Leave St Helier by the main road – La Route St Aubin [A1]; after Millbrook, turn right up Le Chemins des Moulins [A11]. Fork left up B89 when the main road curves sharply round to the left – signposted German Underground Hospital.

★ **German Underground Hospital** ⊘ – This large complex of tunnels is kept as a compelling memorial to the forced labourers (Spaniards, Moroccans, Alsatian Jews, Poles, Frenchmen, Russians) who worked on its construction for 3.5 years under the severest conditions. Note that some visitors may find the visit rather harrowing, others may suffer from claustrophobia.

Hohlgangsanlagen 8 was intended as a secure, bomb-proof artillery barracks, complete with accommodation and a storage facility for ammunition. In January 1944, still incomplete, it was converted into a hospital equipped with an operating theatre, 5 100-bed wards, X-ray room, mortuary, stores, kitchen, staff quarters etc. On entering the long dark galleries hewn deep into the solid rock, the temperature drops, the air is damp, the sound of footsteps is amplified through the concrete emptiness. Wartime films, archive photographs, newspaper cuttings, letters and memorabilia document the personal suffering and trauma of those caught up in the events.

The **Occupation Walk** up onto high ground opposite the complex leads to an area fortified by genuine anti-aircraft gun positions, crawl trenches, barbed wire entanglements and personnel shelters *(leaflet available from Visitor Centre)*.

Return back downhill to the main road [A11], turn right uphill along La Vallée de St Pierre for Quetivel Mill.

Moulin de Quetivel ⊘ – The **mill** (pre-1309), on a bend in St Peter's Valley, is one of several which once operated by the stream until they were made obsolete by steam power. During the German Occupation the machinery was restored for temporary service before being largely destroyed by fire (1969). Since 1979, re-equipped with parts from other disused Jersey mills, Quetivel has been in operation grinding locally-grown grain and producing stone-ground flour for sale. From the mill pond the water is channelled by the mill leat down through the wood (inhabited by red squirrels and woodpeckers) to the mill wheel, a pitch-back overshot wheel. The tour shows each stage of the process from the arrival of the grain by hoist in the loft to the production of stone-ground flour for sale on the ground floor. Most of the grinding stones are made of French burr, quarried near Orly Airport south of Paris; these are composed of segments set with plaster of Paris and last a hundred years. A pair of stones will produce 25 tons of flour before needing to be dressed, when the grooves are recut to the required depth using a tool called a "bill" – this process can take a miller about a week.

Return to the main road [A11] and take second turning on the right La Route de Laleval [C124] for the Living Legend.

Living Legend ⊘ – Inside the granite buildings unfurls the entertaining multi-sensory experience that relates the history and myths of Jersey. The time traveller explores his way along a labyrinth of mysterious chambers, through castle towers and across the decks of a Victorian paddle steamer to discover the various aspects of past islanders' lives and stories told of heroes and villains. Atmosphere is enhanced by visual and sound effects (holograms, lasers, wind machines...).

St Peter's Village

Leave St Helier by the main road La Route St Aubin [A1] and drive through Millbrook and Beaumont; turn right up Le Beau Mont [A12] to St Peter's Village.

St Peter's Church – The Parish church has a remarkable 124ft high steeple which by chance escaped from being faced with cement; at its apex is a red navigation light used by aircraft coming in to land at the airport nearby. Behind the altar is a reredos by George Tinworth, commissioned in the 1880s from Royal Doulton.

Jersey Motor Museum ⊘ – This collection of veteran and vintage vehicles, all in working order and appearing at rallies in Jersey and elsewhere, includes the 1936 Rolls-Royce Phantom III used by General Montgomery in 1944 during D-Day preparations and the 1964 Hillman Husky which belonged to Sir Winston Churchill. Cars by Ford, Austin, Talbot, Triumph, Bentley and Jaguar contrast with Allied and German military vehicles, bicycles (*c*1869 Boneshaker) and motorbikes. Other items include several period brass lamps, classic pedal and petrol-driven children's cars, toys, an old AA callbox and a car from the Jersey steam railway.

On the opposite side of the square is an underground bunker built by the German Organization Todt in 1942, strategically placed so as to keep surveillance over the airport and access roads to the west of the island.

TOUR OF THE ISLAND

☐ From St Helier to Corbière *10 miles (18km) – about 2 hours.*

Leave St Helier by the main road La Route de St Aubin [A1] going west.

Millbrook – The Villa Millbrook was once home to Sir Jesse Boot, the first Baron Trent of Nottingham and founder of Boots the Chemists, who is buried at St Brelade.

St Matthew's Church ⊘ – The **Glass Church**, as it is also known, was unexceptional until 1934 when **René Lalique** (1860-1945), the French specialist in moulded glass, was invited by Lord Trent's widow to redecorate the interior with distinctive **glasswork★**: the entrance doors are made of panels presenting a row of four angels guarding another behind the main altar. The other decorative element is the flowering lily which appears in the windows, screens and in the Lady Chapel. The luminescent, ethereal quality is most apparent at dusk when the lights are switched on.

Follow the main road La Route de La Haule then La Neuve Route [A1].

St Aubin – The little town, which faces east across St Aubin's Bay, is particularly picturesque with its long sandy beach, fishermen's cottages and tall granite merchants' houses lining steep, narrow streets or clinging to the cliffs along the shore. The name is auspicious as

Lalique angel, Millbrook

St Aubin, besides being Bishop of Angers (*d* 550AD) during the lifetime of St Helier, was invoked as protector against pirates.

The local church (1892) has a fine stained-glass window made by the William Morris & Co.

St Aubin's Fort on the island *(access at low tide)* was built in the reign of Henry VIII to protect the town which enjoyed considerable prosperity during the 17C. The Corbière Walk from Charing Cross to Corbière follows the line of the old **Jersey Railway** which opened in 1870 and ran from St Helier to St Aubin before being extended.

Turn left off the main road onto La Route de Noirmont [B57] for access to the promontory and Portelet Bay.

★ Noirmont Point – *Quand Nièrmont met san bonnet, Ch'est signe de plyie (when Noirmont or Black Hill dons his cap, it signals rain)*: the local saying warns of the onset of gales from the southwest. Beyond the pebble beach nestling in

Belcroute stretches the headland, still scarred by the remains of substantial German fortifications (1941 and 1943-44) including the **Command Bunker** ⊙ – a post for the naval coastal artillery battery. The most advanced bastion gives fine views of the rocks immediately below and round westwards to the Ile au Guerdain, surmounted by a defensive tower, in the centre of Portelet Bay.

The southern-most parts of the promontory have revealed an important Bronze Age burial ground, not far from the site of the famous cave of La Cotte de St Brelade.

Return to the main road La Route des Genets [A13] and then fork left down Le Mont Sohier [B66].

St Brelade – This favourite seaside resort is situated in a sheltered bay, its sandy beaches and safe waters ideal for swimming and water skiing. A waterfall tumbles over the rocks on the wooded slopes of the **Winston Churchill Memorial Park** which backs the bay.

At the western end of the beach, behind a screen of trees, the parish church and detached medieval chapel are surrounded by gravestones at one time the resting place for 337 German servicemen who were in the islands as prisoners during World War I or on active duty during the Occupation: in 1961, they were re-interred at Mont de Huisnes at St Malo.

Parish Church – *Light switch inside on the left of entrance.* The cherished Church of St Brelade is built of granite from the cliffs of La Moye (meaning rocky headland). The earliest parts of the structure – the chancel, nave and belfry – date from the 11C. In the 12C the church became cruciform with the addition of a transept; the aisles were added later. Inside, the altar is a solid slab of stone, marked with five crosses representing the five wounds of the Crucifixion. The 15C font is made of granite from the Chausey Islands, which lie south of Jersey and belong to France.

Fishermen's Chapel – *Light switch inside on the left of entrance.* The family chapel, which is built of the same granite as the church, is decorated in the interior with delicate medieval **frescoes★**. At the east end is an *Annunciation* – dated as *c*1375 from the medieval attire of the donors at prayer; the other paintings are from a second phase of work *c*1425: the south wall (right of the altar) shows *Adam and Eve* followed by *The Annunciation* and *The Adoration of the Magi,* the west wall bears *The Last Judgement,* on the north wall fragments have been deciphered as *Scenes from the Passion.* The survival of the paintings is largely due to the fact that from *c*1550 to the mid-19C the chapel was used as an armoury, housing the parochial cannon, and as a carpenter's shop. The windows, by a local craftsman H T Bosdet (1857-1934) narrate the story of St Brendan. Behind the chapel a short flight of steps leads to a path through the churchyard to the beach; this is the only surviving example of a *perquage*: once commonplace in medieval Europe, these paths were intended as escape routes from a chapel or church traditionally a place of sanctuary to the shore and away out to sea.

Continue along the road back into town and turn left along the main road La Route Orange [A13]; fork left down La Route du Sud [B83] to Corbière.

Corbière – All that remains of the terminus of the Western Railway is the concrete platform. As the road descends, a magnificent view is steadily revealed of the rock-strewn point and the white lighthouse rising from its islet: a good place to watch the sun set over the Atlantic. Before the lighthouse *(access on foot at low tide but closed to the public)* was built in 1874, this was a perilous stretch of water where a number of ships foundered, lost to the tide; in clear weather the electric beam carries 17 miles.

② From Corbière to Petit Etacquerel *8 miles (13km) – 1 hour.*

Follow the road round to the junction with La Rue de Sergentes [B35] and turn left back towards the coast.

St Ouen's Bay – The major part of this coastline is taken up with this magnificent, open five mile stretch of sand backed by sand dunes. The deep surf which rolls into the bay makes it a favourite spot for experienced surfboard and windsurf enthusiasts. The firm sand attracts motor and motorcycle racing fans. In the middle of the bay sits **La Rocco Tower**, the last round tower to be built in Jersey (1800); having been severely damaged during the war, the tower was finally restored during the 1970s.

Beyond the beach, the landscape is wild and uncultivated, the vegetation sparse. **La Pulente** used to be the main centre for gathering seaweed *(vraic)* which was traditionally used as fertiliser. La Sergenté, also known as the Beehive Hut, is another important Neolithic tomb near to which a large hoard of coins from Brittany was found. The **St Ouen Pond**, on the right of the road is also known as La Mare du Seigneur as it once belonged to the Seigneur of St Ouen (the most senior of the island seigneurs resident in St Ouen's Manor). This stretch of fresh water is a haven for birds and wild flowers, notably the Jersey or loose-flowered orchid. The three upright stones Les Trois Rocques are presumed to be part of a dolmen.

Kempt Tower ⊙ – This defensive tower has been converted into an Interpretation Centre with maps, photographs and pamphlets about the region: geological features, archeological remains, flora and fauna. The area around it has been made into a nature reserve called **Les Mielles** (the Jersey dialect word for sand dunes) to monitor and protect indigenous plants, birds and butterflies.

Follow La Route des Laveurs [B35] and take the left turn called Le Mont des Corvées [C114].

Birds to be seen around Les Mielles

Besides such common birds as blackbirds, thrushes, wrens, robins and tits, the sand dunes harbour colonies of kestrels and skylarks and attract such migrants as willow warblers, stonechats and wheatears. Stretches of fresh open water and reed beds provide popular habitats for moorhens, coots, ducks (mallard, tufted, shoveler), kingfishers, sandpipers, lapwings, herons and snipe. Please show consideration by not disturbing pairs or fledglings through the nesting and breeding season (April to July).

During the summer, the coastal footpath from Plemont to Grève de Lecq affords good sightings of seabirds: fulmar petrels (May to September), puffins and razorbills – notably early morning and early evening. In winter, Brent geese, plovers, redshanks, turnstones, dunlin, bar-tailed godwits, curlews, oystercatchers, teal, snipe, lapwings and herons may be seen feeding on an incoming tide.

Battle of Flowers Museum ⊙ – The **Battle of Flowers**, held on the second Thursday in August along Victoria Avenue in St Helier, was started in 1902 to celebrate the coronation of Edward VII. Traditionally, the floats were broken up after the parade and the crowd pelted one another with the flowers, then mostly hydrangeas. Today, a collection of floats which over the years have been entered in the wild flower category, is here presented by their creator. The tableaux are made up of different grasses and concentrate on animal subjects.

Return to the coastal road, forking right along La Route de l'Étacq [B35].

Petit Etacquerel – A defensive tower guards the point which marks the northern end of St Ouen's Bay. It is here that in 1651 Admiral Blake landed with the Parliamentary forces which forced the Royalists to surrender.

③ From Grosnez Point to Rozel Bay *17 miles (28km) - 2.5 hours.*

The northern coast of the island is less densely populated than other parts of the island as steep rocky cliffs alternate with small sandy bays. Cliff paths, which stretch from Plémont Bay to Sorel Point and beyond, provide spectacular views of the uneven coastline and the open sea to France, Guernsey and Alderney (although they say that a clear view of Alderney heralds rain). Early crop potatoes are grown on the steeply sloping hillsides *(côtils)*.

Continue north by forking left along La Route du Ouest [B55]: fork left again to reach the car park and look out point at Grosnez.

★ **Grosnez Point** – An area of desolate heathland, covered with gorse and heather and known as Les Landes, extends from Etacquerel to Grosnez Point. South west of the racecourse sits **Le Pinacle**, a strange yet impressive rock that has been found to be associated with pagan rituals since Neolithic, Bronze Age, Iron Age, even Roman times.

Dramatically positioned overlooking the sea are the ruins of a medieval stronghold which must have provided a place of temporary refuge against invasion. Little remains of **Grosnez Castle** (c1373-1540) besides the curtain wall with ditch, gateway and drawbridge; however it enjoys magnificent views out to sea, of Sark and the other islands (northwest).

Return to B55; in Portinfer turn left into La Route de Plémont [C105]. The road forks: to the left it leads to Grève au Lançon. If continued to the end, it skirts the holiday village to end in a car park from where a footpath runs along the coast to Grève de Lecque.

Steep cliffs containing caves shelter this attractive small bay, **Grève au Lanchon**, which has a sandy beach at low tide. The rocky promontory **Plémont Point** projects into the sea providing a fine view of the cliffs.

Return back along La Route de Plémont and turn left onto the road from Grosnez. La Route de Vinchelez [B55] leads to Leoville in the parish of St Mary. Before the Leoville Hotel, take the road left: Le Mont de la Grève de Lecque [B65].

Grève de Lecq – This charming sandy bay with its stream and mill was defended against invasion most recently by the Germans in the Second World War and earlier against the French in the 18C-19C. The defensive tower was built in 1780 although the conical hill behind is from an Iron Age fortification.

The **barracks** ⊙ were built between 1810 and 1815 to accommodate the 150 British soldiers who manned the gun batteries on the slopes around the bay – although blocks were built at Bonne Nuit Bay, Rozel Bay and St Peter's Parish these are the only ones to survive. There were two blocks, each consisting of four rooms for the soldiers and two for the NCOs; the central building was for the officers. Behind stood the ablutions block and two prison cells; to the south was the stabling. In spring and early summer the area is abloom with wild flowers: gorse, daffodils, bluebells, foxgloves.

The water's edge is broken by jagged rocks locally known as **Paternoster Rocks** after the many prayers uttered through time by passing fishermen, remembering colleagues who perished there. Far out to sea is the French coast.

Leave Grève de Lecq by continuing along the road La Mont de Ste Marie [B40], turn left into La Verte Rue [B33] and left again before the West View Hotel into C103.

La Mare Vineyards ⊙ – The estate of an 18C farmhouse has been planted with the only vineyards and cider orchard in Jersey. An introductory video film, describing its history, the vineyards, the harvest and the wine-making process, adds to the interest of touring the vineyards and the gleaming modern vintry, where German-style white wines are produced and may be tasted: Clos de la Mare, Clos de Seyval and Blayney Special Reserve.

Continue along C103 to the Priory Inn.

★ **Devil's Hole** – *Park by the inn and take the concrete path down to the cliff.* The blow hole is an impressive sight dramatised by the amplified thunder of the sea entering the cave below. The name is thought to derive from the old French Creux de Vis meaning screwhole, although other stories tell of the wreck of a French ship in 1871, whose figurehead resembled a devil.

Minor roads run east to St John's Parish and north to the coast.

Sorel Point – The section of road named **La Route du Nord** is dedicated to the islanders who suffered during the German Occupation (stone in car park). It runs from Sorel Point where a mysterious pool (24ft wide, 15ft deep) is revealed in the rocks at low tide: disputes continue as to whether it is a natural or man-made phenomenon; the pool is known as the Fairies' Bath (Lavoir des Dames). To the east is Ronez Point, a headland scarred by granite quarries.

Drive through St John, turning left into La Route des Issues [A9], and then forking left again after the Jersey Pearl Centre into La Route de Mont Mado [B67]. Minor roads off to the left [C99] lead to Bonne Nuit Bay and Giffard Bay.

Bonne Nuit Bay – This bay that must at one time have been haunted by smugglers and pirates, is a favourite place for swimming and sailing. Charles II is supposed to have returned from exile to England from this attractive bay where a stone jetty shelters the tiny harbour. The fort, La Crête, at the east end was built in 1835.

From here a footpath follows the coast round to Bouley Bay. By car, it is easiest to follow the minor roads [C98, B63, C97 – Rue des Platons] to Bouley Bay.

Bouley Bay – In the 19C it was proposed that the deep sandy bay protected by a jetty and backed by high granite cliffs should be transformed into a sheltered harbour. Today it is a safe, popular place for swimming.

Return back towards Trinity; turn left into La Rue ès Picots [B31] past Jersey Zoo before turning sharply left along La Rue du Rocquier [C93] to Rozel Bay.

Rozel Bay – Part of the bay is taken up with a fishing port where the boats go aground at low tide. Above the bay, at the northern end, traces of a great earth rampart survive from the Castel de Rozel, an Iron Age settlement. Many coins from different eras have also been recovered from the area. At the opposite end, sits **Le Couperon**, a Neolithic passage grave (2500BC). Below it, at the water's edge among the rocks at low tide, are a profusion of pools inhabited by small crustacea making it a wonderful place for amateur zoologists and children to explore.

4 **From Rozel Bay to St Helier** *13 miles – 90min.*

The road turns inland before returning to the coast above Fliquet Bay and finally meandering down to the water line: from the Martello Tower runs a submarine cable to France. **Fliquet Bay** is a rocky bay between La Coupe and Verclut Points: an ideal place for deciphering the volcanic evolution of the island. *Either follow the road to St Martin, or explore the country roads like La Grande Route de Rozel [B38], La Rue des Pelles [B91], La Route du Villot [B91], Le Mont des Ormes [B29] to Verclut Point to the left and to Gorey Harbour to the right.*

★ **St Catherine's Bay** – The long breakwater (half a mile), which protects the bay to the north, was part of a British government scheme (1847-55) to create a huge naval "harbour of refuge" as the French developed coastal stations around Cherbourg: work to build a second breakwater was abandoned in 1852 as relations with Napoleon III improved. From the lighthouse at the end there is a magnificent **view★★** of sandy bays alternating with rocky promontories along the coast southwards. Out to sea lie the Ecrehous islets administered by St Martin's Parish – once a favoured trading bank for smugglers and now a popular spot for a Sunday picnic.

Faldouet Dolmen – *Fork right off the coastal road (La Route d'Anne Port).* A tree-lined path leads to this dolmen, which is 49ft long and dates from 2500 BC. The funeral chamber (20ft wide) is covered by a block of granite weighing 25 tonnes. Excavation has revealed a number of vases, stone pendants and polished stone axes.

Gorey – This charming little port at the northern end of Grouville Bay is dominated by the proud walls of Mont Orgueil Castle set on its rocky promontory. Attractive old houses line the quay where yachts add colour to the scene in summer. In the days of the Jersey Eastern Railway (1873-1929) there was a steamship service from Gorey to Normandy.

Mont Orgueil, Gorey

★ **Mont Orgueil Castle** ⊘ – *45min.* Gorey Castle received its present name in 1468 from Henry V's brother, Thomas, Duke of Clarence, who was so impressed by the castle's position and its defensive strength that he called it Mount Pride (Mont Orgueil in French). Over the centuries the castle has served as a residence to the Lords and Governors of the island, including Sir Walter Raleigh (1600-03), a prison for English political prisoners, and a refuge for a spy-network during the French Revolution.

The earliest buildings date back to the 13C when King John lost control of Normandy and built a castle to defend the island from invasion; new fortifications were added over the years as assaults from bows and arrows evolved into mortar attack and cannon fire. It was subsequently used as a prison and eventually ceded by the Crown to the States of Jersey in 1907; in 1996 Queen Elizabeth II handed the castle to the islanders.

The castle is built on a concentric plan, each system of defence being independent of the other. The solid walls founded on the granite rocks are a formidable obstacle. It is like threading a maze to walk up the complex network of passages and steps to the summit. The **view★★** from the top is extensive: down into Port Gorey, south over the broad sweep of Grouville Bay, north to the rocks of Petit Portelet and west to the French coast.

A series of waxwork tableaux in the rooms of the castle illustrates significant events in the history of Mont Orgueil including one of Charles II during his exile in Jersey as the guest of the Governor George de Carteret, to whom he granted the land in Virginia that became New Jersey.

Take the Gorey Coast Road [A3] along the waterfront.

Royal Bay of Grouville – The Parish of Grouville is graced with Jersey's finest bay, a magnificent crescent of sand stretching from Gorey harbour to La Rocque Point. The skyline is punctuated by a series of Martello towers and forts which were constructed during the Napoleonic Wars: of these the Seymour and Icho towers (1811) may be reached on foot at low tide.

Jersey Pottery ⊘ – *45min*. A paved garden, hung with baskets of flowers and refreshed by fountains, surrounds the workshops where the distinctive pottery is produced. Each stage in the process is explained on large panels and the visitor can stand and watch the craftsmen at work at their various skills. The show room displays the full range of products for sale.

Royal Jersey Golf Club – The local golf course enjoys a particularly picturesque position; founded in 1878, it was granted its Royal Charter by Queen Victoria.

Grouville Church – Originally dedicated to St Martin of Tours, the church has an unusual 15C granite font and a number of early examples of locally-made church plate.

St Clement's – St Clement is Jersey's smallest parish, named after the church dedicated to Clement I, the third Pope (68-78AD); it was here that Hugo wrote two volumes of poetry: *Les Chatiments* and *Les Contemplations*, before departing to Guernsey...

The dolmen at Mont Ubé, the 11ft menhir known as **La Dame Blanche**, and a tall granite outcrop called Rocqueberg suggest that this section of the island was well inhabited by Neolithic man. The earliest priory on the site belonged to the Abbey of Mont St Michel.

The oldest extant parts of the present church date from the 12C; the wall paintings from the 15C *(St Michael slaying the Dragon;* the legend of the *Three Living and Three Dead Kings).*

St Clement's Bay – This sandy bay stretches from Plat Rocqe Point, past Le Hocq Point, marked by a defensive tower, to Le Nez Point *(2 miles)*. Out to sea strong tides sweep through, continually churning the water. In 1781 Baron de Rullecourt landed with 600 French troops at the eastern end of the bay in the last French attempt to capture Jersey.

Turn off La Grande Route de St Clement [A4] along La Rue du Pontille [B48]; this road leads into St Clement's Road [A5]. Samarès Manor is ahead on the right.

Samarès Manor ⊘ – The name Samarès is probably derived from the Norman *salse marais*, the saltpans which provided the lord of the manor with a significant part of his revenue.

The history of the estate began in the 11C when William Rufus granted the Samarès fief to his faithful servant Rodolph of St Hilaire. In the 17C Philippe Dumaresq decided to give the estate a new look; he drained the marsh by building a canal to St Helier and imported trees and vines from France. The gardens were landscaped and largely replanted by Sir James Knott who acquired the property in 1924; the herb garden is later still. Of particular interest in the grounds is the rare 11C dovecote; in the house there is the Norman undercroft or manor chapel crypt and the walnut-panelled dining room.

Le Rocher des Proscrits (Z) – *Take Pier Road going south, skirt Mount Bingham and continue along Havre des Pas to Dicq Corner (1.25 miles).*

The road follows the shoreline along the south coast. On the east side of the White Horse Inn, a slipway descends to the beach and a group of rocks: Le Rocher des Proscrits (The Rock of the Exiles), where **Victor Hugo** (*see* GUERNSEY – Hauteville House) used to regularly meet with fellow exiles, is marked by a small plaque *(facing the road)*.

GUERNSEY★

Population 58 867
Michelin Atlas p 5 or Map 403

Guernsey is the second largest of the Channel Islands (24sq miles 63sq km): less sophisticated than its larger neighbour, it has its own particular charm: a slower tempo, the Regency elegance of the capital St Peter Port, the proximity of other islands – Sark, Herm and Jethou. Since the Second World War its main sources of income have been tourism, offshore finance and insurance, and tomatoes.

Geography – Guernsey is shaped like a right-angled triangle; the west coast forms the hypotenuse, the south coast the base and the east coast the perpendicular. There is little open country; from the air the whole island seems to be covered with glasshouses, small fields and dwellings, linked by a network of narrow lanes. The only wild country is to be found along the southern cliffs where flowers abound in spring, while the sandy beaches and rocky promontories of the west and north coast are excellent for bathing, surfing and exploring rock pools. The water lane, where a stream runs in a channel down the side of the road, is a special feature of Guernsey as through Moulin Huet Valley, Petit Bot Valley.

Local economy – As the island slopes from south to north away from the sun, most of the crops are grown under glass. The most famous export, the Guernsey tomato, was first grown in 1893 among the grapes in the greenhouses, hence the name vinery for a tomato farm. Grapes are still grown as well as melons, peas, potatoes and, of course, flowers.

Fishing is still an important activity: in the past the ormer or sea ear (oreille de mer) was a local delicacy prepared by stewing or pickling after being well beaten to make it tender. The shell is lined with mother-of-pearl and sometimes contains pearls. This mollusc is now rare and fishing is severely restricted in all the islands.

The abundant and varied supply of **local granite**, particularly from the Clos du Valle, has provided the islanders with an excellent and attractive building stone, although it is hard to shape or carve: pink or brownish-red from Côbo and Albecq, golden-yellow from L'Ancresse and grey, blue and black from other northern quarries.

Historical notes – Like its neighbours, Guernsey was inhabited in prehistoric times and is rich in Bronze and Iron Age monuments such as dolmens. Traces of the Romans' presence are slight, however, consisting mainly of a Roman vessel and amphora raised from the sea off St Peter Port.

Christianity may have come in the 6C with St Sampson who arrived from South Wales with his nephew St Magloire, although there are indications that the ten island parishes may have been established earlier, based on agricultural units.

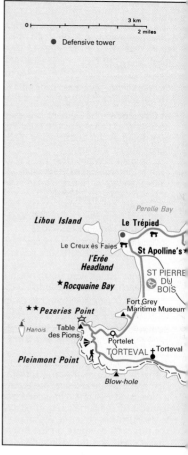

In 933 Guernsey was annexed by the Duke of Normandy and after 1066 was attached to the English Crown; all the charters granted to the island since 1394 are housed in the Greffe in the Royal Court House in St Peter Port. Despite the loss of Normandy to the French in 1204, the link with the Crown was not severed until the Civil War when Guernseymen, angered by the exacting behaviour of the previous English Governor, declared their loyalty to Parliament, although under the Constitution they had no right to do so. At the Restoration a petition was presented to Charles II humbly begging a royal pardon, which was granted.

Although the Channel Islanders are not obliged to fight except to defend their islands and the monarch, many have served with the British forces: the Royal Guernsey Light Infantry suffered heavy casualties at Cambrai in 1917. Since 1939 201 Squadron of the RAF has been affiliated to the island, confirming the link established in the 1920s when it operated flying boats from Calshot.

World War II – On 30 June 1940, German aircraft executed a raid on St Peter Port. The day after, a German plane landed at the airport, its passengers charged with taking possession of the island. For Hitler, this would be the first step to invading mainland Britain. Over the ensuing five years, Guernsey became one of the most heavily fortified outposts of occupied Europe: many scars were left by the compact reinforced concrete fortifications that made up the Atlantic Wall, although not all are accessible to the public (the headquarters of the Luftwaffe are located in the garden of a private house). Guernsey was finally liberated on 9 May 1945.

Constitution – The Bailiwick of Guernsey comprises the islands of Guernsey, Alderney, Sark, Herm and Jethou. The local parliament, known as the States of Deliberation, consists of 33 deputies, elected by public suffrage for three years: 10 Douzeniers nominated by the Parish Councils for one year, 12 Conseillers elected for 6 years by the States of Election, the Attorney-General and the Solicitor-General. It is presided over by the Bailiff who is also president of the Royal Court which consists of 12 Jurats, appointed by the States of Election, and the Crown Officers. Proceedings are in English although French is still used for the formalities.

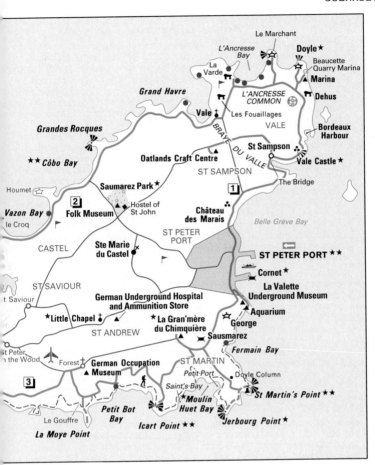

★★ ST PETER PORT

The island capital is built on a most attractive site on a hillside on the east coast overlooking a safe anchorage protected from high seas by Herm and Sark. The medieval town by the shore was rebuilt after bombardment during the Civil War. Another building boom, financed by the profits earned from privateering in the late 18C, produced a delightful Regency town built in a variety of local granite embellished by elegant garden railings. Guernsey's popularity as a tourist destination in the Victorian era was assured by a visit made by Queen Victoria in 1846, commemorated two years later by the 100ft Victoria Tower designed by William Collings.

★ **Castle Cornet** ⊙ **(Z)** – *2 hours.* The castle suffered its greatest misfortune not in war but in a storm in 1672 when a lightning strike ignited the gunpowder store in the old tower keep. The explosion decapitated the castle, destroying not only the tower but the medieval banqueting hall and the Governor's house, and killed his wife and daughter.

History – The original castle (*c*1206) was reinforced under Elizabeth I and again under Victoria. The **Prisoners' Walk** is the original barbican – an unusual and most effective piece of defence work. The castle was occupied by the French from 1338 to 1343 and attacked on various occasions including in 1356, 1372 and 1380 (during the Hundred Years War after Edward III had ordered that the town's defences be improved). The fortress was further reinforced in the 16C while the French occupied Sark (1549-1553). During the Civil War the islanders sided with parliament but the castle remained loyal to the king the last of the royalist strongholds to surrender (1651) after holding out for eight years; many of the 10 000 cannonballs fired into St Peter Port were retrieved by young boys who sold them back to the castle. The hospital and married quarters were added between 1745-1750 to improve living conditions for garrison forces engaged in the French wars.

The castle was superseded as principal defensive stronghold when Fort George was built shortly after the outbreak of the French Revolution. During the 20C, the citadel was fitted with two 12-pounder quick-firing guns

Famous Guernseymen

Despite its size, Guernsey has nurtured several famous men: two Lord Mayors of London – Paul Le Mesurier (1793-94) and Peter Perchard of Hatton Garden (1804-05); Admiral Lord James de Saumarez (1757-1836) who fought against the French in the Napoleonic Wars; Major-General Sir Isaac Brock (1769-1812) who fought under Nelson and died in the defence of Canada against the Americans at Queenstown Heights; Thomas de la Rue (1773-1866) who made his fortune in London printing playing cards, postage stamps and currency notes.

Famous residents include **Victor Hugo** (1802-85) who lived in St Peter Port from 1855-70 while working on several of his most important writings: *Les Miserables; Les Contemplations (Contemplations); La Légende des Siècles (The Legend of the Centuries), Les Chansons des Rues et des Bois (The Songs of the Streets and the Woods)* and *Les Travailleurs de la Mer (The Toilers of the Sea)*. This latter work is set in Guernsey and carries the dedication: 'I dedicate this book to the rock of hospitality, to this corner of old Norman land where resides the noble little people of the sea, to the island of Guernsey, severe and yet gentle...'

Anthony Trollope as an official of the UK postal services recommended a system of pillar boxes – one of which continues to be used.

and equipped with searchlights: these were fitted so as to monitor defences at water level. The Germans further installed a series of concrete shelters and anti-aircraft emplacements. An exhibition in the Lower Barracks graphically relates the **Story of Castle Cornet** from prehistoric to present times.

In the guardroom at the entrance of the castle built in Victorian times, is a display relating to the history of **201 Guernsey's Own Squadron.**

on the Saluting Platform in the outer bailey the ceremony of the **noonday gun** is performed by two men dressed in the Guernsey Militia uniform; one trains a telescope on the town clock and the other fires the cannon (beware of the extremely loud bang!). From the Citadel there is a fine **view★** of the harbour and town *(west)*, St Sampson, Vale Castle and Alderney *(22 miles north)*, Herm, Sark and the French coast *(east)* and Jersey *(south)*.

Gardens – Based on historic records, efforts have been made to recreate gardens from the 16C (Sutler's Garden outside the resident keeper's house), 17C (Lambert Garden created by Sir John Lambert, 'The Knight of the Golden Tulip', one of Cromwell's favourites, who won acclaim growing tulips in Wimbledon) and 18C (Governor's Garden and Master Gunner's Garden as laid out in 1735).

Museums – The **Maritime Museum** relates the island's maritime history from the Gallo-Roman period to the present day. Exhibitions centre on the harbour, Roman and medieval trade, fish and fishing, smuggling, privateering, the Royal Navy; there is a gallery of marine art, a carpenter's workshop, displays on ship building and cross-Channel steamers, divers and lifeboats. A **militia Museum**, housed in the Hospital Building (1746), contains two collections: the Spencer Collection *(lower floor)* of uniforms and insignia of the Channel Islands militias, and on the upper floor, regimental silver, musical instruments and mementoes of the Royal Guernsey Militia which was disbanded in 1939. Collections of weapons used by the militia and other regiments connected with Guernsey; Civil War armaments are housed in the **Armoury**.

Harbour (YZ) – The large modern harbour is a scene of constant activity bustling with car and passenger ferries to the mainland and neighbouring islands, fishing boats and private yachts. The north pier was added in the 18C to the original 13C pier to form the Old Harbour. The Castle Pier and St Julian's Pier out to White Rock were built between 1835 and 1909; the Jetty was added in the 1920s. The North Marina is destined to accommodate more private craft.

It is worth strolling out to White Rock or visiting the Castle for a fine **view** of the town, the harbour and the neighbouring islands.

★ **St Peter's** – The Town Church, as it is known, was begun by William the Conqueror in 1048, and completed around 1475. The nave and west door are part of the original Norman structure. In those days it doubled as a fort and in the past it has housed the guns of the artillery, the fire engine, and the flower market on wet days. The interior is furnished with an interesting range of stained glass and a handsome collection of memorials and monuments commemorating famous Guernseymen.

Market Halls (Z) – On the right is the first covered market to be built comprising Les Halles with the Assembly Rooms above, completed in 1782. Opposite is the single-storey Doric-style meat market (1822). "Les Arcades, 1830" *(on the left)* is very handsome despite the loss of the final bay. The Fish Market, with its row of round windows like great port-holes was finished in 1877. Finally, the Vegetable Market was constructed in 1879. All stand on the site of the Rectory Garden.

26 Cornet Street ⓥ (Z D) – This Victorian shop, complete with period reeded shutters in the bay windows carefully recreates a sweet-shop and parlour as it would have been in 1900. It also serves as the headquarters of the National Trust for Guernsey.

Continue up Cornet Street some distance (numbering system is deceptive).

★ **Hauteville House** ⓥ (Z) – *38 Hauteville.* **Victor Hugo** was exiled from his native France for political reasons in 1851. After a year in Brussels and three in Jersey, from which he was expelled for dis-

Firing the Noonday Gun, Castle Cornet

paraging remarks about Queen Victoria, he came to Guernsey. He bought this great white house – supposedly haunted – in 1856 for a derisory sum.

Set back from the street, the plain façade gives no hint of the incongruous and eccentric décor inside. During his fourteen years' residence Hugo re-decorated the interior, doing much of the work himself: every inch of wall and ceiling is covered with wood carvings or tiles (from Delft or Rouen), tapestries or silk fabric. In the dining room a soup tureen serves as a finger bowl and iron stands are incorporated into the 'ancestors' armchair' to give it a Gothic look; in the Red Drawing Room the torches of liberty held by the negro slaves are simply upturned candlesticks supporting copper scale pans. Mottoes and inscriptions abound and mirrors are placed so as to enhance the effect of various features. Hugo used to work on his poems and novels standing at a small table in the **Glass Room** on the third floor overlooking the sea about which he wrote: "there is nothing more peaceful than this creek in calm weather, nothing more tumultuous in a heavy sea. There were ends of branches perpetually wet from the foam. In the spring, it was full of flowers, nests, scents, birds, butterflies and bees". Regularly, he would take a break from his work by going down to Havelet Bay to swim. From the **Look Out** where he sometimes slept, he could see the house up the road (La Fallue at 1 Beauregard Lane) into which his faithful mistress, Juliette Drouot settled in November 1856. In April 1864, she moved down the road (No 20 Hauteville).

Candie Gardens (Y) – A dramatic statue of the French Romantic poet and novelist Victor Hugo looks out over the sloping lawn. Splendid gardens extend below the museum and the Priaulx Library (formerly Candie House); these were laid out in 1898 as public pleasure gardens with exotic plants (maidenhair tree), replacing the walled orchard and vegetable garden. In the Lower Garden are preserved two glasshouses – the first heated glasshouses to be erected in Guernsey (1792).

Guernsey Museum ⓥ (Y M) – A cluster of modern octagonal structures arranged alongside a former Victorian bandstand (now a tea room), houses the Lukis archeological collection of artefacts retrieved from La Valle chambered tomb in 1811 and the Wilfred Carey Collection of paintings, prints and ceramics. The recreation of a Victorian domestic interior features the pioneer archeologist and eclectic antiquarian collector Frederick Corbin Lukis and his daughter Mary Anne. Certain items were assembled by Wilfred Carey who served several years as a diplomat in the Far East.

An excellent display traces the chronological development of Guernsey complete with geological, archeological and natural history exhibits from the earliest settlers, through the ages to modern day – the broad range of information given is further supplemented by touch-screens.

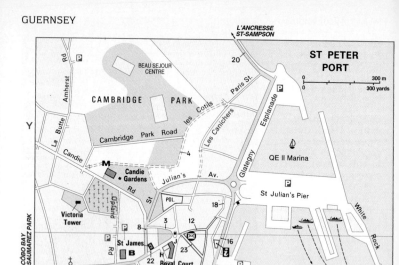

B Elizabeth College   **D** 26 Cornet Street   **M** Guernsey Museum

Other buildings (Z) – **Elizabeth College** (**B**), the public school for boys, was founded as a grammar school in 1563 by Elizabeth I to foster a supply of local English-speaking clergymen. The pseudo-Tudor style building by John Wilson dates from 1826-29.

The elegant Neo-Classical Church of **St James'** ⊙, designed by John Wilson in 1818 for services held in English for the British garrison, is now a concert hall.

The law courts and the States of Deliberation hold their sittings in the elegant **Royal Court House** ⊙ (1792); its archives go back 400 years.

EXCURSIONS

★ Saumarez Park

From St Peter Port take the main road St Julian's Avenue uphill opposite the harbour; continue straight past the St Pierre Park Hotel on the left, and straight over at the crossroads with Rectory Hill (left) and La Rue du Friquet (right). Follow the one-way system by forking left, turning right and immediately left (signposted) along La Route de Côbo. From the car park walk back parallel with the main road to reach the museum.

The trees and shrubs of this beautiful park are matched by the formal rose gardens; the pond is alive with wildfowl. **The Battle of Flowers** is held here every year on the fourth Thursday in August; most of the floats which compete in the different classes are made of real flowers grown locally.

The house (**St John's Residential Home** ⊙) dates from 1721 and was the home of Admiral Lord James de Saumarez; today it is a residential home. It was here that François Truffaut filmed a number of sequences for his film *Adèle H* about the daughter of Victor Hugo.

★ **Guernsey Folk Museum** ⊙ – Inside the farmstead buildings of Saumarez House are recreated a series of Victorian interiors: downstairs, the kitchen and parlour, heated by a great open fireplace fuelled by seaweed, dung or furze, were known as *la tchuisaene* which, in dialect, alludes to it being the heart of the family home; upstairs are the bedrooms and nursery. Carefully selected period furniture and furnishings are complemented by the fascinating and unusual, old fashioned accoutrements (kettles, cauldrons) and toys. Elsewhere are displayed a selection of clothes and textiles retrieved in excellent condition from grandmothers' attic chests. Across the courtyard, additional outbuildings display items from the **Langlois Collection of Agricultural Implements** used to furnish a washroom, dairy, cider barn, plough shed – with illustrations and explanations of the different harvesting methods applied to gathering parsnips, potatoes, wheat and corn given in the room above. Other traditional tools common to the quarrymen, tin-smith, blacksmith, cooper, wheelwright, carpenter are also preserved.

Castel

From St Peter Port take the main road St Julian's Avenue uphill opposite the harbour; continue straight past the St Pierre Park Hotel on the left, and turn left down Castle Hill / Les Rohais de Haut. The church is on the right before the crossroads.

Parish Church – Early documents list the Church of St Mary of the Castle (**Ste Marie du Castel** or Our Lady of Deliverance) as belonging to the Abbey of Mont St Michel in 1155; before then, the site may have had a pre-Christian sanctuary and Roman fort hence its rectangular churchyard.
The 12C church contains 13C frescoes of the *Last Supper* and the fable of the *Three Living Kings* (on horseback going hawking) *and The Three Dead* (skeletal figures). The timed lightswitch is next to the organ.
Outside the church entrance stands a granite statue menhir found beneath the chancel in 1878. It represents a female figure, probably the mother-goddess of the Neolithic and Bronze Age cults; the stone seats were probably used at the former medieval court of Fief St Michael.
Fine **views** extend to the coast and across to Vale Church.

St Andrew

From St Peter Port take the main road St Julian's Avenue uphill opposite the harbour; fork left along the Queen's Road and continue straight along Mount Row/Le Vauquiedor/Mauxmarquis Road. Past the church on the left a signpost indicates the left turn to the German Underground Hospital.

German Underground Hospital and Ammunition Store ⊙ – *La Vassalerie, St Andre's. 20mins.* This is the most extensive project undertaken by the Germans during their occupation of Guernsey: it comprises a series of tunnels over an area of 75 000sq ft, 45-75ft down into the granite bed-rock, and took nigh on 3.5 years to build. When complete, the 500-bed hospital section was used for only nine months to treat French casualties wounded in action against the

The Little Chapel

Liberating Forces. Today the miles of hollow corridor and interlocking wards echo with dripping water, one's own footsteps and silent thoughts: ducts from the central heating and air-conditioning units rust in the confined emptiness, rows of narrow hospital beds furnish the odd ward, signs identify each compartment: operating theatre, X-ray room, and laboratory (9); dispensary (2); staff sleeping quarters; store rooms; cinema (15); mortuary (16)...

Return to the main road, turn left and follow westwards: as the road descends the hill a sign to the right indicates a turning to the Little Chapel and Guernsey Clockmakers.

★ **Little Chapel** – *Les Vauxbelets. 20mins.* Nestling in a shrubbery, 'The Unknown Little Jewel' is a unique model of the grotto and shrine at Lourdes. It was the third in fact to be built in 1925 by Brother Deodat, a Salesian monk from Les Vauxbelets College. Its clinker walls are faced, within and without, with a brilliant mosaic of shells, fragments of glass and bone china: much of which flooded to the site following an article in *The Daily Mirror.*

TOUR OF THE ISLAND

☐ Clos Du Valle: St Peter Port to Vale Church

5 miles/8km – Half a day

Until 1806 the northern part of Guernsey, known as Clos du Valle, was cut off by the Braye du Valle – a tidal channel of mudflats and saltmarsh, now protected as a nature reserve, which runs from St Sampson to Grand Havre.
The channel was crossed by a bridge in St Sampson and by a causeway at low water near Vale Church. For reasons of military security it was filled in by Sir John Doyle; the 300 acres of reclaimed salt pans and mud flats are now covered in glasshouses. The Clos du Valle is densely populated owing to the many quarries which were worked in the area in the 19C.

Leave St Peter Port by the coast road (Glategny Esplanade) north towards St Sampson. Turn left in Belle Greve Bay into Le Grand Bouet and then second right.

Château des Marais – The ruined medieval **Castle in the Marshes** crowns a low knoll: it was first used in the Bronze Age, protected by the surrounding marshy ground. An outer wall encloses a ditch and inner fortification. Excavations in 1975-77 uncovered 13C coins in a chapel dedicated to Our Lady of the Marshes. The castle was refortified in the 18C and was later known as Ivy Castle owing to the creeper which covered it.

St Sampson – Guernsey's second port, which has taken all bulk cargoes since 1964, lies at the eastern end of the Braye du Valle *(see below)*. Shipbuilding in the 18C was eclipsed as the main industry in the 19C by the export of granite for road building; the first of the handsome granite quays was built in 1820. The harbour and its environs feature in Hugo's novel *The Toilers of the Sea* as La Durande.
The first **bridge** originally spanned the Braye du Valle *(see below):* when it became blocked in 1806, it was faced with stone to form a mooring.
St Sampson, the oldest church in Guernsey, was allegedly built where the saint came ashore (*c*550) either from Llantwit Major in South Wales or from Dol in Brittany. The oldest section is the early Norman saddleback tower. Its attractive churchyard overlooks the disused Longue Hougue Quarry.

From The Bridge take Vale Avenue north and keep to the main road (left – La Route du Braye). Oatlands Craft Centre is located opposite a garden centre in Gigandis Road.

Oatlands Craft Centre ⓥ – *Braye Road, St Sampson.* An old brick farmstead and its thatched outbuildings arranged around a courtyard houses a craft centre where craftsmen exercise their skills in pottery, glass blowing, silversmithing and engraving. The two distinctive kilns were used from 1800 to the 1930s to produce bricks for fortifications, chimneys and boiler pits for heating glasshouses, and clay pots for tomatoes.

Vale Castle – The medieval castle, now in ruins, was built on the site of an Iron Age hillfort (*c*600 BC) on the only high point in Clos du Valle, overlooking St Sampson harbour. Most of the extant masonry dates from work undertaken after the American Wars of Independence when France ratified her alliance with the independent American colony and it was considered necessary to consolidate artillery defences and provide additional barracks. These were used by the Island's Militia and by Russian troops evacuated from Holland at the end of the 18C.
There is a fine **view** inland, along the east coast and out to sea to the reef, Alderney *(north)*, Herm and Sark *(west)* and Jersey *(south)*.

Bordeaux Harbour provides mooring for fishing boats; the sheltered bay which provides the only safe swimming in the area, is described by Victor Hugo in his novel *The Toilers of the Sea.*

Defensive towers

In 1778-79 a chain of fifteen loopholed granite towers was built around Guernsey's shoreline: 30ft (9m) high, 20ft (6m) in diameter, with a wall thickness of 4ft (1.22m). The twelve that survive, numbered in an anti-clockwise sequence, illustrate how advanced they were for their period – an adapted design was later used when similar towers were built in Jersey. The ground level was used for storage; entrance to the first floor was by a retractable wooden ladder and gave access to two levels of accommodation loopholed for musketry defence; the open roof was subsequently altered to make room for a 12-pounder gun. The shortcomings of the design, however, were soon realised by Royal Engineers who advocated a different format for the Martello Towers built at Fort Saumarez, Fort Grey and Fort Hommet (1804), in keeping with those being constructed on the south coast of England.

Detached magazines were built alongside in which kegs or barrels of black powder would be stored protected from the damp sea winds and where muskets could be serviced.

Follow the main road north; as it gently swerves to the left, turn down the minor road right. This forks into two: take the left fork: park by the rundown glasshouses on the right opposite the passage tomb.

Dehus Dolmen ⊙ – *Light switch on left inside the entrance.* This, the second largest passage grave in Guernsey, has four side chambers covered by seven capstones: crouch down to see Le Gardien du Tombeau, the figure of an archer *(switch for spotlight)*. It was first excavated in 1837 by Lukis whose finds are in the Guernsey Museum in St Peter Port.

Several minor roads meander northwards to the coast.

★ **Fort Doyle** – From the fort there is an excellent **view** of the Casquets reef and Alderney *(north)*, the French coast, Herm and Sark *(west)*.

Beaucette Quarry Marina – A breach was blasted in the side of this old diorite quarry to turn it into a sheltered marina. Even at high tide only the tops of the masts can be seen.

Fort Le Marchant – This promontory is the most northerly point in Guernsey. The fort is named after the founder of the Royal Military College at Sandhurst in England. Fine view, particularly of L'Ancresse Bay and L'Ancresse Common.

L'Ancresse Bay – The bay is very popular for bathing and surfing particularly at the western end near Fort Pembroke. **L'Ancresse Common** is the only extensive open space on the island and is much used for strolling, dog-walking, horse racing, cattle grazing, kite flying and as a golf course. The area is rich in archeological sites: **La Varde Dolmen** is the largest passage grave in Guernsey; human bones and limpet shells were found beneath the 6 capstones. **Les Fouaillages** burial ground is 7 000 years old; excavations as recent as 1978-81 produced very interesting material. The coastline is well defended by forts and seven defensive towers.

Vale Church – St Michael du Valle was consecrated in 1117 on

Golfing on L'Ancresse Common

Th. Jullien/DIAF

the site of an earlier chapel dedicated to St Magloire, who with St Sampson brought Christianity to Guernsey in the 6C. Until the end of the 19C the church stood at the edge of a tidal inlet, the Braye du Valle which divided the Clos du Valle from the main island. The church is irregular in alignment, suggesting that it was built in stages by Benedictine monks from Mont St Michel who had founded a priory nearby in 968; the priory was in ruins by 1406 and finally demolished in 1928.

Inside, the chancel is decorated with Arts and Crafts tiles; the window in the Archangel Chapel is from the William Morris studio; to the right of the altar is an unusually large piscina.

Outside stands a 7C monument unearthed in 1949 beyond the west door. In the churchyard rest a number of pirates and smugglers shipwrecked nearby.

Past the southeast corner of the Vale churchyard runs the Military Road, the first to be built by Sir John Doyle, which crosses the island north of St Peter Port to the east coast.

② West Coast: Grand Havre to Pezeries Point

10 miles/15km – About half a day.

The **Grand Havre**, an ample inlet at the west end of the Braye du Valle, is best admired from the Rousse headland with its tower and jetty. A more extensive horizon including the many sandy bays which scallop the west coast in both directions is visible from the German gun battery strategically situated on the granite headland the **Grandes Rocques**.

★★ Côbo Bay – The bay is a charming combination of sand for swimming and surfing, and rocks for exploring marine life.

Vazon Bay – The huge beach between Fort Houmet *(north)* and Fort le Crocq *(south)* is excellent for swimming, sunbathing, surfing, horse riding and motor and motorcycle racing. Beneath the sands lie the remains of a submerged forest; at dusk, the rocks assume animal-like shapes such as lions and camels.

★ St Apolline's Chapel – In 1394 a charter was granted for a chantry chapel which is decorated with a **fresco** *(light switch)* of *The Last Supper*. The original dedication to Ste Marie de la Perelle was changed in 1452 to St Apolline (or St Apollonia), whose cult became very popular in Europe at that time. She was an elderly deaconess who was burned to death in an anti-Christian riot in Alexandria in 249; as she was first struck repeatedly in the face and lost many teeth she is invoked against toothache; she is often represented bearing forceps.

After the Reformation the chapel was used as a barn; it was restored in 1978.

Le Trépied Dolmen – This burial chamber at the southern end of Perelle Bay was excavated in 1840 by Frederic Lukis, whose finds are in the Guernsey Museum. In past centuries the site was used for witches' Sabbaths on Friday nights.

L'Erée Headland – The tall defensive tower on the headland is called Fort Saumarez. To the south stands **Le Creux ès Faies Dolmen**, a passage grave said locally to be the entrance to Fairyland; other local myths talk of it being a meeting place for witches. Excavation has produced items dating from 2000-1800 BC.

Lihou island – *Accessible by causeway at low tide.* The semi-detached character of the island is inviting to those seeking the contemplative life. In 1114 a priory was founded and dedicated to Our Lady of the Rock (now in ruins). Earlier this century there was a burst of activity from a factory making iodine from seaweed. The predecessor of the present lonely farmhouse was used by the Germans for target practice. On the west coast a 100ft rock pool provides excellent bathing.

★ Rocquaine Bay – The grand sweep of the bay, which is protected from erosion by a high sea wall, is interrupted by the Cup and Saucer, originally a medieval fort to which a defensive tower was added in 1804. It is painted white as a navigation mark.

Fort Grey Maritime Museum ⊘ – The tower presently accommodates a small museum on two floors dedicated to the history of the fort, and to the many shipwrecks in Guernsey waters, the Hanois Reef and Lighthouse; displays also include artefacts salvaged by marine archeologists from a hundred ships which have run aground along the west coast between 1750 and 1978 – a video explains the disaster involving the loss of the *Orion* and the ensuing difficult rescue operation.

Portelet – The picturesque harbour full of fishing boats is backed by the houses of the Hanois Lighthouse keepers. Nearby is the **Table des Pions**, a circle of turf surrounded by a ditch and a ring of stones, where the *pions* or footmen of the Chevauchée de St Michel ate their lunch sitting at the grass table with their feet in the trench.

La Chevauchée de St Michel

Until 1837 this medieval ceremony, which probably originated in pagan Normandy, took place every three years just before the Feast of Corpus Christi with its procession of the blessed sacrament. The cavalcade (chevauchée) consisted of the Crown Officers and the officials of the feudal court of St Michel du Valle who made a tour of inspection of the island highways; they were dressed in costume and mounted on horseback, armed with a sword and attended by one or two footmen (pions). The pions were usually handsome bachelors and it was their privilege to kiss any young women they met. They lunched at Pezeries; dinner was provided out of the fines levied on the owners of any obstructions; Le Perron du Roi near to the Forest Church served as a mounting block for dignitaries.

★★ **Pezeries Point** – This is the most westerly point in all the Channel Islands, a remote and unfrequented place. The fort was built in the Napoleonic era. The name Pezeries is a corruption of *eperquerie (see INTRODUCTION: Livelihood)*.

3 Southern Cliffs: Pleinmont Point to St Peter Port

16 miles/26km – Half a day.

These cliffs which extend along the south coast and round to St Peter Port provide some of the most wild and dramatic scenery in the island (beware of the cliff face: it is often unstable and dangerous); a footpath runs from the western end to the town, tracing its steep path up and down into the valleys and bays.

Pleinmont Point – The headland which is crowned by TV masts provides an extensive **view**: along the southern cliffs *(east)*, out to the Hanois Lighthouse and its surrounding reefs *(west)*, across Rocquaine Bay to Lihou Island *(north)*. The headland is still dominated by a coastal artillery direction finding tower with wide observation openings, imposed by the Germans upon an existing Martello Tower: others were constructed at Fort Saumarez, Chouet, La Corbière and L'Angle. From here to La Moye Point the cliffs are bare and rugged, indented by small bays and inlets and pierced by many caves. A footpath stretches all along the clifftops through National Trust land, past all the watch houses before coming out by the Aquarium.

The roof of a cave in La Forge Bay has fallen in to form a **blow-hole** *(souffleur)*; the best time to see and hear it in action is about 2 hours after low tide.

La Moye Point, the smallest of the three promontories on the south coast, is wild and beautiful. Le Gouffre, a charming steep valley, flanks it on the west. On the east side precipitous steps lead down to a three-tiered mooring for fishing boats in the shelter of the headland.

Return to the main road – La Route de Pleinmont and continue eastwards back towards St Peter Port. Torteval Church is off to the left.

Torteval – The unusual name of Guernsey's smallest parish is thought to derive from the twisting valley that runs down to Fort Grey. The original Church of St Philippe was demolished in 1816. The present church, intended as a Calvinist chapel is very plain – its distinctive round spire being its most interesting feature.

La Rue de la Villiaze forks right into La Rue des Landes; turn right towards Forest Church (St Margaret's or Ste Marguérite de la Forêt) and then left or right around it. The German Occupation Museum is then well signposted.

German Occupation Museum ⊘ – *1hr.* This museum has grown out of a private collection of artefacts from the Nazi occupation of the Channel Islands. A short video *(7mins)* serves as an introduction to the period of occupation. A series of rooms displays various aspects of life at that time: military hardware (weaponry, radio telephones); vehicles; clothing, uniforms and associated paraphernalia (badges, buttons, mending kits); a field kitchen, food parcels, food substitutes and rationing; personal mementos of German soldiers and forced labourers, newspapers and posters; video of the occupation and the liberation. All vehicles and mechanical artefacts are carefully maintained in working order – hence the smell of motor oil!

A number of small roads lead southwards to the coast; otherwise, return to the main road and turn first right as if for the Manor Hotel: this roads leads to Petit Bot Bay.

Petit Bot Bay – This attractive bay which has good bathing and sand at low water lies at the foot of a green valley guarded by a defensive tower (1780). The stream used to turn a corn and a paper mill but they and two hotels were destroyed by the Germans after a British Commando raid in July 1940.

Across the bay is Icart Point which may be reached by road: return back up the hill to the main road and turn right down La Rue de la Villette. This same road turns inland to rejoin the valley that leads down to Moulin Huet Bay.

★★ **Icart Point** – This is the highest and most southerly headland with very fine **views** of the coast. The view west reveals a string of quiet sandy beaches, some difficult of access, curving round to La Moye Point. On the east side is **Saint's Bay**, a favourite mooring for fishermen.

Moulin Huet Bay – A water lane runs down the valley, one of the most beautiful in Guernsey, to the bay where the stream plunges down the cliff face to the sea. This is where the French Impressionist painter **Renoir** used to come (1883), fascinated by the rocks that glow pink in the setting sun. Both this bay and its eastern neighbour are good for bathing but the sandy beach at **Petit Port** is superior.

Renoir in Guernsey

The French Impressionist painter spent a month in Guernsey late in 1883 during which time he painted some 15 canvases with views of the bay and beach of Moulin Huet – heralded in contemporary guidebooks as the island's finest scenic attraction. Little is known of the reasons why Renoir visited the island – which Hugo later described as having "the singular attraction of combining a climate made for leisure with a population made for toil". For the Victorian Englishman, the place provided idyllic holiday conditions blessed with a gentle climate and exotic vegetation including the sweetest grapes, ripened under glass and harvested from July to September. For the French, Guernsey was a secluded retreat from the bustle of the Brittany coastal resorts.

St Martin – The parish occupies the south eastern section of Guernsey and is principally residential, well served by former military roads to its jagged coastline.

★ **La Gran'mère du Chimquière** – At the gate into St Martin's churchyard stands a Stone Age menhir carved to represent a female figure; her facial features were chiselled later. Known as the Grandmother of the Cemetery, she is supposed to guarantee fertility and receives gifts of coins and flowers. The statue was broken in two in the 19C by an over-zealous churchwarden but re-erected by the parishioners. The church itself dates from 1225-50; the south porch was added in the 1520s. Inside, it has a pre-Reformation font; the lectern and oak pulpit are worked in the Breton style and date from 1657.

Return to the main road; turn right to Jerbourg.

The road passes the **Doyle Column** which commemorates Sir John Doyle, Lt Governor (1803-15); plaque showing distances to other islands. From here the clifftop footpath provides some spectacular views through the pine trees of the coastline. At the southern tip sit the Pea Stacks – the third outcrop of rock, resembling the form of a monk, is called Le Petit Bonhomme Andriou.
The ramparts of a Bronze Age hillfort still crown the headland *(beyond the car park)* together with the remains of 20C German gun batteries.

★★ **St Martin's Point** – There is a magnificent **view** down to the lighthouse on the point, north up the coast to St Peter Port and seawards to the other islands.

★ **Jerbourg Point** – From the Pea Stacks rising from the sea just off the point the view swings northwest into the broad sweep of Moulin Huet Bay. The Jerbourg peninsula is Guernsey's southeastern extremity: excavations have revealed that it was inhabited in Neolithic times, that earthern ramparts and ditches were reinforced during the Bronze Age and that a defensive castle, the Château de Jerbourg was built here to shelter islanders through troubles in the Middle Ages when the French occupied Castle Cornet.

Fermain Bay – *Access on foot from car park or cliff path from Jerbourg; or by boat (summer only) from St Peter Port*. This charming bay with its pebbled cove, backed by densely wooded cliffs and an 18C defensive tower, offers a sandy beach and good bathing at low tide. The pepperpot tower is a Napoleonic sentry box. At low spring tides the remains of German anti-landing barriers can be discerned.

Set back from Sausmarez Road as the main road curves left, entrance beyond main gate into shaded car park.

Sausmarez Manor ⊘ – *1hr.* The elegant Queen Anne house was built in 1714-18 by Sir Edmund Andros, the Seigneur of Sausmarez and onetime Governor of New York. The roof-top 'widow's walk' is a traditional East Coast American feature implemented to provide a view far out to sea. The later Regency additions at the rear were largely rebuilt in the 1870s by General George de Sausmarez who served with the East India Company.

The welcoming interior displays portraits and souvenirs of the Seigneurs of Sausmarez's 750 years of occupation: fine antique tapestries hang in the dark and cosy dining room; handsome family furniture and objects are scattered through the spacious drawing room and larger dining room; the log of the round-the-world voyage of *HMS Centurion* in which Philip Saumarez served is kept with the Inca silver from a captured Spanish treasure ship which was turned into coin of the realm in the great beamed hall...

In an outbuilding are displayed a **collection of doll's houses** ⊙, several of which meticulously recreate typical Guernsey household interiors.

The wooded **grounds** through which passes a **model children's railway** ⊙, is planted with various strains of tall bamboo and camellias.

The park gates, with sculptures by Sir Henry Cheere, celebrate the return of the Manor to the de Sausmarez branch of the family in 1748.

Fort George – This modern luxury housing estate occupies the site of the British garrison, Fort George, built from 1782 to 1812 and destroyed by Allied bombers the day before D-Day having been adapted by the Germans to serve as the wartime headquarters of the Luftwaffe early warning service. The garrison troops used to bathe in the sea below, hence the name Soldiers' Bay. The military cemetery on the clifftop below the fort harbours the only German war graves still on the island.

As the main road drops down towards the waterfront a road leads off sharply to the right: look out for signposts for the Aquarium.

La Valette Underground Military Museum ⊙ – The museum occupies five tunnels that were excavated to hold fuel tanks *(Höhlgang)* for refuelling U-boats: one tunnel was never completed. The four metal containers in situ at the end of the occupation were manufactured in Bremen, and had a capacity of 30 000 gallons; on examination they were found to contain a kind of oil extracted from coal. Today the area has been adapted to accommodate displays of uniforms and apparel belonging to the Guernsey Militia (officially constituted in 1203); German artefacts and mementoes of the occupation.

Guernsey Aquarium ⊙ – Installed in a disused tunnel is a series of water tanks housing a variety of aquatic creatures: tropical and indigenous fish, conger eels, sharks, lobsters, reptiles and amphibians. The tunnel housing them was excavated in 1860 to carry a tramway south along the coast; work was abandoned after a rock fall; the Germans extended it in 1940-45.

ALDERNEY

Population 2 297

Michelin Atlas p 5 or Map 403

Alderney is the most northerly of the Channel Islands and lies eight miles west of the tip of the Cotentin Peninsula in Normandy, separated from the Cap de la Hague headland by the treacherous tidal current known to wary sailors as the **Alderney Race**. Three and a half miles long by no more than one and a half miles wide, the island slopes gently from a plateau (296ft - 90m) of farmland skirted by high cliffs in the southwest to a tongue of low-lying land in the northeast, fringed by rocky spits and sandy bays, and bristling with ruined fortifications.

Historical notes – Owing to its key position, nearest to England, France and the Channel shipping lanes, Alderney has frequently been fortified. The Romans seem to have used it as a naval base; there are traces of a late Roman fort at the Nunnery. The first English fortifications date from the reign of Henry VIII who started to construct a fort on the hill south of Longis Bay. Faced with the threat of invasion in the Napoleonic period, the British Government strengthened the existing defences and sent a garrison of 300 to assist the local militia.

The most impressive fortifications were built between 1847 and 1858. Alarmed by the development of a French naval base at Cherbourg, the British Government decided to create a safe harbour at Braye by constructing a huge breakwater and to defend the island by building a chain of 10 forts along the north coast from Clonque in the west round to Longis Bay in the east. There was also a plan to build another harbour at Longis and link it to Braye with a canal, thus strengthening the defence of the northeastern sector and providing a safe harbour whatever the wind. The forts were constructed of local stone with white quoins and dressings; several stood off-shore and were reached by causeways at low tide.

In June 1940 almost all the population left the island and the livestock was evacuated to Guernsey. During their five-year occupation the Germans re-fortified most of the Victorian forts and built masses of ugly concrete fortifications. When the islanders began to return late in 1945 they found their possessions gone and the houses derelict or destroyed. It took ten years and substantial government aid to make good the damage.

Constitution – Alderney is part of the Bailiwick of Guernsey. Since the introduction of the new constitution on 1 January 1949, the budget and other financial matters have to be approved by the States of Guernsey. Otherwise all island business is decided by the Committees of the States of Alderney, which consists of 12 elected members and an elected President, who serve for three years. The Court consists of six Jurats under a Chairman, who are appointed by the Home Office.

The pre-1949 constitution which had evolved down the centuries included two other bodies, the Douzaine, an assembly of 12 heads of families, and the Court of Chief Pleas. All offices were then elective. The feudal system under a seigneur was never established in Alderney and the later Governors, appointed by the Crown from the 16C to the 19C, often met with opposition from the independent-minded islanders.

Survival – Two constants in the economy of Alderney are fishing and farming; providing the visitor with a delicious variety of fresh fish and crustaceans; before the Second World War this was supplemented by income from exporting cattle, granite and gravel. Tourism, which began after the defeat of Napoleon when people came to visit the many retired military personnel who settled on the island, was given a boost when Queen Victoria visited the fortifications in 1854.

Modern tourism – Alderney supports a small prosperous community, a significant portion of which has settled there since the German occupation. The air is friendly as everyone knows each other and seems happy to welcome visitors in search of a quiet holiday away from the more sophisticated and popular resorts. This, rather, is a haven for nature-lovers in search of wild broom, thrift, sea campion and ox-eye daisies; hoopoes and golden orioles, birds of prey and the occasional white stork or purple heron, and the sea birds, especially the colonies of gannets and puffins. At low tide the rock pools reveal a variety of marine life; anemones, corals and ormers.

Easy access is provided via the airport, which was completed in 1935, by ferry from Guernsey or by private boat. Road traffic is minimal, although taxis are on hand to ferry passengers from the harbour and the First and Last Restaurant uphill as required! Although building development is carefully restricted to safeguard the island's infra-structure, the island provides a range of informal accommodation (hotels, bed and breakfast), and excellent restaurants.

ST ANNE

The charm of St Anne lies in its cobbled streets and smart whitewashed granite houses; its appearance is reminiscent of villages in Cornwall and Normandy. The Town, as it is called by the islanders, lies about half a mile from the north coast on the edge of the best agricultural land, known as La Blaye.

The original medieval settlement of farmhouses was centred on **Marais Square** which was then unpaved and had a stream running through it where the washing was done. As in ancient times, narrow lanes or *venelles* lead out to the un-enclosed fields divided into *riages*, each consisting of a number of strips: Alderney is one of the few places in the British Isles still to operate this archaic system of managing open agricultural land, although electric fencing is occasionally used.

Another settlement grew up at **Le Huret**, where the people gathered to decide when to gather the seaweed *(vraic)* used to fertilise the land. In the 15C more houses were built to the east of the square, to accommodate settlers from Guernsey, and the Blaye was extended to support a population of 700. In the 18C the huge profits made from privateering led to a building boom; thatch was replaced by tiles, the first Court House was built and the Governor spent money on improving the communal buildings as well as his own residence. The northern part of the town – **Queen Elizabeth II Street, Victoria Street and Ollivier Street** – developed in the early Victorian era when the population of the island trebled with the introduction of a military garrison and many immigrant labourers brought in to build the harbour. Utilitarian workmen's cottages were built of local sandstone at Newtown and elsewhere. Many attractive houses and gardens line the green lanes, such as La Vallée, which run from St Anne down to the north coast.

St Anne's – The church, consecrated in 1850, was designed by Sir Gilbert Scott in the transitional style from Norman to Early English cruciform and built in local granite dressed with white Caen stone. The cost was borne by Revd Canon

John Le Mesurier, son of the last hereditary governor of Alderney, in memory of his parents. The church is unexpectedly large as it was intended to hold not only the local population, then swollen by immigrant labourers, but also the military garrison.

English was then replacing Norman French as the local language; the lectern holds two Bibles and the texts in the apse and near the door appear in both languages. Below the west window, which shows children of all races, are six brass plaques commemorating the Le Mesurier family who governed the island from 1721 to 1825. Queen Elizabeth II's visit to Alderney in 1957 is recorded in the window in the Lady Chapel.

During the war the church was damaged by being used as a store and the bells were removed; two were recovered on the island and the other four were found in Cherbourg. The churchyard gates in Victoria Street, erected as a memorial to Prince Albert, were removed by the Germans but replaced by a local resident.

Museum ⊘ – The Alderney Society's Museum presents a comprehensive view of the island: geology; flora and fauna; archeology, particularly finds from the Iron Age Settlement at Les Hughettes; domestic and military history, including the Victorian fortifications and the German Occupation.

The collections are displayed in the old school which was endowed in 1790 by the Governor *(inscription over the gate)*.

The **Clock Tower** (1767) standing nearby is all that remains of the old church which was pulled down when the present one was built. The original dedication to St Mary, and the name of the town too, was changed to St Anne early in the 17C.

Royal Connaught Square – This elegant square, which was renamed in 1905 on the occasion of a visit by the Duke of Connaught, was the centre of the town in the 18C.

Island Hall *(north side)*, a handsome granite building which is now a community centre and library, was enlarged in 1763 by John Le Mesurier to become Government House. The first house on the site was built by Captain Nicholas Ling, who was appointed Lt Governor in 1657 and lived there until his death in 1679. **Mouriaux House** was completed in 1779 by the Governor as his private residence.

Court House ⊘ – The present building in Queen Elizabeth II Street (formerly New Street) dates from 1850. Both the Court and the States of Alderney hold their sessions in the first-floor Court Room which was restored in 1955.

Victoria Street – This, the main shopping street, runs north past the church gates and the war memorial, which records the dead of both world wars. Its name was changed from Rue du Grosnez to celebrate Queen Victoria's visit in 1854.

Butes – The recreation ground, formerly the Butts, provides fine views of Braye Bay *(northeast)*, across Crabby Bay and the Swinge to the Casquets *(northwest)* and the English Channel.

Les Casquets

The sandstone reefs lie 7 miles west of Alderney, close to the main Channel shipping lane: its name is a corruption of The Cascades, derived, it is thought, from the turbulent waters encountered there. The first lighthouses to be built there were powered by coal, then oil and finally by electricity generated on the reef itself. The present 120ft tall beacon, managed by Trinity House, is clearly visible from Guernsey. Throughout history the Casquets have been a notorious hazard to seamen, most especially when thick fog prevails.

TOUR OF THE ISLAND *9 miles; 1 day.*

It is possible to walk round the island following the cliff-top footpath or to drive round making detours on foot to places of interest.

In summer there are boat trips round the island from Braye Harbour; tours ⊘ of the fortifications are organised once a week.

Braye – The harbour is protected by Fort Grosnez (1853) which was built at the same time as the massive **breakwater** (1000yds long plus another 600yds submerged) by the British Government in 1847, just as the French were consolidating their defences at Cherbourg. As with St Catherine's Bay in Jersey, the ambitious plans for harbours of refuge were never completely realised. The first quay, the Old Jetty, was built in 1736 by the Governor to provide a safe landing stage for the privateers and smugglers he 'protected'. The modern concrete jetty dates from the turn of the century.

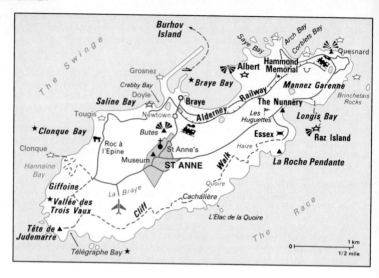

Alderney Railway ⊙ – Formed in 1978, the Alderney Railway Society operates the only standard-gauge railway to survive in the Channel Islands. The line was opened in 1847 to carry sandstone to the harbour; now steam and diesel trains run from Braye Road to Mannez Quarry.

★ **Braye Bay** – The largest bay on the island offers a sandy beach with good bathing and a fine view of the ferries, yachts and fishing boats in the harbour. Skirting the beach is a strip of grass, Le Banquage, where the seaweed *(vraic)* was left to dry.

Fort Albert – Mount Touraille, at the east end of Braye Bay, is crowned by Fort Albert (1853), the most impressive element in the Victorian chain of forts and German fortifications. From the seaward side there is a fine **view** inland to St Anne, westwards across Braye Bay to Fort Grosnez and the breakwater with Fort Tourgis in the background, and eastwards over the northern end of the island.

Hammond Memorial – *At the fork in the road east of Fort Albert.* The labourers of the Todt Organisation – paid volunteers from Vichy France, political refugees from Franco's Spain, Ukraine, Russia, North Africa who worked under duress on the fortifications during the Nazi Occupation are commemorated in a series of plaques inscribed in the languages of the prisoners. There were three camps on Alderney, each holding 1 500 men.

North Coast – Three excellent sandy bathing bays cluster round the most northerly headland beneath the walls of Fort Chateau à l'Etoc (1854), now converted into private flats: **Saye Bay**, nearly symmetrical in shape; **Arch Bay**, named after the tunnel through which the carts collecting seaweed reached the shore; **Corblets Bay**, overlooked by Fort Corblets (1855), now a private house with a splendid view.

Mannez Garenne – The low-lying northern end of the island, known as Mannez Garenne (Warren) is dominated by the remains of a German Observation Tower on the edge of the quarry.

Quesnard Lighthouse ⊙ (1912) stands 121ft high and casts its beam nearly 17 miles. From the lantern platform there is a magnificent **view**★ of the coast and the Race and, on a clear day, of the nuclear power station on the French coast. Many ships have come to grief on this rocky coast where the strong currents of the Swinge and the Race (Raz) meet. The most famous was the *Liverpool*, which ran aground in a fog in February 1902.

Three forts command the coastline; Les Homeaux Florains (1858), now in ruins, was approached by a causeway; Fort Quesnard, on the east side of Cats Bay, and Fort Houmet Herbe, another offshore fort reached by a causeway, were built in 1853.

Longis Bay – The retreating tide reveals a broad stretch of sand backed by a German tank trap which provides excellent shelter for sunbathing. The shallow bay was the island's natural harbour from prehistoric times until it silted up early in the 18C. Traces of an Iron Age settlement were discovered at **Les Huguettes** in 1968 when the golf course was being laid out on Longis Common; the finds are displayed in the museum. Various relics (coins, tiles, pottery and brickwork) indicate the existence of a Roman naval base protected by a fort (*c*2C-4C AD).

Raz Island – A causeway, which is covered at high tide, runs out to the island in the centre of Longis Bay. The fort (1853) has been partially restored and there is a fine view of Essex Castle and Hanging Rock (southwest).

The Nunnery – This building, which is thought to be the oldest on the island, stands on a rectangular site enclosed within a 16ft high wall. John Chamberlain converted it to his use when he became Governor in 1584. Its name was supplied by the British soldiers who were garrisoned there in the late 18C. It is now private dwellings owned by the States of Alderney.

Essex Castle – The first fort on Essex Hill overlooking Longis Bay was begun in 1546 by Henry VIII but abandoned in 1553. It consisted of an outer bailey, to hold the islanders and their flocks, around a central fort divided into four keeps. All but the north and west sides of the outer wall were razed in 1840 when the present structure was built, to be used first as a barracks and then as a military hospital; it is now private property. The pepperpot gazebo was added by the Governor, John Le Mesurier, who started a farm to feed the garrison at the Nunnery and called it Essex Farm; the name ascended the hill to the castle. At this point, the coastline to the west and south becomes ruggedly rocky.

Hanging Rock – The tilt of the 50ft column of rock projecting from the cliff face is said to have been caused by the people of Guernsey hitching a rope to the rock and trying to tow Alderney away.

Cliff Walk – From Haize round to Giffoine there is a magnificent cliff walk served by frequent paths running inland back to St Anne. The cliff edge is indented by a series of small valleys sloping seawards and a few narrow bays, difficult or impossible of access; bathing is not advisable owing to the swiftly-flowing currents in the Race. The view of the steep cliffs plunging into the rock-strewn sea is magnificent.

Cachalière – A path leads down past the old quarry to a pier, built early this century for loading granite but abandoned owing to the dangerous offshore currents. The name derives from Chicago where the Alderney man who paid for the pier had made his fortune. From here the rocks of **L'Etac de la Quoire** can be reached at low water.

★ **Telegraph Bay** – *Access by path and steps; beware of being cut off from the base of the steps by the rising tide.* The Telegraph Tower (1811), which provided communication with Jersey and Guernsey via a repeating telegraph signal on Sark, has given its name to the bay below. Except at high tide there is excellent bathing, sheltered from all but a south wind, and a fine view of La Nache and Fourquie rocks.

Tête de Judemarre – The headland provides a fine view of the rock-bound coast and of the islands of Guernsey, Herm and Sark.

★ **Vallée des Trois Vaux** – This deep cleft is in fact three valleys meeting on a shingle beach.

Giffoine – From the cliff it is possible to see the birds on their nests in the gannet colony on Les Etacs. The remains of a German coastal battery crown the headland above Hannaine Bay, where sandy spits between the rocks provide reasonable bathing. Fine view of Burhou, Ortac and the Casquets (north).

★ **Clonque Bay** – A zig-zag path descends the gorse and heather-clad slope above the attractive sweep of the bay. A causeway runs out to Fort Clonque (1855) which was designed by Captain William Jervois, the same military architect as for most of the other forts on Alderney, now converted into flats belonging to the Landmark Trust. Seaweed from Clonque was highly prized as fertiliser and two causeways enabled the 'vraicing' carts to descend to the beds of seaweed. Just south of Fort Tourgis (1855), now largely derelict, at the northern end of the bay, is the best preserved burial chamber on the island, **Roc à l'Epine**, which consists of a capstone supported on two upright stones. Alderney was once rich in such megaliths but all the others seem to have been destroyed when the Victorian fortifications were built.

Saline Bay – The shore, which is exposed to heavy seas so that bathing can be hazardous, is commanded by a gun battery and Fort Doyle, now a youth centre; beyond lies **Crabby Bay** in the lee of Fort Grosnez.

Burhou Island ⊘ – The island, which lies across The Swinge (about 1.5 miles – 2km), is extensively riddled with rabbit warrens and supports large colonies of puffins, razorbills, gannets and storm petrels as well as other sea birds. A hut provides simple accommodation for an overnight stay for birdwatching.

Accommodation in the West Country may be scarce during festivals or at the height of the summer season: to ensure peace of mind, book well in advance.

SARK★★

Sark is the last feudal fief in Europe and also the smallest independent state in the Commonwealth; its traditions date from the reign of Elizabeth I when its colonisation was permitted so as to stop pirates using it as a safe haven. These are maintained by the inhabitants, half of whom are descended from the first settlers.

The 3.5 miles long by 1.5 wide island, which consists of a green plateau bounded by high granite cliffs dropping sheer into the sea, is located at the very heart of the Channel Islands (7.5 miles east of Guernsey, 19 miles south of Alderney, 12 miles northwest of Jersey). Access is by boat from St Peter Port, this passes south of Herm and Jethou before skirting the impressive cliffs at the north end of the island which is a haven of rural peace. Its two parts, Great Sark and Little Sark, are linked by La Coupée, a high narrow neck of land which inspired Turner, Swinburne and Mervyn Peake, who set the closing scenes of his novel *Mr Pye* here.

Just off the west coast across the Gouliot Passage lies the island of Brecqhou, a dependent of the fiefdom of Sark since 1565, and now on perpetual lease to the reclusive multi-millionaire Barclay twins who have built a massive neo-Gothic mansion there.

History – It seems that St Magloire, the nephew of St Sampson, landed in Sark from Brittany in the middle of the 6C with 62 companions and founded a monastery. In the 9C the island was prey to Viking raids but little is known of the island's history before it became part of the Duchy of Normandy. In 1042 Sark was given to the Abbey of Mont St Michel by William the Conqueror, the Duke of Normandy. A few years later the island was attached to the diocese of Coutances. In 1336 Sark was invaded by a party of Scotsmen under David Bruce, a king in exile. Two years later Sark was attacked by Frenchmen. In 1349 the monks abandoned the island and for several years it was a lawless place, the haunt of pirates. The French regained it in 1549 but were thrown out by an Anglo-Dutch force which returned it to England. In 1565 Elizabeth I granted Sark to Helier de Carteret, Lord of the Manor of St Ouen in Jersey, on condition that he established a colony of 40 settlers prepared to defend the island. This Helier became the first Lord of Sark who set about dividing the land into 40 holdings, attributing one to each of the 40 families who

Visiting Sark

had accompanied him from Jersey, on condition that each tenant build and maintain a house and provide an armed man to defend the island. The number of holdings has not changed since then.

Constitution – At its head is the hereditary Lord (seigneur) who holds the fief of Sark; the present holder is Michael Beaumont, grandson of Sybil Hathaway, the Dame of Sark, whose long reign from 1927 to 1974 saw the island through difficult and changing times. The Seigneur of Sark has retained a number of privileges from the feudal period: the right to keep pigeons and to own a bitch. He also receives one thirteenth of the sale price of all island property.

Sark has its own parliament, the Chief Pleas, composed of the 40 tenants and 12 deputies elected for three years. The Seneschal is responsible for justice, together with the Clerk of the Court (Greffier) and the Sherriff (Prévôt). Law and order are upheld by the Constable assisted by the Vingtenier. A person under arrest is held in the tiny prison (2 cells) for 48 hours. In summer the local force is supplemented by a policeman from Guernsey. Serious cases are heard by the Guernsey courts.

TOUR OF THE ISLAND *1 day.*

One of the charms of Sark is the absence of cars: the only motor vehicles allowed being farmers' tractors, which are limited to one per landholding. In summer horse-drawn carriages and wagonettes provide transport for visitors; there are also bicycles for hire, although the preferred means of exploring the cliffs, bays and headlands is by foot.

Great Sark

Maseline Harbour – The light-house (1912) looks down over the harbour from the cliffs on Point Robert as the boat docks inside the modern concrete jetty which was inaugurated in 1949 by the Duke of Edinburgh when he and the then Princess Elizabeth visited Sark.

★ **Creux Harbour** – Opposite the tunnel to Maseline Harbour is a second tunnel to Creux Harbour, an older and picturesque little harbour, which is dry at low tide.

La Collinette – A short tunnel leads to the local 'bus' which takes passengers up Harbour Hill *(half a mile)* to the crossroads at the top called La Collinette. Straight ahead stretches **The Avenue**, once the drive to the original manor house and lined with trees but now the main street lined with shops. The small

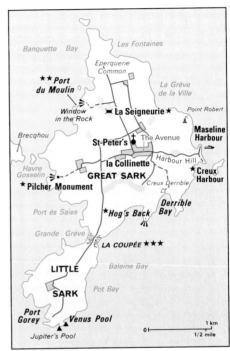

barrel-roofed building on the left at the far end is the island prison built in 1856. **St Peter's Church** dates from the 19C. The embroidered hassocks are the work of the island women; the designs incorporate the motifs and some of the names of the landholdings with which the seats are traditionally associated.

★ **La Seigneurie** – The present beautiful stone and granite manor house, the residence of the Seigneur of Sark, stands on the site of St Magloire's 6C monastery, after which the house is named La Moinerie. Begun in 1565, it was considerably enlarged in 1730 by the Le Pelley family who then held the fief of Sark. The square tower, which provides a splendid view of the island, was built as a signalling tower in 1860.

The house is sheltered from the wind by a screen of trees and high walls. The **gardens** ⊘ on which the Dame of Sark lavished so much attention, are luxuriant with flowers and shrubs, some brought from foreign parts, and maintained with undiminished care.

★★ **Port du Moulin** – A road along the north side of the Seigneurie grounds soon turns into a path following the windings of the clifftop. The sign 'Window and Bay' marks the way to the **Window in the Rock**, which the Revd William Collings had made in the

1850s to provide an impressive **view** of Port du Moulin. *Return to the fork in the path and take the other branch to Port du Moulin.* The bay, which is popular with bathers in summer, is flanked by stark rocks in strange shapes; at low tide huge arches in the rock appear. On the right stand **Les Autelets**, three granite columns accessible as the sea retreats.

Pilcher Monument★

This granite column was raised in memory of a London merchant, F Pilcher, who died at sea in 1868 with three companions while returning to Guernsey. From the plinth there is a fine view of the west coast and of Brecqhou, Herm, Jethou and Guernsey. A path runs down to Havre Gosselin where yachts moor in the summer months.

Derrible Bay – At Petit Dixcart turn left into a stony path, then right into a path beside a field; a left fork leads down through the trees to Derrible Bay which a retreating tide will reveal to contain a large sandy beach.

Part way down, a turning to the right leads to the **Creux Derrible**, an enormous hole in the granite cliffs.

Return to the first fork and bear left, for at the seaward end of this high ridge known as the **Hog's Back★** stands an ancient cannon, from which there is a magnificent **view**: to the left Derrible Bay and Derrible Point; to the right Dixcart Bay with La Coupée and Little Sark in the background.

★★★ **La Coupée** – The concrete roadway and the guard rails were constructed in 1945 by German prisoners of war working under the direction of the Royal Engineers: the narrow isthmus joining the two parts of Sark is unique as it is impressive for on either side steep cliffs drop some 260ft into the sea. The view is magnificent: to the right lie Brecqhou, Jethou, Herm and Guernsey; to the left the coast of Jersey can be made out before the more distant shadow of the French coast. At the foot of the cliff is Grande Grève Bay, a good place for bathing.

Grande Grève Bay

Little Sark

On the southern headland are the chimneys of the old silver mines, now overgrown, which were started in the 19C but had to close because of the infiltration of water into the workings. A footpath to the left of the old mine chimney runs down to **Venus Pool**, a circular pool under the cliffs formed by the sea visible at low tide.

At low tide *(to prevent being stranded, check for tides and allow plenty of time)*, visitors can walk from the Venus Pool westward round the headland via **Jupiter's Pool**, several caves and the rocks in Plat Rue Bay, to **Port Gorey** which served the silver mines.

The clifftop path is always open and provides a fine view down into Port Gorey.

HERM

Michelin Atlas p 5 or Map 403

Herm (1.5 miles long by 0.5 mile wide) lies half-way between Guernsey and Sark. The broad sandy beaches on its north coast contrast with the steep cliffs at the southern end of the island. Herm is a haven of tranquillity having neither roads nor cars; there are however many footpaths among the profusion of wild flowers across the dunes, through the woods and along the cliffs. The deep fringe of rocks which lies offshore is most impressive at low tide.

Southwest of Herm, across a narrow channel, the islet of Jethou *(private property leased from the British Crown)* rises like a hillock in the sea, the home of many sea birds.

Historical notes – Prehistoric tombs made of granite slabs found in the north of the island are evidence of human settlement in 2000 BC; little remains, however, of a Roman presence other than a few coins and pottery. In the 6C Christianity was introduced by St Magloire who founded monasteries in Sark and Jersey. The monks of Sark built a small chapel on a reef between Herm and Jethou, but this was engulfed in the 8C during a violent storm which separated the two islands. In the 17C pirates used the island as a base from which to prey on the many shipwrecks in the area; it was later deserted until the 19C when, for a brief period, granite was quarried for export.

As Crown property the island has been leased to various tenants: in 1890 a German prince, Blucher von Wahlstatt, built the manor house and planted the pine and eucalyptus trees; in 1920 Sir Compton Mackenzie settled there and wrote several novels on and about the island, including *Fairy Gold*, before finally settling on Jethou. During the Second World War the island was occasionally occupied by German troops and appeared in a German propaganda film called *The Invasion of the Isle of Wight*; the British mounted a commando raid in February 1943 before abandoning it to neglect. In 1947 Herm was sold by the Crown to the States of Guernsey and since 1949 the tenant has been Major Peter Wood, who has introduced basic services such as running water and electricity and a limited amount of commercialisation consistent with the obligation to preserve Herm's natural attractions and peacefulness. There is a small permanent community of ten families living and working on Herm throughout the year.

TOUR OF THE ISLAND

3 hours.

At high tide the boat docks at the jetty in the only harbour, where an ancient crane is still in service; at low tide the boat docks by the landing steps at Rosière. A footpath running right round the island leads to the sandy bays, the rocky coast and the outlying reefs, and the high cliffs. From Herm the other islands are visible: Jethou and Guernsey *(west)*, Alderney *(north)*, Sark *(east)*. Jersey lies twenty miles south and the French coast is usually in view to the east.

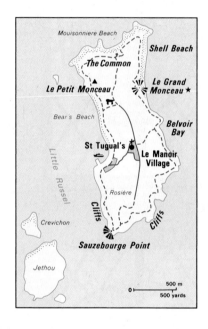

Le Manoir Village – A surfaced road climbs up to the farm and the handful of cottages which make up the hamlet next to the 18C manor house with its square tower.

St Tugual's Chapel was built of island granite in the 11C when Robert the Magnificent was Duke of Normandy. There is a handsome stained-glass window depicting Christ stilling the Tempest.

The Common – The northern end of the island is composed of sand dunes, known as the Common, covered by prickly vegetation and fringed by sandy beaches which are very popular in summer (Bear's Beach, Mousonniere Beach, **Shell Beach** so called because it is composed of millions of shells deposited by the tides and currents from the Gulf Stream).

Half-way along the north coast stands a stone obelisk which replaces the menhir that mariners once used as a landmark.

★ **Le Grand Monceau** – From this hillock there is a splendid panoramic **view** of the sands, the rocks and the islands. North on the horizon lies Alderney; to the east the French coast. **Le Petit Monceau** beyond is a smaller hillock, overlooking the Bear's Beach.

The Cliffs – In contrast with the low land in the north, the southern end of the island is composed of steep granite cliffs dropping sheer into the sea. In **Belvoir Bay** nestles a small sheltered beach, good for bathing. The southern headland, **Sauzebourge Point**, provides a view of Jethou *(southwest)* with Guernsey in the background *(west)* and Sark *(southeast)*.

Practical
Information

Travelling to Britain

Passport – Visitors travelling to Britain must be in possession of a valid national passport. In case of loss or theft report it to the relative embassy or consulate and the local police.

Visas – Entry visas are required by Australian, New Zealand, Canadian and US citizens (if their intended stay exceeds three months).
US citizens may find the booklet *Your Trip Abroad* (US$1.25) useful for information on visa requirements, customs regulations, medical care, etc. when travelling in Europe: this is available from the Superintendent of Documents, PO Box 371954, Pittsburgh, PA 15250-7954, ☎ (202) 512 1800.

Embassies and Consulates
Australia: High Commission, Australia House, Strand, WC2B 4LA.
☎ 0171 379 4334.
Canada: High Commission, Macdonald House, 1 Grosvenor Square, W1.
☎ 0171 258 6600.
New Zealand: High Commission, 80 Haymarket SW1Y 4TQ. ☎ 0171 930 8422.
South Africa: South Africa House, Trafalgar Square, WC2N 5DP. ☎ 0171 930 4488.
United States: Embassy, 24 Grosvenor Square, W1A 1AE. ☎ 0171 499 9000

Medical treatment – Visitors to Britain are entitled to emergency attention at Accident and Emergency departments of National Health Service hospitals; other forms of treatment may incur costs. It is therefore important to take out medical insurance prior to departure.
In cases of emergency, dial 999 and ask for Fire, Police, Ambulance or Coastguard services.

Customs – It is prohibited to import into the United Kingdom any drugs, firearms and ammunition, obscene material featuring children, counterfeit merchandise, unlicenced livestock (birds or animals), anything relating to endangered species (furs, ivory, horn, leather), certain plants (potatoes, bulbs, seeds, trees). It is also an offence to import duty-paid goods over a maximum value of £145 from outside the EC.
A Guide for Travellers outlines British customs regulations and duty-free allowances; it is available from the HM Customs Office (UK) ☎ 0171 202 4227.
Know Before You Go is distributed by the US Customs Service, PO Box 7407, Washington, DC 20044, ☎ (202) 927-5580.

British Tourist Authorities – The BTA has some 43 offices worldwide providing brochures, maps, information and other assistance for a visit to Great Britain.

Australia: 210 Clarence Street, Sydney, NSW 2000. ☎ (2) 267 4555; Fax (2) 267 4442.

Canada: 111 Avenue Road, Suite 450, Toronto, Ontario, M5R 3J8. ☎ (416) 925 6326; Fax (416) 961 2175.

New Zealand: Dilworth Building, corner of Customs and Queen Street, Auckland 1. ☎ (9) 303 1446; Fax (9) 377 6965.

South Africa: Lancaster Gate, Hyde Park Lane, Sandton 2196 (visitor); PO Box 41896, Craighall 2024 (mail). ☎ (11) 325 0343; Fax (11) 325 0344.

United States: 625 North Michigan Avenue, Suite 1510, Chicago, IL 60611. (Personal callers only).
551 Fifth Avenue, New York, NY 10176-0799. ☎ (212) 986 2200 or 1 800 GO 2 BRITAIN

There are also BTA offices in Belgium, Brazil, Denmark, France, Hong Kong, Ireland, Italy, Norway, Netherlands, Spain, Sweden and Switzerland.

A. Taverner

Kingswear Ferry, Dartmouth

Great British Heritage Pass – This ticket (7-day, 15-day or one-month version validated from first day of use) gives free access to over 600 stately homes, castles and gardens throughout Britain (including some owned by the National Trust): it is available exclusively from British Tourist Authority offices (Bath, London, Salisbury) and from points of entry to Britain including airports (Heathrow, Gatwick), seaports (Dover, Plymouth) and stations (Liverpool Steet and Victoria in London). It is only open to visitors visiting from abroad.

Motoring – The most flexible way of exploring the West Country is by car. Its very rural nature also means that visitors can rest assured that large conurbations and complicated traffic systems can easily be avoided as on the outskirts of the large cities (Bath, Bristol, Exeter, Plymouth) "Park and Ride" schemes are in operation: these comprise large car parks from where buses shuttle regularly to the city centre. To assist in route planning consult the **Michelin Map** 403 and the **Michelin Road Atlas** of **Great Britain and Ireland** which show the major (A) roads and many of the minor (B) roads in the West Country.

Documents – Nationals of EC countries require a valid national **driving licence**; nationals of non-EC countries require an international driving licence (obtainable in the US from the American Automobile Club). For vehicles registered abroad it is necessary to have the **registration papers** (log-book) and a nationality plate of the approved size. **Insurance** cover is compulsory; although no longer a legal requirement, the International Insurance Certificate (Green Card) is the most effective proof of insurance cover and is internationally recognised by the police and other authorities.

Car Rental – There are car rental agencies at airports, railway stations and in large towns throughout Britain. European cars usually have manual transmission; automatic cars should be reserved in advance. An **international driving licence** is required for non-EC nationals.

Parking – Be vigilant: parking restrictions vary with each county council: special parking discs for particular zones in the old city centre of **Bath** should be purchased from newsagents in the vicinity; elsewhere, timed tickets may continue to be valid in several different car parks – check listed conditions.

Remember the Highway Code!

The **minimum driving age** is 17 years; children under the age of 14 must travel in the rear of the car.

Seat belts are required to be worn by passengers in the front of vehicles at all times; they are also compulsory for back-seat passengers in vehicles where they are fitted. This includes taxis.

Traffic drives on the left.

Speed limits in towns or built-up areas: 30mph – 48kph; other roads: 60mph – 96kph; dual carriageways: 70mph – 112kph; motorways: 70mph – 112kph.

The regulations on **drinking and driving** (limited to 0.80 mg / 100 ml of blood) and speeding are strictly enforced by fine and/or confiscation of the vehicle.

Priority is given at junctions with major roads (STOP sign) and to vehicles coming from the right at roundabouts.

Vehicles must stop when the traffic-lights turn red at road junctions and may filter to the right only where indicated by a green arrow.

Parking in urban areas tends to be zoned for restricted use by residents or subject to a fee payable in advance (parking meters, disc systems and paying parking zones) or on leaving (multi-storey car parks). In the case of timed tickets, dispensing machines only accept small change; failure to display valid tickets may result in a fine, clamp, or being removed.

Road markings: It is an offence to stop anywhere along **"red routes"** marked with double red lines. No parking is allowed on **white zig-zag markings** immediately before and after a pedestrian "zebra" crossing; remember to give way to pedestrians at zebra crossings and when traffic lights flash amber.

In addition to yellow lines parallel to the kerb, painted markings on the kerb reinforce loading restrictions which should be indicated by a separate sign: 3 lines means no loading at any time.

Petrol – 4 types of fuel (US: gas) are sold in Britain: 4 star leaded, Super unleaded, unleaded and diesel.

Do not leave anything of value in unattended vehicles at any time!

Michelin maps to use in Great Britain and Ireland:
401 for Scotland
402 for the Lake District and Northern England
403 for the West Country and Wales
404 for South East England, the Midlands and East Anglia
923 for Ireland
Keep current Michelin Maps in the car all times.

Travelling in the West Country

By air – Regular domestic flights operate to the following airports.
Bournemouth ☎ 01202 593 939
Bristol ☎ 0117 474 444
Exeter ☎ 01392 367 433
Newquay ☎ 01752 705 151
Plymouth ☎ 01752 705 141

By rail – All the principal cities are networked by the railways with express services to Bath Spa, Bournemouth, Bristol (Bristol Parkway and Bristol Temple Meads), Exeter St David's, Penzance, Plymouth, Salisbury, Swindon, Taunton, Torbay, Weymouth.
Services from London run to Salisbury, Bournemouth and Plymouth from Waterloo; to Swindon, Bath, Bristol, Exeter, Plymouth and Penzance from Paddington: ☎ 0345 484 950.
It is well worth enquiring after **special saver tickets** for off-peak travel, families, the over-60s and under-12s. Eurorail Pass, Flexipass and Saver Pass are options available in the US for travel in Europe and must be purchased in the US ☎ (212) 308 3103 for information.
Other versions exist for foreign visitors; they must be purchased in the visitors' home country. For further information on this and other regional rail passes consult the British Rail International office or sales agents.

By coach – National Express operates a regular service between the major towns in the UK including 30 destinations in the West Country. Special discount tickets available: contact local National Express agents or **National Express**, Victoria Coach Station, Buckingham Palace Road, London SW1, ☎ 0990 80 80 80.

By sea – Details of passenger ferry and car ferry services to Poole, Weymouth and Plymouth from France or Spain can be obtained from travel agents or from the main carriers:
Brittany Ferries ☎ 0990 36 03 60
Stena Line ☎ 01233 647 047

For services to the Channel Islands see separate section.

Tourist Information – The addresses and telephone numbers of the local Tourist Information Centres in large towns and at tourist resorts in the West Country are printed in the Admission Times and Charges section. These operate an accommodation booking service (refundable fee) and supply town plans, timetables and information on local entertainment facilities, sports and sightseeing.

The West Country Tourist Board (WCTB), 60 St David's Hill, Exeter, Devon EX4 4SY. ☎ 01392 425 426; Fax 01392 420 891.
Email: postwctb.co.uk; http://www.wctb.co.uk

Tourism for the Disabled – Many of the sights described in this guide are accessible to people with special needs; these are tagged with the wheelchair sign under Admission Times and Charges: it is recommended, however, that individual enquiries are made as to wheelchair accessibility, special parking arrangements and toilet facilities available.

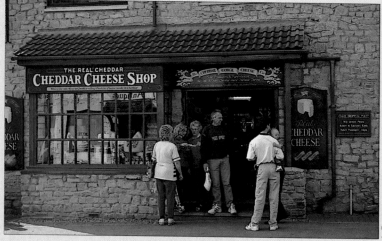

Cheddar Cheese Shop, Cheddar

A. Taverner

The **Michelin Red Guide Great Britain and Ireland** indicates hotels with facilities suitable for disabled people. Otherwise, the Royal Association for Disability and Rehabilitation **(RADAR)** publishes an annual guide with detailed information on hotels and holiday centres; apply to RADAR, 25 Mortimer Street, London W1N 8AB. ☎ 0171 637 5400.

OFFSHORE ISLANDS

Cars are not permitted on Lundy Island, Brownsea Island or the Isles of Scilly. For passenger ferry times to **Lundy Island** (from Ilfracombe, Bideford) and **Brownsea Island** (from Poole, Bournemouth, Swanage), contact local tourist information centres as sailing times may depend on the tides.

Isles of Scilly – Travel to St Mary's and Tresco is occasionally hampered by adverse weather conditions: in the event of fog transfers from the heliport at Penzance may be made to the ferry terminal. It is always advisable to warn the hotel or B&B of one's intended means of travel so that they may know when to expect their guests.
Isles of Scilly Travel Centre: ☎ 0345 105 555.
By air – Advance booking is essential for travel at weekends, most especially during the summer months. It is advisable to keep luggage to a minimum as baggage allowances are strictly enforced. Transfer from the airport on St Mary's to one's accommodation or the harbour for transfer by sea to another island is provided (for a fee) by a bus.
Services operate from Exeter and Newquay, Plymouth (in summer); full details are available from the Isles of Scilly TIC. More regular services to St Mary's (15min) are provided by small **Skybus** aircraft from Land's End Aerodrome: ☎ 01736 787 017.
British International amphibious helicopters fly from Penzance heliport to St Mary's and Tresco (20min). ☎ 01736 363 871.
By Boat: The *Scillonian III* sails daily from Penzance to St Mary's (2.75 hours) from April to October; telephone for winter schedules. ☎ 0345 105 555; 01736 362 009.
Transfers to the smaller islands are provided by launch from the harbour daily at 10am and 2pm.

Before you go...

The Isles of Scilly are a wonderful place to enjoy a peaceful holiday away from the rat-race. Remember to take comfortable shoes suitable for climbing in and out of boats and for walking everywhere. Sun hats and sunscreens are essential protection from the effects of the sun at sea; warm wind-cheaters and a water-proof layer are advised for crossing between islands.
There are branches of Barclays Bank and Lloyds Bank (cash point) on St Mary's, but none on the offshore islands; there are Post Offices on all the islands offering National Girobank and National Savings facilities. It is therefore advisable to take plenty of money if staying on the islands at weekends; public telephones tend to take coins rather than cards.
Before booking full board at a B&B it is well worth checking at what time evening meals are served given that most evening activities (slide shows, wildlife lectures, gig-racing) begin early in the evening.

Accommodation

There are hundreds of options when planning a trip to the West Country, depending on whether the visit is part of a touring programme or a weekend away. A complete range from the most sumptuous hotel to the most modest B&B (Bed and Breakfast) may be gleaned from the many specialist accommodation guides. For advice on facilities, either consult the **Michelin Red Guide Great Britain and Ireland** or call the West Country Tourist Board for their relevant brochures: in both cases, recommended establishments will have been approved by specially appointed inspectors. Most local Tourist Information Centres operate an accommodation booking service for those who prefer to tour freely and are happy to make last-minute arrangements.

Holiday Cottages – The other popular alternative is to opt for a self-catering unit which might include a remote stone cottage, a wing in some Romantic castle, a long boat or horse-drawn canal barge: details from the regional Tourist Boards or from one of the national conservation institutions listed below: for details of facilities, cost and availability contact each individual organisation; the charge for brochures is usually refunded at the time of confirming a booking.

The West Country Tourist Board publishes its own *Inspected Holiday Homes* listing the privately-owned properties they have inspected and categorised as approved, commended, highly commended and de luxe. Details from the WCTB, 60 St David's Hill, Exeter EX4 4SY. ☏ 01392 425 426; Fax 01392 420 891. Email: postintwctb.co.uk

Landmark Trust – Special properties (sleeping one to 16 people) include a flat in The Wardrobe overlooking the Close and Salisbury Cathedral, the Old Light and Millcombe House on Lundy Island, the elegant 18C Library near Great Torrington, Kingswear Castle near Dartmouth, Crownhill Fort outside Plymouth, Frenchman's Creek at Helford; Fort Clonques on Alderney (sleeps 13 and is cut off at high tide), Nicolle Tower on Jersey (once occupied by the Germans as a strategic lookout)...

Barges at Pewsey Wharf, Kennet and Avon Canal

Prices vary depending on whether the stay is over a weekend, mid-week, full-weeks or peak holiday rates. Details from The Landmark Trust, Shottesbrooke, Maidenhead, Berks, SL6 3SW. ☏ 01628 825 925; Fax 01628 825 417.
The Landmark Trust (USA), 28 Birge Street, Brattleboro, Vermont 05301. ☏ (802) 254 6868.

National Trust – Properties in the NT portfolio include apartments on some of the historic estates in their care (Cotehele, Trelissick, Corfe Castle) a former isolation hospital overlooking the Purbeck Hills in Dorset (suitable for wheelchair users) and the remote Doyden Castle in Cornwall.
NT Holiday Cottage Booking Office, PO Box 536, Melksham, Wilts. SN12 8SX. ☏ 01225 705 676; booking office ☏ 01225 791 199; Fax 01225 790 617.

Youth Hostels – Britain's youth hostels are open to members of the Youth Hostel Association or to those with an international membership card. Package holidays are available comprising youth hostel vouchers, rail and bus pass or hostel vouchers, return rail fare and cycle hire.
Details from YHA, Trevelyan House, St Albans, Herts AL1 2DY, ☏ 01727 855215.

Camping and caravanning – The West Country Tourist Board publishes the *West Country camping and caravan touring map*; the British Tourist Authority publishes *Camping and Caravanning in Britain*; local Tourist Information Centres supply lists of camping and caravan sites.
The Caravan Holiday-Home Campaign publishes *Freedom*, a brochure of the holiday parks in the West Country. This is available from PO Box 26, Lowestoft, Norfolk NR32 3LM. ☏ 01452 413 041.

Michelin on the Net: www.michelin-travel.com.

Our route planning service covers all of Europe – twenty-one countries and one million kilometres of highways and byways – enabling you to plot many different itineraries from wherever you are.
The itinerary options allow you to choose a preferred route – for example, quickest, shortest, or Michelin recommended:
The network is updated three times weekly, integrating ongoing road works, detours, new motorways, and snowbound mountain passes.
The description of the itinerary includes the distances and travelling times between towns, selected hotels and restaurants.

Sightseeing

This guide to the West Country is designed to assist visitors to plan their stay in the towns, villages, seaside resorts or private estates with plenty of attractions: not only does it describe places of interest (located on the Principal Sights map), it also indicates some of the many outdoor activities that are freely available to visitors (see map entitled Activities: sea, sand, birds and rambling). For the varied coastline and countryside of the West Country, its temperate climate, combined with its lack of heavy industry, make it ideal for a perfect holiday.

National Art Collections Fund – Britain's leading independent art charity provides grants towards the purchase of works of art of all kinds for the nation. Subscribing members are able to visit almost 200 permanent collections in galleries, museums and historic properties throughout the United Kingdom free of charge; they may also have access to temporary exhibitions at reduced rates. Institutions offering concessions are listed in the Admission times and charges section.

NACF members also receive a review of the year's acquisitions and the magazine *The Art Quarterly* which charts news and comment about the arts, and lists invitations to attend private views and special talks organised at a regional level. Annual membership costs £25.

For information on how to become a member, write to National Art Collections Fund, Millais House, 7 Cromwell Place, London SW7 2JN or call ☎ 0171 225 4800.

English Heritage – EH restores, conserves and maintains over 400 properties representing the wide range of England's architectural heritage; it also has reciprocal arrangements with **Historic Scotland** and **Cadw**. Their **Overseas Visitor Pass**, valid for a period of 14 or 21 days, benefits visitors with easy access to all EH properties for a fixed fee; enquire at any property for further details or at head office: Fortress House, 23 Savile Row, London W1X 1AB, ☎ 0171 973 3000.

For a diary of events (archery displays, battle re-enactments, medieval music etc) held at English Heritage properties, apply to their Special Events Unit ☎ 0171 973 3457. For details of summer concerts (often with fireworks displays) apply to their Concerts Unit : Keysign House, 429 Oxford Street, London W1R 2HD, ☎ 0171 937 3427 or 937 3428.

National Trust – The NT owns and conserves places of historic interest or natural beauty, including stretches of coast and countryside properties. There are reciprocal arrangements between NT and similar overseas organisations like the Royal Oak Foundation in the US. NT Head Office, 36 Queen Anne's Gate, London SW1 9AS, ☎ 0171 222 9251.

National Gardens Scheme – The National Gardens Scheme publishes an annual guide to

Village bakery, Lacock

A. Taverner

private gardens which open to the public for a limited time, in aid of charity; available through bookshops or by post from Hatchlands Park, East Clandon, Guildford, Surrey GU4 7RT, ☎ 01483 211535.

The WCTB publishes a leaflet entitled *Glorious gardens of the West Country*.

Please note that photography may be prohibited inside historic houses and buildings, it is advised to ask staff on duty before assuming that it is permitted.

The great outdoors

Coastal areas – The coastline is edged with a continuous path: a fabulous resource for walkers and ramblers alike. Tidal estuaries provide favoured locations for birdwatchers attracted by both resident and migrant **birds**.

The north coast of Cornwall and Devon is renowned as one of the best places in the south of England for **windsurfing** owing to the great swell of Atlantic waves which rolls along the shore. The more protected coast further up the Bristol Channel and the south coast, with their miles of fine **sand beaches** and rows of colourful beach huts, are ideal places for the archetypal English holiday with buckets and spades, sand castles, ice creams, donkey rides, while in secluded coves and inlets, **rock pools** invite the curious to delve for pebbles or fossils, and explore the marine life.

Small picturesque harbours and bustling marinas throughout the region provide excellent facilities for the more intrepid: **fishing** expeditions, scuba **diving**, yachting, dinghy **sailing**, **jet-skiing** and water-skiing in addition to which there are regular nautical events such as gig-races, regattas and powerboat races.

Inland – Romantics can trace the **literary heritage** of Hardy's Wessex or King Arthur's realm, or explore the more ancient mysteries of prehistoric man. Botanists and horticulturists have a wide choice of fine **gardens** to visit, and lovers of architecture or history may tour some of the many historic houses and fine churches in the region. Steam trains and beam-engines fascinate the mechanical-minded while zoos and animal sanctuaries entertain the young.

Canals and navigable waterways present perfect conditions for **barging** and leisurely cruises. The great moors, meanwhile, have an aura of their own, their broad open spaces providing ample opportunities for rambling, **orienteering** and **pony trekking**. The limestone hills around Cheddar are exploited by enthusiasts who enjoy rock-climbing or **pot-holing** and caving underground.

Information on the activities listed below is available from WCTB (which publishes a booklet *"the edge"*) free from them.

Safety – Legislation has been introduced to ensure certain safety standards are applied to activity associations offering facilities to the under-18s. For additional information contact the Adventure Licensing Authority in Cardiff. ☎ 01222 755 715.

For a general introduction to activity centres in Britain, contact the **British Activity Holiday Association**: 22 Green Lane, Hersham, Walton-on-Thames, Surrey, KT12 5HD. ☎ 01932 252 994.

RAMBLING AND HIKING

The many long-distance footpaths and countryside trails include the South West Coast Path which snakes some 550 miles around the peninsula, the Ridgeway Path (Wiltshire), the Two Moors Way (Devon), the West Mendip Way (Somerset) and the Leland Trail (Somerset). There are also the canal towpaths: Kennet and Avon Canal; Grand Western Canal (Devon) and the routes followed by many disused railways.

Maps – All footpaths are precisely marked on **Ordnance Survey maps** in the Pathfinder series (1:25 000 scale) and in slightly less detail but covering a larger area in the Landranger series (1:50 000 scale).

Walking the Ridgeway

A. Taverner

The Ridgeway: the Countryside Commission publishes a comprehensive *National Trail Guide to the Ridgeway* by Neil Curtis; this gives details of the entire length, recommended sections, maps, information on accommodation, public transport, background history, flora and fauna, archeology, geology of the area. Details from the **Countryside Commission**, John Dower House, Crescent Place, Cheltenham GL50 3RA, ☎ 01242 521381.

The Saints Way, inaugurated in May 1986, runs from Padstow to Fowey: 26 miles marked with wooden posts bearing a little Celtic cross; with an alternative southern section that extends the route to 35 miles. Details are included in a booklet from **Restormel Borough Council**, Tourism and Leisure Department, 39 Penwinnick Road, St Austell, PL25 5DR.
Otherwise, *The Saints' Way – Forth an Syns* (the Cornish name) is published by **Cornwall County Council** and is available from the Countryside Access, Transportation and Estates Department, Castle Canyke Road, Bodmin, Cornwall PL31 1DZ (or from TICs).

The South West Coast Path is well signed along its entire length through private land or coastal route managed by the National Trust. Main source of published information available from the Ordnance Survey. Otherwise, advice, tide tables, maps and information on the 613 miles of coastal path from Minehead in Somerset to Poole in Dorset, managed by most in 6 weeks, is provided by the **South West Way Association**, 1 Orchard Drive, Kingskerswell, Newton Abbot, Devon TQ12 5DG.

The Tarka Trail threads its way through the area extending north from Dartmoor to Exmoor and the coast with reference to places mentioned in Henry Williamson's novel *Tarka the Otter*. Most of the walking and cycling trails are promoted by **The Tarka Country Tourism Association** (TCTA), PO Box 4, Chulmleigh, Devon EX18 7YX. ☎ 01837 833 99.

Protected areas – Large parts of the West Country have been designated Areas of Outstanding Natural Beauty. Regularly updated details about visiting birds, butterfly sightings etc is often available locally; for information about special events and nature trails organised by the national parks, contact the relevant authority.
Dartmoor National Park, The High Moorland Visitor Centre, The Old Duchy Hotel, Tavistock Road, Princetown, Yelverton, Devon PL20 6QF ☎ 01822 890 414.
Exmoor National Park, Fore Street, Dulverton, Somerset TA2 9HL. ☎ 01398 323 841.
RSPB South-West Office, 10 Richmond Road, Exeter EX4 4JA: ☎ 01392 432 691.

Fishing options

WATER SPORTS

Fishing – The West Country offers enormous variety for anglers, in its rivers, lakes, estuaries and harbours or in the sea itself. Information on seasons, fisheries, price of licences and permits may be obtained from local Tourist Information Centres and tackle shops.
Independent operators also advertise on the waterfront for day-trips, notably in Bideford, Brixham, Clovelly, Lyme Regis, Weymouth...

Canal cruises – A variety of operators cater for cruises on the **Kennet and Avon Canal** from Bristol, Bath, Bradford on Avon, Devizes, Pewsey, Newbury, Reading... Comprehensive ranges of information from the Kennet and Avon Canal Trust , Couch Lane, Devizes, Wiltshire SN10 1EB. ☎ 01380 721 279 or from local TICs.
Horse drawn barge trips are also available on the **Grand Western Canal**: details from The Grand Western Horseboat Co, The Wharf, Canal Hill, Tiverton, Devon EX16 4HX ☎ 01884 253 345.

Information and leaflets on boating, barging and cruising are also available from the **Association of Pleasure Craft Operators**, 35a High Street, Newport, Shropshire TF10 8JW. ☎ 01952 813 572.

Boating and sailing – There are marinas and yacht clubs, some with sailing schools, all round the coast of Dorset, Devon and Cornwall, and offshore racing throughout the season *(see Calendar of Events);* details of local facilities and annual waterway rallies, regattas and festivals are available from local Tourist Information Centres or from the Royal Yachting Association, RYA House, Romsey Road, Eastleigh, Hampshire. ☎ 01703 629 962. RYA sailing courses from:

Hengistbury Head Outdoor Education & Field Studies Centre, Broadway, Southbourne, Bournemouth, Dorset BH6 4EN. ☎ 01202 425 173; Fax 01202 430 132;
Island Cruising Club, Salcombe, Devon TQ8 8DR. ☎ 01548 843 481;
The Watersports Centre, Loe Beach, Feock, Truro, Cornwall TR3 6RP. ☎ 01872 862 555.

Surfing – With average winter sea temperatures in Cornwall of 9ºC, fanatical surfers are ensured a year-round pastime. The most popular surfing beaches include Perran Beach at Perranporth; Porthmeor Beach at St Ives; Polzeath Beach tucked inside Hayle Bay; Widemouth Bay below Bude. Whitesand Bay at Sennen near Land's End is perfect for novices while Porthcurno (south of Land's End) is swept by strong currents and therefore suitable for strong and experienced surfers only...

The **British Surfing Association**, based in Penzance, offers lessons on Newquay's Fistral Beach: ☎ 01736 60250.
Harbour Sports Windsurfing (RYA windsurfing school), The Harbour, Paignton, Devon TQ4 6DT. ☎ 01803 550 180; Fax 01803 558 084.
Holiday courses offered by **Outdoor Adventure**, Atlantic Court, Widemouth Bay, Nr Bude. EX23 0DF. ☎ 01288 361 312; Fax 01288 361 153.

OTHER ACTIVITIES

Cycling – Brochures indicating the designated cycle-ways in the West Country are available from WCTB. Ferry companies and the rail network will transport accompanied bicycles; bicycles may also be hired locally.

Golf – Golf courses which welcome visitors are marked on the **Michelin Atlas Great Britain and Ireland** and on **Michelin Map 403**.

Heritage Railway Association – The **Association of Independent Railways and Preservation Societies Ltd** publishes an annual free guide to Steam Railways and Museums, available through Tourist Information Centres or by sending a stamped addressed envelope to Mr R Williams, 16 Woodbrook, Charing, Ashford, Kent TN27 0DN, ☎ 0123 371 2130.

Hot air ballooning – Flights, weather permitting, are made early in the morning or late in the afternoon. Dress should be practical – comfortable flat shoes, no skirts or kilts, man-made fibres please. Remember binoculars, cameras and plenty of film... Safety standards are carefully policed by operators, the best will be certified by the CAA (Civil Aviation Authority).

Bristol Balloons/Balloon Club is perhaps the largest operator in the South West with flights arranged from Ashton Court (Bristol Avon Gorge) and the Royal Victoria Park (Bath). Advance booking is essential, no facilities, alas for the disabled. ☎ 0117 963 7858; Fax 0117 963 9555.

For information about the hugely successful hot-air balloon fiesta at Ashton Court, contact **Bristol Balloon Fiesta** ☎ 0117 953 5884; Fax 0117 953 5606.

Riding and pony trekking – Details of private stables, residential centres and trail riding are available from local Tourist Information Centres. There are excellent opportunities to ride on Dartmoor and Exmoor: contact their information departments for details:

Dartmoor National Park, The High Moorland Visitor Centre, The Old Duchy Hotel, Tavistock Road, Princetown, Yelverton, Devon PL20 6QF ☎ 01822 890 414.

Exmoor National Park, Fore Street, Dulverton, Somerset TA2 9HL ☎ 01398 323 841.

R. Besse/MICHELIN

Bowling

General information

Climate - Owing to the Gulf Stream, the West Country enjoys relatively mild weather throughout the year. The sunny and bright days of spring may be interspersed with sudden showers; in summer (especially in July and August) the warm weather and splendid beaches attract thousands of visitors, and in autumn the countryside mellows to mild days between cool mornings and evenings. Winter in the West Country can be dramatic, with gales and storms; calmer weather brings crisp mornings and invigorating days but temperatures in the far southwest are never extreme.

Time - In winter standard time throughout Britain, including the Channel Islands, is Greenwich Mean Time (GMT). In summer (mid-March to October) British clocks are advanced by one hour to give British Summer Time (BST) which is the same as Central European Time.

Medical treatment - Visitors from EC countries should apply to their own National Social Security Offices for Form E111 which entitles them to medical treatment under an EC Reciprocal Medical Treatment arrangement anywhere in the UK (ie not the Channel Islands).
Nationals of non-EC countries should take out comprehensive insurance. American Express offers a service, "Global Assist", for any medical, legal or personal emergency - call collect from anywhere ☎ 202 554 2639.

Money - English decimal currency (£1 = 100 pence) is used throughout Britain.

Banks - Banks are open from Monday to Friday (except public holidays, *see* Admission Times and Charges), 9.30am to 3.30pm or 4.30pm. Most have cash points which accept international credit cards.
Exchange facilities outside normal banking hours may be available at hotels, bureaux de change and travel agencies. Some form of identification is necessary when cashing travellers cheques or Eurocheques in banks. Commission charges vary; hotels usually charge more than banks.

Credit Cards - The major credit cards - Visa/Barclaycard (Carte Bleue), Access (Mastercard/Eurocard), American Express and Diners Club - are widely accepted in shops, hotels and restaurants and petrol stations.

Post - Postage stamps are available from Post Offices and some shops (newsagents, tobacconists, grocery stores and supermarkets). Post Offices are generally open Monday to Friday, 9am to 5.30pm and Saturday morning, 9am to 12.30pm; sub-post offices may close at lunch-time on Wednesday or Thursday.

Telephone - In an **emergency** phone **999** and ask for fire; police; ambulance; coastal, mountain and cave rescue.
Pre-paid phonecards **(British Telecom, Mercury)** for national and international calls from public phones are available from Post Offices, newsagents, tobacconists etc.
Most countries can be dialled direct: 00 for international exchange followed by country code:

61	Australia	45	Denmark
809	Bermuda	31	Netherlands
64	New Zealand	47	Norway
27	South Africa	46	Sweden
1	USA and Canada		

For queries apply to the Operator (☎ 100), Directory Enquiries (☎ 192), International Directory Enquiries (☎ 153), International Operator (☎ 155).

Shopping - Shops in towns are generally open Monday to Saturday, 9am to 5.30pm or 6pm; smaller stores may close for an hour in the middle of the day. Most towns have an early closing day - usually Wednesday, Thursday or market day - when shops close at midday (see the **Michelin Red Guide Great Britain and Ireland**).

Retail outlets- Factory shops offering goods at a slightly reduced price from the high street are to be found at Swindon and Street.

West Country Specialities- Toffee, fudge and clotted cream (Totnes); local cider, scrumpy and wines (Taunton); Dorset knobs (Dorchester); cheese (Bath, Cheddar, Totnes).

Mail order - Flowers may be sent by post (payable by credit card) from the Isles of Scilly Association of Growers; Jersey and Guernsey growers: contact the relevant Tourist Information Centre for relevant phone numbers.
Other local specialities include **smoked fish** (Newlyn, Kinsgbridge) and **Saffron Cake** from Cornwall...

For information on the regional specialities of the region consult the relevant section in the Introduction.

Books for reference

The *Archaeology of South West Britain* S M Pearce (Collins 1981)

Bath by Sitwell (Century Hutchinson 1987)

Roman Bath Discovered B Cunliffe (Routledge and Kegan Paul 1984)

English Parish Churches as Works of Art by A Clifton-Taylor (Oxford University Press 1989)

National Trust Book of Ruins by B Bailey (Weidenfeld and Nicolson 1984)

The Making of the English Landscape by W G Hoskins (Penguin 1986)

The Buildings of England (Cornwall, Devon, Dorset, Somerset and Bristol, South and West Somerset, Wiltshire) by N Pevsner (Penguin 1950s/1990s)

The Fortunate Islands: The Story of the Isles of Scilly by R L Bowley 1945 (1996)

Blue Guide: Channel Islands by P McGregor Eadie (A & C Black Ltd 1987)

The Model Occupation: The Channel Islands under German Rule, 1970-1945 by Madeleine Bunting (Harper Collins 1995)

The Shining Sands: Artists in Newlyn and St Ives 1880-1930 by Tom Cross (Lutterworth Press 1994)

Arts and Crafts in Newlyn 1890-1930 by Hazel Berriman (Newlyn Art Gallery 1986)

Cryséde: The Unique Textile Designs of Alex Walker by Hazel Burston (Royal Institution of Cornwall 1993)

The Leach Legacy: St Ives Pottery and its Influence by Marion Whybrow (1996)

Thomas Hardy: His Life and Landscape by Hawkins (National Trust 1990)

Wessex – A Literary Celebration by Hawkins (Barrie and Jenkins 1991)

National Trust Book of Long Walks by Nicolson (Weidenfeld and Nicolson 1981)

... and for pleasure

The Mousehole Cat by Antonia Barber

Betjeman's Cornwall

Hound of the Baskervilles by Arthur Conan Doyle

In Time of Flood by James Crowden

Whatever Happened to Margo? by Margaret Durrell

The French Lieutenant's Woman by John Fowles

The Poldark Novels by Winston Graham

Bath Triangle by Georgette Heyer

Westward Ho! by Charles Kingsley

Stalky and Co by Rudyard Kipling

A Murder of Quality by John Le Carré

Last Ditch by Ngaio Marsh

Frenchman's Creek by Daphne du Maurier

Rebecca by Daphne du Maurier

Jamaica Inn by Daphne du Maurier

Vanishing Cornwall by Daphne du Maurier

Moonfleet by Meade Falkner

Mr Pye by Mervyn Peake

Wolf Solent by John Cowper Powys

A Glastonbury Romance by John Cowper Powys

Weymouth Sands by John Cowper Powys

Maiden Castle by John Cowper Powys

Rodmoor by John Cowper Powys

Mr Weston's Good Wine by T F Powys

Mazaran by Nevil Shute

The Camomile Lawn by Mary Wesley

Harnessing Peacocks by Mary Wesley

Tarka the Otter by H Williamson

The Alfoxden Journal: January – May 1798 by Dorothy Wordsworth

For a list of other literary works associated with the West Country see INTRODUCTION: Literary Associations.

Filmed on location

1963 **Tom Jones:** Based on Henry Fielding's enduring novel (1749) set in Somerset, John Osborne's screenplay of the hero's rollicking life is wittily portrayed by Albert Finney and Susannah York. Filmed on location at Nettlecombe Court, near Williton, in North Somerset.

1964 **A Hard Day's Night:** 36 hours in the lives of the Beatles, giving an exaggerated idea of the pressure they bore; filmed in Newton Abbot, Devon; at Crowcombe, Taunton, and Minehead in Somerset.

1965 **Help!** The Beatles try to evade a gang of Eastern thugs and a nutty powerdrunk scientist all after Ringo's ring, partly filmed at Knighton Down, Larkhill on Salisbury Plain.

1967 **Doctor Dolittle:** Leslie Bricusse's musical adaptation of Hugh Lofting's story of the gentle, loving Doctor who has a special way with his animal friends; starring Rex Harrison and Samantha Eggar; filmed in Castle Combe, "England's most beautiful village in 1966", which was transformed into Puddleby-on-the-Marsh: the river was widened, and piers and wharves built. Everything returned to its original state.

1967 **Far From The Madding Crowd:** John Schlesinger directs Julie Christie, Terence Stamp, Peter Finch and Alan Bates in MGM's famous adaptation of Thomas Hardy's classic 19C story of Bathsheba Everdene's love for three men and the tragedy that precedes her final happiness. Filmed on location in Devizes, in the Vale of Pewsey, Wiltshire, Durdle Door, Maiden Castle and in Weymouth, Dorset.

1972 **Kidnapped:** A combination of Robert Louis Stevenson's adventure story and its sequel *Catriona* telling of the dying Jacobite struggle between King George and a few remaining Scottish clans; Michael Caine and Trevor Howard star at Bayards Cove (Dart Estuary), and at Dartmouth which doubled as a Scottish village.

1979-81 **To The Manor Born:** Long-running comedy series about a lady who is forced to sell her stately home and live in the estate's tiny lodge with her butler and beagle: Penelope Keith and Peter Bowles on the Cricket St Thomas estate, near Chard, Somerset.

1981 **The French Lieutenant's Woman:** Harold Pinter's screenplay of John Fowles' romantic novel uses the film-within-a-film method to convey two parallel love stories, the historic and the modern. Starring Meryl Streep and Jeremy Irons; filmed on location in Lyme Regis and Weymouth, Dorset, at Kingswear in Devon, just across the Dart estuary from Dartmouth with its famous naval background.

1981-91 **Only Fools and Horses:** BBC comedy series about a dodgy but likeable spiv, his brother and their grandfather starring David Jason and Nicholas Lyndhurst. Filmed in parts in Bristol, Hull and Brighton. Whitemead House in Duckmore Road, Bristol, is used as the exterior of Del's flat in Nelson Mandela House.

1991 **Truly Madly Deeply:** Anthony Minghella directs Juliet Stevenson and Alan Rickman in a BBC production about a woman who wishes her partner back from his grave; filmed on location in Bristol.

1991-94 **The House of Eliott:** BBC adaptation of a story about love, jealousy and trials of an Edwardian couture house; starring Stella Gonet and Louise Lombard. Filmed on location in Bristol (Berkeley Square, Bristol University and Clifton Girls School) and in Bath (Assembly Rooms).

1993 **The Remains of The Day:** Merchant Ivory/ Columbia Pictures epic starring Anthony Hopkins and Emma Thompson about the perfect English butler who ignored his feelings for an attractive young housekeeper until it was too late. Filmed at Dyrham Park (Darlington Hall), in the Pavilion in Weston-Super-Mare and at Badminton House, Chipping Sodbury.

1995 **The Madness of King George:** Starring Nigel Hawthorne and Helen Mirren, directed by Nicolas Hytner, sequences from the life of King George III, precisely when he appears to go insane, putting the English Throne at risk were filmed at Wilton House, Wiltshire.

1995 **Pride and Prejudice:** BBC adaptation starring Colin Firth, Jennifer Ehle and Alison Steadman. Filmed on location in Wiltshire (Luckington and Lacock).

1995 **Sense and Sensibility:** Ang Lee directs Emma Thompson, Kate Winslet and Hugh Grant in an adaptation of Jane Austen's classic novel about two sisters, one with good sense and the other with an excess of romantic sensibility, and their dramas. Filmed on location at Montacute House, in Montacute Village, at Saltram House near Plymouth, Berry Pomeroy, Mompesson House in Cathedral Close, Salisbury, Wiltshire.

1995 **Restoration:** Michael Hoffman follows a novel by Rose Tremain set in the post-Cromwell age of Charles II. Starring Robert Downey Jr, Meg Ryan and Hugh Grant; filmed in Somerset (Jacobean manor of Brympton D'Evercy), at Mapperton House gardens and Forde Abbey.

Travelling to the Channel Islands

Formalities – Holders of British and Irish passports do not require passports or entry visas for travel between Britain, the Republic of Ireland and the Channel Islands. Members from other EU countries require ID cards only. Citizens from non-EU countries should check whether they need visas, and clear customs when entering the UK.

There are quarantine regulations for the transportation of domestic animals from anywhere but Britain; ie no animals from the Continent are allowed to land on the islands.

Access by air – Direct to Jersey, Guernsey and Alderney from most airports in the UK by Air UK, Aurigny Air Services Ltd, British Air Ferries, British Airways, British Midland, Brymon, Guernsey Airlines and Jersey European Airways.

Aurigny also have flights from Cherbourg and Dinard (passport required on check-in). Note: Aurigny operates a restricted luggage allowance of 15kg per bag, with excess charges for heavier items. ☎ 01481 822 886; Fax 01481 823 344.

Access by sea – A high-speed catamaran service is available from Poole. Sea connections to France include a fast ferry from St Malo or otherwise from Diélette, Carteret and Granville. Average travel time: Poole to Guernsey 2.5 hours then 1hr to Jersey before returning to Poole via Guernsey. Irregular tide conditions may mean vessels land at Jersey and then Guernsey (or vice-versa): check at time of boarding.
Condor Ferries Ltd, Condor House, New Harbour Road South, Poole, Dorset, BH15 4AJ. Reservations: ☎ 01305 761 551; Port arrival information ☎ 01305 761 556; 01534 601 000; 01481 729 666.
Emeraude Lines Jersey ☎ 01534 856 792 (for Sark); Guernsey ☎ 01481 711 414; St Malo ☎ 02 99 40 48 40.
Isle of Sark Shipping Co Ltd for sailings (55min) throughout the year, weather permitting, from Guernsey to Sark: Guernsey ☎ 01481 724 059; Fax 01481 712 081 or Sark ☎ 01481 832 450; Fax 01481 832 567.
Herm Trident for daily catamaran sailings (20min) to Herm from Weighbridge Clock Tower Kiosk in St Peter Port ☎ 01481 721 379

Motoring information – Private cars may be taken to Jersey and Guernsey. Hire cars are available in Jersey, Guernsey and Alderney. No cars are allowed on Sark and Herm.

Although **petrol stations** operate on Jersey throughout the week, all Guernsey petrol stations are closed all day on Sundays.

No **caravans** or mobile homes are allowed on the roads of Jersey or Guernsey – exception may be made for vehicles especially equipped to carry handicapped persons but permission must be approved by the authorities in advance. Contact Tourist Information Services.

The **speed limit** on open roads in Jersey is 40mph (35mph in Guernsey), 30mph (25mph in Guernsey) in built-up areas, 20mph where indicated and 15mph in Green Lanes or where signposted.

Seat-belts must be worn at all times. **Children** under the age of 14 should travel in the rear of the car.

A **yellow line** painted across the road at a junction commands drivers to stop before emerging onto the more major road as if marked with a STOP or HALT sign.

A **yellow grid** at an intersection requests that drivers do not enter the box unless their way ahead is clear.

Filter and Turn at roundabouts request drivers give way to the first car from the right before engaging onto the circuit themselves.

Parking in Jersey's municipal parking blocks or spaces is payable by scratch cards or clock disc: these are on sale from newsagents – and beware, wardens are vigilant; parking is usually free between 5pm and 8am, and all day Sunday.

In Guernsey, vehicles should display a set parking clock (provided in hire cars or available from newsagents).

All **accidents** involving any vehicle should be reported to a policeman (in uniform or honorary: ask a local person): vehicles should not be moved from the scene before being reported.

General information – The local **currency** is Sterling: English money is freely accepted although both Jersey and Guernsey have their own coins and notes which are not legal tender outside the Channel Islands.

All the major UK clearing **banks** are represented on both Jersey and Guernsey (closed Saturday and Sunday): most cash points are situated in town (St Helier and St Peter Port) and at the airport. There are no cash points on the outlying islands. Cheques drawn on a UK bank are widely accepted if supported with a valid bank card. All the major credit cards are also widely accepted.

Emergency telephone numbers – 999 and ask for required service: fire, ambulance, police.

Licensing hours – Public bars in **Jersey** may open to adults (over 18) between 9am (11am Sundays) and 11pm; children under 18 are permitted in public bars until 9pm if accompanied by an adult.
10.30am 11.45pm.
In **Guernsey**, licensed bars open from 10.30am to 11.45pm; on Sundays they may only serve alcohol as an accompaniment to food: 11am-3pm in summer, at landlords' discretion in winter. This rule also applies to licensed restaurants.

Medical care – Be aware that the Channel Islands do not extend the facilities of a free National Health Scheme to visitors from mainland Britain; it is therefore of utmost importance that all personal travel insurance is taken to cover costs of unforeseen medical treatment and eventual repatriation.

Jersey: Advice and treatment is available free of charge from the morning medical clinic at the General Hospital in St Helier (Jersey); charges are otherwise made for consultations and prescriptions.

Postage and telephone charges – Postage stamps and telephone cards for public phone boxes are issued by each Bailiwick for use in Jersey and Guernsey respectively; rates to the English mainland, the other islands and to the Continent vary so enquire locally.

Telephone calls to the UK require the same STD codes as apply at home; international calls require OO (international exchange) followed by the relevant country code: *see General Information for UK.*

Shop openings – In Jersey, most shops and businesses in St Helier open Monday to Saturday; elsewhere the smaller family concerns may close at lunch-times and on Thursday afternoons.

Honesty boxes along the road side should be used when buying the home-grown produce offered for sale.

Time – The Channel Islands follow the same time as the UK, all year round: GMT in winter, BST in summer.

Telephone and post box on Alderney

Tourist information centres. Jersey Tourism Office, 35 Albemarle Street, London W1X 3RP; ☎ 0171 493 5278.
Jersey Tourist Information Office, Weighbridge, St Helier, Jersey; ☎ 01534 500 700.
Guernsey Tourist Board, PO Box 23, White Rock, St Peter Port, Guernsey. ☎ 01481 723 552. Internet : http : // tourism.guernsey. net/
Contact number in France; ☎ 03 88 94 12 12
Contact number in Germany; ☎ 050 43 98 038
Contact number in Switzerland; ☎ 052 202 691
Alderney Tourist Board, St Anne, Alderney; ☎ 0148 182 2994.
Sark Tourist Board, Sark; ☎ 0148 183 2345.

Join us in our constant task of keeping up-to-date. Please send us your comments and suggestions.

*Michelin Tyre PLC
38 Clarendon Road
WATFORD
WD1 1SX
Tel.: 01923 415000
Fax: 01923 415052*

Calendar of events

Market days are indicated in the main text listed in the Sites section. Horse Racing: Flat races and steeplechases are held throughout the year at racecourses in Wiltshire, Somerset and Devon.

February
River Exe . . . . RSPB one-day birdwatching cruises
Shrove Tuesday
St Columb Major . . . . Game of Hurling
March
Cornwall . . . . St Piran's Day (5 March)
April
Devizes to Westiminster . . . . International Canoe Race
St Endellion . . . . Music Festival
Camborne . . . . Trevithick Day
April/May
Minehead . . . . Hobby Horse Celebrations
Newquay . . . . Great Cornwall Balloon Festival
May
Padstow . . . . 'Obby 'Oss Celebrations (1 May)
Helston . . . . Flora Day Furry Dance (8 May)
St Mary's, Isles of Scilly . . . . International Gig Racing Championships
Badminton . . . . Horse Trials
Chippenham . . . . Folk Festival
May/June
Bath . . . . International Festival
Royal Bath and West Show
May/September
Porthcurno . . . . Minack Theatre Summer Festival
June
Bristol to Bournemouth . . . . Vintage Vehicle Run
Glastonbury . . . . Music Festival
Brixham . . . . International Trawler Race and Quay Festival
Bath . . . . Steam and Vintage Vehicle Festival
Truro . . . . Three Spires Festival: Celebration of the Arts
Glastonbury . . . . Glastonbury Pilgrimage
**St Keverve, Bodmin,
Launceston** . . . . Keskerdh Kernow: in memory of 1497 rebellion
Wadebridge . . . . Royal Cornwall Show
July
St Helier, Jersey . . . . St Helier's Day Procession
Tolpuddle . . . . Tolpuddle Martyrs Rally
Devizes . . . . Kennet and Avon Canal Boat Rally
Shaftesbury . . . . Gold Hill Fair
Stourhead . . . . Summer Music Festival
Bristol . . . . Harbour Regatta
Penzance . . . . Golowan Festival
Helston . . . . Air Day, RNAS Culdrose
July/August
Weymouth . . . . International Firework Festival
Sidmouth . . . . International Festival of Folk Arts
St Endellion . . . . Music Festival

August

Newquay	RAF St Mawgan International Air Day
Taunton	Flower Festival
Bristol	Balloon Festival
Truro	International Festival of Music and Dance
Channel Islands	Battle of Flowers (Guernsey: 2nd Thursday; Jersey: 4th Thursday)
Tarrant Hinton	Great Dorset Steam Fair
Weymouth	Carnival
Christchurch	Regatta, fireworks and carnival procession
Dartmouth	Royal Regatta
Poole	The Needles International Powerboat Race
Torbay	Royal Regatta
Newlyn	Fish Festival
Isles of Scilly	Annual pilgrimage to St Helen's Puffins leave Britain on migration

September

Long Ashton	International Kite Festival
Widecombe-in-the-Moor	Widecombe Fair
Bodmin	Cornish Gorsedd: ancient Cornish ceremonies

October

Isles of Scilly	Peak birdwatching season (mid-month)

November

5th November	Guy Fawkes Carnivals, with bonfires and fireworks

December

Monsehole	Tom Bawcock's Eve: torchlight procession

Tall Ships' Race off Falmouth

A. Taverner

Admission times and charges

As admission times and charges are liable to alteration, the information printed below – valid for 1997 – is for guidance only.

⊙: Every sight for which times and charges are listed below is indicated by the symbol ⊙ after the title in the Sights Section of the guide.

&: Facilities for the disabled with impaired mobility, sight and hearing; (&): limited facilities for the disabled; access but no toilets/ toilets but limited access, please phone for details.

Order: The information is listed in the same order as in the Sights Section of the guide.

Dates: Dates given are inclusive. The term holiday means bank and public holidays.

Last admission: Ticket offices usually shut 30min before closing time; only exceptions are mentioned below. Some places issue timed tickets owing to limited space and facilities.

Charge: The charge given is for an individual adult. Concessionary rates may be available for families, children, students, old-age pensioners and the unemployed. Many places offer special rates for group bookings and some have special days for group visits. Large parties should apply in advance.

Abbreviations: EH = English Heritage. NT = the National Trust; the National Trust has reciprocal arrangements with the National Trust in Scotland and in Northern Ireland; NACF = National Art Collections Fund.

Tourist Information Centres: The addresses and telephone numbers are given for the local Tourist Information Centres, which provide information on local amenities, access, advice and a booking service for accommodation in the area.

Public and Bank holidays

On the following days, banks, museums and other monuments may be closed or may vary their times of admission; it is also advisable to check boat, bus and railway timetables for changes in services.

> New Year's Day – 1 January
> Good Friday – Friday before Easter
> Easter Monday – Monday after Easter
> May Day – First Monday in May
> Liberation Day – 9 May (Channel Islands only)
> Spring Bank Holiday – Last Monday in May
> August Bank Holiday – Last Monday in August
> Christmas Day – 25 December
> Boxing Day – 26 December

The term 'school holidays' refers to the breaks between term-time over Easter, the summer months and Christmas, and also to the short mid-term breaks usually in February and October.

A

AVEBURY

🖹 The Great Barn – ☎ 01672 539 425

Alexander Keiller Museum (NT, EH) – & Open all year, daily, 10am to 6pm (4pm October to March). Closed 1 January, 24 to 26 December. £1.50, 80p (child). ☎ 01672 539 250.

Avebury Manor – Open April to October, Tuesday, Wednesday, Sunday and bank holiday Mondays, 2pm to 5.30pm. **Garden:** Open April to October, Tuesday, Wednesday, Friday, Saturday, Sunday and bank holiday Mondays, 11am to 5.30pm. House and garden: £3.50, £1.75 (child); garden only £2.20, £1.40 (child). ☎ 01672 539 250.

B

BARNSTAPLE

🖹 Tuly Street – ☎ 01271 388 583

Parish Church – Open Monday to Friday, 9am to 3pm. **Services:** Sunday 10.30am; third Sunday in the month 6pm; Wednesday 10am; Friday 12noon. ☎ 01271 73837 (Vicar), 01271 44589 (office).

Barnstaple Guildhall – Guided tour (30min) all year, daily, on application to the Tourist Information Centre (see above).

Museum of North Devon, Barnstaple (NACF) – ♧ Open all year, Tuesday to Saturday, 10am to 4.30pm. Closed public holiday. £1, 50p (concession); Saturday mornings no charge. Guided tour (1hr) by appointment. ✆ 01271 46747.

Excursion

Arlington Court (NT) – ♧ **House and Carriage Collection:** Open April to October, Sunday to Friday, holiday Saturday, 11am to 5.30pm. Leaflets in (only house in Dutch) French, German. **Gardens and Park:** Open April to October, Sunday to Friday, holiday Saturday, 11am to 5.30pm; November to March, daily, sunrise to sunset; last admission 30min before closing. House and gardens: £4.90, £12.20 (family ticket); gardens only £2.60. Parking; refreshments; restaurant; shop. ✆ 01271 850 296; Fax 01271 850 711.

BATH

⃣ Abbey Chambers - ✆ 01225 477 101

Bus Tours – Scenic open-top bus tours (45mins) of Bath depart from the Grand Parade and the Abbey. **Regency Tours:** ✆ 01225 891 174.
From the Bus Station and offering discounted rates on entrance fees to most attractions: **Guide Friday Tours:** ✆ 01225 444 102 and **Badgerline Travel Centre:** ✆ 01225 464 446.

Bath Abbey – ♧ Open all year, Monday to Saturday, 9am to 6pm (4.30pm November to Easter), Sunday, 1pm to 2.30pm and 4.30pm to 5.30pm. Closed Good Friday, 24 and 25 December (except for services). Donation £1 per person. Leaflet (Dutch, French, German, Italian, Japanese, Spanish). ✆ 01225 422 462; Fax 01225 429 990.

Bath Abbey Heritage Vaults – ♧ Open Monday to Saturday, 10am to 4pm. £2, £1 (concession), no charge (child). Leaflet (French, German). ✆ 01225 422 62; Fax 01225 429 990.

Pump Room – Open April to September, daily, 9am to 6pm; October to March, daily, 9.30am (10.30am Sunday) to 5pm. Closed 25 nd 26 December. Brochure (French, German). Audio guide (six languages). ✆ 01225 477 785; Fax 01225 477 743.

Roman Baths Museum – ♧ Open April to September, daily, 9am to 6pm; October to March, daily, 9.30am (10.30am Sunday) to 5pm. Closed 25 and 26 December. £6. £15.60 (family), £3.60 (child); combined ticket with Museum of Costume £8. Guided tour (1hr). Audio guide (French, German, Italian, Japanese, Spanish). Guidebook (French, German). Refreshments. ✆ 01225 477 785.

Cross Bath – Open Friday, Saturday and Sunday at variable times depending on volunteers available. Donation. ✆ 01225 310 198.

Royal Photographic Society – ♧ Open all year, daily, 9.30am to 5.30pm (4.45pm last admission). Closed 25, 26 December. £2.50, £5 (family), £1.75 (concession), no charge (child under 7 and disabled people). Licensed restaurant. ✆ 01225 462 841. Fax 01225 448 688.

Building of Bath Museum – Open mid-February to late November, Tuesday to Sunday, 10.30am to 5pm. £3, £1.50(child), £2 (concession). ✆ 01225 333 895.

Assembly Rooms (NT) – ♧ Open (pre-booked functions permitting) daily, 10am (11am Sunday) to 5pm. Closed 25 and 26 December. No charge. Audio guide (French, German, Italian, Japanese, Spanish). ✆ 01225 477 789; Fax 01225 444 793.

Museum of Costume (NACF) – ♧ Open all year, daily, 10am (11am Sundays) to 5pm. £3.60, £2.50 (child); combined ticket with Roman Baths £8. Guided tour (1hr). Audio guide (French, German, Italian, Japanese, Spanish). ✆ 01225 477 789; Fax 01225 428 184.

Museum of East Asian Art – ♧ Open, daily, 10am to 6pm (5pm November). Closed 25-26 December and 1 January. £3.50, £1 (child), £3 (OAPs), £2.50 (students). Wheelchair available on site, induction loop, handling collection. ✆ 01225 464 640.

Bath Industrial Heritage Centre – (♧) Open April to November, daily, 10am to 5pm; December to March, weekends, 10am to 5pm. Closed 24 to 26 December. £3.50, £2.50 (concession), £10 (family ticket). Guided tour (30min); leaflets (Dutch, French, German, Italian, Spanish, Portuguese). Refreshments. ✆ 01225 318 348.

Corsham Underground Quarry – Open, April to June, Sunday and holiday Mondays; July to September, Saturday to Thursday (closed Friday); October, Sunday only; November to March by appointment. Underground tours at 11.30am, 2pm, 3.30pm. ✆ 01249 716 288.

Georgian Garden – Open May to October, Monday to Friday. Admission free.

BATH

No 1 Royal Crescent (NACF) – Open mid-February to October, daily, 10.30am to 5pm; November and March, daily except Monday, 10.30am to 4pm. £3.50. Leaflet (French, German, Japanese). ☎ 01225 428 126.

Sally Lunn's House and Museum – Museum open Monday to Saturday, 10am to 6pm; Sunday 12noon to 6pm. Tea rooms open Monday to Saturday 10am to 11pm; Sunday 12noon to 11pm. 30p. ☎ 01225 461 634.

Victoria Art Gallery – (&) Open all year, Monday to Friday, 10am to 5.30pm (5pm Saturday). Closed bank holidays. No charge. ☎ 01225 477 772; Fax 01225 477 231.

Holburne Museum (NACF) – & Open, Monday to Saturday, 11am to 5pm, Sunday, 2.30pm to 5.30pm. Closed on Mondays from November to Easter. £3.50, £7 (family ticket), £2 (OAPs), £1.50 (students). Guided tour (1 hour). Parking; restaurant; garden. ☎ 01225 466 669; Fax 01225 333 121.

Bath Postal Museum – Open all year, Monday to Saturday, 11am (2pm March to December, Sunday) to 5pm. Closed 1 January, Good Friday, 25, 26 December. £2.50, £1 (child), £1.75 (concession). Refreshments. ☎ 01225 460 333.

William Herschel Museum – Open March to October, daily, 2pm to 5pm; November to February, weekends, 2pm to 5pm. £2, £1 (child), £5 (family). Guided tour (1 hour) by appointment. ☎ 01225 311 342.

George Baytun Book Museum – Open all year, Monday to Friday, 9am to 1pm, 2pm to 5.30pm; Saturday 9.30am to 1pm. Closed holidays. Donation. ☎ 01225 466 000; Fax 01225 466 000.

Beckford Tower and Museum (NACF) – Open Easter to October, weekends, holiday Mondays, 2pm to 5pm. £2, £1 (concession). Guided tour by arrangement. Parking. ☎ 01225 338 727; Fax 01225 481 850.

Prior Park (NT) – Open daily except Tuesday, from 12noon to 5.30pm (or dusk if earlier). Closed 1 January, 25 and 26 December. £3.80, £1.90 (child) with £1 reduction for those able to produce a valid public transport ticket. Limited parking bays for disabled drivers available by appointment only. ☎ 01225 833 422; 0891 335 242 (recorded information).

Excursions

American Museum, Claverton Manor – (&) Open late March to early November, daily except Monday, 2pm to 5pm; bank holiday Monday and preceding Sunday, 11am to 5pm. **Museum, grounds and galleries:** £5, £4.50 (concessions), £2.50 (child); **grounds and galleries:** £2.50, £1.25 (child). ☎ 01225 460 503; Fax 01225 480 726.

Claverton Pumping Station – Open Easter to late October, Sunday, 10.30am to 4.30pm. Pumps in steam (river conditions permitting): telephone for times. £1, 50p (concession); pumping days £2, £1 (concession). Limited parking; refreshments. ☎ 01380 721 279.

Dyrham Park (NT) – **House:** & Open April to late October, Friday to Tuesday, 12noon to 5.30pm. **Garden:** Open April to October same days as house, 11am to 5.30pm. **Park:** Open all year, daily, 12noon to 5.30pm or sunset if earlier. Closed 25 December. **House and park** £5.20, £2.60 (child), £12.90 (2A+3C). **Park and garden** £1.60, 80p (child). Parking; refreshments, shop; picnics in the park. ☎ 0117 937 2501 (house), 01225 891 364 (Warden).

Horton Court (NT) – Open April to October, Wednesday and Saturday, 2pm to 6pm or sunset. £1.60, 80p (child). Guided tour (30min). Parking. ☎ 01985 843 600.

BIDEFORD

🖪 The Quay – ☎ 012370 477676

Burton Art Gallery – & Open all year, Tuesday to Sunday, 10am to 5pm (4pm winter); also mid July to early September, Sundays and certain Mondays, 2pm to 5pm. No charge. Craft shop, café. ☎ 01237 471 455.

The Big Sheep – Open, daily, 10am to 6pm. £4.25, £3.25 (child), £15 (Family ticket). ☎ 01237 472 366.

Excursions

Great Torrington 🖪 1 East Street, South Molton – ☎ 01769 574 122

North Devon Maritime Museum, Appledore – (&) Open May bank holiday to September, Monday to Friday, 11am to 1pm (12.15pm last admission); Easter to October, daily, 2pm to 5pm (4.30pm last admission). £1. Guided tour (1 hour) by appointment; hand boards in French, German, Spanish, Dutch. ☎ 01237 474 852; school groups ☎ 01271 44610.

Northam Burrows Country Park – ☎ 01237 479 708; Fax 01237 423 613.

Tapeley Park Gardens – (&) Open Easter to September, Sunday to Friday, holidays, 10.30am to 6pm. £2.80, £1.80 (child), £2.30 (concession); additional 70p for guided tour (40min) of gardens. Parking; tea room; plant sales. ☎ 01271 860 528/ 01271 860 897.

Dartington Crystal – ♿ **Factory:** Open all year, Monday to Friday, 9.30am to 4pm. **Glass Centre:** Open all year, Monday to Saturday, 9.30am to 5pm; Sunday, 10.30am to 4.30pm. Closed public holidays. £2.75. Parking; licensed restaurant. ☎ 01805 626 266; Fax 01805 626 263.

Great Torrington Town Hall Museum – Open May to September, Monday to Friday, 10.15am to 12.45pm and 2.15pm to 4.45pm; Saturday, 10.15am to 12.45pm; October to April, by appointment. Closed public holidays. No charge. Guided tour by appointment. ☎ 01805 624 324.

Rosemoor – ♿ Open daily, April to September, 10am to 6pm; October to March, 10am to 5pm. Gardens closed 25 December; Visitor Centre closed 24 December to 1 January. £3.20, £1 (child); free to RHS members. Car park. ☎ 01805 624 067; Fax 01805 624 717.

South Molton Museum – Open March to November, Monday, Tuesday and Thursday, 10.30am to 1pm and 2pm to 4pm, Wednesday and Saturday, 10.30am to 12.30pm. No charge. ☎ 01769 572 951.

BLANDFORD FORUM

🛈 West Street – ☎ 01258 454 770

St Peter and St Paul – Open daily, 8.30am to 12.30pm. Sunday services 9.45am Holy Communion, 6.30pm Evening worship.

Blandford Museum – Open, April to September, Monday to Saturday 10am to 4pm. £1. ☎ 01258 450 388.

Cavalcade of Costume – Open Monday, Thursday to Sunday, 10am to 4pm. £2.50. ☎ 01258 453 006.

Excursions

Royal Signals Museum – Open all year, Monday to Friday, 10am to 5pm; also June to September, weekends, 10am to 4pm. Closed public holidays and 10 days at Christmas. £3, £1.50 (child), £2 (concession). Parking; refreshments. ☎ 01258 482 248.

Chettle House – Open April to October, Monday, Wednesday to Sunday, 11am to 5pm. £2. Parking. ☎ 01258 830 209; Fax 01258 830 380.

Milton Abbas – **Abbey Church:** Open normally all year, daily, 9.30am to 6.30pm. **House:** Open Easter and school summer holidays, daily, 9.30am to 6.30pm. £1.75. Leaflet (Dutch). Parking; refreshments (summer). ☎ 01258 880 489.

Fiddleford Manor (EH) – Open all year, daily, 10am to 6pm (4pm October to March).

Sturminster Newton Mill – Open Easter to September, Sunday, Monday (Market Day), Thursday and Saturday, 11am to 5pm. £1, 50p (child). Parking, shop.

BODMIN

🛈 Mount Folly – ☎ 01208 76616

Bodmin Museum – Open April to September, 10am to 4pm; October, 11am to 3pm. No charge. Parking.

Bodmin and Wenford Railway – Open, mid-June to mid-September, Mondays to Fridays. Special timetables apply for special events. ☎ 01208 736 66.

Excursion

Pencarrow – (♿) **House:** Open Easter to mid October, Sunday to Thursday, 1.30pm (11am June to early September) to 5pm. **Gardens:** Open Easter to mid October, daily. £4 (house and gardens). Guided tour (45min) also in Dutch, French, German, Italian, Spanish. Parking; refreshments. ☎ 01208 841369.

BODMIN MOOR

🛈 The Clease, Camelford – ☎ 01840 212 954
Launceston 🛈 Market Street – ☎ 01566 772 321

North Cornwall Museum of Rural Life – (♿) Open April to September, Monday to Saturday, 10am to 5pm. £1.25, 75p (child), £1 (concession). Guided tour by appointment. ☎ /Fax 01840 212 954.

Launceston Castle (EH) – (♿) Open April to October, daily, 10am to 6pm (6pm/dusk, October); Closed 1 January, 24 to 26 December. £1.50, 80p (child), £1.10 (concession). ☎ 01566 772 365.

Lawrence House Museum (NT) – Open April to September, Monday to Friday, 10.30am to 4.30pm; otherwise by appointment. Donation. ☎ 01566 773 277, 01566 774 518.

Merlin Glass, Liskeard – ♿ Open February to December, Mondays to Saturdays, 10am to 5pm. Call for times of glass-blowing demonstrations. ☎ 01579 342 399.

BODMIN MOOR

Dobwells – Open Monday to Saturday, 11am to 4.30pm; Saturday and Sunday 10.30am to 5pm. ☎ 0800 521 812.

Restormel Castle (EH) – Open April to October, daily, 10am to 6pm (6pm/dusk, October). £1.50, 80p (child), £1.10 (concession). Parking, picnic area. ☎ 01208 872 687.

Lanhydrock (NT) – ♿ House: Open April to October, Tuesday to Sunday and bank holiday Monday, 11am to 5.30pm (5pm October). House guide (Dutch, French, German). **Gardens**: Open March to October, daily, 11am to 5.30pm (5pm October); November to February, daily, daylight hours. Garden guide (French, German). House, garden and grounds £6, £15 (2A+2C); garden and grounds £3. Parking (600metres); refreshments; shop; plant sales. Licensed restaurant. ☎ 01208 73320; fax 01208 74084.

BOURNEMOUTH

🛈 Westover Road – ☎ 01202 451 700

Russell-Cotes Art Gallery and Museum – ♿ Closed for refurbishment until end 1998. ☎ 01202 451 800.

Shelley Rooms – (♿) Open all year, Tuesday to Sunday, 2pm to 5pm. Closed Good Friday, 25 and 26 December. No charge. Parking. ☎ 01202 303 571.

Excursions

Christchurch 🛈 High Street – ☎ 01202 471 780

Red House Museum – (♿) Open all year, Tuesday to Sunday, holidays, 10am (2pm Sunday) to 5pm. Closed 25 December and throughout January; Good Friday. £1. ☎ 01202 482 860; Fax 01202 481 924.

Highcliffe Castle – Open daily, end May to August, 1pm to 5pm. £1. ☎ 01425 278 807.

BRADFORD-ON-AVON

🛈 34 Silver Street – ☎ 01225 865 797

Bradford-on-Avon Museum – Open Easter to October, Wednesday to Sunday, 10.30am to 12.30pm, 2pm to 4pm (Sunday: afternoons only); November to Easter, Wednesday to Sunday, (Saturday mornings only 10.30am to 12.30pm) 2pm to 4pm. Donation. ☎ 01225 863 280.

Bridge Chapel – Closed for restoration. ☎ 01225 865 797 (Tourist Information Centre).

Saxon Church of St Laurence – ♿ Open all year, daily, 10am to 7pm (4pm winter). No charge. ☎ 01225 865 797.

Tithe Barn (EH) – ♿ Open April to late October, daily, 10.30am to 5pm; November to late March, daily, 10.30am to 4pm. Closed 25 December. No charge. Parking. ☎ 01345 090 899.

Excursions

Westwood Manor (NT) – Open April to September, Tuesday, Wednesday, Sunday, 2pm to 5pm. £3.30. ☎ 01225 863 374.

Iford Manor Gardens – Open April to October, Tuesday to Thursday, Saturday and Sunday, 2pm to 5pm. £ 2.20, £1.60 (concessions). ☎ 01225 863 146.

Great Chalfield Manor (NT) – Open April to October, Tuesday to Thursday: visit by guided tour only at 12.15pm, 2.15pm, 3pm, 3.45pm, 4.30pm. Closed public holidays. £3.50. ☎ 01985 843 600.

BRIDGWATER

🛈 Town Hall, High Street – ☎ 01278 427 652

Admiral Blake Museum – (♿) Open all year, Tuesday to Saturday, 10am to 4pm. Closed 25 December to 1 January. Donation. Guided tour by arrangement. ☎ 01278 456 127.

Excursions

Barford Park – Open by appointment only, May to September. ☎ 01278 671 269.

Coleridge Cottage (NT) – Parlour and reading room only open April to September, Tuesday to Thursday, Sunday, 2pm to 5pm; otherwise by appointment. £1.70, 80p (child). ☎ 01278 732 662.

Hinkley Point – Open daily (except Saturdays between October and March), 10am to 4pm. Closed 1 January, 25-26 December. No charge. ☎ 01278 654 334.

Stembridge Tower Mill – Open April to September, Sundays, Mondays and Wednesdays, 2pm to 5pm. £1.60, 80p (child). Parking. ☎ 01458 250 818.

Willows and Wetlands – Open all year, Monday to Saturday, 9am to 5pm. Guided tours (1 hour), Monday to Friday, 10am to 12noon, 2pm to 4pm, every 30min. £2.50. Leaflet (French, German). **Shop**: Open all year, Monday to Saturday, 9am to 5pm. ☎ 01823 490 249.

BRIDPORT

Bridport Museum (NACF) – Open April to October, Christmas and New Year, Autumn and Spring half-terms, Monday to Saturday, 10am to 5pm. £1. Guided tour (45-90min) by appointment. ☎ 01308 422 116; Fax 01308 420 659.

West Bay Harbour Museum – Open April to October, daily, 10am to 6pm (8pm in August). £1. ☎ 01308 420 997; Fax 01308 420 659.

Excursions

St Mary's Church, Beaminster – Open, daily, 9am to 5pm. Services Sunday at 8am, 11am, 6.30pm; Saints Days at 10am. ☎ 01308 862 150.

Parnham House – Open April to October, Sunday, Wednesday, bank holidays, 10am to 5pm. £4, £2 (child), £2 (concession). ☎ 01308 862 204.

Mapperton Gardens – Open March to October, daily, 2pm to 6pm. Admission charge. ☎ 01308 862 645; Fax 01308 863 348.

BRISTOL

Christchurch – Open all year, Monday to Friday, 10am to 3pm; Saturday, by appointment. ☎ 0117 927 7977.

St Stephen's City – Open all year, Monday to Friday, 8am to 5pm; Saturday, by appointment. ☎ 0117 927 7977.

St John the Baptist – Open April to October, Tuesday, Thursday, 12noon to 3pm. No charge. ☎ 0171 936 2285 (Churches Conservation Trust).

John Wesley's New Room – Open all year, Monday to Saturday, 10am to 1pm and 2pm to 4pm. Closed Wednesdays in Winter and public holidays. Suggested donation £1. ☎ 0117 264 740.

St Mary Redcliffe – Open daily, 8am to 8pm (6pm September to May). Daily services: 9.15am Morning Prayer, 5pm Evening Prayer; Sunday 8am Holy Communion, 9.30am Sung Eucharist, 11.15am Sung Matins, 6.30pm Sung Evensong. Guided tour by appointment. Brochure (Dutch, French, German, Italian, Spanish). ☎ /Fax 0117 929 1487.

"Exploratory" – ♿ Open all year, daily, 10am to 5pm. Closed 1 week at Christmas. £5, £15 (family 2A+2C), £3.50 (child). Science shop. Café (weekends and school holidays). ☎ 0117 907 9000, 0117 907 5000 (information line); Fax 0117 907 8000.

Arnolfini – ♿ Open all year, Monday to Saturday, 10am to 19.00; Sunday, 12noon to 19.00. Telephone to confirm holidays. Variable charge to exhibitions. Guided tour (45min). Café, licensed bar. ☎ 01272 299 191.

Industrial Museum – (♿) Open April to October, Saturday to Wednesday, 10am to 5pm; November to March, Saturday and Sunday, 10am to 5pm. £1, 50p (concession), no charge (child under 16/student). ☎ 0117 925 1470.

SS Great Britain and Maritime Heritage Centre – (♿) Open all year, daily, 10am to 5.30pm (4.30pm winter) Closed 24, 25 December. £3.90, £2.70 (child), £3 (OAP). Guided tour (1 hour) by appointment. Parking; refreshments. ☎ 0117 926 0680.

Bristol Blue Glass – Great Western Dock, Gas Ferry Road, Bristol BS1 6TY. Open, daily, 10am to 5.30pm (4.30pm in winter). ☎ 0117 929 8900.

Bristol Cathedral – Open all year, daily, 8am to 6pm. Closed afternoon of 25 December. Suggested donation £1. Guided tour (French German) by appointment. Brochure (Chinese, French, German, Italian, Japanese, Russian, Spanish). Refreshments. ☎ 0117 926 4879; Fax 0117 925 3678.

Wills Building, University of Bristol

A. Taverner

BRISTOL

Lord Mayor's Chapel – Open all year, Tuesday to Saturday, 10am to 12 midday and 1pm to 4pm; Sunday, for services only. Donation. ☎ 0117 929 4350.

Harvey's Wine Cellars – Open all year, Monday to Saturday, 10am to 5pm. Closed Sunday and bank holidays. £4, £3 (concessions), £8 (family). Guided tour (French, Spanish) and tutored wine tasting by appointment, from £6.50. Leaflet (French, German, Spanish). Gift shop. ☎ 0117 927 5036; Fax 0117 927 5002.

Georgian House (NACF) – (&) Open all year, Tuesday to Saturday, 1pm to 5pm. Closed 1 January, Good Friday, 25-27 December and the last week in January. £1, 50p (OAP); combined ticket with Red Lodge available. ☎ 0117 921 1362.

Cabot Tower – Open all year, daily, 8am to dusk. No charge.

Red Lodge – Open, Tuesday to Saturday, 1pm to 5pm. £1, 50p (OAP). ☎ 0117 921 1360.

City Museum and Art Gallery (NACF) – (&) Open all year, daily, 10am to 5pm. Closed 1 January, Good Friday, May Day holiday, Spring bank holiday, 25, 26 December. £2, £1 (concession), no charge (child under 16 and students). Café. ☎ 0117 922 3571.

Clifton Observatory – Open, daily (weather permitting), 11am to 6pm summer; Monday to Friday, 12noon to 3pm, Saturday and Sunday, 11am to 4pm in winter. Closed 24-26 December. Camera obscura £1, 75p (child); caves £1. Refreshments. ☎ 0117 974 1242.

Bristol Zoo – & Open all year, daily, 9am to 6pm (5pm September to May). Closed 25 December. £6.50, £3.50 (child), £5.50 (concession). Parking; restaurant. ☎ 0117 973 8951.

Clifton RC Cathedral – Open all year, daily, 7am to 9pm (8pm in winter). Brochure (French, German, Italian, Spanish). ☎ 0117 973 422; Fax 0117 974 4879.

Excursions

Stanton Drew Stone Circles (EH) – Access is at the discretion of the owner who may levy a charge. ☎ 0117 975 0700.

Blaise Castle House Museum – Open all year, Tuesday to Sunday, 10am to 1pm, 2pm to 5pm. Closed 1 January, Good Friday, 25, 26 December, and Mondays. No charge. ☎ 0117 950 6789.

BUDE

🛈 The Crescent – ☎ 01288 354 240

Bude-Stratton Museum – Open daily Easter to September, 11am to 4.30pm. 50p; 25p (concession).

C

CAMBORNE-REDRUTH

Mineral Tramways Discovery Centre – Open Monday to Friday, 10am to 1pm and from 1.30pm to 4pm. Admission free. ☎ 01209 612 917.

Cornish Industrial Heritage Centre Taylors Shaft 11-5pm. ☎ 01209 2166 57 Wheelchair friendly.

Cornish Pumping Engines and East Pool Whim (NT) – Open April to October, daily, 11am to 5pm. £2.50, £2 (concession), £7.50 (2A+3C). ☎ 01209 216 657. Out of season contact the Trevithick Trust ☎ 01209 612 142.

Camborne School of Mines, University of Exeter – Museum of Minerals: Open all year, Monday to Friday, 9am to 5pm. Closed holidays. No charge. Parking. ☎ 01209 714 866; Fax 01209 716 977; Email L.Atkinsoncsm.ex.ac.uk

Excursion

Poldark Mine – Open April to October, daily, 10am to 5.30pm (6pm August). Guided tour (3 hours). Parking; refreshments. ☎ 01326 563 166 (24 hour information line).

CHARD

🛈 The Guildhall, Fore Street – ☎ 01460 67463

Chard Museum – Open early May to mid October, Monday to Saturday, also Sunday from July to August, 10.30am to 4.30pm. £1.70, £4 (family), 60p (child), £1.20 (concession). ☎ 01460 65091.

Excursions

Cricket St Thomas World of Wildlife and Adventure – (&) Open April to October, daily, 10am to 6pm (5pm or sunset, November to March). £5.50. Adventure playground. Parking; restaurant. ☎ 01460 307 55; fax 01460 306 68.

Clapton Court Gardens – Open April to September, Tuesday to Thursday, 2pm to 5pm. £3, no charge for children under 16. Parking. ☎ 01460 732 20.

Forde Abbey – & House: Open April to October, Sunday, Wednesday and holidays, 1pm to 4.30pm. Gardens: Open all year, daily, 10am to 5pm. House and gardens £5; gardens £3.75. Parking; refreshments (April to October). ☎ 01460 220 231; Fax 01460 220 296.

CHEDDAR GORGE

🛈 The Gorge - ☎ 01934 744 071

Cheddar Showcaves – Open all year, daily, 10am to 5pm (10.30am to 4.30pm October to Easter). Closed 24, 25 December. Jacobs ladder, Gough's cave, Cox's cave, Heritage centre, Crystal quest, Lookout tower, Gorge walk £6.50; £18.50 (family ticket 2A+2C), £3.95 (child). Parking; refreshments. ☎ 01934 742 343.

Adventure Caving – Open all year, daily. Guided trip (90min) by prior booking; minimum age 12 years; helmets, caving lamps and overalls provided; waterproof footwear preferable; basic English essential. ☎ 01934 742 343.

Excursion

King John's Hunting Lodge, Axbridge (NT) – Open Easter to September, daily, 2pm to 5pm. No charge. ☎ 01934 732 012.

Chewton Cheese Dairy – Open all year, daily, 9am to 4.30pm. Cheese-making : Monday to Wednesday, Friday, Saturday. £2.50, £1.50 (child), £2 (concession). Guided tour (45min) at 11.30am 12.15pm and 1pm. Parking; refreshments. ☎ 01761 241 666.

CHIPPENHAM

🛈 The Citadel, Bath Road - ☎ 01249 657 733

Yelde Hall – Open mid March to October, Monday to Saturday, 10am to 12.30pm, 2pm to 4.30pm. Closed bank holidays. No charge. ☎ 01249 653 145, 01249 651 488.

Excursions

Corsham Court – & Open Good Friday to October, Tuesday to Sunday and bank holiday Monday, 11am to 5.30pm; November to Maundy Thursday, weekends, 2pm to 4.30pm. Closed throughout December. £4.50, £2.50 (child), £3.50 (OAPs); gardens only £2, £1 (child), £1.50 (OAPs). Guided tour available. Parking. ☎ 01249 701 610, 01249 701 611; Fax 01249 444 556.

Sheldon Manor House and Gardens – & Open Easter to early October, Sunday, Thursday, holidays, 2pm (12.30 gardens) to 6pm; early October to Easter by appointment. £3.25 (open day), £4 (private day). Guided tour (1 hour). Parking; refreshments. ☎ 01249 653 120; Fax 01249 461 047.

CLOVELLY

Visitor Centre – & Open July to September, daily, 9am to 6pm; October to June, daily, 9.30am to sunset. Closed 25 December. £2, no charge (child under 7). Audio visual show. Parking. Refreshments. ☎ 01237 431 288.

Hobby Drive – Open to pedestrians only Easter to mid-October, daily, 10am to 6pm. ☎ 01237 431 200.

Excursions

Hartland Abbey – Open from May to September, (Tuesdays in July and August), Wednesday, Thursday, Sunday and bank holidays between 2pm and 5.30pm. House and grounds: £3.25, £1.50 child; grounds only £1.50, 50p (child). ☎ 01237 441264; Fax 01237 861134.

Docton Mill – Open daily March to October from 10am to 6pm (November and February by appointment). £2.50; 50p (child). ☎ 01237 441 369.

This guide, which is revised regularly,
incorporates tourist information provided at the time of going to press.
Changes are however inevitable owing to improved facilities and
fluctuations in the cost of living.

D

DARTMOOR

Castle Inn, Lydford – Restaurant ☎ 01822 820 241, 01822 820 242.

Lydford Gorge (NT) – (&) Open late March to October, daily, 10am to 5.30pm; November to March, daily, 10.30am to 3pm (from entrance to waterfall only). Short walk to White Lady Waterfall (1 hour; 1.5 miles); long and arduous walk through gorge (2 hours; 3 miles; suitable only for the able-bodied wearing stout shoes). Guided tours on application. £3.10, £1.50 (child). Parking; refreshments. ☎ 01822 820 320 or 01822 820 441.

Okehampton Castle (EH) – Open April to October, daily, 10am to 6pm (6pm/dusk, October). £2.20, £1.10 (child), £1.70 (concession). Parking. Picnic area. ☎ 01837 52844.

Museum of Dartmoor Life, Okehampton – (&) Open Easter to November, Monday to Saturday, holidays, 10am to 5pm. £1.50, 80p (child), £1.30 (concession). Parking; refreshments. ☎ 01837 52295.

Finch Foundry, Sticklepath (NT) – Open April to October, daily except Tuesday, 11am to 5.30pm. £2.40. Parking; refreshments; walks. £2.50. ☎ 01837 840 046.

Castle Drogo (NT) – (&) **House:** Open April to October, daily except Friday (open Good Friday), 11am to 5.30pm. **Garden:** Open April to October, daily, 10.30am to 5.30pm. Leaflet (Dutch, French, German, Italian, Japanese, Spanish). Castle, garden, grounds: £4.90, £12.20 (family); garden £2.30. Parking; licensed restaurant; plant centre. ☎ 01647 433 306; Fax 01647 433 186.

Devon Guild of Craftsmen, Bovey Tracey – (&) Open all year, daily, 10am to 5.30pm. Closed winter holidays. £1.25, 75p (concession). Café. ☎ 01626 832 223; Fax 01626 834 220.

House of Marbles and Teign Valley Glass – Open Easter to September, daily, 9am to 5pm. **Glassmaking:** Easter to September, Monday to Friday, 9am to 4.30pm, Sunday and holidays, 10am to 3pm. No charge. Restaurant. Parking. ☎ 01626 835 358; Fax 01626 835 315.

Becky Falls – Open Easter to November, daily, 10am to 6pm. £2.75, £1.50 (child). Attended parking; licensed restaurant; picnic area; ice cream parlour; shop. ☎ 0164 221 259.

Buckfast Abbey – & Abbey Church and grounds: open all year, daily, 5.30am to 7pm. Monastic services: daily at 5.45am, 6.45am, 1pm, 6.30pm (Saturday at 6.15pm), 9pm. Mass: weekdays at 8am, 12.05 pm; Sunday at 9am, 10.30am, 5.30pm; Holy days at 8am; 12.05pm, 7.15pm.
Visitor facilities: open daily, 9am to 5.30pm (10am to 4pm in Winter). Exhibition £1. Shops open on Sundays at 12noon. Parking; refreshments. ☎ 01364 642 519.

South Devon Railway – & Open March to September, daily, 9.30am (9am holidays) to 6pm. £5.90, £17.50 (family ticket 2A+2C). Guided tour by appointment. Parking; refreshments. ☎ 01364 642 338.

DARTMOUTH

Britannia Royal Naval College – Open most Wednesday and Saturday afternoons, by guided tour (90min) only from 2.30pm to 4.30pm. £3. ☎ 01803 677 120; Fax 01803 677 015.

Newcomen Engine – Open all year, Monday to Saturday, (Sunday, April to October) 10am to 4pm. 50p. ☎ 01803 834 224; Fax 01803 835 631.

Dartmouth Museum (NACF) – Open April to October, Monday to Saturday, 11am to 5pm; November to March, 12noon to 3pm. Closed 24 to 26 December. £1, 30p (child), 50p (concession). ☎ 01803 832 923.

Dartmouth Castle (EH) – Open April to October, daily, 10am to 6pm (6pm/dusk, October); November to March, Wednesday to Sunday, 10am to 1pm, 2pm to 4pm. Closed 24 to 26 December, 1 January. £2.20, £1.10 (child), £1.70 (concession). Limited parking. ☎ 01803 833 588.

Excursion

River Dart boat service – Open late March to October, daily, times according to the tides; November to late March, limited service. Circular cruise 1hr £3; 1hr 30min cruise £3.80; Dartmouth to Totnes single £3.80, return £5.40. Brochure (Dutch, French, German, Spanish). ☎ 01803 834 224.

DEVIZES
🏠 39 St John's Street – ☎ 01380 729 408

Devizes Museum (NACF) – Open Monday to Saturday except public holidays, 10am to 5pm. £2. ☎ 01380 727 369; Fax 01380 722 150.

Kennet and Avon Canal Centre – Open all year except January, daily, 10am to 5pm (4pm winter). £1. ☎ 01380 721 279.

DORCHESTER
🏠 Antelope Walk, DT1 1BA – ☎ 01305 267 992; Fax 01305 266 079

Old Crown Court – Open all year, Monday to Friday except public holidays, 10am to 12noon and 2pm to 4pm. No charge. Guided tour of cells August, Wednesday, 10.15am to 12.15pm; Tuesday to Friday, 2.15pm to 4.15pm. Audioguide (Dutch, French, German, Welsh). 50p. ☎ 01305 252 241; Fax 01305 257 039.

Dorset County Museum (NACF) – Open all year, Monday to Saturday, 10am to 5pm; Sundays in July and August. Closed Good Friday, 24 and 25 December. £2.75, £1.50 (concession). ☎ 01305 262 735; Fax 01305 257 180.

Dinosaur Museum – (&) Open summer, daily, 9.30am to 5.30pm; winter, 10am to 4.30pm. Closed 24 to 26 December. £3.50, £9.95 (family ticket 2A+2C). ☎ 01305 269 880; Fax 01305 268 885.

Tutankhamun Exhibition – (&) Open April to October, 9.30am to 5.30pm; November to March, Monday to Friday, 9.30am to 5pm, Saturday and Sunday, 10am to 3pm. Closed 24 to 26 December. £3.50, £9.95 (family ticket 2A+2C). ☎ 01305 269 571; fax 01305 268 885.

Keep Military Museum – Open all year, Monday to Saturday and public holidays, 9.30am to 5pm. Closed 24-26 December, 1 January. £2, £1 (concession). Parking. ☎ 01305 264 066; Fax 01305 250 373.

Excursions

Maiden Castle Earthworks (EH) – Open all year, daily. No charge. Parking.

Hardy's Cottage (NT) – Open April to October, Sunday to Thursday, 11am to 5pm or sunset; also Good Friday. £2.50. Parking. ☎ 01305 262 366.

Athelhampton House and Gardens – (&) Open Easter to October, daily except Saturday, 11am to 5pm. Brochure (Dutch, French, German). £4.50. Parking. Restaurant. ☎ 01305 848 363; Fax 01305 848 135.

Tolpuddle Martyrs' Museum – (&) Open all year, Tuesday to Sunday, 10am (11am Sunday) to 5.30pm from April to October (4pm November to March). Closed Monday except bank holidays; 24 December to 1 January. No charge. Limited parking. ☎ 01305 848 237.

Methodist Chapel – Open Easter to September, Monday to Saturday, 9.30am to 6pm.

Clouds Hill (NT) – Open April to late October, Wednesday to Friday, Sunday and bank holiday Mondays, 12noon to 5pm or dusk if earlier. Guide books (Braille). £2.20. Parking. ☎ 01929 405 616.

Wolfeton House, Charminster – Open May to September, Monday, Tuesday, Thursday, 2pm to 6pm; October to April; groups by appointment. £3. Parking. ☎ 01305 263 500; Fax 01305 265 090.

E

EXETER
🏠 Paris Street ☎ 01392 265 700; Fax 01392 265 260

Exeter City tour – Programme available from the Tourist Information Centre, Civic Centre. **Redcoat walking tours** ☎ 01392 265 212; Fax 01392 265 260.

Exeter Cathedral – & Open all year, daily, 7.30am to 6.15pm (5pm Saturday,

Carved bench end, Exeter Cathedral

B. Kaufmann

7.30pm Sunday). Donation £2. Guide book (French, German). Leaflet (Czech, Dutch, French, German, Hungarian, Italian, Japanese, Portuguese, Russian, Spanish, Swedish). Guided tour: April to October, daily except Saturday afternoons and Sunday, 11am to 2.30pm. ☎ 01392 55573 (cathedral office), 01392 214 219 (guided tours); Fax 01392 498 769.

Royal Albert Memorial Museum (NACF) – ♿ Open all year, Monday to Saturday, 10am to 5pm. No charge. Café, shop. ☎ 01392 265 858; Fax 01392 421 252.

Rougemont House – Open to pre-booked school parties only. ☎ 01392 265 360.

Underground Passages – Open July to mid-September during school holidays, Monday to Saturday, 10am to 5.30pm (4.45pm last tour); mid-September to June, Tuesday to Saturday, 2pm (10am Saturday) to 5pm. September to June £2.50, £1.50 (child), £6 (family ticket); July to August £3.50, £2.25 (child), £9 (family ticket). Guided tour (40 min) available. ☎ 01392 265 887, 01392 265 858; Fax 01392 421 252.

Exeter Guildhall – Open (civic functions permitting) all year, Monday to Friday, 10.30am to 1pm, 2pm to 4pm (1pm alternate Saturday mornings in winter). Closed public holidays. Donation. Guided tour available. ☎ 01392 265 500.

St Nicholas Priory – (♿) Open Easter to October, Monday, Wednesday, Saturday, 3pm to 4.30pm. ☎ 01392 265 858 (Exeter Museum).

Tucker's Hall – Open (civic functions permitting) June to September, Tuesday, Thursday and Friday, 10.30am to 12.30pm; October to May, Thursday 10.30am to 12.30pm. No charge. ☎ 01392 436 244.

Quay House Interpretation Centre – Open Easter to October, daily, 10am to 5pm. No charge. ☎ 01392 265 213.

Excursions

Topsham Museum (NACF) – Open end March to September, Monday, Wednesday and Saturday, 2pm to 5pm; also Sundays, June to September. £1.50, check for concessions. ☎ 01392 873 244.

Killerton (NT) – ♿ **House:** Open mid March to October, daily except Tuesdays, 11am to 5.30pm. **Garden :** Open all year, daily, 10.30am to sunset. Braille guides; scented garden; wheelchair. £4.80 (house), £12 (2A+2C); £3.20 (garden and park). Parking; refreshments; shop; plant centre. Licensed restaurant. ☎ 01392 881 345.

EXMOOR

Lynmouth 🛈 The Esplanade – ☎ 01598 752 509
Combe Martin 🛈 Seacot, Cross Street – ☎ 01271 883 319
Dunster 🛈 Dunster Steep (limited winter opening) – ☎ 01643 821 835

Exmoor Glass – Glass-blowing demonstrations on application. ☎ 01643 863 141.

Cliff Railway – Open mid March to 26 December, Monday to Saturday, 8am to 7pm; also Easter, holiday weekends, June to September, Sunday, 10am to 7pm. 50p, 30p (child). ☎ 01598 753 486.

Combe Martin Motorcycle Collection – ♿ Open Easter week and mid May to October, daily, 10am to 5pm. £2.50, £1.50 (child and concession). ☎ 01271 882 346.

Dunster Castle (NT) – ♿ **House:** Open late March to October, daily except Thursday and Friday (including Good Friday), 11am to 5pm (4pm October). **Garden and Park:** Open all year, 11am to 4pm (10am to 5pm, April to September). Closed 25 December. Castle, garden and park £5.00, £2.60 (child), £13 (2A+3C); garden and park only £2.70, £1.30 (child), £6.50 (2A+3C). House guide (Braille, Dutch, French, German, Italian). Shop. ☎ 01643 821 314; 0891 335 250 (24hr information line); Fax 01643 823 000.

Dunster Water Mill (NT) – Open April to October, Sunday to Friday (also open Saturday before Easter and Saturdays throughout July and August), 10.30am to 5pm. £1.60. Tearoom; shop. ☎ 01643 821 759.

Dunster Dolls Museum – Open Easter to October, daily, 10.30am to 4.30pm. 50p, 25p (child). ☎ 01643 821 220.

Combe Sydenham Hall – **House and Garden:** Guided tour Easter to October, Thursdays and bank holiday Mondays, at 2pm; additional tours at peak periods. £4, £2.50 (child).
Country park: Open Easter to October, Sunday to Friday, sunrise to sunset. No charge. Parking. ☎ 01984 656 284.

EXMOUTH

🛈 Alexandra Terrace – ☎ 01395 222 299

A La Ronde House (NT) – Open April to October, Sunday to Thursday, 11am to 5.30pm; last admission 30min before closing time. £3.20, £1.60 (child). Parking; refreshments; shop. ☎ 01395 265 514.

Bicton Gardens and Museum – Open April to October, daily, 10am to 6pm (4pm October); November to March, weekends, 10am to 4pm. £4.95, £14 (family 2A+4C), £3.95 (concession); woodland railway 85p. ☎ 01395 568 465.

Otterton Mill – Open Easter to October, daily, 10.30am to 5.30pm; November to Easter, 11am to 4pm. £1.50. Audio-visual presentation (hourly). Restaurant. ☎ 01395 568 521, 01395 568 031, 01395 567 041; Fax 01395 568 521.

F

FALMOUTH
🛈 28 Killigrew Street – ☎ 01326 312 300

Falmouth Municipal Art Gallery – ♿ Open all year, Monday to Saturday, 10am to 4.30pm (1pm Saturday). Closed 25 to 26 December, 1 January and public holidays. No charge. ☎ 01326 313 863; Fax 01326 312 662.

Cornwall Maritime Museum – Open daily, Easter to end October, 10am to 4pm; November to March, Monday to Saturday, 10am to 3pm. £1. Guide (Dutch, French, German, Italian). ☎ 01326 316 745.

Pendennis Castle (EH, NACF) – Open daily, 10am to 6pm (4pm November to March). Closed 24 to 26 December, 1 January. £2.50, £1.30 (child), £1.90 (concession). Parking; refreshments (summer only). ☎ 01326 316 594.

Excursions

Glendurgan Garden (NT) – Open March to October, Tuesday to Saturday and bank holiday Mondays, 10.30am to 5.30pm (4.30pm last admission). Closed Good Friday. £3. Parking; refreshments; plant sales: lower valley paths too steep for wheelchairs. ☎ 01326 250 906 (opening times), 01208 74281 (enquiries).

Trebah Gardens – Open all year, daily, 10.30am to 5pm. £3 (free to RHS members at all times and to NT members November to February); £1 (child); £2.80 (concession). Guided tours by appointment; group concessions. Parking; refreshments; shop; plant sales. ☎ 01326 250 448; Fax 01326 250 781.

Trelissick Garden (NT) – Open March to October, Monday to Sunday, 10.30am (12.30pm Sunday) to 5.30pm (5pm March and October). Woodland walks also open November to end February. £4, £10 (2A+2C). Parking; licensed restaurants; shop and plant sales; arts and crafts gallery; wheelchairs and electric buggy for hire. ☎ 01872 862 090; Fax 01872 865 808.

King Harry Ferry – Operates from Feock to Philleigh (5min) April to September, daily; October to March, Monday to Saturday. Telephone for timetable. Car £2 (single), £3 (day-return). ☎ 01872 862 312; Fax 01872 863 355.

St Mawes Castle (EH) – Open April to October, daily, 10am to 6pm (dusk, October); November to March, Wednesday to Sunday, 10am to 1pm, 2pm to 4pm. Closed 1 January, 24 to 26 December. £2, £1, (child), £1.50 (concession). Parking. ☎ 01326 270 526.

FOWEY
🛈 4 Custom House Hill – ☎ 01726 833 616

Town Hall Museum – Open Easter and Spring holiday to early October, Monday to Friday, 10.30am to 12.30 and 2.30pm to 4.30pm. £1, £2 (family). ☎ 01726 833 616.

Excursions
Looe 🛈 Fore Street – ☎ 01503 262 072

Polperro Heritage Museum – Open daily 10am to 6pm. £1. ☎ 01503 272 423.

Monkey Sanctuary – (♿) Open over Easter holidays, May to September, Sunday to Thursday, 10.30am to 5pm in peak season, 11.30am to 4.30pm in off peak season. Closed Friday and Saturday (except Easter weekend). £3.50. Parking; refreshments. ☎ 01503 262 532.

Paul Corin's Magnificent Music Machines – Open Easter week and early April to late October, daily, 10.30am to 5pm. £3, £1.50 (child). Parking; picnic area; dogs on leads welcome. ☎ 01579 343 108.

FROME
🛈 Justice Lane – ☎ 01373 467 271

Excursions

Rode Bird Gardens – ♿ Open all year, daily, 10am to 6pm (Summer) or sunset (Winter); last admission 1 hour before closing. Closed 25 December. £4.30, £2.30 (child), £3.80 (OAP), £12.80 (2A+2C). Parking; licensed cafeteria. ☎ 01373 830 326; Fax 01373 831288.

Farleigh Hungerford Castle (EH) – (&) Open April to October, daily, 10am to 6pm (6pm/dusk, October); November to March, Wednesday to Sunday, 10am to 1pm, 2pm to 4pm. Closed 24 to 26 December, 1 January. £1.50, 80p (child), £1.10 (concession). Parking. ☎ 01225 754 026.

East Somerset Railway, Cranmore – & Station, museum, locomotive shed, workshops **and gallery:** open daily 10am to 3pm (later on train running days). £2, £1 (child), £1.25 (OAP).
Steam trains in operation: January to March and November, Sundays; April, May and October, Saturday and Sunday; June to September, Wednesday to Sunday; July and August, daily; December, Santa Specials. £5.50, £3.50 (child), £4.50 (OAP). Parking; licensed restaurant; picnic and play areas. ☎ 01749 880 417; Fax 01749 880 764.

Downside Abbey Church – & Open all year, daily, 6.30am to 8.15pm. No charge. Guided tour (45min) on written application to the Guestmaster, Downside Abbey, BA3 4RH. Parking. Fax 01761 232 973.

G

GLASTONBURY   ⊟ 9 High Street – ☎ 01458 832 954; Fax 01458 832 949

Glastonbury Abbey Ruins – & Open all year, daily, 9am (9.30am September to May) to 6pm or sunset if earlier. Closed 25 December. £2.50, £1 (child), £2 (concession). Audio guide (French). Brochure (French, German). Leaflet (Japanese). ☎ 01458 832 267.

Lake Village Museum, Glastonbury Tribunal (EH) – Open same times as TIC, Monday to Saturday, 10am to 5pm (5.30pm Friday, Saturday) in summer; 10am to 4pm (4.30pm Friday, Saturday) in winter. £1.50, 75p (child), £1 (concession). ☎ 01458 832 954.

Lake Village (EH) – (&) Open Easter to September, daily 10am to 5pm (5.30pm Friday and Saturday); October to Easter, daily, 10am to 4pm (4.30pm Friday and Saturday). Parking. ☎ 01458 832 954.

Peat Moor Visitor Centre – Open daily, April to October, 10am to 5pm; November to March on application. ☎ 01458 860 697.

Somerset Rural Life Museum – & Open all year, Tuesday to Friday, 10am to 5pm (4.30pm Friday); also April to October, weekends, 2pm to 6pm; November to March, Saturday, 11am to 4pm. £2. Parking; refreshments (summer only). ☎ 01458 831 197.

Chalice Well – (&) Open April to October, daily, 10am to 6pm; November to March, daily, 12noon to 4pm. £1, 50p (child, OAP). Limited parking. ☎ 01458 831 154; fax 01458 835 528.

Excursion

Shoe Museum, Street – & Open January to December, Monday to Friday, 10am to 4.45pm; Sunday, 11am to 5pm. ☎ 01458 443 131 ext 2169.

H

HONITON   ⊟ Dowell Street Car Park – ☎ 01404 43716

All Hallows Museum (NACF) – Open April to October, Monday to Saturday, 10am to 5pm (4pm October). **Lace-making demonstrations:** June to August. £1, 30p (child), 80p (concession). ☎ 01404 44966.

Excursions   Axminster ⊟ Church Street – ☎ 01297 34386

Cadhay House – (&) Open July to August, Tuesday to Thursday, 2pm to 5.30pm; also late spring and summer holidays, Sunday, Monday, 2pm to 5.30pm. £3. Guided tour (75min). ☎ 01404 812 432.

Farway Countryside Park – Open Good Friday to September, daily, 10am to 5pm. £2. ☎ 01404 87224. Guided tour (2 hours) by appointment. Parking; refreshments. Facilities for the disabled.

The Minster Church, Axminster – Open, daily, 9am to lunchtime and then until 5pm. Services: Sunday at 8am, 10am, 6pm; Tuesday and Friday at 10am. ☎ 01297 32264.

I

ILFRACOMBE

St Nicholas' Chapel – Open late May to mid-October, daily, 10am to 1pm and 2.30pm to 5pm; also May to August, 7.30pm to sunset. No charge.

Tunnels Beach – ♿ Open May to September, daily, 9am to sunset. 90p, 50p (child). Guided tour. Refreshments; picnic area.

Excursions

Hele Corn Mill – Open daily, 10 am to 5pm. ☎ 01271 863 185.

Chambercombe Manor – ☎ 01271 862 624

Braunton Great Field and Braunton Burrows – For leaflets on Nature Trails apply to the Tourist Information Centre, The Bakehouse Centre, Caen Street, Braunton, North Devon, EX33 1AA. ☎ 01271 816 400.

L

LACOCK

St Cyriac's Church, Lacock – Open daily, 10am to 5pm. **Services** : Sunday, at 8am, 10.30am, 6.30pm. ☎ 01249 730 272.

Fox-Talbot Museum, cloisters and grounds (NT) – ♿ Open March to October, daily except Good Friday, 11am to 5.30pm; Museum only also open November to February, weekends only, 11am to 4pm. £3.50, £2 (child), £10 (family); museum winter opening £2, £1 (child). Parking. ☎ 01249 730 459; Fax 01249 730 501. Special events ☎ 01985 843 601.

Lacock Abbey (NT) – (♿) Open late March to October, daily except Tuesdays and Good Friday, 1pm to 5.30pm. Brief guide (Braille, Dutch, French, German, Italian, Japanese, Spanish); guided tour by appointment. Abbey, museum and grounds £5.20, £3 (child), £14 (family). ☎ 01249 730 227.

Excursion

Bowood House and Gardens – ♿ Open April to October, daily, 11am to 6pm or sunset. £5, £2.80 (child), £4.20 (OAP). Information sheet (Arabic, Braille, Dutch, French, German, Italian, Japanese, Spanish). Parking. Refreshments. **Rhododendron Walks** – Open May to mid June, daily, 11am to 6pm. £2.50. No dogs. ☎ 01249 812 102.

LANGPORT

Excursions

Muchelney Abbey (EH) – (♿) Open April to September, daily, 10am to 1pm, 2pm to 6pm. £1.50, 80p (child), £1.10 (concession). Parking. ☎ 01458 250 664.

Muchelney Parish Church – Open April to October, daily, 9.30am to 6pm. Churchwarden ☎ 01458 253 114.

Priest's House, Muchelney (NT) – Open April to September, Sunday and Monday, 2.30pm to 5.30pm. £1.50. ☎ 01458 252 621.

Muchelney Pottery – Open all year, Monday to Friday, 9am to 1pm, 2pm to 5pm; Saturday, 9am to 1pm. £1.50 (please phone in advance for demonstration). Parking. ☎ 01458 250 324.

Midelney Manor – Guided tour May holiday to mid September, Thursdays and holiday Mondays, 2.30pm to 5.30pm (4.30pm last tour). £2.50. Parking. ☎ 01458 251 229.

LIZARD PENINSULA

Helston Folk Museum – Open all year, Mondays, Tuesdays and Thursdays to Saturdays, 10.30am to 1pm and 2pm to 4.30pm, Wednesdays, 10.30am to 12noon. ☎ 01326 564 027.

Flambards Village Theme Park – ♿ Open most days, Easter to October, 10am to 5.30pm (6pm end July and August). £5.00, £3.99 (infants), £4.99 (child), £3.99 (OAP), £17.50 (2A+2C). Parking; refreshments; free wheelchair loan. ☎ 01326 564 093 (24hr information line); Fax 01326 573 344.

National Seal Sanctuary, Gweek – 🦽 Open all year, daily, 9am to 6pm (4.30pm in winter). Closed 25 December. £4.50, £2.95 (child). Feeding talks at 10.30am, 11.30am, 12.30pm, 2.30pm, 3.30pm, 4pm. Guided nature trail walks (summer only). Audio-visual show. Underwater observatory. Parking; shop; café, barbecue, picnic area. ☎ 01326 221 874.

Goonhilly Earth Station – Open Easter to October, daily, 10am to 6pm (last admission 5pm). £3.99, £1.99 (child), £2.99 (student, OAP). Audio-visual show; hi-tech interactive displays; guided bus tour, visitor centre; adventure playground. Parking; restaurant. ☎ 0800 679 593.

LONGLEAT

Longleat – 🦽 **House:** Open all year, daily, 10am to 5.30pm (4pm October to Easter). Closed 25 December. Guided tour (45 min) of house; leaflets (French, German). £4.80, £3.50 (child), £4 (concession). Maze £1.50. Narrow gauge railway: £1.50 (☎ 01985 844 579). Butterfly garden. Pets corner. Coarse fishing all year; permits from water bailiff at lakeside. ☎ 01985 844 496. **Safari Park:** Open mid-March to late October, daily, 10am to 5.30pm. £5.50, £4 (child) £3.50 (concession). Parking. Refreshments. ☎ 01985 844 400; Fax 01985 844 885.

Longleat Safari Park

LUNDY ISLAND

Access – All year from Bideford Quay, in summer from Ilfracombe Pier (2.25hr journey time). Sailings in high season almost daily; out of season, irregularly. Should the return passage be into a different harbour a coach service back to the port of embarkation is laid on. ☎ 01237 470 074 (shore office tickets). 01237 470 422 (shore office bookings). Private launches also from Clovelly (90min).

Landing fee – £3.50; included in fare (reduced for NT members booked in advance) on MS *Oldenburg* from Bideford and Ilfracombe.

Accommodation – For information contact Landmark Trust. ☎ 01628 825 925.

LYME REGIS

🅱 Church Street – ☎ 01297 442 138

Philpot Museum – (🦽) Open April to October, Monday to Saturday, 10am to 5pm; Sundays, 10am to 12noon and 2.30pm to 5pm; November to March, weekends, half-terms and over Christmas. £1, 40p (child). Shop. ☎ 01297 443 370.

Dinosaurland Fossil World – Open, daily, 10am to 5pm (6pm in summer). £3.20, £1.90 (child), £2.90 (OAP). Fossil hunting walks tides permitting. ☎ 01297 443 541.

Michelin Green Guides for North America

California
Canada
Chicago
Florida
New York City
New England
Quebec
San Francisco
Washington

MALMESBURY
🚹 Town Hall, Market Lane - ☎ 01666 823 748

Malmesbury Abbey – Open all year, daily, 10am to 6pm (4pm November to Easter).

MARLBOROUGH
🚹 George Lane Car Park - ☎ 01672 513 989

Marlborough College – Tours on application from the Bursar. ☎ 01672 892 207.

Excursions

Littlecote Manor – Open June to October, Sundays and Wednesdays, 11am to 4pm, last admissions 3pm. £3.50, £3 (concessions): includes guide book to Roman villa, guided tour of house, access to gardens and coffeeshop. Parking. ☎ 01488 682 509.

Wilton Windmill – Open Easter to September, Sundays, holidays, 2pm to 5pm; October to Easter by appointment. £1. Guided tour at weekends. Parking. ☎ 01672 870 911.

Stone Museum, Great Bedwyn – Open all year, daily, 24 hours. ☎ 01672 870 234, 01672 870 043.

Crofton Beam Engines – Open Easter to October, daily, 10.30am to 5pm. £1.50, 50p (child), £1 (concession). **Engines in steam:** 6 to 8 April, 4 to 6 and 25 to 27 May, 29 to 30 June, 27 to 28 July and 24 to 26 August (1996). £3, £2 (concession), £1 (child). Parking. ☎ 01380 721 279 (Kennet and Avon Canal Trust) or 01672 870 300 (Crofton Pumping Station). ☎ 01672 851 639 (enquiries and further information).

MINEHEAD
🚹 17 Friday Street - ☎ 01643 702 624

West Somerset Railway – ♿ Open March to December, daily with off-peak, low-peak, peak and high peak services. £2.30 to £8.20, £11 to £20 (family ticket 2A+2C). Timetable at Minehead; bus connection Bishops Lydeard to Taunton on some services. Other bus link via National Omnibus Co (01823 272 033). Parking; refreshments. ☎ 01643 704 996. 01643 707 650 (talking timetable).

Excursions

Somerset and Dorset Railway Museum – Open March to October, daily, 10am to 5pm, when trains are running on the adjacent West Somerset Railway. ☎ 01984 640 869 / 01308 424 630.

Cleeve Abbey (EH) – (♿) Open April to October, daily, 10am to 6pm (4pm/dusk, October); November to March, Wednesday to Sunday, 10am to 4pm. Closed 24 to 26 December, 1 January. £2.20, £1.10 (child), £1.70 (concession). Parking. ☎ 01984 640 377.

NEWQUAY
🚹 Marcus Hill - ☎ 01637 871 345

Animal World – ♿ Open, daily, Easter to October, 9.30am to 6pm; November to Easter 10am to 4pm. Closed 25 December. £4.50 adult, £1 (2-4yr olds), £3 (5 and over), £13.50 (2A+2C). Parking. Refreshments. ☎ 01637 873 342.

Tunnels Through Time – Open Sunday to Friday (closed Saturdays) Easter to October 10am to 5pm. £3.30, £1.65 (child), £2.50 (OAP), £9.50 (2A+3C). ☎ 01637 873 379.

Newquay Sea Life Centre – Open daily, 10am to 5pm. £4.95, £3.50 (child), £3.75 (OAP). ☎ 01637 872 822(recorded information).

Excursion

Trerice (NT, NACF) – ♿ Open April to October, Tuesday and Saturday, daily throughout August, 11am to 5.30pm (5pm in October). Braille guide; audio tour. £3.80, £9.50 (2A+2C). Tearoom; shop; plant sales. ☎ 01637 875 404; Fax 01637 879 300.

P

PADSTOW
🚹 North Quay - ☎ 01841 533 449

Padstow Fishing Trips – Contact Tourist Information Centre for details. ☎ 01841 533 449; Fax 01841 532 356.

Prideaux Place – Open, daily, Easter Sunday to mid October, 1.30pm to 5pm; bank holiday Mondays, 11am to 5pm. Concerts, opera performances, exhibitions. ☎ 01841 532 411.

Bedruthan Steps (NT) – Cliff staircase: Open Easter to October. Telephone for details. ☎ 01208 74281.

Paradise Park – ♿ Open all year, daily, 10am to 5pm (4pm November to March). Flying demonstrations (weather permitting): Easter to September, at 12noon, 3.30pm. £4.95 or £5.50 in high season. Parking; refreshments. ☎ 01736 753 365.

St Maddern Church, Madron – Key available from the Vicarage.

Carn Euny Ancient Village (EH) – Open all year, daily. No charge. Parking. ☎ 01209 719 988.

Newlyn Pilchard Works – Open, Easter to October, daily, 10am to 6pm. £2.50, £2 (child), £2.30 (OAP), £8.50 (2A+3C). ☎ 01736 332 112.

Newlyn Art Gallery – Open all year, Monday to Saturday, 10am to 5pm. Closed Good Friday, 24 to 26 December. Donation. Refreshments. ☎ 01736 363 715.

Museum of Submarine Telegraphy, Porthcurno – Open April to October, Wednesday, Friday, 11am to 3pm. Guided tour every hour from the beach. £3, £2.50 (concession), £1.50 (student), £8 (2A+3C). Parking. ☎ 01209 612 142.

Minack Theatre – **Box office:** Open May to late September, 9.30am to 5.30pm; performances at 2pm and 8pm. Parking; refreshments. £6, £3 (child). ☎ 01736 810 181; fax 01736 810 779.

Rowena Cade Exhibition Centre: Open April to October, 9.30am to 5.30pm (4.30pm October). Closed 12noon to 2pm on matinee performance days. £1.70, 50p (child), £1.30 (concession). Parking; refreshments.

Land's End Visitor Centre and Site – ♿ Open all year, daily, 10am to sunset. Closed 24 and 25 December. All attractions incur separate charges. Right of way for walkers over site. Parking; restaurant; hotel. ☎ 01736 871 220.

Land's End Aerodrome – Scenic flights: £16 (Sennen Cove); £25 (Porthcurno); £50 (Penwith when available). Trial flight lessons. Parking; refreshments. ☎ 01736 788 771.

Levant Steam Engine (NT) – (♿) Open July to October, daily except Saturday, 11am to 5pm; also June, Wednesday to Friday and Sunday; Easter, May and Spring bank holiday Sunday and Monday. £3, £7.50 (2A+2C). ☎ 01209 216 657, 01736 786 156.

Geevor Tin Mine – Open summer, daily; winter, Monday to Friday. Closed Christmas and New Year. £5, £4 (concession), £2.50 (student), £14 (2A+3C). ☎ 01736 788 662; Fax 01736 786 059.

Pendeen Lighthouse – Open April to May, September and October, Wednesday to Saturday; June to August, Monday to Saturday. £1.50, £1 (concession), 75p (student), £4 (2A+3C). ☎ 01736 788 662.

Wayside Folk Museum, Zennor – Open April to September, daily, 10am to 6pm; October, Sunday to Friday, 11am to 5pm. £2, £1.50 (child), £1.75 (concession). Parking; refreshments. ☎ 01736 796 945.

Chysauster Ancient Village (EH) – Open April to October, daily, 10am to 6pm (6pm/dusk, October). £1.50, 80p (child), £1.10 (concession). Parking. ☎ 01326 212 044.

🚉 Station Road – ☎ 01736 362 207

National Lighthouse Centre, Penzance – Open Easter to October, daily, 11am to 5pm. £2.50, £5 (2A+C), £1.50 (concession). Leaflet (French, German). ☎ 01736 360 077.

Cornwall Geology Museum – ♿ Open Monday to Saturday, 10am to 4.30pm. £2, £1, £1.25 (concession). ☎ 01736 332 400.

Penlee House Gallery and Museum (NACF) – ♿ Open, all year, Monday to Saturday, 10.30am to 4.30pm. leaflet (French, German). £2, £1 (concession). Parking; café; shop. ☎ 01736 363 625.

Penzance Maritime Museum – Open Easter to October, Monday to Saturday, 10.30am to 4.30pm. Admission charge.

Excursion

Trengwainton Garden (NT) – ♿ Open March to October, Wednesday to Saturday, holiday Mondays and Good Friday, 10.30am to 5.30pm (5pm March and October). £3. ☎ 01736 363 021 or 362 297; Fax 01736 368 142.

🚉 The Barbican – ☎ 01752 264 849
🚉 Sainsbury's Supermarket – ☎ 01752 266 030/1

Smeaton's Tower – Open Easter to October, daily, 10.30am to 4.30pm. 70p; special rates for combined ticket with Plymouth Dome and Royal Citadel. ☎ 01752 600 608, 01752 603 300 (bookings); Fax 01752 256 361.

Plymouth Dome - Open all year, daily except 25 December, 9am to 7.30pm (6pm Spring and Autumn; 5.30pm winter). £3.95; special rates for combined ticket with Smeaton's Tower and Royal Citadel. Brochure (French, German, Japanese, Spanish). Café. Facilities for people with mobility or sensory impairment. ☎ 01752 600 608 (recorded information), 01752 603 300 (bookings); Fax 01752 256 361.

Royal Citadel (EH) – Guided tour (75mins) May to September, at 2pm and 3.30pm. Tickets from Plymouth Dome or the Barbican TIC. £2.50, £1.50 (child), £2 (concession). ☎ 01752 775 841 or 01752 266 496.

Chapel of St Katharine - Open all year, Sundays at 10am for worship.

Elizabethan House (NT) – Open April to October, Wednesday to Sunday and bank holiday Mondays, 10am to 5pm. £1 (including NT members), 50p (child). Shop. ☎ 01752 253 871.

Elizabethan Gardens - Open all year, daily 9am to 5pm or sunset. No charge.

Plymouth (Coates Black Friars) Gin Distillery - (&) Open Easter to October, Monday to Saturday, 10.30am to 4pm. £2, £1.25 (concession). Guided tour (45min). ☎ 01752 667 062.

Council House - Open by appointment only. No charge. ☎ 01752 264 858.

Plymouth Guildhall - Open (commercial use permitting) all year, Monday to Friday, 10am to 4pm.

St Andrew's Church - Open all year, daily, 9am to 4pm. **Services:** first Sunday in the month, at 8am, 10am, 6.30pm, other Sundays, at 8am, 9.30am, 11.15am, and 6.30pm. Guide boards (French, Spanish, German). ☎ 01752 661 414 (Parish Secretary - mornings only).

Prysten House - Open April to October, Monday to Saturday, 10am to 4pm. 50p. ☎ 01752 661 414.

Merchant's House - Open Easter Monday and April to September, Tuesday to Saturday and bank holiday Mondays, 10am to 5.30pm (5pm Saturday and bank holiday Mondays). 90p, 30p (child). ☎ 01752 264 878; Fax 01752 264 959.

City Museum and Art Gallery (NACF) - (&) Open all year, Tuesday to Saturday and holiday Mondays, 10am to 5.30pm (5pm holidays). Closed Good Friday, 25 to 26 December. No charge. Refreshments. ☎ 01752 264 878; Fax 01752 264 959.

Aquarium - Open Summer, daily, 10am to 6pm; Winter, weekends and school holidays. £2, £1 (child). ☎ 01752 633 333; Fax 01752 633 102.

Boat Trips from Phoenix Wharf - Operate May to October. **Plymouth Boat Cruises Ltd** ☎ 01752 822 797; **Tamar Cruising** ☎ 01752 822 105.

Excursions

Crownhill Fort - Open daily, Easter to November, 10am to 5pm. £2.75, £1.50 (child), £2.50 (OAPs). Parking; refreshments. ☎ 01752 793 754.

Yelverton Paperweight Centre - (&) Open 2 weeks before Easter to October, Monday to Saturday, 10am to 5pm; also mid May to mid September, Sundays, 10am to 5pm; in Winter on application. No charge. ☎ 01822 854 250.

Buckland Abbey (NT) – (&) Open April to October, daily except Thursday, 10.30am to 5.30pm; November to March, weekends, 2pm to 5pm; last admission 45min before closing time. Leaflet (French, German, Spanish). £4.30, £10.70 (family); grounds only £2.20. Parking; licensed restaurant; tea room; picnics in car park; wheelchairs and motorised buggy available. ☎ 01822 853 607; Fax 01822 855 448.

Dartmoor Wild Life Park, Sparkwell - Open all year, daily, 10am to 6pm. £5.95, £3.95 (child), £4.95 (OAP). **Flying displays:** at 12noon, 4pm. **Big Cat feeding:** 3.30pm. **Seal feeding:** 4.30pm. Adventure playground. Parking; licensed restaurant; picnic area; archery. ☎ 01752 837 209.

Saltram House (NT) - (&) **House:** Open April to October, Sunday to Thursday and Good Friday, 12.30pm (10.30am Art Gallery and Great Kitchen) to 5.30pm. Information sheet (Dutch, French, German, Spanish); Braille guide, audio tape, lift to first floor; wheelchairs available. **NB:** timed tickets may be issued in busy periods. ☎ 01752 336 546; Fax 01752 336 474.
Garden: Open April to October, daily, 10.30am to 5.30pm; also in March, Saturday and Sunday only, 11am to 4pm. £5.30; garden only £2.50; concessions for children. Parking; licensed restaurant, tearoom.

Kitley Caves - Open May to October, daily, 10am to 5.30pm. £3.50, £2.50 (concession). Parking; refreshments; playground; gift shop. ☎ 01752 880 885.

PLYMOUTH

National Shire Horse Centre – (♿) Open all year, daily, 10am to 5pm (4pm November to February). Closed 23 to 26 December. **Parade of Horses:** at 11.30am, 2.30pm, 4.15pm. **Falconry displays:** at 1pm, 3.30pm. £5.50. Parking; licensed restaurant; picnic area; adventure playground; Butterfly House; Craft Centre. ☎ 01752 880 268.

PLYMOUTH SOUND – TAMAR RIVER

Mount Edgcumbe – ♿ **House and Earls Garden:** Open April to October, Wednesday to Sunday, holidays, 11am to 5pm. £3.50. **Country Park and Formal Gardens:** Open all year, daily, sunrise to sunset. No charge. **Visitor Centre:** Open April to October, daily, 10.30am to 5pm. No charge. Parking; refreshments. ☎ 01752 822 236; Fax 01752 822 199.

Antony House (NT) – Open April to October, Tuesday to Thursday, holiday Mondays, 1.30pm to 5.30pm; June to August, Sunday, 1.30pm 5.30pm. £3.80. Guided tour available at less busy times until 4.45pm (last tour). Parking; refreshments; shop. ☎ 01752 812 191.

St German's Church – Open all year, daily, 10am to 4pm. Services: Sunday at 10.15am. ☎ 01503 230 275.

Cotehele (NT) – (♿) Visitors to this fragile house are limited to 600 per day, it is therefore advisable to arrive early and be prepared to wait. As there is no electric light in the rooms, visitors should avoid dull days early and late in the season. **House:** Open April to October, daily except Friday (unless Good Friday), 11am to 5pm (4.30pm in October). **Mill:** Open April to October, daily except Friday (unless Good Friday or Fridays throughout July and August), 12noon to 5.30pm (6pm July and August; 4.30pm in October). **Garden:** Open, daily, 11am to dusk. £5.60 (house, garden, mill); £2.80 (garden, mill). Parking; refreshments; shop; plant sales. ☎ 01579 351 346; Fax 01579 351 222.

POOLE

🚉 The Quay – ☎ 01202 673322

Waterfront Museum, Poole (NACF) – ♿ Open April to October, daily, 10am to 5pm; November to March, telephone for details. £1.95 / £2.50, £7 / £8.25 (family), £1.25 / £1.75 (child); seasonal variations, telephone for details. Tea room. Craft shop. **Scaplen's Court :** – Open July and August, daily, 10am to 7pm. £1.45, £1.10 (child). ☎ 01202 683 138; Fax 01202 660 896.

The Aquarium Complex – (♿) Open July and August, daily, 9.30am to 9pm; September to June, daily, 10am to 5pm. Closed 25 December. Admission charges from £1.50. Refreshments. ☎ 01202 686 712.

Poole Pottery – **Factory Tour:** Open summer, daily, 10am to 4pm; winter, Monday to Thursday, 10am to 4pm. **Shop:** Open, April to October, daily, 9am to 9pm; November to March, daily, 9am to 5pm. Factory tour £3.50, £2.50 (child), £2.50 (concession). Coffee shop. ☎ 01202 666 200.

RNLI Lifeboat Museum – Open all year, Monday to Friday, 9.30am to 4.30pm. Closed holidays. ☎ 01202 663 000; Fax 01202 663 167.

Excursions

Brownsea Island Nature Reserve (NT) – ♿ Access by boat from Poole Quay, Swanage and Bournemouth to Pottery Pier (west end of island). Open April to September, daily, 10am to 5pm (6pm July and August); check time of last boat. Landing fee £2.30, £1.10 (child), £5.70 (2A+2C). Braille guide. Refreshments near landing quay; closes 30min before departure of last boat. ☎ 01202 707 744; Fax 01202 701 635.

Open-air theatre and other events in summer: contact 01985 843 601.

Compton Acres Gardens – ♿ Open March to October, daily, 10am to 6pm (5.15pm last admission). £4.50, £3.50 (concession). Parking; licensed café and terrace brasserie. ☎ 01202 700 778.

S

ST AUSTELL

🚉 Southbourne Road – ☎ 01726 76333

Excursions

Wheal Martyn Museum – Open April to October, daily, 10am to 6pm. £4.25. Leaflets (French, German). Parking; refreshments; shop. ☎ 01726 850 362; Fax 01726 850 362.

Mid-Cornwall Galleries – ♿ Open all year, Monday to Saturday, 10am to 5pm. Closed 25 and 26 December. No charge. Parking; refreshments. ☎ 01726 812 131.

Shipwreck and Heritage Museum, Charlestown – ♿ Open March to October, daily, 10am to 5pm. £3.95, £2.95 (concession). Guided tour (90min) by appointment. Audio-visual presentation. Parking; refreshments. ☎ 01726 69897; Fax 01726 68025.

Lost Gardens of Heligan – ♿ Open, daily, 10am to 6pm (last admission 4.30pm). Closed 25 December. Guided group tours on application. £3.40, £2 (child), £2.90 (OAP), £9 (2A+2C). Parking; refreshments; plant sales; wheelchair loan. ☎ 01729 844 157 / 01729 843 566; Fax 01726 843 023.

ST IVES
🚩 Street-an-Pol – ☎ 01736 796297

Tate Gallery St Ives (NACF) – ♿ Open April to September, daily, 11am to 7pm (5pm Sunday and bank holidays); October to March, Tuesday to Sunday and bank holiday Mondays, 11am to 5pm. Closed 24 to 26 December. £3.50, £2 (concession). Brochure (French). Restaurant. ☎ 01736 796 226; Fax 01736 794 480.

Barbara Hepworth Museum – Open April to September, daily, 11am to 7pm (5pm Sunday and bank holidays); October to March, Tuesday to Sunday and bank holidays, 11am to 5pm; restricted admissions occasionally during the high season. £3, £1.50 (concession). ☎ 01736 796 226; Fax 01736 794 480.

St Ives Museum – Open end May to September, daily, 10am to 5pm. 50p. ☎ 01736 796 005.

ST MICHAEL'S MOUNT

Castle (NT) – Open April to October, Monday to Friday, 10.30am to 5.30pm (4.45pm last admission); from November to March it is essential to telephone for information on opening times. £3.90, £10 (2A+2C). The Mount may also be open most weekends during the summer as charity days when NT members will be requested to pay. Audio tour; video introduction; Braille guide; leaflets (Dutch, French, German, Japanese). Restaurant. ☎ 01736 710 507; Fax 01736 711 544. **Access:** by causeway at low tide; by ferry at high tide during summer months (70p).

SALCOMBE
🚩 Council Hall, Market Street – ☎ 01548 843 927

Ferries – To Kingsbridge (30min): May to September; Monday to Saturday, daily, 3 to 4 trips. Sea or river cruise (1 hour 45min). ☎ 01548 853 525, 01548 853 607. To East Portlemouth: all year, daily except 25 December from 8am. ☎ 01548 842 061, 01548 842 364. To South Sands : Seasonal, Easter, then May to October. ☎ 01548 561 035.

Overbecks Museum, Sharpitor – (♿) **House:** Open, late March to June, Sunday to Friday; July and August, daily; September and October, Sunday to Thursday, 11am to 5pm. **Garden:** Open all year, daily, 10am to 8pm or sunset. House and garden £3.60; garden only £2.40. Parking; tea room; shop. ☎ 01548 842 893.

Excursions
Kingsbridge 🚩 The Quay – ☎ 01548 853 195; Fax 01548 854 185

Boat trip from The Quay – To Salcombe (30min), sea or river cruise (1 hour 45min – 2 hour 15min). ☎ 01548 853 525, 01548 853 607.

Cookworthy Museum – Open Easter to September, Monday to Saturday, 10am to 5pm; October, Monday to Friday, 10.30am to 4pm. £1.70, £4 (family ticket). ☎ 01548 853 235.

SALISBURY
🚩 Fish Row – ☎ 01722 334 956

Salisbury Cathedral – ♿ Open all year, daily except Good Friday, 8am to 8.15pm (6.30pm September to April). **Services:** Monday to Saturday, 7.30am Holy Communion, 5.30pm Choral Evensong; Sunday 8am Holy Communion, 10am Sung Eucharist, 11.30am Matins, 3pm Choral Evensong.
Guided tour (French, Spanish, Italian, German): March to October, Monday to Saturday, 9.30am to 4.30pm, Sunday, 4pm to 6.30pm.
Roof tour: (Tower) January to November and 26 December to 1 January, Monday to Saturday, at 11am, 2pm; also May to August, Monday to Saturday, at 3pm and 6.30pm; Sunday, at 4.30pm. **West Front tour:** May to October, Tuesday, Thursday and Saturday, at 10.30am, 11.30am, 2.30pm, 3.30pm. **Magna Carta** on display January to November (not December). Guide book (French, German, Japanese). Leaflet (French, Spanish, Italian, German, Dutch, Japanese). £2.50, £5 (family); Tower tour £2; West Front tour £2. ☎ 01722 323 273.

Salisbury and South Wiltshire Museum (NACF) – ♿ Open all year, Monday to Saturday, 10am to 5pm; also July and August, Sundays, 2pm to 5pm. Closed Christmas. £3, 75p (child), £2 (concession). Leaflet (French, German). ☎ 01722 332 151; Fax 01722 325 611.

Royal Gloucestershire, Berkshire and Wiltshire Regiment (Salisbury) Museum
– (&) Open April to October, daily, 10am to 4.30pm; November to mid-December,
Monday to Saturday, 10am to 3pm; February and March, 10am to 4pm. Closed
January. £2. Limited parking; refreshments. ☎ 01722 414 536.

Mompesson House (NT) – (&) Open April to October, Saturday to Wednesday,
12 midday to 5.30pm. £3.20, £1.60 (child); garden only 80p. Leaflet (Dutch,
French, German, Italian, Spanish). Parking in Cathedral Close (charge); tearoom.
☎ 01722 335 659.

Creasy Collection of Contemporary Art – Open all year, Monday to Saturday, 9am
to 7pm (5pm Thursday, 4pm Saturday). ☎ 01722 324 145.

Fisherton Mill – Open all year, Monday to Saturday, 9.30am to 5.30pm. Parking,
shop, restaurant. ☎ 01722 415 121.

Excursions

Old Sarum Castle ruins (EH) – Open daily, 10am to 6pm (4pm October to March).
Closed 24 to 26 December, 1 January. £1.70, 90p (child), £1.30 (concession).
Parking. ☎ 01722 335 398.

Heale House Garden, Woodford – Garden: Open all year, daily, 10am to 5pm. £2.75.
Parking; plant sales. ☎ 0172 278 2504.

Newhouse, Redlynch – Open August, Monday to Saturday, 2pm to 5.30pm. £2.50.
☎ 01725 20055.

Isles of SCILLY
🛈 Porthcressa Bank, St Mary's – ☎ 01720 422 536

St Mary's Museum – Open Easter to October, daily, 10am to 12 midday, 1.30pm
to 4.30pm; also May to August, daily, 7.30pm to 9pm; also October to April,
Wednesdays, 2pm to 4pm. £1. ☎ 01720 422 337.

Gig Racing – April to September, Wednesdays, Fridays, at 8pm – to follow the
race, check the blackboards on the quay for cost and departure of passenger boats.

Tresco Abbey Gardens – (&) Open all year, daily, 10am to 4pm. £5. Guided tour
(1hr). Café. ☎ 01720 422 868.

SHAFTESBURY
🛈 8 Bell Street – ☎ 01747 853 514

Shaftesbury Local History Museum – Open Easter to September, daily, 11am to
5pm; October to Easter by appointment. 75p. ☎ 01747 852 157.

Shaftesbury Abbey and Museum – Open April to October, daily, 10am to 5pm.
£1, 40p (child), 70p (concession). ☎ 01747 852 910.

Excursion

Old Wardour Castle (EH) – Open April to October, daily, 10am to 6pm (6pm/dusk,
October); November to March, Wednesday to Sunday, 10am to 4pm. Closed 24
to 26 December, 1 January. £1.50, 80p (child), £1.10 (concession). Parking.
☎ 01747 870 487.

SHERBORNE
🛈 Digby Road – ☎ 01935 815 341

Sherborne Abbey – (&) Open all year, daily, 8.30am to 6pm (4pm in winter). No
charge. Brochure (Dutch, French, German, Italian, Japanese, Spanish). Guided tour
by appointment. Shop. ☎ 01935 812 452.

Sherborne Museum – (&) Open April to October, Tuesday to Sunday and bank
holiday Mondays, 10.30am (2.30pm Sundays and bank holidays) to 4.30pm; £1.
Guided tour (45min) by appointment. ☎ 01935 812 252.

Sherborne Old Castle (EH) – Open April to October, daily, 10am to 6pm (6pm/dusk,
October); November to March, Wednesday to Sunday, 10am to 1pm, 2pm to 4pm.
Closed 1 January, 24 to 26 December. £1.50, 80p (child), £1.10 (concession).
Parking; refreshments. ☎ 01935 812 730.

Sherborne Castle – Open Saturday before Easter to September, Thursday,
Saturday, Sunday and bank holiday Mondays, 1.30pm (12.30pm grounds) to
5pm. £4.80, £12 (family 2A+2C), £2.40 (child); grounds only £2.40, £1.20 (child).
Leaflet (Dutch, French, German, Italian, Spanish). ☎ 01935 813 182; Fax 01935
816 727.

Excursions

Sandford Orcas Manor House – Open May to September, Sundays, 2pm to 6pm;
Mondays, 10am to 6pm. £2.50, £1 (child). Guided tour (30min). Parking. ☎ 01963
220 206.

Purse Caundle Manor – Open May to September, Thursday and Sunday, 2pm to 5pm. £2.50. Guided tour (30min). Parking. ☎ 01963 250 400.

Worldlife – Open April to September, daily, 10am to 5pm. Refreshments; picnic area. ☎ 01935 474 608; Fax 01935 429 937.

SIDMOUTH
🛈 Ham Lane – ☎ 01395 516 441

Donkey Sanctuary, Salcombe Regis – ♿ Open all year, daily, 9am to sunset. No charge. Guided tour (2 hours) by appointment; leaflets (French, German). Parking; limited refreshments; picnic area. ☎ 01395 578 222; Fax 01395 579 266. **Slade Centre** ☎ 01395 516 592; Fax 01395 579 266.

Excursions
Seaton 🛈 The Esplanade, Seaton, Devon EX12 2QQ – ☎ 01297 21660

Beer Quarries – Open daily April to September, 10am to 6pm; October 10am to 5pm; last admission 1hour before closing. £3.25, £2.40 child and concessions, £10.30 (2A+2C). ☎ 01297 680 282.

Seaton Tramway – Open Easter to October, daily, 9.40am to 5.20pm (8.40pm July and August). Return £4.20, £2.40 (child), £3.40 (OAP). Tram driving lessons. ☎ 01297 620 375; Fax 01297 625 626.

SOMERTON

Lytes Cary Manor (NT) – Open April to October, Monday, Wednesday, Saturday, 2pm to 6pm or sunset; last admission 30mins before closing. £3.80, £1.90 (child). ☎ 01985 843 600.

Treasurer's House, Martock (NT) – Open April to September, Sunday to Tuesday, 2.30pm to 5.30pm. £1.50. ☎ 01985 843 600.

East Lambrook Manor Garden – Open March to October, Monday to Saturday, 10am to 5pm. £2.50. Parking; refreshments, shop. ☎ 01460 240 328.

Barrington Court (NT) – ♿ **House and gardens:** Open April to October, daily except Friday, 11am to 5.30pm. £4, £2 (child). Braille guide; scented plants and flowers. Parking; shop; restaurant. ☎ 01460 241 938.

STONEHENGE

Stonehenge (EH, NT) – ♿ Open June to August, daily, 9am to 7pm; mid March to May and September to mid October, daily, 9.30am to 6pm; mid October to mid March, daily, 9.30am to 4pm. Closed 1 January, 24 to 26 December. £3.50, £1.80 (child), £2.60 (concession). Audio tours (six languages). Parking, refreshments, shop. ☎ 01980 624 715.

Stonehenge Down (NT) – Open at all times; may be cordoned off during the Summer Solstice (21 June) for up to two days.

Excursion
Amesbury 🛈 Redworth House, Flower Lane ☎ 01980 622 833

Woodhenge (EH) – Open at any reasonable time. Admission free.

STOURHEAD

Stourhead (NT) – ♿ **Gardens:** Open daily, 9am to 7pm or sunset if earlier (5pm 24-26 July). **House:** Open April to October, Saturday to Wednesday (closed Thursday and Friday), 12 midday to 5.30pm. Garden: March to October £4.30, £2.30 (child), £10 (2A+2C); November to February

Grotto river god, Stourhead

A. Taverner

STOURHEAD

£3.30, £1.50 (child), £8 (2A+2C); House: £4.30, £2.30 (child), £10 (2A+2C); house and garden £7.70, £3.60 (child), £20 (2A+2C). Parking; pub and licensed restaurant; picnics in car park and garden. Avoid congested times at weekends and in May and June. ☎ 01747 841152.

King Alfred's Tower: Open late March to October, Tuesday to Thursday, 2pm to 5.30pm; Saturday, Sunday, Good Friday and bank holiday Mondays 11.30 to 5.30pm or sunset if earlier. £1.50, 70p (child).

SWANAGE

🄳 Shore Road – ☎ 01929 422 885

Swanage Railway – Services operate daily June to September, holidays and in some form most weekends throughout the year depending on local volunteers. Talking timetable. ☎ 01929 424 276, 01929 425 800.

Excursions

Studland Ferry – Open all year, daily, 7.10am to 11.10pm (last ferry); 25 December, 8am to 6.10pm. £2 (car), 80p (passenger). Bournemouth-Swanage Motor Road and Ferry Company ☎ 01929 450 203.

Corfe Castle Ruins (NT) – Open late March to late October, daily, 10am to 5.30pm (4.30pm, March and late October); early November to early March, daily, 11am to 3.30pm. Closed 25 and 26 December, 2 days end January. £3.50, £1.80 (child). Parking; refreshments. ☎ 01929 481 294.
Special events: ☎ 01985 843 601.

Blue Pool – (♿) **Grounds:** Open March to November, daily, from 9.30am. **Museum:** Open Easter to October, daily, from 10am. £2.40, £1.20 (child), £1.80 (senior citizen). Guided tour; Braille guide. Parking; refreshments; play area for children. ☎ 01929 551 408.

Lulworth Castle (EH) – Open April to September, daily, 10am to 6pm; October to mid December, daily, 10am to 4pm. £1.50, 75p (child), £1.20 (concession). Parking. ☎ 01929 400 510.

SWINDON

🄳 37 Regent Street – ☎ 01793 530 328

National Monuments Record Gallery – Open Wednesday to Saturday, 10am to 6pm; Sunday, 11am to 5pm. Bookshop. For all information contact. ☎ 01793 414 600; Fax 01793 414 606; E-mail inforchme.gov.uk.

GWR Museum – (♿) Pending the transfer of the collection to the Old Swindon Works (1998): open all year, daily, 10am (2pm Sundays) to 5pm. Closed Good Friday and 1 January. Guided tour by prior arrangement. £2.30. ☎ 01793 466 555; Fax 01793 484 073.

Railway Village Museum – Open all year, daily, 10am (2pm Sundays) to 5pm. Closed Good Friday and 1 January. 85p. ☎ 01793 526 161 ext 4527.

Swindon Museum and Art Gallery – Open all year, daily, 10am (2pm Sundays) to 5.30pm. Closed Good Friday, 25, 26 December and bank holidays. No charge. ☎ 01793 493 188; Fax 01793 484 141.

Richard Jefferies Museum – Limited opening; for times ☎ 01793 493 188.

Lydiard Park House (NACF) – Open all year, daily, 10am to 1pm, 2pm to 5.30pm (4pm November to February). Closed Sunday mornings, Good Friday, 25, 26 December. £1.40. ☎ 01793 770 401. Parking; refreshments (summer only). Facilities for the disabled.

Church – Key available from Lydiard Park House.

Science Museum, Wroughton – Open Event Days only, or by special arrangement for groups with Marketing and Events Officer, D4 Admin Office, Wroughton Airfield, Swindon, SN4 9NS. ☎ 01793 814 466; Fax 01793 813 569.

T

TAUNTON

🄳 Paul Street – ☎ 01823 336 344

Somerset Cricket Museum – Open April to November, Monday to Friday, 10am to 4pm. ☎ 01823 275 893.

Somerset County Museum (NACF) – (♿) Open all year, Mondays to Saturdays, 10am to 5pm. Closed 1 January, Good Friday, 25, 26 December. £1.20. ☎ 01823 320 200; Fax 01823 320 229.

St Mary Magdalene – Open Monday to Friday, 8.30am to 5.15pm; Saturday 9am to 4pm. Services daily at 8.30am, 12noon, 5pm; Sunday at 8am, 10.30am, 6.30pm.

Excursion

Hatch Court - **House:** (&) Open mid June to mid September, Thursdays only, 2.30pm to 5.30pm. **Garden:** & Open mid April to late September, Monday to Friday, 10am to 5.30pm. House £3.50, £1.50 (child); Garden £2, £1 (child). Guided tour (45min). Parking; tea room (Thursday); plant sales. ☎ 01823 480 120; Fax 01823 480 058.

TAUNTON DEANE

Gaulden Manor - & Open May to first Sunday in September, Sunday, Thursday and public holidays, 2pm to 5.30pm. £3.50. Guided tour (30min). Parking; refreshments. ☎ 01984 667 213.

TAVISTOCK   🛈 Town Hall building, Bedford Square - ☎ 01822 612 938

Morwellham Wildlife Reserve - (&) Open daily, 10am to 5.30pm (4.30pm November to Easter, 2.30pm last admissions). Closed 23 December to 3 January. £4, £3.50 (OAP), £3 (6-16yrs).

Morwellham Quay - (&) Open daily, 10am to 5.30pm (4.30pm November to Easter, 2.30pm last admissions). Closed 23 December to 3 January. £7.90, £7 (OAP), £5.50 (6-16yrs) all inclusive (coppermine train ride, horse and carriage ride). Parking; restaurant. ☎ 01822 832 766; Fax 01822 833 808.

TEIGNMOUTH   🛈 Seat Front - ☎ 01626 779 769

Excursions   Newton Abbot 🛈 6 Bridge House, Courtenay Street - ☎ 01626 67494

Powderham Castle - Open Easter to October, Sunday to Friday, 10am to 5.30pm. £4.95, £12.45 (family ticket). ☎ 01626 890 243.

Bradley Manor (NT) - Open April to September, Wednesday, 2pm to 5pm. £2.60. ☎ 01626 54513

Ugbrooke House - & Guided tour (75min) mid July to early September, Tuesday to Thursday and Sunday at 2pm and 3.45pm. **Garden:** Open as for house, 1pm to 5.30pm. £4.20, £2 (child). Parking; refreshments. ☎ 01626 852 179; Fax 01626 853 322.

TINTAGEL

Arthur's Castle (EH) - Open daily, 10am to 6pm (4pm October to March). Closed 24 to 26 December, 1 January. £2.50, £1.30 (child), £1.90 (concession). Parking. ☎ 01840 770 328.

Old Post Office (NT) - Open April to October, daily, 11am to 5.30pm (5pm October). £2. ☎ 01840 770 024.

King Arthur's Great Hall of Chivalry - & Open daily, 10am to 5pm (later in summer months). £2.50, £1.75 (concession), £7.50 (2A+2C). ☎ 01840 770 526.

Excursions

Delabole Quarry - **Showroom:** Open all year, Monday to Friday, 8am to 4.30pm. Closed 23 December to 3 January. No charge. Tours by appointment May to September; £1 to £3 per head. ☎ 01840 212 242; Fax 01840 212 948.

Delabole Wind Farm - Open daily Easter to October, 10am to 5pm. 75p. ☎ 01840 213 377; Fax 01840 213 939.

Pixie House - Open daily March to December from 10am to dusk. Donation. ☎ 01840 212 638.

TIVERTON   🛈 Phoenix Lane
☎ 01884 255 827

Tiverton Castle - Open Easter to June and September, Sunday, Thursday and bank holiday Mondays; July and August, Sunday to Thursday, 2.30pm to 5.30pm; otherwise in a group by prior appointment. £3. Guided tour (90min) by appointment. Parking. ☎ 01884 253 200, 01884 255 200; Fax 01854 254 200.

Wind turbine, Delabole

R. Besse/MICHELIN

TIVERTON

Tiverton Museum – Open February to December, Monday to Saturday, 10.30am to 4.30pm. Closed Christmas to February. £1. Guided tour by appointment. ☎ 01884 256 295.

Excursions

Knightshayes Court (NT) – ♿ Open April to October, daily (House closed on Fridays other than Good Friday), 11am to 5.30pm. House £5; garden and grounds £3.30, concessions available. Parking; refreshments; shop; plant centre. Licensed restaurant. ☎ 01884 254 665; Fax 01884 243 050.

Coldharbour Mill, Uffculme – Open Easter to October, daily, holidays, 10.30am to 5pm; November to Easter, Monday to Friday, holidays, call to check. £5, £13.50 (2A+2C), £2.50 (child). Guided tour (90min). Parking; licensed restaurant (Easter to October). ☎ 01884 840 960; Fax 01884 840 858.

Devonshire's Centre, Bickleigh Mill – Open April to October, daily, 10am to 5pm; November to March 10am to 5pm. Parking; licensed restaurant. ☎ 01884 855 419.

Bickleigh Castle – Open Good Friday to Easter Friday, daily; Easter Saturday to Spring bank holiday, Wednesday, Sunday and public holidays; then to early October, daily except Saturday, 2pm to 5.30pm. £3.50. Guided tour (90min) except during school holidays. Parking; refreshments. ☎ 01884 855 363.

TORBAY

🛈 Vaughan Parade, Torquay – ☎ 01803 297 428
🛈 The Esplanade, Paignton – ☎ 01803 558 383

Torre Abbey (NACF) – Open April to October, daily, 9.30am to 6pm; November to March, Monday to Friday, 10am to 5pm by appointment. £2.70, £5.95 (family ticket (2A+3C), £2.20 (concession). Guided tour (1 hour) by appointment; leaflet (Spanish). Tea room (summer). ☎ 01803 293 593; Fax 01803 215 948.

Torquay Museum – Open, Sunday to Friday, 10.30am (1.30pm Sunday) to 4.45pm, also Saturdays, Easter to October. £2, £2.25 (concession), ☎ 01803 293 975; Fax 01803 294 168.

Kents Cavern – ♿ Guided tour (45min) all year, daily, 10am (9.30am July and August) to last tour at 5pm (5.30pm July and August; 4pm October to March); also evening tours from mid-June to early September, 6.30pm to 9pm. Closed 25 December. Daytime rates: £3.75, £2.40 (child), £3.25 (OAP), £11.30 (2A+3C); evening rates: £4.40, £3.50 (child), £4 (OAP), £14.50 (2A+3C). Parking; refreshments (summer only). ☎ 01803 215 136.

Babbacombe Model Village – ♿ Open Easter to October, daily, 9am to 9pm; November to Easter, daily, 10am to sunset. Closed 25 December. £3.80, £2.15 (child). Parking; refreshments. ☎ 01803 315 315; Fax 01803 315 173.

Bygones – Open, March October, Monday to Friday, 10am to 10pm (6pm March to May and mid-September to October), Saturday and Sunday, 10am to 6pm; November to February, daily, 10am to 4pm (5pm Saturday and Sunday). £2.95, £1.75 (child), £2.50 (concession). Parking; refreshments. ☎ 01803 326 108.

Paignton Zoo Environmental Park – ♿ Open all year, daily, 10am to 6.30pm (5pm November to February). Closed 25 December. £6.60. Guided tour (45min). Parking; restaurant; shop. ☎ 01803 557 479; Fax 01803 523 457; email http://www.paigntonzoo.demon.co.uk

Oldway Mansion and Gardens – ♿ Open May to September, Monday to Saturday, 9am to 5pm, Sunday, 2pm to 5pm; October to April, Monday to Saturday, 9am to 5pm (1pm Saturday). No charge. Guided tour (summer only). Parking; refreshments. ☎ 01803 296 244 ext 2123.

Paignton Parish Church – Open all year, Monday to Friday, 10.30am to 12.30; also April to September, 2.30pm to 4pm. ☎ 01803 559 059.

Paignton and Dartmouth Steam Railway – Operates April to October and early to late December, daily, at regular intervals from 10.15am. Telephone for timetable. Return £6; special tickets combining boat trip and returns. ☎ 01803 555 872. Fax 01803 664 313.

Excursions

Cockington Court – Open April to October, daily, 10.30am to 4.30pm. £1. ☎ 01803 606 035.

Compton Castle (NT) – (♿) Open April to October, Monday, Wednesday, Thursday, 10am to 12.15pm and 2pm to 5pm. £2.70, £1.30 (child). Guide cards (Dutch, French, German). Parking. ☎ 01803 872 112; Fax 01803 875 740.

Berry Pomeroy Castle (EH) – (♿) Open April to October, daily, 10am to 6pm.(6pm/dusk, October). £2, £1 (child), £1.50 (concession). Parking. ☎ 01803 866 618.

TOTNES

Elizabethan Museum, Totnes – Open mid-March to October, Monday to Saturday and bank holiday Mondays, 10.30am (2pm Saturday) to 5pm, Saturdays, 2pm to 5pm. £1.50, £1 (concession). Guided tour (45min) by appointment. ☎ 01803 863 821.

Totnes Guildhall – Open Easter to September, Monday to Friday, 10.30am to 4.30pm. Closed public holidays. 75p. Brochure (Dutch, French, German, Italian, Spanish). Guided tour (20min). ☎ 01803 862 147; Fax 01803 864 275.

Devonshire Collection of Period Costume – Open Spring holiday Monday to September, Monday to Friday, 10am to 5pm, Sundays, 2pm to 5pm. £1.20, £2.50 (family ticket 2A+2C), 40p (child), 80p (concession). ☎ 01803 862 423.

Totnes Castle (EH) – Open April to October, daily, 10am to 6pm (6pm/dusk, October); November to March, Wednesday to Sunday, 10am to 4pm. Closed 25, 26 December, 1 January. £1.50, 80p (child), £1.10 (concession). Parking. ☎ 01803 864 406.

Excursions

Bowden House British Photographic Museum – Open Easter Sunday to late October, Monday to Thursday, also holiday Sundays and Mondays, 12 midday to 5.30pm. Guided tour, summer only, at 1.30pm, 2pm, 3pm, 4pm. £4.50, £2.50 (under 13), 75p (under 10). Parking; licensed café. ☎ 01803 863 664.

Dartington Hall and Gardens – (&) Open all year, sunrise to sunset. £2 (donation). Parking. ☎ 01803 866 688.

High Cross House – & Open March to October, Tuesday to Friday, 10.30am to 4.30pm, Saturday and Sunday 2pm to 5pm; otherwise by appointment. £2.50, £1.50 (concession). Parking, refreshments. ☎ 01803 864 114; Fax 01803 867 057.

Dartington Cider Press Centre – & Open all year, Monday to Saturday, 9.30am to 5.30pm; Sunday from Easter to Christmas, 10.30am to 5.30pm. Closed 1 January, 25, 26 December. Parking; restaurants. ☎ 01803 864 171; Fax 01803 866 094.

TROWBRIDGE

Trowbridge Museum – & Open Tuesday to Friday, 12noon (10am during school holidays) to 4pm; Saturday, 10am to 5pm. Donation. ☎ 01225 751 339.

Excursion

Warminster Dewey Museum – Open Monday to Friday, 10am to 5pm (1pm Wednesday; 7pm Thursday and Friday); Saturday, 9am to 4pm. Closed bank holidays. No charge. ☎ 01985 216 022.

TRURO

Royal Cornwall Museum (NACF) – Open all year, Monday to Saturday, 10am to 5pm. Closed holidays. £2, £1 (concession). Guided tour (60min); printed guide (Dutch, French, German, Spanish). Café; shop. ☎ 01872 272 205; Fax 01872 240 514.

Probus Gardens – & Open Easter to September, daily 10am to 5pm; October to Easter, Monday to Friday, 10am to 4pm. Donation (£2). Guided tour (90min). Parking; refreshments; plant sales. ☎ 01726 882 597; Fax 01726 883 868.

Trewithen – (&) **Garden:** Open March to September, Monday to Saturday and bank holiday Mondays, 10am to 4.30pm; April and May, Sundays only. **House:** Guided tour (35min) April to July, Mondays, Tuesdays and August bank holiday Monday, 2pm to 4pm. Garden £2.80; house £3.20. Dogs on leads. Parking; refreshments; wheelchair access to grounds only. ☎ 01726 883 647, 01726 882 764; Fax 01726 882 301.

W

WAREHAM

Wareham Local History Museum – (&) Open Easter to mid October, Mondays to Saturdays, 11am to 1pm, 2pm to 4pm. No charge. Guided tour (45min). ☎ 01929 553 448.

Toy Museum, Arne – (&) Open April to June and September, Sundays, Tuesdays to Fridays, 1.30pm to 5pm – closed Monday and Saturday; July and August, daily, 10.30am to 5.30pm. £2.25, £1 (child), £2 (OAP). Parking; tea room. ☎ 01929 552 018.

Tank Museum, Bovington – ♿ Open all year, daily, 10am to 5pm. Closed at Christmas. £5, £13 (2A+2C). Guided tour (2 hours) by appointment; Braille and audio tours, good access for wheelchair users. **Firepower and Mobility displays** (1hr) on Thursday at 12noon during July and September, on Thursday and Friday at 12noon throughout August. Armoured vehicle rides daily, except Saturday, July to September. Parking; licensed restaurant; picnic area; assault course for children. ☎ 01929 405 096; Fax 01929 405 360.

Monkey World – Open, daily, 10am to 5pm (6pm July and August). £4.75, £2.75 (child), £3.25 (OAP), £13 (2A+2C). Parking, refreshments. ☎ 0800 456 600, 01929 462 537.

WELLS

🛈 Town Hall, Market Place – ☎ 01749 672 552

Wells Cathedral – Open all year, daily, 9am to 8.30pm in summer, 7pm in spring, 6pm in winter months. Services: weekdays 7.30am Matins, 8am Holy Communion, 1.05pm Holy Communion on Tuesday and Thursday, 5.15pm Evensong; Sunday 8am Holy Communion, 9.45 Sung Eucharist, 11.30am Matins, 3pm Evensong. ☎ 01749 674 483.

Wells Museum – (♿) Open April to October, daily, 10am to 5.30pm (8pm July and August); November to March, Wednesdays to Sundays, 11am to 4pm. Closed 24, 25 December. Room guide (French, German). £2. ☎ 01749 673 477.

Bishop's Palace – (♿) Open Easter Saturday to October, Tuesday to Friday, 11am to 6pm, also Sunday, 2pm to 6pm; bank holiday Mondays and throughout August, 10am to 6pm. £3, £2 (OAP). Refreshments. Available for hire. ☎ 01749 678 691.

St Cuthbert – Open daily 8am to 4pm. **Services**: Wednesday at 10am; Sunday at 8am, 10am, 6.30pm.

Excursions

Wookey Hole Caves – (♿) Open daily, 9.30am (10.30am November to February) to 5.30pm (4.30pm November to February). Closed 17 to 25 December. Guided tour (2hr) of caves and paper mill; caves are not accessible to wheelchairs. Leaflet (French, German, Italian, Spanish). £6.50, £3.50 (child), £5 (OAP). Parking; restaurant; picnic area. ☎ 01749 672 243; Fax 01749 677 749; E-mail adminwookeyhole.demon.co.uk.

WESTON SUPER MARE

🛈 Beach Lawns – ☎ 01934 616 838.

Clevedon Court (NT) – Open April to late September, Wednesdays, Thursdays, Sundays and bank holiday Mondays, 2pm to 5pm. £3.60, £1.80 (child). Guided tour by arrangement. Tea room. ☎ 01275 872 257.

WEYMOUTH and PORTLAND

🛈 Weymouth Esplanade – ☎ 01305 785 747
🛈 Portland – ☎ 01305 861 333

Sea Life Centre – ♿ Open, daily (weekends only in December), 10am to 5pm. £5.95, £3.95 (child), £3.95 (OAP). ☎ 01305 788 255 (recorded information); 01305 761 070.

Tudor House – Open June to September, Tuesday to Friday for guided tours 11am to 3.45pm; October to May on first Sunday of each month and all bank holidays, 2pm to 4pm; group visits may be arranged on other days by appointment. £1.50, concessions available for children and students. ☎ 01305 782 925 or 01305 788 168.

Timewalk Journey – Weymouth Museum and Timewalk: Open daily, 9.30am to 5.30pm (9.30pm school summer holidays); last admission 1 hour before closing. £3.75, £10.95 (family ticket), £2.50 (child), £3.25 (concession); ticket also valid for The Devenish Story. Audio commentary (French, German). Refreshments available within Brewers Quay complex. ☎ 01305 777 622; Fax 01305 761 680.

Discovery – ♿ Open March to December, daily, 10am to 5.30pm (9pm school summer holidays); January and February, Wednesday to Sunday, 10am to 5.30pm. £3.30, £9.80 (family ticket), £2.20 (child), £2.70 (concession). ☎ 01305 789 007.

Nothe Fort – ♿ Open May to September, daily, 10.30am to 5.30pm; October to April, Sundays, 2pm to 5pm. Introductory boards (French, German) £2.50. Parking; refreshments. ☎ 01305 787 243; Fax 01305 787 243.

Boat trips – Operate from the harbourside, cruises and fishing trips around Portland harbour and Fleet.

Chesil Beach Centre – Open 11am to 6pm (4pm October to March). Guided tours. ☎ 01305 760 579.

Abbotsbury Oyster Farm – Sea food bar Easter to September. ☎ 01305 788 867.

Portland Bill Lighthouse – Bird Observatory/ Field Centre: Open March to mid-November or by prior arrangement. ☎ 01305 820 553.

Portland Museum – Open Easter to September, Friday to Tuesday, 10.30am to 1pm, 1.30pm to 5pm. Closed October to Easter. £1.60, 80p (concession). ☎ 01305 821 804.

Portland Castle (EH) – Open April to October, daily, 10am to 6pm. (6pm/dusk, October). £2, £1 (child), £1.50 (concession). Parking. ☎ 01305 820 539.

Excursions

Tithe Barn Children's Farm, Abbotsbury – Open Easter to October, daily, 10am to 6pm (5pm last admission). £3, £9 (family), £2.20 (child), £2.80 (concession). Feeding the lambs : 12noon, 2pm, 4pm. Shop. ☎ 01305 871 817.

St Catherine's Chapel (EH) – Open all year, daily, sunrise to sunset. Services: May to November, certain weekdays only at 8pm.

Swannery – & Open Easter to October, daily, 10am to 6pm (5pm last admission). £4.80, £11 (family), £2 (child), £3.80 (concession). Guided tour (90min). Parking; restaurant; shop. ☎ 01305 871 858.

Sub-Tropical Gardens – & Open mid March to October, daily, 10am to 6pm (sunset, November to February). £4.20, £10 (family), £1.50 (child), £3.80 (concession). Parking; restaurant; plant sales; gift shop. ☎ 01305 871 387.

Hardy Monument (NT) – Open late March to late September, Saturday and Sunday, 11am to 5pm. £1. ☎ 01985 843 600 (National Trust).

WILTON

Wilton Carpet Factory – Open all year, daily, 9am (11am Sunday) to 5pm. Closed New Year, Easter Sunday and Christmas. £3.50, £1.50 (child/student), £3 (OAP). Guided tour (1hr 15min): Monday to Saturday at 10.15am, 11.45am, 2pm and 3.30pm; Sunday, at 11.30am, 2pm and 3.30pm. ☎ 01722 744 919, 01722 742 733; Fax 01722 742 923.

Wilton House – (&) Open Easter to October, daily, 11am to 6pm (5pm last admission). Full access for wheelchairs. £6.50. Leaflet (Dutch, French, German, Japanese). Parking; refreshments. ☎ 01722 746 729.

WIMBORNE MINSTER
🛈 29 High Street - ☎ 01202 886 116

Wimborne Minster Chained Library – Open Monday to Friday, 10.30am to 12.30pm, 2pm to 4pm.

Priest's House Museum – (&) Open April to October, Monday to Saturday, 10.30am (2pm Sundays, June to September) to 5pm. £2, 80p (child), £1.60 (concession). Guided tour (45min) by appointment; leaflet (French, German). Tea room (June to September). ☎ 01202 882 533; Fax 01202 882 533.

Heritage Centre – Open all year, Monday to Saturday, 9am to 5pm. Tape hire £1, 60p. ☎ 01202 888 902.

James Mortimer – The National Trust/Photo Library

Marble console table and Spanish miniatures, Kingston Lacy

WIMBORNE MINSTER

Wimborne Model Town and Gardens – Open Easter to September, daily, 10am to 5pm. Refreshments; under-cover play area. £2.25, £1 (child), £1.75 (concession). ☎ 01202 881 924.

Walford Mill Craft Centre – Open Easter to Christmas Eve, daily, 10am to 5pm; January to March, Tuesday to Sunday.

Excursions

Kingston Lacy (NT) – **House**: Open April to October, Saturday to Wednesday, 12noon to 5.30pm.
Open, (11.30am gardens and park) (6pm gardens and park). Leaflet (Braille, Dutch, French, German). Open special days to disabled: ring to enquire. **Park and garden**: open April to October, Saturday to Wednesday, 11.30am to 6pm; February, March, November, December, Friday to Sunday, 11am to 4pm or sunset. House, garden, park £5.50, £2.70 (child); garden and park £2.20, £1.10 (child). Parking; licensed restaurant; shop; refreshments. ☎ 01202 883 402; Fax 01202 882 402.

Stapehill – Open Easter to September, daily,10am to 5pm; October to December, February to Easter Wednesday to Sunday, 10am to 4pm. Parking; refreshments. £4.80, £3.80 (child), £4.40 (concessions). ☎ 01202 873 060.

Cranborne Manor Gardens – Open March to September, Wednesdays, 9am to 5pm. £2.50. Parking; plant sales. ☎ 01725 517 248.

Y

YEOVIL

🖪 Petter's Way – ☎ 01935 471 279
🖪 Fleet Air Arm Museum Car Park, Yeovilton – ☎ 01935 841 083

St John the Baptist's Church – Open daily, 9.30am to 3pm. **Services** : Sundays, at 8am, 10.30am, 6.30pm, Tuesdays, at 10am. ☎ 01935 475 396 (Rector).

Museum of South Somerset – Open all year, Mondays to Saturdays, 10am to 4pm. ☎ 01935 424 774.

Excursions

Fleet Air Arm Museum, Yeovilton (NACF) – 🚹 Open all year, daily, 10am to 5.30pm, last Flights to Carrier 4pm (4.30pm November to March, last Flights to Carrier 3pm). Closed 24 to 26 December. £6.50, £4 (child), £5.50 (OAP), £18 (2A+2C), £4 (concession). Parking; refreshments. ☎ 01935 840 565; Fax 01935 840 181.

Haynes Motor Museum – 🚹 Open all year, daily, 9.30am to 5.30pm in summer; 10am to 4pm in winter. Closed 1 January, 25 December. £4.50, £2.75 (child), £4 (OAP). Parking, restaurant-café, gift shop; picnic area. ☎ 01963 440 804.

Montacute House (NT) – (🚹) Open March to October, daily except Tuesday, 12noon to 5.30pm. No access for wheelchairs. **Garden and park**: open same as house, also November to March, daily except Tuesday 11.30am to 4pm; early November to late March, Wednesday to Sunday, 11.30 to 4pm. House, garden and park: £5, £2.50 (child), £12.50 (2A+3C); garden only: £2.80 (April to October), £1.20 (child). Parking; licensed restaurant, shop. ☎ 01935 823 289.

Tintinhull House Garden (NT) – (🚹) Open April to late September, Wednesdays, to Sundays, bank holiday Mondays, 12noon to 6pm. £3.50, £1.70 (child). Parking; tea room. ☎ 01935 822 545.

Channel Islands

JERSEY   🛈 Liberation Square, St Helier - ☎ 01534 500 777.

Royal Court House - **States in session** : All year outside August, alternate Tuesdays, 9.30am to close of business; also Fridays from 2.30pm for public property purchases hearings. ☎ 01534 502 101.

Jersey Museum - &. Open all year, daily, 10am to 5pm (4pm winter). Closed 25 December. £3.20, £2.10 (concession). **Passport Saver Ticket:** £ 10, £6.75 (concession) for Elizabeth Castle, Mont Orgueil, Hamptonne, La Hougue Bie, Occupation Tapestry gallery. Guided tour by appointment. ☎ 01534 30511.

Maritime Museum and Jersey Occupation Tapestry - &. Open daily, 10am to 5pm, (4pm winter). Closed 25 December and 1 January. £3.20, £2.10 (concession). **Passport Saver Ticket:** £ 10, £6.75 (concession) for Jersey Museum, Elizabeth Castle, Mont Orgueil, Hamptonne, La Hougue Bie. ☎ 01534 30511.

Fort Regent - &. Open daily, 8.45am to 11pm. Closed 24 to 26 December, 1 January. £2, £1.50 (concession), £1 (child) before 6.30pm; £1.50, £1.05 (concession), 80p (child) to 11pm. Guided tour (30min or 40min) April to October, daily, at 10.30am and 1.30pm. Parking; refreshments. ☎ 01534 500 200; Fax 01534 500 225.

Island Fortress Occupation Museum - &. Open daily, April to October, 9.30am to 10.30pm; November to March, 10am to 4pm. £3, £1.50 (child), £2 (concession). ☎ 01534 34306.

Elizabeth Castle - Open late March to October, daily, 9.30am to 6pm (5pm last admission). £3.20, £2.10 (concession). Guided tour (1hr 30min). **Passport Saver Ticket:** £ 10, £6.75 (concession) for Jersey Museum, Mont Orgueil, Hamptonne, La Hougue Bie, Occupation Tapestry gallery. Restaurant. ☎ 01534 23971.

Jersey Zoo - &. Open all year, daily, 9.30am to 6pm or sunset. Closed 25 December. £5.20, £3.20 (child), £4.20 (concession). Guided tour (2hr) available. Parking; refreshments. ☎ 01534 864 666; Fax 01534 865 161.

Eric Young Orchid Foundation - &. Open all year, Thursdays to Saturdays, 10am to 4pm. Closed 25 December. £2.50, £1.00 (child), £1.50 (concession). ☎ 01534 861 963.

La Hougue Bie - &. Open late March to October, daily, 10am to 5pm. £3.20, £2.10 (concession). **Passport Saver Ticket:** £ 10, £6.75 (concession) for Jersey Museum, Elizabeth Castle, Mont Orgueil, Hamptonne, Occupation Tapestry gallery. Parking. ☎ 01534 853 823.

Hamptonne Country Life Museum - &. Open late March to October, daily, 10am to 5pm. £3.20, £2.10 (concession). **Passport Saver Ticket:** £ 10, £6.75 (concession) for Jersey Museum, Elizabeth Castle, Mont Orgueil, La Hougue Bie, Occupation Tapestry gallery. ☎ 01534 863955.

German Underground Hospital - &. Open early March to early November, daily, 9.30am to 5pm (last admission 4.15pm); November and December, Sundays and Thursdays, 12pm to 5pm (last admission 4.15pm). Closed January and February. £4.40, £2.20 (child). Parking; cafe. ☎ 01534 863 442. Fax 01534 865 970.

Quetivel Mill (NT) - (&) Open April to mid October, Tuesdays to Thursdays, 10am to 4pm. £1.50, 50p (child over 10, student), £1 (concession). Parking. ☎ 01534 45408, 01534 483 193 (NT).

Living Legend - &. Open April to October, daily, 9.30am to 5.30pm; March and November, Saturdays to Wednesdays, 10am to 5pm. Narrative (French, German, Norwegian, Swedish). £4.70, £2.75 (child), £4.20 (senior citizen), £3.15 (student), £3.35 (disabled). Parking; refreshments; shops; adventure golf. ☎ 01534 485 496; Fax 01534 485 855.

Jersey Motor Museum - (&) Open end March to late October, daily, 10am to 5pm. £2.10, £1.00 (child). Parking. ☎ 01534 482 966.

St Matthew's Church (Glass Church) - Open all year, Monday to Friday, 9am to 5.30pm (4.30pm November to March) weekends, for services only. Guide books (French). Parking. ☎ 01534 615 905.

Command Bunker, Noirmont Point - Open June to August, Thursdays, 7pm to 9.30pm; September, Mondays, 10am to 12noon. Parking. £1.00. Further details from the Channel Island Occupation Society, The Chateau, Five Mile Road, St Ouen.

Kempt Tower Interpretation Centre - Open May to September, Tuesday to Sunday, 2pm to 5pm; May and September, Thursday, Sunday and holidays, 2pm to 5pm. No charge. Guided tour (1hr 30min) Thursdays at 3pm. Parking. ☎ 01534 483 651.

Battle of Flowers Museum – (&) Open Easter to mid November, daily, 10am to 5pm. £2, £1.75 (concession). Parking. ☎ 01534 482 408.

Greve de Lecq Barracks (NT) – (&) Open May to mid October, daily except Monday, 11am to 5pm. Now includes North Coast Visitor Centre. Donation. Parking. ☎ 01534 482 238; 01534 483 193 (NT).

La Mare Vineyard – & Open April to September, Monday to Saturday, holidays, 10am to 5.30pm. £3.50. Free wine tasting. Parking; refreshments. ☎ 01534 481 178; Fax 01534 485 210.

Mont Orgueil Castle – Open daily, 9.30am to 6pm (dusk in winter); last admission 1 hour before closing. £3.20, £2.10 (concession). **Passport Saver Ticket:** £ 10, £6.75 (concession) for Jersey Museum, Elizabeth Castle, Hamptonne, La Hougue Bie, Occupation Tapestry gallery. ☎ 01534 853 292.

Jersey Pottery – & Open all year, Monday to Saturday, 9am to 5.30pm. Closed Christmas to New Year. No charge. Parking; licensed restaurant; shop. ☎ 01534 851 119; Fax 01534 856 403.

Samarès Manor – & **Garden:** Open April to October, daily, 10am to 5pm. **House:** Guided tour (40min) April to October, Monday to Saturday at 11.45am and 12.30pm. Gardens £3.50, £1.70 (child), £2.90 (OAP); house £1.75. Herb talks Monday to Friday at 2.15pm. parking, refreshments. ☎ 01534 870 551; Fax 01534 68949.

GUERNSEY

🛈 North Plantation, St Peter Port – ☎ 01481 723 552.
🛈 The Airport, Forest – ☎ 01481 37267.

Castle Cornet – Open April to October, daily, 10am to 5pm. Noonday gun fired daily. £4.00. Guided tour (1hr) available. Parking; refreshments. ☎ 01481 726 518.

26 Cornet Street – Open late March to mid October, Tuesdays to Thursdays and Saturdays 10am to 4pm. ☎ 01481 728 451.

Hauteville House – Guided tour (15 people maximum) April to September, Monday to Saturday, 10am to 11.30am and 2pm to 4.30pm. Closed Sunday and bank holidays. £3, £1.50 (child).

Guernsey Museum – & Open all year, daily, 10am to 5pm (4pm winter). Closed 23 to 26 December. £2.50, £1.25 (concession). Parking; refreshments. ☎ 01481 726 518.

St James' – Open all year, Monday to Friday, 9am to 5pm. Closed holidays. ☎ 01481 711 360.

Royal Court House – **States in session** : January to December (except in August), last Wednesday of the month (second Wednesday in December), 10am to close of business. Details of debates available from the Greffe. ☎ 01481 725 277.

St John's Residential Home – Open all year, daily. Rooms on the ground floor only. Contact Matron for further details. ☎ 01481 56865.

Guernsey Folk Museum – Open late March to late October, daily, 10am to 5.30pm (4pm in winter). £2.50, £1.00 (concession). Parking. ☎ 01481 55384.

Saint's Bay

German Underground Hospital and Ammunition Store - Open May and June, daily, 10am to 12noon and 2pm to 5pm; September, daily, 10am to 12noon and 2pm to 4.30pm; April and October, daily, 2pm to 4pm; March and November, Sunday and Thursday, 2pm to 3pm. £2.50, 60p (child). ☎ 01481 39100.

Oatlands Craft Centre - &. Open all year, daily (except Sundays in winter), 10am to 5pm (reduced hours in winter). Parking; refreshments. ☎ 01481 49478.

Dehus Dolmen - Open all year, daily, sunrise to sunset. ☎ 01481 717 000 (Secretary of Heritage Committee).

Fort Grey Maritime Museum - Open April to October, daily, 10am to 5pm. £2, £1 (concession). Parking. ☎ 01481 726 518.

German Occupation Museum - &. Open daily, 10am to 5pm. £2.50, £1.25 (child). Parking; refreshments. ☎ 01481 38205.

Sausmarez Manor - &. **Garden:** Open all year, daily, 10am to 5pm. **House:** Guided tour Easter to October, Monday to Thursday and holiday Monday, 10.30am, 11.30am; June to September, 2pm and 3pm. **Subtropical Wild Woodland Garden** - Open March to January, daily, 10.30am to 5.30pm. ☎ 01481 35571 (Estate Office); Fax 01481 35572.

Dolls House Collection: Open March to January, Mondays to Fridays, 10.30am to 6.30pm (5pm winter); Sundays, 11am to 5pm. **Manor Railways:** Open March to January, daily, 10.30am to 5.30pm (4.30pm winter). House £4; Subtropical garden £1.50; Dolls' House £1.95; Railway (outdoor 7" gauge train ride) : 90p, 70p (child). Parking; refreshments; play area; pets' corner. ☎ 01481 35904 (Dolls' House). ☎ 0585 237 349 (Railway).

La Valette Underground Military Hospital - Open daily, 10am to 5pm. £2.50, £1.00 (child), £2 (OAP). Parking; refreshments. ☎ 01481 722 300.

Guernsey Aquarium - &. Open all year, daily, 10am till dusk. Closed 25 and 26 December. £2.25, £1.40 (child), £1.90 (concession). ☎ 01481 723 301.

ALDERNEY
🖪 Queen Elizabeth II Street - ☎ 01481 823 737.

Alderney Society Museum - Open Easter to October, daily, 10am to 12pm and Mondays to Fridays, 2pm to 4pm. £1. ☎ 01481 822 655.

Court House - Open all year, Monday to Friday, 9.30am to 12.30pm, with permission from Clerk of the Court.
Court in session: Thursdays, 2.30pm. States in session: first Wednesday in the month, 5.30pm.

Alderney Forts Tour - Operates all year, daily, at 1.45pm. Time 1hr 30min from Butes. Victorian or German forts tour : book daily from 10.am. £4. ☎ 01481 822 992.

Alderney Railway - Operates Easter to September, Saturday, Sunday and holidays, 2pm to 5pm. £1.30, £1.70 (steam trains).

Quesnard Lighthouse - Open (weather permitting) all year, daily.

Burhou Island - Open all year except during the breeding season (mid March to mid July). £3 (per night). Apply for permission from the Harbour Office, daily, 8am to 6pm (5pm winter, Monday to Friday). ☎ 01481 822 620; Fax 01481 823 699.

SARK
🖪 - ☎ 01481 832345.

La Seigneurie Gardens - Open Easter to mid October, Monday to Friday; Saturday in July and August, 10am to 5pm. 80p, 40p (child). ☎ 01481 832 345.

FOLLOW THE COUNTRY CODE

Guard against all risk of fire
Fasten all gates
Keep dogs under proper control
Keep to the paths across farmland
Avoid damaging fences, hedges and walls
Leave no litter
Safeguard water supplies
Protect wildlife, wild plants and trees
Go carefully on country roads
Respect the countryside.

Index

Names of places, houses, streets are in roman type: Camelford, Lanyon Quoit, Tamar...

People, historical events, subjects are in italics: Drake, Sir Francis...

Collective references under Canals, Industrial archeology, Maritime museums, Military museums, Railways etc...

Notes